A SEMINARY SURVEY

A SEMINARY SURVEY

A Listing and Review of the Activities of the Theological Schools and Major Seminaries Located in Africa, Asia and Latin America which are Training Men to Serve as Ordained Ministers and Priests in the Protestant, Roman Catholic and Eastern Churches

by YORKE ALLEN, Jr.

HARPER & BROTHERS PUBLISHERS NEW YORK

"Spes Messis in Semine"

CONTENTS

PART ONE: PROTESTANT THEOLOGICAL SCHOOLS

PART TWO: MAJOR SEMINARIES OF THE ROMAN CATHOLIC CHURCH

PART THREE: THE SEMINARIES OF THE EASTERN CHURCHES

PART FOUR: CONCLUSION

MAPS

The maps on pages 283–289 indicate those localities in Africa, Asia and Latin America in which the theological schools and major seminaries of the Protestant, Roman Catholic and Eastern Churches, as listed in this Survey, are situated.

FOREWORD

The writing of a foreword is a dubious occupation. "Good wine needs no bush"; and a good book needs no prelusory puff. But when Mr. Yorke Allen, Jr., honored me with a request that I should write a foreword to this volume, I accepted readily. I did not do so because I have a burning desire to tell the prospective reader what he can quickly find out for himself—that this is a remarkable book. My purpose is, rather, to describe how this Survey came to be written, and to record some of the far-reaching results which have already accrued from the writing of it. These things cannot be learned from Mr. Allen's text; his modesty has prevented him from telling them. But they ought to be told, and I welcome this opportunity to tell them.

In June 1955, when I was General Secretary of the International Missionary Council, I wrote to Mr. John D. Rockefeller, Jr., to seek his support in the creation of a fund for the improvement of training for the Christian ministry in Africa, Asia and Latin America. The IMC had, for many years, made theological education one of its chief concerns. It had conducted surveys, collected information, and offered advice on the subject. But it was precluded from further action by poverty rather than by principle. Poverty, as Sydney Smith has remarked, is no disgrace; but it is "confoundedly inconvenient." And the lack of resources for strengthening the training of the ministry in the "younger churches" was proving to be a very grave handicap to advance. In advocating a Fund for theological education, I was assured of the moral backing of the Executive Board of the Division of Foreign Missions of the National Council of the Churches of Christ in the USA. I was further fortified by the fact that the representatives of a number of mission boards had indicated their readiness to try to put financial substance behind their moral support, if an ecumenical Fund were established.

The response of Mr. Rockefeller and his advisors to my approach was careful, deliberate and based upon a determination to discover facts. One fact was soon obvious. No comprehensive survey of the institutions training men for the ministry of the "younger" churches in Africa, Asia and Latin America had ever been published. A considerable amount of material on certain areas and on varying aspects of theological education was available. But this material had never been brought together in such a way as to present a complete picture of the activities of the theological schools in all "younger church" areas.

The portions of *A Seminary Survey* relating to the Protestant ministry were prepared as a basis for Mr. Rockefeller's consideration of the IMC's request. Mr. Allen, who is a member of Mr. Rockefeller's staff, set about the formidable task of assembling in a single document all the relevant information he could find on this subject. He brought to this work immense industry and a transcendent capacity for taking trouble. He was relentless in his pursuit of information. In this Survey he reveals great skill in the organization of a mass of detail, and wise discrimination in its interpretation.

What he began as a professional duty, Mr. Allen continued as a personal enthusiasm. When it was later suggested that *A Seminary Survey* might be published, Mr. Allen agreed to this with the understanding that, in order to present a balanced picture, the Survey should include additional material relating to the seminaries and scholasticates training men for the priesthood in the Roman Catholic and Eastern Churches in Africa, Asia and Latin America. The results of this whole effort are embodied in this book. It is, without doubt, the most comprehensive factual review of training for the Christian ministry in these areas which has ever been published.

Mr. Allen has not only surveyed theological education in these great areas of the world. He has cast a searching eye upon the policies of foreign mission boards, particularly in the USA. We sometimes quote the prayer of Robert Burns:

> O wad some Pow'r the giftie gie us
> To see oursels as others see us!
> It wad frae mony a blunder free us,
> And foolish notion.

This book is a partial answer to this prayer, for those of us who are involved in the missionary enterprise. It is a salutory, if startling, answer.

I am sure that Mr. Allen enjoyed writing this book. But he did not write it for his own amusement. It was prepared for a purpose. John Milton has much to say in his *Areopagitica* about the *potency* of the written word. He was, of course, referring to the impact of books after publication. This volume has been potent before publication. A first draft of the Survey, dealing with Protestant theological schools, was submitted in the spring of 1957 to the executives of eight mission boards in the United States to ascertain their initial opinions concerning it. A few months later these boards agreed to contribute a total of $2,000,000 to the proposed IMC Fund for Theological Education, during the five-year period 1958–62. On the basis of these pledges a request for a similar amount was presented to the Sealantic Fund, which was established by Mr. Rockefeller some years ago. When the Assembly of the IMC met at the University College of Ghana from December 28, 1957, to January 8, 1958, it was thus possible to present, not merely a proposal for the establishment of a Theological Education Fund, but the assurance of substantial resources with which to launch it. The Assembly authorized the creation of the Fund. In April 1958 the Sealantic Fund contributed $2,000,000, thereby assuring an initial total of $4,000,000 for this enterprise.

The Ghana Assembly, in inaugurating the Fund and approving the general principles governing its operation, expressed its "profound appreciation" and "deep gratitude" for this initiative. The Assembly recognized that this step represented only a beginning, and urged every member body of the IMC to contribute to the new Fund. An ecumenical committee was appointed to supervise the work of the Fund. Its terms of reference and general operating principles, as approved by the Assembly, together with a list of members, are to be found in Appendix C of this volume.

In the shaping of this train of events, Mr. Allen's Survey has played a notable part. It is not surprising, therefore, that the Theological Education Fund Committee should have expressed a lively interest in its publication. The Committee is not, of course, in any way responsible for, nor governed by, the opinions expressed in the Survey. The Theological Education Fund Committee, and its officers, are responsible solely to the International Missionary Council. This volume is, in the strict sense of the term, an independent appraisal. Its value is enhanced, rather than diminished, by that fact; and the influence which it has already exerted before publication will, I believe, be greatly extended by its wider circulation.

It is a privilege to commend this remarkable piece of work, not only to those who are involved in the task of training candidates for the ministry of the Church, but to all who are concerned with the strategy of the Christian world mission.

C. W. RANSON
Director
Theological Education Fund

PREFACE

It is a rather surprising fact that fewer than 5% of the 581 theological schools, seminaries and scholasticates maintained by the Roman Catholic, Protestant and Eastern Churches in Africa, Asia and Latin America have been mentioned in the standard reference works listing the postsecondary educational institutions training students in those areas. One may search at length in such compendia as the *Index generalis, The World of Learning,* the *Minerva-Jahrbuch der gelehrten Welt* and UNESCO's *World Survey of Education* and find listed therein only a very few of the institutions training men for the Christian priesthood and ministry in the underdeveloped countries. Another example which might be cited is a massive (1,676 pages) and definitive survey dealing with only a part of one continent, i.e., Lord Hailey's *An African Survey*—Revised 1956. This authoritative volume lists and discusses among other things the colleges and universities in Africa south of the Sahara, including postsecondary technical schools training engineers, teachers, bookkeepers, printers, bricklayers, veterinaries, and even midwives, etc. Nevertheless it makes no mention whatever of the 109 Christian seminaries in the same area which are now training 3,168 students to be ministers and priests.

This points to a rather curious and unfortunate dichotomy which exists between the secular activities of business and governments in the underdeveloped countries on the one hand and the religious activities of the Protestants and Roman Catholic foreign missionaries working in those same areas on the other. It is estimated, for example, that there are approximately 234,000 United States civilians living in Africa, Asia and Latin America, most of whom are engaged in business or government activities of one sort or another. Much has been written and is being written about their work, the life they lead, etc. Yet it is not widely recognized that more than one out of every ten of these "overseas Americans" is serving in Protestant foreign missions. Virtually all of them are devoting their entire careers to a life of sacrificial service to the cause of Christ and the needs of man. As representatives of the United States they are usually far closer to the indigenous populations in Africa, Asia and Latin America than are our diplomatic and business officials. Yet their work and accomplishments are largely unrecognized outside of foreign missionary circles.

There would seem to be at least two reasons for this. The first is the principle of the separation of Church from State, which is one of the cornerstones of American political philosophy and governmental practice. This has meant that in the underdeveloped countries Americans working for the United States Government or business interests have trod separate paths from those who are working as foreign missionaries. The second reason is that most foreign missionaries of all nationalities and churches appear to underrate the importance of making their accomplishments known. But if the 339 North American Protestant foreign mission agencies are to continue to raise and disburse approximately $147,000,000 each year, it might be advisable for them to increase the number, "streamline" the contents and broaden the distribution of their reports to the public. Similarly, within the Roman Catholic Church, few of its agencies seem to appreciate the importance of issuing effective missionary publications as do the Society for the Propagation of the Faith and (among the religious institutes) the Jesuits, Maryknoll and the Divine Word Fathers.

The activities of the Protestant, Roman Catholic and Eastern Churches in training their candidates for the ministry and priesthood in Africa, Asia and Latin America have received even less attention than has their work in secular education, hospitals, agriculture, etc. This is odd inasmuch as the lessons of history clearly demonstrate that the training of the clergy is at the core of the process of maintaining any ecclesiastical organization. A part of the reason for this is that among the clergy, the theologians are perhaps the least inclined to draw attention to their daily activities and accomplishments. But unless such attention is gained the theological schools and seminaries are apt to be overlooked and "taken for granted" by both the laity and the clergy alike. The result is that in recent years many of these institutions have received inadequate financial support.

It is hoped that the following chapters may serve to point to the practical importance of training a clergy in Africa, Asia and Latin America which will be able to cope successfully with the problem of meeting the rapidly changing spiritual needs of the people residing in those areas. It should also be noted that, as a result of the developments which are now occurring so rapidly in these three continents, a survey of the current activities of their seminaries must necessarily be out of date in some respects, even before the manuscript has been sent to the printer. Those readers who wish to obtain the most recent and complete information on these institutions should write either to the schools themselves, or to the Theological Education Fund office of the International Missionary Council in New York City, or (with respect to Roman Catholic seminaries) to the appropriate office in the Vatican City.

This Survey could not have been written without the help of many persons.

Because of their number it has seemed best to list them in the bibliography to be found at the end of the Survey. Any comments which are not directly attributed in the text to individual sources represent the author's own views, and do not necessarily reflect the opinions of the author's informants or employers, or approval by them of the author's views or statements. The author would like to express his thanks to each and all who have been of assistance, including one person who is not listed in the bibliography because her help has been and is in a different category: that is his wife, to whom this volume is affectionately dedicated.

YORKE ALLEN, JR.

LIST OF TABLES

A SEMINARY SURVEY

Part One:

PROTESTANT THEOLOGICAL SCHOOLS

CHAPTER 1

INTRODUCTION

A. PURPOSE AND SCOPE OF THE SURVEY

The purpose of this Survey is to present (1) a listing and review of the activities of the theological schools and seminaries training men to serve as ordained ministers and priests in the Protestant, Roman Catholic and Eastern Churches which are located in Africa, Asia and Latin America; and (2) the conclusions and recommendations of this Survey which are the basis for a joint effort which is now being undertaken by the International Missionary Council and a number of Protestant foreign mission boards for the purpose of improving the training of the ministry in the younger Protestant churches.

Until the last few years there has been comparatively little published concerning this field, so that there is not a great deal of public information available on which to draw. Accordingly, even though the attempt has been made to be both complete and accurate, it is recognized that there are without doubt some gaps (and doubtless some inaccuracies) in the picture which is presented, and that some of the information presented herein may already be somewhat out of date.

This Survey is concerned primarily with the organization and financing of the theological schools and seminaries in Africa, Asia and Latin America, and only incidentally with such matters as curriculum content, their philosophy of education, or the theology of missions, etc.

The scope of the Survey is limited to the younger church areas and therefore excludes Europe, Australia and New Zealand, Canada, the United States (and its possessions) and Communist-controlled countries. Since it is simpler to group the remaining countries by areas, this has been done under the following headings:

1. AFRICA: North and South of the Sahara.
2. MIDDLE EAST: Iran, Iraq, Arabia, Jordan, Israel, Lebanon, Syria, Turkey and Cyprus.
3. SOUTHERN ASIA: Afghanistan, Pakistan, Nepal, India and Ceylon.
4. SOUTHEAST ASIA: Burma, Thailand, Malaya, Indonesia, Oceania, Indochina and the Philippine Islands.

5. EAST ASIA: Japan, Korea, Formosa and Hongkong.
6. LATIN AMERICA: Mexico, Central America, the Caribbean area and South America.

B. TYPES OF PROTESTANT THEOLOGICAL SCHOOLS

There is a broad diversity in the type of educational institutions overseas which are training men for careers in the younger Protestant churches. For example, in Japan alone there were listed in 1955 some 167 Protestant educational institutions of one sort or another currently operating in that country. Many institutions operate independently of accrediting authorities and cannot readily be classified in one category or another, especially those which simultaneously offer courses for students at various academic levels. Accordingly the initial portion of this Survey is limited to the seminaries which are providing training for ordinand students, i.e., men (and women) intending to enter the full-time Protestant ministry.

Unfortunately there has been some confusion in the terms used in various reports to describe theological schools in different areas. The 1938 Tambaram Conference, some of the findings of which are discussed later in this Survey, divided theological training into three categories:

1. *Theological Colleges,* in which the *majority* of students have taken a full course in arts or science at a college level before beginning the study of theology. Such a college would compare to a graduate divinity school in the United States which has been fully accredited by the American Association of Theological Schools and which awards a Bachelor of Divinity (B.D.) degree.

2. *Theological Schools,* the standard entrance to which is ordinarily the same as that of matriculation at a college or university. These institutions offer courses at the undergraduate level, and many of them award a Licentiate in Theology (L.Th.) or a Bachelor of Theology (B.Th.) diploma.

3. *Bible Schools,* in which theological teaching is at the prematriculate, i.e., high school, level.

The Tambaram definitions will generally be followed in this Survey, but in a somewhat more flexible manner. According to the Tambaram definitions, in all of Africa, Asia and Latin America there are less than a dozen theological colleges, of which five are in India. Only a handful of the tropical African institutions would correspond in every respect to the Tambaram definition of a theological school, inasmuch as very few of their candidates are matriculates. Therefore the term "theological school" as used herein includes a fairly broad range of institutions at both the college and precollege level, some of which offer liberal arts courses as well as theological studies, but whose principal activity is the training of ordinands for the full-time ministry. The term "seminary" is used, for the sake of convenience, to mean both theological colleges and schools.

This Survey includes only a brief section relating to the many Bible schools which exist almost everywhere throughout Africa, Asia and Latin America. The term "Bible school" is used to mean those institutions at the college, but usually the precollege, level which provide a religious education (or a predominantly secular education in which religious courses are offered) directed primarily for the training of teachers, laymen or others, either for secular careers or for part- or full-time Christian work, exclusive of the full-time ordained ministry.

The distinctions among these three main categories of institutions are not always easy to maintain, inasmuch as some Bible schools which serve primarily to train unordained workers are used by a number of the younger churches for the training of men who may later seek ordination, sometimes without further education. Furthermore, some institutions simultaneously offer courses for both ordinands and religious workers, and statistics showing the breakdown between the courses and the number of students in each category are not readily available. Thus the theological schools listed in this Survey represent a possibly rather arbitrary selection of seminaries which is designed simply to present an over-all picture of the whole field of training men for the full-time ministry. In general, only the seminaries supported by "denominational" foreign mission boards are listed inasmuch as the schools maintained by the evangelist, adventist, pentecostal and non-denominational agencies often focus their efforts on training personnel for religious work other than the ordained ministry, and their academic standards usually are not as high as the former.

The theological schools now in operation in each area are listed, together with a brief discussion of their salient characteristics. In some cases the estimates of the number of the full-time faculty members and ordinand students at an individual school have of necessity had to be rather arbitrary, and may be on the low rather than the high side. Summaries are given of the recommendations which have been made in various reports concerning ways and means of improving theological education in specific areas or countries. No attempt has been made to write a detailed history of any one seminary. Some schools require little or no comment, and on others little or no information seems to be readily available.

C. The Administrative Structure of the Protestant Foreign Missionary Enterprise

In order to obtain a perspective from which to judge the scope of the Protestant foreign missionary effort in general and the relative importance of the support given by mission boards to theological education overseas, it is necessary to relate the activities of the foreign seminaries to the status of Christianity in the countries in which the schools are located.

With respect to the distribution of the Christian population of the world by areas, the data in Table 1 include church-membership figures in Communist countries. These statistics are rounded estimates as of 1957 and are derived from data published by the Catholic Students' Mission Crusade and the Missionary Research Library. The figures are only intended to be indicative and should be treated with reserve inasmuch as ecclesiastical statistics are not always accurate. Also one should take into account the fact that there are considerable differences in the membership reporting methods used by the Protestant and Eastern Churches as compared to the Roman Catholic Church. For example, a case can be made that the Protestant church membership figures in Table 1 should be doubled if they are to be compared accurately to Roman Catholic membership figures (which include children and some adults not classified by Protestant churches as members). In some instances the term "Protestant community" (which includes children and catechumens, as well as communicants) is used later on in this Survey in addition to the term "Protestant membership."

TABLE 1.   WORLD CHRISTIAN POPULATION BY AREAS (1957)
(IN MILLIONS)

| Area | Total Population | Christian Communities | | | | % of Christians to Total Population | % of Protestants to Total Population |
		Protestant	Roman Catholic	Eastern Churches	Total		
Africa	226	13	20	7	40	18	6
Middle East	86		1	1	2	2	
Southern Asia	483	6	6	1	13	3	1
Southeast Asia	184	8	21		29	16	4
East Asia	717	2	4		6	1	
Latin America	183	6	167		173	94	3
Subtotal	1,879	35	219	9	263	14	2
Europe	610	102	234	127	463	76	17
USA and Canada	187	67	41	2	110	59	36
Australia and New Zealand	11	7	2		9	82	64
Subtotal	808	176	277	129	582	72	22
Total	2,687	211	496	138	845	31	8

Insofar as conversions to Christianity over the centuries are concerned, the figures in Table 1 indicate (1) the small number of converts obtained by the Protestant missionary enterprise in the Middle East and in Southern and East Asia in proportion to the total population of each of those areas; and (2) the fact that in the younger church areas there are more than six Roman Catholics to every one Protestant church member. However, if one excludes Latin America, the proportion of Roman Catholics to Protestants in the younger church areas is reduced to slightly less than 2:1. It also is reported that although the Christian population of the world is growing, yet in proportion to the total population of the world it is showing a slow and disturbing decline.

Few statistics are available concerning the total number of missionaries sent out by Protestant mission organizations throughout the world, or of the money spent by these organizations in Africa, Asia and Latin America. The reason is that overseas (as well as in the United States) there are a large number of small religious and secular organizations which operate independently of the larger denominational mission boards, and whose annual reports are seldom collated. There are more than 450 Protestant church groups in all countries of the world conducting missionary activities of one sort or another in foreign lands. Table 2 presents what appear to be the most reliable estimates relating to the total number and origin of Protestant missionaries in recent decades.

TABLE 2. TOTAL NUMBER OF PROTESTANT
FOREIGN MISSIONARIES
(1925–58)

Year	North American	All Countries
1925	14,043	29,188
1936	11,289	27,577
1950	15,039	
1956	23,432	34,692
1958	25,058	38,606

In Table 2 the heading "North American" includes missionaries sent by Canadian as well as American boards. However, of the 23,432 missionaries sent from these two countries in 1956, only 752, or 3% came from Canada. Thus it is likely that in all the years shown at least 95% came from the United States and less than 5% from Canada. It will also be noted that there was a 5% decline in the total of Protestant missionaries sent from all countries between the years 1925 and 1936. This drop was more than accounted for by the decline in the number of missionaries sent from North America during these years.

Table 2 also discloses that at present two-thirds of the total number of Protestant missionaries in the world are sent from North America. The 1958 total of 25,058 is more than double the number of personnel sent from America in 1936. This increase of 13,769 missionaries sent from North America during the period 1936–58 came at a time when the total number of Protestant missionaries from all countries increased by only 11,029. Thus during this period there was a decrease of 2,650 Protestant missionaries sent out from European countries, a reduction of approximately 9%. This shift in the balance of missionary forces has resulted in the United States' becoming since World War II the major missionary-sending country in the world. The predominant role of the Protestant American boards and agencies, however, is vitiated to an unfortunate extent by their fragmented structure and individualistic attitudes.

The number of Protestant missionaries sent out from various countries in Europe, North America and elsewhere in 1957 and 1958 (as reported and estimated by the Missionary Research Library) is shown in Table 3.

With respect to the geographical distribution of the missionaries in the field, the statistics relate only to North American Protestant missionaries. Even this information is incomplete. For example, Table 4 sets forth the distribution of only 19,578 missionaries compared to the 25,058 listed in Table 2. The explanation of the difference is accounted for by the fact that a number of mission agencies did not report on the distribution of their missionary personnel.

TABLE 3. NUMBER OF PROTESTANT MISSION-
ARIES SENT OUT FROM SELECTED COUNTRIES
(1957–58)

United States	24,284
United Kingdom	7,000
Sweden	1,568
Germany	975
Norway	967
Canada	774
Australia	665
Netherlands	600
Switzerland	544
France	350
Denmark	280
Finland	250
New Zealand	182
Belgium	61
Younger Churches, etc.	106
	38,606

TABLE 4. DISTRIBUTION OF NORTH AMERICAN PROTESTANT MISSIONARIES
(1925–58)

	1925		1958		
	Number	%	Number	%	Approx. Number of Protestants per Missionary
Africa	1,487	11	6,356	32	2,000
Middle East	908	6	578	3	100
Southern Asia	2,443	17	2,161	11	3,000
Southeast Asia	844	6	2,252	11	3,500
East Asia	6,040	43	2,499	13	1,000
Latin America	2,153	15	4,825	25	1,250
Other Countries	213	2	907	5	
	14,088	100	19,578	100	1,750ᵃ

NOTE: ᵃ Excluding "Other Countries."

Table 4 discloses the 300% increase in the number of missionaries sent by Protestant agencies to Africa during the period 1925–58. In 1958 there were more American missionaries in Africa than in any other area, with Latin America (up over 100% from 1925) in second place. These two areas account for 57% of the total number of American missionaries in the field. The religious contrast between these two areas is a marked one: Latin America is already a predominantly Christian area, whereas in most of Africa south of the Sahara there is at present no centrally organized religion with which Christianity must compete.

It will also be noted that during this same period the number of missionaries sent to the Middle East has been reduced by one-third. In Southeast Asia there has been a 166% increase in missionaries and in East Asia a decrease of about 60%.

The latter is accounted for by the drop in American missionaries sent to China, from 4,492 in 1925 to one in 1956 (in prison).

The largest number of North American missionaries stationed in any one country in 1958 was India, where the total was 1,883. Japan was second with 1,549, and the Belgian Congo was third with 1,289.

The distribution by missionary groups of the 25,058 North American missionaries who are supported at home and in the field by the 339 North American missionary agencies, and the magnitude of the 1957 income of these groups, is indicated in Table 5. It is possible that in the case of some of the smaller conservative evangelical missionary groups the income totals they report may be somewhat inflated.

TABLE 5. INCOME OF NORTH AMERICAN PROTESTANT FOREIGN MISSIONARY GROUPS (1957)

	Number of Member Agencies	Total 1957 Income	%	Number of Missionaries 1958	%
Division of Foreign Missions, NCCC (DFM)	78	$ 82,981,000	54	10,977	42
Independent: Denominational	28	18.049,000 [a]	12	2,072	8
Educational Institutions	13	1,840,000	1	20	
Evangelical Foreign Missions Association (EFMA)	45	21,951,000	14	4,688	18
Interdenominational Foreign Missions Association (IFMA)	40	13,458,000	9	5,902	23
Assoc. Missions of International Council of Christian Churches (AMICCC)	16	3,123,000	2	851	3
Independent: Non-denominational	36	2,141,000	2	910	3
Canadian Boards	15	5,996,000	4	774	3
Miscellaneous [b]	78	4,092,000	2	207	
	349	$153,633,000	100	26,401	100
Less Duplication [c]	10	6,350,000		1,343	
	339	$147,283,000		25,058	

NOTES: [a] Of which the Southern Baptists accounted for the major part.
[b] Consisting of unaffiliated American branches of international organizations, supporting agencies and specialized services.
[c] Ten agencies are members of or are related to more than one missionary group.

The $147,283,000 income received by the 339 foreign mission agencies in 1957 was 84% more than their total reported income in 1951. In 1955, 77% of their income was expended on appropriations for the salaries and expenses of missionaries and for mission activities overseas. The remaining 23% was devoted to administrative expenses, promotion, travel, furlough salaries, the purchase of supplies and equipment, etc.

It is estimated that an additional $35,000,000 is now being spent each year on foreign mission activities by non-American Protestant boards and agencies, principally those located in Europe and the nations comprising the British Commonwealth. Thus an estimated total of approximately $182,000,000 was spent by all Protestant foreign mission agencies in 1957, of which approximately 81% was income derived from North American agencies.

With respect to the annual budgetary expenditures in each geographic area of the leading individual American foreign mission boards and agencies, Table 6 presents this information for 56 American organizations which in the year 1954 reported a total income of $48,539,000. Of this amount a total of $41,901,000 was spent by them on overseas activities.

TABLE 6. GEOGRAPHIC DISTRIBUTION OF 56 AMERICAN MISSION BOARDS' EXPENDITURES OVERSEAS (1954)

Area	Amount	%
Africa	$ 5,769,000	14
Middle East	2,503,000	6
Southern Asia	7,162,000	17
Southeast Asia	7,186,000	17
East Asia	3,280,000	8
Latin America	7,384,000	17
Europe	2,958,000	7
Miscellaneous	5,659,000	14
	$41,901,000	100

It is of interest to note the correlation (and in some instances the lack of it) between the percentage distribution of the Protestant populations in all the underdeveloped areas, and the distribution in those same areas of the missionary boards' personnel and their expenditures, as derived from the previous tables. This is shown in Table 7.

TABLE 7. DISTRIBUTION OF PROTESTANT POPULATIONS AND MISSIONARY EFFORT (1954–58)

	Column A	Column B	Column C
	Protestant Population	American Missionaries	American Mission Board Expenditures
Africa	37%	33%	18%
Middle East		3	8
Southern Asia	17	12	21
Southeast Asia	23	12	21
East Asia	6	14	10
Latin America	17	26	22
	100%	100%	100%

In view of the approximate character of the Protestant population statistics referred to in Column A in Table 7, and the fact that Column B relates to 339 American agencies, whereas Column C relates to only 56, the information in the table is at best only indicative of the situation. Furthermore the percentages do not reflect the support provided by local sources for mission activities in the younger church areas. However, the table does point to two facts previously suggested, i.e., (1) the disproportionately high percentage of expenditures devoted by mission boards to activities in the Middle East in relation to the Protestant population in that area, and (2) the disproportionately low percentage of expenditures in Africa.

At this point some mention should be made concerning the organization of the missionary enterprise. At the apex of the Protestant missions structure is the International Missionary Council (IMC). Organized in 1921, it is composed of some 35 constituent agencies, a number of whom (like the National Council of Churches in the USA) in turn represent many other organizations. The Council's operating budget in 1956 amounted to $141,000. Of this income, approximately three-quarters was contributed by foreign mission boards all over the world, with American boards' contributing two-thirds of the mission boards' share. The Council's American members are asked to contribute to its operating budget each year 0.375% of their annual overseas expenditures, but a number of its members do not always meet their quota.

The IMC has a General Secretary plus three secretaries in London and a like number in New York City; two secretaries appointed jointly with the World Council of Churches, one of whom is in East Asia; a Commission of the Churches on International Affairs (jointly with the World Council of Churches); an international committee entitled The Christian Approach to the Jews; and a Field Representative for Home and Family Life. The Council also publishes a magazine, the *International Review of Missions.*

The function of the International Missionary Council is essentially consultative, i.e., to coordinate the Protestant missionary enterprise in all areas. Its work is climaxed by conferences held at irregular intervals: Edinburgh (1910), Jerusalem (1928), Tambaram, Madras (1938), Whitby, Canada (1947), Willingen, Germany (1952) and Ghana (1957). The reports of these conferences are replete with broadly worded findings on many topics, but it does not appear that a high proportion of those related to theological education are promptly and concretely implemented by the mission boards and the younger churches concerned.

At the IMC's Quadrennial Assembly which was held in Ghana, the Assembly voted to endorse in principle the proposed integration of the IMC with the World Council of Churches. It is anticipated that the merger will be consummated by 1961, at which time a new Division of World Mission and Evangelism will be created within the World Council and which will carry on the activities formerly conducted by the IMC. The head of the new Division will be an Associate Secretary of the World Council of Churches.

Shortly after World War II the IMC and the World Council of Churches (WCC) established a Joint Far Eastern Office in Asia which was concerned largely with ecumenical rather than missionary matters. As a result of two meetings held in Hongkong in 1954 and 1955 by Asian church leaders and mission board executives (notably the Presbyterians USA) the Asia Council on Ecumenical Mission (ACEM) was formed for the purpose of coordinating the individual missionary activities of the younger churches in Asia. The creation of the ACEM was a source of some concern to the IMC and the WCC, inasmuch as the ACEM proposed to engage in activities which the Joint Office in Asia was believed to be fully capable of conducting.

The ACEM commenced operations in the latter part of 1955 with a bishop of the United Church of Christ in the Philippines as Chairman. It has arranged for the sending of two Korean missionaries to Thailand, and a Filipino missionary to Okinawa, etc. During the first year of its operations, the expenditures of the organization amounted to approximately $5,000, largely to pay the travel expenses of its delegates. These funds came from various sources including the UCCP and the Presbyterian Church in Korea, etc.

At a meeting held in 1957 in Prapat, Sumatra, some 105 delegates, consultants and observers from 14 Asian countries and elsewhere, including representatives of the IMC and WCC, agreed to recommend the formation in 1960 of a continuing body to be known as the Eastern Asia Christian Conference (EACC) whose functions would be largely the same as those of the ACEM. The EACC hopes to raise a general budget of $24,000 for an expansion in operations, of which hopefully the IMC and WCC would provide $17,000 and the member churches and councils of Asia $7,000.

With respect to the various foreign missionary associations within the United States, Table 5 discloses the predominant importance in this field of the agencies which are members of the Division of Foreign Missions (DFM) of the National Council of Churches. In 1957 the DFM mission boards received 54% of the total income of all the American mission agencies and maintained 42% of the total number of American missionaries in the field.

On the other hand, it is also of interest to note that in the four-year period 1952–56 the proportion of DFM missionaries decreased from 50% to 43%. In 1956 member agencies of the DFM sent out a total of 631 more missionaries than they did in 1952. But in 1956 all the other North American Protestant boards and agencies sent out 4,170 more missionaries than four years previously.

The management of the DFM is exercised through an Executive Board under which are many "standing" and "special" committees. Of these, the two main groups are:

5 Area Committees: a. Africa
                               b. Near East

                      c. Southern Asia
                      d. Far East
                      e. Latin America

6 Functional Committees: a. Christian Medical Council
                      b. Rural and Agricultural Missions
                      c. World Literacy and Christian Literature
                      d. Radio-Audio-Visual Education
                      e. Missionary Personnel
                      f. Associated Mission Medical Office.

In 1956 the operating budget of the DFM itself amounted to $1,445,000, or roughly ten times that of the IMC. Approximately 80% of the Division's financial support is derived from contributions to the National Council of Churches made by the DFM member boards and agencies and specifically designated by them for the work of the Division. The Division requests its members to contribute to the central administrative expenses of the DFM each year 0.5% of their annual overseas expenditures.

The DFM has two main functions. The first is to serve as a conduit through which mission boards and other contributors may transfer their gifts to certain united Protestant activities overseas. An analogy to this is the case of Japan in which the United Church (Kyodan) stated after World War II that it preferred to receive its contributions from overseas through one agency. Accordingly the interested boards in the Division established an Interboard Committee for Japan through which most American support for the Kyodan Church is channeled. It should be added that Japan is perhaps not a typical situation, inasmuch as most of the missionary boards' funds for activities in other countries are sent by them directly to the responsible committees or organizations concerned.

The second and most important function of the Division of Foreign Missions is to coordinate the planning of the agencies and mission boards of the churches which are either affiliated with or are members of the National Council. The effectiveness and the planning which is done by the Division reflects the personality of the secretaries and the historical factors which resulted in the formation years ago of the committees which later were merged to form the Division. For example, the Committee on Cooperation in Latin America (which has 37 member agencies and was founded in 1916, thereby antedating the National Council by several decades) has been concerned with many matters, including the preparation of curricula for Protestant grade schools and formulating answers to the comments made by Latin American Roman Catholics against them.

The Executive Secretary of the DFM is not in a position to exercise full authority over some of the area and functional committees in the Division inasmuch as the activities of these committees are often financed primarily by the designated contributions of the individual mission boards. Furthermore, the DFM cannot issue directives, nor can it prevent a mission board from entering into or discontinuing any activity it chooses.

There is no need to discuss in detail here the activities of the Evangelical Foreign Missions Association of North America (EFMA—home office, Washington, D. C.), the Interdenominational Foreign Missions Association of North America (IFMA—home office, New York City), of the Associated Missions of the International Council of Christian Churches (AMICCC—home office, Cleveland). The members of these three associations reported an aggregate income of $38,532,000 in 1957 and supported an aggregate of 11,441 missionaries in 1958. Thus, with a total income of only 46% of that received by the members of the DFM, the three associations nevertheless support a larger number of missionaries (11,441 vs. 10,977). This is accounted for by the fact that the members of these three associations are not interested primarily in supporting institutional services overseas such as hospitals, colleges, etc. The member agencies of the EFMA, IFMA and AMICCC are generally so individualistic and inflexible in their concepts that their coordinating organizations exercise little or no control over them. In 1950 the operating budget of the EFMA amounted to only $39,000. The income of their member agencies is obtained principally from individual contributors having conservative religious outlooks. Only a comparatively few of these agencies are interested in training an indigenous ministry overseas, and such interest as they have is usually manifested in support given to small Bible schools, frequently of low scholastic standing. The EFMA, IFMA and the AMICCC are unwilling to cooperate closely with the DFM.

Among the completely independent denominational foreign mission boards, only one requires detailed comment at this point. The activities of the Southern Baptist Convention in the mission field are of interest, particularly because this denomination is so "isolationist" in its policies that the extent of its work overseas is not widely recognized. In 1954 the total "givings" of this church for all purposes (including the upkeep of local parishes in the United States) amounted to $305,574,000. In 1955, one-quarter of the total income of its foreign mission board was contributed by sources in the State of Texas. The Convention is devoting approximately 4% of its total givings for overseas mission activities. In the same year this Board maintained 1,020 foreign missionaries plus an additional 4,677 "national" personnel, of whom 985 were ordained. In the near future it anticipates the number of its foreign missionaries will rise to 1,750, of whom one-third will be assigned to Latin America. Of the 16 Southern Baptist seminaries now operating in Africa, Asia and Latin America, all but half a dozen or so appear either to have been founded in the years 1950-53 or were upgraded from

Bible institute to seminary status during these same years. A separate list of these schools is contained in Appendix B.

The power of the purse as exercised by the individual mission boards is manifest. Table 8 discloses the very substantial annual income placed at the disposal of the leading mission boards in the United States in 1957. Only those agencies are listed which report that they support at least 100 missionaries from the United States who are stationed overseas. On this basis 55 out of the 324 boards in the United States are qualified to be included in the list.

TABLE 8. INCOME OF THE LEADING FOREIGN MISSION BOARDS AND AGENCIES IN THE USA (1957)

	1957 Income (Thousands)	Number of Mission-aries[b]	Coordi-nating Organi-zation
Denominational (35)			
Southern Baptist	$14,209	1,186	
Methodist	14,038	1,453	DFM
Seventh-Day Adventist	12,819	2,000	DFM
United Presbyterian USA	10,676	1,293	DFM
Assemblies of God	3,835	676	EFMA
United Lutheran	3,702	542	DFM
Presbyterian US	3,576	504	DFM
Christian and Missionary Alliance	3,352	822	EFMA
American Baptist	2,804	407	DFM
Congregational Christian (American Board)	2,687	353	DFM
Protestant Episcopal	2,570	395	DFM
Church of the Nazarene	2,405	367	EFMA
Lutheran Church—Missouri Synod	1,831	241	DFM
Evangelical United Brethren	1,682	143	DFM
Conservative Baptist Foreign Mission Society	1,668	368	EFMA
Baptist Mid-Missions	1,664	479	AMICCC
Disciples	1,506	242	DFM
Reformed Church in America	1,120	158	DFM
Evangelical and Reformed (United Church of Christ)	1,182	143	DFM
Evangelical Lutheran	1,071	315	DFM
Association of Baptists for World Evangelism	1,044	212	AMICCC
Christian Reformed	947	181	EFMA
Augustana Evangelical Lutheran	829	217	DFM
Free Methodist	738	148	DFM
American Lutheran	712	132	DFM
Evangelical Covenant Church of America	562	145	DFM
Mennonite Brethren	450	199	EFMA
Mennonite Board of Missions and Charities	415	170	DFM
Pilgrim Holiness Church	378	109	
General Conference Mennonite Church	377	125	DFM
Church of the Brethren	372	110	DFM
Evangelical Free Church	367	136	EFMA
United Missionary Society	219	108	EFMA
Eastern Mennonite	198	130	DFM
World Mission Prayer League (Lutheran)	171	108	

TABLE 8.   INCOME OF THE LEADING FOREIGN MISSION BOARDS AND AGENCIES
IN THE USA (1957)   (cont'd)

	1957 Income (Thousands)	Number of Mission-aries[b]	Coordi-nating Organi-zation
Nondenominational (22)			
Evangelical Alliance Mission	$2,488	764	IFMA
Sudan Interior Mission[a]	2,215	1,071	IFMA
Oriental Missionary Society	1,223	162	EFMA
Wycliffe Bible Translators	1,190	705	IFMA
Africa Inland Mission	962	492	IFMA
Salvation Army	942	112	
World Gospel Mission	765	166	EFMA
China Inland Mission[a]	578	281	IFMA
World Radio Missionary Fellowship	574	106	IFMA
New Tribes Mission	564	388	
Central American Mission	490	168	IFMA
Unevangelized Field Mission	443	203	IFMA
Latin America Mission	431	123	IFMA
Gospel Missionary Union	429	201	IFMA
South Africa General Mission[a]	300	203	IFMA
Far Eastern Gospel Crusade	295	134	IFMA
International Missions	251	131	IFMA
European Evangelistic Crusade	238	109	IFMA
West Indies Mission	235	132	IFMA
International Child Evangelism Fellowship	226	114	EFMA
South America Indian Mission	221	112	IFMA
Worldwide Evangelization Crusade	204	189	EFMA

NOTE: [a] An international agency
having an American branch.
[b] As of 1958.

It is of interest to note that in terms of their income available for foreign missionary activities, the Southern Baptists (with $14,209,000 in 1957) head the list, followed closely by the Methodists. Of the 55 agencies listed, 25 had 1957 incomes which were in excess of $1,000,000. There are a number of other American missionary agencies having an annual income of more than $1,000,000, but these are not included in the list because the nature of their activities is such that they either have none or fewer than 100 Americans stationed in the field.

The affluence of the individual American foreign mission boards as compared to their European counterparts may be judged by comparing the figures in Table 8 with those in Table 9. The latter lists the annual expenditures (actual and estimated) in a typical recent year of the leading foreign missionary societies and countries in Europe and the British Commonwealth. From this comparison it will be noted that there are three foreign mission boards in the United States (the Southern Baptists, Methodists and Seventh-Day Adventists) each of whose expenditures in 1957 were larger than the aggregate expenditures of all the leading missionary societies in Great Britain. On the other hand, such a comparison is not necessarily indicative of the relative quality or importance of the work being done by these boards and societies.

TABLE 9. ANNUAL EXPENDITURES OF THE LEADING PROTESTANT FOREIGN
MISSIONARY SOCIETIES AND COUNTRIES IN EUROPE AND THE BRITISH COMMON-
WEALTH (1953–57)

British Missionary Societies[a]		
Methodist Missionary Society		$2,253,000
Church Missionary Society (Low Anglican)		1,529,000
Society for the Propagation of the Gospel (High Anglican)		877,000
London Missionary Society (Congregational)		780,000
Baptist Missionary Society		642,000
Church of Scotland Foreign Missions Committee (Presbyterian)		450,000
Universities Mission to Central Africa (Anglican)		308,000
Other Societies, etc. (estimated)		4,271,000
	Subtotal	$11,200,000
Continental Missionary Societies[b]		
Netherlands Reformed Church		$ 624,000 [c]
Paris Evangelical Missionary Society[e]		506,000
Basel Mission		496,000 [g]
Berlin Mission		241,000 [d]
Danish Missionary Society		290,000
	Subtotal	$2,157,000
European Countries		
Sweden		$3,456,000
Norway		2,299,000
Denmark[f]		349,000
Switzerland[g]		679,000
	Subtotal	$6,783,000
Canadian Missionary Societies		
United Church of Canada		$2,495,000
Anglican Church of Canada		1,052,000
Canadian Baptist Foreign Mission Board		561,000
Pentecostal Assemblies of Canada		490,000
Presbyterian Church in Canada		451,000
Other Societies, etc.		947,000
	Subtotal	$5,996,000
Australia and New Zealand		
Australia		$1,128,000
New Zealand		883,000
	Subtotal	$2,011,000
	Total	$28,147,000

NOTES: [a] Average annual expenditure (1953–55).
[b] Fiscal year not specified, presumably 1955.
[c] Ordinary and capital expenditures
exclusive of governmental and
special subsidies.
[d] Expenditures in South Africa and
Tanganyika only.
[e] Serves most of the Protestant denominations in France, notably the
French Evangelical Reformed
Church.
[f] Exclusive of the Danish Missionary
Society.
[g] Exclusive of the Basel Mission.

In addition to mentioning the diversity of organization and the magnitude of
resources of the over-all missionary enterprise, it is also worth noting briefly the
increasingly sharp impact which is now being made upon mission activities by
the rising tide of nationalism among so many of the countries in Africa, Asia and
Latin America. Within the limited time in which this Survey has been compiled,
no attempt has been made (nor would such be appropriate) to evaluate the progress and current status of all the elements comprising the missionary enterprise
as a whole. On the other hand, since theological education is such an integral
part of this effort, an observer of foreign missions and seminaries cannot help but
note the constantly increasing difficulties under which missionaries overseas are
working. Thus while the number and expenditure of such missionaries are currently at an all-time high, the orbit in which their operations are being permitted

to continue is constantly shrinking. Numerous instances of this trend in recent years could be cited, particularly the collapse five years ago of the missionary enterprise in China which formerly was America's major mission field.

The following is a sample of half a dozen news items culled from those which have appeared in dispatches published in 1956 alone:

1. The debacle of the British and French invasion of the Suez Canal area resulted in the enforced withdrawal of many of their missionaries from Egypt and some other Near Eastern countries.

2. In May, 1956, the Sudan Minister of Education announced that the Government would soon take over all Christian missionary schools in the South Sudan.

3. In India it is reported that missionary organizations are not allowed to open new centers or institutions without the permission of the Government of India. They cannot set up new work for which additional foreign personnel has to be engaged. Existing institutions may expand but the opening of new branches must have the Government's permission.

4. In the summer of 1956 the Government of Madhya Pradesh (formerly the Central Provinces in India) published a report made by the Investigation Committee headed by M. B. S. Niyogi (the former Chief Justice of the Nagpur High Court) in which it is stated: "A vile (Christian) propaganda against the (Hindu) religion of the majority is being systematically . . . carried on. . . . This increase (in American missionary personnel in India) is obviously due to the deliberate policy of the International Missionary Council to send evangelistic teams to areas of special opportunities in some of the newly independent nations." While the Committee is reliably reported to have been composed of persons selected because of their known anti-Christian views, and their findings were discredited with the Central Government because of the procedures followed during the hearings, nevertheless the Niyogi report was the subject of wide discussion and may be indicative of the trend of thinking on the part of many Indians.

5. In Ceylon the Commission of the All-Ceylon Buddhist Congress recently complained bitterly concerning the fact that a majority of Buddhist children on the island are being educated in Christian schools and demanded that all educational facilities be vested in the State.

6. In Burma there is a rigid screening of all missionaries before a visa is granted. No non-Burmese missionaries are allowed to work in the unevangelized tribal areas. This has obliged the Baptist Church in Burma (350,000 members) to reconsider its whole home missionary program.

In the minds of multitudes of Africans and Asians the activities of foreign missionaries are, in all probability, rightly or wrongly considered as a vestige of a dying or extinct colonialism. This equating of missionary activity with Western imperialism is a heavy handicap for the European and American missionaries in their work.

As examples of the trends in the missionary world, two comments relating to the African scene might be cited. The first is by Mbonu Ojike, a Nigerian (which appears in his book *My Africa* published in New York in 1956): "For the good of humanity a gradual withdrawal of Western missionaries from Africa is highly desirable. . . . At present the idea of Western Christian missionaries is comparable to that of European imperialists—to perpetuate Africa as a child who must be led by the adult hand. Unless the Western Church is practicing religious imperialism, it will now leave African churches to be ruled and administered freely by African Leaders." The second statement is by Dr. George W. Carpenter, formerly Secretary of the Africa Committee of the DFM : "The fact that missionaries are of the same race and often of the same nationality as the foreign rulers in colonial Africa, and that the Gospel has been couched in Western terms, involves serious consequences. To the African it all seems foreign. . . . The rise of nationalism and African self-consciousness expose the danger of these identifications. But it is clear that nationalists have no time for fine distinctions, they lump us all together and reject us for our foreignness. . . ."

It is not suggested that all of the recent developments in the foreign mission field are adverse, as those cited above; nor can extracts chosen at random from the newspapers and elsewhere be regarded as presenting a balanced picture of the situation. On the other hand, it does not seem unreasonable to envision the possibility that in the next two or three decades considerable numbers of foreign missionary evangelists may come to be withdrawn from Africa and Asia, voluntarily or involuntarily.

The growing pace at which events are moving in the underdeveloped countries is recognized by the mission boards. However, for a variety of reasons they do not seem to be able voluntarily to redeploy their personnel and activities to a significant extent in order to take advantage of opportunities which arise when changes in the political and social scene overseas occur. All too often Christian strategy appears to be determined by external events rather than as a result of the initiative and planning of the churches.

It is against this background of a fragmented Protestant missionary effort, annually spending large sums of money in countries where nationalism is seething and Communism is on the march, that one may appraise the effort being made to train the future ministers of the younger churches.

CHAPTER 2

AFRICA

A. NORTH OF THE SAHARA

This area, along with the Middle East, is the heartland of Islam, from which religion it has always been the most difficult for Christianity to gain converts. Of the 23,000,000 population of Egypt, 90% are Muslims, and less than 10% (i.e., approximately 2,000,000) are members of the Coptic Orthodox Church. The only Protestant denomination of importance in the country is the Evangelical Church in Egypt which now has approximately 30,000 members and a community of 60,000 persons.

The strength of Islam is due to a combination of several factors. As Dr. Glora Wysner has pointed out, "Islam has made its appeal to the African because it has been presented to the Africans by Africans and is looked upon as an African religion, while Christianity is looked upon as a 'foreign' religion." Officially sponsored radio stations in Egypt have broadcast to other countries in Africa the theme that Islam is the true religion for the black races while Christianity is the religion of the whites.

Islam is gaining in Africa because it often seems easier for a pagan to become a Muslim than to become a Christian. Christianity is a complex doctrine for Africans to appreciate easily. Furthermore, it can be something of a disruptive force in a tribal society because of its stress on the spiritual importance of the individual. The Koran is explicit and concrete in its doctrine, in general permits its believers to have more than one wife, and draws no color line in the Mosque. Islam is spreading south of the Sahara as commerce and trade with northern Africa continue to increase. In Central Africa south of the Sahara the number of Muslims is said to be about equal to the number of Christians.

The fountainhead of Islam is the University of Al-Azhar in Egypt which was founded in Cairo almost a thousand years ago in the year 970. It was reported in 1957 to have as many as 25,020 students enrolled in institutes in 14 different locations in the country (Assiut, Cairo, etc.). These students were engaged in studies ranging from the secondary to the graduate level. Instruction is free and pupils receive modest cash allowances for their maintenance. Some 3,798 students were said to be enrolled in the three university faculties of the Arabic language, Islamic jurisprudence and theology. Among the Institutes two are noteworthy: The Islamic Mission Institute (3,826 students) and the Queraat Institute (for the study of the Holy Koran—438 students).

Approximately 2,000 of the students at Al-Azhar are said to come from 25 foreign countries, and in recent years young Muslims from Central and East Africa have been encouraged to attend the University in order that the prestige of Islam and Egypt may be increased throughout Negro Africa. In 1953 the University sent out 112 professors and teachers to serve in other Muslim countries. According to one estimate, since 1945 the Al-Azhar has sent out 2,000 Muslim missionaries to various parts of Africa.

The majority of the Protestants in Egypt are said to be converts from the Greek Orthodox and Coptic Orthodox Churches rather than from Islam. It is stated that the loss of Christians converted to Islam each year in Egypt is comparatively large (while in Africa south of the Sahara the loss of Christians to Islam is very small). Put in a different way, it appears that in a typical year in Egypt more Christians become Muslims than vice versa. During the past 60 years the percentage growth in the number of Egyptian Protestants has been less than the comparable increase in the number of Roman Catholics or even that of the population as a whole.

There is only one Protestant seminary in Africa north of the Sahara, as shown in Table 10.

TABLE 10. THEOLOGICAL SCHOOLS IN AFRICA NORTH OF THE SAHARA (1957)

		Approx. Number of		
		Full-Time	Theol.	Denominational
Name	Location	Faculty	Students	Support
Evangelical Seminary	Cairo	2[a]	25	Coptic Evangelical

NOTE: [a] Plus part-time faculty.

Evangelical Seminary: The President of this institution, the majority of the voting members of its faculty and almost all of its students are Egyptians. Founded by the United Presbyterians in Cairo in 1863, the school was later transferred to Assiut for 20 years and then moved back to Cairo. Nearly all of the Seminary's financial support now comes from the Coptic Evangelical Church of the Nile Valley. The latter is an indigenous body which for nationalistic rather than ecclesiastical reasons formally separated itself in 1958 from the United Presbyterians. (The latter denomination merged with the Presbyterians USA in 1958.)

The Evangelical Seminary has been offering a three-year course to graduates of high schools. The school's academic standards are not high, and it is said to have been adversely affected by the general decline in the educational level as a whole which has taken place in Egypt during the past decade.

Some of the Seminary's students occasionally take courses at the American University in Cairo, particularly to improve their knowledge of the English language. At one point it was proposed to link the courses at this school with those at the University into a four-year curriculum at the end of which a student would be awarded an A.B. degree. However, the plan did not prove to be successful, in part because the University's admission standards were higher than those of the Seminary.

This school has always been quite conservative in its theological outlook, and one gathers the impression that it has the atmosphere of a lonely outpost rather than that of a dynamic educational institution.

B. EAST AFRICA

Part I of the *Survey of the Training of the Ministry in Africa* sponsored by the International Missionary Council deals with the seminaries in East and West Africa. It was written by Bishop Stephen Neill, formerly the Anglican Bishop of Tinnevelly in India, who during the past decade has been active in the London office of the IMC and was formerly an Associate General Secretary of the World Council of Churches. In 1950, Bishop Neill visited most of the institutions training men for the ministry in East and West Africa. In his report a number of thoughtful comments are made concerning the curricula offered to African theological students, but few statistics are given as to the size of the schools' faculties or student bodies. The author has little or nothing to say concerning what it would cost to carry out his recommendations.

The membership of the more important Protestant churches in East Africa is approximately as shown in Table 11.

The theological schools in East Africa are listed in Table 12.

TABLE 11. MEMBERSHIP OF PROTESTANT CHURCHES IN EAST AFRICA (1956)

	Kenya	Uganda	Tanganyika
Population	6,000,000	5,000,000	7,500,000
Protestant Community	300,000	450,000	300,000
Churches			
Anglican	40,000	100,000	100,000
Lutheran			100,000
Presbyterian	20,000		
Friends	20,000		
Moravian			20,000

TABLE 12. THEOLOGICAL SCHOOLS IN EAST AFRICA (1957)

Name	Location	Approx. Number of Full-Time Faculty	Approx. Number of Theol. Students	Denominational Support
Sudan				
Bishop Gwynne College	Mundri	4	20	Anglican, Presbyterian, etc.
Kenya				
St. Paul's United Theological College	Limuru, Nairobi	3	25	Anglican, Presbyterian, etc.
Uganda				
Bishop Tucker Theological Seminary	Mukono, Kampala	8	40[b]	Anglican
Buwalasi Diocesan College	Mbale	5	35	Anglican
Tanganyika				
St. Cyprian's Theological College	Namasakata, Tunduru	2	18	Anglican
St. Phillip's Theological College	Kongwa	2[a]	28	Anglican, Moravian
Makumira Lutheran Theological School	Makumira, Arusha	4	55	Lutheran
Total: 7[c]		28	221	

NOTES: [a] Plus part-time instructors and lecturers. [c] See also Table 70A, Supplementary List of Theological
[b] Plus students at lower level of training. Schools.

1. *Sudan*

Bishop Gwynne College: This Anglican Seminary was established by the Church Missionary Society in 1944 and opened in 1946. According to Rev. David Brown (who was appointed in 1954 to serve as its principal),

Bishop Gwynne College is at Mundri in the Moru district of Equatoria Province (approximately 100 miles from the Uganda border). The College is built on a slight hill, close to the main road from Juba to Nzara and to Wau. The soil is not good and although plantations and gardens have been planted their growth is hindered by lack of water. Students come from most of the southern tribes and a few from the Nuba Mountains. . . . Students come for a year's preliminary Bible training which aims to help them to be better witnesses in their own employments, whether as teachers, dressers or the like. Alternatively there is a vocational course which gives a man the opportunity to test his vocation to the ministry. The two years deacons' course is followed by a year's parish work as deacon, after which a further year's training is given before ordination as priest. Not all these courses are given in any one year. Students attend the college with their wives and any children up to school age, after which the children are expected to stay in their schools as boarders. Each family is given a three-roomed cottage; bachelors in due course will sleep in dormitories and dine communally. . . . It is not easy for students from many different tribes to become a united community — the Zande and Moru tribes fought their last great battle at Jebel Mundri little more than fifty years ago. . . ."

In 1958 a special course for government teachers was inaugurated by the College at the request of the Ministry of Education. These teachers were to be given instruction and training in how to teach Christianity and the Bible to students in government schools. The College also added one member to its faculty in order to extend its "apprentice schools" which take students on tours to villages where they engage in preaching and evangelism.

Since 1954, Bishop Gwynne College has been offering joint training courses for the ministry with the American Mission in the Upper Nile. The latter has been supported on a denominational basis by the United Presbyterians (USA), the Reformed Church in America, and the Coptic Evangelical Church in the Nile Valley. In 1957 the Mission became the Church of Christ in the Upper Nile.

2. Kenya

St. Paul's United Theological College: One of the oldest of the seminaries in East Africa is St. Paul's United Theological College which is located in Limuru, a residential suburb of Nairobi, the capital of the colony. In 1896 the Church Missionary Society founded St. Paul's Divinity School, and for many years it served as the seminary of the Anglican diocese of Mombasa in Kenya. Some time after its establishment, the Church of Scotland and the English Methodists commenced to send students to the school. In 1927 it was suggested that the training of the Presbyterian and Methodist students should be conducted jointly with the Anglican seminarians, but the plan was not carried out. Thus for many years it was necessary to maintain within the seminary's premises two technically separate institutions with two principals, independent arrangements, and to a large extent different planning in their curricula. Twenty-two years later, in 1949, joint training of the students was started on a trial basis. After six years of this experiment, plus two more spent in "constitutional deliberations," in July 1957 the formal ratification of the College's new constitution took place. Thus the history of this institution reflects in microcosm the travails and progress of the Protestant missionary effort as a whole.

Some of the students at St. Paul's come from Tanganyika. A three-year course for ministers is offered. The school has been strengthened as a result of its multidenominational support, but it is still not a strong institution. In the fall of 1958 St. Paul's had only three men on its faculty (one of whom was about to go on furlough). The seminary is situated on an attractive campus but is beset by financial stringencies. It is also said to have been benefited by the realization on the part of some of its faculty members that the revolt of the Kikuyu tribesmen in the 1952–56 Mau Mau incident (an estimated 14,000 killed, 62,000 imprisoned, and 1,000,000 persons resettled in 850 new villages) calls for a fresh approach to the study of Christianity and its relevance to life in Africa today.

3. Uganda

Bishop Tucker Theological Seminary: Virtually all of the Christians in Uganda are members of either the Roman Catholic or the Anglican Churches. Bishop

Tucker College, located at Mukono, is the stronger of the two Anglican seminaries in Uganda.

Writing in 1955 the Principal of the Seminary (Rev. John V. Taylor of the Church Missionary Society) commented that this institution is

primarily a theological college though it also contains a separate teacher training department. At present the theological college contains five separate classes of students. The old style senior catechists (we call them lay readers) are given a year's training in the vernacular. The new style lay readers, young men of 20, fresh from the Secondary School Standard 3 or 4, are given two years' training in English after which they will go to specially chosen clergy to help in their parishes especially with the youth work and evangelism for two years or three, before coming back to the College for ordination training. Then we have the old style ordinands, mostly vernacular lay readers or school teachers, who study for ordination in the vernacular, and the new style ordinands, more highly educated men who can be taught in English, though we never allow them to drop the vernacular for their essays and discussion work. Both these classes of ordinands come for a two years' course and bring their wives and youngest children with them. They live in a model village and the unit of our training is not the individual pastors but the Christian family which is to go out as witnessing agent. Finally we have what is always the toughest and most difficult class of all, the deacons who have already done two years' work after their first ordination and who return to the College for two terms before they are ordained as priests.

Thus a student's theological training at this Seminary may be spread over eight or nine years divided between academic studies and practical work in the field. The school has an excellent program whereby its faculty and students are brought into contact with local churches over weekends, or for periods of a week at a time, studying their needs and opportunities at first hand. Other faculty-student teams visit catechetical schools periodically for the same purpose. The caliber of the Bishop Tucker faculty is said to be good, but the multiplicity of their courses and activities places an unduly heavy burden upon them.

According to the warden of this school, Rev. D. K. Nsubuga, writing in 1958,

the annual operating budget of the Seminary is 2,500 pounds to sustain a student body of up to seventy-five men. This money is raised and contributed by the Diocese of Uganda. Apart from the allowances for missionary staff members all (this) money comes ultimately from the pockets of our village Christians. . . . Unfortunately, the Seminary budget is not sufficient to provide many articles of equipment that we need. The following things would assist us tremendously in our task: a tape recorder, typewriter, mimeograph machine, adding machine, money to buy additional text books, a sound motion picture projector, a tractor for the Seminary farm and a station wagon to deliver students, teachers and priests to far away places where, for lack of transportation, no work is now being done. But we thank God that the day-to-day running of the Seminary has been seen and accepted as the responsibility of the Diocese itself.

The Bishop Tucker Seminary, like most of the theological schools in East Africa which are supported by Anglican missionary societies, receives little or no financial assistance from the latter for its budgetary needs. The societies' annual aid is usually contributed in the form of faculty personnel provided by them. The local dioceses and churches are thus more concerned and involved with the day-to-day needs and operations of the seminaries than they otherwise might be. While this has many advantages, the concomitant is that the schools' capital needs are often beyond the available resources of the local churches. In the fall of 1958, for example, the roof of the classroom building at Bishop Tucker College had fallen in to the point where one classroom was no longer available for use, and the prospect was that the remaining classrooms might also have to be abandoned. The estimated cost of the necessary repairs was said to be approximately $1,000—a sum which apparently could not be raised within the diocese, even on an emergency basis. Consequently, in the absence of special support from abroad, the school was contemplating the possibility of closing for a period of six months or so in order to be able to accumulate the needed repair funds within its own regular budget.

Buwalasi Diocesan College: This Anglican institution is located at Mbale in the Upper Nile area of Uganda. Bishop Neill recommended that the theological education of Anglican ordinand students should be concentrated at Bishop Tucker Seminary and the training of catechists at Buwalasi. His recommendation was not fully carried out, in part at least because of the rapid increase in recent years in the number of converts to Protestantism in this area. The Buwalasi school is, however, concentrating the bulk of its efforts on training catechists, for which there is a strong demand.

4. *Tanganyika*

St. Cyprian's Theological College: Tanganyika is a large, sparsely settled territory in which Protestant missions are widely scattered. St. Cyprian's trains theological students sent to it from the three Anglican dioceses in Tanganyika (Zanzibar, Masasi and Southwest Tanganyika) which are supported by the Universities Mission to Central Africa.

St. Phillip's Theological College: Often known simply as the Kongwa College, this Anglican seminary is located in a town of that name which is 60 miles east of Dodoma, the capital of the central province of Tanganyika. According to Bishop Alfred Stanway of the Diocese of Central Tanganyika,

Kongwa College was founded somewhere at the turn of the century. In those days some men would be brought in and trained and then there would be a period before others were brought in. Since 1927, however, it has had a permanent existence training clergy and evangelistic teachers. Of recent years, except for an occasional short evangelistic course, it has been used for the training of clergy and has always had a full time European Principal plus an African priest and others helping, as well as visiting lecturers.

Our usual plan now is to start a course and men stay in for two years and then go back after being out for a refresher course. We try and get a full batch and in the intervening year we send some candidates to Limuru and others to Australia and England.

The present course, which began in 1957 and ends in 1958, is a combined course with the Moravian Mission of the Southern Highlands and the Moravian Mission of Tabora. It consists of an equal number from both missions, fourteen from this Diocese and fourteen from the Moravians.

Makumira Lutheran Theological School: This institution was founded in 1947 at Lwandai in the Usambara Mountains and was transferred to the Makumira Estate on the Usa River near Arusha in northeastern Tanganyika in 1954. The seminary has good building facilities, and its faculty consists of four full-time instructors (a Swede, Finn, American and an African). The School offers a three-year course and is a joint institution for all the Lutheran missions working in Tanganyika. About two-thirds of its financial support comes from Lutheran churches in America. In the period 1954–57 the School's faculty was increased from two to four, and its enrollment was expanded from about a dozen students to the present number (55). The 10-year plan for the seminary (1957–66) calls for an enrollment of 55 students annually until 1960, at which time the total will be increased to about 70. Ultimately the entering classes will have 34 students each. During this decade it is estimated by the Lutherans that an aggregate of 168 men will be graduated, or an average of about 17 a year. This suggests that the attrition rate in the seminary is expected to be in the neighborhood of 30–40% of each entering class. The Lutherans' projections for Makumira constitute one of the few examples of this type of long-range planning which one can cite. The seminary as a whole is one of the strongest in East Africa.

5. *General Comments*

The principal recommendation for East Africa in the 1950 IMC report was based on a unanimous conclusion of a conference of theological teachers convened by Bishop Neill when he visited Mukono in Uganda. This was that the next step forward in theological training in East Africa should be the setting up of one church theological college to serve the churches in the three territories. This theological college, it was suggested, should be located near to, but in complete independence of, the new University College which was then being formed at Makerere, near Kampala in Uganda. The new college would not replace the two schools operating in Uganda, and it was agreed that such a college could not successfully be maintained, except as a united effort of the Churches. It would require a staff of four qualified theological teachers who hopefully would be supplied by the Anglicans, Lutherans, Methodists and Presbyterians. Although "it was frankly recognized that the creation and maintenance of such a college would make heavy financial demands upon the Churches," it was felt that such a college should nevertheless "start work sometime in 1953."

No concrete action was taken in the period 1950–58 by the mission boards and churches concerned to implement this recommendation. At a conference of Anglican missionaries held in May 1956 at St. Paul's Theological College in Limuru it was suggested (1) that the courses at St. Paul's in Kenya and those at the Lutheran seminary at Makumira in Tanganyika should be coordinated; and (2) that a certifying board should be established to set up curriculum standards for seminaries in East Africa. But no agreement was reached whether advanced theological training should be offered at Limuru in Kenya or at Makerere in Uganda. In the discussion there were two different schools of thought concerning the future needs of the theological schools in East Africa. The delegates from Kenya gave first priority to postordination training for special situations, i.e., rural or urban work, whereas those from Uganda emphasized the need to improve the training furnished students before their ordination. In the words of one observer, "as both schemes call for considerable staff and finances, they can be said to be in conflict (with each other) for they are in competition for the same resources."

Meanwhile the Lutherans held an All-Africa Lutheran Conference at Marangu on the slopes of Mount Kilimanjaro (near Arusha) in Tanganyika in November 1955. Approximately 116 African Lutheran delegates were in attendance. They were asked: "What are the burning issues facing the African churches today?" The matter of theological education was agreed to be the most urgent. The African laymen present stated they believed their pastors were not sufficiently trained. After two days they unanimously resolved: "The African delegates feel that it is very desirable that an institution for advanced theological education be established as soon as possible in Southern Rhodesia, Liberia or Ethiopia. . . ." The Africans did not suggest that the institution should be solely Lutheran. A delegate from Sweden, Dr. Bengt G. M. Sundkler (coauthor of Part II of the IMC Survey) recommended the Lutherans start a school offering a postordination course of two to three years, possibly at a master's degree level, but not leading to a doctoral degree. It was felt that such an institution might be organized in East Africa or possibly in connection with the new University at Salisbury (Southern Rhodesia) with a faculty of two professors and a select group of some 12 to 15 students. Subsequently it was decided that the courses (seminars) should be given at Marangu, and an addition to the local hotel building was constructed for this purpose. The first seminar is to commence in February 1959 under the direction of a German missionary professor. He will be assisted by a full-time young American tutor and by lecturers from Europe and America who will stay at Marangu for periods of from three to six months each. The seminars will serve as a postordination refresher course for experienced pastors coming from Lutheran missions in various parts of East, West, Latin and Southern Africa.

Makerere College, which is located on Makerere Hill on the outskirts of Kampala in Uganda, was favored in 1950 by Bishop Neill as the site near which a new, independent theological college should be established. Founded in 1922 as a technical school, Makerere now has six faculties (arts, sciences, medicine, veterinary science, agriculture and education). In 1949 the College was enabled to grant degrees through an examining arrangement established with the University of London. Now also known as the University College of East Africa, Makerere is reported to have received a total of £1,087,223 ($3,044,224) for its capital needs in governmental grants in the period 1945–55 under the terms of the Colonial Development and Welfare Acts. From other nongovernmental sources it is stated to have received an additional £1,010,000 ($2,828,000) during the period 1949–54. In 1957 the College had a full-time teaching and research staff of over 90 persons. One-third of its students come from Kenya, a third from Uganda and a third from Tanganyika. The College's operating expenses are defrayed by the governments of these territories in the same proportion. Its enrollment has been steadily increasing, with a total of approximately 700 students in residence in 1957 (compared to 500 in 1955). By 1970 or thereabouts it is hoped that 2,000 students will be enrolled.

These statistics related to Makerere are cited as an indication of the strong growth in secular education at the college level which has taken place in East Africa since World War II. This has been made possible through the substantial grants received by the College from the British Government and from private foundations in Great Britain and the United States. The recent growth of Makerere is in sharp contrast with the very small progress made in improving the theological schools in East Africa during this same period.

In 1956 Makerere established a Department of Religious Studies within its Faculty of Arts. The Department offers two series of courses, "A" and "B," which are taught by the Roman Catholic and Protestant chaplains respectively. Each lasts three years and leads to the award of a Certificate in Religious Studies. In April 1957, seven Roman Catholic students and one Protestant student successfully completed the first year of the course. Only those students in the College who have previously completed a degree, diploma or certificate course in one of its faculties may take courses in this Department.

One of the problems confronting those who wish to raise the level of theological education in East Africa and elsewhere on the continent is whether this can best be accomplished through (a) strengthening the departments of religion in the university colleges, or (b) moving existing seminaries to plots adjacent to the campuses of the university colleges, or (c) strengthening existing seminaries at their present locations. It has been suggested, for example, that the course "B" at Makerere might be expanded into a full-fledged Protestant faculty of theology with a staff of up to five professors, etc., offering courses leading to a B.A. degree in which theology would be one of three subjects in which a student specializes. Owing in part to a lack of sufficient funds for such use, this proposal continues in the discussion stage. Some of the Lutherans in Tanganyika are inclined to hesitate about sending their students to be trained by a predominantly Anglican faculty in Uganda. Some of the Anglicans in Kenya would prefer to try to improve their present seminary.

C. WEST AFRICA

Nigeria has a population (31,000,000 persons) which is more than 50% larger than that of Kenya, Uganda and Tanganyika combined. It is the most populous individual country in Africa. Poverty and disease are still major problems. There are over 500,000 lepers in Nigeria alone. Nevertheless Nigeria and Ghana are relatively prosperous countries when compared to other areas in Africa. Fifty years ago there was no entity called Nigeria. Today Nigeria is emerging from a colonial status and may achieve its independence by 1960, with Liberia's having done so in 1847 and Ghana in 1957.

The general educational level in West Africa is somewhat higher than in East Africa. In the former region the Christian churches have had a longer history than those in East Africa, primarily as a result of a closer connection with Europe and a more widespread European influence. In the northern, interior portions of Nigeria and Ghana, Islam is strong. The approximate membership of the more important younger churches in West Africa is shown in Table 13.

The theological schools in West Africa are listed in Table 14.

TABLE 13.   MEMBERSHIP OF PROTESTANT CHURCHES IN WEST AFRICA (1956)

	Nigeria	Ghana	Liberia	Sierra Leone
Population	31,000,000	4,000,000	2,000,000	2,000,000
Protestant Community	1,000,000	300,000	50,000	50,000
Churches:				
Anglican	100,000			11,000
Methodist	40,000	60,000	20,000	7,000
Lutheran	38,000			
Baptist	30,000			
Presbyterian	15,000	40,000		
Ewe (Scot. Presb.)		13,000		
Episcopal			5,000	
Evang. United Brethren				3,000

TABLE 14. THEOLOGICAL SCHOOLS IN WEST AFRICA (1958)

Name	Location	Approx. Number of		Denominational Support
		Full-Time Faculty	Theol. Students	
Nigeria				
Trinity College	Umuahia	3	35	Anglican, Presbyterian, Methodist
Theological Training Center	Nyasoso	2	14	Lutheran & Reformed (Basel Mission)
University College, Ibadan, Department of Religious Studies	Ibadan	3	24	(Government)
Immanuel College	Ibadan	6	35	Anglican, Methodist (English)
Nigerian Baptist Theological Seminary	Ogbomosho	10[a]	100[b]	Southern Baptist
Theological College of Northern Nigeria	Jos	[c]	[c]	Sudan United Mission, etc.
Ghana				
University College of Ghana, Department of Divinity	Achimota, Accra	5[a]	24	(Government)
St. Augustine's College	Accra	[d]	[d]	Anglican
Trinity College	Kumasi	4	25	Methodist, Presbyterian
Liberia				
Cuttington College Divinity School	Suacoco, Gbanga	3[a]	3[e]	Episcopalian, Methodist, etc.
Sierra Leone				
Fourah Bay College, Department of Divinity	Freetown	4[a]	9	(Government), Anglican
Total: 9 (in operation)[f]		40	269	

NOTES: [a] Plus others teaching part time or at a lower level of instruction.
[b] Plus other students at lower level of training.
[c] Opening in 1959 (see text).
[d] Closed in 1957 (see text).
[e] See text.
[f] See also Table 70A, Supplementary List of Theological Schools.

1. *Nigeria*

Trinity College: Located at Umuahia in eastern Nigeria, Trinity College is a union school supported by the Anglicans (Church Missionary Society), Presbyterians (Church of Scotland) and the Methodists (British Conference). It was founded in about 1939. A three-year course is offered.

This seminary was visited by Dean Frost (of the Faculty of Divinity at McGill University) who lectured at Trinity for three weeks in 1957. He comments: "The College sets its own entrance examination, the aim being that of university entrance standard but I have strong reservations about its effectiveness. The examination tended to be too factual in a rather narrow, stereotyped manner. Good men I suspect were failed by the examiner because they did not know the right dates or could not master sufficient book-knowledge. . . . The men (students) are intelligent and keen, but their knowledge is second-hand, bookish and unrelated to their experience. The college needs . . . a proper dining hall . . . and more adequate feeding arrangements." Both Bishop Howells and Dean Frost comment that the greatest need at Trinity is to strengthen its faculty.

Of the 35 students enrolled at Trinity in 1957, 28 were Anglicans, three were Methodists and three were Presbyterians. Furthermore there were said to be at least a dozen qualified students who were unsuccessfully seeking to be admitted to the school. They could not be enrolled owing to the shortage of faculty personnel. There are only three full-time teachers on the staff—one from each of the supporting denominations. Many of the students seeking admission come from Anglican churches. It is possible that the Anglicans might be willing to provide a second Anglican teacher on the faculty. However, some of the Presbyterians and Methodists are inclined to believe that if half of the faculty and four-fifths of the students were Anglicans, the seminary would no longer be truly interdenominational in character. This has led to something of a stalemate and provides one more example of the difficulties which sometimes arise in operating a union institution.

Theological Training Center: In 1927, the Basel Mission founded a catechists' school in Nyasoso in the British Cameroons, an area which is now the southeastern portion of Nigeria. In 1952 the Mission established a center for training ordinand students at the same location. A three-year course is offered, and 14 students graduated from it during the period 1954–57. The Basel Mission is a Swiss missionary society supported by Lutheran and Reformed Churches in Switzerland and Germany. In the winter of 1958–59 the European missionary on the faculty was scheduled to go on furlough. Since no replacement was available, the seminary was to be closed down during his absence.

University College, Ibadan, Department of Religious Studies: Ibadan in the western portion of Nigeria has a population of about 500,000 persons and is the largest city in West Africa. The University College was empowered in 1948 to grant degrees in conjunction with the University of London. In 1957 it had 563 students enrolled in over a score of academic departments, and it was predicted that by 1963 the enrollment would total 1,500 students. During the period 1945–55 a total of £1,710,864 ($4,790,419) was contributed to the University College for its capital needs in the form of governmental grants made to it under the terms of the Colonial Development and Welfare Acts.

In 1950 this institution inaugurated within its Faculty of Arts a Department of Religious Studies with one full-time professor and two lecturers (all English). Bishop Neill concluded at that time that the Department would create "more problems than it solves . . . (because) students will not be receiving direct ministerial training planned to fit them for their work as ordained ministers."

In 1957 the Department had a total of 24 students enrolled in courses distributed over a four-year period. While the College's Faculty of Arts awards a B.A. and B.A. Honours degree in a number of fields, it was not until 1958 that the College was empowered to award a B.D. degree (for which the honours course will commence in 1959). It is not likely, however, that the Department of Religious Studies will soon be expanded into a faculty of divinity since the University College is a government institution and Islam is strong in the northern part of Nigeria. On the other hand, the students in the Department of Religious

Studies are receiving theological instruction of a higher caliber than that prevailing in some of the seminaries located elsewhere in West Africa.

Immanuel College: This theological school is located in Ibadan and consists of a merger of two seminaries, Melville Hall (Anglican-Church Missionary Society) and Wesley College (English Methodists), both of which had previously been training students in Ibadan for a number of years.

Bishop Neill commended the excellence of the training provided for theological students at Melville Hall. In 1957 it had a full-time faculty of five and a total of 28 students enrolled in a two-year theological course. It suffered, on the other hand, from inadequate buildings and a lack of sufficient funds with which to build up its staff.

Wesley College was primarily a teacher-training institution with a small seminary attached to it. Between 50 and 100 students planning to be teachers were enrolled in the College in 1957, and it also operated a large high school. A faculty of two persons taught theology to half-a-dozen ordinand students. Dean Frost commented that Wesley College constituted "a good example of how theological training should not be done—though the present Tutor (who had no experience in theological training before going to Nigeria) is making as good a job of his task as the situation allows."

Bishop Neill recommended in 1950 that the theological students at Wesley College should be trained at Melville Hall. Subsequently others suggested that the two seminaries should be merged into the Department of Religious Studies at the University College, Ibadan, in order to form a full-fledged faculty of divinity at that institution. It was felt that the University College might provide a broader training for ministerial students than would an individual seminary, even if the latter were located close to the University's campus. Bishop Neill, however, recommended alternatively the establishment of a church college on a site adjacent to that of the University College but in full independence from it. This was similar to his recommendation for the establishment of a comparable church college near Makerere University College at Kampala, Uganda.

After seven years of discussion and negotiation, the Bishop's recommendation was followed. An agreement was reached whereby commencing on January 1, 1958, Melville Hall and Wesley College would be united under the name of Immanuel College. Immanuel is under the control of a Board of Governors responsible to the synods of the two supporting churches. The same academic courses are being offered to the Anglican and Methodist students, with the classes being held at (the former) Melville Hall. Some of the students may attend lectures at the University, and some of the University's staff occasionally lecture at the seminary. The full-time faculty at Immanuel numbers six, of whom three are Anglican missionaries, two are Methodists and one is African. Of the six, five hold B.A. degrees.

Immanuel offers three courses leading to (1) two-year ordination, (2) a London

University diploma in theology, and (3) a London University B.D. degree. A few Immanuel students are studying for their B.D. degree. Consequently, when the University College, Ibadan, commences its B.D. course in the fall of 1959, this will result in there being two institutions in the same city training men for the London B.D. degree. Since there are only two other institutions in the entire continent of Africa (i.e., the University Colleges of Ghana and Fort Hare) in which nonwhite students may study for a B.D. degree, it would appear to be a needless duplication of effort to have two more such institutions competing with each other in Ibadan.

With a view toward working out a basis for closer cooperation between Immanuel and the University College, a tract of land located about one mile from the campus of the University College was acquired in 1957 as the future site for Immanuel. The cost of the land was shared by the Anglicans and the Methodists. It is estimated that £80,000 ($224,000) will be needed to finance the cost of constructing the new buildings for Immanuel, none of which had been started as of the fall of 1958. Some of this amount might be obtained through the sale of the plant presently occupied by Immanuel, but the total cost of the project seems high.

Nigerian Baptist Theological Seminary: One of the more strongly organized schools in Nigeria is the Nigerian Baptist Theological Seminary located at Ogbomosho, which is on the railroad 50 miles northeast of Ibadan. The Seminary is supported by the Southern Baptists and was established by them in 1897. During its early years the school was "moved around quite a bit . . . being located at various times in Ogbomosho, Abeokuta, Shaki and Oyo. For a while it was combined with the Baptist College, but the two emerged as separate schools in 1938."

In 1955 the Southern Baptist Mission in Nigeria had a total of 189 foreign missionaries serving on its staff, a larger total than in any other country in Africa, Asia or Latin America in which this denomination is conducting missionary activities. In 1957 the Ogbomosho Seminary had a total of 14 persons serving full time on its faculty, of whom about ten were teaching students destined for the ministry. In the same year a total of 163 students were enrolled in all its courses, of whom an estimated 100 were ordinands engaged in theological studies. Thus, in terms of the number of members of its faculty and student body, it is the second largest Protestant seminary in Africa. Its graduates serve in Southern Baptist churches in the Cameroons and Ghana, as well as in Nigeria.

The Southern Baptists report: "In 1948, after several years of experimentation, the Nigerian Seminary became affiliated with the Southern Baptist Theological Seminary, Louisville, Kentucky, thus enabling it to offer the Bachelor of Theology degree. During the centennial celebration of Baptist work in Nigeria in 1950, the Seminary awarded the degree for the first time. Eight men were the recipients." The course of study leading to this degree lasts four years. The Seminary also offers three-year and two-year certificate courses and refresher courses of one year. A women's training department was recently opened, and the wives of students are required to enroll in it. Some attempts have been made by the faculty in recent years to orient the school's curriculum more closely to African as contrasted with Western Christian concepts.

In 1954 a new $120,000 building was completed on the Ogbomosho campus to house the Seminary's administrative offices, chapel, library, and classrooms. This is said to be one of the finest buildings possessed by any Protestant seminary in Central Africa. In recent years three new dormitories for married students, a dining hall and a new student center have also been erected.

While the theological outlook of this school is conservative, its officials have nonetheless been active in the past in promoting the work of the Christian Council of Nigeria.

Theological College of Northern Nigeria: This institution was planned to be opened in January 1959 and a site in Bakuru near Jos was purchased for this purpose. Bishop Neill advocated the establishment of one united theological school to serve all of northern Nigeria, an area in which the influence of Islam is strong. This College has been founded to meet this need.

According to Dr. Frank Short, the proposed new school is being supported by

the five Sudan United Mission branches in Nigeria, the Church of the Brethren Mission and, almost certainly, the Dutch Reformed Church Mission in Nigeria. . . . The purpose is to take the ordinands to a higher level than at present so that they can cope with the more educated folk who are now in the congregations. Two courses are pictured, viz., the Diploma Course will recruit from those who have finished Secondary School, or have a higher Elementary Teaching Certificate; and the Certificate Course will recruit from a somewhat lower level than that, though higher than is at present customary in Northern Nigeria. The College will be interdenominational and the teaching staff will be drawn from a number of Church backgrounds. It is expected that the College will begin with at least three members of staff.

The Sudan United Mission is an association of several missionary societies with headquarters in London. It has a branch in the United States which is a member of the Interdenominational Foreign Missions Association of North America (IFMA).

2. *Ghana*

University College of Ghana, Department of Divinity: The University College is located at Legon Hill, Achimota, which is near Accra, the capital of Ghana. The College was established in 1924 and thus has been in existence for a considerably longer period than either of the University Colleges at Makerere in Uganda or Ibadan in Nigeria. Organizationally the College at Achimota is patterned after Cambridge University in England. In 1957 it had a total enrollment of approximately

400 students. Degrees are granted in conjunction with the University of London. During the period 1945–55 a total of £400,000 ($1,120,000) was contributed to the College for its capital needs in the form of governmental grants under the terms of the Colonial Development and Welfare Act. This and other financial support has enabled the institution to create a beautiful campus situated on the rolling country-side, with formal gardens, reflecting pools, etc. Its buildings are designed according to a relatively expensive style of architecture.

Since the University College was founded, it has continuously maintained a small Department of Divinity within its Faculty of Arts. In 1957 the Department had 16 students enrolled in it, of whom 11 were studying for an A.B. degree (preparatory to their B.D. work) and five were taking theological courses. Of the latter, two were enrolled in the four-year B.D. course. Partly owing to the closing of St. Augustine's College in 1957, and partly as a result of active recruitment of students undertaken by the Department's faculty, the number of B.D. candidates in the fall of 1958 rose to 24. Eight of these were planning to be ministers, and 16 expected to become teachers in secular schools.

Several visitors to the University have commented on the comparatively high quality of the instruction given in this Department. On the other hand, it has been training only a small number of theological students, possibly due in part to its relatively high standards. Rev. Christian G. Baëta, who is the Senior Lecturer in the Department, was a coauthor of Part II of the *IMC Survey of the Training of the Ministry in Africa.*

The costs of operating the Department of Divinity have been defrayed entirely from the University's over-all budget to which the Government contributes annually. No mission board or local church in Ghana supports the Department, and its influence on the other seminaries in the country has been small. One problem which may arise is whether the Government will wish to continue to subsidize its cost. So far, there has been no threat to close the Department, but the majority of the government leaders are not practicing Christians and are said to be highly nationalistic in their outlook. It has been suggested that if the mission boards were to volunteer a modest amount of support over and above the government subsidies to the Department, such action might tend to forestall the Government from cutting off its support of the Department.

St. Augustine's College: Originally this Anglican seminary was located in Kumasi. With a faculty of one missionary (plus occasional part-time assistance) it has not had more than half a dozen students enrolled in it at any one time. Supported by the Society for the Propagation of the Gospel, the seminary according to one observer carried on a tradition "of a rather extreme Anglo-Catholicism." Its admission standards were lower than those maintained at the other theological schools in the country.

In 1954 or thereabouts the Anglicans decided against having any link with Trinity College in Kumasi and moved St. Augustine's to Accra where its classes were held for two or three years in the bishop's house. This was done partly at the insistence of some of the African members of the Anglican Church and partly because more Anglican priests were available in Accra to serve as part-time lecturers. Later, some of the university-grade ordinands were sent to the Department of Divinity at the University College of Ghana for their training; and the Society for the Propagation of the Gospel offered to provide free training at Kelham Theological College in England, to any qualified theological student (below university grade) from Ghana who could afford to defray the transportation costs involved. In 1957 two African students were enrolled at Kelham (which grants no degree), but it was recognized that this arrangement would be useful for only a small number of students. Accordingly late in 1957 St. Augustine's was finally closed and its students are now being sent to the University College at Achimota.

The fate experienced by St. Augustine's is indicative of the trends which are prevailing in Africa today.

Trinity College: This seminary was founded in 1942 in Kumasi, which is the second-largest city in Ghana and the capital of the Ashanti region some 150 miles northwest of Accra. The College is a union institution formerly known as Wesley College. The earlier seminary was supported by the English Methodists. The English Presbyterians formerly maintained a catechists' school at Akropong, 35 miles from Accra, which they established in 1848. In 1942 they decided its graduates should receive their theological training at Trinity College in Kumasi. Accordingly the Presbyterian Church of Ghana and the Ewe Presbyterian Church (which has an evangelical, Calvinist tradition) now share in the support of this school.

In the decade leading up to the proclamation of Ghana's independence in 1957, it was realized that the long-term future of Trinity College would be far better assured if it were moved to or near the campus of the University College at Achimota. Furthermore Trinity's site in Kumasi had become noisy and somewhat unsuitable. It was hoped that it might be possible to enlist the cooperation of St. Augustine's College in Kumasi for such a move, but the Anglicans declined to enter into such a venture and moved their College to Accra in 1954 on their own accord. Another factor which delayed matters was the thought that if Trinity were to build a new campus near the University College, the style of its buildings should conform to those belonging to the University. This would have entailed an expenditure far in excess of the resources of the seminary's supporting church bodies which were available for this purpose.

Accordingly in 1956–57 the College's long-range program was reviewed. New architectural plans were drawn up by a missionary architect along simpler lines, though in conformity with the general plans of the University. The new cost estimates were considerably lower than the original ones. This encouraged the Methodists and Presbyterians to apply for, and obtain, a tract of land from the University which it is leasing to the seminary at a token rent of one shilling a year. Trinity will move to the new site whenever sufficient funds can be obtained to construct the new buildings for its campus. The latter would have a dormitory capacity of approximately 60 students, housing facilities for six faculty members, four classrooms, a chapel seating 200 persons, administrative offices, a library, dining hall, etc.

The total cost of the new project is estimated at £100,000 ($280,000). Toward this amount the three supporting churches in Ghana have set for themselves the task of raising £47,000 in the three-year period 1958–60; and in mid-1958 they had made a start toward attaining their goal.

According to Rev. G. Thackray Eddy, Chairman and General Superintendent of the Methodist Church in Ghana,

the union theological college will be established under its own administration, and initially no relationship, academic or otherwise, with University College itself is being planned. Whether some kind of relationship between the theological College and University College will emerge, we and the University authorities feel it wise to leave to the future. But it will be obvious, for example, that the right to read in the University College library, and the presence within the University of a Department of Divinity whose staff is engaged in theological teaching and research, and is wholly sympathetic to our needs, will provide the theological College with a stimulating environment.

One of the difficulties in engendering a close working relationship between Trinity and the University College's Department of Divinity arises as a result of the higher academic standards maintained by the latter. The Department's B.D. graduates tend to enter into teaching careers in the field of religion, whereas Trinity's emphasis has been placed on educating pastors, many of whom serve in rural areas. Furthermore the salaries paid to the Department's faculty are higher than those paid by Trinity to its faculty members.

One plan which has been suggested as a means of linking the academic effort of the two institutions while Trinity is still located at Kumasi calls for the latter to divide its students into two groups. The first might spend half a year or so at Kumasi and then the remaining three or four years at Achimota studying for a B.D. degree. The second, less capable and more numerous group of students would remain for the full three-year course at Kumasi.

General Comments: Both Rev. Christian Baëta and Rev. Peter K. Dagadu (Secretary of the Christian Council of Ghana) comment on the difficulty which the churches in Ghana are currently having in recruiting capable young men to choose careers in the ministry. With the withdrawal of the British administrative and technical personnel, most of the better trained young students in the country are seeking careers in government and industry in order to replace the Europeans. Formerly a number of ministers were recruited each year from the ranks of school teachers, but the recent expansion in the nation's educational system has tended to dry up this source of ministerial candidates also. The problem is said to be a serious one.

3. Liberia

Cuttington College Divinity School: A number of sources consider Cuttington College and Divinity School to be the best general educational institution in Liberia today. The College was named after Robert Fulton Cutting of New York City who made a $5,000 gift in 1888 to the Protestant Episcopal Mission Board in order to establish it. From that year to 1929 it was operated as a high school and school of theology at Cape Palmas in the southeastern coastal area of the country. One of its former students was President William V. S. Tubman, and the College established an excellent record in developing leaders for the country.

In 1929 the College and its Divinity School were closed: its buildings had become so dilapidated that they were unsafe for use, and funds to repair them were not available. The institution remained closed for 20 years. In 1949 it was reopened at Suacoco, largely on the initiative of a Negro bishop, Dr. Bravid W. Harris, Missionary Bishop of Liberia of the Protestant Episcopal Church. Collaborating with him in this project was a Negro Bishop of the Methodist Church in Liberia, Dr. Willis J. King.

The Episcopalians decided that Cuttington, when reopened, should be located in a more healthful area. Accordingly a 2,000-acre tract situated at Suacoco was purchased. Suacoco is at a 1,500-foot elevation, some 125 miles inland from Monrovia, "a four-to-six hour drive, depending on the weather." Inasmuch as some of the work at Cuttington is in agriculture, the College now has 1,500 acres planted in cocoa, coffee, rubber, Nigerian palm oil and citrus trees. Its catalogue states that "these crops are expected to contribute heavily to the support of this institution in later years." The institution has 19 concrete buildings, the total cost of which has been approximately $500,000, of which the Episcopalians have contributed the major share.

Of the 96 students at Cuttington in 1957, 91 were studying in its Liberal Arts College, and approximately one-half of them were reported to be Episcopalians. In 1955 the Divinity School had about 15 theological students enrolled in it. This number dropped to five in 1957 and three in 1958 but was expected to recover to nine in 1959 and remain at that level for several years.

Students are required to have completed at least two years of study in the College (or its equivalent elsewhere) before being admitted to the seminary. The Divinity School awards a B.A. degree (major in theology) and a B.D. degree, the latter requiring three years of postgraduate work after the A.B.

The College as a whole has a well-trained staff of 16 teachers and grants B.A. and B.S. degrees. The Episcopalians have three and the Methodists one missionary assigned to the Divinity School faculty. Of the four men, three are serving full time. The Methodists have plans under way to build a student building and a missionary home on the campus. The Lutherans have not as yet been willing to cooperate in supporting the seminary. However, they recently decided to join with the Episcopalians and Methodists in establishing a new hospital and nurses training school within one mile of Cuttington and also are proposing to build a school for missionary children on the Cuttington campus. It is hoped that ultimately the Baptists may join in the work at Cuttington also.

4. Sierra Leone

Sierra Leone is the oldest mission field of the Protestant churches in tropical Africa and is the one in which these missions have in a number of respects made the least progress. The country is small and backward, and the Protestant community is still less than 3% of the total population. This failure is partially due to the influence of Islam in the north and east, and to social distinctions which exist between the Africans residing in the colony of Sierra Leone and those living within the Protectorate in the interior.

Fourah Bay College, Department of Divinity: The only seminary in Sierra Leone is the Department of Divinity at Fourah Bay College which is located in the capital, Freetown. The College as a whole has had, in the words of Bishop Neill, "an erratic and glorious career, but its downs have been more frequent than its ups."

Founded in 1827 by the Church Missionary Society (Anglican) as a training college for African teachers, catechists and ministers, it subsequently added other departments, and its curriculum became primarily secular in content. In 1876 it entered into an affiliation with Durham University in England for the purpose of granting degrees.

As the 1955 report of Ruth Sloan Associates points out, until 1948 Fourah Bay was the only place in British West Africa where a student could obtain a university degree in residence. "In 1947 the college was unendowed; the Sierra Leone Government paid only £200 towards the expenses of its degree courses; the finances remained the responsibility of the Church Missionary Society. . . . In 1944, Fourah Bay College, with only 17 students (in all its departments) was in a sad state." The Elliott Commission recommended in that year that Fourah Bay become "a territorial college of Intermediate University Status. . . . A national protest movement resulted. A Fourah Bay College Fund Committee . . . was formed to organize country-wide support. . . ." Finally an agreement was reached whereby the College would become partly "a college of arts, science and technology" and in part a "university college." Whereupon a Colonial Development and Welfare grant of £350,000 ($980,000) was made to Fourah Bay for its new construction needs.

In 1954 there were a total of 357 students enrolled in the College as a whole, of whom only nine were undergoing ministerial training. Since then the number of theological students has fluctuated between six and nine. Some of the students are being sent to Fourah Bay by the Evangelical United Brethren Church mission.

The four full-time faculty members in the Department of Divinity are said to be well qualified for their tasks but have a teaching load of 56 hours a week. Their time is divided between teaching and giving lectures in four courses: (1) a four-year undergraduate course in religious knowledge leading to the Durham B.A. degree in general studies, (2) a two-year postgraduate degree leading to the Durham diploma in theology, (3) a three-year course for students who have not completed secondary school but wish to prepare for the ministry, and (4) lectures in religious education.

Dr. Theodore L. Tucker (who visited Fourah Bay in 1958) comments that one of the principal difficulties is persuading the graduates of the Department to accept very low-paying careers in the church when far more lucrative positions with the Government are available to them.

D. LATIN AFRICA

Part II of the *IMC Survey of the Training of the Ministry in Africa* discussed the seminaries in the majority of the countries in Latin Africa listed in Table 15. They were visited in 1953 by a commission of which the Chairman was Dr. M. Searle Bates, Professor of Missions at Union Theological Seminary, New York City. The other three members were Rev. Christian G. Baëta, Senior Lecturer in Theology at the University College of Ghana; Dr. Frank Michaeli, Professor of Old Testament in the Faculté libre de théologie protestante de Paris, which is supported by the Reformed Church of France; and Dr. Bengt G. M. Sundkler, Professor of Missions and of Church History in the University of Upsala in Sweden. The report which they wrote is concerned primarily with curricula content and the philosophy of religious training, etc. Only five of its 95 pages deal with seminaries as individual entities. Little data is furnished concerning student enrollments or faculty personnel, and no financial information is supplied.

1. *Dahomey*

The combination of Muslim influence among the natives in the northern (Saharan) portion of French West Africa and the strength of the Roman Catholic Church supported by the French colonists and officials living in the coastal regions

TABLE 15. THEOLOGICAL SCHOOLS IN LATIN AFRICA (1957)

Name	Location	Approx. Number of Full-Time Faculty	Theol. Students	Denominational Support
Dahomey				
Protestant Seminary	Porto Novo	2	6	Methodist (English)
Cameroons				
Protestant Theological School	Ndoungue	2[a] [d]	29[d]	French Evangelical Reformed Church, Baptist
Dager Biblical Seminary	Bibia, Lolodorf	6[d]	27[d] [e]	Presbyterian (USA, Cameroons)
Lutheran Seminary	Meganga	2	8	Lutheran (various)
Belgian Congo				
Pastors School	Kimpese	3[c]	21[d]	Baptist (American, English, Swedish)
Springer Institute	Mulungwishi	4[b]	15	Methodist (USA)
Pastors School	Bolenge	4[a]	20	Disciples, etc.
Morrison Institute	Kabinda	2	15	Presbyterian US
Ruanda-Urundi				
Diocesan Divinity School	Ibuye, Ngozi	1[a] [d]	10[d]	Anglican
Angola				
Emmanuel Theological Seminary	Dondi, Bela Vista	4[a]	20	Congregational, Methodist, etc.
Mozambique				
Theological College	Vila de João Belo	1[a]	10	Anglican
Union Seminary	Ricatla	3[a]	15	Swiss Reformed, Methodist
Madagascar				
Ambatomanga Theological School	Tananarive	2[a]	32	French Evangelical Reformed Church
Arivonimamo Theological School	Tananarive	3	13	English Quakers
Ambohipotsy College	Tananarive	2[a]	25	English Congregational
Imerimandroso College	Lake Alaotra	3	25	English Congregational
Fianarantsoa College	Fianarantsoa	2[a]	13	English Congregational
Ivory Theological College	Fianarantsoa	8	78	Lutheran
St. Paul's College	Ambatoharanana	2[b]	6	Anglican
Total: 19[f]		56	388	

NOTES: [a] Plus part-time faculty.
[b] All part-time.
[c] The assumed equivalent of nine part-time teachers (see text).
[d] 1958.
[e] Plus students at a lower level of training.
[f] See also Table 70A, Supplementary List of Theological Schools.

do not make this area an attractive field for Protestant missionary work. Health conditions have also been bad. One result is that many of the Protestant missionaries working in French West Africa have been sent there by the more independent and fundamentalist American agencies.

Protestant Seminary, Porto Novo: The small, old and weak theological school at Porto Novo is supported by the Methodist Missionary Society of Great Britain. It was closed in 1953 but subsequently was reopened. Some thought has been given in the field to forming a new union institution to be sponsored by the Methodists, the Paris Missionary Society (French Evangelical Reformed Church) and some of the conservative missions active in West Africa. It would be located at Abidjan, the capital of the Ivory Coast, and would serve the three French colonies of Dahomey, Togo and the Ivory Coast. At present the Evangelical Church of Togo sends its ministerial candidates to be trained at the French Reformed Seminary in Ndoungué.

2. *Cameroons*

In the Cameroons, the autonomous Cameroon Presbyterian Church has about 75,000 members, and the Reformed Evangelical Church (of French background) has about 65,000 members.

Protestant Theological School: This seminary is supported by the French Evangelical Reformed Church and is located at Ndoungué near Nkongsamba about 100 miles northeast of Douala. It was originally established in 1921 at Douala and was moved to Ndoungué in 1926. In 1935 its name was changed to "École de théologie," and in 1937 the two-year course was lengthened to three years. The School was closed in 1939 and reopened in 1947. The seminary's course of studies was being extended to four years commencing in October 1958. Two men were serving full time (and one man part time) on its faculty in 1958. Most of its students come from the Cameroons, with a few from Gabon and Togo. Following their graduation they are usually ordained after a period of two to four years' practical experience in the field.

Dager Biblical Seminary: The Dager Biblical Seminary was organized in 1922, and its buildings were erected in 1926. By 1931 it had four full-time instructors, a number which was not exceeded until 1958. In 1954 its course was extended from three to four years.

The Dager Seminary is supported by the Cameroon Presbyterian Church and the Presbyterians USA. It is located at Bibia, Lolodorf, not far from the French Reformed seminary at Ndoungué. The two schools had a combined total of 56 theological students in 1958 and eight full-time faculty members, of whom three were Africans. Both schools teach the Calvinist tradition in the French language. Nevertheless these two seminaries have long been in the doldrums because it has never been possible to work out a basis of cooperation between them, and the two mission boards supporting them were unwilling to increase their contributions unless they did cooperate.

In 1955 the Dager Seminary was visited by Dr. Charles T. Leber, General Secretary of the Presbyterian USA Foreign Mission Board who reported on it as follows:

The facilities . . . particularly the faculty and student hovels (I cannot call them residences), are not only deplorable and degrading but a shame upon the Presbyterian Church. Shacks in a low-type refugee camp are better. Standing on the campus of the only theological seminary of the Presbyterian Church in the Cameroun, we thought of the beautiful and well-equipped Princeton Seminary campus (in the USA) and the new million dollar library that is to be built in the name of Robert E. Speer. And we wondered. We wondered, too, that, still after many years, indecision as to a proposed union with the French Reformed Church Seminary has been drawn out so as to contribute to the desolate conditions at Dager. And wondered, too, at the 55 relatively new buildings at (the medical station at) Batouri, when we looked shamefully at Dager. What price strategy?

The situation illustrates the power exerted by the missionaries in the field over their own home boards. In this instance the French Evangelical missionaries are said to consider their neighboring Presbyterian USA missionaries as "rich outsiders" operating in French territory where French missionaries are short of funds. They also consider the American Presbyterians are "modernists." It is stated by some observers that some of the American Presbyterians in the Cameroons are critical of the French missionaries because the latter smoke tobacco and drink wine.

In October 1956 the Dager faculty was seriously depleted by furloughs, and the Seminary needed $20,000 to renovate its dormitories. Since something had to be done about the situation, it was planned at one point to move this Seminary in 1957 to Libamba where the Presbyterians have been operating the Cameroons Christian College, a secular institution at the high school level. However, the situation subsequently improved. The number of full-time faculty members rose from two in 1956 to six in 1958, and the theological students from 12 to 27. The Seminary also purchased a plot of land on the edge of Yaoundé, the capital of the Cameroons, to which it would like to move its campus.

The Cameroons are scheduled to become fully independent in 1960. The following passage appeared in the 1956 annual report of the Presbyterian USA Foreign Mission Board:

French Camerouns, as all parts of Africa, is being flooded with literature of every description. Anti-colonial attacks concocted in East Berlin find their way by devious routes to Cameroun; articles published in Budapest are flown to Yaoundé, the capital of the country. . . . Revolt broke out during the month of May (1955) and military forces were called upon to suppress the rioting, resulting in several deaths and many injuries. Tanks patrolled the streets of Yaoundé and Douala for several days and curfew was imposed in troubled areas. . . . It could be expected that in the medical services of the Mission this universal restlessness would be least apparent. On the contrary, that was where violence was first experienced when the Sakbayeme Hospital had to be closed for two months in 1954 because of union disturbances. . . . Union organizers, generally under the direction of the nationalist movement, seek to organize the teachers and militantly attack Mission and Church as enemies of progress. . . . During the Easter vacation this year a group of these (native) teachers (in missionary grade schools) assembled to form an organization of their own, outside the national labor union, still loyal to the Church but indicating their desire to be free from ecclesiastical control. The unsettling atmosphere created by much of this activity has impaired the effectiveness of classroom work.

The "partial" answer of the Presbyterian missionaries in that colony to meet this situation is of interest. The report states : "A partial answer to this problem was the creation of a mobile unit composed of two missionary women who visited many of the schools, some of them located in almost inaccessible villages, where they were entertained by the teachers and their families, and conducted courses in teaching methods."

Lutheran Seminary, Meganga: This school was first opened in June 1958. It is supported by the Norwegian Missionary Society and by two Lutheran church bodies in Minnesota, the Evangelical Lutheran Church (Minneapolis) and the Lutheran Brethren Mission (Fergus Falls). The Seminary is one of the first joint Lutheran ventures in which the Lutheran Brethren Mission has participated. Their interest stems from the fact that they (along with the Norwegian and the Evangelical Lutherans) have been active in missionary work in the Northern Cameroons, including the operation of one or two Bible schools. The new Seminary is located at Meganga, near Ngaoundere in the Ganga Mountains area. Meganga is a smaller town than Ngaoundere but was chosen as the site for the school because it is centrally located in relation to the various Lutheran mission stations in this part of the Cameroons and because some buildings were available there which could be used for this purpose. A four-year course is offered. A Norwegian and an American missionary are serving on its faculty. One of their principal long-term problems is dealing with the increasing Muslim influence in this district originating from the Lake Chad and the Sudan areas. The local kings and tribal chiefs are generally Muslims, and their people are for the most part pagans. It is among the latter that the missionaries usually obain their ministerial candidates.

3. *Belgian Congo and Ruanda-Urundi*

In the Belgian Congo and Ruanda-Urundi there are approximately 16,000,000 people of whom about 1,100,000 are members of the Protestant constituency. Roman Catholics outnumber Protestants by about four to one. The Protestant constituency in the Belgian Congo is shown in Table 16 .

TABLE 16. MEMBERSHIP OF PROTESTANT CHURCHES IN THE BELGIAN CONGO (1956)

Baptists	80,000
Presbyterians	80,000
Disciples	80,000
Seventh Day Adventists	48,000
Methodists	30,000
Christian and Missionary Alliance	25,000
Covenant	25,000
Anglicans	20,000
Conservative Baptists	14,000

Some idea of the extent of the foreign missionary activity in *secular* educational work in the Congo may be gained from the fact that Protestant missions administer 9,400 schools and Roman Catholic missions operate approximately 14,500. From 1922 to 1954 the Government pursued a policy of furthering the education of the Congolese through mission schools. However, in 1955 the Government reversed this policy and is now developing a long-term program of promoting lay schools in urban and rural areas. The Methodists report that increases in Government subsidies to mission schools will be kept to a minimum and that eventually subsidies will be reduced.

There are over 1,650 Protestant foreign missionary personnel assigned to 280 main stations in the Congo. These missionaries are maintained by numerous organizations, including the Africa Evangelistic Band; the American Baptist Foreign Mission Society; the Association of Free Churches of Norway; the Berean African Missionary Society; the Baptist Missionary Society (British); Unevangelized Fields Mission; the Methodist Church, Board of Missions; Worldwide Grace Testimony; the Presbyterian Church in the US, Board of World Missions; the Svenska missionsförbundet (Swedish Congregationalists); the United Christian Missionary Society (Disciples of Christ); the Evangelical Mission Covenant Church of America; the Salvation Army; the Belgian Society of Protestant Missions to the Congo; the Westcott Mission; Pentecostal Missionary Union of Great Britain and Ireland; the Africa Inland Mission; the Assemblies of God; the Christian and Missionary Alliance; the Christian Missions in Many Lands (Plymouth Brethren); the Congo Evangelistic Mission; the Congo Inland Mission; the Congo Balolo Mission of the Regions Beyond Missionary Union; the Seventh Day Adventists; the World Gospel Mission; Svenska baptist missionen (Swedish); American Mennonite Brethren; the World-Wide Evangelization Crusade; the Church Missionary Society; Danish Baptists; Evangelical Mission of the Ubangi; British and Foreign Bible Society; Free Methodist Church of North America; Friends Africa Gospel Mission (Kansas); and Svenska friamissionen, etc.

Thus Protestantism.

In contrast to the extensive, fragmented and variegated activities of the Protestant missions in the field of secular education, medical training and evangelism in the Congo, it is of interest to note that there are only four small and comparatively weak Protestant seminaries for the training of Congolese ministers. These schools are maintained by older and larger mission boards inasmuch as the more evangelical and smaller missionary groups prefer to concentrate their activities in the Congo along other lines.

Pastors School, Kimpese: The Pastors School at Kimpese (École de pasteurs et d'instituteurs) is on the railway line one-third of the way from Matadi to Leopoldville. The seminary was founded in 1908 and is maintained by the American, British and Swedish Baptists. It has two divisions, one concerned with the education of ministers, and the other with training secular school teachers. A second and adjacent institution is engaged in training nurses and medical assistants. In addition there are primary, secondary, adult and trade schools maintained as part of this educational complex. The total number of the faculty at all the units at Kimpese is 20, of whom one is a Congolese. These faculty members divide their time teaching the courses in their own field which are given at the various schools. Thus the Pastors School has no full-time teachers and nine part-time teachers. A four-year course is offered by it.

In June 1958 there were a total of 825 students in all the Kimpese schools. Of this number only 21 were enrolled in the Pastors School, and the latter is having some difficulty in maintaining even this level of enrollment. In the past the seminary has had to suspend its theological course from time to time owing to a lack of applicants. At the meeting of the School's Board of Managers in July 1956 it was noted with regret that there were only 11 candidates for the "cours de théologie."

This seminary was one of the pioneering institutions in providing training for all members of the students' families, rather than for the ministerial candidates alone.

In 1957 the School's capital needs were as follows:

Classroom	$10,000
Auditorium	5,000
Power line to new dam on Inkisi River	10,000
Equipment	5,000
	$30,000

Springer Institute: The Springer Institute at Mulungwishi is maintained by the American Methodists. It is located on an 1,800-acre tract at a 3,600-foot elevation, 110 miles north of Elizabethville in the Haut Katanga province (the center of the uranium mining area) in the southeastern corner of the Congo. The school is quite remote from the other seminaries in the colony and is supported by two Congolese Methodist conferences which are 1,000 miles apart. It offers a three-year course at a high secondary level, and its faculty of four is said to be in need of strengthening, particularly since all serve part time only. The Springer Institute is located adjacent to the Congolese Christian Institute which trains teachers for secular schools. There is some interchange of faculty between the two institutions.

Pastors School, Bolenge: This seminary is located a few miles from Coquilhatville in the northwestern corner of the colony, some 650 miles up the Congo River from its mouth. The School is supported by the Disciples, the Swedish Baptists, etc. It was founded later than the Pastors School at Kimpese and, like the latter, its four-year course is said to be at a high secondary level.

Morrison Institute: Formerly a Bible school located at Bulape, the Morrison Institute was moved several years after World War II to Kabinda in the central Congo where it would be closer to the center of the colony's population. At that time its curriculum was upgraded to a theological school level. The seminary is supported by the Presbyterians US.

A four-year course is offered, of which three years are spent in studies. The fourth (intervening between the second and third years of study) is spent in internship or field work in Luluabourg, a city which is 125 miles from Kabinda. An unusual feature is that during this "clinical year" the seminary students spend one-half of their time assisting in pastoral and youth work in individual churches; the remaining half is devoted to courses in church administration, religious education, etc., which are conducted for them by missionaries residing in Luluabourg. The success which has been achieved in this way has caused the seminary to contemplate the possibility of moving its campus to Luluabourg.

Diocesan Divinity School: Located at Ibuye near Ngozi (50 miles northeast of Usumbura) in Ruanda-Urundi, this seminary was founded by the Anglican Mission in Uganda prior to World War II. The emphasis of its training is said to be on the evangelical aspects of the ministry. In addition to educating ten theological students in 1958 the school was also conducting a catechists course for 24 students. The generally low educational level in Ruanda-Urundi has made it difficult to upgrade the work being done at this institution.

General Comments: In July 1956 the first Consultative Conference on the Training of the Ministry in Africa was held in Leopoldville. It was sponsored by the IMC and the Africa Committee of the DFM and was the first such conference held in Latin Africa devoted solely to this purpose. Most of the 17 delegates represented Congolese seminaries of various denominations. Among the recommendations of the Conference were: "(1) . . . That the teaching, direction, financing and planning of the theological schools (in the Congo) be undertaken jointly by the missions. . . . (2) That . . . there . . . be a union theological seminary of an advanced academic standard, comparable to similar institutions elsewhere, to serve the Protestant Church in all the French-speaking areas of Central Africa." The Africans present were particularly in favor of these recommendations. Even the Southern Baptist missionaries voted for them. But no decision was reached as to where such a union seminary should be located, or which school might be built up to serve as such, or whether it should be a new institution altogether.

The second Consultative Conference was held from May 29 to June 1, 1958, at Douala in the French Cameroons. It was concluded that a union theological seminary should be established at Yaoundé, the capital of the French Cameroons. Its purpose would be to train ministers for French-speaking Africa at a level which would be above that of the existing seminaries in the Cameroons. Entering students would be required to have passed their baccalaureate (school-leaving certificate after seven years in the secondary school) or its equivalent. It was believed that the institution should be located near a center of learning and in an area with a large Protestant population. The first site choice was Yaoundé because it may become a university town and is centrally located in relation to other French-speaking areas in Central Africa. The suggestion was made that at least half of the teaching staff should be French speaking. The course of study would be of four years' duration. It was hoped that the date of the opening of the seminary might take place in either 1960 or 1961. The first estimate of the capital cost of the proposed institution was $240,000. The second made by the Conference noted that after "taking into consideration the increase in prices and other factors, it would be necessary to allow . . . $360,000" for the establishment of the seminary. It was hoped that five-sevenths of its annual operating budget would be defrayed by mission boards active in French West and Equatorial Africa (including the Cameroons) and two-sevenths by mission boards working in the Belgian Congo.

The Conference report also states that the delegates from the Belgian Congo suggested Elizabethville and Leopoldville as the site for the proposed seminary. However, it was concluded that these cities were too remote from French territories. Another factor was the belief that the students from the Belgian Congo who would be qualified to enter the projected theological school would be very few in number as compared to those coming from other areas. Nevertheless the Douala Conference concluded that "the founding of a faculty (seminary) at Yaoundé implies the opening as soon as practicable of a second faculty to be situated in the Belgian Congo to meet the needs of students when they are in sufficient numbers. . . . In order to avoid any discrimination between these two faculties, they are to be considered as sister institutions and to be governed by one and the same governing body."

The capital costs involved in establishing a new union theological seminary at Yaoundé seem high, without even taking into consideration the possibility of a similar institution being founded in the Congo in the next few years. In the case of Yaoundé a complicating factor is the desire of the Cameroon Presbyterian Church to devote its resources to moving the Dager Biblical Seminary to the plot it had previously purchased at Yaoundé for this purpose: some elements in that Church would accord first priority to strengthening Dager in its new location and then devote their remaining available resources (if any) to the proposed union institution in that city. Here again problems remain to be solved if duplication of effort is to be avoided, not only at Yaoundé but also between the Protestants in the Cameroons and those in the Congo.

4. *Angola*

Emmanuel Theological Seminary: In 1934 the American Congregational mission established a ministerial and catechists' training course at Dondi in central Angola. By 1947 it had developed into a small theological school. It was also supported by the United Church of Canada. Meanwhile the American Methodists had also been active in Angola, having maintained a Bible school at Quessua, about 300 miles away. Conversations between these boards over a period of several years finally led to the Methodists' joining in supporting the school at Dondi as of September 1957 (and the changing of its name to Emmanuel Theological Seminary). Its full-time faculty was increased from three to four, and the enrollment of its theological students rose from 15 to 20. Furthermore the outreach of Emmanuel, which formerly was limited to training ministers for the Ovimbundu people (approximately 1,500,-000), has now been extended to include theological education for the Kimbundu people in Angola (1,000,000 persons) as well. Of the four teachers on its faculty, two are Africans. Considerable effort is being made to provide training for all the members of the students' families. The school's plant facilities are said to be comparatively good.

5. Mozambique

In Mozambique the total population of this large Portuguese colony is only 6,-500,000 persons. The Protestant community numbers 50,000. The Church of Christ in Mozambique (Methodist and Swiss Evangelical) has 20,000 members, and the Anglicans 15,000.

Union Seminary: The Union Seminary is located at Ricatla, a mission station of the Swiss Reformed Church which is 16 miles north of Lourenço Marques, the capital of Portuguese East Africa. The Swiss Mission in South Africa had trained groups of ministers from time to time in Mozambique but lacked the resources to develop this pastors school at Ricatla into a full-fledged seminary. For over a decade plans were discussed for forming a united institution by bringing in the American Methodists. The Swiss Mission was to provide the land, some vacant buildings and sufficient funds for rehabilitating the latter. The project was delayed for several years because the Methodists criticized the plans on the grounds that an insufficiently advanced course of studies would be offered. Then staffing difficulties arose, and it was not until November 1957 that a final agreement was reached. The Seminary was to open in March 1958 with a full-time faculty of three plus three part-time professors. A four-year course was planned, of which the first year would be at a pretheological level. The American Board (Congregational Church) and the Church of Manica and Sofala are also contributing toward the costs of the school and are each sending one or two students to be trained there. An enrollment of 15 students was envisaged.

6. Madagascar

In the fall of 1956 a survey of the Protestant ministry in Madagascar was made by an international team sponsored by the IMC. Its members were:

1. Dr. Charles W. Ranson, General Secretary, IMC; Chairman of the Commission,
2. Dr. Fridtjov Birkeli, Director of the Department of World Missions, Lutheran World Federation (Geneva),

3. Dr. Frank Michaeli, Professor of Old Testament, Free Faculty of Protestant Theology (Paris), and

4. Rev. T. Rasendrahasina, General Secretary, Imerina Synod of the London Missionary Society (Tananarive).

The survey noted that Protestant missionary activities in Madagascar have been carried on principally by five denominations:

1. The Friends Foreign Mission Association (Society of Friends), Great Britain,
2. The London Missionary Society (English Congregational Church),
3. The Lutheran Church of Madagascar (and its associated Norwegian and American missions),
4. La Mission protestante française (Paris Evangelical Missionary Society), and
5. The Anglican Church of Madagascar.

The population of Madagascar amounts to approximately 4,700,000 persons, of whom about 2,000,000 are said to be members of the Christian community. Thus almost one-half of the Malagasy people are Christians, with the remainder largely animist. This is a higher proportion of Christians than in most other countries of Asia and Africa. Among the 2,000,000, approximately one-half, or 925,000, are reported to be Roman Catholics. The estimated size of the various Protestant denominations is shown in Table 17.

TABLE 17. MEMBERSHIP OF PROTESTANT CHURCHES IN MADAGASCAR (1956)

	Adherents[a]	Members[b]
Lutherans	400,000	200,000
English Congregational	300,000	50,000
French Evangelical Reformed Church	260,000	40,000
English Quakers	56,000	30,000
Anglicans	30,000	30,000
	1,046,000	350,000

NOTES: [a] Estimate of IMC survey.
[b] Estimate of Missionary Research Library.

The number of pastors currently serving in all the Protestant churches in Madagascar is estimated at 1,000, which is a relatively high figure for a younger church. The survey report states:

From the sociological point of view, there has been a considerable change in the recruiting of pastors over the years. In the beginning, the most gifted among the young men were eager to enter the theological schools, and very often these came from the highest castes. The missions were thus able, during the first decades, to enlist the services of the best elements in the population and so profit by the respect inspired by these men who were reckoned amongst the most cultivated in the nation. Later, the situation changed. The French administration opened new possibilities of employment and young Malagasy (men) found an outlet for their ambitions by entering government service, whilst the churches had to be content with somewhat second-grade recruits. Later still, private enterprises offered new outlets to an intelligent and dynamic youth. So it can be said that the Church had to make do with the residue, after government service and commerce had skimmed off the cream. The pastor was no longer the only well-educated and cultured personality; he was very often recruited from the humblest levels of society. Because of this, his profession was no longer so highly esteemed and respected as in the past. . . .

One remarkable feature of church organization in Madagascar is the financial autonomy which has already been achieved, to a very large extent, in the inland regions. Not only have the churches been able to pay all the salaries of the pastors and other agents in their service, but they have also been able to build schools and churches and find the requisite budgets for many institutions such as theological colleges. Financial progress has led, in the central region of Imerina, to an advanced level of financial independence.

Ambatomanga Theological School: This seminary was founded in 1902 by the Paris Evangelical Missionary Society of the French Evangelical Reformed Church. It trains theological students for approximately 200 churches of this denomination on Madagascar which are served by 175 qualified pastors. Most of the entrants have previously graduated from the four Bible schools conducted in Madagascar by the same denomination. Its students have usually also had previous experience as catechists. The educational level of the School is said to be of high quality, and the course of study lasts for four years. The Paris Missionary Society has for some years been sending graduates of Ambatomanga to France for more advanced theological study in order to obtain a B.D. degree. On the debit side, however, is the fact that the staff of two full-time teachers is too small and should be increased by at least one more full-time person. Furthermore, although a new class is admitted each year, yet in a given year only one class in each subject is held. This results in third- and second-year men being instructed alongside of first-year men, to the detriment of the former.

The school building containing two classrooms and a modest chapel appears to be inadequate for the number of students and the activities carried on there. The students' families live in houses forming a kind of village community which is situated on a pleasant site some miles outside of the capital, Tananarive.

The survey reports that one of the buildings at Ambatomanga (the library) was partly destroyed "during the events of 1947." (These events were a large-scale rebellion of the Malagasy people against French rule, a fact which received scant notice in the American press. At the height of the fighting it was reported that some 38,000 French and other white colonists were obliged to vacate their farms and take refuge in the garrisoned towns. Before the revolt was finally suppressed it is conservatively estimated that 40,000 of the Malagasy population were slain.)

Arivonimamo Theological School: There are more than 300 churches in Madagascar founded by the English Friends (Quakers). These are served by only 41 pastors plus a large number of evangelists and catechists. Thus this denomination has less than one-quarter as many fully trained pastors serving a 50% larger number of churches than does the French Evangelical Reformed Church on Madagascar. From 1913 to 1934 the Quakers' Arivonimamo Theological School was a Bible school, and students wishing to take a full theological course were sent to the Ambohipotsy College (Congregational—see below). However, for doctrinal and ecclesiastical reasons this arrangement was terminated in 1934. Since that time pastors for the Quaker Church have been trained at Arivonimamo. Few of its entrants possess a scholastic certificate, and the educational level of the School corresponds to that of the top class of a primary school or the first two years of a secondary school. Future pastors are given a four-year course.

Ambohipotsy College: Of the three seminaries supported by the London Missionary Society (LMS) (English Congregational Church), the Ambohipotsy College, founded in 1869 in Tananarive, is the most important. It is also the oldest theological school in Madagascar. This College has a rather ancient plant with lecture rooms, a library and study room, chapel, etc. However, according to the survey,

the general standard and quality of the students do not seem to correspond to what might be expected of an institution situated in the centre of the country and drawing its students from an urban and progressive population. For the most part they do not spring from the intellectual élite of the people . . . and very few young men with qualifications ranging as high as the baccalauréat . . . think of training for the ministry. Is the syllabus too modest to attract such recruits? . . . . A higher scholastic level might well give back to the College its former prestige. . . . Staffing difficulties and inadequate maintenance of the teaching staff probably constitute this college's weak point. . . . The principal obstacle . . . is financial; to change the existing situation, it would be necessary to re-adjust the teachers' salaries and align them to those paid to many of the town pastors.

Imerimandroso College: The second LMS school is the Imerimandroso College which was founded in 1922 and serves a synod comprising approximately 140 churches. "Pleasantly situated on a hill overlooking the eastern shore of Lake Alaotra, the largest lake in Madagascar, in the northern part of the Central Region, Imerimandroso College receives students from the various neighboring districts, though the majority come from the Sihanaka and Betsimisaraka tribes. . . . Students are only received every other year to follow a four-year course of study."

Fianarantsoa College: The third LMS school, Fianarantsoa College, is located in the south central region of Madagascar and is the weakest of the three. "The college has undoubtedly suffered a good deal from the lack of continuity in its direction in recent years. The Governing Committee, reduced to two or three people, has not been able to assume real responsibility for this institution, either in the material or the academic spheres. Consequently the buildings are in a bad state and there is no rebuilding plan in prospect. Certain improvements have been put in hand, but work has been stopped, making it impossible to use half the building. . . . The teaching is suffering from inadequate staffing and the overloading of those who are trying to cope with too many hours a week teaching and too heavy duties outside the college."

Ivory Theological College: The strongest Protestant seminary on Madagascar is the Ivory Theological College serving the Lutheran Church of Madagascar. One Norwegian and two American Lutheran missions have long been active in the entire southern portion of the island. Their churches were united some years ago, and the theological training of their pastors was concentrated in the one theological college at Ivory (pronounced Ee-voo-ry). The Lutheran Church in Madagascar has more than 700 places of worship, 300 ordained pastors, and 1,600 catechists. "The buildings housing the College (are spacious, well planned, kept in good repair and) represent a real achievement; the central building with its classrooms and chapel is surrounded by a regular village of students' and teachers' houses. Plans have been drawn up, and are already being carried out, for the rebuilding by stages, along more modern lines, of the present rather ancient blocks of houses occupied by the students' families. . . . The community life of the students (there are nearly 300 people, including women and children, within the one community) is fostered by the appointment of village leaders and a pastor who acts as a student chaplain." A total of 78 theological students was enrolled in 1956. The syllabus of the College is closely coordinated with those of the seven Bible schools maintained by the Lutherans in Madagascar which send most of their students on to Ivory. The teaching staff of the College numbers eight full-time personnel, the largest of any Protestant seminary in Latin Africa. The entrance standards permit an ambitious program of study to be carried on, including Greek and Hebrew. The one adverse comment made by the survey team concerning Ivory was that this College is the only one which is governed by an exclusively missionary committee having no Malagasy members. Furthermore the proportion of the College's budget defrayed by the mission appears to be much higher than in the case of the other theological schools on the island.

St. Paul's College: Located at Ambatoharanana, 50 miles north of Tananarive, this Anglican seminary is "set in a peaceful country side, remote from the main roads and housed in strong buildings. . . . This village obviously helps silent meditation and prayer, even if it suffers nowadays from material disadvantages, such as the lack of a water-supply and motor-roads." Only two years of study are offered at St. Paul's. The student body now numbers six, having dwindled from 17 in 1954. "It is obvious that the general academic level . . . corresponds more closely to a Bible school rather than to a school for training pastors. . . . A general improvement in the academic work of the College ought . . . to be based on the following points:

extending the course of studies to three or four years at least; raising entrance standards. . . ."

General Comments: Concerning the seven Protestant theological schools on Madagascar, the IMC survey team pointed out that "with one exception all these schools lack adequate teaching staff, and in order to carry out their task, have to wrestle with the problem of inadequate resources. . . . This dispersion of available resources very largely explains why the quality of pastoral training in Madagascar is below what it ought to be. . . . We consequently recommend a reduction in the number of theological schools." The report concluded that such a reduction would be a reasonable possibility because Madagascar is a relatively united and homogeneous country using one language and has a tradition of cooperation among the Protestant denominations there—although somewhat limited in the case of the Anglican Church of Madagascar. Furthermore the total number of Christians on the island and their available resources are insufficient to justify seven separate institutions. The LMS Church with three schools was thought to be particularly in need of concentrating its teaching facilities.

After considering various possibilities the Commission decided against recommending that there should be three main colleges (one in the northern, one in the central and one in the southern part of the island) in favor of setting up two principal institutions. The first already in existence in the south is the Lutheran institution, Ivory College.

The second institution, for the northern part of the island, ought to be a new foundation, which would require a complete revision of the churches' present organization. . . . The churches and missions of the LMS, Friends and the French Evangelical Reformed Church should pool all their resources allocated for training pastors in a single institution which would supply pastors for all the areas within their care. . . . The three churches in question are already engaged in active negotiations for organic union, which will, we hope, be fulfilled by the setting up of a United Church in the North of Madagascar. . . . The members of the Commission have been very much impressed by the strongly held opinion of Malagasy Christians holding office in the Church as to the urgent necessity of having only one school for training pastors.

As for the cost of setting up the proposed new institution, the survey states:

The purchase of a site, the erection of buildings and the maintenance of a teaching staff would naturally entail a financial plan and heavy responsibilities. The Churches and Missions interested in this project are alone able to decide how they will collect and use such resources. But if they are prepared to pool what they spend at present on each of the colleges they support separately, the financial problems created by the existence of a united college will not be insoluble. An initial capital outlay will doubtless be necessary, especially for buying the new site and developing it, but this obligation ought to be thought of as an exceptional contribution in which the churches would be ready to join if they were clearly shown the advantages of a single college, to which they look forward very keenly.

The Commission made a final recommendation: it was against attempting to establish a faculty of theology in Madagascar at this time. Such a faculty would imply that most of the teachers had obtained a doctoral degree and that a regular and sufficient flow of students was available who had already passed the baccalauréat. "None of these conditions is at present fulfilled in Madagascar. . . . The Commission consequently came to the conclusion that the time was not ripe for a project of this order. The immediate, primary task is the setting up of the two main schools for training pastors. . . . The result of this undertaking will be the gradual raising of the standard of theological education. Then, later on, the conditions will probably have been created which will make it possible to consider the founding of a Faculty of Theology in Madagascar."

After the publication of the Committee's report in 1957, its findings were in general favorably received. Some progress was made by the three local churches involved in attempting to implement the principal recommendation that their three seminaries in the northern part of Madagascar should be merged into one institution. However, the committee which was appointed to deal with this matter has encountered many problems. These relate to the minimum number of scholarships needed, the emphases which should be placed on the differing aspects of church polity and liturgy, and the method of placement of the seminary graduates (e.g., should they be permitted to select on their own initiative rural parishes where the need for ministers is great? Or should they be directed toward the larger and better paying pastorates in the towns and cities?).

E. The Relations Between the Protestant and the Roman Catholic Churches in Africa

One of the reasons for the comparative lack of success on the part of Protestant missions in Latin Africa, as contrasted with their achievements elsewhere in Africa south of the Sahara, is due to the competition which they experience in this area with the missionary clergy of the Roman Catholic Church.

Parts I and II of the IMC report point out that the

state power and the authority of individual officials and police are used by the Roman Catholic system in discriminatory and oppressive fashion only on the Portuguese territories. . . . In Belgian territory, there is some natural preference, arising from the Roman Catholic strength in the metropolitan country. . . . French administration is essentially secular and impartial, though individual officials may have their inward or political preferences for Roman Catholic interests. (However) in every one of the territories there are some officials who declare to Protestants their disgust with cases of wrongful acts by Roman Catholics such as excessive demands for public aid, falsification of school reports, and pressure upon administrators. . . . The Belgian, French and Portuguese administrations in Africa dislike Protestant fragmentation. . . . Protestant pastors feel keenly the better status, vis-à-vis the government . . . enjoyed by African priests of the Roman Catholic Church. . . . There are areas in which the Roman Catholic missionaries outnumber the Protestants by ten to one, and the number is still increasing. It can hardly be doubted that the Roman Church consciously aims at turning tropical Africa into a Roman dominion.

With respect to the Belgian Congo, it would seem that the most important factor accounting for the success of the Roman Catholic Church (which has received as many as 250,000 new members annually there during the past few years) has been the concentration of missionary personnel. In 1954 there were 4,800 European priests, sisters and brothers in the Congo, or four times the number of Protestant missionaries. Within the colony, the Roman Catholics have placed great stress in fostering not only theological but more particularly primary and secondary education. As John Gunther notes,

the Roman Catholic Church owes its terrific power to several factors. Belgium itself is more than 90 per cent Catholic, and naturally the local administration reflects this strong preponderance. . . . The first missionaries to penetrate into the Congo (in 1878) were British Protestants. The Catholics began to enter in the early 1880's, but for a generation most educational work was done by the Protestants, not the Catholics. In 1925 came a measure by the Belgian government giving the Catholic church an absolute monopoly on governmental subsidies to education for twenty years. Money (state money) poured in to aid the Catholic missions, whereas the Protestants had to keep afloat and maintain *their* schools by their own efforts. So they were rapidly outdistanced. No full accounting has ever been made of the billions of francs the Catholic missions received. They spent them well. Their educational plant is magnificent by African standards. In 1945 the twenty-year monopoly expired, and since that date the Protestant missions have received a share of government funds for education. The fact remains that for twenty critical years, when the Congo's educational system as it exists today was being established, the Catholics had everything their own way.

Perhaps the largest number of restrictions have been placed on Protestant missionaries working in the Portuguese colonies in Africa. This has taken the form of occasionally not granting (except after prolonged delay) return visas to Protestant missionaries on furlough, and also in other measures. In Angola a fair amount of freedom is said to be accorded to the activities of Protestant missionaries, but in Mozambique (where the Roman Catholics have a smaller over-all preponderance) the situation is more tense.

The Roman Catholics on their part believe that their missionary activities in tropical Africa have been hampered during the past century by the attitude and actions of the government officials in those areas. A Jesuit historian, Father Martin P. Harney, S.J., comments as follows on Protestant-Roman Catholic relations in the early days in Madagascar:

Father General Roothaan in 1844 sent six Jesuits of the Lyons province (of the Society) to the island; such was the control which the Protestant missionaries possessed that little could be accomplished, so the fathers moved off to work in the islands of Réunion and Mauritius. Not until 1855 did a member of the Society return to Madagascar; then Finaz, unrecognized, labored at Tananarivo to prepare the way for later missionaries. His technical skill in constructing a small railway, a telegraph system and a gas balloon gained him the favor of the Court; two of his brethren were permitted to come to Tananarivo. The Protestants, however, so worked on the ruling Queen that the fathers had to leave the capital city and were unable to return until after her death in 1861. Despite much continued opposition—Protestantism was declared the state religion in 1869—the Jesuits successfully developed their missions until 1883. . . . The French, now rulers of the island, lent their support to the Catholic missions.

In the late 1880s in Uganda the relations between native Protestants and Roman Catholics deteriorated to the point of armed conflict between them: this culminated in a pitched battle early in 1892, following which government forces restored order.

Fortunately in recent decades this animosity has become very considerably tempered. However, in general the tendency for Roman Catholic missionary personnel to concentrate their activities in Latin Africa (rather than in the present and former British areas in East, West and Southern Africa) continues. At a conference of Catholic mission specialists held at Fordham University in 1954, Father John J. Considine, M.M., a recognized expert in this field, stated: "Although (Roman Catholic) missionaries in the interior may not be aware of it, a strong anti-Catholic bias is common at headquarters, and it is reflected in such matters as educational subsidies, scholarships, etc. A Catholic, either white or black, has little chance of success in the British colonial service."

The differences in the results of the training given to theological students in Roman Catholic as compared to Protestant seminaries in Africa was commented on at the 1954 Fordham conference by Professor Kenneth S. Latourette of the Yale Divinity School as follows: "As between the two great wings of Christianity, some differences in effect were seen. In general, the Roman Catholic black was more docile, more dependent on the white man, and more submissive to him. The Protestant black was inclined to be more independent, to think for himself and to be more self-reliant. The Roman Catholic regarded the Protestant attitude as breeding rampant individualism, vagaries and rebellions. The Protestant adjudged the Roman Catholic methods to be producing automata, to be cramping the rightful development of human life, and to be making for a continuation of servitude, even though in a mild and benevolent form."

In July 1958 the International Fides Service of the Roman Catholic Sacred Congregation "De propaganda fide" in Rome published an article relating to the religious developments in recent years at the University College, Ibadan. The following is an excerpt from that article:

... At present about 500 of the students are nominally Protestant (and) about 160 are Catholics. ... One might notice in the college—as elsewhere in Nigeria—a tendency among Protestants to sink their sectarian differences to some degree and to try and come together in the fellowship of one Christian grouping. This leads to a doctrinal position that is apparently closer to the Catholic one and removed from Low Church Protestantism that has prevailed up to the present in Nigeria. In this lies much Catholic hope, especially since both in the College and in the country in general Catholicism with its strong structure, its insistence on high moral standards and its trust in God's promises can look forward increasingly to be seen both by Protestants and pagans as the one, universal Church of God, a church which does not have its origins in nationalistic squabbles and which is not confused with doctrinal anarchy.

Finally one might note the comment made in 1956 by Dean Norman A. Horner (of the Presbyterian Theological Seminary in Louisville, Kentucky) after he had spent ten years observing in detail and at close range the Protestant and Roman Catholic missions among the Bantu in the Cameroons: "It is well to remember that much of anti-Catholicism as well as anti-Protestantism is intolerance without rational basis. ... It is better for both sides to face their differences squarely and intelligently, and then maintain that they must coexist in spite of these differences."

F. SOUTHERN AFRICA

Part III of the *IMC Survey of the Training of the Ministry in Africa* discusses the seminaries in the British colonies in southern Africa and in the Union of South Africa. The authors were Dr. Norman Goodall, a Joint Secretary of the IMC and the World Council of Churches; and Rev. Eric W. Nielsen, a Secretary in the Department of Missionary Studies of the IMC. They visited the schools in this area in the latter part of 1953. Their survey excluded those seminaries in the Union of South Africa, chiefly belonging to the Dutch Reformed Church, which admit only white students.

Southern Africa can be divided between those areas which are under British control and those which comprise the Union of South Africa. Table 18 lists the leading younger churches and their membership in the British protectorates.

Table 19 lists the Protestant seminaries now being operated in the British territories in southern Africa.

1. *Northern Rhodesia*

Madzimoyo Theological School: This small school was established by the Dutch Reformed Church in 1940 as a training center for evangelists who formerly were

TABLE 18. MEMBERSHIP OF PROTESTANT CHURCHES IN THE RHODESIAS AND
NYASALAND (1956)

	Northern Rhodesia	Nyasaland	Southern Rhodesia
Population	2,000,000	2,500,000	2,000,000
Protestant Community	50,000	250,000	200,000
Churches:			
Church of Central Africa[a]		150,000	
Anglican	8,000	20,000	25,000
Methodist	1,500		30,000
Seventh Day Adventist	5,000	8,000	15,000
Reformed	15,000		5,000
Church of Central Africa in Rhodesia[b]	5,000		5,000
Evangelical Lutheran			5,000

NOTES: [a] Presbyterian.
[b] Presbyterian and Congregational.

TABLE 19. THEOLOGICAL SCHOOLS IN THE RHODESIAS, NYASALAND AND BASUTOLAND (1956–57)

		Approx. Number of		
Name	Location	Full-Time Faculty	Theol. Students	Denominational Support
Northern Rhodesia				
Madzimoyo Theological School	Fort Jameson	3	8	Dutch Reformed Church
St. John the Baptist Seminary	Lusaka	2[a]	20	Anglican
Kashinda Bible School	Kashinda	1	10	Congregational (English), Church of Scotland
Nyasaland				
Overtoun College	Livingstonia	2	9	United Free Church of Scotland
St. Andrew's College	Likoma Island	1	7	Anglican
Theological College	Mkhoma	2	12	Dutch Reformed Church
Mlanje Mission Seminary	Blantyre	2	8	Church of Scotland
Southern Rhodesia				
Theological Seminary	Old Umtali	1[a]	4	Methodist (USA)
Epworth Theological College	Salisbury	2	6[b]	Methodist (English, USA)
Theological College	Morgenster	2	5[b]	Dutch Reformed Church
African Baptist Theological Seminary	Gwelo	2	25	Southern Baptist
Basutoland				
Morija Theological School	Morija	2[a]	12	French Evangelical Reformed
Total: 12		22	126	Church, etc.

NOTES: [a] Plus part-time lecturers or assistants.
[b] Plus students at lower level of training.

trained in the Dutch Reformed seminary at Mkhoma in Nyasaland. Theological
training at Madzimoyo was commenced in 1951, and the first three-year course was
completed in 1953. The level of training has been low and the instruction intermittent.

St. John the Baptist Seminary: The St. John the Baptist Seminary is located in
Lusaka, the capital of Northern Rhodesia. This school is the Provincial Seminary
for the Anglican Province of Central Africa and was opened in 1954. It is not a
large seminary, but its enrollment of 20 theological students is more than double
that of either of the other two Protestant schools in the Protectorate.

Kashinda Bible School: Though called a Bible school, this institution is in effect a theological school inasmuch as it trains men primarily for the ministry and its graduates are ordained without further education. The lack of adequate planning in the Protestant missionary effort is seen in the comment made in Part III of the IMC 1953 survey concerning the Kashinda School to which the London Missionary Society (Congregational) had recently made some capital contributions for new facilities: "In spite of the capital fairly recently invested in admirable buildings at Kashinda, it seems inevitable that the question of location will have to be reconsidered. Uneasiness as to the rightness of the present site for the essential purposes of the college is widespread and persistent. This is based on the conviction that, for better or for worse, the key to the future of Northern Rhodesia lies in the Copper Belt. . . . The strategic place for the training of the ministry and the study and discussion of Christian theology in Northern Rhodesia, particularly during the next twenty-five years, is closer to the revolutionary forces gathered on the Copper Belt."

2. Nyasaland

Overtoun College: This small seminary has offered only intermittent instruction to theological students in recent years. Affiliated with the Livingstonia Institution, its location is scenic and its facilities are good. However, the College is very small in size. It is supported by the United Free Church of Scotland.

St. Andrew's College: When the IMC team visited Nyasaland in 1953 this Anglican seminary on Likoma Island had no classes in progress. The College offers a four-year course of instruction over a six-year period: the first two years at St. Andrew's lead to the diaconate, the next two are spent in practical work in the field, and the last two at the college lead to ordination to the priesthood. It was planned to send the more promising students to St. John the Baptist Seminary in Lusaka for further training, retaining St. Andrew's as a diocesan college teaching in the vernacular.

Theological College, Mkhoma: This small school in central Nyasaland has a good plant and is supported by the Dutch Reformed Church. "Little use is made of textbooks."

Mlanje Mission Seminary: Supported by the Church of Scotland, this institution serves the Blantyre Presbytery in southern Nyasaland. It offers a three-year course and "the students live with their families in small students' houses (in a very bad state of repair)." Part III notes that the small remote area of Nyasaland is served by three seminaries of Calvinist background (two Scottish Presbyterian and one Dutch Reformed), one for each of the three Presbyteries in the Protectorate. "The differences between the . . . (three Calvinist) groups with regard to mission policy . . . are real. They have been seriously enhanced of late. . . ." The two seminaries supported by the Scottish Presbyterians are in the northern and southern parts of Nyasaland. The Dutch Reformed seminary at Mkhoma is located in the center of the colony and differs from the Scottish seminaries on the subject of racial segregation.

3. *Southern Rhodesia*

In the two Rhodesias and Nyasaland, the African population totals approximately 6,270,000 persons. In the 12 seminaries in these three areas there were in 1956 fewer than 125 theological students, or one for every 50,000 Africans in the population. This compares to the ratio of one American theological student per 10,000 in the USA. The low level of general education in the Rhodesias is indicated by the fact that while there are several hundred thousand pupils attending primary schools, nevertheless in 1950–51 in Northern Rhodesia and Nyasaland combined there were only 436 pupils attending secondary schools. Of the latter number, presumably very few continued their studies at a college level.

In 1953 the Rhodesian Government commenced plans to establish a new university to be located in Salisbury, Southern Rhodesia, and the vital step was taken of declaring that the university's student body would be multiracial. A total of £1,250,000 ($3,500,000) was allocated for the capital costs of the project under the terms of the Colonial Development and Welfare Acts. In 1955 a royal charter was granted, and the institution was named the University College of Rhodesia and Nyasaland. The first students commenced their studies there in March 1957. The founding of this University College has an important bearing on the development of the seminaries in this portion of the continent, even though the University College at present does not offer any courses in religion.

Theological Seminary, Old Umtali: Part III of the IMC survey pointed out in 1953 that in Southern Rhodesia

there are two theological colleges of the same Confession: Old Umtali belongs to the American Methodists and Epworth to the British Methodists. Both colleges are small with a very limited number of students and small staffs. It seems to us very difficult to justify . . . the continued separation of these two colleges. . . . The question of uniting the two colleges has been discussed on various occasions over a number of years. At one time a case could be made out for maintaining a rural emphasis in the one place, Old Umtali, and a more urban emphasis nearer Salisbury (Epworth). . . . In any case rapid urban developments around Umtali deprive this arrangement of such strength as it once possessed. . . . Everything should be done to secure the unification of the two colleges, especially before capital commitments (now contemplated) on either side makes the position still more difficult. In our judgment the best location for the united college would be Epworth. . . .

Despite this clear-cut and emphatic recommendation, three years elapsed before the English and American Methodists reached some agreement on the matter. It appears that the English Methodists were reluctant to cooperate; and some American Methodist missionaries in Southern Rhodesia reportedly disapproved of some of their English brethren (among other reasons) for smoking tobacco.

In 1955 the American Methodists reported: "It continues to be a matter of great concern . . . that desirable candidates for the ministry are not forthcoming. This year no new student entered the seminary (i.e., Old Umtali). We rejoice, however, over the fact that we shall be able to dedicate a beautiful and adequate plant for the seminary. . . ." Thus in 1954–55 the American Methodists invested in a new plant at Old Umtali, despite the fact that (1) no student entered the seminary in 1955 and (2) the IMC report had urged that such a capital commitment be postponed. It appears that the funds for this project had been contributed to the mission board for this purpose just prior to the publication of the IMC recommendation, and it was decided it would be unwise not to carry through the original plan.

Another visitor to Old Umtali comments that the seminary has a number of secular schools in its vicinity and that the foreign missionaries teaching in them are more effective than the members of the seminary's faculty. In many other places in Africa, he feels, the clergy do better instructional work in secular institutions than they do in theological schools.

Epworth Theological College: In 1956 the English and American Methodists agreed to link the training of Epworth Theological school near Salisbury with the seminary at Old Umtali. The school at Epworth was previously attached to the Waddilove Training Institution. It is to be upgraded to a theological college by 1959 for the training of ministerial students in close association with the new university at Salisbury. Old Umtali will train evangelists and unordained ministers for both the English and American Methodist missions, and it will become a training center for religious education workers, local preachers and accepted supply pastors. Epworth will have a faculty of four teachers (two Europeans and two Africans), and the Presbyterian Church of Southern Rhodesia is already sending some of its students to be trained there.

Theological College, Morgenster: Established by the Dutch Reformed Church (Cape Synod) in 1936, this has always been a small seminary with seldom more than five native theological students enrolled at any one time. Some evangelists are also trained here. Despite the clear need for more ministers, the Dutch Reformed Church (according to Part III) has been "very strict in its acceptance of new men; perhaps it verges on excessive caution. . . . The course for ordination at Morgenster covers four years. . . . There is little dependence on textbooks of any kind. The dictation method is generally used. . . . The staff consists of two Europeans, nominally whole-time."

African Baptist Theological Seminary: The Southern Baptist seminary at Gwelo was opened in February 1955 with a class of 12 students meeting in a remodeled farmhouse on a 250-acre site. Most of the students had previously served as pastors and evangelists. A classroom building, chapel, a missionary residence and quarters for married students have since been completed. A three-year course is taught in English, and the 1958 enrollment was expected to reach 30 students.

4. *Basutoland*

Morija Theological School: Although it is a small enclave surrounded by the Cape Province, Natal and the Orange Free State (all of which are part of the Union of South Africa), Basutoland is a British Protectorate and not a part of the Union. The small seminary at Morija is located in the center of the Lessouto Plateau in the western part of the Protectorate. The school was founded in 1887 and is supported by the Paris Evangelical Missionary Society and the Swiss Mission in South Africa. A three-year course is offered, but owing to a lack of sufficient faculty personnel it has been impossible to have separate classes. The result is that all its students must be instructed together, regardless of their stage in training.

The 1953 recommendation of the IMC survey team was that in view of the generally low educational level in Basutoland and the slender resources then available to support theological education in the Protectorate, it might be wiser to downgrade the Morija School to a center for training evangelists and send its ordinand students to Fort Hare College in the Cape Province for their theological education.

This recommendation was not followed. On the contrary, with the increasing racial tensions in the Union of South Africa, the Morija seminary is being strengthened. Commencing in 1958 its faculty had two full-time professors rather than one, and the course was lengthened from three to four years. Five part-time teachers assist in the instruction. However, only about a dozen students are enrolled. This number may increase, and it is of interest to note that the Roman Catholic Church has centered much of its missionary activity in southern Africa since World War II in Basutoland rather than in the Union.

5. *Union of South Africa*

There are approximately 14,200,000 persons in the Union of South Africa, of whom 3,000,000 are Europeans and 11,200,000 are non-Europeans. Of the latter about 9,500,000 are Bantus, and 1,700,000 either East Indians or Cape-coloured (i.e., of mixed stock). In recent years the European population has remained comparatively stable in numbers and is likely to continue to do so. On the other hand, the South African government predicts the Bantu population will exceed 20,000,-000 by 1996, a prospective increase of over 100% during the next four decades.

The 1946 Government census reported the data relating to the total community of persons affiliated with the various Protestant denominations (and with the Roman Catholic Church) as shown in Table 20.

Since 1946 the constituencies of the churches in South Africa have grown. However, it should be noted that the number of "full members" or "communicants" in the Protestant churches are only a small fraction of the number of persons listed as being members of their constituencies. In addition to the 3,669,000 nonwhites accounted for in Table 20, another 1,000,000 persons (chiefly Bantus) are adherents of one or another of some 900 sects (indigenous separatist churches) which are so suffused with animism and pagan superstitions that they can scarcely be called Christian.

TABLE 20.   CONSTITUENCIES OF CHURCHES IN SOUTH AFRICA (1946)

	Europeans	Non-Europeans	Total
Dutch Reformed Church[a]	1,075,000	534,000	1,609,000
Methodist Church of South Africa	181,000	1,099,000	1,280,000
Anglican Communion[b]	375,000	742,000	1,117,000
Roman Catholic Church	118,000	434,000	552,000
Lutheran Churches[c]	23,000	442,000	465,000
Presbyterian Churches[d]	95,000	169,000	264,000
Congregational Churches	12,000	223,000	235,000
Nederduitse hervormde Kerk van Afrika	127,000	17,000	144,000
Reformed Church in South Africa[e]	76,000	9,000	85,000
	2,082,000	3,669,000	5,751,000

NOTES: [a] Nederduitse-gereformeerde Kerk. [b] Principally the Church of the Province of South Africa. [c] Various. [d] Principally the Presbyterian Church of South Africa and the Bantu Presbyterian Church of South Africa. [e] Gereformeerde Kerk in Suid-Afrika.

From Table 20 it will be noted that approximately one-third of the persons affiliated with the Dutch Reformed Church are non-Europeans, whereas the constituencies of the other two Reformed Churches are almost entirely white. On the other hand, the Methodist, Lutheran and Congregational constituencies are overwhelmingly nonwhite, with the same being true to a lesser extent in the case of the Anglicans, Roman Catholics and Presbyterians. Virtually all of the population of Dutch extraction are members of one or another of the Reformed Churches, and those of English descent are for the most part Anglicans.

The multiplicity of churches in the Union of South Africa which include the words "Dutch Reformed" in their names is not only a source of confusion to those not familiar with them, but also constitutes a rather extreme example of the fissionary tendencies of Protestantism.

The Dutch Reformed Church (Nederduitse-gereformeerde Kerk) is the oldest Protestant denomination in the country, having been founded shortly after the establishment in the Union of the first settlement by the Dutch East India Company in 1652. In some respects the Dutch Reformed Church today occupies somewhat the same position in the Union that the Roman Catholic Church does in Spain. This Church is divided into five principal synods whose jurisdictions correspond to the four principal states or provinces in the Union of South Africa (Transvaal, Orange Free State, Natal and Cape Province) plus South-West Africa. These synods are separate and autonomous church organizations which are loosely linked together by means of the Federal Council of the Dutch Reformed Church.

The second-largest Reformed Church in South Africa is the Nederduitse hervormde Kerk van Afrika (whose title, when translated into English, is the Dutch Reformed Church of Africa). This Church split off from the original Dutch Reformed Church in 1853. There were several reasons for this, among them the belief that the Dutch Reformed Church was too rigidly Calvinist in its outlook and too inflexible in its discipline.

By contrast, the third-largest Reformed Church, the Reformed Church in South Africa (Die gereformeerde Kerk in Suid-Afrika) split off from the Dutch Reformed Church in 1859. The Reformed Church in South Africa was initially composed for the most part of conservative, Calvinist Boer farmers residing in outlying districts. They were opposed (among other things) to the singing of evangelistic hymns (but not psalms) during the services held by the Dutch Reformed Church. Today the largest community of members of the Reformed Church in South Africa reside in and near Potchefstroom in the Transvaal.

In Table 20 the 1946 constituency of the largest of the three main Reformed Churches—the Dutch Reformed Church (Nederduitse-gereformeerde Kerk)—was shown as amounting to 1,609,000 persons. This is a combined total of the constituency of the four principal autonomous synods of that Church in the Union together with their nine mission churches. The latter are the Dutch Reformed Churches for nonwhites which administer their own affairs. Occasionally these mission churches send out missions of their own, which in turn form new churches. Thus one of the parent synods, The Dutch Reformed Church of the Orange Free State, formed the Dutch Reformed Mission Church of the Orange Free State in 1910 for nonwhites. The latter sent out a mission to the Anyasa and Barotse areas in the Rhodesias which was organized into an autonomous church in 1943 under the name of The Orange Free State Dutch Reformed Mission Church in Rhodesia. A complete list of the nine nonwhite mission churches formed under the auspices of the four parent synods (in the Union) of the Dutch Reformed Church is shown in Table 21.

The nine Dutch Reformed Mission Churches, though autonomous, are largely financed by one or another of the parent synods of the Dutch Reformed Church. In recent years as the racial tension in the Union has increased, the parent synods of the Dutch Reformed Church have increased their missionary efforts among the Bantu and coloured people in South Africa. The total amount of funds spent by this Church for this purpose rose from £506,000 in 1954 to over £1,000,000 in 1957, an increase of 100%. However, there has not been much progress achieved in the formation of an indigenous clergy among the Dutch Reformed Mission Churches. For example, the largest of them (The Dutch Reformed Mission Church of South Africa—which has been serving the coloured population in the Cape Province for over 75 years) has 130 congregations staffed by 111 European missionaries and only eight coloured pastors.

TABLE 21.   NONWHITE MISSION CHURCHES OF THE DUTCH REFORMED CHURCH
(1956)

Date Founded	Name	Adherents	Members
1881	Dutch Reformed Mission Church of South Africa (for the coloured)[a]	243,000	84,000
1910	Dutch Reformed Mission Church of the Orange Free State	103,000	35,000
1926	The Church of Central Africa (Presbyterian)[b]	180,000	60,000
1932	Dutch Reformed Mission Church of Transvaal	162,000	48,000
1943	The Orange Free State Dutch Reformed Mission Church in Rhodesia	50,000	18,000
1951	Dutch Reformed Bantu Church of South Africa[c]	23,000	7,000
1952	Shona Reformed Church[d]	70,000	27,000
1952	Dutch Reformed Mission Church of Natal	17,000	6,000
1956	The Reformed Church of Benue, Nigeria	3,000	1,000
		851,000	286,000

NOTES: [a] Founded at Wellington, Cape Province.
[b] Founded in Nyasaland, together with the Scottish Presbyterian Missions of Blantyre and Livingstonia. The number of adherents and members shown here relate only to those persons associated with the Dutch Reformed Church Mission.
[c] Founded at East London for the Cape Bantu.
[d] Morgenster, Southern Rhodesia (Mashonaland Mission).

The American Congregationalists report: "In South Africa we are in the midst of an explosive (i.e., racial) situation. One of the few places where South Africans have any freedom or opportunity to show their individuality is in the churches and schools of our traditions. . . . Under the Bantu Education Act, the government withdrew the funds which formerly provided 75% of the support of our (secular) schools. As a result we have had to give up about 110 primary schools, which have been taken over by the government." Thus what is foreshadowed in the Congo is now taking place in the Union of South Africa, namely the transfer of secular education from the hands of the missionaries to the Government. It is estimated that 75% of the secular education in Africa south of the Sahara is in missionary hands. It would seem almost inevitable that fifty years from now the governments will be controlling at least 75% of the secular schools, or more.

With respect to the Union Government's apartheid racial policy, the Dutch Reformed Church as a whole does not officially endorse these measures on Biblical or other grounds, and has sought in a number of instances to influence Government officials to modify the implementation of these measures as they have affected the activities of this Church. The Anglican Church of the Province of

South Africa has officially condemned the practice of apartheid, and some of its bishops have resisted the attempts of the Government to enforce it within their dioceses.

Part III of the IMC survey found that "as far as theological training is concerned, the churches in South Africa are probably better off in most cases than several of the churches in other parts of Africa farther north. The churches and missions have long since accepted ministerial training as an important and integral part of their work. . . . All this is to a large degree a reflection of the long history of Christianity in the Union of South Africa. Here Christianity is not of yesterday, as it is to some degree farther north. . . . There is need for very considerable improvement both in the standard and depth of the theological training as at present given. . . ."

Writing in 1958, Dr. G. B. A. Gerdener (Professor Emeritus of the History of Missions in the Dutch Reformed Church Theological Seminary at Stellenbosch) points out that almost half a century ago, one of his predecessors in this post,

Prof. J. du Plessis summed up a paragraph on a "better qualified Native ministry" with these words: "Better staff-training schools and theological colleges are the great missionary desideratum in South Africa to-day." Although the position has been greatly improved during the first half of the twentieth century, the words of the writer in 1910 are still true. Perhaps the need of Christian literature for the Bantu must be added to-day as an equally important or, at least, urgent desideratum. . . . The number of ordained non-Europeans seems to be advancing satisfactorily. Whether the standard and co-ordination of their training is keeping pace with their numbers, is another question.

Each of the three principal white Dutch Reformed Churches, and three of the nine mission churches of the Dutch Reformed Church, maintain their own seminaries. Two of the white Dutch Reformed Churches support parallel but separate theological faculties at the University of Pretoria. In addition, the Anglicans and Lutherans conduct a number of theological schools in this area training European and non-European students. Table 22 lists the seminaries of the various denominations active in the Union of South Africa (and in South-West Africa) at the present time.

TRANSVAAL

University of Pretoria: This University offers a B.D. degree to white students for three years' work after the A.B. degree. Ministerial candidates take either Course A or Course B. Course A is the only "seminary" of the Nederduitse hervormde Kerk which established this theological faculty of four professors in 1917. Course B is the only "seminary" in the Transvaal which is supported by the Dutch Reformed Church, and this theological faculty has five professors. Course B has an enrollment of 45 students, or three times the number enrolled in Course A. Both the Nederduitse hervormde Kerk and the Dutch Reformed Church nominate their

TABLE 22. THEOLOGICAL SCHOOLS IN THE UNION OF SOUTH AFRICA (1958)

Name	Location	Approx. Number of			Denominational Support
		Full-Time Faculty	White	Theol. Students Nonwhite	
Transvaal					
University of Pretoria	Pretoria				
Theological Faculty A		4	15		Nederduitse hervormde Kerk
Theological Faculty B		5	45		Dutch Reformed Church
Marang Lutheran Theological Seminary	Rustenburg	2		12	Lutheran (German)
College of Resurrection and St. Peter	Rosettenville	4		25	Anglican
Dube Theological School	Johannesburg	1		6ᵉ	Reformed Church in South Africa
Potchefstroom University Seminaryᵃ	Potchefstroom	5ᵇ	55		Reformed Church in South Africa
Orange Free State					
Stofberg Memorial School	Viljoensdrift	5		30ᵉ	Dutch Reformed Church
Adams United Theological School	Modderpoort	3		19	Congregational, African Presbyterian
Natal					
Oscarsberg Lutheran Theological Seminary	Rorke's Drift	3		31	Lutheran
Hermannsburg Seminary	Greytown	1		7?	Lutheran (German)
Dingaanstat Theological School	Dingaanstat	3		ᶜ ᵉ	Dutch Reformed Mission Church of Natal
Cape Province					
St. Bede's Theological College	Umtata	2		25	Anglican
Decoligny Theological School	Transkei	3		3ᵉ	Dutch Reformed Bantu Church of South Africa
St. Paul's College	Grahamstown	5	60		Anglican
Rhodes Universityᵈ	Grahamstown	3	12?		(Government)
University College of Fort Hareᶠ	Alice	3		30	Methodist, Presbyterian
Moravian Theological Seminary	Port Elizabeth	2		10	Moravian Church of South Africa
Theological Seminary	Stellenbosch	5	176		Dutch Reformed Church
Zonnebloem College	Cape Town	2ᵇ	2	7	Anglican
Missions Institute	Wellington	4ᵇ	40		Dutch Reformed Church
Training College	Wellington	2ᵇ		13ᵉ	Dutch Reformed Mission Church of South Africa (for the coloured)
South-West Africa					
Finnish Mission School	Onajena	2		15	Lutheran (Finnish)
Paulinum School	Karibib	2		7ᵉ	Lutheran (German)
Total: 23		71	405	240	

NOTES: ᵃ Potchefstroom University for Christian Higher Education, and its associated seminary. ᵇ Plus other instructors on part time or at lower level of instruction. ᶜ First class of students entering in 1959. ᵈ Department of Divinity. ᵉ Plus students at lower level of training. ᶠ Faculty of Theology.

own professors to these faculties, and they are then appointed by the University Board. Some of these professors teach combined classes at the pretheological level containing students preparing to enter either Course A or Course B. However, there are differences in the theological emphases of the two supporting churches. Consequently at the theological level a student takes all his work in either Course A or Course B which are taught separately by professors belonging to the respective churches. It is said that the teaching in Course A tends to be somewhat more liberal and objective than that in Course B, with a greater reliance being placed on the latest findings in higher criticism, etc. Some of the Course A faculty members come from Holland. In general, however, the academic level of the two faculties is about the same.

It might be noted here that the Faculty of Divinity at the University of South Africa (which is also located in Pretoria but is an examining body rather than a teaching institution) offers a three-year correspondence course leading to a B.D. degree

Marang Lutheran Theological Seminary: This small theological school was founded at Berseba in South-West Africa in 1876. Subsequently it was reopened in 1938 in connection with the Bethel Training College at Bodenstein in the Lichtenburg district in the southeastern portion of the Transvaal. However, Bethel College was a teacher-training institution and its administration was taken over by the Government in 1956 in accordance with the terms of the Bantu Education Act (passed in 1953). Accordingly in 1958 the Seminary was opened once again at its present location, Rustenburg, a city some 60 miles west of Pretoria. The school is supported by a German Lutheran mission society, the Hermannsburger Mission. In addition to a four-year course for pastors, a few part-time courses for evangelists and lay workers are given.

College of the Resurrection and St. Peter: Located at Rosettenville near Johannesburg, this high-church Anglican seminary has four full-time lecturers which in theory is one of the strongest theological faculties in the Union teaching nonwhite students. However, according to Part III, "with perhaps one outstanding exception among the present students, signs of a capacity for advanced theological study . . . are rare." The discipline is strict and a comparatively heavy emphasis is placed on liturgics. The buildings were erected with funds provided by the Community of the Resurrection (Mirfield, England) and training was commenced in 1903. A three-year course is offered for deacons, followed by six months' practical work in the field, after which a short course is given leading to ordination and the awarding of an L.Th. degree.

Dube Theological School: This seminary of the Reformed Church in South Africa is situated in the Dube Location at Johannesburg. It trains nongraduate native students at a Bible school and a theological level. Of its total enrollment of 30, an estimated half-dozen are studying to be pastors, and the remainder are preparing to be evangelists. It has been only during the past few years that the Reformed Church in South Africa has undertaken missionary activities among the Bantus in the Transvaal.

Potchefstroom University Seminary: The Potchefstroom University for Christian Higher Education was founded in 1869 in Burgersdorp (Cape Province) and later was moved to Potchefstroom in the Transvaal. Originally a seminary, it subsequently developed into a university college, and in 1951 achieved full university status. The University has a total of 1,350 white students taught by six faculties in the arts and sciences. Its Faculty of Theology consists of a dean and four professors teaching approximately 55 students at the theological level. The B.Th. degree (four years' work after the B.A. degree), M.Th. and Th.D. degrees are awarded. After the students have received their theological degrees, they receive further training in church work at the Seminary of the Reformed Church in South Africa which is closely associated with Potchefstroom University. The University's Board appoints the professors on its Faculty of Theology, subject to the approval of the Church. The latter appoints the Seminary professors. The same professors lecture in both institutions. The Seminary is the only one training men for the ministry in the Reformed Church in South Africa. It is said to place a strong emphasis on the teaching of dogmatics and church doctrines.

ORANGE FREE STATE

Stofberg Memorial School: Founded in 1908 on the Orange Free State side of the Vaal River, a few miles from Vereeniging, this seminary has been the principal training center for the Bantu ministry of the various Dutch Reformed Mission Churches in the Union. Coloured students are also trained here. Its affairs have been administered by the Orange Free State synod of the Dutch Reformed Church. The seminary was formerly closely associated with secondary and teacher-training schools. It trains men to be ordained ministers, catechists and evangelists. The ordination course lasts three years. The School is said to be well staffed with five lecturers. The teaching is in Afrikaans and many of the faculty have been graduates of Course B at the University of Pretoria. The Memorial School was named after Rev. Pieter B. J. Stofberg, a mission secretary of the Dutch Reformed Church synod in the Orange Free State. In the 50-year period 1908–58 it graduated 65 pastors, 625 evangelists and 993 fully qualified teachers. Stofberg's primary, secondary and teacher-training schools were taken over by the Union Government's Department of Bantu Education in 1955. In 1958 it was anticipated that the theological department at Stofberg would soon be "decentralized" and "moved to Bantu areas." Thus the future of this seminary is uncertain.

Adams United Theological School: This seminary is supported by the American Board of Commissioners for Foreign Missions (Congregational) and the Bantu Presbyterian Church of South Africa. The School is a direct outgrowth of the former Theological Training Department of Adams College in Durban, Natal, which was closed when the College was liquidated at the end of 1956 in accordance with the terms of the Bantu Education Act.

Adams College was founded on the banks of the Amanzimtoti River in Natal in 1853 by missionaries of the American Board. It was a pioneering institution in a number of respects and was successful in educating a number of African leaders in civic and church life, including Chief A. J. Luthuli (the first African to be appointed to the staff of a high school in the Union) and Professor Z. K. Matthews (the first African to be appointed principal of a high school having Europeans on its staff). The College developed along interdenominational lines, and like a number of other institutions in Africa, most of its students in recent years were being educated for careers as teachers in secular schools and colleges rather than for careers in the church. In fact, when the IMC survey team visited Adams in 1953, the Theological Training Department had no students enrolled in it (owing to the absence of applicants) but planned to resume instruction in 1954. In 1955 the African Methodist Episcopal Church closed the seminary (Wilberforce Training College, founded in 1938) which it was then operating in the Union and transferred its nine theological students and their teachers to Adams.

In accordance with the prevailing custom, none of the missionaries on the Adams faculty could eat a meal with a native, or reside in the same compound with them. The result was the white teachers lived some 20 miles from the campus.

The IMC survey team recommended that theological instruction should be discontinued at Adams and its divinity students and faculty school be transferred to the University College of Fort Hare, provided that the facilities at Fort Hare were improved. The team envisaged a four-year course, with three years spent at Fort Hare leading to a Certificate of Theology, and a fourth year spent at Adams in postgraduate supervised field work and pastoral theology. This recommendation was never implemented owing to the demise of Adams College as a whole.

In 1953 the Bantu Education Act was passed, the purpose of which was to transfer the control and administration of native education from the Provincial Education Boards to the Native Affairs Department of the Government of the Union. All institutions training teachers (whether supported by mission boards or not) were to become state institutions, while the Government's subsidies toward the salaries of faculty members teaching other secular courses to Bantus enrolled in private institutions were to be progressively reduced. Theological schools were not affected by the Act, but Adams College as a whole became one of the main targets of the Government's interest. Adams' request that it be reclassified as a private school (foregoing the subsidy it had previously received from the Government) was denied by the Government in July 1956. Accordingly at the end of that year, the College closed its doors.

The American Board was concerned that the work of Adams' Theological Training Department should be continued and recognized that from henceforth only the Government could legally use Adams' facilities to operate a secular college for the Bantus. Since it did not seem desirable to operate a seminary connected with a Government institution, the Board sold the Adams campus to the Government and the latter opened a new school on this site called The Amanzimtoti Zulu College.

With the proceeds of this sale Adams United Theological School was established in 1957 at Modderpoort in the Orange Free State. Modderpoort is a small railway junction town near Ficksburg and close to the Basutoland border. It was chosen as the site for the new seminary because it was close to the geographical center of a number of Congregational missionary activities in the Union and because some mission-owned buildings were available there for use. The School is a union institution supported by the American Board, the London Missionary Society (Congregational), the Bantu Congregational Church, the African Presbyterian Church, and the United Church in the Goldfields. It has a full-time faculty of two Europeans which is soon to be expanded to three. Approximately 19 nonwhite students are enrolled.

There has been some thought given to the possibility of merging the Adams School with the theological school maintained by the French and Swiss missions at Morija in Basutoland. However, it seems likely that both of these seminaries will remain at their present locations for some time and for the same reason: Bantu theological students from the Union might not be granted passports to enter Basutoland, and Basuto students might not receive visas to enter the Union.

NATAL

Oscarsberg Lutheran Theological Seminary: This school is located at Rorke's Drift, 25 miles southeast of Dundee. It is the main training center for pastors for the Lutheran missions and churches throughout southern Africa. Established in 1912, it is supported by four Lutheran missions which also send students to it: the Berlin Lutheran Mission, the Norwegian Mission Society, the American Lutheran Mission and the Church of Sweden Mission. In 1956 two similar and concurrent four-year courses were inaugurated so that one class would graduate and one class would enter the school every second year. The 31 students enrolled at that time were taught by three Europeans. According to Part III the teaching at Oscarsberg in 1953 was "generally of the more strictly conservative type. . . . There have been discussions with a view to developing the course to (a) B.D. standard. Our impression is that the standard is nowhere near the foundation on which the B.D. course can be built. . . . We could not help sensing some dangers in attempting to speed up the raising of standards, especially in a formal curriculum modelled too rigidly on the accepted pattern of western theological colleges. The fact is there is not a sufficient number of qualified students available at present. . . ."

Hermannsburg Seminary: This small Lutheran school is located at Greytown, 40 miles northeast of Pietermaritzburg (and only 50 miles south of the main Lutheran seminary at Rorke's Drift). It was originally established in 1877 and currently is offering courses for men planning to be ordained pastors or evangelists, as well as refresher courses for lay workers. The pastors take a five-year course. One missionary from the Hermannsburger Mission serves on the faculty.

Dingaanstat Theological School: Located at Dingaanstat in Zululand, this institution has been training Bantu students at a Bible school level. The first class of students to be taught at a theological level will commence in 1959. Its graduates serve in the ministry of the Dutch Reformed Mission Church of Natal.

CAPE PROVINCE

St. Bede's Theological College: Located at Umtata in the eastern section of the Province, St. Bede's offers a three-year course to native students preparing for the priesthood in the Anglican Church of the Province of South Africa. According to Part III, "the general academic standard is fairly low . . . the main emphasis is on devotional training and pastoralia. . . . The teaching limitations (i.e., a faculty of two) are serious. . . ." The student body of 25 is drawn almost entirely from rural areas. St. Augustine's Ordination Test School, which was founded at Modderpoort in the Orange Free State by the Society of the Sacred Mission in 1956, serves as a two-year preparatory school for St. Bede's.

Decoligny Theological School: The Decoligny seminary is located at Transkei, near Umtata. It trains men for the ministry of the Dutch Reformed Bantu Church of South Africa. Prior to 1953 this institution offered courses only at a Bible school level. Since then it has added courses at a theological level in which only a very small number of students (three or so) are as yet enrolled. Approximately 35 students are being trained to be catechists and evangelists. A number of the faculty have been graduates of the Stellenbosch seminary.

St. Paul's College: Located in Grahamstown, this College is the only institution maintained by the Anglican Church of the Province of South Africa exclusively for the training of white priests to serve in its ministry in the Union. It was founded in 1902 and in many ways St. Paul's resembles the typical theological college in England. The school offers a two-year course to entrants possessing an A.B. degree, at the end of which an L.Th. diploma is awarded. Approximately 60 theological students are now enrolled, which is close to the College's maximum capacity. Despite this, in recent years St. Paul's has graduated only about one-half of the white priests annually ordained in this Church. The remainder have been emigrating to South Africa from abroad, principally from Great Britain.

Rhodes University: In 1958 the Department of Divinity at Rhodes University in Grahamstown had approximately a dozen white students enrolled in its courses. The University offers a diploma in divinity and also a B.D. degree for two years' work after the B.A. degree. Rhodes became an independent university in 1951, but (like the seven other residential universities in South Africa) approximately two-thirds of its budget is defrayed by grants received from the Government.

University College of Fort Hare: This College is located at Alice, 60 miles northeast of Grahamstown. It is the only predominantly non-European university college in

South Africa. Within a 30-mile radius of Alice there are no less than 80 schools of various types for African students, and the area surrounding Fort Hare constitutes the most important center of Bantu education and culture in the Union today.

The College was originally called the South African Native College and was opened by General Louis Botha, the Prime Minister, in 1916. Originally it had a score of students instructed by two full-time teachers in a small bungalow. From 1924 to 1937 Fort Hare functioned both as a secondary school and a university college, not dropping the former courses until 1937. Its degrees were awarded under the authority of the University of South Africa. When Rhodes University assumed an independent status in 1951, Fort Hare became affiliated with it and now confers degrees under Rhodes' authority.

In 1958 there were 430 students enrolled in 19 departments at Fort Hare, and it was anticipated that by 1959 the total would reach 500. About 93% of its students (Bantu, East Indian and coloured) came from various parts of South Africa, with the balance coming from beyond the borders of the Union.

The fees paid by the students are low and constitute only about 12% of the College's current income. Originally the main financial support for Fort Hare was provided by missionary sources. In recent years the South African Government has made annual grants to the College amounting to two-thirds of its operating budget. These grants have risen from an average of £25,575 for the years 1947–50 to £87,000 in 1957, an increase of more than 200% in less than a decade. Including farm lands, the property of the College totals some 1,500 acres which, together with the buildings thereon, are valued at approximately £500,000.

Unless they can live in the neighborhood with their parents or relatives, the students are required to live in one of five hostels. Of these, three are for men and are operated under church auspices, as follows:

Hostel	Opened	Church
Wesley House	1921	Methodist Church of South Africa
Iona House	1924	Church of Scotland (Presbyterian)
Beda Hall	1934	Anglican Church (Province of South Africa)

Originally the cost of building these hostels was paid for by the churches. However, in recent years Government grants have defrayed one-third of their construction costs, and the College Council has contributed another third. When Wesley House was opened by the Methodists in 1921 they transferred their theological training to Fort Hare. The wardens of Wesley and Iona serve as theological tutors to the Methodist and Presbyterian ordinand students residing in those hostels. There are no Anglican theological students at Fort Hare, but occasionally some students have been sent there by the Congregational and Moravian missions and churches.

In 1958 only about 30 students (or 7% of the total student body) at Fort Hare were enrolled in theological studies. This was approximately the same number as in 1949. The divinity faculty consists of one full-time professor plus two lecturers. Four courses in the field of theology were being offered:

Course	*Type*
Certificate in Theology	A two-year course open to nonmatriculated students
Diploma in Theology	A Rhodes diploma taken by many of the ordinand students
B.A., divinity options	A three-year course which (up to 1953) only six Fort Hare students had been able to take
B.D.	Up to 1953 no Fort Hare student had taken this course

In the years up to and including 1957, a total of 55 students had obtained the Diploma in Theology at Fort Hare. Most of the theological students have not been academically qualified for this course. As a result they have studied for the Certificate, which does not carry any recognition from Rhodes University.

In 1953 the IMC survey team concluded that for nonwhite students Fort Hare "should be developed as the acknowledged centre in South Africa for theological training of an academic standard." It was recommended that a separate hostel for theological students should be built at the College instead of having these men reside with other students in Wesley House and Iona House. The theological students constituted only a small minority in the general hostels, and, without alienating them from the student body, it was felt a separate hostel would make possible "a much stronger and more ordered devotional life than is at present possible."

The survey team hoped that it might be possible to transfer the seminaries at Morija and Adams College to Fort Hare in order to concentrate as much theological training as possible at one center in the Union. This suggestion was predicated on the assumption that the Basuto students from Morija would be able to obtain visas to enter the Union and that the suggested new hostel at Fort Hare would be built. The team also recognized, however, that Alice is a rather isolated site and that a number of observers considered the "atmosphere" at Fort Hare too politically conscious to be congenial for seminary work.

Subsequent events made it impracticable to carry out any of the team's recommendations. In May 1955 the unrest among the students at Fort Hare was such that they went on strike and the College was temporarily closed on the charge that a "secret authority" existed in the student body. A governmental commission of inquiry commented on the institution's over-strict regulations and the fact that its isolated location tended to enhance a sense of segregation and a self-conscious racialism. Fort Hare was subsequently reopened, but in 1956 the theological students are reported to have manifested their discontent by refusing to sing in chapel, to read prayers, etc.

In 1957 the Government proposed the enactment by the South African Parliament of a Universities Bill, the purpose of which would be to eliminate all non-European students from European universities in the Union. This would be made possible through the establishment of five exclusively non-European university colleges of which one would be for coloured students, one for East Indians and three for Bantu students. All five universities currently exist only on paper. Whether Fort Hare would qualify as one of the three Bantu colleges is debatable. The President of Fort Hare was arrested on the charge of sedition and some believe the Government's aim is to close the College (or administer it directly) as a means of counteracting the emotional tendencies among its students which rise to the surface in matters involving racial discrimination.

Thus the future of Fort Hare and its theological department is obscure. Conceivably the Methodists and Presbyterians may be confronted with the necessity of transferring their theological students elsewhere, as was done when Adams College was closed.

Moravian Theological Seminary: Located at Fairview, a suburb of Port Elizabeth, this school was established in January 1952. During the period 1955–57 six of its graduates were ordained as pastors. The majority of its students are Cape-coloured. Two missionaries of the German Moravian Mission serve full time on its faculty. A three-year course is offered to full-time students. A four-year "afternoon" course is also available for students who have previously had teacher training and who teach in primary and secondary schools in the mornings. The Seminary's operating expenses are met by the Moravian Church in South Africa. Some of its students are sent to it by churches located in South-West Africa—such as the Evangelical Church (Rhenish Mission) and the Ambokawango Church (Finnish Mission).

Theological Seminary, Stellenbosch: This school is the principal seminary of the Dutch Reformed Church. It is a separate institution from the University of Stellenbosch whose campus is located in another part of the town. The University and the Seminary exert an important influence among the members of the Cape Synod of the Dutch Reformed Church, and these two educational institutions work in close cooperation with each other.

The Seminary was founded in 1859 for the purpose of helping to ensure the orthodoxy of the Dutch Reformed Church at that time through providing training for its ministerial candidates which would not be influenced by the rationalistic philosophy espoused a century ago by some of this Church's ministers who had been educated in universities in Holland. The seminary now offers a four-year course in theology leading to a diploma. More than one-half of the students entering the Seminary have previously received an A.B. degree (or two-year diploma) from the University. Examinations at the Seminary are conducted by a Church Committee which authorizes the successful candidates to engage in service in the Church or in the mission field. In some recent years, up to one-half of the Seminary graduates have elected to enter missionary work, formerly for the most part outside of the Union, but now increasingly within the Union.

Those seminary students who wish to continue their theological studies can read for a B.D. or a D.D. degree. *Cum laude* students commence their final year of B.D. work after their third year at seminary. The D.D. is awarded for two years' work after the B.D. degree to students who have had at least three to five years interim experience as parish ministers. Both the B.D. and the D.D. degrees are awarded by the University of Stellenbosch. However, the University's Faculty of Theology is composed only of men serving full time on the Seminary's faculty. Most of the B.D. and D.D. students are in residence at the Seminary rather than at the University, because all their lectures and classes are held at the Seminary. The University appoints some of the professors serving on the students' thesis and examination committees. In 1958 approximately 40 of the 176 students at Stellenbosch were said to be candidates for the B.D. and D.D. degrees.

Zonnebloem College: It is estimated that 90% of the coloured population in the Union live in the Cape Province. They tend to reside in towns and follow a European way of life as compared to the Bantus dwelling in the outlying districts. Approximately 90% of the coloured population are Christians, and in general, their educational level is considerably above that of the Bantus. The small Zonnebloem Institute in Capetown is maintained by the Anglican Church primarily to train coloured priests for this Church. It has both white and nonwhite students enrolled in its courses. Its full-time faculty of two is supplemented by five part-time instructors.

Missions Institute, Wellington: The Dutch Reformed Church established this Institute in 1870 or thereabouts for the purpose of training white ministers for missionary work among the coloured population in the Cape Province. This Church spends approximately £100,000 or more each year for the various phases of its missionary work among the coloured population. The Missions Institute at Wellington has a faculty of four full-time persons and about 40 white theological students. The four-year curriculum offers the usual subjects taught in a seminary, with a somewhat greater stress being placed on anthropology and local languages, and less emphasis on Greek, etc. The Cape Synod of the Dutch Reformed Church recently voted to merge the Missions Institute into this Church's Theological Seminary at Stellenbosch by 1961. It was felt that the Institute would be strengthened through such a merger and concentration of faculty personnel.

Training College, Wellington: The Dutch Reformed Mission Church in South Africa is the unit of the Dutch Reformed Church which is supported by the coloured population in the Cape Province. This training college was founded in Wellington in 1917 to train evangelists. In 1930 it inaugurated courses for pastors. In 1954 the college moved into a new building, and at present it has approximately 13 students enrolled in its theological courses. In the 20-year period 1933–53 only 11 candidates completed the course. In the past there has been some interchange of faculty with the Missions Institute in Wellington.

SOUTH-WEST AFRICA

Since 1920 this large and sparsely populated territory has been held by the Union of South Africa as a mandate from the League of Nations. The Union, however, has pursued a policy of integrating South-West Africa as closely as possible within its own political and administrative structure, including (among other measures) the application to the territory of the current policy in regard to the Bantu Education Act.

Finnish Mission School: Originally established by German Lutherans prior to World War I, this School was reopened by the Finnish Mission in 1922. At first its courses were offered intermittently. The present seminary was established in Onajena in 1953 and offers a three-year course to about 15 Lutheran theological students, most of whom have previously been teachers. There are two full-time Europeans on the faculty. The language of instruction is the vernacular, although increasing emphasis is being placed on the use of Afrikaans. (See Chapter 8, C, for later information.)

Paulinum School: The Rhenish Mission established the Paulinum School in 1938. It is located at Karibib in the central portion of South-West Africa on the railroad 100 miles east from Walvis Bay. The course lasts for four years for pastors, and a shorter period for evangelists and church teachers.

G. Over-all Aspects

Parts I, II and III of the *IMC Survey of the Training of the Ministry in Africa* and subsequent reports make largely the same comments on certain over-all aspects of theological education in Africa. These relate to:

1. Recruiting students.
2. Sending students overseas for training.
3. Improving existing seminaries.
4. The shortage of the local clergy.
5. The action taken to date in response to previous survey recommendations.
6. The missionary opportunity.

1. Recruiting Students: If the seminaries in Africa are to be strengthened, it would appear that a necessary first step would be the institution of recruitment programs aimed at obtaining both a greater number of theological students and, more importantly, students of higher quality. According to Part III,

where are the students for training? We met the question everywhere, and it was often put bluntly: "It is hardly realistic to discuss theological training as long as this prior question is still largely unsolved." Again, we do not want to present too dark a picture but the situation seems to be almost desperate. The number of new recruits nowhere grows to any appreciable extent; in many places it is decreasing. . . . Churches and missions which have placed great emphasis on the creation of an African ministry have often been unable to carry on a continuous theological training scheme simply because there have not been enough students available. Most of the churches find some difficulty in financially supporting their present number of ministers; to add to the number appears to many to be entirely out of the question. The recruitment problem is therefore mainly discussed in terms of existing vacancies; yet even within these limits there is a shortage of men.

One result of this failure on the part of seminary administrators to cope adequately with the recruitment problem has been the closing down from time to time of a number of theological schools for lack of students. Part II comments: "One important higher training school in the Belgian Congo was suspended from 1937 to 1950. In Liberia, the highest training institution was closed from 1927 to 1948; and the two leading missions secured practically no pastors in that time. . . . A mission in Angola had no training, even for catechists, for fifteen years. There are many other instances of this sad lack of continuity in training programmes. So often it is said, 'We stopped in the depression, and just didn't get started again until after the war'."

2. *Sending Students Overseas for Training:* The question arises: to what extent is it advisable to send African students abroad for training? Part II states: "A student who goes abroad rather young and stays several years to do secondary education— or its upper levels—and then a theological course, secures the maximum of disadvantage, or nearly so. This practice . . . seems uncalled for and should be discouraged. An African is better advised to use any possible time abroad for work above what he can get in his own territory. Missions and churches are tending, with due caution and limited funds, to send a few very carefully chosen men, already prepared as well as they can be in Africa by school and private study, for a period of one or two years in European and American seminaries."

Bishop Neill stated in Part I: "Almost without exception, the most useful African leaders whom I was privileged to meet were men who had had some period of training in some country other than their own. . . . On the whole it can be said that the African students (overseas) have done remarkably well."

However, the 1956 Presbyterian USA Foreign Mission Board report, when discussing this same point, apparently disagreed: ". . . higher education on the field is costly and most of those (Africans) who went abroad to study never returned, or came back with minds and souls distorted."

3. *Improving Existing Seminaries:* Dr. Charles Forman notes that with respect to the seminaries in Equatorial Africa and Madagascar, "the European-supported schools derive practically all their budget, except the salaries of foreign teachers, from the African churches themselves. American schools still depend almost completely on foreign funds. The reverse side of this coin is that European schools are

nearly all suffering from an acute shortage of funds which puts even the most urgently needed improvements beyond their reach. . . . Some schools, most strikingly the one at Limuru in Kenya, are so pitifully short-staffed that they can scarcely carry on a proper program at all, especially when one member goes on furlough and thereby cuts the faculty in half !"

According to Part II, "the facts record not only start and stop, and start again. Some starts are frankly without a plan for more than the first year. . . . Again, when Mr. A goes on furlough, as he is expected to very frequently, the school is transferred to Mr. B's station. Mr. B regards the school as an additional duty put on top of all his previous exhaustion. He has no time to prepare for courses; and furthermore, he is not trained. . . . Some missions have surprisingly few missionaries with theological training."

The small size of almost all the faculties of the seminaries in Africa is evident from the statistics contained in the tables previously presented. The tendency of mission agencies to establish one-man seminaries can hardly be defended. Part III states: "In our opinion a theological college needs at least two, preferably three, full-time men on its staff. This requirement is not conditioned essentially by the number of students; there is the same theological task to be done whether there are five or fifteen students. With three men on the staff a desirable division of labour would apportion the main subjects as follows:

1. Old Testament; Church History.
2. New Testament; Doctrine.
3. Ethics; Pastoral Theology."

It seemed evident to Bishop Neill (in Part I) "that each institution was trying to do far too many things, and therefore could not possibly do any of them well, especially in view of the chronic shortage of staff under which they labour."

The Bishop was also "struck . . . by the isolation in which theological teachers in Africa live. Distances are very great and therefore conferences are very expensive." The authors of Part III declared: "We were surprised to discover how slight is the contact between the theological colleges of the different areas and churches. Some college principals, even, were unaware of the existence of certain other colleges. Few theological teachers have ever met their colleagues in other institutions; rarely does there seem to have been a thorough and widely representative discussion of common problems, methods of work, literature resources and needs, etc. . . . We recommend that a Standing Committee on theological training be established."

Concerning the general inadequacy of the education of the clergy in Africa, the following quotations have been extracted from Parts I, II and III, respectively:

Most African clergy have started life as village catechists. After a brief course of elementary training, they have begun their work as preachers of the Gospel. They have then been brought in again for one or two periods of training as catechists; and then finally for a further period of training for the ordained ministry. On the whole, this theological training is well done, within the limits of what is possible under present conditions. The weakness is not so much in the training itself, as in the inadequacy of the general educational foundation on which it rests. . . . The majority of the men currently received as ministers and put in charge of churches are getting in general education a more or less satisfactory four to six years in primary (elementary) school, followed by two or three years of ministerial training. More run below this level than above it. . . . Proportionately the number of Africans who go beyond Standard VIII or X is very small indeed. . . . (There is a) general acceptance by practically all the churches and missions concerned that the standard of theological training must be raised. Almost invariably this is assumed to mean that the academic structure of the course must be advanced . . . raising the entrance standard of the colleges from say, Standard V or VI to Matriculation; this seemed to be regarded as the sine qua non for any improvement in theological training. We clearly recognize the need for this raising of entrance standards; with the rapid growth of a more educated African population there is pressing need for African ministers whose formal education does not lag behind that of those to whom they will minister."

At the same time, improvement of the instruction given at all levels is needed. Part III adds: "Theological training is not necessarily improved by raising the college entrance from Standard VI to Matriculation and providing a theological road which promises a B.D. on the horizon. . . . The improvement most urgently needed is in another dimension; it is the need to improve, deepen and make more living the theological training at *any* educational level, even one which begins, as in many instances and for a long time to come it must begin—well below a Matriculation entrance standard."

Another factor, according to Part III, is the need to make a greater use of African teachers: "In all the training centres visited by us—including the Union of South Africa and the three Central African territories—we met only two African tutors engaged in theological teaching. . . . One of the most important steps . . . will be taken when the teaching of theology to Africans is made, far more than at present, the responsibility of Africans. . . . In general, theological education in Africa has so far been conceived almost wholly in terms of transferring to Africa the kind of pattern which has long been familiar to the West."

Following his trip throughout Central Africa in 1958, Dr. Charles Forman reported:

Laymen are probably more concerned and more vociferous as to the needs of theological education in Africa than in any other continent. . . . Everyone is agreed that the big new forward step which is required is the provision of theological education on a new and higher level, the level of university instruction. It is pointed out again and again that general education has outstripped theological education and the latter must now catch up. The Church is losing the interest of the city people and the educated classes, the very groups which control the future of Africa, because it has no ministers capable of dealing with their problems and answering their questions. If the church cannot provide theological training at the level of the highest intellectual life of the continent it will most certainly lose the mind of Africa.

4. *The Shortage of the Local Clergy:* The growing need for a larger number of indigenous Protestant ministers is pointed out by Bishop Neill in Part I: "In almost every area which I visited, the shortage of trained and ordained ministers is one of the most serious weaknesses in the equipment of the Church. . . . We find that in Uganda, for example, there is on the average only one ordained minister for 5,000 baptized Christians. In Eastern Nigeria, the situation is on paper rather better, one ordained minister being provided for 3,000 baptized Christians."

The same situation, according to Part II, exists in Latin Africa: "One large mission in Belgian Congo reports eighteen pastors for 75,000 communicant members and slightly more than 1,000 places of worship. . . . The Anglican Church in Ruanda-Urundi has eight pastors—prospectively twenty-two—for 17,500 baptized Christians and 95,000 additional adherents, in 1,400 small village churches. . . . A large church body in the Camerouns has seventy-four pastors for 72,000 communicants and a total of 120,000 believers. . . . A circuit in the Ivory Coast has 16,000 members gross count, in eighty-nine villages, under the charge of two pastors (no missionary, twenty-four catechists)."

And in South Africa (according to Part III) the typical

ordained theologically-trained minister is in charge of a considerable area with anything from five to fifty local congregations. He is usually assisted by evangelists, catechists or deacons (according to the various church systems). For the itineration of his parish— which commonly measures, say, 25 by 45 miles and may even be much larger—he either cycles or walks. His main tasks are administrative. . . . It results in the local congregation seeing the ordained minister two or three times a year; very often the visits are less frequent than this. . . . The result is that—to put it drastically—the ordained minister has become an organizer, an administrator and an itinerant celebrant of the Sacraments.

The Anglican Church of the Province of South Africa has several hundred ministers, of whom only one is an African who has received an A.B. degree plus some theological training.

Parts I and II point out: "To some extent, the shortage of African ministers is compensated for by the work of lay ministers. These are numbered by thousands. . . . In the many thousands of small villages . . . it is the catechist who has carried the daily and weekly burden. . . . The catechist has conducted or provided for the Sunday service, usually preaching himself. Commonly, he has conducted brief morning prayers, or evening prayers, or both. . . . Where a Sunday school exists, he is responsible for it. . . . He conducts Christian funerals. . . . The catechist is not authorized to perform the sacraments of marriage, baptism, or the Lord's Supper. Thus, his ministry is conspicuously incomplete."

The weaknesses inherent in this system, according to Part II, stem from the fact that "many catechists barely read, and have the equivalent only of two to four years of primary school in general education. . . . Most catechists are very poorly paid by the churches, and are expected to secure . . . other income from teaching or a trade. Few give full time to the church work."

Part III asks a question and suggests an answer: "Is there not something deeply wrong with a situation in which ordination is available to a man who has reached a certain academic standard, even though he will become more of an administrator than a pastor, while ordination is withheld from the man who exercises the daily cure of souls if he lacks a prescribed educational standard? . . . The proposal for a part-time, *ordained* ministry should be considered in this connection. . . . The development of a part-time ministry would bring the sacraments within reach of many remote congregations who are at present denied them except on rare occasions."

The factors which have resulted in there being such an inadequate supply of African pastors are listed in Part II as follows:

1. The past adequacy or the presently assumed adequacy of missionaries as pastors;
2. The insufficient supply of men deemed earnestly committed, spiritually worthy, appropriately trained, and generally competent;
3. The apparent inability of the churches to support well-trained men giving full time to their service.

Part III ascribes the shortage primarily to the low salaries paid to African ministers:

When discussing with missionaries, African ministers and theological students the shortage of new recruits, the reason invariably given was that the salary is too low. . . . For any educated African, the Christian ministry involves a financial sacrifice out of all proportion to anything called for in the West. . . . Another factor which is seriously complicating the problem . . . of the support and recruitment of the ministry, is the rapid increase in teachers' salaries. . . . Teachers with Matriculation plus a professional certificate (are paid) from £168 to £336 a year. This has to be compared with the average minister's salary which is usually somewhere between £50 and £75 a year, with little possibility of a real increase.

Furthermore, as Principal Taylor of Bishop Tucker College at Mukono points out,

the reasons for the shortage of educated men for the ministry are not only financial, but are closely connected with the structure of Church authority under which the ministers are expected to serve. One young university graduate said to me, "I believe I am quite ready to become poor. But what would be the use of it? If I had any new ideas to offer I would never be allowed to try them out; if I had any fresh insight into the needs of my Church, they would never be listened to." The Church which is so institutional has a far too rigid control over its younger ministers. Their salary comes to them through an elderly African Rural Dean, their housing is the responsibility of poor and unsympathetic

Church elders; and the older, less-educated clergy are naturally a bit envious and a bit afraid of the younger more privileged men. When we first launched the new-style lay readers in the Church we sent out from Mukono a group of young men filled with enthusiasm and a crusading zeal. At the end of a year half of them were broken with disappointment and frustration, and two had left the work for other jobs. One of them called me to visit him and I found that he and his wife and two children had been given one room in a disused sports pavilion as their home, and the verandah they were expected to use as a two-class school. The older, conservative clergy do not know how to use the young educated men; and the young men know it and most of them stay away.

5. *The Action Taken to Date in Response to Previous Survey Recommendations:* At the All-Africa Church Conference which was held at Ibadan, Nigeria, in January 1958 an attempt was made to summarize the progress achieved to date in implementing the recommendations contained in Parts I, II and III and in the IMC Madagascar Survey. These developments have been commented on previously in this chapter. In general the response has been slow and hesitant. With a few exceptions it appears that the major obstacle has been the attitude of the foreign missionaries stationed in Africa rather than that of either the Africans themselves or of most mission board executives. A Preliminary Progress Report of the Conference states that in French West Africa

one obstacle to regrouping was the fact that most of this work is done by each mission in the vernacular of its region, so that a common school using French as a medium seemed scarcely probable. Another obstacle to joint work is the fact that certain missions have several schools within their own organization and seem unable to unite them on a denominational basis; the factor of the vast distances between these schools is not the only element preventing their unions. . . . Although perfecting ministerial training through union schemes has apparent favor at executive levels and at international conferences . . . the fact of field resistance, and financial considerations which block cooperation are worth noting. Certain boards also seem inclined to finance talks about union, whereas actual union schemes are slow in getting their support.

According to one observer with wide experience in the field, the average length of time which elapses between the making of a formal recommendation by a survey and its implementation in the field is seldom less than six years, and usually more.

6. *The Missionary Opportunity:* Dr. Henry P. Van Dusen has commented that Africa is "the neglected continent" with "backward missions," and that it "presents an opportunity of winning more converts than anywhere else in the next 25 years." One of the primary reasons for this is that in the countries south of the Sahara most non-Christian Africans believe in various forms of animism rather than in a comparatively well-developed religion such as Islam.

Bishop Neill states in Part I: "There is no area in the world in which the church is faced with so unexampled an opportunity as in tropical Africa. . . . In Uganda thousands of people are still being admitted to the church every year. . . . From the

Christian point of view, what immediately impresses the visitor is the newness of everything. The first baptism among the ... Kikuyu took place only in 1906. ... In India, after four centuries of missions, slightly more than two per cent of the population is Christian. In tropical Africa, the proportion of Christians seems to be not less than one in ten. ... The rapidity of progress is one of the greatest causes of weakness in the African churches."

The authors of Part III state that beneath a constantly growing sense of nationalism

there is taking place a resurgence of old pagan beliefs and traditions. ... There are indeed indications of a growing African consolidation as a defence mechanism against white aggression. ... It was said in South Africa somewhat sharply: "The Church gets the ministry it deserves." ... The decreasing respect for the African minister within his own community has been mentioned. ... The African Christian community seldom sees the office of the ministry as an integral part of the life of the church itself. It is regarded as belonging to the pattern of western missionary activity. ... Some of the young nationally and politically self-conscious Africans disparage the ministry as belonging more or less to the realm of white missionary domination.

A member of the faculty at Fourah Bay College, with previous teaching experience on the faculty of St. John's College in India, has noted the differences in attitudes which have prevailed in recent years among African as contrasted with Indian students. In the case of the latter, particularly among those enrolled in secular colleges and universities in India, there is often said to be a lack of self-discipline and a feeling of frustration which occasionally leads to student strikes. By contrast, the typical African college student (outside of the Union of South Africa) is found to be receptive, eager to learn, and imbued with a confidence in the future which is based in part on the comparative ease with which college and technically trained students finds secular employment in most parts of the continent.

The final conclusion of Bishop Neill was:

I ended my tour, and I remain burdened with a sense of immense opportunity and immense peril. Not even the famous mass movements in India have brought into the Churches such masses of people as are now pressing in in every part of Africa. It is hardly an exaggeration to say that in fifty years time, tropical Africa might well be in the main a Christian country. ... For the most part, the Churches are wholly unable to deal with those who are coming in. ...To bring converts into a superficial level of Christian emancipation is no difficult task. ... To lead them forward into steadiness and sobriety of Christian thinking and living is a very different matter. There lies the peril. ... The danger becomes acute, when the situation begins to become static, low standards are accepted as normal, and the Church settles down to a complacent half-Christianity. ... Young Africa is asking questions, and will not stay long for an answer. If the pastor cannot give the answer, the Communist, the secularist, the political agitator are ready with very seductive and appealing answers.

CHAPTER 3

THE MIDDLE EAST

The total population of the Middle Eastern countries (as of 1957 as listed in chapter 1 of this Survey) was approximately 86,000,000 persons, of whom virtually all are Muslims. Protestantism has had little success in obtaining a significant number of converts. Furthermore Protestant and Roman Catholic missionaries in the Middle East rub shoulders with the various Eastern Churches in this area. In the past this has often been a source of irritation to the latter churches which, understandably enough, consider themselves to be in the direct line of succession from the original Christian church.

Lebanon is the only Christian country in the Middle East, with 55% of its 1,320,-000 population Christians and 45% Muslims. Of the approximately 450,000 Lebanese who are members of Christian churches, about 68% are members of one of the various Eastern Churches, 25% are Roman Catholics of the Maronite, Armenian and Syrian rites, and the remaining 7% (about 30,000 persons) are members of the Protestant community.

As shown in Table 23 there is only one small Protestant seminary in the Middle East.

TABLE 23.   THEOLOGICAL SCHOOLS IN THE MIDDLE EAST (1958)

		Approx. Number of		
	Location	Full-Time Faculty	Theol. Students	Denominational Support
Lebanon				
Near East School of Theology	Beirut	4[a]	12[b]	Congregational, Presbyterian USA, etc.

NOTES: [a] Plus one additional faculty member to be named.   [b] Plus three other students at lower level of training.

During the 19th and 20th centuries the American Board of Commissioners for Foreign Missions (the Congregational Church) focused its missionary activities in Turkey. In the latter half of the 19th century the Board established four seminaries or clergy training schools in that country. Three of them trained Turkish-speaking students. The first was at Marsovan (in the western portion of Turkey), the second was at Marash (in central Turkey), and the third at Kharput (in the eastern part of the country). The fourth school was founded in Mardin in the southeastern section of Turkey in order to train Arabic-speaking ministers. According to Julius Richter, the training provided at these institutions was "confined to the more important theological studies, exposition of the Scriptures standing in the center of the whole course. . . . Little attention (was) devoted to foreign languages, either English, Greek or Hebrew. . . . While the first students in the seminaries were half-developed men, without much preparatory training, it became necessary later to provide a better preliminary training in order that the work in the theological seminaries might be more thorough and fruitful. Accordingly, intermediary schools were instituted between the primary schools and the seminaries. . . ."

A good number of the students at these seminaries were of Armenian origin who might otherwise have been destined to be trained in the priesthood of the Armenian Orthodox Church. These four schools never made much progress and during World War I it was necessary to close them. The massacres of the Armenians by the Turks during those years served to scatter the constituency from which the four seminaries drew their students.

In 1922 the American Board resumed the training of ordinand students at Constantinople in the vicinity of Robert College. This seminary was known as the School of Religion, and in 1922–23 its enrollment consisted of 10 students from Turkey, four from Bulgaria and 12 emigré students from Russia. After the catastrophe of Smyrna, the Armenian and Greek students were moved to Athens, and the School of Religion functioned both at Constantinople and in Athens until 1925 when the branch at Constantinople was closed.

Meanwhile, in 1873 a seminary was opened in Beirut which ten years later was moved to the campus of the Syrian Protestant College (now known as the American University of Beirut). Subsequently the seminary sold its building to the College and for some years it functioned as a summer school in Suk el-Gharb. Reopened in another section of Beirut in 1905, its name was changed in 1926 from the Beirut Theological Seminary to the School for Religious Workers.

In 1930 it was proposed that the School of Religion in Athens should be merged into the School for Religious Workers at Beirut. Two years later the Congregationalists and the Presbyterians USA agreed to this, and the name of the new institution was changed to The Near East School of Theology. In 1945 the Evangelical Synod of Syria and Lebanon (Presbyterian, with approximately 6,000 members) and the Union of Armenian Evangelical Churches in the Near East (with about 3,000 members) became cooperating bodies with the seminary. In 1950 (two years after the creation of the State of Israel) the Anglicans discontinued the clergy training class they had been conducting in Jerusalem, and the Evangelical

Episcopal Community of Jordan and Lebanon (3,000 members) also affiliated itself with the School. These five church bodies are now represented on the Board
of Managers of the NEST.

A total of 15 students were enrolled in the NEST in 1958, of whom 12 were
destined for the full-time ministry. The student body was composed of 13 Armenians from Lebanon and Syria, and two Arabs from churches associated with
the Presbyterian mission in Iraq. There were no Arab students from either Syria
or Lebanon. The predominance of Armenian students in the seminary over the
years presents something of a problem inasmuch as the Armenians occupy somewhat the same economic and social position in the Middle East today as do the
Jews in Eastern Europe and the Overseas Chinese in Southeast Asia. It is difficult
for Armenian ministers to serve in Arab pastorates. All three Protestant Churches
in the Levant are said to be facing a critical shortage of ministers, owing largely
to their inability to recruit a sufficient number of candidates for this work. In part
this is due to the migration of Protestants and other Christians from Lebanon to
North and South America, and in part to the fact that many of the Protestant
ministers in the Middle East are paid such low salaries by their congregations that
they must supplement their income through nonreligious employment.

The NEST offers courses for men and women at both the undergraduate and
graduate levels. Several courses in Islamics are listed in the catalogue. The School's
diploma in theology or Christian education is awarded to graduate students possessing a B.A. degree for three years' work at the NEST. It may also be obtained
in four years' time by students entering the NEST who are seniors or juniors at
the American University of Beirut (AUB), and in five years' time by those entering the NEST as sophomores. The School's certificate is awarded for three years'
work to students who upon their admission have completed work only as far as
freshman year in college or its equivalent. The curriculum for the certificate is
similar to that of the diploma course except that it omits the courses taken at the
AUB. The certificate students are trained to enter Christian service of one sort or
another, as are the recipients of the School's certificate for its short course for
women.

Since 1926 the NEST has cooperated with the AUB in an arrangement whereby
students of either institution may take courses in the other. Students enrolled in
the diploma course of the NEST attend both institutions, and they receive the
diploma from the School and an A.B. degree from the University. Neither the
diploma nor the degree is granted until the requirements of both institutions have
been satisfactorily met. During each semester the NEST also offers several courses
in religion on the campus of the University.

While there are a number of advantages to this arrangement between the NEST
and the AUB, there are certain disadvantages as well. The NEST is located about

two miles away from the University, so that when a student is taking the combined course it is necessary for him to spend considerable time each day traveling by bus or tram between the two institutions. Furthermore the students at the NEST tend to be less mature than they would be if they had previously completed their courses in the arts and sciences.

Another problem which has confronted the NEST is that it is occupying somewhat unsuitable quarters on property which originally was the old missions compound outside the walls of Beirut. The city has since expanded beyond the walls, and the NEST finds itself located in what is now downtown Beirut. The seminary's principal building is Colton Hall, which was erected in 1912. It contains a chapel, library, and administrative offices on the ground floor, with the classrooms and dormitory rooms for men on the second floor. Accommodations for women are provided in the Stiger Building, and the common room and refectory occupy the ground floor of the parish house of the National Evangelical Church, which is Beirut's largest Protestant church.

Despite the exchange of courses, etc., between the NEST and the AUB, the distance which separates the two campuses is said to preclude the possibility of a truly close relationship between the two institutions. During the past ten years constant consideration has been given to the possibility of relocating the NEST on or near the campus of the University. Plans were developed for the purchase of a plot of land near the medical gate of the University in Ras Beirut which would cost approximately $35,000. It was estimated that a building for the seminary would cost $65,000, making a total investment of $100,000 needed to finance the move. However, none of the mission boards or churches supporting the NEST had sufficient funds available to pay the cost of such a move.

The School has planned both a short-range and a long-range development program. The former would require ca. $14,000 to set up a new library room and alter the present library space in order to make it suitable for administrative offices and classrooms. The long-range program anticipates relocation costs of as high as $300,000 and a recurring annual income of $81,000 to cover (among other items) the salaries of seven or eight full-time faculty members at a minimum annual salary of $5,000.

The dependence of the seminary upon foreign sources of income is evidenced by the fact that approximately 80% of its 1957–58 budget was met with contributions (approximately equal in amount) from the Congregational and the Presbyterian USA mission boards. The remaining 20% was provided by the three local churches, with the Union of Armenian Evangelical Churches contributing the largest share of the three.

In 1957 the Presbyterian USA Board of Foreign Missions sent a survey team to Syria and Lebanon in order to assess the various activities of this Board in these countries. After reviewing the work of the NEST, the team's report commented as follows on the School's administration and faculty:

The Near East School of Theology seems to have had a rather rapid turnover of its principals since the union of the two Schools in 1932. In the past ten years there have been two principals and now they have another, acting principal. . . . The lack of adequate full-time faculty is the weakest factor in the Near East School of Theology at present. This criticism does not refer especially to individual teachers on the present faculty, but to the situation as a whole. One critic went so far as to advise that apart from the acting principal, all the present faculty members should be dismissed. . . .

According to the printed "Catalog" for 1957–58, there were five full-time members of the faculty, including a young man who acts as student counsellor and teaches New Testament and Greek. Whether he teaches all ten of the courses outlined in the Catalog under the field of New Testament is not clear. No teachers are specifically assigned to these courses in the Catalog and one gets the impression that they are taught, if taught at all, if and when a teacher can be found to teach them. There is no teacher on the present faculty, nor on the list of lecturers, who is responsible for the seven courses in Old Testament described in the Catalog. . . . The important department of Theology, consisting of ten courses, is now the responsibility of two part-time lecturers. From a personal interview with one of these lecturers, it is evident that only some of these courses are being taught. . . .

Another aspect of the faculty situation is the evidently inadequate preparation of many of the teachers, whether full-time or lecturers, to teach their subjects. There is only one teacher holding a Ph.D. degree on the whole full and part-time faculty. . . .

The survey team recognized the desirability of relocating the NEST on or near the AUB campus. However, in view of the shortage of funds available for such a purpose, it was recommended that

the pressing needs of the School for faculty, students, revised curriculum and library space now take precedence over relocation. . . . For more than a decade the School of Theology has struggled with limited resources, a diminishing student enrollment, and inadequately trained and underpaid faculty. . . . It is evident that if the . . . School . . . is to live up even to its Catalog, not to speak of its responsibilities for training the Christian ministry of the Near East, its faculty must be radically improved and increased. One statement of the School's needs proposes the addition of five new professors, one each in the departments of Old Testament, New Testament, Theology-Ethics, Church History, and a single man for librarian and dormitory supervision. . . .

The team concluded that not only would it be necessary for the NEST to have at least five full-time men on its faculty, but that the School should (1) inaugurate a program for recruiting students and (2) enlarge its library space.

Beirut is considered by many to be the cultural center of the Arab World, whereas Cairo is the religious center of Islam. At the foreign missions conference held at

Lake Mohonk, N.Y., in April 1956 by the Presbyterian Church USA, the thought was expressed that the NEST might consider the possibility of merging with the Evangelical Seminary in Cairo whose plant facilities are somewhat superior. However, the conclusion was reached that "further investigation" of this possibility would be needed.

At this point in world affairs, it would be difficult to think of a less attractive place than Cairo in which to endeavor to establish a strong Protestant seminary.

There is no cooperation among the seminaries of the Protestant and Eastern Churches in the Middle East. In this connection Rev. Pitt S. Willand, who has had extensive contacts with some of these seminaries, wrote in 1957:

The whole field of theological education in the Middle East needs re-examination, reorientation, and strengthening. . . . There is virtually no contact between the theological students of the various churches. None of the seminaries maintains high academic standards. The entire ecumenical cause . . . would be immeasurably strengthened by, first, the reorganization of the Near East School of Theology and, then, its development into a regional center for theological study with a faculty of trained scholars from various churches and adequate funds. Admittedly, there are many problems involved in the establishment and conduct of a theological institution training both Protestant and Orthodox ordinands. Before such an institution could take form, a careful study would have to be made and painstaking negotiations entered into, in the field and at home. I am convinced that this is a propitious time to begin such a study, and that it should be begun forthwith. I very much fear that if an attempt is not made to establish such a regional center for theological education, we will see before much longer a proliferation of underequipped and poorly staffed seminaries in the area which can only perpetuate and deepen the chasms existing among the churches and continue to condemn the clergy of the area to insufficient training for the work they are called to do.

CHAPTER 4

SOUTHERN ASIA

A. India

1. *Introduction*

In round figures, of the 360,000,000 people in India about 85% are Hindus, and 10% are Muslims. Of the remaining 5% one-half (i.e., about 9,000,000 persons) are members of the Christian community. Of the Christians approximately one-half are Roman Catholics and one-half Protestants. The majority of the latter have been converted from the low-caste Hindus in the population. Roughly 57% of all the Christians in India are to be found in the four southern states of Madras, Kerala, Mysore and Andhra. As many as one-third of the Christians reside in the small state of Kerala and constitute one-third of the population of that state. Kerala has one of the highest literacy rates in India (between 30 and 50%). (It is also the first Indian state to have placed the control of its government in the hands of the Communist Party.)

Excluding the ancient Syrian Orthodox (Jacobite) Church in India having a total community of about 750,000 persons, the membership status of the more important younger Protestant churches is approximately as shown in Table 24.

TABLE 24. MEMBERSHIP OF LEADING PROTESTANT CHURCHES IN INDIA (1957)

Federation of Evangelical Lutheran Churches in India	500,000
Church of South India	350,000
Baptist Union of India, Pakistan, Burma and Ceylon	300,000
United Church of Northern India	150,000
Methodist Church of India	150,000
Church of India, Pakistan, Burma and Ceylon (Anglican)[a]	100,000

NOTE: [a] Excluding dioceses merged into the Church of South India.

The Church of South India consists of a union of Anglican, Presbyterian, Methodist, Congregational and Reformed Churches located in the southern part of India. It was established in 1947. This Church has 14 dioceses, seven Indian bishops, 1,200 ordained ministers, and a community of about 1,000,000 persons. The merger is unique in that it was the first time that the Anglicans (i.e., the dioceses in

TABLE 25. THEOLOGICAL SCHOOLS IN INDIA (1956)

Name	Location	Approx. Number of				Denominational Support
		Full-Time Faculty	Part-Time Faculty	Theol. Students	Nontheol. Students	
Theological Colleges (affiliated with Serampore Senate)						
Serampore College	Serampore	8		25	2	Baptists, etc.
United Theological College	Bangalore	8	6	30	14	Church of South India, etc.
Leonard Theological College	Jabalpur	11	2	64	20	Methodist, etc.
Bishop's College	Calcutta	4		22		CIPBC[a]
Gurukul Theological College	Madras	4		11		Lutheran
Subtotal: 5		35	8	152	36	
Theological Schools (affiliated with Serampore Senate)						
Union Theological Seminary	Bareilly	8	3	26		Methodist, English Baptists, etc.
Tamilnad Theological College	Tirumaraiyur	5	4	30	4	Church of South India
Gujerat United School of Theology	Ahmedabad	4		9		Irish Presbyterian, etc.
Kerala United Theological Seminary	Trivandrum	4	4	16		Church of South India
North India United Theological College	Saharanpur	8	4	23		United Church of Northern India, etc.
Mar Thoma Theological Seminary	Kottayam	1	4	9		Mar Thoma Syrian Church
Lutheran Theological College	Ranchi	3		30		Lutheran
Basel Mission Theological Seminary	Mangalore	3	5	10		Basel Evangelical Mission, etc.
Luthergiri Theological Seminary	Rajahmundry	9	3	23	20	American Evangelical Lutheran Church, etc.
Andhra United Theological College	Dornakal	4	4	14	9	Church of South India, etc.
Baptist Theological Seminary	Kakinada	11	2	25	6	Canadian Baptist
United Theological College of Western India	Poona	5	5	22		Scottish Presbyterian, etc.
Cherta Theological College	Cherrapunji	3	3	14	18	Welsh Presbyterian, etc.
Union Kanarese Seminary	Tumkur	3	3	9		Church of South India, etc.
Union Theological College	Indore	3	2	4	6	Church of Scotland, etc.
Subtotal: 15		74	46	264	63	
Theological Schools (not affiliated with Serampore Senate)						
Union Biblical Seminary	Yeotmal	10	6	59	13	Free Methodist, etc.
Assam Baptist Theological Seminary	Jorhat	8	7	40		American Baptist
Theological Seminary	Kotapud	6	3	17	30	Lutheran (German)
Christian Training College	Cuttack	2	4	14		Baptist (English and Canadian)
Andhra Baptist Theological Seminary	Ramapatnam	4	3	12	19	American Baptist
Allahabad Bible Seminary	Allahabad	3	5	15	2	Oriental Mission Society
Santal Theological Seminary	Benagaria	6	1	20		Lutheran (Danish)
United Theological School	Calcutta	2	3	[b]	7	CIPBC[a]

TABLE 25.   THEOLOGICAL SCHOOLS IN INDIA (1956)   (cont'd)

Name	Location	Approx. Number of				
		Full-Time Faculty	Part-Time Faculty	Theol. Students	Nontheol. Students	Denominational Support
Karnataka Bible Seminary	Gadag	2	2	21		Oriental Mission Society
Concordia Seminary	Nagercoil	3	1	25	8	Missouri Synod Lutheran
Nimasarai Bengali Divinity School	Old Malda	2	1	8?		Lutheran (Danish)
Tamil Evangelical Lutheran Seminary	Tranquebar	2	3	15	10	Tamil Evangelical Lutheran Synod
Subtotal: 12		50	39	246	89	
Total: 32ᶜ		159	93	662	188	

NOTES: ᵃ Church of India. Pakistan, Burma and Ceylon   ᶜ See also Table 70A, Supplementary List of Theological
(Anglican).   Schools.
ᵇ No theological students in ministerial courses offered.

southern India of the Church of India, Pakistan, Burma and Ceylon—which were
the most numerous among the merging bodies) had ever been drawn into such
a union. The Church of England, the Protestant Episcopal Church and a number
of other churches or provinces in the Anglican Communion now recognize the
Church of South India, but with certain reservations.

The United Church of Northern India consists of a union of Presbyterian, Congregational, Reformed and Moravian Churches located in northern India. Negotiations for a larger union with Anglican, Methodist and Baptist churches in this
area are proceeding well, with the hope of consummation by 1960. If this is
achieved, it is planned to call the new church the Church of North India, and
steps will be taken to establish close relations with the Church of South India.
Thus, of all the countries in Africa, Asia and Latin America which have a significant number of Protestants, the greatest progress has been made in India in achieving organic denominational unity on a purely voluntary basis.

One of the principal sources of information on the theological schools in India
is *The Christian Ministry in India* by Dr. Charles W. Ranson. This study was based
on a survey made by him in the years 1943–45 for the National Christian Council
of India, Burma and Ceylon, of which he was then Secretary. Extensive questionnaires were issued, followed by regional conferences. The report was published in
1945 and accordingly is now out of date in some respects, but valuable in others.

The list of theological colleges and schools shown in Table 25 was derived from
and corresponds fairly closely with the list contained in a second important source
of information—the survey *After Ten Years—A Report on Theological Education in
India* which was prepared by Professor M. H. Harrison for the National Christian
Council of India and which was adopted by its Board of Theological Education
in 1956. The phrase "After Ten Years" in its title refers to the period which had
elapsed since the publication of the Ranson report.

It will be noted from Table 25 that there are located in India today five theological colleges, as this term was previously defined in chapter 1. This is a larger number than is to be found in most of the other individual countries in Africa, Asia and Latin America. It reflects the fact that theological education in India has had a considerably longer history than in the other younger church countries. Serampore and Bishop's College, for example, were founded over a century ago.

Under the heading "Denominational Support" in Table 25 there is listed only the name of that denomination which has been most active in contributing to the needs of a given theological school. However, in India and elsewhere in Asia there has been a tendency toward multidenominational support of the seminaries. For example, Serampore College is listed as "Baptist, etc." Actually this seminary now receives budgetary contributions from 12 denominational bodies (The British Baptists, Church of Scotland, American Baptists, American Methodists, Canadian Baptists, Arcot Lutheran Church of Madras, London Missionary Society [Congregational], American Evangelical Mission, United Church of Northern India, Baptist Churches of the Northern Circars, Mar Thoma Syrian Church, the Church of India, Pakistan, Burma and Ceylon, and the Australian Baptists). Similar lengthy lists might be compiled for some of the other theological schools listed in the table. Unfortunately the number of donors to the seminaries is more impressive than the aggregate amount of their cash contributions to them.

2. *The Senate of Serampore College*

The comparatively high standard of theological education in India is due largely to the fact that the five theological colleges and 15 of the leading theological schools are affiliated with the Senate of Serampore College.

The Senate was established in 1918. In the period 1945–56 the number of seminaries affiliated with it rose from 9 to 20.

Through the Senate the five theological colleges confer B.D. degrees somewhat similar to those granted in the United States. These institutions require an A.B. degree as a prerequisite for entrants, teach in the English language and insist on their students' studying the Greek language.

The 15 theological schools affiliated with the Senate do not grant B.D. degrees but confer an L.Th. diploma (Licentiate in Theology). These schools require only a high school diploma of their entrants, teach in the vernacular language of the area in which they are situated (with a few courses occasionally taught in English), and do not require the study of Greek.

The Senate sets the examinations and awards the degrees for all of its affiliated institutions, thereby standardizing theological education in a way which is not done in any other country in Africa, Asia or Latin America. The Senate meets in India and is an interdenominational body whose members are drawn chiefly from the principals of its affiliated colleges and schools.

In 1954 the Senate awarded a total of 38 L.Th. diplomas and 23 B.D. degrees. Since 1911 the Senate has granted a total of 417 L.Th. diplomas and 494 B.D. degrees. Customarily only four or five M.Th. degrees are awarded a year, and so far only one D.D. by thesis has been conferred. Candidates for advanced degrees study in any one of the affiliated institutions which has the professor best qualified to advise him concerning his chosen field. In order to avoid an undue concentration, some effort is made to spread the case load of advanced students evenly among the seminaries.

In 1956 Professor William Stewart of Serampore College wrote:

There are, however, other institutions in India concerned with training for the ministry whose authorities fear that Serampore affiliation might unduly fetter them. Of these some also are suspicious of a "Serampore theology," which they conceive to be dangerously liberal. The best-known of such institutions is probably Union Biblical Seminary, Yeotmal, which in recent years has developed training at a graduate level with a course more satisfying to the "conservative" groups. This Seminary asked the Serampore Senate for some kind of "accreditation" rather than for the affiliation which involves taking the Serampore examinations. This request the Senate found itself unable to grant, partly because its charter would not permit it to grant degrees to students whom it had not examined. . . . Yeotmal has now acceded to requests that it should itself "accredit" certain smaller institutions and help them to maintain a good standard. . . . There is thus the possibility that India may have two separate systems of theological education. . . .

It has been suggested that the Serampore Senate might become the examining body and award degrees to students in seminaries outside of India. However, this does not at present appear to be an active possibility. A few years ago the Djakarta Theological College inquired concerning the possibility of its becoming affiliated with the Senate. This query was never carried beyond the discussion stage inasmuch as language difficulties appear to raise important obstacles: the Senate conducts its work in English, which is not the primary language of most of the seminaries in Indonesia or in the other countries in southern and southeast Asia.

3. The Five Theological Colleges

Serampore College: This institution is composed of two departments: Arts and Sciences, and Theology. It has approximately 850 students (mostly non-Christians) studying in the former department, and only about 30 students enrolled in the theological college. The Arts and Sciences Department is affiliated with the University of Calcutta. The Serampore Theological College acting through the Serampore Senate exercises the degree-granting powers of a university itself.

Serampore is located on the banks of the Hooghly River, 15 miles upstream from Calcutta. It was founded in 1818 by an English Baptist missionary, William Carey. He chose the town of Serampore, which was then a "factory" colony under the Danish flag, because the (British) East India Company had refused to admit him and his fellow missionaries into Calcutta. In 1827 King Frederik VI of Denmark granted Serampore its charter under which it might confer degrees in theology. When the Danish "factories" at Serampore were sold to the British Government in 1845, the royal Danish charter at Serampore continued in force and the first theological degree was granted under its authority in 1915. Serampore College (i.e., the institution as a whole) is governed by a council which meets in London and on which several denominations are represented.

With the endorsement of the Indian Government, the Principal of Serampore, Dr. C. E. Abraham, endeavored in 1955–56 to raise $225,000 in the United States for its capital needs. Of this sum $150,000 was designated for the needs of the Arts and Sciences Department and $75,000 was earmarked for the seminary at Serampore (for a new chapel, classrooms and residences). The Southern Asia and Near East Committee of the Division of Foreign Missions (National Council of Churches, USA) voted to ask the Division's member mission boards for contributions for this purpose. The American Methodists contributed $15,000 to the project in 1956 and indicated their willingness to contribute an additional $5,000 provided other mission boards gave to it according to their means. This condition was not met, and the Committee was obliged to express its disappointment that the members' response was poor—"not through lack of interest but because of other heavy commitments (of the boards)." Serampore has also been seeking to obtain $19,500 annually for its seminary's operating and scholarship needs.

United Theological College of South India and Ceylon: This institution is located at Bangalore and was established in 1910 as a union institution. Many consider the UTC has the strongest faculty and is the strongest single institution of all the seminaries in India. Of its eight full-time faculty members, three are Indians. The College has had a comparatively good faculty since it was founded, and it has trained more post-B.D. students than any other theological college in India. A YMCA Secretarial School, the Missionary Language School and the Christian Institute for the Study of Religion and Society are affiliated with the UTC.

In 1953 two-thirds of the school's budget was furnished by mission boards, principally the English Methodists and Congregationalists. In 1955 churches in India contributed approximately $200 to the seminary's budget. Two years later this total had risen to $1,400.

The College has drawn up a comprehensive building plan providing for an increase in the capacity of its library and chapel, enlarging the student hostel, and increasing the number of married students' quarters, staff residences and classrooms. The UTC's present facilities can house 40 single and six married students, and these accommodations are now in full use. The school has only two scholarships (amounting to $180 a year) to offer to its B.D. students. Recipients retain them for each of the three years in this course. More of such scholarships are needed. In addition the seminary believes the number of its full-time faculty members should be increased to 12. Finally the UTC has as one of its aims the establishment of a center of graduate theological studies at Bangalore.

In 1954 the College elected its first Indian Principal, Dr. J. Russell Chandran, who is also serving as General Editor of the Christian Students' Library: this project (which is described in chapter 11) was launched by Rev. Marcus Ward, who was also a member of the Bangalore faculty. Professor M. H. Harrison, whose 1957 survey of the seminaries in India entitled *After Ten Years* has already been cited, serves as a professor at the UTC.

Rev. P. D. Devanandan, who formerly was a professor on the UTC faculty, is now the Director of the Centre for the Study of Hinduism. It was intended in 1957 that the Centre should be established in the city of Bangalore: it would not become a part of any one seminary in India, but rather would cooperate with a number of them in research in the Hindu religion. As such it would be a counterpart in this field of the Henry Martyn School of Islamic Studies which was begun as a joint enterprise in India of several churches and mission boards well over a decade ago.

Leonard Theological College: Located at Jabalpur, Leonard is Methodism's premier theological institution in India. It is also the largest of the five theological colleges in this country.

This school was established as an outgrowth of the Union Theological Seminary at Bareilly—another Methodist institution and one of the 15 theological schools affiliated with the Serampore Senate. The seminary at Bareilly had been founded in 1872, and its courses were given in Hindustani. English as a medium of higher instruction in India did not become widespread until several decades later. During World War I the quality of the students at Bareilly declined to the point where it was decided in 1918 to establish an English Department there. In the next few years it became evident that Bareilly was not the most convenient location for an institution aimed at serving all the Methodist conferences in India. Accordingly it was decided that the English Department should be set up as a separate theological college, which in 1923 was established in Jabalpur.

During the period 1945–56 the Methodists contributed $250,000 toward the cost of erecting new buildings at Leonard which changed the entire aspect of the college, turning it from a "compound" of scattered unplanned buildings to an integrated institution. The most recent addition to the Leonard buildings was the chapel and administration building made possible mainly by American Methodists' "Week of Dedication" offerings. From the same source of funds there was contributed the cost of a cafeteria and auditorium. The school also has excellent equipment for training students in audio-visual techniques. Leonard has more of an American theological tradition than the other seminaries in India, and its comparatively modern facilities reflect the financial support it has received from the United States.

From 1954 to 1955 its total student enrollment increased from 87 to 105, divided among four departments: the School of Theology, Post Graduate Studies, Religious Education, and the School for Women. In 1956 the School of Theology was training 64 students at a theological level. It grants both a B.D. and a G.Th. (Graduate in Theology) degree, the latter being equivalent to an L.Th. degree. Both courses require three years of work. Each student studying the rural church attends a short course in agriculture at the Allahabad Agricultural Institute.

The number of students registered in the Post Graduate School at Leonard has fluctuated between three in 1949-50 (its first year of operation) and a high of six in 1954-55. The size of this School is intentionally kept small inasmuch as it is aiming to achieve a level of academic excellence. Only students having a B.D. degree are admitted, and they read for an M.Th. degree. Leonard's graduate students have made an extensive survey of religious institutions in the Jabalpur area. However, little has been done to analyze this material.

Leonard became a union institution in 1949 in the sense that at least four other denominations, including the Presbyterians USA, Evangelical and Reformed Church and the Disciples, now contribute to its support. Recently Dr. George S. Sahai, formerly a professor at Lucknow Christian College, was elected Principal, succeeding a Westerner in this position. Now that Leonard's building program is largely completed, he believes the seminary should increase its emphasis on recruiting students of higher caliber. He further believes that the members of its faculty should spend more time in translating theological texts into the local languages of India.

Bishop's College: This Anglican seminary was founded in the Calcutta area in 1824, six years after the founding of Serampore. It was moved to the city of Calcutta in 1880 where it now occupies an excellent site, has a substantial chapel and rather aged residential facilities. For many years the College included both an Arts and a Theological Department. During one period of its history the theological work ceased altogether. However, in 1918 the College became an exclusively theological institution training men for the Anglican ministry. The main emphasis of its training is said to be on deepening the spiritual life of its students.

Since the independence of India, this College has been governed by the Episcopal Synod of the Church of India, Pakistan, Burma and Ceylon. Bishop's College is only 13 miles' distance from Serampore College, and at one point a merger of the two seminaries was proposed. The suggestion was declined on denominational grounds.

Gurukul Lutheran Theological College and Research Institute: This is the most recently established of the five theological colleges in India. Originally a theological school, it was reopened on a 21-acre site in Madras in July 1953. The United Lutherans were already supporting the Luthergiri Seminary at Rajahmundry. Various Evangelical Lutheran churches were supporting the Lutheran Theological College at Ranchi (which is an L.Th. school), and also the Tamil Evangelical Lutheran Seminary at Tranquebar. These three seminaries are all located in the northeastern and southeastern portions of the Indian peninsula where Lutheran missionary activities have long been centered.

After World War II the need for training Lutheran ordinand students at the theological college level became apparent. Various sites for a new Theological College were considered. At one point discussions were held with the United Theological College at Bangalore with a view toward exploring the possibility of the Lutherans' establishing their new college on or adjacent to the UTC campus. However, the latter serves the Church of South India which the Lutherans at that time had declined to join on the ground of their different interpretation of the nature and structure of the Church. Accordingly in 1953 the United Lutherans, along with 11 other Lutheran agencies and churches in India and Europe, established the Gurukul College at Madras.

The opening of Gurukul drew some sharp criticisms in the local press at that time. For several months *The Guardian* newspaper in Madras printed adverse comments contained in letters to the editor, in one of which the question was asked: "Is it wise today to launch on a venture which is so hopelessly dependent on foreign funds and which must, therefore, crash when such funds dry up—as they must some day?"

The student body at Gurukul numbered only nine in 1954-55 and 11 in 1956. Thus the seminary is still in an early stage of its existence and faces a number of problems. Its faculty of four professors are missionaries sent by the Swedish and German Lutheran Churches.

The Research Institute, the name of which is included in the College's title, is also still in its formative stages. The aim of the Institute is to create an indigenous Indian Christian theology and to conduct research at the graduate level in the fields of Hinduism and some of the other religions of India. A few projects have been initiated.

4. The Twenty-Seven L.Th. Theological Schools

Because of their large number there is no need for a detailed discussion in this Survey of each of the 27 theological schools at the L.Th. level in India. Concerning many of them there is little or no information which is readily available outside of India.

In 1955 on the initiative of Serampore College a conference on ministerial training was held at Dornakal which was attended by the principals—or their representatives—of 14 seminaries. The L.Th. curriculum was reviewed in such a way as to strengthen the balance between disciplined study and practical training.

The 15 L.Th. schools affiliated with the Serampore Senate are often larger and at a somewhat higher academic level than are the 12 which are not so affiliated. In 1956 the Senate permitted the former to spread their courses over a four- rather than a three-year period in order that more courses in pastoralia might be offered by them.

Concerning the 12 schools which are not affiliated with the Serampore Senate, even fewer facts are generally available. It will be noted from Table 25 that eight of these institutions are Lutheran or Baptist seminaries, and that two of them are supported by the Oriental Mission Society. The 12 seminaries are for the most part more conservative in their theological outlook than are the 20 seminaries affiliated with the Serampore Senate. The best known among the 12 has already been referred to above, namely the Union Biblical Seminary at Yeotmal. This institution is classified in the Harrison report as a "theological college" because in June 1955 it started a class of students looking forward to the awarding of a B.D. degree. However, the Seminary is still training most of its students at the L.Th. level and is so classified herein. The Yeotmal Seminary receives support from 14 different church groups.

Each of the 27 seminaries at the L.Th. level in India usually serves only one language area. The implications of this fact are discussed below and in chapter 10 of this Survey.

Bishop Newbigin stresses the importance of the 27 schools at the L.Th. level as compared to the five theological colleges. Because the plant facilities of the former are more simple, and their instruction is given in the regional languages, he believes they are more in tune with the needs of the Indian ministry than are the colleges. The latter teach in English and, it is said, tend to "westernize" the theological concepts of their students. With the exception of the Union Theological Seminary at Bareilly and a few others, the typical L.Th. school, on the other hand, is even more understaffed and underequipped than are the colleges.

B. PAKISTAN AND CEYLON

The constitution of Pakistan describes the country as an Islamic Republic. It also guarantees religious freedom. There are more Muslims in Pakistan than in any other nation in the world. Of the 83,000,000 persons in Pakistan 0.3% (i.e., 250,000 persons) constitute the Protestant community after a century of missionary effort.

Before the partition of India in 1948, many of the Christians living in what is now West Pakistan were day laborers. After partition, the influx of Muslims into Pakistan caused such acute economic distress that the employment opportunities for these Christians were greatly reduced. One result has been that they are not able to support their Christian churches to the same extent as before, and this in turn has discouraged young men from choosing the ministry as their career. Also, at the time of partition, many of the promising Indian Christian leaders who formerly lived in what is now Pakistan elected to migrate to India, thereby further weakening the Christian churches in Pakistan.

The strongest of the younger Pakistani churches are in the Punjab in West Pakistan. Their membership is approximately as follows:

Methodist	25,000
Presbyterian	20,000
Church of India, Pakistan, Burma and Ceylon (Anglican)	10,000

As shown in Table 26, there are only two Protestant seminaries in Pakistan. These are both located in the western segment of the country.

TABLE 26.   THEOLOGICAL SCHOOLS IN PAKISTAN (1956)

		Approx. Number of		
Name	Location	Full-Time Faculty	Theol. Students	Denominational Support
Gujranwala Theo-logical Seminary	Gujranwala	5	25	United Presby-terian, etc.
Theological Seminary of Pakistan Lutheran Church	Mardan	1	6?	Lutheran (Danish)
Total: 2		6	31	

Gujranwala Theological Seminary: Founded by the United Presbyterians in 1877, this institution is the most important seminary overseas supported by this denomination (which merged with the Presbyterians USA in 1958). The city of Gujranwala is located 40 miles north of Lahore. The school has also received financial support from the Presbyterians USA, American Methodists, the United Church in Pakistan, and the Church of India, Pakistan, Burma and Ceylon (Anglican). However, the latter four denominations did not commence to support Gujranwala until after the partition of Pakistan and India. The United Presbyterians are said to have been somewhat reluctant at first to accept their support; and this denomination has continued to exert a major influence in the seminary through its eight representatives on the board (which numbers 15).

Some of the work at this Seminary is conducted in English at the theological school level. The rest is in Urdu at the L.Th. level. Some courses are also conducted for the wives of the students.

The Report of the 1956 General Assembly of the United Presbyterian Church included this comment on Gujranwala: "There has been a steady decrease in the number of students over the past several years. In 1954, we had 37 on the roll; in 1955, 32 were reported. This year we report 25, and there will be, according to present indications, a further reduction this year, since less will be entering than are leaving. Of the 25 on the roll, 11 are in the third year class, 8 in the second year class and 6 in the first year. . . . We should look into this matter of decrease. It is certainly not because there is any lack of need."

Despite the declining enrollment at Gujranwala, ground was broken in 1956 for a new classroom and library building, and three new homes for professors were built in recent years. The new classroom building will also house a chapel and administrative offices, and its construction was planned for completion by the autumn of 1956. The building replaced by it was to be converted into a social and conference center.

Theological Seminary of the Pakistan Lutheran Church: This school was founded by the Danish Pathan Mission in April 1956. It offers a three-year course and has a principal and six part-time instructors on its faculty. The Seminary is located in Mardan which is about 30 miles east of Peshawar in the Northwest Frontier Province.

Ceylon is a stronghold of Buddhism, and the Government is following a policy of deliberately favoring this religion, in part because Christians had supposedly been favored by the former colonial authorities. Of the 8,000,000 persons on the island, only about 100,000 are Protestants. The leading Protestant churches are:

Church of India, Pakistan, Burma and Ceylon (Anglican)	20,000
Methodist	15,000
Church of South India	5,000

There is only one small Protestant seminary on the island as shown in Table 27.

TABLE 27.   THEOLOGICAL SCHOOLS IN CEYLON (1956)

| Name | Location | Approx. Number of | | Denominational Support |
		Full-Time Faculty	Theol. Students	
Diocesan Divinity School	Colombo	2	9	Church of India, Pakistan, Burma & Ceylon (Anglican)

Comparatively little missionary progress has been made among the dominant Sinhalese people in Ceylon who are strongly Buddhist. As a result the Christian churches on the island are composed principally of Tamil members whose forebears were immigrants from southern India. A consequence of this is that the Protestant churches for the most part send their candidates for the ministry to the mainland of India for their training—the Anglican students going to Bishop's College in Calcutta, the Methodists to the United Theological College at Bangalore, and the Baptists to Serampore. In 1958 some discussions were being held with a view toward establishing an interdenominational theological school in Ceylon, using Sinhalese and offering the Serampore L.Th. course.

C. Over-all Aspects

1. *Conclusions*

The report issued in 1932 by the Commission on Christian Higher Education in India states: "If one considers the state of theological education, as a whole, one is impressed by its elementary character, its denominational character, and its isolation from the general trend of academic education." Concerning this indictment, Dr. Charles W. Ranson states in *The Christian Ministry in India* (written in 1945): "Much talk has flowed across the conference tables since . . . this somewhat drastic judgment, yet little has happened in the field of theological education which would compel a radical revision of the critical estimate offered thirteen years ago."

The over-all conclusion of the Ranson report on the state of theological education in India is a scathing one:

It is impossible to evade the conclusion that the education of the ordained ministry represents one of the weakest points in the whole Christian enterprise in India, and that its present defects are primarily the result of a long period of hesitant policy and haphazard practice regarding ministerial recruitment and training. . . . Most theological institutions have never achieved the stability and security of the Christian Arts Colleges. . . . The available evidence appears to indicate that the Home Boards spend annually on Christian Arts Colleges alone, more than six times the amount of their cash grants to the institutions which are directly engaged in training men for the ministry. This disturbing disparity is but one indication of hesitancy in policy regarding theological education.

A prominent Indian comments that the seminaries in India have been of only secondary interest to many of the foreign missionaries stationed in this country because the latter are often fundamentally more interested in the social service aspects of their work. Could this be a by-product of the "social gospel" theories which were popular in American seminaries a few decades ago?

Shortage of Ministers: In the mid-1950s it was estimated that some 32,000 non-Roman Catholic congregations in India were being served by approximately 7,000 ordained pastors. Thus there was one pastor for each 4.5 congregations. In some parts of India one ordained pastor may be responsible for Christians in as many as 30 or 40 villages. Despite the fact that this situation appears to have been deteriorating rather than improving during the past decade, there is not a unanimous opinion concerning the ways and means of overcoming this shortage of ministers. According to the Harrison report, the union seminaries generally believe that the number of theological students being trained is not adequate. On the other hand a number of the denominational and smaller provincial seminaries in India consider that an adequate number of men are now being trained, or that as many are being trained as their churches can afford to support.

Trends in Curricula: Coincident with the withdrawal of the British from India, there has been some change in the curricula of the Protestant seminaries. While there is still a preponderant emphasis on the main theological disciplines (Old and New Testament, theology and church history), nevertheless there is a growing emphasis on religious education, practical theology and homiletics, a trend favored by the Americans in the field.

Poor Quality of Faculties: The Ranson report states:

There is no tutorial system and very little individual contact between teachers and students in theological work. . . . The majority of the members of staff, particularly in theological schools, are forced to attempt far too much. Most of them are teaching in two or three different courses. . . . Part-time teaching is very common and is yet another reflection of the rather sketchy manner in which provision is made for theological instruction. . . . This problem of understaffing is more serious in the theological schools than in the colleges. . . . The tendency toward hack work is increased (by the fact) . . . that many teachers in these institutions teach a wide variety of subjects without having had the chance to acquire a specialized knowledge of any of them.

Another weakness cited in the same report is that too high a proportion of the faculties are foreigners:

The Indian staff of the theological institutions is not nearly so strong either numerically or in quality as it ought to be. There is a mere handful of nationals of first-rate quality teaching theological subjects. . . . The Bombay regional report (made in response to the Ranson questionnaire) suggests three main reasons why qualified nationals have not been attracted by the challenge of this type of service in Christian work. One is that the financial arrangements are far from satisfactory. The grade of salary offered is discouraging; there are no arrangements for (a) Provident Fund or Pension Scheme in most schools. . . . A second reason . . . is that . . . the Indian member on the staff . . . has little voice in the direction of the life and activity of the school. In very few instances is the Indian member a colleague who shares fully with his non-Indian fellows on the staff the responsibility for the administration of the life and discipline of the school. A third reason is that there is no feeling of security or tenure; at short notice he may be transferred or his services dispensed with.

During the past decade there has been some improvement in this situation. The Harrison report mentions that about one-half of the 32 seminaries now have Indians as principals, and that 57% of their faculty members are Indians. Only about 40% of the faculty of the five theological colleges are Indians. On the other hand, the Harrison report states that

in several of the smaller schools the teachers are clearly insufficiently qualified for satisfactory work at the theological school level. . . . In regard to taking one class at a time, it is certainly asking superhuman attainments in general erudition to expect that three or four men will cover adequately the whole curriculum even of the L.Th. standard by preparing for the teaching of new subjects each year. . . . Salaries are in many cases far too low to enable teachers to live without preoccupation with financial worries or to secure the books which are essential for their personal use. . . . Some schools showed . . . by the responses of their staffs to questions that they were content to live as isolated Christian groups in the midst of a non-Christian culture. . . .

Poor Quality of Students: The Ranson report is outspoken in its adverse criticism of the poor quality of theological students in India:

. . . It may be said without hesitation that the standard of work both in colleges and in schools is much below what can be regarded as satisfactory. . . . This dissatisfaction . . . relates not merely to general educational attainment but also to the religious knowledge of the students. . . . One college lecturer points out that even when they have passed the B.D. examination many students possess only the most sketchy knowledge of the substance of the Scriptures. . . . The (secular) colleges impose more or less uniform standards of entrance. Not so the theological schools. In most cases they have to be content with what they can get (in the way of students) or what the supporting churches send them. . . . One of the most disturbing features of the situation in India, however, is the extreme rarity of candidates of first-class intellectual capacity and the very general impression, both among theological teachers and those who observe their work from outside, that the ability of theological students is rather below that of Christian students in training for other vocations. . . . On the whole, men of limited general education and meagre theological equipment predominate.

Once again it is the Methodists who (in their 1956 report) strike a more optimistic note: "A notable development is the steadily higher . . . standard of the theological students. Not many years ago an arts or science graduate was scarcely found among the numerous high school 'pass' students (in seminaries). Last year (by contrast) in the largest first year class in Leonard's history . . . all except one (student) had finished four years of College." The Harrison report also indicates there has been some improvement in recent years in the academic qualifications of the men admitted to Indian seminaries.

Nevertheless it appears that few, if any, of the theological schools in this country have effective recruitment plans for attracting capable young students to attend seminary. This is considered by some prominent Indians to be one of the weakest features in theological education in the country. A part of the difficulty, as Dr. David G. Moses points out, is due to the fact that church officials in India are not sufficiently aware of the problem. Many Protestants in India are members of the lower middle class for whom the low salaries paid to pastors are an effective deterrent with respect to the possibility of their choosing the ministry as a career. Many congregations are unable to pay adequate salaries and, not recognizing the importance of adequately trained men, engage Bible school graduates instead. The salary of a YMCA secretary in Madurai, for example, is said to be three times that paid to a pastor by the typical congregation in the Church of South India. The higher paying governmental positions which are now open to Indians also serve as a counterattraction away from a career in the church. One of the solutions which have been suggested is for the seminaries to inaugurate vigorous recruitment programs aimed at promising students in the colleges and in the high schools.

The Excess Number of Seminaries: The Ranson report is critical of the small size of most of the seminaries in India and states that "a theological school should not normally attempt to train more than forty men at one time. . . . For (such) a school . . . a minimum staff of four well-qualified lecturers is considered necessary. Where new admissions are made oftener than once in three years, a staff of six is regarded as the minimum required for efficient work."

The 1957 Harrison report states:

. . . Although the Church in India is comparatively poor both in financial resources and in the possession of personnel qualified and available for theological teaching, yet the number of institutions maintained appears greatly to exceed what is really required for meeting the actual needs effectively. Not only was the number large at the time of the Ranson Report, but, despite his plea for concentration of effort in fewer institutions, the total has further increased at the present both in the groups of colleges and schools. The result of this growth in the number of institutions is that nearly all with very few exceptions have smaller enrollments than could be readily provided for in teaching arrangements. Staffs are in most cases smaller than is desirable, and financial resources do not make possible adequate library and other facilities. Despite the fact that theological education appears often to be meagrely provided for, it is probably true to say that in no other type of education given in India is the cost per student, if all items of expenditure are included, higher than in ministerial training. . . .

2. *Recommendations of Previous Reports*

Postgraduate Study Center: At a meeting of the Principals of the five theological colleges which was held in March 1957 in Nagpur, it was agreed that it would be desirable to establish a post-B.D. study center in India. It was recommended that three of the five colleges (i.e., Serampore, Bangalore and Leonard) should join together and in 1957–58 offer an M.Th. degree, each college specializing in those branches of the curricula in which it is strongest.

With respect to the need for graduate theological work being done in India rather than abroad, an Indian comments that the students at this level should have their thinking oriented primarily on church problems of India rather than those typically discussed at Harvard and Yale. The difficulty is that if such work is to be done in India, the instruction will need to be carried on largely by visiting professors from abroad, since most of the experienced theological professors in India now have their time completely devoted to their work with B.D. students.

Theological Colleges: Neither the Ranson nor the Harrison report favored an increase in the number of theological colleges in India. These five institutions serve the areas shown in Table 28.

TABLE 28. AREAS SERVED BY THE FIVE THEOLOGICAL COLLEGES IN INDIA
(1958)

Theological College	Location	Area
Serampore	Serampore	Eastern
Bishop's	Calcutta	Eastern
Leonard	Jabalpur	Central
United Theological College	Bangalore	Southern
Gurukul	Madras	Southern

Theological Schools: In the year 1930, the National Christian Council of India recommended the establishment of one "Union Theological Seminary of the L.Th. grade in all the main language areas and that the vernacular should be the main medium of instruction." In the succeeding 15 years there was no implementation of these recommendations, nor was there any marked improvement in the quality of many of these provincial institutions.

The 1945 Ranson report advocated much the same plan: "Wise strategy clearly indicates a policy of concentration as the first step toward a real advance in the quality of theological education." Accordingly it was recommended that there should be an extensive realignment in the provincial seminaries, as shown in Table 29.

The Ranson report received serious attention. However, progress in implementing its recommendations during the ensuing eleven years, 1945–46, was slow and hesitant. There were a number of reasons accounting for this, some of which were foreseen by the author himself, as follows:

1. Differences in the thinking of the various denominations.
2. Nationality differences among foreign missionaries in India.
3. Local loyalties to individual seminaries, including alumni pressure and faculty pride.

At a meeting of the Theological Education Committee of the National Council of Churches in India held in 1952, it was decided it would be desirable to find out how far the Ranson recommendations had been carried out. Two years later a questionnaire was circulated by the Council among the Indian seminaries. Four years later, in 1956, Professor M. H. Harrison issued some preliminary conclusions concerning the results of this inquiry. This was followed by the issuance of his final report in 1957 (as previously noted).

Table 29. Realignment of L.Th. Seminaries Recommended in Ranson
Report (1945)

Language Area	Recommended Union School	Location
Bengali	Diocesan Divinity School at Ranaghat[a]	Ranaghat
Gujarati	Gujarat United School of Theology	Ahmedabad[d]
Hindi	Union Theological Seminary	Indore
Kanarese	Tumkur Union Kanarese Seminary[b]	Tumkur
Malayalam	Kerala United Theological Seminary	Trivandrum
Marathi	St. Andrew's Divinity School[a e]	Nasik
Oriya	Christian Training College	Cuttack
Santali	None: suggests a new union Bible school	Dumka
Tamil	Bishop's Theological College	Tirumaraiyur
Telugu	A new union theological school	Bezwada
Urdu	Assuming one union school were not feasible, then the L.Th. schools at Bareilly, Khatauli[e] and Saharanpur should be strengthened	
Assamese	Theological College	Cherrapunji

Notes: [a] Apparently not operating under this name in 1953–54.
[b] Subsequent to 1945 this institution was raised from a Bible school to an L.Th. theological school level.
[c] Now out of existence.
[d] This seminary, formerly located in Baroda, moved to Ahmedabad subsequent to 1945.
[e] In the Marathi area the United Theological College of Western India at Poona has been strengthened instead.

In 1956 the only example Dr. Harrison had found of a united regional theological school doing all of the L.Th. level of work in a single language area in India was the United Theological College of Western India at Poona (in the Marathi language area). Even this conclusion was questioned by the Principal of the Union Biblical Seminary at Yeotmal.

The 1957 Harrison report states: ". . . The continuing validity of Ranson's main recommendations seems to be clearly confirmed. . . . The present survey has already made it abundantly clear that the plans of the Ranson report are very far from being realized as a whole . . . the bulk of theological education at the (L.Th.) school level is not at present being done in the so-called regional schools. . . ."

Dr. Harrison cited a number of reasons for the failure of the L.Th. seminaries to unite into single, regional institutions:

1. The linguistic areas of India are not all homogeneous but are broken up into sub-areas which differ to some extent, at least, in language, culture and social structure. Thus the Kannada-speaking Christians of the Basel Mission on the West Coast have hitherto found it somewhat difficult for historic and geographical reasons to feel they are quite at one with those of the Mysore plateau.

2. Some seminaries have valuable properties which cannot readily be transferred to a union institution. "Thus the Mar Thoma Seminary at Kottayam has a fine, modern

building, the cost of which was raised by local effort, and it might be thought that it would show a lack of responsibility to the donors to fail to use their gifts for their intended purpose."

3. The educational standards in some union institutions appear to be lower than those in denominational seminaries in the same area.

There have been efforts to unite the three seminaries in the Andhra area in India (at Dornakal, Kakinada and Ramapatnam), but to no avail. It seems to be the case that unless a seminary is originally founded as a union institution, it is exceedingly difficult under normal conditions to persuade other denominations voluntarily to join in its support.

Another example of the difficulties inherent in endeavoring to merge seminaries in India is cited in the transcript of the 1956 Presbyterian USA Conference at Lake Mohonk, which states: "We consider it tragic that the union of the Union Theological Seminary (at) Bareilly (Methodist) and (the North India United Theological College at) Saharanpur (Presbyterian USA) . . . was not effected two years ago, and it is our desire to renew the effort to bring about union of the two." Both the Saharanpur and Bareilly seminaries are union institutions teaching in the Urdu language. Despite this fact, the possibility of merging them has been discussed off and on for decades, but without concrete result.

The Harrison report suggests that "in some cases the problem of using available property without duplication of effort may be solved by making one institution (in a given region) the place for education of the L.Th. standard, while using another for a Bible school for the entire linguistic area."

With respect to the conclusions and recommendations for mergers contained in most over-all surveys of theological education, it seems fair to say any such report which is imposed upon individual seminaries by outside agencies, and in which the schools themselves have had little or no direct part in their preparation, is not likely to be implemented. The seminaries affected may have an academic interest in such a survey but are not apt to feel that merger recommendations are binding upon them.

A gap in the Ranson report, the IMC surveys of the training of the ministry in Africa, and in virtually all of the other publicly available reports on theological education elsewhere, is their failure to include reasonably detailed estimates of the costs of implementing their recommendations.

With respect to the proposed merger of regional seminaries in India, the Ranson report did not consider such costs would be serious, and suggested that the pooling of resources might largely take care of the matter. The report continues:

It is clearly impossible at this stage to present a detailed estimate of the cost of the proposals. . . . The proposals regarding the institutions of collegiate grade will certainly involve greatly increased expenditures. . . . One of the first tasks of the regional committees

... should be to work out in detail the financial implications of the proposals in each language area, (and) to estimate ... the extent of the need for additional finance for capital and recurring expenditure. .... When detailed financial proposals covering the whole area of the plan have been worked out, and it is known what churches and missions are able and willing to do in the pooling of present resources, it will be necessary to launch a campaign to secure for the plan the support of the whole Church of India and of supporting missions.

It seems to be the case that if a survey leaves to "others" the task of preparing reasonably detailed estimates of the cost of implementing their recommendations, and also the task of demonstrating how and from whom such funds are to be obtained, the "others" are apt to neglect to compile such cost estimates, etc., and there the matter "rests." This statement is not intended to be an adverse criticism of the authors of the various surveys. Rather it is suggested that in the future such surveys should place a greater emphasis on the financial aspects of what is recommended.

A special committee of the Board of Theological Education of the National Christian Council of India met in Kodaikanal in April 1957 to compile a joint fund-raising appeal on behalf of the Indian seminaries. Some of these institutions had been planning expansion programs, but several had failed in their attempts to obtain financial assistance from foundations or from their supporting mission boards owing to the multiplicity of the different requests.

The committee resolved, among other things, that: (1) the appeal for capital funds should be made roughly on a fifty-fifty basis on behalf of the five theological colleges and the 27 theological schools, and (2) certain askings should be earmarked for the more conservative schools, such as the Allahabad Bible Seminary, etc. The committee formulated a consolidated appeal schedule. It included requests for annual budgetary support to six institutions totaling $16,900 a year, together with requests for capital contributions totaling $1,480,000 which would be used for the major needs of the B.D. and L.Th. seminaries as shown in Table 30.

There is no need here to attempt to assess the scope of this rather ambitious program, or to analyze the relationships of the various items which comprise the total of the askings. Two conclusions, however, are apparent. The first is that the National Christian Council of India (as is the case with its counterparts elsewhere) is virtually obliged (a) to include a large rather than a small number of institutions in such a consolidated appeal, and (b) to agree that such undesignated contributions as are received should be apportioned among the recipients on more or less of a formula basis which is not directly related to the specific individual needs of one institution as against those of another. This may reflect realistic thinking of a sort, but points to the difficulty councils have in trying to reach an agreement concerning the priorities to be established among the capital needs of their constituent members.

TABLE 30. CONSOLIDATED 1957 FUND-RAISING APPEAL OF THE BOARD OF
THEOLOGICAL EDUCATION (INDIA)

Institution	Needs		
	Current Budgetary	Capital	Endowment
Serampore Senate	$ 4,200	$ 40,000	$ 60,000
Serampore College	2,000	95,000	60,000
United Theological College, Bangalore	8,300	95,000	60,000
Leonard Theological College		25,000	20,000
Union Biblical Seminary, Yeotmal		90,000	60,000
L. Th. Schools			
Andhra (for one union school)		40,000	60,000
Tamilnad (for one union school)		40,000	60,000
Kerala (for one union school)	400	10,000	60,000
Karnataka (for one union school)		10,000	60,000
Hindi (for one union school)	600	40,000	40,000
Marathi (Poona)		40,000	60,000
Gujerat (Ahmedabad)	1,400	10,000	20,000
Assam (for one union school)		40,000	60,000
Other schools		85,000	100,000
Women's training		20,000	20,000
	$16,900	$680,000	$800,000

The second conclusion is that with respect to the L.Th. schools the committee apparently predicated its formula upon the hope that the prospect of capital contributions would cause a number of them to agree to merge into one union school for each of the major language areas in the country. A review of the comparatively lengthy record to date suggests that the realization of such a hope in the near future may not be justified.

Finally one might cite the statement in a report by Dr. R. Pierce Beaver (Professor of Missions on the Federated Theological Faculty at the University of Chicago), which he made upon his return from a visit to India in 1956–57 where he studied Christianity and the major religions of that country in some detail: "There is no way in which the Western missions can help the Church in south Asia more effectively than by providing resources for the strengthening of theological education in the region. Moreover, since India is so far advanced in theological education in comparison with adjoining areas in Asia, strengthening the Indian colleges could advance ministerial training over a much wider area."

CHAPTER 5

SOUTHEAST ASIA

A. Burma, Thailand and Malaya

For the Southeast Asian area, one of the most important sources of information is the Anderson-Smith *Report on Theological Education in Southeast Asia—The Report of a Survey Commission, 1952–53* (hereinafter referred to as the AS Report) which was published by the Board of Founders of the Nanking Theological Seminary. The survey was undertaken by Dr. Sidney R. Anderson, a church administrator, and Dr. C. Stanley Smith, a theological professor. Dr. Smith was a member of the Weigle survey team in China in 1934–35 and also served in recent years as Field Representative in Southeast Asia for the Board of Founders.

The membership status of the more important younger Protestant churches in Burma, Thailand and Malaya is approximately as shown in Table 31.

TABLE 31. MEMBERSHIP OF PROTESTANT CHURCHES IN BURMA, THAILAND AND MALAYA (1957)

	Burma	Thailand	Malaya
Population	19,000,000	19,000,000	6,000,000
Protestant community	400,000	25,000	50,000
Churches:			
Baptists	200,000	3,000	
Anglicans	12,000[a]		6,000[b]
Assemblies of God	8,000		
Methodists	5,000		12,000
Church of Christ in Thailand[c]		17,000	
Presbyterian			4,000

NOTES: [a] Church of India, Pakistan, Burma and Ceylon, Diocese of Rangoon. [b] Anglican Church, Diocese of Singapore. [c] Presbyterian, Baptist (Karen) and Disciples.

The reason for the small number of Christians in Burma and Thailand is the great strength of Buddhism. The royal family of Thailand is the head of the Buddhist religion in that kingdom and regards this function as an important one. The Hinayana branch of Buddhism which is predominant in Southeast Asia is a stronger and more moral religion than the Mahayana Buddhism of China. The Roman Catholics, also, have made little missionary progress in the area, except among the Shan tribes in Burma.

TABLE 32.   THEOLOGICAL SCHOOLS IN BURMA, THAILAND AND MALAYA (1957)

Name	Location	Approx. Number of		Denominational Support
		Full-Time Faculty	Theol. Students	
Burma				
Burma Divinity School	Insein	4[a]	62[b]	American Baptist, Methodist
Holy Cross College	Rangoon	2	17	Anglican
Thailand				
McGilvary Theological Seminary	Chiengmai	5[a]	9[b]	Presbyterian USA
Thailand Baptist Theological Center	Bangkok	2[a]	9[b]	Southern Baptist
Malaya				
Trinity Theological College	Singapore	8[a]	27[b]	Methodist, Anglican, etc.
Malaya Baptist Theological Seminary	Penang	4	12[b]	Southern Baptist
Total: 6		25	136	

NOTES: [a] Plus part-time faculty.
[b] Plus other students at lower level of training.

The theological schools now operating in Burma, Thailand and Malaya are listed in Table 32.

1. *Burma*

Burma Divinity School: In Burma, 80% of the population are native Burmese, and the remaining 20% are tribespeople—Karens, Chins, Kachins, etc. About 90% of the Christians in Burma are Karens, and the Karen Baptist Church is one of the strongest and most missionary-minded of the indigenous Protestant churches of Asia.

The American Baptists commenced their missionary work in Burma in 1813, mainly among the Karens and other Shan tribes. The Insein Theological Center maintained by the Baptists is located on Seminary Hill near a village which is eight miles outside of Rangoon. It consists of six institutions at various academic levels—the Burma Divinity School plus five separate Bible schools for Karen, Pwo Karen and Burmese men and women.

According to the AS Report, "the Burma Baptist Divinity School . . . aims to take students who have had full high school education, including eligibility for matriculation into the Rangoon University. All too often, however, it has to be satisfied with an 'equivalent' preparation. . . . The Insein Theological Center must have been an impressive place before the recent fighting in Burma between the Karen revolutionaries and the Government. During this time, however, the buildings were heavily shelled and damaged."

In 1955 there were approximately 21 theological students enrolled in the Divinity School. By 1957 the number had grown to 62. This was the largest number in the 25 years during which the seminary has been operated. However, this school suffers from the fact that most of the work of the faculty is done through part-time teachers. The faculty members at all six institutions at Insein numbers 28 full-time instructors teaching 334 students at various levels and in various languages.

The AS report commented that one of the difficulties of achieving a closer union between the Baptists and the Methodists at Insein has been caused by the fact that the Methodists have been carrying on work among the Chinese in Burma, and they were not certain that they wanted to send their candidates for the ministry to be trained at Insein. Many of the Methodists felt it would be better to send them to Trinity College in Singapore which is strongly Methodist. Nevertheless in 1956 the seminary adopted a new constitution as a result of which its Board of Trustees now include Methodist and Anglican members. Furthermore the word "Baptist" was dropped from its title (which previously had been The Burma Baptist Divinity School). In 1957 it was anticipated there would also be a Methodist on the seminary's faculty.

The Divinity School grants a Th.B. degree on the authority of the Central Baptist Seminary in Kansas City, Kansas. Its first post-war commencement took place in October 1955 when seven ordinand students were graduated.

Holy Cross College: This Anglican seminary was reopened in Rangoon in 1955 after several years of inactivity. Approximately 17 students are reported to be studying for the priesthood there. An acute shortage of trained leaders is one of the most critical problems confronting this Church in Burma. The level of training at Holy Cross is said to be below that provided by the Burma Divinity School at Insein.

2. *Thailand*

After 128 years of Christian missionary activity in Thailand, there are only about 25,000 Protestants and about 35,000 Roman Catholics. The first Protestant missionaries worked for 13 years in the country without obtaining a single convert. Out of 35 ordained ministers in the Church of Christ in Thailand, only eight are high school graduates. Many Protestant congregations appear to be satisfied with the services of an unordained preacher, instead of an ordained minister to whom a salary must be paid.

McGilvary Theological Seminary: Located in Chiengmai in the hills of northern Thailand, this school was opened in 1949 and graduated its first postwar class of five students in 1952. Of the five full-time faculty members, only one is an Asian. In addition three Asians and four missionaries teach part time in the Seminary.

One of the most serious problems confronting McGilvary is the small number of theological students it has enrolled in its courses—11 in 1956, and 9 in 1957. There has been little or no growth in the student body during the past five years. The Seminary requires its entering students to have graduated from senior high school. It is planned to have McGilvary cooperate more closely with the Prince Royal Academy which is a boys' high school located less than a half mile away.

Thailand Baptist Theological Center: This Southern Baptist seminary was opened in Grace Baptist Church in Bangkok in 1952. Since 1954 it has been renting private houses pending the construction of a campus of its own. The school offers courses in both the Thai and the Chinese languages because more than half of the population of Bangkok is Chinese (although this nationality is a small minority in the country as a whole). Unfortunately only one member of the faculty speaks both languages, so this necessitates having two sets of full- and part-time teachers for the instruction of only nine theological students (five Chinese and four Thai). Despite its small size and brief history, this institution is classified by the Southern Baptists as a theological school rather than a theological institute: its academic standards are below those of most of the other seminaries in this area.

3. Malaya

There is in Malaya a rather bewildering religious diversity. The Malays are Muslims; the Chinese are Confucianists, Buddhists and Taoists; the East Indians are largely Hindus; the Burmese, Singhalese and Siamese are Buddhists; and the tribes of the remote forest are animists. Islam is the strongest single religion in Malaya, although the Chinese comprise about one-half of the total population (and 80% of the population of Singapore). Among the Protestants the Methodists and Anglicans are engaged in the largest number of activities in this country which only recently gained its independence.

Trinity Theological College: This institution is the successor to the Malaya Methodist Theological College which was closed when the Japanese occupied Singapore in 1942. The AS report states that this "College was conceived in a Japanese internment camp when members of the English Presbyterian, Church of England and Methodist churches, forced to live together there, decided to try to carry cooperative living into their religious work after they emerged from their confinement. . . . Early in 1948 . . . it was decided to establish a union theological college to be called 'Trinity College'." The seminary opened in that year with seven theological students. In 1954 Trinity established a Bible school department course for those not seeking to qualify for the licentiate of theology. It now also conducts a Bible correspondence course. Dr. C. Stanley Smith served as its head for a number of years prior to his retirement in 1957.

In 1951 Trinity opened a Chinese-speaking department which by 1955 was considerably larger than the English-speaking section. In fact, Trinity is training the largest number of Overseas Chinese students of any seminary, with the exception of the Tainan Theological College on Formosa.

One of the weaknesses at Trinity in the past has been the comparatively few hours devoted by the students to theological study and preparation for classes as against the large amount of time—from four to five hours a day—spent by many of them in teaching in Christian or government middle schools. The students entering Trinity are said to be not well prepared academically so that few of them are equipped to engage in creative thinking while in seminary.

The site on which the Trinity campus is located belongs to the Methodist Church and was leased by it for a 30-year period to the school. The cost of the original buildings was contributed by the Methodist Mission. If Trinity were to relocate its campus nearer the University of Malaya in Singapore, such a move would cost an estimated $150,000.

With respect to the College's operations and budgetary needs, Table 33 lists the approximate measure of the denominational support it receives.

TABLE 33. DENOMINATIONAL SUPPORT OF TRINITY
COLLEGE, SINGAPORE (CA. 1956)

	% of All Students	% of Cost Contributed
Methodist	67	25
Anglican	17	13
Presbyterian (English)	14	14
Other sources	2	27
Board of Founders of NTS		21
	100	100

The Nanking Board of Founders has made the following capital contributions to Trinity in recent years:

1953	$25,000	Remodeling its original building.
1955	50,000	New building for library and offices, etc.
1956	15,000	New residence for Principal.
	$90,000	

The Anglican students at Trinity (about a dozen in number) reside at St. Peter's Hall, a hostel located about a mile away from the College. It was established by the Diocese of Singapore in 1953 with the proceeds of a grant of £10,000 from the Society for the Propagation of the Gospel. Its full-time staff of two priests give lectures at Trinity and provide supplementary instruction at St. Peter's in the Anglican forms of the liturgy, etc.

Malaya Baptist Theological Seminary: This school is located on Penang, an island in the Straits of Malacca (400 miles northwest of Singapore) on which a well-known Roman Catholic major seminary is also located. The Southern Baptists opened the school in January 1954 with five students. In 1957, 20 students were enrolled, some of whom were studying for the Bible school certificate, diploma of theology or bachelor of religious education which the Seminary awards (in addition to the B.Th. and the B.D.). The first graduation was held in January 1957 when two students were awarded diplomas.

B. INDONESIA AND BORNEO

With a population of 81,000,000, Indonesia follows Pakistan as being the second largest predominantly Muslim nation in the world. According to the Indonesian Ministry of Religious Affairs the number of persons in each of the principal religious groups in the country are as shown in Table 34.

The Muslims of Indonesia are more tolerant of Christianity than are the Muslims residing in Islamic countries elsewhere. Even though less than 4% of the Indonesian people are Christians, Indonesia nonetheless has the third highest percentage of Christians (after the Philippines and Korea) of any country in the Orient. The

TABLE 34.   MAJOR RELIGIOUS COMMUNITIES IN
INDONESIA (1956)

Muslims	66,287,000
Buddhists	5,000,000
Protestants	3,286,000
Hindus*a*	1,386,000
Roman Catholics	1,080,000
"Mystics"	440,000

NOTE: *a* Principally on the island of Bali.

Christians on the island of Java are small in number in relation to the island's 50,-000,000 population, yet they constitute the largest group of Christians in any Muslim country.

The AS report states:

In spite of the fact that there has been a greater defection to Christianity among the Mohammedans of Java than in any other part of the world, the strength of Mohammedanism in Indonesia is still very great. . . . The Dutch Colonial Government of the Indies, like the British Colonial Government of Malaya . . . was afraid that missionaries might antagonize the Moslems. . . . One of the reasons why Indonesia seems to be so difficult for Americans to understand is partly . . . the fact that there has been so little mission work carried on in that country by American missionaries.

The large mass movements to Christianity took place on islands other than Java, before Islam had reached them and while they still retained their native animism. . . . There are some 600,000 Batak Christians in Northern Sumatra. . . . The density of Christians in Indonesia varies from ninety per cent of the population in Minahassa, in (the) northern Celebes, and fifty per cent of the population in the Batak areas of northern Sumatra, to only one per cent of the population of Java.

The Batak Church had its origin in the Rhenish Mission which represented both Lutheran and Reformed elements. Since World War II the Batak Church has become a member of the Lutheran World Federation. In the animistic areas, such as Timor and the central portion of the Celebes, there are still mass movements to the Church. For example, the Protestant Evangelical Church of Timor baptizes about 10,000 new members every year.

Prior to 1945 the leading denomination in Indonesia was the Protestant Church of the Netherlands East Indies. This was a state-supported institution with many of its ministers recruited from Holland. With the withdrawal of the Dutch colonial authorities, this Church was disestablished and it does not at present have strong connections with any mission board.

The AS report states that at present in Indonesia the "Protestant churches are of two kinds. First, the ecumenically minded groups which are federated in the (Indonesian) National Council of Churches (NCC), and second, a number of sectarian organizations of American origin. These organizations have no relationship with the NCC. The latest organization to enter Indonesia is the Foreign Mission Society of the Southern Baptist Convention. . . . The clearly avowed aim of the NCC is to establish a United Church of Indonesia."

Owing to the fact that Indonesia as a country is a collection of islands stretching 2,700 miles in length, the individual Christian congregations are grouped in larger church bodies (mostly of the Reformed polity and faith) having a regional rather than a denominational basis. The largest among these are shown in Table 35.

TABLE 35.   MEMBERSHIP OF LEADING PROTESTANT CHURCHES IN INDONESIA (1956)

Church	Community[a]
Batak Protestant Christian Church, Sumatra	650,000
Christian Evangelical Church of Minahassa, Celebes[b]	350,000
Protestant Church of the Moluccas (Church of Ambon)[b]	350,000
Evangelical Protestant Church of Timor[b]	250,000
Protestant Church of Western Indonesia[b]	200,000

NOTES: [a] Includes only communicants, children of Christian families and catechumens.
[b] These four churches are linked together in the Protestant Church of Indonesia which is the successor to the Protestant Church of the Netherlands East Indies.

There are now said to be between 4,000 and 5,000 individual Protestant congregations in Indonesia. The number of ordained ministers (men and women who have completed a theological course and who are active in the parish ministry) probably does not exceed 500. The remaining congregations are served either by local evangelists or on a circuit basis.

The Protestant seminaries now operating in Indonesia and Borneo are listed in Table 36.

According to the AS report, "in Indonesia . . . there has been, on the whole, a higher standard of theological training for the ministry than we found in most other places. . . . One cannot but admire the high grade, constructively planned and effectively carried out system of theological education which the Dutch and their European societies have given to Indonesia."

Dr. Winburn T. Thomas writes that

the Commission on Missions and the Inter-Church Aid Committee of the Indonesian Council of Churches have listed leadership training as the first priority in the church's needs. . . . Since the inauguration of the Comprehensive Program by the Far Eastern Joint Office (of the IMC), theological education has been allocated a larger proportion of American funds than any other aspect of the operation in Indonesia. . . . All the Indonesian staff at these two institutions (Djakarta and Makassar) are being paid from American funds; large numbers of the students enrolled at these two institutions as well as smaller numbers at the Theological Schools in Jogjakarta, Malang and Ambon, are being subsidized by scholarships from individual American donors and church bodies.

Nommensen University Theological Faculty: Nommensen University was founded in Sumatra in 1954 under the auspices of the Batak Church. This Church has a German Lutheran background. The University was named after Ludwig Nommensen of the Barmen Missionary Society under whose guidance the Rhenish Mission achieved a mass movement to Christianity in the late 19th century among the Batak

TABLE 36.   THEOLOGICAL SCHOOLS IN INDONESIA AND BORNEO (1957)

Name	Location	Full-Time Faculty	Theol. Students	Denominational Support
Sumatra				
Nommensen University Theological Faculty	Pematang-Siantar	8[a]	25[b]	Batak, Lutheran
Java				
Djakarta Theological College[d]	Djakarta	9[a]	80	Reformed Church, Presbyterian USA, etc.
Jogjakarta Theological Seminary	Jogjakarta	5[a]	50[b]	Church of Mid-Java, etc.
Baptist Theological Seminary of Indonesia[d]	Semarang	3	15[b]	Southern Baptist
Theological School Balewijoto	Malang	5[a]	27[b]	Church of East Java, Mennonite
Borneo				
Bandjermasin Theological School	Bandjermasin	3[a]	15[b]	Church of Kalimanten, Basel Mission
House of the Epiphany	Kuching, Sarawak	1[c]	10[c]	Anglican
Celebes				
Union Theological School	Makassar	7[a]	70[b]	Presbyterian USA, Dutch Reformed, etc.
Timor				
Theological School	So'e	2	15	Evangelical Protestant Church of Timor
Moluccas				
Ambon Theological School	Ambon	5[a]	46[b]	Moluccan Protestant Church
Total: 10		48	353	

Notes: [a] Plus part-time faculty.   [c] As of 1956; closed in 1957 (see text).
[b] Plus other students at lower level of training.   [d] As of early 1958.

people in Sumatra. Since then they have had to survive the active hostility of their strongly Muslim neighbors, the Atjeh tribes to the north and the Minangkabau peoples to the south. The comparative insecurity of their position has served to heighten the spiritual devotion of the Batak people to their church. Since the Dutch colonial authorities from time to time sought to discourage Protestant missionaries from entering parts of Sumatra, the Bataks were required to a large extent to rely on their own efforts in developing their church leaders.

Nommensen University was originally established by the Bataks with little or no outside financial assistance. Initially an Economics and Engineering Department was set up in Pematang Siantar in the Lake Toba region of northern Sumatra. The site was a 63-acre tract of land which had previously been a hospital compound bordering on the Harrison and Crosfield Rubber Estate. The old hospital wards were reconditioned for use as classrooms and dormitories. The theological faculty was also established at Pematang Siantar at this time. Shortly thereafter it was decided that the students in the Economics and Engineering Department would be better taught if that Department were moved to Medan (a commercial center about 80 miles distance to the north) where Sumatran businessmen would be available to serve as part-time lecturers and the students would have more opportunity for practical in-job training experience. Accordingly the transfer was made, leaving the theological faculty the complete use of the Pematang Siantar facilities.

The latter buildings were augmented by considerable new construction undertaken in 1955–57, including a $50,000 building, the cost of which was largely contributed by the Lutheran World Federation. It contains classrooms, a faculty meeting room, and an auditorium seating 300 persons. A new refectory and eight new faculty residences were also built. In 1955 the seminary's dormitories were requisitioned by the Indonesian army and were returned to the school a year later.

The Nommensen theological faculty conducts three types of courses for a total of approximately 100 students. The first is a four-year B.D. course for about 25 men who are college graduates. The second is a five-year pretheological preparatory course (middle school) for approximately 30 students. The third is a refresher course for about 45 students, most of whom are either pastors in the Batak Church or are lay teacher-preachers. Nommensen has trained some outstanding Batak Church leaders. On the other hand, up until 1957 the Batak Church sent more of its students to the Djakarta Theological College for their seminary training than it did to Pematang Siantar. In 1957 the Nommensen seminary exchanged one professor with the Djakarta College.

The progress made by this school and by the Batak Church in the four-year period 1954–58 is encouraging.

Djakarta Theological College: Formerly known as the Higher Theological School (HTS), this seminary changed its name in September 1954 to the Djakarta Theological College (STT). Its academic standards are higher than those maintained by most of the other Protestant seminaries in Africa, Asia and Latin America.

The HTS was founded in 1934. It is the oldest (and the only union seminary at the university level) in Indonesia. The School was organized through the joint action of the Board of Foreign Missions of the Dutch Reformed Church (Oegstgeest), the Rhenish Mission and the (then established) Protestant Church of the Netherlands East Indies. It was first located at Bogor where it was housed for a time in the *ashrama* (retreat center) of a former Methodist school. Subsequently it was transferred to Djakarta.

During the Japanese occupation of Indonesia in World War II this institution was closed. Up to 1953 the HTS was governed by a Board which included both representatives of the mission societies and of the Indonesian churches. When the HTS became the STT in 1954, the administrative authority over the seminary was transferred to the National Council of Churches in Indonesia. Thus in some respects the STT might be considered as a national higher theological school. The STT retained a Board of Curators which includes representatives from its supporting church bodies.

In March 1958 the College's faculty consisted of nine full-time professors (three Indonesian, two Dutch, two Swiss, one German and one American professor), all from the Reformed tradition. In addition, there were approximately a half-dozen part-time instructors and lecturers. The three Indonesian professors (Dr. Pouw Ie Gan, the rector in 1958, Dr. Sudarmo, and Rev. Peter Latuihamallo) have had their salaries provided for by the Board of Founders of Nanking Theological Seminary, the Missionary Center of the Reformed Churches in the Netherlands (Baarn), and the Far Eastern Office of the Division of Foreign Missions of the National Council of Churches (USA), respectively. A number of its faculty members are studying for advanced theological degrees in Germany and the United States, including Rev. Latuihamallo, who was the rector of the seminary up to 1957.

The entrance requirements at the STT specify that incoming students must have completed three years of upper-middle school. This is the same requirement as is set for students entering the University of Indonesia. (A higher institution for pre-university training, such as a college of arts, does not exist in the country.)

According to Rev. Latuihamallo and Rev. S. Marantika (the General Secretary of the National Council of Churches in Indonesia, who also serves as Secretary to the Board of Founders and the Board of Curators of the STT), the first two years of the five-year curriculum are given over largely to a survey course of a general collegiate character. The last three years are spent in theological studies. "Greek, Hebrew, Latin, Arabic, English and German are taken by most of the students" during the five-year period. Two-year courses at the STT in English, Hebrew and Greek are compulsory, and entering students must previously have had six years of English. Students specializing in the Old or New Testaments must take an additional three years in either Hebrew or Greek. German and Dutch are optional courses at the STT, and during the last three years electives in Latin, Arabic and Sanskrit are given. Lectures and examinations are conducted in Bahasa Indonesian, English and German. Formerly most of these languages were compulsory for all the HTS students. It still is not unusual for the College's graduates to be able to use eight languages as tools for additional research and study.

While this is a remarkable and unique situation as compared to the other seminaries overseas, in the opinion of some observers the STT may be exacting unduly heavy language requirements from its students at the expense of other courses in its curriculum. An indication of this is seen in the fact that in 1956 the college was considering adding a sixth year to its curriculum in which its graduates would return to the STT after a period of active service in the church in order to obtain special training in pastoralia and religious education.

At the end of the five-year period the students take comprehensive examinations which are mostly oral and extend over a three-day period. The STT is now conferring a B.Th. degree upon its own authority. The institution is also planning to add an M.Th. course to its curriculum. If the STT should become a faculty of theology in the new Christian University in Djakarta, as has been contemplated, this would increase the trend toward the college's becoming more of a postgraduate course and eventually would enable it to award a Th.D. degree if it chose to enter this field.

Rev. Latuihamallo comments that the course of studies at the STT is a rigorous one, based on a continental European background, and perhaps is overcrowded. The college has introduced reading periods to enable the students to engage in occasional individual research projects, the writing of papers, etc. One of the concomitants of the heavy work schedule is that the STT students tend to lose touch with the typical citizen of Indonesia. As a means of counteracting this, the College is placing increasing stress on more practical work on weekends in local churches. During his first year a student is sent back to his home and under the guidance of his pastor or of a foreign missionary he must make a study of the cultural history of his people and write a paper on this topic. In later summer vacations a student must engage in research in the character of the indigenous religions in Indonesia and the special problems confronting the Christian churches in this country. Carefully drafted reports must be submitted upon his return to the College each autumn. In this program the STT pays for the travel expense involved. The College is also instituting annual retreats for the faculty and student body as a means of deepening their devotional life. Finally the STT is conducting refresher courses (ministerial conferences) for its own graduates each year: these last from ten days up to three weeks.

In March 1958 the total enrollment at the STT was 80 students, an increase of approximately 100% over 1950. Subsequent to 1954 the College has had no recruitment problem; and in the academic year 1956–57 only 22 students out of 37 applicants were admitted to the entering class. In 1957–58, 30 students were admitted. The students come from all parts of the Indonesian archipelago. They represent about 27 of the 31 individual churches affiliated with the National Council, plus some pentecostal churches. As many as one-quarter of each class are of Chinese descent.

According to Dr. Winburn T. Thomas, the STT students are active in the Student Christian Movement in Indonesia and this helps to "account for the strength of this movement among the universities of the nation. During the Christmas holidays in 1955, the first national interseminary conference was conducted in a Djakarta suburb, with the Theological College students taking the leadership in its organ-ization and financing. Of the six students who attend the Southeast Asia Theologi-cal Conference in Bangkok . . . five of them were from this body. . . . Most of them . . . (later) move into leadership posts within the Indonesian Christian community."

Because of its academic standing, the Djakarta College exerts an influence in the country which is out of proportion to the number of its graduates. In 1958 either one or two STT men were serving on the faculties of six of the seminaries in Indo-nesia and Borneo. Others among its graduates occupy administrative posts in the National Council of Churches and nine of the individual church synods, as well as the pulpits in a number of the leading city churches. Both of the commanding offi-cers of the chaplain corps in the Indonesian army and in the navy are STT men. The other side of the coin is the fact that the remaining seminaries in Indonesia which are at the junior-college level are the schools at which most of the ordained minis-ters have received their training.

A problem confronting the college is the fact that it cannot finance more than a small portion of its operations from income it derives from within Indonesia. Only half-a-dozen of the 31 churches which are members of the National Council con-tribute annually to the seminary's budget: a few other churches have been willing to make contributions in the form of rubber or copra, but these offers cannot be ac-cepted because of the clerical and administrative details involved. Approximately 75% of the STT's annual income is received from overseas, principally from church bodies in the USA. The Depok Endowment in the Netherlands has also been a sub-stantial contributor to the College's capital needs.

In the two-year period ending April 30, 1955, the Board of Founders of Nanking Theological Seminary contributed $45,000 to the STT for construction purposes. Of these funds, $10,000 was used for new classrooms and administrative offices, and $35,000 was used for a new dormitory. In recent years the College has also been able (with assistance from various sources) to construct a library, refectory and houses for five of its professors. In 1958 its objective was to obtain $60,000 for a new classroom building and a like amount for a chapel. The STT would also like to establish (at a cost of $50,000) an ecumenical center in Indonesia which might func-tion along the lines of the Bossey Institute near Geneva.

Perhaps the outstanding feature of the Djakarta Theological College is the fact that, as a result of having maintained a good faculty which has faithfully adhered to high academic standards over the years, this institution has been successful in at-tracting not only good students from within its own country but also considerable financial support from abroad.

Jogjakarta Theological School: In Central Java the Christian Reformed Church is fairly strong and largely controls the Theological School at Jogjakarta. This School is probably the second-strongest seminary on the island of Java, and a larger proportion of its classroom work is carried on in Bahasa Indonesian than is the case at the Djakarta Theological College.

This seminary was visited in August 1956 by Dr. C. Stanley Smith who commented:

> The School seems to be well organized and administered. . . . The presence of this large student population (Gadjahmada University, 4,672 students) in Jogja makes it an important place for a good theological institution. . . .
>
> The Theological School at Jogja . . . (is) ambitious to raise the standard of their theological course, if not equal to that of the HTS in Djakarta, at least to . . . a course based upon junior middle school; . . . with a three-year preparatory course after junior high school, then a three-year course in theological subjects, the whole course leading to a degree of L.Th. . . . At present they have only a five-year course above junior middle school and give no degree or recognition other than a diploma. . . .
>
> Because of lack of dormitory space they are unable to take in a new class each year, but only one every two years. . . . The School is very much in need . . . of additional class rooms, library room and (an) administration office. . . . I was impressed with the good quality of the student body and . . . need of a more adequate staff if the School is to develop as they hope. . . .
>
> I found . . . there was real hope of a union between the Theological School (Balewijoto) at Malang and the Jogja School . . . (but) in 1952, this same hope of a union . . . was (also) held out (to me). . . . Four years ago the plan was for one good theological school in Djakarta and a number of secondary schools (theological training schools) in other areas. Theological education, however, has advanced so rapidly during these four years that it is now realized that it may be possible to raise the general level of these secondary schools to that of at least senior high school preparation.

In 1957 the Jogjakarta seminary added a sixth year of courses to be taken by the graduates of its five-year course, leading to a B.Th. degree.

Baptist Theological Seminary of Indonesia: The first Southern Baptist missionaries entered Indonesia on Christmas Day in 1951. This Seminary was opened by them in October 1954 in temporary quarters on a hill outside of Semarang overlooking the city. A new main building for the Seminary was constructed on this site in 1955. A four-year course is offered to high school graduates. The Southern Baptists report that "due to a shortage of seminary teachers, first-year students have had to enter advanced classes with second- and third-year students. Some have taken advanced courses in Old and New Testament before they could take the basic survey courses. . . . Many of these young people are making real sacrifices to follow Christ. . . . Some of the 19 enrolled this year have been totally cut off from family support or even family contact. The only charge at the seminary is for food and laundry. Therefore, students do most of the work, serving meals, cleaning buildings, etc."

Theological School Balewijoto: The Church of East Java is the dominant Protestant church in the eastern portion of the island. With some support from Dutch missionary societies, it operates this small seminary at Malang, "a beautiful, quiet cultured place. . . . The school (is) located in a very beautiful spot on the side of a hill. It is on the same campus as a Christian hospital and while its buildings are old and in rather great need of modernization, yet on the whole they seem fairly adequate for their present needs." This seminary is said to lack the stimulation provided by neighboring universities as is the case with the seminary in Jogjakarta. At the opening of the school year 1955 the "theological school" of the Mennonite Church of north-central Java was united with the Malang seminary.

Bandjermasin Theological School: The Bandjermasin Theological School was established on the South Coast of the Island of Borneo by the Basel Missionary Society in 1931. It is supported by the 31,000 members of the Evangelical Christian Church of Kalimanten (the latter being the Indonesian name for Borneo). The Dyak Church supplies all of the total enrollment of 59 students at the Bandjermasin School, and its Rector is a Dyak Christian. The instruction is in Indonesian and English, inasmuch as all but one of the German-Swiss members of the faculty speak Indonesian.

According to Dr. Smith,

there are at present only two classes in the School. . . . Only two of the entering class this year had been able to secure their graduating certificates from SMP—most of them had completed the Junior Middle School course but failed their final examinations. So they entered the Theological School! I was told that they hoped to take the exams again with better success. A new class is taken into the Theological School every two years. . . .

The cause of this lack of space for dormitory, library and classrooms is not due to the smallness of the School property, but to the continued occupation of perhaps the major part of it by the military. . . . If these (facilities) could be regained, the School would be adequately housed for any foreseeable future. . . .

Two-thirds of the support of the School . . . comes from the Basel Mission. The total budget is about Rs. 60,000 of which 10,000 per year comes from the Government's Department of Religion. The (Church's) Synod contributes 8,000. The Synod's contribution comes from all the churches in the Synod, each one of which gives from 15 to 50 rupiahs per month to the School, according to the size of its membership. . . .

House of the Epiphany: This theological "college" is supported by the Anglican Church and is located in Kuching, Sarawak, a British colony on the north coast of the island of Borneo. The seminary "opens as required." It was closed in 1957. In the year previous it had one full-time staff member and several part-time instructors engaged in training approximately 10 ordinand students. The school will be reopened when a new group of ordinands are ready for seminary. In the interim some students are occasionally being sent to Anglican theological schools elsewhere in Australasia.

The Anglicans in Sarawak number about 10,000 members, compared to about 15,000 Methodists. In 1956 the Methodist Church (USA) selected Sarawak as a point of special missionary emphasis in the quadrennium 1957–60. In the previous year they opened a Bible school at Sibu.

Union Theological School, Makassar: One of the fastest growing seminaries in Indonesia is the Union Theological School at Makassar in the Celebes Islands. Makassar is 900 miles east of Djakarta. According to the President of this seminary, the city of Makassar "is the cultural, religious and economic center of Eastern Indonesia. . . . 1½ million Christians live in Eastern Indonesia in the area served by the Makassar Theological School. Before the war there were 14 theological training schools in this area, and since the war these colleges . . . united to form the Union Theological School at Makassar" (UTSM).

Established in 1947, the UTSM encountered opposition from local Muslim groups when it initially attempted to obtain a site in Makassar. Consequently the seminary was located during its first two years in some rather makeshift quarters at So'e on the island of Timor. The Lutheran Church in Holland contributed some funds to enable it to obtain a permanent site. Then approximately $85,000 was pledged by American mission boards under the leadership of the IMC to help the UTSM match some available Dutch funds, thereby enabling it to locate on its present site at Makassar in the Celebes. There is said to be a growing hostility to the School arising largely from jealousy on the part of Muslim leaders owing to the rapid growth of the Theological School. It is reported there has even been some thought given to establishing a Muslim school in the vicinity.

The total enrollment at Makassar in 1957 was about 80 students. The capacity of the School is approximately 150 students at all levels of instruction. An increase in its enrollment during the next few years is anticipated as the level of secondary school standards in Indonesia are raised. In 1957 the duration of the courses at the UTSM was lengthened from four years to five.

In the summer of 1956 two key Dutch missionaries of outstanding ability who were serving on the faculty resigned from the UTSM, leaving one Hollander temporarily serving as Rector and one American and one Filipino on the faculty (in addition to the Indonesian instructors). In 1957 Mrs. C. L. Manuputti Manusamma, the first Indonesian woman to be ordained to the ministry, was appointed Rector of the seminary.

With respect to more recent gifts, it appears that approximately $100,000 has been raised by the UTSM in the last few years, with substantial contributions having been received from the Presbyterians USA and the Methodists. At one point the School had incurred an overdraft of $16,000 occasioned by the effects of inflation upon its building construction costs. However, the Nanking Board of Founders appropriated $14,000 in 1957–58 to enable the UTSM to liquidate the remainder of this indebtedness and to install its own Delco electric light system.

The School now has a large hostel, recreation and dining room, kitchen and washroom, four teachers' homes, and two classrooms. The UTSM is seeking to raise an additional $50,000. If obtained, these funds will be used for additional classrooms and housing, a new chapel, main office and a library. Dr. Smith reported that the water supply of the School has been threatened, and that a new well system is needed. On his visit to the UTSM in 1955 he had been depressed as he looked at the School's dormitory in the evening, "because it had no electric lights. The students were attempting to study under the feeble light of small oil lamps. This year (1957) all has changed, the whole dormitory was ablaze."

Theological School, So'e: In July 1957 the special assembly of the Evangelical Protestant Church of Timor was reported to have voted to raise this Church's Bible school at So'e to the junior college level and to extend its course of theological study from two to four years, followed by ordination. Christianity reached the island of Timor before Islam, and the indigenous animism is disappearing rapidly. Approximately 10,000 converts to Protestantism are being obtained by this Church each year, a rate which is reportedly being exceeded by the Roman Catholic Church in this area.

Ambon Theological School: The Ambon Theological School on the Island of Ambon is controlled by the Church of the Moluccas. The Moluccas are a large, remote island chain 600 miles east of Makassar. When the Dutch took over the administration of these islands, they tried to suppress Roman Catholicism and to introduce Protestantism. Today Ambon is about 50% Christian. When Indonesia became independent, the islands comprising the northern part of the nation, including the Celebes and the Moluccas, revolted in favor of a federated rather than a centralized form of government with headquarters in Java. In 1958 Ambon was still a military zone requiring special military permission to enter.

Dr. Smith reports:

The faculty of the School is composed entirely of Indonesians with five full-time teachers and five part-time ones. . . . The Theological School at present is entirely supported by the Ambonese Church . . . (and there is a) very intimate relationship between the Church and the Theological School. . . . Its faculty, with the exception of the rector who receives his salary from the budget of the institution, receive their salaries directly from the treasurer of the Synod. . . . The Synod . . . has been reluctant to ask for aid from outside sources. However, it is increasingly aware . . . that if it is to have a theological school at all adequate to meet the growing needs of the Church, it must accept some aid from abroad. . . . By itself the Synod of Molucca is not a sufficiently large body to maintain a special Theological School . . . but if the large area of New Guinea could be restored to the Synod . . . then . . . the Theological School at Ambon would have a much greater significance than it does now. . . .

The Theological School which is close to the beach on which the Japanese landed, shows the signs of the invasion, the bombing, and a later pos.war period of revolution against the . . . Government in Djakarta. . . . I was deeply impressed by the poor condition of the School plant. . . . The roofs of most of the buildings are in a poor state of repair and leak so badly that often classes have to move from one part of the room to another to find shelter during heavy rain. . . .

In 1957–58 the Board of Founders of Nanking Theological Seminary contributed $10,000 to this seminary to enable it to repair these buildings. At one point there was some consideration given to the possibility that the Ambon School might unite with the Union Theological School at Makassar. However, this did not take place, and it is doubtful that such a merger will occur within the foreseeable future.

Over-all Comments on Indonesian Schools: Concerning theological education in Indonesia, Dr. Smith believes "the standard required for entrance in all but two of the theological schools is too low. . . . In view of the strongly rural character of Christian communities in Indonesia I would suggest that some of the theological schools at least should be prepared to offer special training in rural life, sociology, economics and methods of evangelism to non-Christians. . . ." It is also his "conviction that the organization of theological education in Indonesia is sound and generally effective (and) that the advance of theological education has been unusually rapid, especially during the past four or five years. . . ."

C. OCEANIA

Because of (1) the small size of most of the islands of Oceania, (2) the wide distances which separate them, and (3) their comparatively sparse populations, the various mission stations tend to be more isolated from the rest of the world than are those even in "darkest" Africa. With respect to the field of higher education as a whole, the generally low cultural level prevailing in Oceania has been such that it has been more feasible to send the most gifted theological students to Australia and New Zealand to complete their education for the ministry, rather than attempt to build up one or two comparatively strong seminary centers in the islands. As a result, the theological schools in Oceania are for the most part small. It would also appear that as a group they are teaching at a lower level of instruction than are the seminaries in the other areas of Asia, Africa and Latin America. Table 37 lists the theological schools which were training students in Oceania as of 1957.

Newton Theological College: This Anglican institution is the diocesan seminary for the training of the Papuan clergy in the southeastern (Australian) portion of New Guinea. The Anglican mission stations extend along the northeastern coast of Papua from Chad's Bay to Finschhafen. Their headquarters are located at

Dogura, so that the Bishop and other priests are available to give lectures to the students at the Newton Theological College. Most of this seminary's financial needs are met through funds raised in Australia and England. According to the secretary of the New Guinea Mission, entering students have in all cases served as teacher-evangelists for several years with the care of an outstation and school.

TABLE 37.   THEOLOGICAL SCHOOLS IN OCEANIA (1957)

Name	Location	Approx. Number of		Denominational Support
		Full-Time Faculty	Theol. Students	
Papua, New Guinea				
Newton Theological College	Dogura	1[a]	11	Anglican
Lutheran Theological Seminary	Locgaweng, Finschhafen	2	6?	Lutheran
Lawes College	Fife Bay	3[a]	20	Congregational (English)
British Solomon Islands				
St. Peter's Theological College	Siota	2	15	Anglican
New Caledonia				
Pastors School	Houailou	1[a]	13	French Evangelical Reformed Church
Gilbert Islands				
Rongorongo College	Beru	3[a]	24	Congregational (English)
Western Samoa				
Malua Theological College	Malua	4	48	Congregational (English)
Cook Islands				
Takamoa College	Rarotonga	2	10	Congregational (English)
Society Islands				
Pastors School	Papeete, Tahiti	1[b]	7[c]	French Evangelical Reformed Church
Total: 9[d]		19	154	

NOTES: [a] Plus part-time faculty.   [d] See also Table 70A, Supplementary List of Theological
[b] Equivalent of three part-time faculty members.   Schools.
[c] Plus students at lower level of training.

Prior to their being licensed as teacher-evangelists they have had four years' training at St. Aidan's College (Dogura). The course at Newton for the diaconate usually last four years. After serving as deacons for two or three years the students must complete a further two-year course at Newton before being ordained priests.

Lutheran Theological Seminary: German missions have long been active in New Guinea, dating back to the pre-World War I period when the northeastern section of New Guinea was a German colony known as Kaiser Wilhelmsland (which is now an Australian mandate). In 1957 the Lutherans established a new seminary at Finschhafen. Cooperating in this venture are the American Lutheran Church, United Evangelical Lutheran Church in Australia, the Neuendettelsau and the Leipzig Mission Societies in Germany, and the Lutheran World Federation. The faculty includes a total of six persons, half of whom are missionaries.

Lawes College: First established by the English Congregational mission at Vatorata in 1894, this seminary was transferred to Fife Bay (50 miles west of Samarai) in 1924. At that time its name was changed to Lawes College. Up until 1947 the theological training of its students was supplemented by practical instruction in carpentry, house and boat building, etc. In recent years the school's educational standards have been raised somewhat. Lawes College's older buildings were constructed with local materials using sago bark walls for the students' houses. Since World War II some new buildings have been erected with contributions provided by a war memorial fund in Australia.

St. Peter's Theological College: St. Peter's is located at Siota. The latter is on the north coast of Florida (Gela) Island (which is directly north of Guadalcanal). Commenting on this Anglican seminary, the Secretary of the Melanesian Mission states that during World War II "Siota was wrecked through enemy action and there are hardly any permanent buildings left. We are now starting to rebuild these at great cost. . . . Normally the staff consists of two European priests, one of whom is married. . . . When students come to read for Orders, it means very often that they bring four, five or even six of a family with them. This of course adds greatly to the expense of running the College. Although we try to grow as much food as possible at Siota, we are not blessed with good garden land, so our costs are something like £700 per annum, the greater part of which is spent on supplementing the students' meagre diet."

Pastors School, Houailou: This seminary is an outgrowth of the Bethany Bible School originally established in 1862 by the English Congregational mission at Chepeneke on the island of Lifu. The latter is one of the Loyalty Islands (100 miles east of New Caledonia). In 1878 this mission also established a pastors school on the neighboring Mare Island. However, the latter institution was closed down in 1887 as a result of political disorders. In 1897 the French Evangelical Reformed Church missionaries took over the Pastors School on Mare Island and operated it until 1902. At that time it was transferred to Do-Néva at Houailou (sometimes known as Ponerihouen, on the east coast of New Caledonia, 100 miles northwest of Noumea). This seminary was closed in 1922 (with all the pastors being trained at Bethany) and was not reopened until 1939. In 1942 the Bethany Bible School (also administered by the French Evangelical Reformed mission) was renamed The Bible School of Lifu: it now provides a three-year preparatory course for students who then transfer to the Pastors School at Houailou for a further three years of training. The one full-time missionary on the faculty of the Pastors School is assisted by a local minister serving part time.

Rongorongo College: The islands of Micronesia, of which the Gilbert Islands are a part, are located midway between those of Melanesia to the south and west and those of Polynesia to the east. Both Micronesia and Polynesia have been areas in which English Congregational missionaries have been active for many years. The Rongorongo College was founded by them in 1901. It is located on Beru, a small island 40 miles southeast of Tarawa. The seminary trains Gilbertese pastors for the Gilbert Islands, Nauru (to the west), the Phoenix Islands (to the east), Ocean Island, and pastors for the Banaban people of Ocean Island who are now settled on Rabi in the Fiji group. In 1957 some of the seminary's buildings were seriously damaged by typhoons.

Malua Theological College: The College was originally established in 1844 as the Malua Institute and has had an unbroken record of providing education for the ministry ever since. It is located at Malua, 10 miles west of Apia, on Upolu Island in Western Samoa. The seminary trains men for the churches in Samoa, the Ellice Islands and for Papua (New Guinea). In 1957 the College's buildings were being reconstructed in a modern style, and the local church in Samoa undertook full responsibility for financing the cost of this work. In terms of the total number of students enrolled in its courses, this is the largest seminary in Oceania.

Takamoa College: Originally established in 1839, this is one of the oldest Protestant seminaries in the Orient. Located on Rarotonga, it trains ministers for the churches in the Cook Islands. Some of its graduates have also served with distinction in Papua.

(The English Congregational mission also maintains the Vailahi Institute on the small island of Niue which is 580 miles west of Rarotonga and is a New Zealand dependency. Niue has only 12 churches, each of which follows a very old practice of sending one student to the Institute. As a result there is usually a "surplus" of "trained" ministers on the island. The educational level at the Institute is much lower than that at the four other seminaries in Oceania supported by this mission. The result is that it can hardly be classified as a theological school.)

Pastors School, Papeete: This tiny seminary is located at Papeete, the capital of Tahiti in the Society Islands group (a French colony). The school is supported by the Paris Foreign Mission Society of the French Evangelical Reformed Church. The Director and two Tahitian pastors all serve part time on its faculty. After completing the four-year course, its graduates must spend at least two years in supervised field work in parishes before they may be ordained.

D. Philippine Islands

The Republic of the Philippines is the only Christian nation in Asia. Of its total population of approximately 19,500,000, some 17,325,000 persons are estimated to be religious believers, as shown in Table 38.

TABLE 38. MAJOR RELIGIOUS COMMUNITIES IN THE
PHILIPPINE ISLANDS (1956)

Roman Catholic Church	14,500,000
Philippine Independent Catholic Church	1,500,000
Protestants	600,000
Muslims	675,000
Buddhists	50,000
	17,325,000

In addition to the religious communities listed in Table 38, one might mention the Monoloan sect. Under the leadership of Paul Luther Monolo (who calls himself "the Third Angel"), this group claims to have as many as 2,000,000 followers.

The dominant position of the Roman Catholic Church in the Philippines is a heritage of the days when the Philippines were a Spanish colony. However, Protestant sources claim that only one out of every ten Roman Catholics in the Republic is a practicing churchman. Protestant missions did not gain a foothold in the Islands until they were ceded in 1898 by Spain to the United States.

The 1956 report of the Methodists' Division of Foreign Missions is quite explicit in its comment on the present policy of the Roman Catholic Church in the Philippines: "The Roman Church is determined, if at all possible, to surround, isolate and then eradicate the Protestant communities. They view Protestants as 'heathens' in the same category with Communists, Muslims and pagans. In recent years they have particularly attacked the YMCA, the YWCA, the Masons and Rotary." Protestant churches in the Philippines have sometimes been stoned, their services interrupted, and boycotts of Protestant schools have been proclaimed. On the other hand, according to a Presbyterian USA missionary with long experience in the Philippines, Rev. Henry Welton Rotz, there has been a "rather remarkable absence of the viciousness and violence that has been seen in other parts of the world," and he concludes that the "persecution pattern in the Philippines is usually one of irritation rather than violence." In many localities in the Philippines friendly relationships are said to exist between the individual Roman Catholic and Protestant churches and their members.

The Philippine Independent Catholic Church was founded in 1902 by Rev. Gregorio Aglipay. The latter was a Filipino who had been ordained a Roman Catholic priest in Manila in 1890 and had subsequently risen rapidly in church circles. However, he became dissatisfied with the Roman Catholic Church's policy of appointing only Spaniards as bishops in the Philippines. He personally appealed to the cardinals in Spain, without success, and then to the Pope, who declined to intervene. For this action he was censured by the Roman Catholic Church hierarchy in the Philippines and was excommunicated in 1899.

In 1902 Father Aglipay outlined his plans for forming a new church to Bishop Charles H. Brent of the Protestant Episcopal Church and to other American clergymen then stationed in the Philippines: they declined to cooperate with him on the grounds that Protestants generally did not desire to disrupt the membership of the Roman Catholic Church. Nevertheless in that same year Father Aglipay founded what is now often known as the Aglipayan Church. Its membership rapidly grew and reached approximately 1,500,000 persons. Since that time there has not been much growth in the Aglipayan Church, and it has suffered through a lack of an adequately trained ministry. In the early days the American Unitarians sent some material aid which could not be accepted without some of their spiritual influence making itself felt as well. This tended to widen the gulf separating the Aglipayan Church from orthodox Protestant churches. The Unitarian influences gradually died out and eventually the Aglipayan Church elected its own bishops.

The Independent Catholic Church has had no seminary of its own. After the death of Bishop Aglipay in 1940, the Aglipayan Church in 1948 obtained apostolic succession for its episcopate through the consecration of three of its bishops by bishops of the Protestant Episcopal Church. In a generation's time it seems likely that the polity of the Aglipayan and the Protestant Episcopal Churches will become identical, and the latter Church has been active in helping to provide theological training for Aglipayan students.

The membership of the larger Protestant churches in the Philippines is approximately as shown in Table 39.

The Protestant seminaries in the Philippines are listed in Table 40.

TABLE 39. MEMBERSHIP OF LEADING PROTESTANT CHURCHES IN THE PHILIPPINES (1956)

United Church of Christ in the Philippines[a]	100,000
Methodist Church[b]	85,000
Seventh Day Adventists	41,000
Convention of Philippine Baptist Churches	25,000
Churches of Christ (Disciples) of the Philippines[b]	15,000
Episcopal Church	12,000
	278,000

NOTES: [a] The UCCP is a merger of the missions of the Presbyterians, Disciples (in part), Methodists (in part), Evangelical United Brethren and Congregational Churches. It is served by more than 400 ordained pastors and 525 evangelists and deaconesses. [b] Exclusive of churches in the UCCP.

TABLE 40. THEOLOGICAL SCHOOLS IN THE PHILIPPINES (1957)

Name	Location	Approx. Number of Full-Time Faculty	Theol. Students	Denominational Support
Luzon				
Union Theological Seminary	Manila	7[a]	58[b]	United Church of Christ in the Philippines, Methodist, etc.
St. Andrew's Theological Seminary	Manila	6[a]	44	Protestant Episcopal
Lutheran Seminary	Manila	2	5	Lutheran (Missouri Synod)
Philippines Baptist Theological Seminary	Baguio	5[a]	18[b]	Southern Baptist
Laoag College of Theology	Laoag	4	10[b]	Disciples
Negros				
Silliman University College of Theology	Dumaguete	7[a]	41[b]	Congregational, Presbyterian USA
Panay				
Central Philippine University College of Theology	Iloilo	4[a]	21[b]	American Baptist
Total: 7		35	197	

NOTES: [a] Plus part-time faculty. [b] Plus other students at lower level of training.

Union Theological Seminary: Of the seven theological schools in the Philippines, the most important is the Union Theological Seminary (UTS) in Manila. It was founded in 1907 with the merger of the Ellinwood Bible Training School (of the Presbyterian Mission) and the Nicholson Seminary (of the Methodist mission). The United Brethren commenced supporting the UTS in 1911, the Disciples of Christ in 1916, and the Congregational mission in 1919.

In the past, the UTS offered three courses in theology: one of three years to college graduates who were candidates for a B.D.; one of four years to high school graduates who were candidates for a B.Th. degree; and to candidates who had completed only the first two years of the B.Th. course, the Seminary awarded an A.Th. (Associate in Theology). However, commencing in 1955 the UTS required all preministerial and religious education majors to have had two years of liberal arts college work as a prerequisite for admission. This raising of entrance requirements resulted in a small decrease in its enrollment of theological students in 1956. The Seminary also grants a B.R.E. (Bachelor of Religious Education) degree.

In October 1955 the total enrollment in the Seminary was 186, including the women students who are enrolled in the affiliated Harris Memorial School (Methodist). In that same year there were only eight students enrolled in the B.D. course. By the first semester of 1956–57, the number of ordinand students totaled 58, of whom 18 were at the B.D. and 40 at the B.Th. level. The theological students are divided about equally between the Methodists and the UCCP Church, with smaller numbers coming from other denominations. Most of the students are Filipinos since the immigration restrictions of the Philippine Government make it rather difficult for Chinese and other foreign students to come to the Islands for graduate study.

A number of the UTS professors have been B.D. students at the Union Theological Seminary in New York City, and the President, Dr. Benjamin I. Guansing, and five others of the UTS faculty have also done graduate work there. The UTS is an affiliated member of the American Association of Theological Schools, and some consider it is operated very much on an American rather than an indigenous pattern.

The AS report commented adversely on one aspect of the UTS curriculum: "Because of the shortage of qualified teachers and the demands upon the time and energy of its faculty made by the large number of students in the lower courses, it has often been necessary to put the B.D. students into some at least of the lower classes. . . ."

To the UTS in 1950–51 the Methodists contributed $6,262, and the UCCP (United Church) $6,812, making a total of $13,074. Of the sum contributed by the UCCP, the Presbyterian Mission gave $4,287, the Evangelical United Brethren Mission, $1,425, and the Disciples Mission, $1,100. The total budgeted income of the UTS in that year was $16,350. Thus approximately 80% of the Seminary's 1950–51 income came from missionary sources. However, in its fiscal year ended 5/31/56 the total operating budget of the UTS amounted to $40,692, of which mission boards contributed $18,700, or 46%.

During World War II the UTS buildings were used by the Japanese for a radio station and were partially damaged by American artillery fire. They were rebuilt shortly thereafter, and the school was reopened in July 1946. In 1954 the Seminary decided that it would be desirable for it to move from its present location on Taft Avenue in a noisy section of downtown Manila to a suburb, Quezon City, now the capital of the Republic. A high percentage of its students come from rural areas for whom the city was not attractive; and it was proving difficult to find housing for the increasing number of married students. By September 1955 a "preliminary" ten-year plan costing a grand total of $1,037,000 was worked out by the Seminary in connection with the plans for its new campus, as shown in Table 41.

TABLE 41. TEN-YEAR PLAN OF UNION THEOLOGICAL SEMINARY, MANILA
(1955–65)

Land	$ 150,000
Administration Building (Library and Classrooms)	200,000
60 Cottages	258,000
2 Dormitories	123,000
Chapel, Infirmary	40,000
Miscellaneous	216,000
Rehabilitation of Present Building	50,000
	$1,037,000

In June 1956 the Nanking Board of Founders voted to set aside $80,000 for the purchase of property in Quezon City as a future site for the UTS, but this did not involve a final commitment of the Founders to donate it to the Seminary and was made contingent on approval being obtained from the Executive Board of the UCCP and from the interested mission boards in New York City. Some delay in obtaining these approvals was caused by a number of factors. One of these was a desire on the part of the Seminary to establish a large, agriculturally self-sufficient campus in Quezon City—whereas it was believed that in a decade this city will have been absorbed by the fast-expanding city of Manila. Finally the Methodists and the Presbyterian USA boards in New York agreed in principle and voted to try to raise $75,000 each toward these needs, with the hope that an additional $100,000 would be furnished by other boards and donors, as well as by the UCCP.

In August 1956 the Seminary's Trustees decided to adopt a $236,000 program as a first step in its move to the suburbs. After using the Nanking Founders' $80,000 to purchase a site, the UTS proposed to spend:

Academic Building	$164,000
Men's Dormitory	33,500
Dining Hall and Women's Dormitory	38,500
	$236,000

At the end of 1957 the UTS purchased a 242-acre tract of land 20 miles south of Manila on the highway leading to Tagaytay City (after deciding against the purchase of a more costly 275-acre tract somewhat closer to the city). It was planned that the first construction would involve a commitment in the amount of $150,000, whenever such funds could be raised.

St. Andrew's Theological Seminary: When World War II began, the Protestant Episcopal Church had (in addition to its American personnel) only two Filipino priests, one native deacon and two Chinese priests stationed in the Philippines. When all foreign missionaries were interned by the Japanese, these five, plus the Filipino catechists and seminarians, were the only ones left to lead the 10,000 members of the Episcopal Church. Not only were they successful in holding this Church together, but in some areas they even were able to enroll new members.

Prior to 1942, the Episcopalians operated a small clergy training school in Sagada. After V-J Day the school was reopened on a temporary basis, pending its transformation into St. Andrew's Theological Seminary in the autumn of 1947. St. Andrew's is now said to be "Exhibit A" among the schools overseas which are supported by the Protestant Episcopal Church. One-half of its students are sent to it by the Aglipayan Church. A four-year course is offered, and the growth of the Seminary has been much faster than anticipated.

The Episcopalians have been developing a $2,000,000 project on a 36-acre tract which was purchased by them in 1947. It is near the University of the Philippines and is half-way between downtown Manila and Quezon City. The largest institution in the project is St. Luke's Hospital, costing well over $1,000,000. The Seminary's new buildings were among the first to be built on this site. The funds for this project are being obtained from various sources, with a major share coming from reparation funds. The latter are available because the buildings which formerly belonged to these institutions were destroyed in World War II. Up to the present, the Episcopalians have advanced approximately $300,000 for St. Andrew's Seminary, and the board has accorded this school a high priority in its allocations. A decade from now it is possible that the Seminary may become even more closely related to the Aglipayan Church. On the other hand, this factor tends to prevent St. Andrew's from achieving a close cooperation with the Union Theological Seminary in Manila.

Lutheran Seminary: In 1955 the Missouri Synod Lutherans established this theological school in rented quarters on the outskirts of Manila. Five students were enrolled initially under a faculty of three pastors, one or two of whom were serving part time.

Philippine Baptist Theological Seminary: This school was opened by the Southern Baptists in temporary quarters in 1952. The first class was graduated from its three-year course in 1955. In the latter year the Seminary was moved into substantial new buildings on a hillside campus near Baguio. The City of Baguio is the chief health resort and summer capital of the Philippines. It is situated over 4,500 feet high in the Benguet Mountains, 160 miles north of Manila. A number of rest homes for various Roman Catholic orders are also located there. A recent visitor (Dr. C. Stanley Smith) comments that the married students' apartments at the Southern Baptists' school "offer the best facilities of any seminary in Southeast Asia. . . . The Baguio seminary also conducts a Bible school at the end of which the students are awarded a certificate. The faculty consists of eight teachers, all Westerners. Students total 22, of whom 16 are Filipinos and six are Chinese."

Laoag College of Theology: This seminary is a part of the Northern Christian College (NCC) which is located in Laoag, a town in Ilocos Province in the northern tip of Luzon, approximately 125 miles north of Baguio. The NCC was visited by Dr. C. Stanley Smith in 1956–57 whose report to the Board of Founders of Nanking Theological Seminary commented on it as follows:

The NCC was founded by the Disciples Mission in the Philippine Islands and follows the patterns of Disciples' seminaries in the United States in that it combines college and theological study fairly closely. The NCC offers courses from kindergarten to college. Its (the seminary's) B.Th. course runs for three years. Of the 350 students (at the NCC), 22 are taking a pretheological course, and an additional 10 are studying for the B.Th. degree. After completing the pretheological course, the students take one year of field work before commencing studies in the Laoag College of Theology. This year serves as a screening period to see whether the young men are qualified or sufficiently interested to continue their work toward a B.Th. degree. The College occupies two main buildings on a campus which comprises a good share of a city block. The faculty of the Laoag College of Theology consists of four teachers (two Filipinos) all of whom also teach in the NCC College of Arts. This (theological) school trains ministers for the United Church of (Christ in) the Philippines.

The College of Theology, Silliman University: This College is a department of Silliman University which is located at Dumaguete on the island of Negros. The seminary was originally established in 1921 as the Silliman Bible School and achieved college status in 1931. It occupies a large building not far from the center of the University campus.

The enrollment in the seminary dropped to as low as 15 in 1940–41, and the school was closed during World War II. Reopened shortly after V-J Day, its enrollment rose to 121 in 1954–55, of whom approximately 41 were men training for careers in the ordained ministry. The emphasis of its teaching and practical work is decidedly rural. At first, the Congregational Church furnished most of the support for the school, but now it also receives budgetary assistance from the Presbyterians USA.

In 1954–55 Dr. William P. Fenn, Executive Secretary of the United Board for

Christian Higher Education in Asia, was loaned by that organization to make a detailed survey of the program of Silliman University. The published report of his survey team includes some comments on the Silliman College of Theology describing it as one of the University's most important units:

> We hope that the day is not too distant when government educational authorities will recognize its legitimate status as one of the colleges of Silliman University. . . . The College serves a real need . . . and provides an environment peculiarly suited to the preparation of ministers for rural parishes. . . . If we were to make any criticism of the curriculum it would be of what seems to us an excessive emphasis on methods at the expense of content. . . . We urge that every effort be made to strengthen the Filipino element on the faculty. We particularly welcome plans for typical rural residences for married couples studying in the College. . . . There is need for increased support of the College by the Church so that it may be a more nearly self-supporting unit of the University. There is special need for funded scholarships to provide for all ministerial students who need help.

In 1951, Mr. Arthur L. Carson, who was then President of Silliman University, proposed that the seminaries in the Philippines should be reorganized so that there would be one school on the graduate level, presumably the UTS at Manila, a part of whose course would include one year's training in the rural ministry at Silliman. He also suggested that with respect to the three main local languages in the Philippines, the UTS should concentrate on training students in Tagalog, the Central Philippine University College of Theology at Iloilo in Ilongo, and Silliman in Cebuano Visayan. These recommendations in some respects resemble those made in the Ranson report on India. Similarly, they have not been implemented.

Central Philippine University College of Theology: At the Central Philippine University at Iloilo on the island of Panay, there is a College of Theology which is supported by the American Baptists. The College was started in 1933 and places emphasis on training for rural pastorates. The course is four years in length and in 1955 it admitted its first class under a new plan requiring an "Associate in Arts degree, or its equivalent, for admission."

The increase in the enrollment at the University as a whole from 243 in 1955 to 1,793 in 1956 has been impressive in view of the reported campaign of the Roman Catholic hierarchy in the pulpit, press and on the radio to spread word that Filipino families would be excommunicated if any of their members were to attend Iloilo.

General Comments (Philippine Islands): In 1955 a Presbyterian USA missionary, Rev. Henry Welton Rotz, wrote a doctoral dissertation relating to the recruitment, training, support and performance of church leaders in the Philippines. This report was based upon 886 returns to questionnaires he sent out in 1952 to 1,024 ordained ministers and lay church workers in the Republic. Of the 373 ordained church leaders who replied to the questionnaire, 38% were seminary graduates, 36% had received some seminary or Bible school training, and 26% had obtained no professional training of any sort. The author commented as follows concerning the state of theological education in the Philippines:

The seminaries have been guilty of paralleling American seminaries and considering the school good that is most like an American school. . . . A Philippine seminary should be considerably different. . . . The ordained leaders . . . are in insufficient supply, and at the present rate of training and expansion of Protestant Christianity in the Philippines there seems to be no indication that there will ever be enough seminary trained ordained leaders. . . . A high percentage of the church leaders, especially the ordained ones, have already reached a point beyond the normal Filipino life expectancy. As a consequence, the necessity to recruit new leaders is of an emergency nature. . . . It is suggested that intensified programs of recruitment be conducted in church related schools. . . . Probably the greatest single factor slowing the recruitment of leaders is the inability of the churches to pay an adequate salary. . . . Economic factors create the largest amount of frustration, dissatisfaction, and unhappiness among church leaders. . . .

E. OVER-ALL ASPECTS

Concerning the Protestant seminaries in the five countries comprising Southeast Asia, the AS report has this to say:

In spite of the almost complete support of theological education from mission funds, it is still true that this support is very inadequate to meet the needs of modern theological education. This is especially true of denominationally supported schools; union seminaries are generally in better financial condition. Some of the schools which we visited have annual budgets of less than US $3,000. It is not to be wondered at, therefore, that theological schools are woefully understaffed as to national teachers. With few exceptions, national teachers are paid from the current budget of the school, missionary teachers receive their salaries from their Home Boards. Governing Boards, therefore, do not need much persuasion to accept a missionary rather than call a national whose salary must come from their meager budgets.

As for the equipment of these schools, the AS report states: "While some of the plants are not bad in comparison with national church buildings, if the comparison is made with other educational plants and equipment the contrast is startling; if compared with theological seminaries in America the contrast is so great that it is painful to contemplate, e.g., there is no theological school in all Southeast Asia that has a whole plant equal in cost and utility to the new student center now nearing completion at Princeton Theological Seminary—but only one of the minor buildings of a great institution."

A European who recently visited Southeast Asia commented on the classroom attitude of the seminary students. He pointed out that if he presented facts to the students, the latter seldom criticized them; or, if he presented criticisms, the students were likely to adopt such criticisms *in toto* without attempting to weigh their merit. Thus the problem of upgrading theological education involves more than merely improving the caliber of the teachers, the content of their curricula and the facilities within buildings: there is also a need to stimulate the constructive critical faculties of the students.

Another recent visitor comments on the fact that a surprisingly high proportion of the enrollment in the seminaries and Bible schools in Southeast Asia (exclusive of Formosa and Hongkong) consists of overseas Chinese students. Christianity appears to have a more ready appeal for the overseas Chinese (who are an energetic group but somewhat insecure as a consequence of their displacement) as compared to the Burmese, Malay and Javanese peoples, etc., who are devoted in their support of Buddhism or Islam. This disproportionate representation of the Chinese in the seminaries' enrollment sometimes causes linguistic problems to arise.

In 1953 Dr. Henry P. Van Dusen stated:

The most grievous, unnecessary, and inexcusable weakness of theological education in Southeast Asia is that each school works in relative isolation without knowledge of what others have tried and learned, without mutual interchange and profit. . . . There is need that there be in Southeast Asia at least one higher grade theological college beyond the B.D. degree. . . . If there is need for at least one such college, it is equally clear that there is room for not more than one. The language of instruction at that level would need to be in an ecumenical tongue, and today that is English. The books needed are also largely in English. . . . There is urgent need for higher theological conferences in Southeast Asia. . . . There should also be a Theological Educational Council for Southeast Asia. . . .

There is need of a theological education cooperative training program for Southeast Asia. There should be summer institutes for theological teachers. Such institutes should take up the problem, for instance, of the best way of teaching the Old Testament. We should send the best Old Testament teacher from the United States and some from Asia. Let these teachers attack their problems in common. Then deal with the New Testament in the same way. Audio-visual education is another subject for common study. The problems are essentially the same for all the churches and all of the theological seminaries.

The Bangkok Theological Conference: A Conference on Theological Education in Southeast Asia was held in Bangkok, Thailand, from February 21 to March 8, 1956, under the auspices of the International Missionary Council, the World Council of Churches and the Board of Founders of Nanking Theological Seminary. About 70 educators were in attendance, including representatives of 19 theological institutions. The membership of the Conference was almost equally divided between Asian nationals and western missionaries. Dr. Rajah B. Manikam, the Lutheran Bishop of Tranquebar and formerly the Southeast Asia Secretary for the IMC and WCC, was associated with Dr. C. Stanley Smith in planning for the Conference.

Dean Liston Pope of the Yale Divinity School commented at the Conference: "Of approximately twenty theological schools (in East Asia) which I have visited to date, nearly all are less than fifty years old. Nearly all were either destroyed or badly damaged during the second World War, and nearly all were closed down for five or six years, with the attendant loss of faculty, students, libraries and nearly every other asset. . . . The actual situation is that the present system of theological education in Southeast Asia is less than ten years old!"

Addresses were given by western theologians on the "continental," the British, and the American seminary traditions. These "underlined the continental emphasis on 'thoroughness' in the theological disciplines, the British ideal of training based on a more general cultural course, and the American awareness of man's various needs." By contrast, two comments of Asian theologians are worth noting: "We must have our own development in systematic theology and Christian ethics," said Rector Peter Latuihamallo of the Djakarta Theological College. Principal J. Russell Chandran of Union Theological College, Bangalore, told the Conference that the Christian faith commends itself to Asian people provided it is expressed in their forms of thought.

With respect to the 19 seminaries whose representatives met at the Conference, 69 full-time members of their faculties were reported to be non-Asians. Only 46 faculty members were Asians, or about 40%.

There was general agreement that a Journal of Theology should be started, to be published under the auspices of one of the leading seminaries and which might help lay the foundation for a distinctive Christian theology for the Asian churches.

The Conference voted (a) to found an Association of Theological Schools and Colleges in Southeast Asia; (b) to establish standards of accreditation; and (c) to appoint a committee to report on standardization of degrees; and it agreed on a nomenclature for classifying training institutions.

The hope was expressed that the Association of Principals which was created at the Conference would ultimately become an Association of Theological Schools and Colleges which would be helpful in promoting the interchange of programs and students, producing bibliographies of textbooks, and voicing appeals to the WCC and IMC for the needs of theological education in Southeast Asia.

"The Conference (also) appointed a committee to carry out the proposal made by Dr. Ranson that 'a higher theological faculty for the advanced training of carefully selected students from all countries of Asia which are in a position to take advantage of it' be established. . . . President Benjamin Guansing of Union Theological Seminary, Manila, was named chairman of a committee of six Asians to bring in proposals on the matter."

Dr. Guansing's committee recommended the establishment of such a graduate divinity school, particularly since it would serve as a training center for future members of Asian theological faculties. In its report, the committee stated it had "decided to recommend the choice of Bangalore in India, and Kyoto or Tokyo in Japan in this order of priority."

Bangalore was given first priority because of its temperate climate, easy accessibility, the presence of a graduate level theological college with a fairly good library, the medium of instruction being English, the contact with many non-Christian religions, the proximity to good university libraries, the easy availability of language pundits for languages like Pali and Sanskrit, the possible location of a Buddhist University in Bangalore, comparatively low cost of living and its location in the midst of a fairly strong Christian Church.

Kyoto and Tokyo also have the advantage of a good climate, easy accessibility, graduate level theological colleges, and good library facilities. They have the added advantage of Christian universities, International Christian University in Tokyo and Doshisha University in Kyoto. However, Japan was given the second place because (the) normal medium of instruction of their theological faculties is Japanese and this fact is likely to limit the scope of the Higher Theological Faculty.

It was agreed that to begin with the subjects chosen for specialization should be History of Religions and Sociology. This is because at present there are better experts in Asia for these subjects than for the other branches of theological learning. It was agreed that, to begin with, we choose two professors and ask them to travel in different Asian countries to acquaint themselves well with the specific issues in the region. As soon as possible after the first two years attempts will be made to enlarge the Higher Theological Faculty to five members.

The Committee estimated that the establishment of such a graduate divinity school would entail the following expenses:

Nonrecurring capital expense	$125,500
Annual budgetary expense (five years @ $29,500)	147,500
	$273,000

It was hoped that churches in Asia, the Nanking Board of Founders and foreign mission boards would contribute toward these costs. It was also suggested that at least one-sixth of the total budget should be raised in Asia, with the Asian support gradually increasing over the years.

No agreement was reached at Bangkok as to the location of the proposed higher theological faculty. A number of those present, including Dean Pope, were skep-

tical as to the feasibility of the project on the grounds that it might prove difficult at this time to launch a separate institution in Asia devoted solely to theological studies at the postgraduate, Ph.D. level.

The holding of the Bangkok Conference stimulated the interest of religious
leaders in the subject of theological education in their own countries. One specific
result was the decision to hold a conference in Indonesia in 1957 on theological
education in that country, with the emphasis of the discussion to be placed on
the content of their seminaries' curricula. Also, the Nanking Board of Founders
planned to hold a two-month theological seminar in Singapore in 1957.

CHAPTER 6

EAST ASIA

A. JAPAN

In Japan only 0.6% (approximately 460,000 persons) of the total population of about 88,000,000 are enrolled in Protestant and Roman Catholic churches. The comparable figures for other leading countries in Asia are China 0.25%, India 2.5%, Indonesia 4% and Korea 7%. On this basis it would be fair to say that in relation to the time and money spent by Christian missionaries in Japan during the past century, the mission boards have obtained proportionately fewer converts in that country as compared to most of the other major Asian nations. The growth of Christianity in Japan during the years 1904–53 was as shown in Table 42.

TABLE 42.   GROWTH OF CHRISTIANITY IN JAPAN (1904–53)

	1904	1953	Increase
Total Population	50,000,000	87,000,000	74%
Protestants	53,000	237,000	347%
Roman Catholics	58,000	185,000	220%
Orthodox	27,000	33,000	22%
Total Christian Community	138,000	455,000	230%
Percentage of Population	0.28	0.59	

On the other hand, it also appears that among the Japanese Christians there is a disproportionately large number of leaders in the Government and in the arts and sciences, etc. This is indicated in Table 43.

In 1941 the Japanese Government required all the Protestant churches in Japan

TABLE 43.   OCCUPATIONAL DISTRIBUTION OF JAPANESE CHRISTIANS (CA. 1955)

	Population	Christians
Farmers	50%	2.0%
Laborers	27%	2.5%
Fishermen	3%	0.5%
Middle Class and Intelligentsia	20%	95.0%
	100%	100.0%

to unite into one organization, the Kyodan Church, in order that their activities might be more easily supervised by the Government during World War II. Groups within some denominations, including about one-third of the Episcopalians, refused to join the Kyodan and, in effect, went "underground" instead.

At present the Kyodan includes the following denominations: Congregational, Evangelical and Reformed, United Brethren, Methodist, Presbyterian USA, Dutch Reformed, Disciples and (to some extent) the American Baptists. During the war the Kyodan also included the Episcopalians, Lutherans, some Presbyterians and the "Holiness groups": however, late in 1945 and in 1946 these Protestants withdrew from it in order to re-establish their own separate denominational activities.

During the past decade American influence has been strong in Japan, and many new small sects from the United States have entered the country, including nine different groups of the Baptist confession alone. There are now a total of about 80 denominations in Japan compared to 33 before the war.

Approximately 70% of the Protestant church members in Japan are related directly or indirectly to the Kyodan. In this organization there are some 1,400 individual churches and 1,300 pastors. The Lutherans and Episcopalians, etc., maintain contact with it through the National Christian Council of Japan. In 1957 the membership status of the leading Protestant churches in Japan was as shown in Table 44.

TABLE 44.   MEMBERSHIP OF PROTESTANT CHURCHES IN
JAPAN (1957)

Church of Christ in Japan (Kyodan)	170,000
Episcopal Church of Japan	39,000
Convention of Baptist Churches in Japan	10,000
Evangelical Lutheran Church of Japan	8,000
	227,000

After World War II the Kyodan requested the American mission boards contributing personnel and financial aid to its support to channel such assistance through one agency. Accordingly the Interboard Committee for Christian Work in Japan was established in New York City, made up of representatives from eight denominations: Congregational, Disciples, Evangelical and Reformed, Evangelical United Brethren, Methodists, Presbyterian USA, Reformed Church in America, and the United Church of Canada. The Interboard Committee receives annual estimates of the financial aid required by the Kyodan in Japan. These estimates are compiled by the Council of Cooperation which is the Interboard Committee's counterpart in Japan and is composed of representatives of the recipient agencies in that country. During the past few years the Interboard Committee has received approximately $2,000,000 a year in contributions from its member denominations. For 1957, approximately $750,000 was asked of its members for the operating expenses of various projects in Japan, plus approximately $1,190,000 for special projects of the Kyodan.

The following are the priorities of interest of the Interboard Committee as stated in its literature: (1) rehabilitating the buildings of Japanese secular educational institutions run down or destroyed during World War II; (2) constructing new church buildings; and (3) evangelism. Among its other projects the Committee hopes to raise by 1959 the sum of $100,000 for the endowment of professorial chairs in four of the Kyodan seminaries.

There are over 150 Protestant-sponsored secular and religious schools of one sort or another now being operated in Japan. A list of the 12 theological schools is presented in Table 45.

TABLE 45.   THEOLOGICAL SCHOOLS IN JAPAN (1956)

		Approx. Number of		
Name	Location	Full-Time Faculty[d]	Theol. Students	Denominational Support
Tokyo Union Theological Seminary	Tokyo	19[a]	130[c]	Kyodan
Japan Lutheran Theological Seminary	Tokyo	5[a]	35[c]	Evangelical Lutheran Church of Japan
Rikkyo (St. Paul's) University Theological Faculty	Tokyo	3?	26	Episcopal Church of Japan
Episcopal Seminary	Tokyo	8[a]	23	Episcopal Church of Japan
Aoyama Gakuin University Theological Faculty	Tokyo	3?	30?	Kyodan
Japan Biblical Seminary	Tokyo	20[a]	60[c]	Kyodan
Lutheran Theological Seminary	Tokyo	3?	13	Lutheran (Missouri Synod)
Doshisha University School of Theology	Kyoto	15[a]	116[c]	Kyodan
Kwansei Gakuin University Theological School	Nishinomiya	14[a]	55[c]	Kyodan
Kanto Gakuin University Institute	Yokohama	8[b]	20	American Baptist
Osaka Kirisutokyo Gakuin Theological Department	Osaka	5[a]	37[c]	Free Methodist
Seinan Gakuin University Theological Department	Fukuoka	5[a]	45	Southern Baptist
Total: 12[e]		108	590	

NOTES: [a] Plus part-time staff.
[b] Also teaching in affiliated junior college.
[c] Plus students at lower level of training.

[d] Actual or equivalent.
[e] See also Table 70A, Supplementary List of Theological Schools.

Of the 12 institutions listed in Table 45, five have been accredited by the Bureau of Education of the Japanese Government as universities and are qualified to award degrees beyond the B.D. level, as shown in Table 46.

TABLE 46.   ACCREDITED SEMINARIES AWARDING ADVANCED DEGREES IN JAPAN (1957)

Name	Degrees	Field of Doctoral Degrees
Tokyo Union Theological Seminary	M.Th., D.Th.	Systematic Theology, Biblical Theology
Doshisha University Theological School	M.Th., D.Th.	Historical Theology
Kwansei Gakuin University Theological School	M.Th., D.Th.	Biblical Theology
Rikkyo (St. Paul's) University Theological Faculty	M.Th.	
Aoyama Gakuin University Theological Faculty	M.Th.	

Tokyo Union Theological Seminary: The Tokyo Union Theological Seminary (UTS) was established in 1943, two years after the organization of the Kyodan. The UTS was originally intended to be the only seminary of that denomination. However, some schools declined to be merged into it so that, as shown in Table

45, the Kyodan is now supporting four other schools as well. However, the UTS is the official school of the Kyodan and receives the largest single share of this Church's support for its seminaries.

The creation of the UTS, according to its catalogue, was brought about by the merger of several theological institutions, including chiefly the former Theological Department of Aoyama Gakuin University (Methodist), the Japan Baptist Seminary and the Japan Theological Seminary (Presbyterian), each of which represented previous mergers of a number of training schools. The Japan Theological Seminary represented an earlier merger of the Theological Departments of the Tohoku Gakuin, the Meiji Gakuin and the Tokyo Shingakusha Seminary. The UTS is the largest of the five Kyodan seminaries, and its trustees are all ministers and elders of that church.

During the first six years of its existence, the UTS occupied the buildings and campus of the Japan Lutheran Theological Seminary which had been closed during the War. In 1949, when the Lutherans desired to reopen their own school, the UTS moved to a site in Mitaka, 12 miles west of the center of Tokyo (and three miles' distance from the site where the International Christian University was later established). The UTS now occupies a wooded campus of six acres within the city limits. With seven new buildings, the Seminary is one of the best housed of the theological schools in the Orient. It is rivaled in this respect only by the Higher Theological School in Djakarta and Trinity College in Singapore.

According to the UTS catalogue, "the basic theological course consists of six years: the first two years for general cultural studies, and the next four years entirely theological. However, in conformity with the new government requirements, the first four years constitute a college course, and the last two years a graduate school course. Students may graduate at the end of the college course with the bachelor of arts degree (major in theology) but practically all students take the bachelor of divinity degree as well. In 1955, a three-year doctoral course for advanced graduate study in theology (Th.D.) was also recognized and accredited by the Department of Education." The UTS has a rural center for practical training in the ministry located some 40 miles east of Tokyo. It also operates a summer school offering refresher courses for pastors.

The Anderson-Smith report points out that since World War II the Government has

required an independent theological seminary to maintain a college of its own, if it is not a part of a College or University. The Theological School in Kyoto, being part of the Doshisha University, does not have to maintain a college of its own, but the UTS, being independent, must maintain a college. . . . The (UTS) Seminary faculty does not like this system very much. They feel that it burdens them with maintaining a college of arts and science which is expensive, taxes their teaching staff, and also crowds the

Seminary buildings with young college students. . . . Personally, I think that the UTS is to be congratulated in having this arrangement. After seeing the difficulty which most theological schools in the Orient have in getting adequately prepared students for their theological courses, the opportunity of having preparation of the students for their theological work directly under the control of the Seminary and taught by teachers chosen by the Seminary . . . is greatly to be desired. . . . If the seminaries in Southeast Asia could be assured of students as well prepared as these Japanese students would seem to be, there would be great rejoicing. . . . (The UTS) may well be on its way to becoming the leading theological seminary in the Orient. Were it not for the language difficulty, this Seminary might be a place where theological students in Southeast Asia desiring to secure a good, advanced theological education could go. At present . . . its student body (is almost entirely of) Japanese nationality."

President Hidenobu Kuwada of the UTS is a graduate of Auburn Theological Seminary (now united with the Union Theological Seminary in New York City), and Dr. Charles W. Iglehart, formerly Professor of Missions at UTS-NY, has also served as a member of the Tokyo UTS faculty. The eminent Swiss theologian, Dr. Emil Brunner, taught a course at this school during the two years (1953–55) he was on the faculty of the nearby International Christian University. On the other hand, in the opinion of some, the UTS has not yet achieved the highest status as a graduate school in the eyes of the Japanese. Many of its faculty are said to be strongly influenced by Barthianism to the point of minimizing other theological systems.

A somewhat less optimistic view of the position of the UTS is expressed by a number of other persons familiar with Japan. They consider it is the leading seminary of the Kyodan and potentially may become the outstanding school in the country. However, they also point out that it is seriously weakened by the fact that the members of the UTS faculty who serve "full time" actually spend a considerable portion of their days eking out their income with salaries paid to them by one or more churches for which they are serving as pastors. The President of the UTS, for example, has been receiving a salary from the Seminary which is the equivalent of approximately $50 a month. The monthly compensation paid to an assistant professor on the faculty of the Meiji Gakuin College (which is not a wealthy institution), for example, is said to be equal to or greater than this. There is some question as to how far this situation can be cured, and on this account some believe the Theological School of Doshisha University is a stronger seminary. At Doshisha the seminary has the support of the University and does not have to divert its funds for the pretheological training of its students.

The UTS catalogue states that the financial support of the UTS comes from the sources listed in Table 47.

TABLE 47.   FINANCIAL SUPPORT OF THE UNION THEOLOGICAL
SEMINARY OF TOKYO (CA. 1956)

Interboard Committee for Christian Work in Japan	45%
Student fees	30%
Donations	14%
United Church of Christ in Japan (Kyodan)	9%
Endowment	2%
	100%

The same document flatly declares that this institution is "unable to pay its professors an adequate living wage. Consequently, all of the professors must supplement their income in some way, and they cannot give full time to the Seminary. At present all but two of the professors are teaching part time in other schools. Several are teaching in five or six different institutions. This means that there is little time or energy left for all-important student consultations, student fellowship, or continued study in the professor's own field. In an earnest attempt to solve this problem, friends of the Seminary have started a campaign to raise funds, through the member boards of the Interboard Committee, for the endowment of four professors' chairs at $10,000 each. The interest from these endowments would provide a more adequate income for the Seminary professors, enabling them to give time to the Seminary work, including the very necessary personal contacts with students."

The UTS catalogue continues:

A student's annual expenses, including fees, room and board at the Seminary, and small personal expenses, come to about 75,000 yen ($210 a year). Nearly all the students are severely limited financially. Many of them (21%) come from ministers' families, who live on subsistence incomes. About half come from non-Christian families, and so cannot count on help from home in their preparation for the Christian ministry. About 80% are working to help put themselves through school, and a few are helping to support their families as well. These outside jobs, which are difficult to find in this overpopulated land and which pay very little, include such work as that of night watchman, interpreter, janitor, clerk, nurse, teacher and tutor. This work is done, of course, in addition to the student's field work in a church.

Japan Lutheran Theological Seminary: The Lutherans commenced missionary work in Japan somewhat later than did many other Protestant denominations. Their Seminary was originally founded in 1909 as part of the Kyushu Gakuin (a secondary school for boys) and was moved to Tokyo in 1925. During World War II the school was closed and its campus loaned to the then newly created Union Theological Seminary of the Kyodan. The latter occupied the buildings until 1950 when the Lutherans decided to re-establish their own seminary there. In order to conform to the Government's postwar educational regulations, the Seminary has had to offer two years of undergraduate work in liberal arts courses, plus three years in theology. A major share of its capital and budgetary expenditures have been defrayed by the United Lutherans, with the balance being met through contributions from three other Lutheran church bodies. All but two of the faculty are Japanese.

Episcopal Seminary: After World War II the three Episcopalian dioceses which joined the Kyodan in 1941 split off from it and merged with the seven dioceses which had been "underground" during the war. The ten dioceses then formed the autonomous Episcopal Church of Japan. The latter receives support from the Protestant Episcopal Church (USA), the Church of England in Canada, the Anglicans in Australia and the Church of England.

Established in 1926, the Episcopal Seminary trains students for the Episcopal Church of Japan. The school has received more support from the Protestant Episcopal foreign missions board than has been furnished by it to any other Episcopalian-sponsored seminary abroad with the exception of St. Andrew's in Manila.

During World War II the buildings which the Seminary had occupied in Tokyo for over 40 years were destroyed. In 1948 the Episcopal Church of Japan was enabled by the Protestant Episcopal board to purchase for the Seminary at a cost of approximately $44,000 the private mansion of Baron Iwasaki in the Hongo Ku residential section of Tokyo. Shortly thereafter it became apparent that it was inappropriate to train impecunious Japanese ordinands in a palatial mansion. Accordingly the estate was sold at an advantageous price and a new campus was acquired in the Setagaya Ku section in the outskirts of Tokyo (next door to the residence of General Tojo). The new buildings were dedicated in 1953 and can accommodate 50 students.

In the past the Episcopal Seminary has been known as the Central Theological College. Prior to 1941 it was part of Rikkyo (St. Paul's) University. The school is still related to the University but has its own board of directors. Its entrants must be college graduates, and it offers a three-year graduate course to them. Its scholastic standards are said to be not as high as those of the Tokyo UTS. When the school was moved in 1953, some thought was given to transferring it to the campus of St. Paul's. However, it proved impossible either to have the Seminary become part of Rikkyo University or even to work out a close practicable affiliation between the two institutions.

Aoyama Gakuin University Theological Faculty: There is a tendency for the universities in Japan which lack affiliated theological schools to open up Departments of Religion, the graduates of which are not as well trained for the ministry as are the seminarians. An example of this is the Aoyama Gakuin University whose Theological Department was merged in 1943 into the Tokyo Union Theological Seminary. In 1956 or thereabouts the University opened a new department of religion, concerning which some mission boards have not been enthusiastic.

Other sources report that a fair proportion of the students enrolled in the theological courses offered in some of the university-related theological faculties, departments and Christian institutes in Japan are not intending to follow a career in the ordained ministry. Some of these students ultimately enter into Christian work of one sort or another. Others, however, are said to be enrolling in theological courses primarily for the purpose of continuing their general education at the graduate level—in some cases after having failed to gain admittance into graduate schools specializing in other fields and disciplines.

Japan Biblical Seminary: This school was established by the Kyodan in 1946 and has an evangelical background. The main emphasis of the Japan Biblical Seminary is on classes in the late afternoon and evening, and many of its students are preparing for Christian service as laymen or in religious education, etc. Its academic standards are below those of the Episcopal Seminary and only moderately higher than those of a Bible school.

Lutheran Theological Seminary: Originally a Bible school, this institution was upgraded by the Missouri Synod Lutherans into a theological school in 1953. Only university graduates are admitted, and in 1956 the first class of three seminarians were graduated. It is located in a building in Tokyo in which this denomination has its headquarters for its activities in Japan.

Doshisha University School of Theology: Located in Kyoto, one of the oldest cultural centers in Japan, the Doshisha School of Theology is one of the strongest, if not the strongest, seminaries in Japan. Doshisha University was founded in 1875 by the Congregational mission board. Later the Presbyterians USA and the United Brethren joined in supporting it. The University now has about 20,000 students, of whom 15,000 are enrolled in its colleges and graduate schools. It is the largest and oldest Christian institution of higher learning in the Far East.

The University's School of Theology was one of the first of its graduate schools to be founded. It has been in continuous operation despite (1) the vicissitudes subsequently experienced by the country as a whole, and (2) the greater interest shown by most educated Japanese in the academic and scientific (as contrasted with the theological) achievements developed in the West.

At the end of 1956, the Dean of this School commented: "With 174 students enrolled, the tuition receipts are entirely inadequate to cover even a major part of the salary schedule of the staff. By pooling the budgets of all parts of the university, the inordinately large enrollments of other departments can pay for the considerable deficit run by the School of Theology each year. This imbalance is used by other college deans to prevent the desired expansion of offerings and facilities which are much desired by the faculty of the School of Theology."

The Doshisha School is the second-largest Protestant seminary in Japan in terms of its over-all enrollment, the Union Theological Seminary in Tokyo having a total enrollment in the neighborhood of 200 students. Of the 174 Doshisha students, approximately one-third are considered to be studying at a pretheological level.

The School's curriculum covers a full six years of study, divided into three parts: first, a general cultural, liberal arts program for the first two years of university enrollment; second, two years of basic "pastoral" studies; third, two years of "theological specialization." These studies lead to the degree of Bachelor of Theology for the first four years of "undergraduate work" and Master of Theology at the end of the last two years. The four-year and the subsequent two-year courses are considered to be two parts of the same curriculum and not separable except in the case of those students who do not desire to enter the ministry.

There are reported to be a total of 15 full-time members on the School's faculty (10 full professors, 3 assistant professors and 2 instructors) plus 15 part-time lecturers. Of the full-time personnel, 11 are Japanese and four are Westerners.

The School's faculty members are paid directly by the University and are said to be given adequate time in which to engage in research activities. The emphasis of the seminary's training is on evangelism, with increasing attention being given to equipping its students to spread the gospel in industrial and urban areas. The School continues to follow a "socially liberal" trend in its teaching. The original impetus for this came from some of its American faculty personnel who were members of the Congregational Church and who were influenced by the "social gospel" theories espoused in the first three decades of the 20th century by Walter Rauschenbusch and Harry Ward.

In 1923 the seminary commenced to issue a quarterly magazine entitled *Studies in the Christian Religion,* and it has been published continuously since that time.

The buildings used by the Doshisha School are rather old and are said to be in need of renovation.

The financial difficulties confronting the students enrolled in this seminary (whose students presumably do not differ in this respect from those enrolled in most other seminaries in Japan) have been described by the Dean at Doshisha as follows:

Students in the School of Theology are under greater financial handicaps, by and large, than students in the other parts of the university. . . . Whereas there is a student loan fund available, it is not granted to theological students due to the assumption that unlike business or economics students, when theological men graduate the chances of their earning a salary which will allow them to repay any loan is considered to be nil. . . . Tuition and university fees, books, room, board and miscellaneous costs total a minimum of $285 per student per year, outside of travel expenses. Should a student be granted a partial scholarship giving him $200 a year, he must earn the additional $85 or more by working an equivalent of no less than 141 full days. . . . Working in a department store pays theological students 56¢ a day and other "arbeit" is almost as low. . . . The difficulty is great considering that he is expected to spend part of Saturday and all day Sunday in his field work for some church. . . . Field work, or church service for theological students in this country pays nothing more than the cost of travel or other out-of-pocket expenses of the students: there is no such thing as holding a church pastorate to put yourself through seminary. Neither is it possible for a student to spend his summer in work whose earnings will carry him through the following year—there just is no such work available, because of the labor situation in Japan. There is, however, a self-support job open to each of Doshisha's theological students for special evangelistic or other church work that gives him invaluable experience for his life work, and that is where they go each summer, almost without exception.

Kwansei Gakuin University Theological School: Kwansei University was established outside of Kobe in 1889 by the Methodist Church South (now part of The Methodist Church). The Canadian Methodists, who later were merged into the United Church of Canada, joined in supporting this University. In 1929 it moved to a spacious campus in Nishinomiya, which is half way between Kobe and Osaka. The university now comprises a graduate school and five colleges with a total of 8,491 students. The theological department is the oldest in the University. Its standards are said to be somewhat lower than those of Doshisha. Kwansei is reported to favor "a warm, emotional Methodist approach" and stresses rural evangelism in its teaching.

Kanto Gakuin University Institute: The total enrollment of Kanto Gakuin University in Yokohama, which is supported by the American Baptists, is more than 5,000 students. However, only about 20 men are studying in its undergraduate theological department for full-time service in the Christian ministry. At one time this department was a part of the theological department of Aoyama Gakuin University (Methodist) which was merged with other seminaries in 1943 to form the Tokyo Union Theological Seminary. Those members of the Aoyama Gakuin faculty who declined to join the UTS transferred to Kanto, and the Kanto Institute of Christian Studies, as it is now known, resumed operations in 1950. Of its enrollment of 35 students, about 15 are being trained for work in religious education. Those students having special ability are encouraged to continue their studies at the UTS in Tokyo. The American Baptists made a $26,000 grant in 1955 toward the cost of a new building at the Kanto Institute which contains a chapel, library and five classrooms.

Osaka Kirisutokyo Gakuin Theological Department: The level of work done at this school is considered to be about the same as that at the Japan Biblical Seminary.

Seinan Gakuin Theological Department: Seinan Gakuin University in Fukuoka City on the southern island of Kyushu is supported by the Southern Baptists. It has a total of approximately 4,000 students. Of this number about 45 are men studying in its Theological Department for full-time careers in the ministry.

In 1958 the Southern Baptists reported that this seminary

which has (had) an intermittent history dating back to 1910, was re-established at the close of the Pacific War (World War II) as a part of Seinan Gakuin ... University. ... It continues to be affiliated with Seinan Gakuin because only universities may grant degrees in Japan. However, its campus is on the outskirts of the city about three miles from the college ... in the midst of an evergreen forest at the foot of Mount Abura. ...

About 70 students, a few of whom are women, are enrolled in the seminary course which consists of two years of general education and two years of theological subjects, normally culminating in a bachelor of theology degree accredited by the Japanese Government. In addition, an extra year of study is provided for advanced seminary work. The administration plans in the near future to extend the seminary course one year to allow for more intensive graduate work and a large number of electives. Plans also call for the expansion of courses in religious education. ... The full-time faculty includes five Japanese and four missionaries. There are also a number of part-time lecturers and teachers.

In 1952 a dormitory capable of accommodating 60 students was erected, and in 1955 the seminary completed the construction of a $100,000 building housing its administrative offices, classrooms, library and a chapel seating about 150 persons.

General Comments: Dr. Harold A. Bosley, Pastor of the First Methodist Church of Evanston, Illinois, visited Japan and Korea on behalf of the Methodist Division of World Missions in the months of October through December 1955. His report contains the following remarks on the general status of Protestant theological education in Japan:

1. The process of early specialization in all fields is the general weakness of education in Japan, and it is clearly apparent in the seminaries.

2. It is most regrettable when for whatever reason a major seminary is located away from a college or university campus.

3. Most (seminary) faculty members are very well trained (having received such training) not alone in the seminaries of Japan and Korea but also in the United States, Canada, England and the Continent. ... But the faculty is overworked and underpaid even by present standards in Japan. ... In order to make a living, they must be a pastor of one or two churches in addition to their Seminary task. ... It is becoming the accepted thing in Japan.

4. Unless we are careful we will have more seminaries than we can staff or support. The tendency to develop legitimate departments of religion in colleges into quasi-seminaries is clearly evident in some cases. ... The need is for better seminaries, not more of them.

Another observer comments that there is a real need to improve the intellectual caliber of the men serving on seminary faculties in Japan. While it is difficult to persuade the graduates of Japanese universities to engage in pastoral activities at the grass-roots level, yet the greatest need is for top-quality ministers to attract more of the intellectual lay leadership of Japan to membership in the Kyodan. The work at the grass-roots level can doubtless best be carried on by the graduates of the Bible schools. It is important that the efforts to evangelize the Japanese be carried on by Japanese rather than foreign missionaries; and that Japanese rather than Americans serve on seminary faculties, not only because of the language problem, but also because of the understandable desire on the part of the Japanese to run their own institutions.

Seminarians in Japan are said to have a predilection for continental dialectics rather than for American pragmatism, despite the preponderance of American missionaries in Japan. There is also reported to be a trend among the students toward a form of Barthianism adapted to Japanese culture. The tendency on the part of Japanese seminaries to emphasize instruction in the intellectual aspects of Christianity results in their providing insufficient training in the practical aspects of the ministry. It has been suggested that the way to correct this would be to send over leading American theologians from time to time for limited service on Japanese faculties. However, it is believed that only well-known professors should be assigned to such missions inasmuch as scholars of lesser caliber do not readily obtain the intellectual respect of the Japanese.

Writing in 1957, Dr. Hidenobu Kuwada (the President of the Tokyo Union Theological Seminary) commented on the Japanese theological schools as follows: "In proportion to the total number of believers, which is rather small, the number of seminaries and Bible training schools is large. . . . The leading teachers in the seminaries and in university schools of religion are Japanese. . . . At various points the theological education of Japan can now be regarded as having reached the stage of standing upon its own feet. . . . We should be supplying some teachers for certain neighbouring countries such as Formosa and Korea, possibly short-term visiting professors who can help to strengthen the Church in these lands. . . ."

B. KOREA

This country is now emerging from a belief in animism dating back, it is stated, to the year 2333 B.C. Many of the people believe in either Mahayana Buddhism or Confucianism, or in both. Of the estimated 22,000,000 persons in South Korea, about 1,500,000, or approximately 7%, are members of the Christian community. Thus, after the Philippines, Korea has the highest proportion of Christians of any nation in Asia. In addition Christianity exerts a stronger influence in this country than these statistics might suggest. For example, all of the 400 chaplains in the armed forces of the Republic of Korea are Christians.

The growth of Christianity in Korea was impeded during the period of the Japanese occupation (1910–45), and the general educational level of the Korean people today is below that of the Japanese. The withdrawal of the Japanese occupation authorities enabled the Koreans to inaugurate a policy of permitting a greater degree of religious freedom and admitting a larger number of foreign missionaries than hitherto.

The complete disruption caused by the Korean War of 1950–53 had the double effect of (1) disarranging the new educational system set up in South Korea subsequent to World War II, and (2) providing a further impetus among the population toward Christianity. With over 1,000,000 casualties and 4,000,000 refugees from the north, the South Korean population today is reported to have an annual income of approximately $85 per capita, or roughly 30% of the comparable figure for Japan. Along with their quest for a modicum of material security, many Koreans are said to be turning to Christianity as a source of spiritual support and solace.

Four additional factors might be cited as helping to account for the present strong trend towards Christianity in Korea: (1) many of the leaders in the Independence Movement against the Japanese occupation in the 1910–45 period were Christians who today have considerable prestige in the country; (2) there is no strongly organized local religion opposing the Christian missionaries in Korea; (3) the relief goods and services provided by the American and other churches after the Korean War were of very tangible benefit, for which the population (particularly the youth) are grateful; and (4) the South Koreans are constantly exposed to the danger of further Communist attacks, and in the cold war for men's minds, the philosophy and rationale of Christianity is for them an appealing alternative to that of Marxism.

The Roman Catholic Church has not made as much progress in its missionary efforts in Korea as elsewhere in Asia, and its membership comprises only about one-sixth of the Christians in this country. Korea is regarded by a number of mission board executives as one of the most promising mission territories in Asia today. Before World War II there were about 30 churches in Seoul. Now there are more than 400. In the City of Pusan there were seven churches before 1945, and now there are nearly 200. The membership of the leading churches in Korea is shown in Table 48. The differences between the number of communicants and the num-

TABLE 48.   MEMBERSHIP OF LEADING CHURCHES IN KOREA (1957)

Protestant	Communicants[a]	Total Number of Adherents[b]
Presbyterian Church in Korea	150,000	551,000
Methodist Church	50,000	247,000
Presbyterian Church in the Republic of Korea	20,000	173,000
Presbyterian Church in Korea (Koryu)	30,000	140,000
Holiness Church	30,000	102,000
Other Protestant Churches	—	111,000
		1,324,000
Roman Catholic Church		242,000
		1,566,000

NOTES: [a] Source: Missionary Research Library.   [b] Source: National Christian Council of Korea (as of March 1, 1957).

ber of adherents for these churches is accounted for in part by differences in the method of computing or estimating membership totals, and in part because of the fact that in Korea, in addition to being baptized, one must also become a catechumen in a church before being admitted to full communicant membership.

According to Dean Hahn, the Presbyterians and the Methodists commenced their missionary activities in Korea at approximately the same time several decades ago, and in the early years they are said to have provided roughly equal numbers of foreign personnel and contributions in carrying out their respective efforts. Yet to-day the total number (864,000) of adherents of the three Presbyterian Churches in Korea amounts to approximately two-thirds of the total Protestant community, and for every one Methodist in Korea there are almost four Presbyterians. One of the reasons for this disparity is ascribed to the fact that the Methodists formerly subsidized all of the costs of their work, including the salaries of many of their Korean ministers. The Presbyterian missionaries, on the other hand, placed their stress on creating a "self-supporting, self-propagating and self-governing" church. In the beginning, the latter policy resulted in difficulties for the Presbyterians. But when these were overcome, it enabled them to forge ahead in their conversion efforts. It is also probably fair to say that the policy of emphasizing local control made it easier for the liberal and conservative elements among the Presbyterians to secede and form churches of their own.

TABLE 49. THEOLOGICAL SCHOOLS IN KOREA (1957)

Name	Location	Approx. Number of		Denominational Support
		Full-Time Faculty	Theol. Students	
Theological Seminary of Presbyterian Church in Korea	Seoul	18[a]	625[b]	Presbyterian Church in Korea, USA, US, etc.
Han-Guk Theological Seminary	Seoul	14	200	Presbyterian Church in the Republic of Korea
Methodist Theological Seminary	Seoul	15[a]	125[b]	Methodist
Yonsei University College of Theology	Seoul	12	75[b]	Presbyterian USA, Methodist, United Church of Canada
St. Michael's Theological College	Seoul	1	6	Anglican
Koryu Presbyterian Seminary	Pusan	4	100	Presbyterian Church in Korea (Koryu)
Korean Baptist Seminary	Taejon	4	90	Southern Baptist
Taegu Presbyterian Theological Seminary	Taegu	5[a]	75[b]	Presbyterian Church in Korea
Hannam Theological Seminary	Taegu	4[a]	50[b]	Presbyterian Church in the Republic of Korea
Total: 9		77	1,346	

NOTES: [a] Plus others teaching part time.
[b] Plus other students at lower level of training.

There are nine Protestant seminaries in Korea, as shown in Table 49. It will be noted that by far the largest number of Protestant theological students of any single country in Africa, Asia or Latin America is being trained in Korea. It is of interest that the development of the churches in Korea has to an unusual extent been involved with the formation of their seminaries.

Theological Seminary of the Presbyterian Church in Korea: Before World War II the seminary of the General Assembly of the Presbyterian Church in Korea was located in Pyongyang (which is now the capital of North Korea). This school closed its doors in 1937 in connection with a controversy related to the attendance of Christians at Shinto shrines. A year later some Presbyterians opened a new seminary in Seoul called the Chosun Theological Seminary. This institution is now known as the Han-Guk Theological Seminary.

Ten years later, in 1948, some other Presbyterians established a second theological school in Seoul known as The Presbyterian Seminary. In 1950 a committee of the General Assembly of the Presbyterian Church in Korea sought to reconcile the differences between the two schools. The committee recommended that both institutions should be closed and one official seminary of the General Assembly should be established in Seoul in their stead.

In line with this the Presbyterian Seminary in Seoul was shut and the General Assembly school was established in the capital. However, the members of the Han-Guk faculty declined to accept the committee's recommendation because they felt it would place the Han-Guk Seminary in the control of conservative elements in this Church. With the attack of the North Korean Communists on South Korea, the General Assembly's Seminary was re-established in Taegu, and the Han-Guk school was transferred to Pusan. Since 1953 both institutions have once again been located in Seoul.

Because the Han-Guk Seminary would not become a part of the General Assembly's theological school, the result was that the latter institution did in fact become dominated by the conservatives. The General Assembly became critical of what it considered to be the liberal elements in the Han-Guk faculty and passed a resolution stating that Han-Guk graduates would not be permitted to become ministers in the Presbyterian Church in Korea. The Han-Guk Seminary graduates therefore formed a general assembly of their own and called their church the Presbyterian Church in the Republic of Korea. Much of the discord between these groups took place while the Korean War was still in progress.

Meanwhile, after 1947, some right-wing, conservative elements in the Presbyterian Church in Korea, supported by American groups related to Rev. Carl McIntyre and the International Council of Christian Churches, formed the Presbyterian Church in Korea (Koryu). At present three out of every four Presbyterians in Korea are members of the Presbyterian Church in Korea, with the remainder divided between the more liberal Presbyterian Church in the Republic of Korea and the more conservative Presbyterian Church in Korea (Koryu).

The reason for the conflicts among the Presbyterians in Korea is due to a combination of factors. Among them is the trouble caused by right-wing, conservative Presbyterian groups sent from the United States. Many Koreans also appear to have a rather elementary approach to problems of church organization. They are said to have a tendency to oversimplify theological differences and then quickly resolve them into what seem to them to be diametrically opposed concepts.

The other side of this coin is the fact that the Theological Seminary of the Presbyterian Church in Korea is the largest Presbyterian seminary in the world and is training almost half of the theological students in this country. The total enrollment at this school during 1957 was about 675 students, of whom approximately 625 were taking courses at a theological level. Over 100 students applied for admission to the first-year class in 1956, but because of lack of accommodations only 50 could be accepted. Three types of students are enrolled in the Seminary's five-year course: graduates from colleges, from high schools and from preparatory schools. Because of the pressure of students seeking admission, this Seminary's entrance requirements are being raised. Almost all of its graduates enter the pastoral ministry.

To keep pace with the increase in its enrollment, this Seminary in 1956–57 added five Koreans to its faculty (two of whom had earned their doctorates). The school has also offered refresher courses in the summer for several hundred ministers.

In 1956 the school was operating in temporary quarters in a building which used to be a Shinto temple situated on a small site on top of a hill in the center of Seoul. As many as 139 students were being taught in one classroom, with few books and fewer desks. In that year the Seminary requested the Presbyterians USA for a grant of $100,000 to acquire some adjacent property and to erect a new administration-classroom building. The Presbyterians US were asked to contribute a new dormitory and a library. It is anticipated that many of these projects will be under way by 1959.

Even the large number of students being trained at this school is not too many to keep pace with the new Presbyterian churches that are being established in Korea each year. In two of the cities in South Korea there are more Presbyterian churches than in any other city in the world. If the present growth trends continue, it may be necessary for the Presbyterians in five years' time to establish one or two more seminaries in Korea. In the meantime, despite the present large size of the Seminary in Seoul, the feeling is that it would be preferable not to subdivide it. Furthermore this is the only theological school in Korea which the Presbyterians USA and US support together.

Han-Guk Theological Seminary: In 1945 when the Japanese withdrew from Korea, the Han-Guk Seminary was the only Presbyterian theological school in the country. As previously mentioned it was originally established in 1938. Ten years later it became the nucleus of the Presbyterian Church in the Republic of Korea when the latter split off from the Presbyterian Church in Korea. The General Assembly of the latter church would not recognize for ordination the graduates of the Han-Guk Seminary owing to differences in their theological orientation. Neither the Presbyterians USA nor US support the Han-Guk Seminary, but the United Church of Canada does. The school is the second-largest Protestant seminary in Korea, and it is licensed by the Government as a college. A good number of its graduates enter the teaching profession rather than the ministry.

Methodist Theological Seminary: During World War II the Japanese required the Methodists and Presbyterians in Korea to unite into one church (for the same reason that the Kyodan was formed in Japan). Shortly after V-J Day, however, the two denominations split apart. Today the cleavage between them is such that they will not cooperate even for the joint production of Sunday school literature.

The Methodist Theological Seminary in Seoul was founded in 1905 and serves a Methodist community of some 247,000 persons in Korea organized in 1,000 churches. In 1929 the Women's Bible Training School was merged into the Seminary. The number of its graduates over the years amounts to about 500, compared to its present total enrollment of 350 students.

During World War II the school was closed for several years and subsequently reopened. The Communist invasion of South Korea in June 1950 again brought a sudden stop to the school, and its faculty and students were scattered. In the fall of 1951 the President was able to open the Seminary as a refugee school in Pusan. In the spring of 1954 the Seminary returned to its original campus in Seoul. A four-year course of studies is now being offered.

On Sunday, November 14, 1954, a special collection known as the "Bishops' Appeal for Korea" was held in all Methodist churches in the United States at the request of the Methodists' Division of World Missions. On that and a few succeeding Sundays a total of $1,653,000 was raised for this purpose, of which 70% was allocated to the Division and 30% to the Methodist Committee for Overseas Relief. The Division allocated its funds (approximately $1,100,000) as follows:

Church reconstruction	60%
Schools, hospitals and other institutions	25%
Missionary residences	10%
Constituencies	5%
	100%

Top priority was given to the needs of the Methodist Seminary, but only $50,000, or less than 5% of the funds available to the Division for allocation, were earmarked for this purpose. The reason was that the Division's funds were intended to be used for reconstruction purposes and it happened that the Seminary's building came through the war with comparatively little damage.

Subsequently the Division set aside $150,000 from its regular budgetary funds for the enlargement and rebuilding of the Seminary and committed itself to an additional $100,000 expenditure for the school. However, the transmission of this money to Korea was delayed as a result of uncertainty as to the proper location for the Seminary in Seoul. Dr. Harold Bosley, whose report on Japan has been previously cited, also visited Seoul and reported the following concerning the Seminary's plant:

It is inadequate now and it will be far from adequate when the present building program is completed. And for the reasons: (a) it will be far away from a college campus; (b) not enough money, by one-half, has been allocated to the rebuilding program; (c) the Seminary campus itself will continue to be divided and the crowded condition of the present location does not permit the faculty to locate near the Seminary; (d) the present enrollment will overtop the proposed facilities, which means that there is no provision for expansion of enrollment without weakening the Seminary's program. I cannot conceal my feeling that it is a serious long-range mistake to locate the new seminary building where the present one is. I recommend that the entire matter be reconsidered.

At present (1958) it appears that the Seminary will remain at its present location. Its building program includes plans for a large new main building, a chapel, library and a girls' dormitory costing a total of at least $200,000.

Yonsei University College of Theology: Yonsei University was founded by the Presbyterian Church USA and three other mission boards. It was then known as the Chosun Christian University and it became a union institution in 1915. The Methodists and the Presbyterian Church in Canada (later merged with the United Church of Canada) currently contribute to its support. In 1957 the Severance Union Medical College and Hospital was merged into Yonsei and its present name adopted. The University occupies an attractive campus on the outskirts of Seoul. Its President, Dr. L. George Paik, is a Presbyterian. The Yonsei College of Theology has the highest academic standard of any seminary in Korea. Because of the comparatively high standing of the University, it would have seemed logical for the mission boards to have concentrated their support on its College of Theology. However, because of the strong denominational currents in Korea, such has not proved to be possible.

The Presbyterian and Methodist mission boards contribute comparatively little to the Yonsei seminary as compared to their annual budgetary and capital gifts to their own denominational schools. The reason given by them is that a high proportion of the Yonsei seminary graduates do not subsequently enter the ministry, whereas this is not the case with the graduates of the denominational schools. Perhaps less than 10% of the Yonsei graduates become pastors, and only a few enter church administration work: approximately one-half of the Yonsei seminarians are said to enter the teaching profession.

At one time it was suggested that the Methodists might either merge their seminary with the Yonsei College of Theology or share certain common facilities with it. The Methodist mission board in New York favored the suggestion, but it was blocked by the Methodist Seminary in Seoul. The faculty of the latter felt that such a merger would be at the expense of the prestige of the Methodist Seminary, particularly inasmuch as their scholastic level was below that of the Yonsei seminary.

Commenting on the College of Theology, President Paik wrote in 1957:

We enrolled students in the College with hopes that we would draw all the denominational seminaries into our campus as affiliated institutions. However, new-found nationalism in Korea heightened denominationalism. Denominational seminaries branched off in different sections in the country contrary to our dreams. The Anglican Mission was one of these denominations made concrete request for affiliation, but our Board could not give favorable reply to it on the ground that the Anglican Mission was not a cooperating organization. There was also certain unexpressed apprehensions of proselytism. . . .

[Of the College's total of 50 graduates since 1950] many of these are serving as ordained ministers, mostly in the Korean Methodist Church. . . . Our graduates receive degree upon graduation, while the Presbyterian Seminary is not an accredited school, and does not attract our graduates to meet the Proviso requirement. We, therefore, encourage those who wish to be ordained as ministers to the Gospel to go to denominational seminaries. . . . A large number of our graduates of the school are serving as teachers in church related secondary schools, workers in Religious Education, Christian journalism, audiovisual education and others. One fifth of our graduates have done or are doing graduate work in US. . . .

The College consists of two departments, Theological course and Church Music. The latter is only two years old but is the only one of its kind in Korea, if not in East Asia.

There are no adequate class room facilities and musical instruments such as pianos and organs. We hope that the College of Theology be attached to the new proposed auditorium. We think about change the name of the College to School of Religion with emphasis on Religious Education. If and when we can secure cooperation of YM and YW, we would like to carry on the training program for these two world organizations. . . .

St. Michael's Theological College: St. Michael's Theological College in Seoul went out of existence during the Korean War. In 1952 it was reopened in temporary quarters and at a lower level of training than hitherto. The education of this class of students was completed in 1955. A building fund campaign was launched in order to reconstruct the school's plant on a more adequate site near Seoul. Six students were expected to commence reading for a degree at Yonsei in January 1958, while the new Principal (an American) was learning the Korean language. Thus in 1958–59 the College is expected to be more of a residence hostel than a seminary in its own right, with training at a theological level to be resumed by the College in 1960. This seminary is supported by the Society for the Propagation of the Gospel.

Koryu Presbyterian Seminary: Located in Pusan, this school is the fourth-largest Protestant seminary in Korea in terms of the number of its theological students. As previously mentioned, it is supported by the Presbyterian Church in Korea (Koryu) and receives financial assistance from The Independent Board for Presbyterian Foreign Missions which is a member of the Associated Missions of the International Council of Christian Churches (Rev. Carl McIntyre).

Korea Baptist Theological Seminary: The Southern Baptists now have about 150 churches in Korea. Up until 1954 the Korea Baptist Seminary was essentially a Bible school. However, in that year its curriculum was upgraded to a theological school level and the Seminary was accredited by the Ministry of Education. A new seven-acre site in Taejon, the railroad center of central South Korea, was purchased for it, and in 1957 the construction of a large new administration building was completed. It contains eight classrooms which can accommodate 50 students each. Plans are being made to construct a new dormitory inasmuch as the students are now being lodged in an inn located two miles away from the campus.

The Southern Baptists reported in 1958 that "the school is divided into three departments: the seminary proper, offering a three-year course patterned after seminary courses in the (United) States; the preparatory department, offering a (prerequisite) three-year liberal arts course . . . , and a third department for those who desire training but do not qualify for one of the other courses. Last year there were 135 enrolled in all departments."

General Comments: The Presbyterians USA report that one of the remarkable phenomena in the training of men for the churches in Korea in recent years has been the increase in the number of night schools, some of whose graduates enter the Protestant ministry without further training. These schools for the most part are not recognized by the principal denominations, and their entrance requirements are not high. "It is estimated that there are over 2,000 students in these schools, taking a course that covers three or four years. The limitations and inefficiency of these schools are well known, but the zeal of the students is inescapable and it seems likely this movement may continue for some time."

One effect of inadequate ministerial training in Korea, according to a leading citizen of that country, is that the Korean clergy are having increasing difficulty in commanding the respect and interest of the younger intellectuals.

If the present trend toward Presbyterianism and Methodism is to continue, it would seem essential for these denominations to raise the level of scholarship at their seminaries in Korea. This might be one of the most important means whereby the divisive tendency of the Korean Christians could be counteracted. Dr. Harold Bosley's report also comments (italics his) on the

inadequate provision for faculty support and the encouragement of scholarly work. . . . I have the uncomfortable impression that while the professor is held in high repute by churchmen, the actual act of teaching and study is subordinated to what is regarded as the more necessary work of taking care of some church or mission station. . . .

Inadequate scholarship aid to students. . . . I think the Korean seminarian is having a harder time of it than his counterpart in Japan just now. . . .

Every effort must be made to bring the capabilities of the seminary to the level of offering full ministerial training with a recognized degree. It is a scandal to be content with less. . . .

C. Formosa

According to the Anderson-Smith report:

Since the expulsion of the Dutch, in 1661, Protestant mission work on Formosa has been carried on mostly by the Presbyterian Church of Canada whose missionaries first came to Formosa in 1872, settling in North Formosa, and by the Presbyterian Church of England, whose missionaries began work in 1865. . . . It looks, however, as though the Presbyterian monopoly on Protestant mission work in Formosa is going to be seriously challenged. . . . Some of these mission organizations, new to Formosa, such as the American Presbyterians, North and South, and the American Methodists, are ecumenically minded. . . . Others, however, are divisive. These latter bodies are coming in, in strength . . . and . . . are stressing leadership training in Bible schools. . . . It was reported that there would be at least six new Bible schools on the Island by the Fall of 1952 . . . being built by the Oriental Missionary Society, the Assemblies of God, the Seventh Day Adventists, the Southern Baptists, the Missouri Synod Lutherans, and others. Some of these schools are sizable structures capable of housing some 150 students. . . . Their greatest field . . . will probably be for some time the refugee Chinese from the mainland who as one missionary describes them have been largely as sheep without a shepherd. The Presbyterian Missions, both Canadian and English, have been so understaffed and financially restricted that they have not been able to care adequately even for their own work among the Formosans.

The sociological situation on the island is abnormal. The indigenous population of Formosa, about 8,000,000 persons, was augmented in 1950 by from 1,000,000 to 3,000,000 mainlanders with whom there had been very little contact in previous years. There is a disparity in their educational and cultural backgrounds which places the leadership of the mainlanders in an advantageous position.

Approximately 600 Roman Catholic missionaries and some 350 Protestant missionaries have entered into Formosa since 1949. The Protestant community is estimated at 150,000, and the Roman Catholics at 50,000 persons. Because of their long record of activities on the island, the strongest Protestant church is the Presbyterian Church of Taiwan which was formed in 1957 as a merger of the Synod of North Taiwan (Canadian Presbyterian mission) and the Synod of South Taiwan (English Presbyterian mission). All the other Protestant churches are still very small. The four seminaries now operating in Formosa are listed in Table 50.

Taiwan Theological College: This school was formerly located in the heart of the City of Taipeh, the capital of Formosa. In 1955 or thereabouts it sold its property at a good price and moved to a new site in the hills overlooking the City. The Taiwan College faculty is said to be in need of considerable strengthening. A rather funda-

TABLE 50. THEOLOGICAL SCHOOLS IN FORMOSA (1957)

Name	Location	Approx. Number of		Denominational Support
		Full-Time Faculty	Theol. Students	
Taiwan Theological College	Taipeh	5[a]	52	Presbyterian Church of Canada, US
Taiwan Baptist Theological Seminary	Taipeh	6	35[b]	Southern Baptist
Tainan Theological College	Tainan	12[a]	119[b]	Presbyterian Church of England
Concordia Theological Seminary	Chiayi	3	15	Lutheran (Missouri Synod)
Total: 4		26	221	

NOTES: [a] Plus part-time faculty.
[b] Plus students at a lower level of training.

mentalist viewpoint is espoused by the staff, though some non-Presbyterian students are admitted.

The Anderson-Smith report states that this seminary has a curriculum which "is theoretically based upon senior middle school graduation and gives a four-year theological course. The standard of middle school graduation, however, cannot always be maintained. . . . The College requires an entrance examination in English, Bible, and Mandarin (not too strict). Because the quality of the students is low, many cannot pass these examinations. . . . The Canadian Presbyterian Mission supplies most of the budget of $2,500. Less than $200 comes from the Formosan churches." Financial pressures have been such that some of the houses in the College's compound are rented as income producers rather than used as houses for its faculty.

Taiwan Baptist Theological Seminary: This Southern Baptist school was opened in 1952 and its first class of 14 students was graduated in 1955. In each of the past few years the total enrollment has been about 55 students at various levels of training. In 1954 a new chapel and classroom building was built as part of a long-term construction program on its new campus in the outskirts of Taipeh.

The President of this Seminary commented in 1958 that the Southern Baptist churches and chapels in Formosa "multiply faster than we can supply preachers for them. . . . Fortunately the students don't have to graduate before they can be of help to the Baptist work on the island. They attend classes only four days a week and spend the other three preaching and working in the churches and chapels throughout Taiwan."

Tainan Theological College: The Tainan seminary, located in the southern part of Formosa, is considered to be the strongest of the four schools on the island and one of the strongest in East Asia. It was founded in 1876 by Thomas Barclay of Scotland who set up the College and its Press, and translated the Bible into Romanized Amoy. In 1940 the Japanese tried unsuccessfully to install a Japanese principal, whereupon it was closed and its students sent to the Taiwan Theological College.

The Tainan College was reopened in 1948. By 1957 a total of 191 students were enrolled in this institution, of whom 116 were taking the five-year Bachelor of Theology course (to which a sixth year was to be added). Of the remainder, three students were taking the B.D. course, 42 were enrolled in the three-year Bible school course, and a total of 30 were taking the "higher" and "lower" courses offered in the field of religious education. The Bible school was started in 1953, originally as a temporary measure to meet the evangelistic needs developing in Formosa.

The first two years of the B.Th. courses consist of basic, general studies. In 1957–58 the entire third-year class studied at Tunghai University, an experiment which proved successful. The fourth and fifth years are at the B.D. level, and the first term of the sixth year is spent in internship work.

The teaching staff at Tainan numbered 25 in 1957, of whom 13 were part time. The school's academic standards are considered to be high, and the faculty is said to be strong with respect to the foreign missionaries serving on it. This seminary is also sending some of the Chinese members of its faculty to England and the United States for advanced study.

After World War II the buildings at this school were badly run down and in need of repair. According to Dr. Hwang Chang-hui (the Principal of the seminary), the outstanding event at Tainan in 1955 was its construction program. "The sum of about US $40,000 has been raised locally and from the generous grants of the Presbyterian Church of England and especially the Nanking Theological Seminary Board of Founders. This has been spent on, a) renovating and transforming the 50 year old main building into something almost new . . . b) a new building—ground floor for administrative purposes and the 1st floor for a Library, (and) c) a beautiful College Chapel." The 1955 grant to the seminary by the Board of Founders amounted to $27,000, and further capital grants of $23,000 and $12,000 were made by the Board in 1957 and 1958.

The authors of the Anderson-Smith report were surprised by "the comparatively high degree of (budgetary) support given to the Tainan College by the Synod of South Formosa. . . . The . . . College is one of the few—very few—theological schools in the Orient that has succeeded in tapping the financial resources of the native churches. . . . Last year, some 8,000 Taiwan Dollars were contributed. This year the offerings amounted to some £250; every church in the Synod gave something." Not even in the United States do many Protestant denominations have a "Theological College Sunday" as is the case in southern Formosa. Since February 1957 the college has been under the General Assembly of the Presbyterian Church in Formosa.

In 1951 the budget of the Tainan Seminary amounted to US $3,000–3,500. Of this sum, $1,000–1,200 was being used for the salaries of Chinese teachers at the rate of about $28 per month. The English Presbyterian Mission was contributing approximately $1,600, or about one-half of the operating expenses. Four years later (fiscal 1955) the school's budget had risen to $13,000, or by about four times. Of this sum, about half was being raised locally, and the other half was being contributed by the English Presbyterians and the Nanking Board of Founders. In 1958 tuition fees were charged for the first time.

Concordia Theological Seminary: This school was originally established by the Missouri Synod Lutherans in 1952. It is located in Chiayi which is in the southern part of Formosa and is the center of this denomination's missionary activities on the island. The Seminary's campus now has a library-classroom building, mess hall, dormitory and faculty residences. The students are for the most part mainland Chinese from all walks of life and with an age spread of over 20 years among them.

General Comments: The cities of Taipeh and Tainan are less than 200 miles' distance from each other (and the rail fare between them costs approximately $5.00 US). Inasmuch as both the Taiwan and Tainan Theological Colleges are Presbyterian seminaries, and the two synods were joined together a few years ago to form a single, united Presbyterian Church of Taiwan, logic would suggest that the Taiwan school, as the weaker of the two, should be merged into Tainan. This suggestion was made to the Taiwan Seminary prior to the purchase by them in 1955 of their new campus. The suggestion was declined, primarily, it appears, because the Canadian Presbyterians who support the Taiwan school are theologically more conservative in their outlook than are the English Presbyterians who support Tainan. The suggestion has also been made that both seminaries might consider merging and forming a union theological school at the recently opened Tunghai University founded on Formosa at Taichung with the assistance of the United Board for Christian Higher Education in Asia. Both seminaries declined to do so.

Subsequently the President of Tunghai expressed a desire to establish a theological department for training ministers at Tunghai, with respect to which possibility the United Board was not encouraging. As an alternative the latter suggested the creation at Tunghai of a chair in the study of religions and placing a greater emphasis on pretheological courses for students intending to enter seminary. This plan has been adopted.

D. HONGKONG

As a result of the Communists' capture of China, Hongkong has grown from a city of 800,000 at the end of World War II to a metropolis of approximately 3,000,-000 persons. At present the average *family* income of 80% of the colony's residents is less than $8 per week, and more than 60,000 persons live on the roofs of buildings. The Protestant community is estimated at 100,000 persons. Hongkong is not only the base from which many of the Chinese evangelists in Southeast Asia and Formosa operate, it is also the location of an increasing number of theological training centers. Three seminaries are now operating in this British colony, as shown in Table 51.

TABLE 51.   THEOLOGICAL SCHOOLS IN HONGKONG (1957)

| | | Approx. Number of | | |
| | | --- | --- | |
Name	Location	Full-Time Faculty	Theol. Students	Denominational Support
Hongkong Lutheran Theological Seminary	Hongkong	5[a]	27	Lutheran
Hongkong Baptist Theological Seminary	Hongkong	4[a]	30[b]	Southern Baptist
Union Theological Seminary	Hongkong	1[a]	4	Anglican, etc.
Total: 3		10	61	

NOTES: [a] Plus part-time faculty.
[b] Plus students at lower level of training.

Hongkong Lutheran Theological Seminary: This Seminary moved to Hongkong from Hankow in 1948. At first it rented quarters in a building of the Christian Mission to the Buddhists located high on a hill at Taofongshan overlooking the harbor. When the activities of the Christian Mission expanded, in 1955, the Seminary found and renovated other quarters in a building which had formerly served as an "independent" Chinese university and also at one point as an orphanage. It is located seven miles northwest of the city of Kowloon. The scholastic work at this school is at about the L.Th. level. Its full- and part-time faculty consists of six Europeans and Americans, and two Chinese. The Lutherans report that in the four years 1950–53, 39 students were graduated from this Seminary. Of this number, 32 are doing evangelistic work in Hongkong.

The Anderson-Smith report states that as of 1950 "the highest grade school (in Hongkong) is the Lutheran Theological Seminary . . . a school of high academic and spiritual qualities. . . . Largely because the Lutherans have so little work in Southeast Asia (with the exception of northern Sumatra, this Seminary) is primarily interested in training men—and some women—for work in the growing Lutheran churches in Hongkong. . . . (There is) little desire on the part of the Lutherans to enter into any cooperative enterprise with an outside organization. They were willing to receive some non-Lutheran students, since there were no longer enough Lutheran students to fill the dormitory."

Hongkong Baptist Theological Seminary: This Seminary was opened in 1951 and continues the traditions of the school which the Southern Baptists formerly operated in Shanghai. It is considered by some to be an adequately staffed, vigorous institution. It grants both a B.D. and a B.Th. degree. However, the level of its scholarship is said to be not very high.

The Southern Baptists first operated this Seminary in the Kowloon City Baptist Church and later in buildings they erected at the Village of Brotherly Love, a relief project set up by Hongkong Baptists for the victims of an extensive fire. In 1956 the school purchased a new site on a wooded hill in the center of Kowloon.

More than one-half of this Seminary's graduates have left Hongkong for service in other countries, principally in Malaya.

Union Theological Seminary: This institution was originally intended to be a postgraduate school of Chung Chi Christian College in Kowloon. Chung Chi, however, wished to postpone the development of a theological faculty until its undergraduate school was well organized and the construction of the permanent buildings on its new campus completed. Bishop Hall and others in the Anglican Church concluded that the provision of theological training for college and university graduates in Hongkong should not be postponed. Consequently in 1955 the Union Theological Seminary was founded, and since that time it has admitted only those students holding a B.A. degree or its equivalent.

The course of study lasts for three years and corresponds to a B.D. course at an American divinity school. The Trustees of the Seminary include officially appointed representatives of the Anglican Church, the Church of Christ in China, the London Missionary Society, the Methodist Church (USA) and the YMCA. However, up to 1957–58 only the Anglicans had been able to provide students with the necessary educational qualifications for the full-time course at the Seminary.

The school has one full-time faculty member, and a second teacher (a Chinese) was expected to join the staff in 1958 after completing his studies in the United States. The part-time faculty includes missionaries, parish clergy and ordained professors of the churches represented on the Seminary's Board and from the Evangelical and Reformed mission. Thus even though the Principal is an Anglican missionary priest, the principle of interdenominational sponsorship is maintained in the composition of the faculty.

Although it is still only a very small institution (four students) the Seminary has considered the possibility of purchasing and renovating a large house with considerable grounds adjoining St. John's College of Hongkong University.

E. CHINA

The mainland of China falls outside the scope of this Survey and the statistics below concerning its seminaries are not included in the totals cited elsewhere in this report. However, it is of interest to note briefly the past and present situation of Protestant theological education in that country inasmuch as before World War II China was America's major mission field.

Despite the very considerable effort over a 125-year period on the part of American missions (and others), the Protestant *community* in China in 1950 (one year after the proclamation of the Communists' People's Republic of China) amounted to only 1,500,000 persons, or 0.25% of the country's 600,000,000 population. As of the same year the reported *membership* of the leading Chinese younger churches was approximately as shown in Table 52.

TABLE 52.   MEMBERSHIP OF PROTESTANT
CHURCHES IN CHINA (1950)

Church of Christ in China[a]	177,000
True Jesus Church[b]	125,000
Methodist	103,000
Nei Ti Hui[c]	85,000
Episcopal Church of China	77,000
Lutheran Church of China	65,000
China Baptist Convention	65,000
	697,000

NOTES: [a] A united church of Presbyterian, Congregational, Reformed, Evangelical, Baptist and other churches.   [b] An indigenous church.   [c] Churches founded by the China Inland Mission.

In 1934 an extensive survey of the theological schools in China was made. Its findings were published under the title of *Education for Service in the Christian Church in China—The Report of a Survey Commission,* and the document came to be known as the Weigle report. It recommended that the 24 or more seminaries then being operated in China be consolidated into (a) four union theological colleges to be merged under the name of the Nanking Theological Seminary (but with courses offered at four different locations), (b) three union theological training schools, and (c) two graduate schools of theology. These recommendations were never carried out by the mission boards concerned, nor is it clear that many of the younger churches in China at that time were in favor of such consolidations.

TABLE 53.   PROTESTANT THEOLOGICAL SCHOOLS IN CHINA (1956)

Name	Location	Approx. Number of		Denominational Support
		Full-Time Faculty	Theol. Students	
Nanking Union Theological Seminary	Nanking	30	100[b]	Union
Yenching Union Theological Seminary	Peking	5	21[b]	Union
Canton Theological College	Canton	4[a]	16?	Union
Chungking Theological Seminary	Chungking	7	13[b]	(Fundamentalist)
Total: 4		46	150	

NOTES: [a] Plus part-time faculty.
[b] Plus students at lower level of training.

The Sino-Japanese War disrupted nearly all the theological schools in the country. Since the Communist regime took control of the mainland in 1949–50, their situation has been even more difficult. In 1956 Bishop Rajah B. Manikam of the Evangelical Lutheran Church of India made a visit to Communist China. He subsequently reported that four Protestant seminaries were being operated in that country, as shown in Table 53.

Nanking Union Theological Seminary:

The present Nanking Union Theological Seminary (according to Bishop Manikam) is a union of 11 theological institutions, formerly scattered over China. Since the separate existence of all 11 institutions could not be justified after liberation, the union was effected in the autumn of 1952.

Among the 183 students the following 19 denominations are represented, Church of Christ 59, Anglican 32, Baptist 32, Methodist 23, English Methodist 6, China Inland Mission 6, China Evangelical Church 5, Self-Supporting Church 5, Little Flock (Brethren) 2, Pentecostal 2, Faith of the Apostles 2, Spiritual Work 2, Quaker 1, China Preaching Church 1, Seventh Day Adventist 1, Lutheran 1, Bethel 1, Disciples 1, Independent Local Church 1. About 30 of these students are women.

Instruction is given on three levels: (a) To university graduates for the B.D. degree—in training for 3 years, (b) To Senior Middle students—in training for 4 years and (c) Junior Middle Students in training for 4 or 5 years. The largest number of students come from rural areas and are in the second group. Not only (do) the major denominations cooperate, but also the Seventh Day Adventist and the Apostolic Faith. . . . These . . . are said to learn from each other and they respect each other. The Seminary expects to have about 100 students a year. . . . There is no difficulty in recruitment, only in selection. . . .

Because the faculties of 11 institutions were absorbed by this union institution, the staff of 30 is larger than the student body of 100 would warrant. Fifty per cent of the staff are women. The Seminary is utilizing this large staff for research.

There is no study of Marxism in this institution. A course on current events is given once a week. . . .

Formerly B.D. and B.Th. degrees were granted by Nanking Seminary. Now no degrees are granted. . . .

. . . there was considerable resentment against the continued use of the name of the Nanking Theological Seminary for a Board in the United States which operates outside China. . . . Some were inclined to question the legitimacy of the use of funds earmarked for their institution on seminaries outside China.

Yenching Union Theological Seminary, Peking:

This is a union of 11 theological institutions . . . (as shown in Table 54).

It is interesting to note that this Union institution has bodies like the Fundamentalist, Holiness Church and Assemblies of God cooperating in the support of it. I was naturally interested to know how Theology and Dogmatics were being taught. I was told that parallel courses in Dogmatics were being offered by Baptist, Presbyterian and Methodist professors. . . .

Yenching has today a student body of 76, from 10–12 denominations. . . . Thirty study in the Bible School admitting Junior Middle-pass students, 20 in the Theological School section admitting Senior Middle-passed students, 1 in the Theological College undertaking B.D. courses and 24 in a one-year refresher course for pastors and church-workers.

TABLE 54. INSTITUTIONS MERGED INTO YENCHING UNION THEOLOGICAL
SEMINARY (1956)

Institution	Denomination
Yenching School of Religion	Congregational, Anglican, Presbyterian, etc.
Peking Theological Seminary	Methodist
Peking Bible School for Women	Interdenominational
Baptist Theological Seminary from Honan	Baptist
Bible Institute of Holiness Church, Peking	Holiness
North Eastern Theological College, Mukden	Presbyterian
Lutheran Theological College, Hankow	Lutheran
Honan Bible Institute	Fundamentalist
Central China Theological Seminary	English Methodist, Church of Christ in China
Theological Seminary	Assemblies of God
Devotional Institute	Interdenominational

I was told there were three sources of income: (1) the Institutions that have joined Yenching, (2) the churches that are supporting the Institution and (3) tuition fees. . . . Last year 186 applied for admission, of whom only 30 were admitted.

Canton Theological College:

Canton Theological College is operated by Anglicans, Church of Christ in China and Methodists. Students from other denominations attend . . . Before the liberation the Anglicans had a chapel service of their own but now all worship together . . . Of the 26 students, 6 are doing practical work. . . . This college admits high school-passed students and trains them for 4 years. There is also a three-year training course to which are admitted junior high school-passed students. . . . This institution has existed as a Union for 43 years.

Chungking Theological Seminary:

Founded in 1944 . . . and was formerly operated by the China Inland Mission. . . . (It) is not a Union Seminary. . . . It has an interdenominational staff of seven full-time professors: 3 Methodist, 1 Lutheran, 1 CIM, 1 Anglican and the Principal belonged to the Swedish Alliance Church. . . . This seminary is definitely of the fundamentalist point of view. . . . Last year only 8 students were selected out of 50 or 60 applicants.

General Comments: While one may question the use that Bishop Manikam makes of the word "liberation," it is nevertheless clear that in China it was the Communists, rather than the Protestants, who brought about the consolidation of 22 theological schools into two union institutions.

The Bishop's findings were subsequently confirmed as a result of a visit made to China in November-December 1956 by a deputation of Anglicans from Australia headed by Archbishop W. K. Mowll. According to one of the members of this group, the Nanking Union Theological Seminary had a total enrollment of

232 students, of whom 107 were preparing for Christian service of one type or another, and 125 were pastors taking refresher courses lasting for one term or thereabouts. At the time the group visited the Seminary, only two B.D. students were in residence, and it was stated that in the period 1952–56 a total of 15 B.D. degrees had been awarded. This is an average of three or four per year, which is a small number in relation to the country's total population of well over 600,000,000 persons.

CHAPTER 7

LATIN AMERICA

A. The Relations between the Protestant and the Roman Catholic Churches in Latin America

Of the estimated 191,055,000 people in Latin America as a whole (as of 1957), 170,572,000, or 89% were reported to be Roman Catholics, and only 6,131,000 were Protestants. Thus 97% of the Christians are reported as being Roman Catholics. However, according to the Protestants, the great majority of the people are anticlerical and indifferent to the spiritual aspects of the work of the Roman Catholic Church. The prevailing philosophy of life is said to be a sophisticated realism. This is one of the bases on which Protestant missionary activity in these countries has been undertaken.

Chapter 14 in this Survey discusses the efforts of the Roman Catholic Church to develop a local Roman Catholic clergy in Latin America through the establishment of a considerable number of major seminaries. An evaluation of the Protestant seminaries in Latin America would be incomplete without some reference at this point to the activities of the Roman Catholic Church in these countries insofar as they are related directly or indirectly to the training of Protestant ministers.

There is no need to outline in detail here the political position of the Roman Catholic Church in Latin America, or the reactions against its power which have taken place from time to time in some of these countries. These matters have been comprehensively and objectively discussed, among others, by Professor M. Searle Bates in his book *Religious Liberty* published by the International Missionary Council in 1945.

During the past century the Roman Catholic Church in Latin America has sought from time to time to impede the entrance of Protestant missions into this area. There is *legal* freedom of worship accorded to Protestants in all the Latin American countries, and there are few or no governmental restrictions against Protestant seminaries per se. However, in actual practice the religious freedom enjoyed by the Protestant churches varies from country to country and from time to time. In 1956 a prominent Mexican Protestant, Dr. Gonzalo Baez-Camargo summed up the situation as set forth in Table 55.

From Table 55 it will be noted that the Protestants in Mexico and Colombia are among those who find themselves in the most difficult religious situations in Latin America at this time. In 1934 the Mexican Government confiscated all property that

TABLE 55.   RELIGIOUS FREEDOM OF PROTESTANT CHURCHES IN LATIN AMERICA (1956)

| | Absence of Persecution | | Active Persecution | |
	Complete	Relative	Sporadic	Frequent
Central America	Cuba	Dominican Republic	Nicaragua	Mexico
	Puerto Rico	Guatemala		
	Haiti	El Salvador		
	Panama	Honduras		
		Costa Rica		
South America	Brazil	Venezuela	Ecuador	Colombia
	Uruguay	Paraguay	Peru	Bolivia
	Chile	Argentina		

had at any time served as a Roman Catholic or Protestant place of worship, religious school or seminary. Since then the Government's restrictions have been somewhat relaxed. However, all church buildings are state property and the Government may decide how they are to be used. For example, the Divino Salvador Church in Mexico City was originally a Roman Catholic cathedral but was assigned to the Presbyterian Church by the Government. Foreign priests and Protestant missionaries cannot officiate in religious services attended by the public, and evangelical messages cannot be given over the radio (although the Bible may be read and commented upon).

The opposition of Roman Catholics to Protestantism has been the strongest in Colombia. In 1956 the Presbyterians USA reported that "due to the attitude of the present regime it is almost impossible to secure entry permits for ordained (Protestant) missionaries." An official release issued in June of that year by the Committee on Cooperation in Latin America (of the Division of Foreign Missions of the National Council of Churches, USA) states among other things that during the eight-year period 1948-56, some 46 Protestant church buildings in Colombia were destroyed by fire or dynamite, 75 Protestants were killed because of their religious faith, and more than 200 Protestant primary and secondary schools were ordered by the Government to be closed. In reply to these charges, Roman Catholics in Colombia cite what they consider to be the improper conduct of Protestants in Colombia, particularly on the part of the more evangelistic sects. The Roman Catholic position is set forth in some detail in a release issued by the Information Bureau of the National Catholic Welfare Conference in Washington, D. C., on August 30, 1957. However one may choose to strike a balance between these two releases (which are too lengthy to quote here), it is nevertheless clear that the relationship between Protestants and Roman Catholics in Colombia is far from being a happy one.

In the face of the opposition and in some countries the hostility of the Roman Catholic Church, one might question whether it is wise strategy for Protestant foreign mission boards to send such large numbers of personnel and funds to Latin America. However, as is the case with missions sent by them to Islamic countries, the reply which is given is that the missions must evidence their "Christian witness" everywhere, despite all difficulties. Thus, at the 1956 Presbyterian USA conference at Lake Mohonk, Rev. Gilberto Torres, pastor of the First Presbyterian Church of Bogotá, commented: "In spite of the difficulties suffered by our Colombian churches, I believe that we have an open door." One may wonder how much of this attitude is based on a truly Christian impulse and how much of it is based merely on a desire to wrest Latin American countries from the virtual Roman Catholic monopoly there.

According to the Santiago, Chile, correspondent of the *Christian Century,* in 1957 the Roman Catholic Church in Latin America created

in Bogotá, Colombia, a central office similar to that of the National Catholic Welfare Conference in Washington, D. C. There a common strategy will be developed, and an effort made to coordinate the activities of the episcopacy, the religious orders and the lay organizations throughout Latin America. Commenting on the new enterprise Chilean Cardinal Caro said: "In Vatican circles the progress of Protestantism in Latin America is considered alarming. This (progress) is the outcome of the power of the dollar. The principal factors in the spread of Protestantism in these lands are the well equipped Protestant schools, the widespread distribution of pamphlets and other Protestant reading matter, the powerful Protestant missions, and the possibility that future directors of these missions may study and be trained in Latin America itself."

The last possibility enumerated by the late Cardinal Caro is of particular interest.

It was also in Chile over a decade ago that a distinguished American Roman Catholic missionary leader, Rev. John J. Considine, M.M., evolved the following principles relating to Catholic attitudes and conduct toward Protestant missions. He wrote in a widely circulated book (*Call for Forty Thousand*):

After a prolonged discussion in Santiago with several Chilean friends, I wrote down their conclusions in the following little table of four "don'ts" and one "do" on the question of Protestantism in Chile. They might as well apply to other parts of Latin America. The table reads as follows:

1. DON'T question the sincerity of any considerable portion of those who become Protestants.
2. DON'T presume that any considerable portion of converts become Protestants to get North American financial support.
3. DON'T presume that any considerable number of Protestants hope to make progress by attacks and quarrelling; most of them know they must establish a strong religious life.

4. DON'T trust greatly to civil laws or other nonspiritual aids for the protection of Catholics.

DO meet the peril to our Catholic life with greater Catholic life.

An enlightened policy toward each other of "live and let live" along the lines of the above might well be followed by Protestants and Roman Catholics in all countries throughout the world.

One of the fairest, succinct and most objective accounts of the relations between Protestants and Roman Catholics in Latin America has been written by a Jesuit father, Rev. Peter M. Dunne, S.J., who commented: "But if Catholics only knew it, Protestant activity in Latin America can be a blessing in disguise if it acts as a stimulant to increased activity."

B. MEXICO AND CENTRAL AMERICA

Table 56 lists the Protestant theological schools now operating in Mexico and Central America.

TABLE 56.   THEOLOGICAL SCHOOLS IN MEXICO AND CENTRAL AMERICA (1957)

Name	Location	Approx. Number of		Denominational Support
		Full-Time Faculty	Theol. Students	
Mexico				
Union Theological Seminary of Mexico	Mexico City	4[a]	14	Methodist, Disciples, Congregational
Presbyterian Theological Seminary	Mexico City	4	14	Presbyterian USA, US
Baptist Seminary of Mexico	Mexico City	3[a]	12[b]	American Baptist
Mexican Baptist Theological Seminary	Torreón	5[a]	20[b]	Southern Baptist
St. Andrew's Theological Seminary	Guadalajara	2	4	Protestant Episcopal
Concordia Seminary	Monterrey	1	8	Lutheran (Missouri Synod)
Guatemala				
Presbyterian Seminary of Guatemala	Guatemala City	2	6	Presbyterian USA
Total: 7[c]		21	78	

NOTES: [a] Plus part-time faculty or professors teaching at lower level of training.
[b] Plus students at lower level of training.
[c] See also Table 70A, Supplementary List of Theological Schools.

1. *Mexico*

Mexico has a population of approximately 27,000,000 people, of whom 95% are Roman Catholics and less than 1% are Protestants. The membership of the leading Protestant churches is as follows:

Presbyterian Church of Mexico	80,000
Assemblies of God	25,000
Methodists	20,000

None of the five Protestant seminaries in this country measures up to a high standard. There are several reasons for this. The first is the pressure from the

Roman Catholic Church. The second is the fact that those Mexicans who are or become Protestants tend to be aggressively conservative and isolationist in their attitudes. There is little church cooperation at the local level or with the Committee on Cooperation in Latin America. Thus, Mexican Presbyterians will not cooperate to any important extent with Mexican Methodists, etc., and neither welcome guidance from denominations in the United States. In 1914 several American mission boards tried to set up comity arrangements in Mexico, but failed. The third reason is that since World War II there has been an influx of divisive sects, particularly from the Southwestern United States. It is comparatively simple for these evangelical missionaries to enter Mexico. In the case of the Presbyterians, the International Council of Christian Churches (Rev. Carl McIntyre) has been active.

Union Theological Seminary of Mexico: Established in 1917, about 85% of the students enrolled in the full theological course offered at this Seminary are Methodists. The school is supported by the Methodists, Congregational Church, the Disciples and American Friends. The latter group, however, has for the most part withdrawn its support. The school has never met with great success, and the level of its instruction is considerably below that of the Union Theological Seminary of Buenos Aires, for example. In 1955 this school offered a full four-year seminary course for the first time.

In recent years the UTS has been sending its students to public high schools for their pretheological training, and it has been conducting its own classes in the nearby Gante (Methodist) Church. In 1953 a new dormitory, library, and dining room were erected at a cost of approximately $120,000, of which the major portion was supplied by the Methodists who also support three of the six members of its faculty. One of the reasons for the investment of such a considerable sum of capital funds by the Methodists in this school was that in recent years the Missouri district of this denomination made large grants specifically designated for it. Unfortunately the UTS is located in a different section of Mexico City from the National University, and has little contact with it.

Presbyterian Theological Seminary: This school is the seminary of the National Presbyterian Church of Mexico. There are reported to be only 75 ordained Mexican Presbyterian ministers, and their "salary scale is so low that some of the pastors have had to give up their work and go into more remunerative employment in order to support their families." Other pastors have taken on side jobs in order to be able to continue their ministries. This Seminary is not doing work at a high academic level. The school recently added two years of preparatory school work to extend the course to six years for those men who have not done preparatory work in public schools. Funds have been made available to the Seminary for the construction of a married students dormitory.

Baptist Seminary of Mexico: The American Baptists established this school in

Mexico City in 1947. Because of its low entrance requirements, its scholastic level is below that of the American Baptists' seminary in Cuba.

Mexican Baptist Theological Seminary: Established in Torreón in 1901, this Southern Baptist seminary has had a peripatetic career. Closed in 1913 because of civil war conditions, it was reopened in Saltillo in 1917 jointly by the American and Southern Baptists. Unsettled political conditions caused this Seminary to move to Monterrey, back to Saltillo, to San Antonio (Texas), and to El Paso, and it is now in Torreón. The American Baptists withdrew their support from the school in 1934.

The Southern Baptists reported in 1958 that only

within the last few years have the present adequate and attractive buildings been constructed. According to Mexican law, the teaching of religion must be confined to church buildings. For that reason all seminary classes meet in the educational unit of Calvary Baptist Church (in Torreón), which adjoins the seminary's administration and dormitory buildings.

The 1956–57 (total student) enrollment reached thirty-two. . . . The administration is insisting that applicants under twenty-four years of age finish at least secondary school before entering the seminary. . . . Each year the school program is so arranged as to allow the students to participate in one or more simultaneous evangelistic campaigns in Mexico. To publicize one of these the seminary choir presented, in the spring of 1957, a thirty-minute radio broadcast every day for a week. . . .

St. Andrew's Theological Seminary, Guadalajara: This school can barely be classified as a seminary. Much of its work is at the preseminary level and in practical training for industry and farming. Although it was founded over 30 years ago, it continues to be a weak institution. In the next few years the Episcopalians hope to strengthen it, although the establishment of the proposed new Episcopalian seminary in Puerto Rico has been granted a higher priority in this denomination's plans.

2. *Guatemala*

Presbyterian Seminary of Guatemala: Established as a seminary in 1940, this school was previously a Bible institute. At present its entrance requirements specify that its entrants must have completed sixth grade at school, but the Seminary plans soon to raise its admission standards to a high-school level. Of the 18 men who are enrolled, it is estimated that six are ordinands.

C. THE CARIBBEAN AREA

Dr. E. J. Bingle has written: "The Caribbean is not one of the star areas of present-day missionary enterprise; it was once, a century ago, and it has left an unfinished task and a cluster of difficult and in some ways peculiar problems. . . ." The use of catechists, for example, seems to be very restricted in the English-speaking parts of the area. Prior to the Caribbean Consultation held under its auspices in San German, Puerto Rico, in May 1957, the IMC was not active in the area, and only one of the younger churches there is a member in its own right of the World

TABLE 57.   THEOLOGICAL SCHOOLS IN THE CARIBBEAN AREA (1957)

Name	Location	Full-Time Faculty	Theol. Students	Denominational Support
Cuba				
Union Theological Seminary	Matanzas	9[a]	45[b]	Presbyterian, Methodist, Episcopalian
Baptist Theological Seminary of East Cuba	Santiago	c	5[b]	American Baptist
Puerto Rico				
Evangelical Seminary of Puerto Rico	Rio Piedras	2[a]	23	American Baptist, Disciples, etc.
Haiti				
Baptist Theological Seminary of Haiti	Cap Haitien	2	6	American Baptist
Episcopal Theological Seminary	Mont-Rouis	1[a]	4	Protestant Episcopal
Jamaica				
Union Theological Seminary	Caenwood	6	30[b]	English Methodist, Scottish Presbyterian, etc.
Calabar Theological College	Kingston	2[a]	12	English Baptist
St. Peter's Theological College	Kingston	2	9	Anglican
Barbados				
Codrington College	Bridgetown	6	25	Anglican
Trinidad				
Presbyterian Theological College	Port of Spain	2?	10	Canadian Presbyterian
Total: 10		32	169	

NOTES: [a] Plus part-time faculty.   c 11 faculty members, all part time.
[b] Plus students at lower level of training.

Council of Churches. A number of American denominations contribute their support to activities in the Caribbean through their home rather than their foreign mission boards. With respect to the seminaries in this area, the American influence of freedom of religion is sufficiently strong, particularly in Cuba and Puerto Rico, so that it is a comparatively simple matter to send students to these schools from neighboring countries in Central and South America where Roman Catholic influence on the whole is stronger. Table 57 lists the theological schools now operating in the Caribbean.

1. *Cuba*

Of the 6,000,000 inhabitants of Cuba, only about 100,000 persons (or 2%) are members of the Protestant community. The membership of the leading younger churches in the country is estimated as follows:

Methodists	10,000
Baptist Churches of West Cuba (So. Bapt.)	8,000
Protestant Episcopal Church	7,500
Baptist Convention of East Cuba (Amer. Bapt.)	7,000
Presbyterian Church (USA, Synod of New Jersey)	3,500

Union Theological Seminary, Matanzas: This school is generally considered to be the leading seminary in the Central American and Caribbean areas. Located on the heights above Matanzas Bay, some 60 miles east of Havana, it is an excellent example of how interdenominational cooperation plus strong local leadership can within a comparatively short space of time create a successful institution.

Approximately one-half of its full-time faculty of nine are Americans, of whom three are Methodists, two are Episcopalians, and four are Presbyterians. Of the latter, two are Ph.D.s from Princeton Theological Seminary. In October, 1957, the school had a total enrollment of 59 students, of whom 45 were ordinands and 14 were women preparing for careers in religious education. These students come from seven Latin American countries (Bolivia, Colombia, Costa Rica, Cuba, the Dominican Republic, Puerto Rico and Venezuela). It recently completed its tenth year of operation.

In the past Matanzas required its entrants to have completed five years of schooling beyond eighth grade. Thus its three-year course commences at the sophomore level. In October 1957 the school added an additional year of pretheological work in literature, English and philosophy to be taken by the students before they would be permitted to commence the three-year, regular course.

Recently two new departments were added to the Seminary—one in rural Christian education and the other in music. In addition this Seminary is planning to establish in 1959–60 a program of study leading to a Master of Theology degree.

The President of Matanzas, Dr. Alfonso Rodriguez Hidalgo, was reared as a Roman Catholic. In 1920 he became a convert to the Presbyterian Church. After obtaining a Ph.D. in the University of Havana in 1943, he decided at the age of 36 to enter the ministry. While still a student at Princeton Theological Seminary (and before it was possible for him to be ordained) he was elected the first President of Matanzas. He was recently elected Moderator of the New Jersey Synod of the Presbyterian Church USA (the Cuban and Puerto Rican Presbyteries are constituents of this denomination's General Assembly in the USA). It seems clear that one of the factors accounting for the excellence of this Seminary has been the quality of his leadership.

Among the other reasons for its success is the fact that Cuba is only 90 miles by air from Miami and thus subject to American influences. The ministry in the local Protestant churches are largely indigenous, and there has fortunately been comparatively little in the way of theological dissension with conservative or divisive sects. This Seminary was the setting for the Caribbean leadership training conference which was organized in December 1953 by the World Student Christian Federation and was attended by 80 delegates from nine countries.

During 1956–57 there was considerable construction at the Matanzas school. This included a new men's dormitory costing $40,000, a chapel costing $30,000, a library at $15,000, a dining hall (capacity 150), an administration building, girls' dormitory and professors' residences. The chapel was paid for by the Protestant Episcopal Church and represented their contribution to equalize somewhat the capital investments already made on the campus by the Presbyterian and Methodist Boards. Of the school's current operating budget, one-half is supplied by the Presbyterians and one-fourth each by the Methodists and Episcopalians.

The five-year expansion program formulated by the Matanzas Seminary in 1957 (to cost a total of $1,100,000) would enable it to expand its housing capacity from the present maximum of 10 staff and faculty members plus 60 students to a maximum of 24 staff members plus 150 students. In order to accomplish this, real estate costing an estimated $250,000 would need to be purchased; $621,000 would be spent for new buildings and for additions (plus equipment) to present facilities; the balance would be used for a Faculty Salaries Fund ($110,000) and for scholarships, library acquisitions, etc. (a total of $117,000).

The administrative officials of the Matanzas Seminary make good use of recognized public relations techniques. The school periodically issues leaflets, etc., describing its activities, and the quantity of these publications exceeds those put out by any other theological school in Latin America.

Baptist Theological Seminary of East Cuba: This school was founded by the American Baptists in 1947, approximately two years after Matanzas was established. The latter Seminary was eager to have the Baptists locate their new school on the Matanzas campus. However, the area of the American Baptist activities in Cuba is centered in the two eastern provinces of Camaguey and Oriente. Consequently the American Baptists decided to found their own seminary in Santiago de Cuba, a city which is 400 miles east of Matanzas.

The level of scholarship at this school is much lower than that which obtains at Matanzas or at the American Baptist seminary at Rio Piedras in Puerto Rico. All of its faculty serve part time. Until recently only one class was admitted every four years, so that its second senior class was to graduate in 1957. At present the Seminary is considering the possibility of admitting new classes every two years. Its principal is Dr. Oscar Rodriguez, a Puerto Rican.

2. *Puerto Rico*

Of the 2,250,000 persons in Puerto Rico, the Protestant community numbers 250,000. The estimated membership figures of the leading younger churches is shown in Table 58.

Evangelical Seminary of Puerto Rico: Established in 1919, this school is an example of a union institution which has never made much progress. It is located in Rio Piedras (a suburb of San Juan)—across the street from the University of Puerto Rico (which has an enrollment of 18,000 students).

The Seminary is supported by the American Baptists, Methodists, Presbyterians, Disciples, Evangelical and United Brethren, and the Congregational Church. Of its total expenses of $23,600 in its fiscal year ended May 31, 1956, $22,500 was

TABLE 58. PROTESTANT DENOMINATIONS IN PUERTO RICO
(1957)

Assemblies of God	13,000
Protestant Episcopal	10,000
Baptist Convention	8,000
Disciples	6,000
Methodist	5,000
Presbyterian Church (USA, Synod of New York)	5,000
United Evangelical Church of Puerto Rico[a]	5,000

NOTE: [a] A union of Congregational Christian and United Brethren church bodies

defrayed from subsidies received from mission boards. During that year the school had virtually no receipts from tuition fees. For the most part only Puerto Rican students attend.

In 1955 the principal of the Seminary and two other faculty members resigned as a result of sharp disagreements on matters of policy. The Seminary had reached such a low state that a Survey Committee was appointed to review its operations. The two members of the Committee were Dr. B. Foster Stockwell, President of the Union Theological Seminary in Buenos Aires, and Dr. Lynn Leavenworth, Director of the Department of Theological Education of the American Baptist Board of Education. According to the Committee's report, which was published in June 1955,

the Committee observed a general sense of frustration on the part of trustees, faculty, students and pastors in the face of problems that would not appear insurmountable if there were clear administrative lines and procedures. . . . The general awareness of inadequacy appears to produce tensions and crossed purposes rather than remedial action. . . . The movement appears to be from an institution that was strictly missionary in character to that of a theological seminary governed by an autonomous Board of Trustees. Whereas, the faculty appointments are supposedly by the Board, actually they appear to be controlled by the respective denominational bodies who think in terms of the Baptist, or Methodist, or Presbyterian, or Disciples, or United Evangelical member of the faculty. This tends to make for a Methodist Old Testament chair, a Baptist theology chair, a United Evangelical church history chair, etc. When a vacancy occurs the decision regarding a placement tends to be made in the States.

Subsequent to the publication of the Committee's report, the Seminary replaced some of its former faculty members with temporary professors. A new president (Dr. Thomas Liggett, who formerly taught on the faculty of the Union Theological Seminary in Buenos Aires) took over in August 1957.

The school appears to have "turned the corner" and its outlook is now said to be more favorable. One indication of this is that a new administration building was being erected in 1957 to replace the old and decidedly inadequate structure formerly in use. This building of advanced modern design contains four classrooms, a chapel, library, cafeteria and offices. Toward its $80,000 cost, $50,000 was contributed by the supporting American denominations, and $30,000 was raised locally in Puerto Rico.

Proposed Episcopal Seminary in Puerto Rico: Early in 1957 the National Council of the Protestant Episcopal Church decided it would be advisable to open a seminary in 1959 or thereafter in the vicinity of the University of Puerto Rico in Rio Piedras near San Juan. The new institution was to serve Episcopalian ordinands from all Latin American countries in which this denomination is active. As part of this program it was planned to close the three small Episcopalian seminaries now operating in Mexico, Haiti and Brazil. Ultimately it was hoped that, when fully operating, the new Puerto Rican seminary would provide a four-year course for 50 ordinand students taught by a faculty including five full-time professors. It was also anticipated that its facilities might cost as much as $500,000.

There were several reasons motivating the Episcopal Church along these lines. The first was the language factor and the fact that there are so few suitable theological texts in languages other than English (discussed more fully in chapter 10 in this Survey). The second was the realization that the three Episcopalian seminaries now operating in Latin America are all weak. The third was the fact that it would apparently be easier to develop an international seminary in Puerto Rico than elsewhere in Latin America.

In view of the Episcopalians' budgetary support to Matanzas and their donation of a chapel to that Seminary in 1955, the question arises why they did not choose to locate their proposed new seminary on the campus at Matanzas. The reason given is that the instruction at Matanzas is in Spanish, whereas at the proposed new Puerto Rican seminary English would be used. Also it was felt that the influx of up to 50 Episcopalian ordinands at Matanzas might have changed the denominational balance at the latter school.

Subsequently the plans for establishing this new seminary were referred to the Joint Commission on Theological Education of the Protestant Episcopal Church for its consideration. This is an advisory group of clerics and laymen which, after studying the matter, recommended against carrying out the project for several reasons. First, the language problem was found to be a thorny one in that the Episcopalian seminary students in Haiti speak French and those in Brazil speak Portuguese: neither group would wish to study in the English or Spanish languages. Secondly, the Episcopalian bishops and seminary administrators in Mexico, Haiti and Brazil preferred to train their seminarians in their own countries and send the more qualified students to the United States for their postgraduate work. As a result of the Commission's findings and recommendations, the plans for the proposed Puerto Rican seminary were postponed.

Then in the fall of 1958 the National Council of the Protestant Episcopal Church approved in principle the establishment of the seminary. The funds for this purpose (approximately $250,000) are to be obtained from a Lenten Offering to be held in the United States in 1960. The Episcopalian bishops in Cuba and Mexico agreed to send a limited number of men to the proposed new institution but they will also continue to maintain the seminaries they are now supporting within their own dioceses.

This account illustrates among other things the complexities which may become involved when an attempt is made to consolidate several provincial theological schools into one regional seminary.

3. *Haiti*

With a population of 3,400,000 persons and a Protestant community of only about 200,000, the following are the approximate membership figures for the leading denominations in Haiti:

Baptist	20,000
Protestant Episcopal	15,000
Seventh Day Adventist	13,000
Church of God	10,000

Baptist Theological Seminary of Haiti: The individual American Baptist churches in Haiti are growing quite rapidly. This school was established in 1947 and has a three-year course. Its scholastic standards are comparable with those of the Baptist Theological Seminary of East Cuba, and the school is devoting a large proportion of its time to the training of lay leadership. The Seminary reports that its buildings "do not provide adequate sleeping space for our summer program—Bible camps and conferences—which is an important part of our total program."

Episcopal Theological Seminary: This school was founded not many years ago but has never had more than seven students at any one time. In 1944 it was moved into a former orphanage building in Port-au-Prince, and in 1949 to its present location at Mont-Rouis. It is planned to continue operating this seminary (because its instruction is in French) despite the small Episcopalian constituency in Haiti and the plans for a new Episcopalian theological school in Puerto Rico.

4. *Jamaica*

Jamaica has a population of 1,500,000 persons, of whom approximately three-quarters are Negroes. Along with the other British colonies in the Caribbean it is one of the few places in Latin America where Protestantism is the dominant religion. The size of the membership of the leading denominations is approximately as follows:

Anglicans	35,000
Baptists	23,000
Seventh Day Adventists	23,000
Methodists	17,000
Presbyterians	12,000

Union Theological Seminary, Caenwood: Organized on its present basis in 1954, this Seminary is another example of a comparatively weak union institution, though it is the leading theological school in the British West Indies.

Before 1954 this school was known as the United Theological Colleges and consisted of Calabar College (English Baptist), St. Colmes (Scottish Presbyterian) and Caenwood College (English Methodist). The former two colleges had been in existence for over 100 years, and Caenwood for three decades. In 1954 some of their buildings were crowded and others were deteriorating as a result of inadequate maintenance and financial support from Great Britain. The English Methodists and Scottish Presbyterians (but not the English Baptists, who had already moved their seminary) agreed to merge their "colleges" on the Methodists' campus at Caenwood (a suburb of Kingston) in order to form the present UTS. This institution now is supported not only by these two denominations but also by the Congregational, Disciples and Moravian denominations. The supporting denominations contribute a fixed amount each year, pay fees for each of their students enrolled in the Seminary, and some also pay the stipends of tutors on the faculty. It is hoped that the United Presbyterians USA may add their support (particularly in connection with its building needs) and that the Canadian Presbyterians will also increase their participation in the work of the UTS.

The UTS receives students from all parts of the Caribbean and from British Guiana. Those having sufficient ability can study for either the B.D. degree of London University, or the Diploma of Theology of that institution. No West Indian serves on the UTS faculty. It is said that a greater emphasis needs to be placed on pastoralia and other courses which will prepare the seminary's students more adequately for the daily problems encountered by the people living in the West Indies.

One factor which resulted in the decision of the UTS to move to Caenwood was the opening in 1948 of the University College of the West Indies at Mona, another suburb of Kingston which is three miles from Caenwood. A long-range hope is that the UTS might ultimately serve as a faculty of divinity for the University College.

Calabar Theological College: The English Baptists declined to join in the new Union Theological Seminary at Caenwood because they had already moved their

Calabar Theological College to Half Way Tree, Kingston. The English Baptists still participate in some of the UTS activities, and some UTS students attend lectures at Calabar, which is 25 minutes' driving distance away.

St. Peter's Theological College: This small seminary is sponsored by the Jamaica Diocese of the Anglican Church, and its operating costs are met partly by the Diocese and partly through students' fees. Although St. Peter's is located within one-quarter of a mile of the Union Theological Seminary at Caenwood it nevertheless has little contact with the latter institution.

5. *Barbados*

Codrington College: Codrington College is the only seminary in the Caribbean which has an endowment of any significant size. It still benefits from the estates bequeathed to it by the will of Christopher Codrington in 1710. The school receives students from all parts of the Caribbean except Jamaica, and now has 25 ordinands enrolled. It is affiliated with Durham University in England, so that some of its students study for the B.A. Theological Honours degree of that University.

Codrington is the Provincial Training College for the Anglican Church and at present is staffed by members of a local chapter of the Community of the Resurrection (the Mirfield Fathers). The chapter consists of a prior, a principal, five men on the teaching staff of the College, plus lay brothers. The latter are largely concerned with duties connected with the estates. This seminary is a High Church institution. During the past 300 years the clergy in Barbados of the Church of England have hitherto been appointed and paid for by the Government: they are said to regard the recent influx of the Christian sects as an unwarranted intrusion.

6. *Trinidad*

Presbyterian Theological College: This school, which is supported by the Canadian Presbyterians, is affiliated with Mount Allison University and Pine Hill Divinity Hall in Canada. The latter two institutions permit students from the Trinidad seminary to take a B.A. degree in Canada after two years' residence there, and a B.D. degree after another two years. Thus all advanced training for these ordinands is in Canada rather than in Trinidad.

7. *Over-all*

In his preparatory paper for the IMC Caribbean Consultation in 1957, Rev. Herbert J. Cook commented:

A comparison of the present position of theological training with the position only a decade ago reveals a change of thinking. . . . It used to be thought desirable that in as many cases as possible training should be completed in a British or American college.

Now the emphasis is on training within the area, and colleges which have a preparatory course only, such as the Lutheran, or a preliminary course which has (later) to be completed in Canada, as the Presbyterians, are beginning to question the advisability of their present schemes.

At the conclusion of his 1954 trip through the Caribbean area, Dr. E. J. Bingle wrote: ". . . Whatever else I learned in the Caribbean, I saw more clearly than ever that the ministry, taken in its many aspects of recruitment, instruction, vocation and support, is the unsolved problem of the younger churches."

D. SOUTH AMERICA

Table 59 lists the theological schools now operating in Colombia, the Guianas and Brazil.

TABLE 59.   THEOLOGICAL SCHOOLS IN COLOMBIA, THE GUIANAS AND BRAZIL (1957)

Name	Location	Approx. Number of		Denominational Support
		Full-Time Faculty	Theol. Students	
Colombia				
International Baptist Theological Seminary	Cali	3	11[b]	Southern Baptist
British Guiana				
Bethel College	New Amsterdam	1	5	Canadian Presbyterian
Surinam				
Moravian Theological Seminary	Paramaribo	1	3[b]	Moravian
Brazil				
North Brazil Baptist Theological Seminary	Recife	4[a]	31[b]	Southern Baptist
Presbyterian Seminary of the North	Recife	4[a]	25	Presbyterian USA, US, Brazil
South Brazil Baptist Theological Seminary	Rio de Janeiro	4[a]	60[b]	Southern Baptist
Presbyterian Theological Seminary of Campinas	Campinas	7[a]	92[b d]	Presbyterian USA, US, Brazil
Theological Seminary of Independent Presbyterian Church of Brazil	São Paulo	5[a]	25	Independent Presbyterian Church of Brazil
Theological Seminary of the Methodist Church	São Paulo	8[a]	50	Methodist
Baptist Seminary	São Paulo	[c]	25	Baptist (Brazilian)
Concord Seminary	Pôrto Alegre	6[a]	20[b]	Lutheran (Missouri Synod)
Episcopal Theological Seminary	Pôrto Alegre	3	10	Protestant Episcopal
Theological Seminary	São Leopoldo	6[a]	30[b]	Evangelical Lutheran
Total: 13		52	387	

NOTES: [a] Plus part-time faculty, or professors teaching at the pretheological level.   [b] Plus students at lower level of training.   [c] All part-time.   [d] 1958.

1. *Colombia*

In Colombia only one person in one thousand is a Protestant.

International Baptist Theological Seminary, Cali: As the only Protestant theological school in Colombia, this Seminary faces many obstacles in its path. Opened in 1953, the total enrollment of this Southern Baptist institution in 1957 was 25 students (mostly married), of whom 11 were ordinands. These students come from Colom-

bia and Ecuador. A few of them are residents of San Andres Island (a possession of
Colombia in the Caribbean Sea off the coast of Nicaragua) where English is spoken
by many as their native tongue. The Southern Baptists reported in 1958 that

at present the seminary meets on the third floor of the educational building of Cali's First
Baptist Church. However, twenty-five acres in the city have been bought for the seminary
campus and construction has been started on an administration and three apartment
buildings. Future plans call for a chapel, a kitchen and dining hall, and a dormitory.

In June 1957 the first graduation exercises were held, and two men, one from Ecuador
and one from Colombia, received the degree of licentiate in theology (equivalent to a little more than a bachelor of theology degree in the States). The prerequisite for this course
is the completion of secondary education. The seminary also offers a degree in religious
education for women. It plans to offer a degree in music when suitable candidates present
themselves.

2. British Guiana

Bethel College: The largest church group in this British colony is the Anglican
"Church of the Province of the West Indies." The Guianas as a whole are oriented
more toward the Caribbean than they are toward their South American neighbors,
Venezuela and Brazil. Bethel College is supported by the Canadian Presbyterians
who concentrate their work in the colony among the East Indians who live there.

3. Surinam

Moravian Theological School: Formerly known as Dutch Guiana, Surinam has one
Protestant seminary, the Theological School of the Moravian Church, located in
Paramaribo. Founded in 1902 the School is supported by the Congregation of Evangelical Brethren (Moravian) Church in Surinam which has the largest membership
among the Protestant denominations there. The seminary offers two years of training for ordinands, following which students are sent for $2\frac{1}{2}$ years of study in the
Moravian Seminary at Zeist, Holland, which is connected with the theological faculty of the University of Utrecht. The Surinam School also offers a three-year course
for catechists; and in 1957 it was training (in addition to three ordinand students)
five catechists, plus three other catechists who were to be ordained but who were
taking only some of the courses. The seminary formerly required six years of secondary education for entrance but was compelled to lower this requirement. The
School usually has one full-time faculty member, but in 1957 was being served by
seven part-time teachers instead (one for each of the courses offered).

4. Brazil

Although there are only 2,500,000 Protestants among Brazil's total population of
58,000,000, nevertheless Protestantism in this country has in recent years had a

more rapid percentage growth than in any other country in the world. The largely indigenous Pentecostal churches which are stronger in Brazil than in any other Latin American country, are reported to have a membership of over 300,000, of whom the Assemblies of God number 200,000 adherents. The membership of the leading denominations is shown in Table 60.

TABLE 60. MEMBERSHIP OF PROTESTANT CHURCHES IN
BRAZIL (1957)

Evangelical Lutheran	500,000
Assemblies of God	200,000
Baptists	125,000
Lutherans—Missouri Synod	84,000
Presbyterian Church of Brazil	70,000
Methodists	45,000
Independent Presbyterian Church of Brazil	22,000
Congregational	13,000
Episcopal Church of Brazil	6,000

North Brazil Baptist Theological Seminary: This Southern Baptist institution located in Recife was formerly a Bible school which was founded in 1902. Recently the school raised its entrance requirements in order to achieve a seminary status. A new dormitory is being erected on its campus. In 1957 this institution reported a combined enrollment of 106 students in the day school, night school and correspondence courses which the Seminary offers. Of its total faculty of 10, eight were Brazilian graduates of the Seminary and two were Southern Baptist missionaries from overseas.

In 1955 the Southern Baptists were maintaining 183 missionaries in Brazil, the largest number of mission personnel sent by this denomination to any country, with the exception of Nigeria.

Presbyterian Seminary of the North, Recife: This school is essentially a regional institution serving the Presbyterian constituency in northern Brazil, as far south as Bahia. In recent years the Seminary purchased an estate of approximately 10 acres, located in the outskirts of Recife. The central building which was constructed in 1955 contains a dormitory, classrooms, refectory, a small chapel, etc. An older building on the campus has been in need of renovation for some time. The school wishes to buy an adjoining property of approximately four acres in order to convert the house located thereon into a married students' dormitory. The cost of this acquisition and reconversion would in all probability exceed $50,000.

The theological outlook of this Seminary is said to be very conservative. Its academic level is lower than that of the Presbyterian Seminary at Campinas. This is due in part to the fact that its admission requirements are necessarily lower inasmuch as the general level of education in northern Brazil (particularly in the interior) is below that prevailing in the southern part of the country. A young Brazilian minister was appointed dean of this institution in recent years, and its standards are said to be improving.

This institution is supported in part by contributions from the General Assembly of the Presbyterian Church of Brazil and in part through gifts from local families. It has also received some support from the English Congregationalists.

South Brazil Baptist Theological Seminary: The Baptist College and Seminary of Rio de Janeiro was formally opened in 1908. In 1937 the Seminary, which is supported by the Southern Baptist Convention, was separated from the College, and it is now located on the former estate of the Baron of Itacurussa in the Tijuca section of Rio de Janeiro. In 1953 two new Seminary buildings (including a large administration and classroom building) were dedicated. In 1956 a dormitory was opened, and in 1958 an apartment building for married students was being constructed. The Southern Baptists reported in that year that plans were being made for the construction of a chapel-library building with a seating capacity of 412 in the chapel and space for 30,000 volumes in the library.

This institution is said by some to be rather weak academically. The students are active in field work, especially evangelism. Two nights every week the students, with a loud-speaker mounted on top of a car, preach in the streets or public squares and hand out tracts and Gospels.

Presbyterian Theological Seminary of Campinas: This Seminary, often referred to simply as "Campinas," is located in a city of that name (population: 200,000) which is situated some 60 miles northwest of São Paulo. The São Paulo area is experiencing the greatest population growth in Brazil, due largely to the healthful climate, abundant natural resources, and growing industry in that region. It is stated that the Presbyterian churches cannot supply the demand for ministers, so great is the increase in the number of congregations throughout the country. Although Brazil is predominantly a Roman Catholic country, the Presbyterians and others believe that the large increase in the population in the interior of the southern part of the country offers numerous possibilities for evangelizing efforts. At the 1956 Presbyterian USA Conference at Lake Mohonk, N.Y., the suggestion was made that the Brazilian Presbyterians might establish a third seminary in Brazil to be known as the "Seminario do Centro." This idea appears to have been dropped in favor of a plan to establish a rural pastors seminary, possibly in the State of Espirito Santo (north of Rio de Janeiro). Meanwhile the 1956 Presbyterian USA report states that a partial solution in this situation might be afforded through the establishment of Bible institutes to prepare evangelists and lay workers for paid and volunteer work in sections of Brazil that are developing rapidly.

Founded in 1888 the Campinas Seminary is the leading institution for the training of Presbyterian ordinands in Brazil. In 1958 it had a student body numbering 108, of whom 92 were theological students. Its enrollment increased from about 30 students in the 1930s to 48 in 1949, and then doubled in the period 1950–58. Of its full-time faculty of seven members, the dean and one other are foreigners, and the remaining professors are Brazilians. Some of the latter also teach in other institutions in order to supplement their incomes: for example, the principal teaches 12 hours a week in a nearby secondary school.

The course of study at Campinas lasts five years, of which the first two are the equivalent of a preparatory liberal arts course, and the remaining three consist of theological courses. In 1952 the Seminary inaugurated a program of visiting professorships in accordance with which the Presbyterian USA and the Presbyterian US mission boards send a leading seminary professor from the United States to Campinas every two years for a special lectureship of one to three months' duration. Since 1952 this Seminary has also conducted annual pastors' institutes offering refresher courses each year for approximately 70 ministers.

The operating financial needs of the Campinas Seminary have been met almost entirely since 1917 by the Presbyterian Church of Brazil. The mission boards of the Presbyterian Churches USA and US have occasionally contributed capital gifts. In 1956, for example, each of them gave $10,000 toward the cost of constructing a new auditorium building on its campus. The Presbyterian Church of Brazil is now trying to raise additional capital funds for a new dormitory to accommodate the Seminary's growing student enrollment. Members of the Ferraz family (who are active locally in the cane sugar business) have also made substantial contributions to its needs.

Theological Seminary of the Independent Presbyterian Church of Brazil: This school receives no support from any American mission board. The Independent Presbyterian Church of Brazil split off from the Presbyterians USA about 50 years ago as a result of (1) a clash in personalities, (2) a disagreement concerning the advisability of Presbyterians' being members of masonic organizations, and (3) the belief on the part of the Brazilian Presbyterians that the theological outlook of their American brethren was insufficiently conservative. It appears that, as in Mexico and Korea, the strongly nationalistic converts to Protestantism in Latin America often tend to join the Presbyterian Church and, in line with their isolationist attitudes, they sometimes form independent Presbyterian offshoots.

Located in the center of the City of São Paulo, this Seminary has an all-Brazilian faculty. Its theological outlook is conservative, and its academic level is said to be lower than that of the other two seminaries in the City. In recent years, conversations have been held with a view toward exploring ways and means of merging this institution with the Presbyterian Seminary at Campinas. Such action, however, is related to the possibility of uniting all Brazilian Presbyterians into one church, a goal which is not as yet at hand.

Theological Seminary of the Methodist Church of Brazil: This is the second-largest Protestant seminary in the São Paulo area (located 15 miles east of the City). It is supported by the American Methodists and has recently been greatly expanded at considerable expense, as the approximate figures in Table 61 indicate.

This school has about the same academic standards as the Presbyterian Seminary at Campinas, but there is little in the way of regular faculty or student interchange between the two institutions.

TABLE 61.   DEVELOPMENT OF METHODIST SEMINARY, SÃO PAULO (1940–58)

Date of Construction	Building	Cost Paid by		
		Local Gifts	Methodist Board	Total
1940s	Main building, Faculty Residence	$ 36,000	$24,000	$ 60,000
1957	Administration, Class Rooms	32,500	32,500	65,000
1957	Church and Chapel	90,000	10,000	100,000
1958	Library	30,000	30,000	60,000
		$188,500	$96,500	$285,000

The Methodist Seminary was opened in about 1940, and its enrollment is expanding. Of the school's $10,634 receipts for ordinary operations in its fiscal year ended June 30, 1956, 40% was provided by the Methodists' Division of World Missions which describes the Seminary as the "apple of the eye" of the Methodist Church of Brazil. Methodist students from Portuguese East and West Africa occasionally are trained here.

Baptist Seminary of São Paulo: In February 1956 Brazilian Baptists inaugurated a Baptist Seminary as part of the Baptist College of São Paulo (which was established in 1901). During its first year this Seminary functioned as a night school. As yet it has no full-time faculty members, and four or five professors teach its day school courses on a part-time basis. The enrollment is approximately 25 students who are principally interested in the evangelistic aspects of the ministry. The financial needs of this institution are met by the College, through contributions received from the Baptist Convention of São Paulo, and from individuals.

Concordia Seminary, Pôrto Alegre: In addition to the estimated 20 ordinand students at this school, there are approximately 160 students receiving a pretheological education here. This Seminary is maintained by the Missouri Synod Lutherans.

Episcopal Theological Seminary, Pôrto Alegre: Brazil is the only country in South America in which the Episcopalians are active. This Seminary in the extreme southern part of Brazil was founded in 1900, but from time to time has since closed its doors. As previously noted (in connection with the proposed Episcopal Seminary in Puerto Rico), the Pôrto Alegre Seminary was at one point scheduled to be closed. However, with the changes in this plan it now appears that steps will be taken to keep the Pôrto Alegre school open.

Evangelical Lutheran Seminary, São Leopoldo: As previously noted, the Evangelical Lutheran Church is the largest of the Protestant churches in Brazil. Its membership has been estimated as high as 700,000 persons, most of whom are immigrants from Germany or their descendants residing in southern Brazil.

The Seminary of this Church is located in São Leopoldo which is 20 miles west of Pôrto Alegre. Its enrollment consists of a total of approximately 130 students. However, like the Concordia Seminary in Pôrto Alegre, the great majority of them are studying at the pretheological level. The faculty consists of a total of 10 men serving full time.

During the 1920s a Union Theological Seminary was established in Rio de Janeiro, largely as a result of the efforts of a Brazilian, Erasmo Braga. However, the Brazilian Protestant churches came to believe that this union institution was being imposed upon them by non-Brazilian ecumenical agencies. Accordingly they declined to support the new Seminary, and after a few years it was obliged to close its doors.

Table 62 lists the Protestant theological schools in Argentina and Chile.

TABLE 62.   THEOLOGICAL SCHOOLS IN ARGENTINA AND CHILE (1957)

| Name | Location | Approx. Number of | | Denominational Support |
		Full-Time Faculty	Theol. Students	
Argentina				
Union Theological Seminary	Buenos Aires	7[a]	40[b]	Methodist, Presbyterian, etc.
Lutheran Theological Seminary	Buenos Aires	3[a]	12	United Lutheran
International Baptist Seminary	Buenos Aires	6[a]	40[b]	Southern Baptist
Concordia Seminary	Villa Ballester	5[a]	10[b]	Lutheran (Missouri Synod)
Chile				
Baptist Theological Seminary	Santiago	3	12[b]	Southern Baptist
Total: 5[c]		24	114	

NOTES: [a] Plus part-time faculty, or professors teaching at the pretheological level.
[b] Plus students at lower level of training.
[c] See also Table 70A, Supplementary List of Theological Schools.

5. *Argentina*

Of the 19,000,000 persons in Argentina, only 100,000 are Protestants. The latter are divided among many churches, of whom the largest have memberships as shown in Table 63.

TABLE   63.   MEMBERSHIP   OF   PROTESTANT CHURCHES IN ARGENTINA (1957)

German Evangelical	approx. 35,000
Lutheran Church (Missouri Synod)	15,000
Baptists	11,000
Seventh Day Adventist	6,500
Methodists	6,000
Congregational	6,000
United Evangelical Lutheran	4,000

Union Theological Seminary, Buenos Aires: Founded in 1884, this school was operated in various locations in Argentina and Uruguay until it was finally moved to Buenos Aires in 1916. The Methodists and Waldensians have cooperated in its support from the beginning. In 1917 the Disciples commenced to contribute financial aid, and in 1947 the Presbyterians USA joined in supporting the school.

Of the total enrollment of approximately 70 students in this school, about 40 are men training for the ministry. The remainder are principally women students taking courses to be Christian workers. In addition the UTS has had as many as 200 students enrolled in its correspondence courses and conducts evening classes for pastors and lay workers. The ordinand students come from the six countries in the southern portion of South America.

The faculty includes professors from the United States, Argentina, Bolivia, Italy, Germany and Spain. Its President, Dr. B. Foster Stockwell, is an American Methodist. The professor of pastoral psychology was a well-known Jesuit priest and scientist in Spain before his conversion to Protestantism some years ago. Seven members of its faculty possess doctoral degrees.

This school is generally considered to be the strongest of all the seminaries in Latin America. One of its features are the annual Carnahan lectures which have been given in recent years by a number of outstanding theologians from abroad, including Drs. Visser t'Hooft, Mackay, Van Dusen, etc. The Seminary is an affiliated member of the American Association of Theological Schools and hopes eventually to become fully accredited by this Association.

More than 80% of the school's operating budget is supplied by the Methodists who also are contributing the services of several of its faculty members (whose salaries are paid directly by the Board). The UTS has been experiencing a growth in its enrollment. The main building, which was constructed in 1942 and which seemed to be more than adequate at that time, has had to be enlarged by increasing the dormitory space in it.

In the summer of 1956 the UTS launched a campaign to raise approximately $30,000 from local sources to help finance the cost of a new classroom, library and dormitory building. For this same project, in the ensuing two or three years the Methodist Board plans to contribute $100,000. The remaining $25,000 of the estimated $155,000 total cost is to be furnished by the other participating boards and by the Waldensian Church in the River Plate area.

Lutheran Theological Seminary, Buenos Aires: In 1951 the Lutherans established a preseminary on an attractive campus in Manuel de Pinazo, a suburb located 25 miles from the center of Buenos Aires. The building was so planned that the projected seminary could be housed in it from the start. In 1955 the Seminary itself was launched, and in September 1956 a new building for the school was dedicated.

The Seminary was established to serve Lutheran students from all of South America. The present Rector is Pastor Bela Lasko, a Hungarian who received his theological training in Sweden. The Seminary has on its board of directors representatives from Lutheran churches in Colombia, Venezuela, Peru and Uruguay, as well as in Argentina.

The 1957 operating budget of this school was set at approximately $32,000. In 1956–57 the Seminary had a faculty of three professors teaching 12 ordinand students. However, it was hoped that by 1957–58 the faculty would be double that size and the student body considerably enlarged.

As of October 1955 the United Lutherans had provided $154,000 for buildings for the Seminary, and the Lutheran World Federation's Latin America Committee (on behalf of other Lutheran churches in North and Latin America, and in Europe) had furnished an additional $30,000. It is estimated that the total cost of the land and buildings when completed will amount to $225,000.

Apparently the possibility of the Lutherans' locating their work at the Union Theological Seminary in Buenos Aires was not considered in detail. However, cordial relations are maintained by this Seminary and the UTS, and one professor is exchanged between them.

International Baptist Seminary, Buenos Aires: In 1954 the Southern Baptist Mission in Buenos Aires opened this Seminary for students from the five southern countries on the continent. Replacing a seminary originally opened in 1912, it had an initial total enrollment of 53 men and women. Of this number, 20 were students in the affiliated Training School for Women. A few Mennonite and Brethren students are also taking courses, and in 1957 the enrollment totaled 62 students. A correspondence course was initiated in 1955, and night classes are being planned. The Seminary reports that its main building was constructed at a cost of $450,000. The Southern Baptists are building up their faculty and are said to be creating a good seminary. One criticism which has been made of the school, however, is that not enough of its curriculum is related to Latin American culture.

Concordia Seminary, Buenos Aires: This school was founded in 1942. According to its Rector, Dr. F. Lange, it prepares pastors for the Spanish work of the "Lutheran Church—Missouri Synod in South America. It is fulfilling its purpose so well that for the past 10 years no foreign men have had to be called to serve in this district." Of its 31 students the majority are being trained by the school at the preseminary level. The faculty is largely European and the school's "new buildings are already too small." Dr. Lange believes the greatest need for Protestant leadership in Latin America is "a positive religious approach to biblical study, interpretation and application, as may be contrasted to an ethical and philosophical guide for practical living; the first leads, the second follows." For a short period prior to the founding of the Lutheran Theological Seminary at Manuel de Pinazo, some of the students of the latter institution studied at the Concordia Seminary.

6. Chile

Chile has a somewhat higher proportion of Protestants than most South American countries, i.e., 12%. Of the 750,000 persons in the Protestant community, an estimated 400,000 are adherents of the indigenous Pentecostal churches. The Methodist and Baptist churches, etc., are all small.

Baptist Theological Seminary, Santiago: The Southern Baptists purchased a property in Santiago in 1955 for this school and are now improving their building. It was sold to them by the Presbyterians USA and the Methodist boards who had formerly used it for a joint Bible school which was closed several years previously. The increase in the Southern Baptists' activities in Chile, compared to that of the Methodists and Presbyterians, seems to be due to (1) the much larger funds which have become available in recent years to the Southern Baptists' foreign mission boards; and (2) their decision to place primary emphasis on Latin America (and Africa) even at the expense of reducing some of their activities in India and elsewhere.

More than one-half of the Southern Baptist pastors in Chile—20 out of 37—are graduates of this denomination's Seminary. About one-third of the regular students complete what corresponds to a junior-college level of preparation before they enter the institution.

7. *Over-all*

One factor which has not been noted above is the fact that a large number of the men entering the full-time "ordained" Protestant ministry in Latin America are not being trained in any theological school at all. These young men are members of the numerous and rapidly growing Pentecostal groups which follow the practice of requiring them to serve a long period of apprenticeship (up to 10 or 20 years) with their own congregations before they are admitted to the ministry.

Dean Shaull of the Presbyterian Seminary in Campinas, Brazil, considers the following are the most pressing needs of the Protestant theological schools in Latin America:

1. Higher academic standards.
2. Theological literature written in Spanish and Portuguese.
3. Additional outside contacts through the medium of visiting lecturers, etc., in order that seminary curricula may be made more relevant to current social problems.

He points out that one way in which higher academic standards might be attained would be through the establishment of a center for one year of graduate theological study on the part of ordained ministers. There are some who believe that such a center should be established in Brazil as a joint effort on the part of the existing seminaries. However, the matter of its location is always a thorny problem, and the discussions to date on this matter have been nebulous.

Possibly a precursor of such a center would be the establishment of a Brazilian theological journal. Plans for such a publication have been discussed by a group of younger Presbyterian, Methodist, Baptist and Episcopalian ministers in Brazil. Although it is believed that only a modest sum would be needed to establish a publication fund (possibly $1,000 a year), it has not as yet proved possible to launch the venture. No such magazine exists in the Portuguese language. If such a publication were launched, it might achieve a limited circulation in the Portuguese colonies in Africa as well as in Brazil.

During his visit to a number of seminaries throughout Latin America in 1958 Bishop Neill observed that there was a lack of sufficient rapport between some of the faculty members and their students. Too often the professors were inclined to consider that once having delivered their lectures they had thereby completed their teaching tasks.

Concerning the outlook for Protestant theological education in Argentina, President Stockwell of the Union Theological Seminary in Buenos Aires wrote in 1957 as follows: "It is unfortunate that theological education in Argentina is divided among so many schools with relatively meagre resources. But this is simply a projection of the divisions which exist among the churches which have established outposts in these fields. There is little hope for more inclusive interdenominational theological training here until the North American churches become less insistent on indoctrinating the younger churches in the ways of the older—and on maintaining separations which, though perhaps tolerable in the United States, are tragic in fields like these."

CHAPTER 8

SUMMARY OF THE THEOLOGICAL SCHOOLS

A. QUANTITATIVE ASPECTS

Table 64 presents a tabulation of the number of Protestant theological schools, full-time faculty members and theological students in all of the younger church areas which have previously been listed in this Survey.

From Table 64 it will be noted that there are a total of 202 Protestant theological schools located in the younger church areas in which 6,194 students are being trained for the ministry. The number of ordinand students is about equal in three of the major areas: Southern Asia, Southeast Asia and Latin America. Of the total of 6,194 in Africa, Asia and Latin America, 61% are enrolled in the Asian seminaries. More than one-third of the total (i.e., 36%) are students in schools in East Asia. In fact, one out of every six students is a seminarian in Korea, and the total (1,346) studying in that country alone almost equals the number of ordinands being trained in Southern and Southeast Asia combined (1,542).

These figures also disclose that the average theological school in the younger church areas has four full-time faculty members and an enrollment of 30 theological students. In Africa the average is three full-time faculty members and 23 students. The typical Korean seminary is the largest, i.e., an average of eight full-time faculty members and 150 students.

In quantitative terms, Table 65 indicates the adequacy of the numbers of seminary students being trained in each area in relation to the estimated Protestant population in those areas.

The ratio of theological students to the Protestant population in the younger church areas is about one for each 5,600. If East Asia (notably Korea) is excepted, the ratio becomes one for each 8,250 Protestants. These figures, of course, do not take into account the factor of missionary opportunity inherent in the religious situation in these areas—particularly with respect to the prevalence of a belief in animism, from which it is easiest for Christianity to make converts. For example, in South Korea the 1,566,000 Christians are only 7% of the estimated 22,000,000 peo-

TABLE 64. SUMMARY OF PROTESTANT THEOLOGICAL SCHOOLS IN AFRICA,
ASIA AND LATIN AMERICA (1956–58)

Area	Number of Schools	Approx. Number of Full-Time Faculty	Approx. Number of Theol. Students	% of Students
Africa				
North of the Sahara	1	2	25	
East Africa	7	28	221	
West Africa	9	40	269	
Latin Africa	19	56	388	
Southern Africa	35	93	771	
Subtotal	71	219	1,674	27
Middle East				
Lebanon	1	4	12	
Southern Asia				
India	32	159	662	
Pakistan and Ceylon	3	8	40	
Subtotal	35	167	702	11
Southeast Asia[a]				
Burma, Thailand and Malaya	6	25	136	
Indonesia	10	48	353	
Oceania	9	19	154	
Philippines	7	35	197	
Subtotal	32	127	840	14
East Asia[a]				
Japan	12	108	590	
Korea	9	77	1,346	
Formosa	4	26	221	
Hongkong	3	10	61	
Subtotal	28	221	2,218	36
Latin America				
Mexico and Central America	7	21	78	
The Caribbean Area	10	32	169	
South America	18	76	501	
Subtotal	35	129	748	12
Total	202	867	6,194	100

NOTE: [a] Excluding Australia, New
Zealand and Communist China.

ple in that country. It is likely that the remaining 20,434,000 persons represent more of an opportunity for conversion to Christianity than would a like number of Muslims in the Middle East. Similarly, in Africa south of the Sahara there are approximately 31,000,000 Roman Catholics and Protestants. This total amounts to only 20% of the 147,000,000 people residing in this area, the great majority of whom are reported to be animists.

The figure of 84,000,000 included in the table as the size of the Protestant population in the United States is based on estimates of the constituency of Protestant churches (as contrasted with an estimated enrolled membership of approximately 57,000,000 Protestants). This is the same basis on which the membership statistics of Roman Catholic churches in the United States are compiled. Accordingly it appears that there are in round figures 5,600 Protestants in the United States for each ordinand student in seminaries associated with and accredited by the American Association of Theological Schools. This does not allow for those students who are enrolled in Bible schools in the United States and who ultimately become ministers.

The ratio of 1:5,600 in the United States is the same as that prevailing in Africa, Asia and Latin America. But, again excepting Korea, the ratio of 8,250 Protestants to each seminarian in the underdeveloped countries is considerably higher than that in the United States.

TABLE 65.   NUMBER OF THEOLOGICAL STUDENTS IN RELATION TO PROTESTANT
COMMUNITIES (1956–58)

Area	Approx. Number of Theol. Students	Protestant Population	Number of Protestants per Student
Africa	1,674	13,000,000	7,800
Middle East	12	84,000	7,000
Southern Asia	702	6,000,000	8,600
Southeast Asia	840	8,000,000	9,500
East Asia	2,218	2,000,000	900
Latin America	748	6,000,000	8,000
	6,194	35,084,000	5,600
USA	15,000	84,000,000	5,600

A review of some of the budgets of these schools underscores the inadequate financial support the typical seminary overseas is receiving. In Table 66 are assembled and converted to US dollars the annual budgetary totals reported in recent years by 30 seminaries abroad.

The figures in Table 66 should be interpreted with considerable reserve, for the following reasons:

1. In some instances (as noted) the budgets exclude the salaries which are paid directly to their Western faculty members by the mission boards which contribute their services. Such salaries may also have been excluded by other seminaries without their so indicating in their reports.

2. Those theological schools which are constituent parts of universities (Silliman College, for example) may not have disclosed in their seminary budget the cost of maintaining central services available to them such as the heating plant, library, etc.

3. It appears that seminaries have different accounting methods, particularly as to how they include within their operating income the proceeds of contributions received for capital purposes.

4. The figures cover different fiscal years: in the case of some seminaries there appear to be fairly substantial fluctuations in the size of their operating budgets from year to year.

5. The budgetary totals of some schools include the cost of training nontheological students, whereas in other seminaries this is not the case.

Nevertheless, after allowing for these factors it seems reasonable to assume that by taking an average of these 30 seminaries, a number of the possible divergencies would tend to be cancelled out. It will be noted that the average budget amounts to $15,700. This figure probably should be adjusted slightly upward to reflect the number of instances in which the Western members of the faculties have their salaries paid directly by their mission boards rather than through the school's operating

TABLE 66. ANNUAL BUDGETS OF 30 SEMINARIES (1953–57)

Name	Location	Annual Budget	Fiscal Year
Africa			
Ambatomanga Theological School	Tananarive	$9,100	1956
Arivonimamo Theological School	Tananarive	4,480	1956
Ambohipotsy College	Tananarive	8,400	1956
Imerimandroso College	Lake Alaotra	1,736	1956
Fianarantsoa College	Fianarantsoa	2,016	1956
Ivory Theological College	Fianarantsoa	20,720	1956
St. Paul's College	Ambatoharanana	980	1956
Southern Asia			
United Theological College	Bangalore	9,100	1953
Gujranwala Theological Seminary	Gujranwala	9,475	1954
Andhra Baptist Theological Seminary	Ramapatnam	10,937	1957
Assam Baptist Theological Seminary	Jorhat	6,090	1957
Southeast Asia			
Burma Divinity School	Insein	13,870	1956–57
McGilvary Theological Seminary	Chiengmai	5,750	1954
Trinity Theological College	Singapore	8,330ª	1954
Djakarta Theological College	Djakarta	32,000	1955–56
Baptist Theological Seminary	Semarang	11,000	1954
Malang Theological School	Malang	27,200	1954
Ambon Theological School	Ambon	10,000	1954
Union Theological Seminary	Manila	40,692	1955–56
St. Andrew's	Manila	49,360	1954
Central Philippines University College of Theology	Iloilo	14,609	1954
Silliman College of Theology	Dumaguete	11,663	1954
East Asia			
Union Theological Seminary	Tokyo	27,110	1956
Taiwan Theological College	Taipeh	4,600	1954
Tainan Theological College	Tainan	12,000ª	1954
Lutheran Theological Seminary	Hongkong	20,900	1954
Southern Baptist Theological Seminary	Hongkong	12,000	1954
Latin America			
Evangelical Seminary of Puerto Rico	Rio Piedras	25,500	1955–56
Theological Seminary of Methodist Church of Brazil	São Paulo	10,635	1955–56
Union Theological Seminary	Buenos Aires	50,428	1955
	Average	$15,700	

NOTE: ª Not including salaries of the Western staff.

budget. On the whole, therefore, it seems reasonable to estimate that the typical seminary overseas has expenses of approximately $18,000 a year. Since each school has an average of about 30 theological students, this means that approximately $600 per year is spent to educate each student. It is of interest to note how these figures compare with the expenditures per student in the seminaries which were accredited by and were associate members of the American Association of Theological Schools in 1952–53 as shown in Table 67.

Table 67 indicates that there are about twice as many seminaries in Africa, Asia and Latin America as there are in the United States. But the typical foreign seminary has, when compared to its American counterpart, a full-time faculty which is less than half as large (4 vs. 10), a student body less than one-quarter as large (30 vs. 136), a budget less than one-tenth as large ($18,000 vs. $185,000), and spends per year less than one-half as much per ordinand student. The amount spent by the

Table 67. Comparison of Seminaries in the United States with Those
Overseas (1953–58)

Approximate Number of	United States	Africa, Asia & Latin America
Seminaries	108[a]	202
Full-Time Faculty		
Total	1,100[b]	867
Average per Seminary	10[c]	4[e]
Theological Students		
Total	14,720[d]	6,194
Average per Seminary	136[f]	30[f]
Estimated Current Annual Income		
Total	$19,900,000	$3,636,000
Average per Seminary	185,000	18,000
Average per Student	1,350	600

Notes: [a] 73 fully accredited plus 35
associated members of the AATS
(including estimates for the six
seminaries for which no data is included in the AATS report).
[b] Plus 600 part-time faculty members.
[c] Plus an average of six part-time
faculty members.

[d] Assuming 20% of the 18,400 total
enrollment of students were not
ordinand students.
[e] Plus an estimated average of two
part-time faculty members.
[f] Plus others at lower level of training.

typical foreign seminary each year in training each of its students is only about one-
quarter as much as that spent annually by the Union Theological Seminary in New
York City ($600 vs. $2,277).

B. Qualitative Aspects

Since there are no reliable accreditation standards in use among the seminaries in
Africa, Asia and Latin America (with the exception of the members of the Serampore Senate), it is difficult to compare the merits of the individual schools except on
an arbitrary basis of appraisal. The comments made in the various reports suggest

Table 68. Comparative Standing of Theological Schools in Africa,
Asia and Latin America (1957)

Below Average	Average	Above Average
Africa[a]	Burma, Malaya	Union of South Africa
Middle East	Indonesia	India
Thailand	Philippines	Japan
Central America	Korea	
Caribbean Area	Formosa	
	South America	

Note: [a] Exclusive of those in the
Union of South Africa.

that the academic standards of the typical seminaries in some countries and areas are
on the average higher than in other areas. These comments are summarized in
Table 68.

After allowing for differences in the general academic level prevailing in one area
as compared to another, the 13 schools listed in Table 69 might be cited as the leading institutions.

TABLE 69. THE LEADING THEOLOGICAL SCHOOLS IN AFRICA, ASIA AND
LATIN AMERICA (1957–58)

Africa	Middle East
University of Pretoria (A & B Faculties)	None
Stellenbosch Theological Seminary	

Southern Asia	Southeast Asia
Serampore College, Calcutta	Trinity Theological College, Singapore
United Theological College, Bangalore	Djakarta Theological College
Leonard Theological College, Jabalpur	Union Theological Seminary, Manila

East Asia	Latin America
Union Theological Seminary, Tokyo	Union Theological Seminary, Matanzas
Doshisha University Theological School	Union Theological Seminary, Buenos Aires
Tainan Theological College	

Of the 13 schools listed in Table 69, eight (excluding the South African seminaries) have appointed as their principals theologians who are outstanding nationals in their own countries. These men are listed in Table 70.

If to these eight schools is added a ninth (Doshisha, of which the Chancellor of the University and the Dean of its Theological School are both Japanese), the importance of having foreign seminaries run by nationals of those countries is manifest. Only national principals are in a position to solicit with vigor the financial support of the younger churches for their seminaries which is so essential.

TABLE 70. PRINCIPALS OF LEADING SEMINARIES OVERSEAS (1958)[b]

C. E. Abraham	Serampore College
J. Russell Chandran	United Theological College, Bangalore
George S. Sahai	Leonard Theological College
Peter Latuihamallo[a]	Djakarta Theological College
Benjamin Guansing	Union Theological Seminary, Manila
Hidenobu Kuwada	Union Theological Seminary, Tokyo
Hwang Chang-hui	Tainan Theological College
Alfonso Rodriguez Hidalgo	Union Theological Seminary, Matanzas

NOTES: [a] On leave in the USA in 1958.   [b] Excluding those in the Union of South Africa.

No over-all figures are available indicating the extent to which the faculties of the seminaries in Africa, Asia and Latin America are staffed by local personnel. However, an inspection of the 1954–55 *Handbook of Serampore College* and the handbook prepared for the 1956 Bangkok Theological Conference discloses the following:

	Full-Time Faculty Members			
	Western	Asian	Total	% Western
19 Schools in Serampore Senate	51	52	103	50
19 Schools in Southeast Asia	69	46	115	60

It seems reasonable to estimate that more than one-half of the faculty members of the African seminaries are Westerners. On the other hand, the seminaries in East Asia in all probability have fewer than 50% of their faculty composed of Westerners. Accordingly it would appear that roughly one-half (or 433) of the 867 full-time faculty members of the seminaries in all of Africa, Asia and Latin America are nationals of those countries.

Concerning the relationships between the Western and local members of the theological school faculties, the Anderson-Smith report states:

The missionary in theological education still holds a position of authority that he has generally given up in other spheres of missionary work. . . . Probably in no other field of education can a man rise to high position in his institution, with so little professional preparation, in such short time, as in a theological school on the "Mission Field." Men just out of theological seminaries in the West with an ordinary B.D. degree have had to become the heads of departments and sometimes even the heads of theological schools. . . . But just as the younger missionaries often rise too rapidly in position and responsibility on the Mission Field, so it is true that nationals rise all too slowly. Theological seminaries are the last stronghold of missionary domination in the whole missionary enterprise. As a rule, there is a larger proportion of Westerners to national teachers in theological schools than in any other phase of missionary work; whereas nationals have generally replaced missionaries in administration, and often as heads of departments in other forms of education, in theological education, the majority of the schools are still under Western administration . . . (this is) the result of a failure to plan far enough in advance for national leadership so that adequately prepared men and women will be available. Part of this failure may be due to that often unconscious sense of superiority on the part of the Westerner which has marred so much of our service as missionaries in the Orient. In other forms of education, the shallow basis for this sense of superiority has long since been revealed by the ability and often even superiority of national leadership; but the field of theological education still seems to provide a special sphere for Western leadership.

Since the Anderson-Smith report was written (i.e., in 1953) there has been a considerable increase in the number of nationals serving on seminary faculties. However, as Mr. Winburn T. Thomas recently wrote: "Mission subsidy for theological education is most easily arranged when missionaries serve on the teaching staff. Sending societies that would not justify an annual subsidy of $20,000 for a theological training school will assign 3 or 4 top ranking missionaries to teaching and administrative posts in the institution." Mr. Thomas also believes that "if Protestant Christianity is to become indigenous to Asia, theological education must be committed to Asian Christians who have not become de-culturalized by extended contacts with the West, and the curriculum of Asian seminaries must interpret the Gospel in the several psychological, sociological and cultural languages."

The level of the salaries paid to seminaries' faculty members is one indication of the strength of these institutions. These salary scales vary from country to country, particularly as the cost of living varies. One might cite as an example one of the stronger institutions among the 202 which is located in one of the countries in Africa, Asia and Latin America where the cost of living is among the highest. In a recent fiscal year it paid the following annual salaries (which would seem high in some other countries):

President	$3,000
Secretary	1,140
Treasurer	1,050
Professor, Practical Theology	2,160
Professor, Church History	1,980
Professor, Sacred Music	2,082
Librarian	1,290

It is not within the competence of this Survey to attempt to analyze and compare the strengths and weaknesses of the ministries of the younger churches in one area or another. However, it probably is fair to say that the indigenous Protestant ecclesiastical leadership in the younger church areas is generally weak everywhere with the possible exception of two or three countries. As Dr. David G. Moses, the Principal of Hislop College in Nagpur, India, has commented concerning the churches of Southern Asia, "barring a few notable exceptions, they are all pale and anemic imitiations of the churches of the West."

One of the chief difficulties experienced by Protestant seminaries overseas in obtaining students of high quality is the fact that such young men are understandably concerned by the prospect of being paid unduly low compensation during their entire careers. In addition to the quotations already cited in the IMC surveys of Africa and the Ranson report on India, the comment of one more observer might be cited, indicating that this condition is a characteristic weakness of Protestantism in most countries:

A second difficulty is the financial one. This is said of countries as far apart as India and Bolivia: "Lack of financial security. Low salary." This is remarked of the Philippines: "As a capable person well trained, who might accept the leadership of a seminary or an educational institution, can receive a much larger salary elsewhere, it is difficult to find some one who will take the smaller salary of the church institution." This is reported from across the Rio Grande: "In Mexico some national leadership has been developed but many have moved to the United States where salaries are higher and educational opportunities greater. If the salaries in Mexico were sufficient to give a minister a comfortable living, we probably would not have lost more than 50% of our trained leadership." How familiar all such statements sound! The financial difficulty is ever with us and world wide.

There would seem to be little need to summarize or repeat at this point the virtually unanimous chorus of indictments which have been quoted earlier in this

Survey concerning the poor quality of the work being done as a whole at the seminaries overseas. One may conclude with the findings, published in 1932, of a report which has not as yet been quoted in this Survey. This is the *Laymen's Inquiry,* whose Commission of Appraisal inspected missionary enterprises in India, Burma, China and Japan in 1932:

To a student of the religious needs of the countries of the Orient, the theological seminaries as they stand today seem strikingly inadequate for training the type of spiritual leaders most needed at the present time. They are reproductions on a small scale of the American denominational seminaries of a former generation. There are some excellent scholars at work in the best of them, but these institutions have not been uniquely planned to meet the peculiar problems and tasks of the countries where they exist, nor are they well adapted to fit the spiritual needs of the time. . . .

The number of weak Christian institutions and of merely nominal Christians throughout the Orient is a reproach to the missionary enterprise. Moreover, they represent in the aggregate an enormous waste of men and money. Denominational interests, institutional pride, and lack of cooperative planning have contributed to the development of conditions which should no longer be tolerated.

The fact that only 2% of the 3,050 pages of the full report of the *Laymen's Inquiry* touch on theological education gives some indication of the increase in the importance of the role of the seminaries overseas which has occurred during the 25 years since the report was published.

Commenting in 1957 on the *Laymen's Inquiry* in an article entitled *Re-thinking Missions after Twenty-five Years,* Dr. Kenneth Scott Latourette wrote:

Re-thinking Missions put its finger on some of the clamant inadequacies of theological education in Asia, but it failed to appreciate fully either the major importance of that phase of the world mission or one of its fundamental problems, the economic base of the churches. If the churches are central to the world mission, an able and adequately prepared clergy is absolutely essential; and modifications, even drastic departures from the forms of preparation current in the West, are imperative. Confronted with a quite different society and with much smaller economic resources than the churches of the West, the churches of Asia—and Africa and Latin America—and the missions which assist them would be guilty of major neglect if they were to fail to place much more emphasis than in the past on theological education and on experimenting with forms of the ministry and of church organization adapted to conditions in these continents.

C. SUPPLEMENTARY LIST OF THEOLOGICAL SCHOOLS

After the manuscript of *A Seminary Survey* had been sent to the publisher, several informants forwarded to the author the names of some additional theological schools which had come to their attention as a result of returns from questionnaires, etc. This information was received at too late a date for it to be included in the text, tables and maps appearing elsewhere in this Survey. Consequently, rather than omitting all mention of them, it has seemed best to set forth the names of these institutions in a supplementary list, which is presented in Table 70A.

TABLE 70A.   SUPPLEMENTARY LIST OF THEOLOGICAL SCHOOLS (1958–59)

| | | Approx. Number of | | |
| | | Full-Time | Theol. | |
Name	Location	Faculty	Students	Denominational Support
Africa				
Tanganyika				
All-Africa Theological Seminary[a]	Moshi	3	17	Lutheran World Federation
Nigeria				
Evangelical Lutheran Seminary of Nigeria	Obot, Idim	2[b]	27	Lutheran (Missouri Synod)
Cameroons				
Evangelical Seminary	Ngouedi, Loutété	3[b]	12[c]	Swedish Covenant
Southern Asia				
India				
Chota Nagpur Diocesan Theological Class[d]	Murhu, Ranchi, Bihar	2	15	CIPBC[e]
Oceania				
Torres Strait				
St. Paul's Theological College	Moa Island[f]	1	8	Anglican[f]
British Solomon Islands				
Goldie College	Banga	4	2[c]	Methodist (New Zealand)
Fiji Islands				
Methodist Theological Institution	Nausori	3[b]	3[c]	Methodist (English)
Tonga Islands				
Sia'toutai College	Nuku'alofa	3[b]	9[c]	Free Methodist (English)
West Samoa				
Piula Training College	Lufilufa	4	8[c]	Methodist (English)
East Asia				
Japan				
Central Theological College	Tokyo	6[b]	24	Anglican[h]
Latin America				
Costa Rica				
Latin American Bible Seminary	San José	7[b]	27[c]	Latin American Mission
Bolivia				
Baptist Theological Seminary	Cochabamba	5	5[c]	Baptist (Canadian)
Chile				
Bible Seminary	Santiago	5	2[c]	Methodist
Total: 13		48	150	

NOTES: [a] See comments in Chapter 2, B, concerning the All-Africa Lutheran Conference held at Marangu in 1955.
[b] Plus part-time instructors.
[c] Plus students at lower level of training.
[d] Not affiliated with Serampore Senate.
[e] Church of India, Pakistan, Burma and Ceylon (Anglican).
[f] Moa Island is within Australian territorial limits, and this school is administered by the Diocese of Carpentaria.
[g] No ordinand students enrolled in 1958–59.
[h] Japanese Province.

Similarly, two other recent developments might be noted here. (1) The Finnish Mission School at Onajena in South-West Africa (listed as such in Table 22 and in the subsequent comment) is now known as the Ovambokavango Lutheran Theological Seminary. In 1959 it had five full-time (plus one part-time) instructors teaching a theological class of 10 nonwhite students at Elim (and a preliminary class of 16 students at Oshigambo) in Ovamboland. (2) Subsequent to 1956 (the date of the information presented in Table 25), the Concordia Seminary at Nagercoil, Kanyakumari, Madras, India, became affiliated with the Serampore Senate.

CHAPTER 9

THE NUMBER AND ROLE OF THE BIBLE SCHOOLS

A. The Number of the Bible Schools

In the preceding chapters relating to the theological schools in Africa, Asia and Latin America, little mention has been made of the number of Bible schools which exist throughout the underdeveloped countries.

Reliable facts and figures concerning these institutions are not readily available. One reason for this has already been cited in the comment in chapter 1 relating to the types of theological schools, namely, the difficulty of distinguishing between them and the Bible schools. The latter term is used in this Survey to mean those institutions, usually at the precollege level, which provide a religious education (or a predominantly secular education in which religious courses are offered) directed primarily toward the training of teachers, laymen or others, either for secular careers or for part- or full-time Christian work exclusive of the full-time ordained ministry. As also noted, some Bible schools are used by a number of the younger churches for the training of men who in later years may seek ordination without further education.

A further source of confusion is the fact that the term "Bible school" has been applied to two different types of institutions. In most younger church areas the older and well-established missions and churches maintain Bible schools for the training of lay personnel, e.g., catechists, evangelists, etc. The term used in that context denotes an institution for the training of unordained church workers. On the other hand, many of the newer fundamentalist missions use the term "Bible school" to denote their own type of theological school where the institution is based on a conservative interpretation of the Scriptures, and where candidates for the ordained pastorate as well as lay students are trained.

Accordingly the comments below are intended to be indicative only, and no attempt has been made to provide a complete or even a comprehensive listing of all the Bible schools now being operated in Africa, Asia and Latin America.

Africa: As is the case in the United States, the Bible schools in Africa are even more loosely organized and heterogeneous in their activities than are the seminaries. Little information is available concerning their number, but it seems likely that there are proportionately fewer of them than is the case in India. In part this may be true because at present so many of the theological schools in Africa are themselves little above the Bible-school level.

In Ethiopia there is a theological "seminary" located at Nakamte, in Wollega Province, which is maintained by the Evangelical National Missionary Society of Stockholm. This institution has a full-time staff of two teachers but trained no ordinand students during the years 1954–57. Thus, despite its name, it is in effect a Bible school.

Part II of the IMC Africa Survey lists a small school at Atakpame in Togo (approximately 100 miles north of the Gulf of Guinea, on the railroad line from Lomé to Blitta). It was founded prior to World War I by the North German Mission which was active in this area when it was a German colony. It is currently supported by the French Evangelical Reformed Church which describes it as a Bible school. Most of the ordinand students from Togo are sent to the French Reformed Seminary located at Ndoungué in the Cameroons, with the result that the Atakpame Bible school is concentrating on instructing catechists and lay leaders, using the Ewe language. The library of this Bible school is described as "very poor, especially in Biblical literature." The school has two classrooms "which permits studies to be carried on in two sections and which complicates life when there are several classes and sections of students enrolled in the school at the same time."

In Northern Rhodesia, the Zambezi Mission maintains a Bible school for the training of evangelists at Sefula. Those students who are judged as being worthy of education at the theological level with a view toward becoming pastors are sent to Overtoun College in Livingstonia (Nyasaland) or to the seminary at Morija in Basutoland, or to the theological school at Kashinda in Northern Rhodesia. The Church of Sweden Mission maintains a Bible school at Masingo near Belingwe in Southern Rhodesia: because of the shortness in the supply of missionary teachers available in 1957, this institution was offering "only short courses" for evangelists, Sunday school teachers and lay workers.

The IMC Madagascar Survey Commission reported on the 12 Bible schools being operated on that island. Of this number, seven were being conducted by the Lutheran churches which had the most complete and systematic organization of these schools. Four others were being operated by churches supported by the Paris Missionary Society, and one by the London Missionary Society.

In 1958 Professor Gerdener of the Dutch Reformed Seminary at Stellenbosch listed a number of Bible schools which were being operated in the Union of South Africa, together with some seminaries which also might be classified as Bible schools. The list is shown in Table 70B.

TABLE 70B.   BIBLE SCHOOLS IN THE UNION OF SOUTH AFRICA (1956)

Name	Location	Approx. Number of Students	Financial Support
Transvaal			
Wilberforce Training College	Johannesburg	15?	African Methodist Episcopal Church
Fred Clark Memorial Training Institute	Nancefield	12?	Salvation Army
Lovedale Bible School	Lovedale	?	Presbyterian, Methodist, etc.
Natal			
Union Bible Institute	Sweetwaters	63	13 mission agencies
Maqhamusela Lutheran Bible School	Eshowe	12?	Lutheran
Cape Province			
Tigerkloof School[a]	Vryburg	6	English Congregational
Bible Institute of South Africa	Kalk Bay	45	7 mission agencies
Bechuanaland[b]			
Kanye Bible School	Kanye	6?	English Congregational
Swaziland[b]			
Bible School	Stegi	20?	Church of the Nazarene

NOTES: [a] To be closed by the Native Affairs Department   [b] British Protectorate.
in 1958.

Southern Asia: The *Christian Handbook of India,* 1954–55, lists some 72 Bible schools in that country, of which five are "theological schools which cater also for training at the Bible school level." Of the 72 schools, 55 were for men and 17 for women. At the time the Ranson report was written (1945), available statistics indicated that for every ordained minister in India there were at least four unordained church workers.

Because the Ranson report was unable to include a consideration of the Bible schools in India, the National Christian Council of India convened a conference in August 1956 at Bangalore to consider the findings of a survey made under the Council's auspices during the previous month of 13 Bible schools in Tamilnad and Karnataka. These two districts are in the southern tip of the Indian peninsula. The institutions listed in Table 71 were visited by the committee.

Several of the Bible schools listed in Table 71 also offer courses at the theo-

TABLE 71.   BIBLE SCHOOLS IN TAMILNAD AND KARNATAKA (1956)

Name	Location	Approx. Number of Full-Time Faculty	Students	Financial Support
Advent Christian Bible School	Velacheri	1	16	American Advent Mission
Darisanapuram Bible School	Cuddalore	1	10	Danish Missionary Society
Hindustan Bible Institute	Madras	3	14	Nondenominational
Men's Bible School	Dharapuram	2	12?	Church of South India
Tamil Bible Institute	Madurai	5	19	Assemblies of God
Village Training Center	Dharapuram	4	20	Church of South India
Women's Evangelical School	Karunakarapuri	2	10	Tamilnad Evangelical Lutheran Synod
South Asia Bible Institute	Bangalore	3	33	Assemblies of God
Arcot Theological Seminary	Vellore	4	35	Church of South India
Madras Bible Seminary	Kilpauk	2?	10?	Oriental Mission Society
Union Theological Seminary	Pasumalai	4	20?	Church of South India
South India Bible Institute	Bangarapet	8	48	World Gospel Mission

logical school level. Of the 13 Bible schools discussed by the committee at the
1956 conference, only 12 are listed in the table inasmuch as the remaining institution (the Tamil Evangelical Lutheran Seminary at Tranquebar) was classified
in the 1953–54 NCCC list and the 1957 Harrison report as a theological school
and is so classified in this Survey. On the other hand, the South India Bible Institute of the World Gospel Mission at Bangarapet was listed in the 1953–54 and
1957 reports as a theological school but was classified at the 1956 conference as a
Bible school and is so classified in Table 71. Thus it is evident that the dividing
line between lower level theological schools and Bible schools is not easy to de-
fine precisely.

The committee stated that of the 13 schools it visited, four were quite conservative in their theological outlook. The courses at these institutes varied from one to
four years in length. In addition most schools offer refresher courses each year of a
few weeks' duration. The emphasis of their teaching is on preaching and tract distribution. They are training rural pastors, evangelists, volunteer workers, village
teachers and catechists, women church workers, etc. The range of their curricula
is indicated by the fact that the Village Training Center at Dharapuram offers
courses in handicraft training for which illiterates are eligible. The Madras Bible
Seminary at Kilpauk "seeks to be evangelistic in emphasis, evangelical in doctrine . . . bibliocentric in method, and practical in aim."

The purpose of the 1956 survey and conference "was to try to determine the
place of Bible schools in the changing situation today." Accordingly it is of interest to note the findings and recommendations which the conference made. With
respect to the place of Bible schools today, the conference confined its recommendation to the suggestion "that they (i.e., the Bible schools) be studied by the
churches" with a view to determining the best use to be made of them.

Concerning "the place of paid, unordained pastors and evangelists," the conference resolved "to record two opposing points of view. On the one hand it
was argued that these categories should be omitted in any new pattern since their
employment:

1. impedes self-support in the church where giving in rural areas yet fails to cover
the total cost of the ordained ministry;

2. impedes the development of a voluntary ministry;

3. perpetuates the old authoritative pattern where ordained ministers are tempted to
regard these workers as subordinates to undertake a great part of the pastoral care which
is really their own responsibility;

4. further, there is a continual pressure put upon Church authorities by unordained
pastors seeking ordination.

"On the other hand, it was held that in many areas the number of ordained ministers was so small that the main burden of pastoral care in the villages devolved upon

unordained pastors, catechists and evangelists, and that at least for a period of ten years . . . suitable candidates . . . with two years Bible training should be employed."

With respect to the courses offered by these Bible schools, "the conference decided that it was not possible to form and recommend detailed curricula for the various types of training in Bible schools." As for cooperation among these institutions, "the conference was convinced that it was not practicable, as in the case of theological schools, to plan for one regional Bible school in each language area operated on cooperative lines."

If the experts attending the conference were unable to reach more sharply defined conclusions and recommendations than these concerning the way in which the Bible schools in India should be developed, it would appear that little could be done by an outside agency in this situation at the present time, despite the great need for improving the level of instruction at these schools.

Southeast Asia: The authors of the Anderson-Smith (AS) report had not intended to study Bible schools, but the increasing number of these institutions in this area required some comment by them. At Insein, Burma, they observed four such schools closely related to the Burma Divinity School. In Thailand they found that the Bangkok Bible School was related to the Chinese Presbytery and the Presbyterian Mission in that city, and was meeting the needs of students unable to use the Thai language.

In Malaya the Methodist Church has a Bible school at Ipoh which is said to be unique in that it sends its graduates to the rubber estates for further work. In Singapore there is the nondenominational Singapore Theological Seminary which is financed by the Overseas Missionary Fellowship of the China Inland Mission. It has also had some support from the International Council of Christian Churches (Rev. Carl McIntyre). It is said to be highly critical of Trinity College and will have nothing to do with the IMC. All of its 14 students are Chinese, and it is reported to have a full-time faculty of six. Despite its title, this institution appears to be essentially a Bible school.

In Indonesia there are a number of Bible schools. Rev. Winburn T. Thomas reports that "the Board of Missions of the Reformed Churches in the Netherlands at Oegstgeest admitted in 1951, that 'we probably are allocating too large a share of funds relatively to regional Bible schools. . . .' In that year the Board . . . was allocating approximately \$12,000 to the regional Bible schools, \$5,500 to the middle-grade theological schools, and \$1,000 to the Djakarta Theological College."

The new Methodist Theological School at Sibu in Sarawak, which was opened in 1955 for junior middle school graduates, is still essentially a Bible school. In 1957 the Evangelical Lutheran Mission Society of Neuendettelsau (near Ansbach, Germany) established two Bible schools in Kalasa and Zaka in New Guinea. It appears that there are 70 pastors within the Lutheran Church of New Guinea who, despite the fact that they had previously had no special training, served for many years as teachers or evangelists. These men were ordained after taking a special course lasting one or two years in these Bible schools.

With respect to the situation in the Philippines, the authors of the AS report comment: "In Manila, there were at least six Bible schools open. We visited one of them. It is called the FIBIAS Bible School and was established in Quonset huts by ex-G.I.s, members of Pentecostal Baptist churches in America who had returned to the Philippines after serving there in the last World War. This School is very Fundamentalist and noncooperative. . . . It . . . aims to train men and women who will go out into active evangelistic work rather than settle down in pastorates." The Methodists report that "since World War II 'splinter groups' of an exceedingly conservative and divisive type have invaded the Philippines and this has caused considerable frustration to the larger churches."

The Rotz report comments on the Bible schools in the Philippines as follows: "Now that there are seminaries, some feel the Bible schools should focus on lay education. Originally the Bible schools were often operated by one person (often a US missionary) who set the admission standards, the tuition, the curriculum and the daily schedule. Consequently the Bible schools were unalike and their dissimilarity caused them to become suspect. However, the Bible schools are now tending to become more alike each other."

East Asia: The 1956 *Japanese Christian Yearbook* lists approximately 50 Protestant Bible schools of various sorts in Japan.

Recent reports of the Presbyterian and Methodist boards contain the following comments on the growth in the number of Bible schools in Korea: "Bible institutes have been growing phenomenally during the past year. . . . These . . . institutes . . . (are) one of the big assets of the Church in Korea. They supply a very thorough Biblical background of training to the students who go on to seminary." "The need for more trained Christian leadership has compelled the establishment of a new Bible institute and training center at Taejon, about 120 miles south of Seoul. . . . It will be coordinated with the (Methodist) Seminary in administrative relationships."

Another tendency in Korea has been the development of night school seminaries for students who must work for their living in the daytime. These students generally are not as apt pupils as those trained by the theological schools. Some thought has been given to coordinating the work in both types of institutions, i.e., a student might take three years' work in a night school seminary and two years in a regular seminary.

On Formosa, according to the AS report, there are "a rapidly growing number of Bible schools. There would be six by the fall of 1952, and seven if the Canadian Presbyterians opened a second school. . . . These Bible schools are being established mostly by the more sectarian missionaries and societies coming from the mainland of China." Two years later (1954) Dr. C. H. Hwang reported that there were 16 Bible schools set up in Formosa training 500 students, or an average of about 30 students. Only two or three of them were under church auspices, but he felt the Bible schools were needed because of the shortage of ministers on the island.

Latin America: The July 1, 1955, *Partial Report of the Latin America Theological and Bible Schools,* issued by the Committee on Cooperation in Latin America, lists approximately 100 Bible schools operating in Central and South America. The Presbyterians USA report that in rural areas in Mexico and elsewhere the Bible school movement has been an important factor in the growth of the church, particularly in the training of evangelists.

In Latin America the Southern Baptists are operating theological "institutes" which occasionally are called "theological seminaries." The July 1958 issue of *The Commission* which is published by their foreign mission board states: "There is considerable variation in the level of work at the different schools. Some of them are doing work on a Bible school level. However, we call most of them seminaries because the goal is to lift the academic standing as rapidly as possible to full seminary level. And already some of the schools are able to grant seminary degrees." The list of the theological schools (as defined in this Survey) which were being maintained in Africa, Asia and Latin America in 1958 by the Southern Baptists appears in Appendix B. A number of their seminaries in Latin America were institutes a few years ago, and only recently were elevated to the status of a theological school. In addition to the six theological schools in Latin America listed in Appendix B, this denomination is operating eight additional theological seminaries or institutes in Latin America which are still at the Bible school level. These eight institutions are listed in Table 72. If present trends continue, it would seem likely that some of them will be upgraded to a theological school level in the next few years.

TABLE 72. SOUTHERN BAPTIST "INSTITUTES" IN LATIN AMERICA (1958)

Location	Country
Guatemala City	Guatemala
San José	Costa Rica
Havana	Cuba
Nassau	Bahamas
Caracas	Venezuela
Belém do Pará	Brazil
Asunción	Paraguay
Montevideo	Uruguay

Over-All: From the above it would appear that there are in the neighborhood of at least 325 Bible schools now operating in Africa, Asia and Latin America. Thus there are three Bible schools for every two theological schools and colleges previously listed in this Survey as currently operating in these same countries. Assuming that there are an average of at least 15 students per Bible school who are training for full-time religious work of one sort or another in the younger churches, this suggests that there may be in the neighborhood of 3,900 such students in the under-developed countries, or two-thirds of the number of ordinand students enrolled at the various seminaries. On the other hand, some estimates place the total number of Bible schools in Africa, Asia and Latin America as high as 500, with a total enrollment exceeding that of the theological schools. In either event, the total of the students enrolled at both the Bible schools and the seminaries in these areas represents only a small fraction (probably about one-quarter) of the 38,606 Protestant missionaries from all countries currently stationed in the field.

B. THE ROLE OF THE BIBLE SCHOOLS

The Bible schools have been described as "the stepchildren of theological training on the mission field." The IMC Madagascar Commission reported they considered the task of the Bible schools in Madagascar is to

1. prepare the church workers (catechists) who lead and sustain the local communities, without whose services it would be impossible to think of church life in wide areas of Madagascar;
2. provide a recruiting ground, in part at least, for candidates for theological schools;
3. train the teachers in village schools; and
4. help train lay workers in the churches.

The AS report comments that the challenge of the Bible schools to the ecumenical church lies in several factors, among which are:

a. their independence of and control by the larger, more cooperatively minded, churches and missions;
b. their fundamentalist character in theology and their Biblical literalism;
c. their appeal to youth because of
   1. a short-cut education for church work and the ministry,
   2. generally low standard for entrance,
   3. an aggressive, dogmatic, bibliocentric approach, and
   4. their challenge to a more evangelistic, adventurous, and less traditional and ritualistic ministry.

The above comment presumably refers to the Bible schools of fundamentalist organizations in Southeast Asia, rather than to the training institutions for lay workers which are a feature of church life elsewhere.

Rev. Winburn T. Thomas has written that nine-tenths of the ministerial functions in Indonesia are performed by unordained, part-time preachers who earn some or all of their income as teachers, farmers, etc. With respect to Indonesian Bible schools he believes "their graduates are at this stage the backbone of the local congregations. Criticisms abound that training in Djakarta or in the middle-grade theological schools separates the student from the rural environment. Upon their return, if they return, they frequently want a standard of living above that of most of their parishioners. These village evangelists are trained in an environment not unlike their own homes, and more readily adjust themselves to its limitations upon their completion of the two-year course. Said the Stated Clerk of one of the larger Synods, who is himself a graduate of Djakarta, 'The evangelists, underpaid and sometimes not paid at all, are doing the pioneering work.' "

A view which is contrary to that of Mr. Thomas concerning the capabilities of the graduates of the Bible schools is presented by Rev. Keith Bridston: ". . . It is disturbing to see that the most indigenous ministry which these churches in Asia and Africa possess—the catechists, the lay evangelists, the teacher-preacher—are declining in importance and numbers and they are, because of their inadequate education and theological training, gradually becoming irrelevant to the new groups of educated, progressive, and politically self-conscious people who are in the Church but feel restive and dissatisfied with its conservatism and lack of cultural and political sensitivity."

In the address he made at the 1956 Bangkok Conference, Dean Liston Pope stated:

Denominationalism and sectarianism compound the confusion. While the outstanding seminaries in Southeast Asia tend to be union institutions or representatives of national churches, the situation has been complicated recently by the multiplication of Bible schools and missionary efforts on the part of innumerable sectarian groups, most of them deliberately or even belligerently noncooperative and fundamentalist in character. Nowhere is the situation worse than in Taiwan, but it is prevalent in most countries. Unfortunately most of these groups represent marginal religious bodies in the United States, and I therefore feel free to talk candidly about them. . . . Unable to commend itself widely at home, this kind of religion, financed by the tithes of a few devout people and large gifts from affluent people who think that such religion would be good for other people— such religion is now rampant in Southeast Asia. One might almost say that the former mission fields are fundamentalism's last stand. . . . Needless to say, the standards and curricula of most of these schools will hardly bear intelligent investigation; fundamentalism has never succeeded in establishing even one excellent educational institution in America, and it is hardly to be expected that it will do so in Asia. But it can dilute all theological education very badly, and it can confuse the struggling Christian churches. It might be argued that there is enough work for everybody to do in Asia, but this is like arguing that patent medicine salesmen should be welcomed because disease is widespread.

At the same conference, Dr. C. H. Hwang (Formosa) stated that he favored those Bible schools which are lay training institutes. On the other hand he would oppose those which are institutions offering lower grade theological education leading to ordination because (according to the conference report)

(1) The students are too young and of poor intellectual caliber. (2) The Bible schools compete financially with the more necessary schools of higher theological education. (3) They are ecclesiastically divisive.

However, he admitted, in the present situation in S.E. Asia, the development of Bible schools may be a temporary necessity, for two reasons: (1) As a defense against the spread of the divisive sects, and (2) To meet the present critical needs for trained leadership in churches which are expanding too rapidly to be cared for by seminary graduates alone.

He concluded with two proposals: (1) That each country survey objectively its present situation as to the urgent need for leadership and set up Bible schools, or not, accordingly. (2) That where Bible schools are founded, they be placed under the same Board of Directors as the seminary, to insure adequate supervision and church control.

Dr. Chou summarized the brief discussion that followed: (1) We all agree that there is a need which the Bible schools may meet for lay training, the training of pioneer rural workers, and the training of women for Christian service, or even for the training of regular church workers where there is no seminary; and (2) there should be over-all planning to meet this need to determine what part of the need may best be met through the Bible schools, and what part should be met by the seminaries.

The AS report concluded that in many places the Bible schools are filling a vacuum, and Dr. Smith suggested that "a study might show that the Bible school ought to play a larger part in the theological system of the Orient. Should this prove to be the case, the churches should re-examine their policies to see whether a grade of workers of Bible school training grade could be integrated into the whole ministry of the Church. Bible schools should have the same relationship to the churches as the theological seminaries, and the faculty of the latter should teach in them and help to maintain high standards. Ordinarily, graduates of the Bible schools should not be allowed to enter a seminary without further general education, but the door should be left open, and the means of acquiring a broader general education should be provided."

Because of their number and diversity, it seems likely that the Bible schools are meeting a need not otherwise being met, and that they will continue to develop in their individual, unsystematic way regardless of what is said about them, pro or con. Since many of the present theological schools first began as Bible schools, this evolutionary trend may continue.

Some of the recommendations quoted above may be sound. Nevertheless, it is difficult to see how effective institutional assistance could be provided to more than a handful of the 325 Bible schools, and it would be difficult to pick and choose among them. A fundamentally different approach toward helping the Bible schools is suggested later on in the present Survey.

CHAPTER 10

THE LACK OF TEXTS

A. The Condition of the Libraries

With respect to the libraries of the theological schools in Asia, Dr. Henry P. Van Dusen has stated:

Libraries are, generally speaking, pitifully inadequate. The books are antiquated and obsolete. They are almost all Western books and in English. The most serious lack is precisely in the most essential teaching tools. It is a shocking shame and our greatest sin that we have not equipped the Asian theological schools with the most fundamental and essential teaching tools for their basic work. It is difficult to understand why we have failed. . . . There is a desperate need for fundamental textbooks which should be prepared in Asian countries. I believe it can be done in such a way as to serve all of our denominations. If the theological schools can be welded together as one enterprise doing one essential job, is it not possible that the theological schools in the mission field can pool their resources for the essential tools?

The above observation may be applied to virtually all of the libraries in the theological schools in Africa, Asia and Latin America. The following statements and quotations have been obtained from various sources and demonstrate the accuracy of this observation.

1. *Africa*

The Bishop Tucker College at Mukono in Uganda has a fairly good library of approximately 5,000 volumes. On the other hand, the typical seminary library in Africa (including the personal collections of the faculty members) probably has an average of only 1,000 books in it. Mimeographed lecture notes are said to be the best substitute, but these are decidedly inadequate.

In Nigeria, Trinity College at Umuahia (according to Dean Frost) "needs a much larger library appropriation." The library at Melville Hall (now part of Immanuel College) in Ibadan is described by Bishop Howells as "very poor" and contains only about 500 books. Two or three theological magazines are received. By contrast the theological section in the library at the University College, Ibadan, is said to have an excellent collection of books by African standards: this is because the government contributes £1,000 annually for their purchase.

Similarly in Ghana the collection of books on theological topics in the library at the University College, Achimota, for the use of its Department of Divinity is better than the libraries of any Protestant seminary in that country. Governments not only have more funds to spend on education than do missionary societies, but it would also appear that they have a keener appreciation of the role of the library in the educational process. On the other hand it is also true in Ghana (e.g., at Trinity College in Kumasi) that the local denominations contribute books to the theological students for their own personal use while in seminary and afterwards in their pastorates.

The 1954 and 1956 catalogues of Cuttington College state that the college library contains about 8,000 volumes on all subjects. The College ultimately hopes to have a capacity of 25,000 volumes when a new wing for the library is completed. It is anticipated that approximately 1,000 volumes will be added each year. Nearly 70 periodicals are currently being received. The library has a growing collection of Africana and standard reference works. "To facilitate the work of seminarians special emphasis has been placed upon the collection of theological material. . . . The total cost for tuition, room and board is $120 for each school year. The cost (to each student) of books and other supplies varies from about $15 to $40. Students who have to conserve their money may keep down the expenses of books by borrowing books from their friends."

At the Fourah Bay College in Freetown the library contains approximately 11,000 volumes on all subjects. The Dager Biblical Seminary in the Cameroons is said to have "a small library building" which is "almost empty of books."

The library at the Pastors School at Kimpese in the Belgian Congo is said to be one of the weakest in all of the seminaries in Africa. Perhaps "nonexistent" might be a better term to describe it. It is reported to consist of one bookcase (about six feet high) containing four shelves (each about three feet wide) on which are kept a collection of antiquated books, many of which tend to fall apart when taken off the shelves. A half dozen or so recently published texts in French have been purchased, but it would appear that the current acquisition program of the smaller Pastors School at Bolenge is considerably larger than the one at Kimpese.

The report of the IMC team which surveyed the Protestant ministry in Madagascar in the fall of 1956 contains the following comments concerning the condition of the libraries in the seven theological schools on the island:

1. *Ambatomanga:* The library, partly destroyed during the events of 1947, is now almost re-stocked, especially with French books . . . its stock of Malagasy books might well

be improved; it might also offer greater facilities for consulting books by including a reading or study room. . . .

2. *Arivonimamo:* The equipment and facilities for private study (library) are certainly inferior to what they might be, especially in theological literature in French, which comprises a few Christian biographies.

3. *Ambohipotsy:* The students are able to use a good library, well stocked with English theological books, though the number of French books is rather meagre.

4. *Imerimandroso:* . . . the students' library is thinly stocked and in very poor shape. . . .

5. *Fianarantsoa:* The library, containing a good number of out-of-date English books, ought to be completely reorganized, classified and considerably improved.

6. *Ivory Theological College:* The French section of the library ought also to be developed alongside the works in English and German, of which the students can only make a very limited use. If the plan to build a new library, in a special building with reading rooms, is carried out in the near future with the help of the American Missions, we hope this comment will not be forgotten.

7. *St. Paul's College:* . . . although it is not very extensive, (the library) is one of those containing (the) most theological books in Malagasy. . . .

The IMC Survey team noted that in one of the seven theological schools in Madagascar, some Roman Catholic books were being used as textbooks even though suitable Protestant books were available. The team's report included within its comments and recommendations the following statement: "The creation of a true theological library ought to be one of the first concerns of those in charge of schools for training pastors. They should endeavour: (a) to acquire an adequate number of books in Malagasy, French, and in some cases, English. People seem only too ready to make do with a minimum stock of out-of-date books, when excellent recent works are readily available; (b) to classify these books, keep them in a good state of repair and house them properly. In many places, books are not kept under cover and are spoilt all too soon. One or more students might be made responsible, provided they are given a clear method to follow."

During his visit to Madagascar in the fall of 1956, Dr. Charles W. Ranson noted the contrast which exists between the libraries of the Protestant institutions and the library of the one Jesuit seminary on that island: "The large and beautifully kept (Jesuit seminary) library presents a marked contrast to all the libraries which were seen in non-Roman institutions. This is the only theological library we have seen in Madagascar which could compare with an average college library in the West. I was stirred to envy on behalf of the institutions which are our immediate concern. . . . There was an impressively wide range of periodicals both in the (Jesuits') Staff and Student Common Rooms. . . . Here (in the students' rooms) one noticed again the large number of books." The total number of books in the Jesuit seminary library is reported to be over 10,000 volumes.

Little information is readily available concerning the condition of the libraries in the Protestant theological schools in Southern Africa. It would seem to be fair to assume, with respect to those in the Union of South Africa, that (1) the libraries available for use by the white students being trained by the various Dutch Reformed Churches are probably excellent by African standards, and (2) the opposite is the case in the seminaries training Bantu students.

Indeed (except in the case of the Madagascar report) so little mention is made in the various surveys of Protestant theological education in Africa concerning the libraries maintained by the seminaries, it seems likely that they are generally either so small in size or so seldom used as not to be of much importance in the daily life of the students. A part of the reason accounting for this situation is the low academic level of the students in most of the schools. On the other hand this level is now rising, and a first step in improving the poorer libraries would be to increase their purchases of simpler theological texts and their subscriptions to suitable periodicals.

2. *Middle East*

The library of the Near East School of Theology, according to the report of the survey team which visited the seminary on behalf of the Presbyterian USA board in 1957, "contains more than 21,000 volumes, mostly in the English and Arabic languages. Of special note are old Arabic manuscripts, and an extensive Islamic section." Books in Turkish, Syriac, Armenian and Aramaic are included, and approximately 800 new volumes are being added each year. Periodicals are available in English, Arabic and Armenian, and the School's reference room is open daily during the school year for general use. The seminary students also have the privilege of using the library of the American University of Beirut which contains over 50,000 volumes on all subjects, the majority of which are in English, Arabic and French. The survey team recommended that the Near East School of Theology obtain the services of a full-time trained librarian or, if this should prove to be impracticable, that a member of the faculty be placed in charge of the library. There is also a considerable need for more space in the library, both for books and for places where the students may carry on their studies.

3. *Southern Asia*

India: The Serampore College library in 1954 had a total of approximately 25,000 books. This is one of the largest collections possessed by any of the Protestant seminaries in Africa, Asia or Latin America. However, the conditions in which these books are housed have been so poor that in the fall of 1956 the Board of Founders of the Nanking Theological Seminary was considering the possibility of making a special grant to Serampore to improve this situation, even though India is outside the Southeastern Asian area with which the Board has been especially concerned.

The 1956–57 yearbook of the United Theological College at Bangalore comments as follows concerning the library of this institution as of the year 1955–56:

> During the year under review we have acquired many new books for the library. Our budget, however, does not permit us to get all the important books we would like to add to the library. There are many gaps in each section and the library is far from adequate for studies beyond the B.D. standard.
>
> The library needs more attention than it gets now. Mere physical extension of the library is not enough. For more efficient organization of the library we need a trained librarian and adequate assistance. Even much smaller colleges have a larger library staff. Here a member of the Faculty has had to take care of the library with the help of a student librarian. The result is that we have not been able so far to provide for a detailed subject catalogue of the books. If the library is to become more useful for advanced students, we should take immediate steps to provide for adequate library staff.

According to the Principal of the United Theological College, Dr. J. Russell Chandran, the library of this institution contains approximately 15,000 volumes and thus is one of the most extensive possessed by any Protestant seminary in Asia. Dr. Chandran considers that it has fairly adequate holdings for work at the Master of Theology level in the fields of Old and New Testament and in theology, but that it is inadequate in the field of church history, and in the history and philosophy of religion. Two mission boards have deposited their archives in this library, but owing to the lack of staff personnel this material has not as yet been catalogued. The acquisition budget of the UTC library is approximately $250 a year. About a dozen of the leading European and American periodicals are subscribed to, but Dr. Chandran points to the lack of significant Indian journals describing the noteworthy cultural and religious developments in India.

The library at Leonard Theological College numbered 15,000 books in 1956 (some 2,000 more than in 1945). A librarian and a full-time assistant are employed, the latter having been engaged "for many months" in the task (begun in 1949) of recataloguing the books. In 1950 the Brenton T. Badley Memorial Historical Library was moved from Bombay to Jabalpur to be incorporated as a section of the library at Leonard, which is now the central depository for the archives of Methodism in India.

When the Gurukul Theological College was founded by the Lutherans at Madras in 1953, it was necessary to create its library *de novo*. In April 1955 the Principal, Dr. P. David, sent to all the Lutheran seminaries in the United States a list of 650 books, many of them out of print, which his faculty believed its library should have. Dr. David hoped duplicate copies of these might be sent to Gurukul from America. At present the Gurukul library is stated to have about 1,000 volumes, but the quality of these holdings is not specified.

At the North India Union Theological College at Saharanpur a visitor has commented: ". . . The theological library had many good basic theological books though many of them were in bad condition, mildewed or worm-eaten." A somewhat contrary appraisal was expressed in the 1957 report of a committee which visited the schools awarding the L.Th. degree in India and which inspected the Saharanpur library: "The library has a good room. . . . The books are well kept. The reading desks, lights and fans are comfortable. There are 3,000 English books. An effort is made to secure all available Christian literature in Hindi and Urdu. Urdu and Hindi grammars and dictionaries are in the library. There is a lack of classical books in Urdu and Hindi."

The same committee reported as follows concerning the library of the Union Theological Seminary at Bareilly: "The library is reported to contain about 1,000 Hindi, 1,500 Urdu and 5,000 English volumes. Included are large numbers of duplicate (and even triplicate) copies of a considerable number of books that would be of interest for historical research rather than for the ordinary work of the Seminary. . . . We are of the opinion that the usefulness of the library would be greatly enhanced if it were recatalogued and a card index provided which would give ready information on the books available under author, title and subject."

The committee considered that the library of the Union Theological College at Indore (containing 3,443 volumes in English and Hindi) was "well organized and is fairly adequate for L.Th. needs."

A 1958 report of the National Christian Council of India notes that the acquisition budgets of the libraries of the Tamilnad Theological College at Tirumaraiyur and the Tamil Evangelical Lutheran Seminary at Tranquebar each amount to approximately $100 a year.

The Luthergiri Theological Seminary at Rajahmundri reports it has a library of 6,500 volumes. This school is said to be very much in need of "solid" theological literature written in the vernacular.

In the 1954 handbook of the Serampore Senate, each of the 19 members of the Senate contributed descriptions of their own facilities. The comment contributed by the Lutheran Theological College at Ranchi concerning its library is wistful, but doubtless an accurate one: "There is a library, but it is rather poor."

In the same handbook the comment furnished by the Basel Evangelical Mission Theological Seminary at Mangalore is perhaps even more revealing: "(Our) library is fairly adequate and in recent years several new volumes in biblical studies have been added."

The survey entitled *After Ten Years—A Report on Theological Education in India* which Professor M. H. Harrison prepared for the Board of Theological Education of the National Christian Council of India in 1957 states:

. . . The existing libraries are in a great many cases disappointing. Particularly in view of the fact that most of the theological schools are teaching through the medium of the regional language, it was surprising to see what a poor assortment of books in the language of the area their libraries contained, usually little more than a shelf or two of meagre pamphlets. It is doubtless true that theological literature in the regional languages adequate for teaching purposes does not yet exist, but one would have expected to find at least the tools for systematic study, grammars, dictionaries, editions of the classics of the language, etc. It was quite clear that in many cases the majority of the students were unable to make effective use of more difficult books in English, and one would have expected to find that English books would be chosen with the ability of students to make use of them in mind. New books were frequently selected with a view rather to the needs of the staff. Most libraries are attempting to introduce the Dewey Decimal system of library classification, but many are thus far rather half-hearted in the use of it. It would be well if all libraries, even in small institutions, which employ this system would purchase the necessary tools for its use, viz. Dewey's Decimal Classification in the latest edition, and the Cutter-Sanborn table of author numbers. These tools are expensive, but once purchased make possible the accurate classification of a library even where no trained librarian is available.

Among the recommendations in the Harrison report were the following three:

1. That in the larger theological libraries provision be made for the services of a trained librarian.
2. That libraries be made more useful in the arrangement of books on the shelves by separating materials of merely historic interest from books which it may be expected that students will normally use. Further, that wherever possible adequate reading rooms and current periodical literature be provided.
3. That a system of inter-library exchanges be instituted so that books may be located where they will be of greatest service.

Finally one might cite the succinct remark made by Dr. Luther Gotwald, Executive Secretary of the DFM (and who was previously for many years a missionary in India): "In India the (seminary) libraries have always been a second thought."

Pakistan: According to the Principal of the Gujranwala Theological Seminary in Pakistan, Dr. James D. Brown, its "library expansion has been greatly limited because of lack of space. With our new building, this will no longer be a limiting factor, and we will need to expand. . . ."

4. *Southeast Asia*

Except where otherwise noted, the following comments in quotations concerning the libraries of the theological schools in Southeast Asia (and Formosa) were all made by Dr. C. Stanley Smith in various reports he made to the Board of Founders of the Nanking Theological Seminary in the period 1952–57. Those concerning the libraries of Indonesian seminaries were made by him as a result of his visit to that country in the summer of 1956.

Burma Baptist Divinity School: "The library was looted very badly either at this time (i.e., the Karen revolution in 1951–52), or during the Japanese occupation." The School reports it recently obtained the "religion" section of the library of the former Baptist-supported Judson College which was nationalized by the Burmese Government after World War II.

At the McGilvary Seminary in Chiengmai, Thailand, the library has been assisted with grants from the Board of Founders. One result is that it is outgrowing its present quarters and needs to be moved to a more suitable location.

The library of Trinity Theological College in Singapore "though far from being adequate for a first-class theological college is still one of the best in Southeast Asia, (and) has most of its books in English—some 2,000 out of its 2,500 or so volumes. . . . While I was principal . . . I had not dared to put new theological books, and especially expensive reference books, on the open shelves of what was called the library because with five unguarded doors the books could very easily disappear, especially as there was no one in charge during a good part of the day."

In 1956 the Nommensen University Theological Faculty listed its future needs, other than for property, for the next five years in the following order of priority: library books, first; audio-visual equipment, second; and maps and charts for classroom use, third.

The library at the Djakarta Theological College contains approximately 15,000 books and subscribes to a dozen periodicals from Europe and the United States. "It was a joy to visit the new library of the STT in Jakarta; to find there a growing collection of good books covering the main subjects of the theological curriculum properly classified and catalogued with a faculty member in charge." A somewhat contrasting view is expressed by Dean Pope who found on a recent visit to this library that it was lacking in books in some fields such as social ethics and pastoral counseling. The former Rector of the School, Dr. Peter Latuihamallo, is also concerned by the need to augment its holdings of standard reference works.

At the Theological School Balewijoto in Malang, "Dr. Akkeren's concern was not so much for property improvement as for some help in building up the library and in scholarships."

At the Bandjermasin Theological School in Borneo

the library was very easy to inspect as it consisted of one book case about $3\frac{1}{2}'$ x 6' in size. When I went to inspect it I found it locked, but a key was procured. The case was largely occupied with books in German or Dutch. There were few, if any, books in English and also very few in Indonesian. I should say that for all practical purposes a theological library hardly existed in this school. Since the Basel Mission has, on the whole, been rather generous in the support of the school, it would seem that the lack of library books does not arise from a lack of funds. It probably arises from the lack of an adequate library room. . . . There is a rather general feeling in Indonesia that students . . . should receive most of their knowledge through lectures and dictation by the teachers and that the students are unable to do any independent reading or thinking during their course.

At the Union Theological School, Makassar,

I was interested in the lack of an adequate library . . . in 1955 and recommended a grant of $500 to be used . . . largely for theological books in English . . . (which would be) not too difficult for students who were beginning their English education. . . . I was interested in visiting the library and to see what use had been made of the funds granted. The library is located in one of the student dormitory rooms. It is opened only one day a week for the loan of books and there are no provisions for the students to study in this room. There were many new books in Dutch, but I could find only a few new acquisitions in English.

The library at the Ambon Theological School "consists of part of a room containing two bookcases about 5' x 6' each. These two cases contain theological books largely in Dutch and German. There are very very few books in English and if anything even less in Indonesian. When I visited the library I found a bed in the other part of the room divided by the two book cases. . . . There seemed to be some dispute as to how much time the library was opened. The student in charge . . . said that the library was opened only one day a week. . . . One of the teachers . . . said that the library was open every day. . . ."

Indonesia—General Comments:

One of the most distressing things about my visit . . . was the lack of anything approaching an adequate library. How these theological schools can operate with such poor library facilities is a question I cannot answer. It means, I think, that the work in the school is purely one of an indoctrination, the student receiving all of his information through one professor with little or no opportunity or requirement to do any individual study or reading to get different points of view.

The librarian is all too often a member of the faculty whose full time is given to his work of teaching or administration so that he has to delegate his library responsibility to a student. Usually both faculty member and student are without any special knowledge of library science in its most elementary form.

In the procurement of new books there is a general lack of organization in obtaining the suggestions of members of the faculty as to books which should be purchased. Not only the ordering of the books, but the selection of them is left in the hands of one person, often the rector, who sometimes has to add the work of librarian to his already overburdened schedule of responsibilities. In many cases the budgets of the schools are so low that nothing, or little, can be devoted to building up a library. Fortunately, there is a growing improvement in this respect.

The idea of a library as a place not only where books may be housed but also a place where students may study and browse about among a collection of books so that he may become familiar with their general nature and content and be stimulated to read more generally seems to be foreign to most of the theological schools of Indonesia. Something should be done to give the library a more recognized place in theological education even in the secondary level of theological schools.

Some would say that the students are too immature and are untrained to do any private study in a library; others would add that proper text-books are so scarce that the teacher has to give the students all the information he will receive. While these things are undoubtedly true, yet they should be considered as obstacles to be overcome rather than conditions to be accepted as incurable or to be passively borne.

If students are to be able to make use of better library facilities, then the number of hours spent in the class-room listening to lectures of which they take notes, must be shortened. A student cannot attend classes for twenty-five or thirty periods a week and have any time or strength left for adequate preparation of his lessons, not to speak of time for reading and individual pursuit of subjects of intellectual interest in a library.

Students have said to me, not infrequently, during my recent visits that they wanted to do more reading but there were neither the books to read nor the time to read them. Might it not be possible that if the faculty members of these schools had fewer hours of preparation to make each day and fewer hours to teach each week, that they might be able to give some time, or more time, to the production of theological literature in the form of text-books, reference books, commentaries or even homiletical material than is now possible.

The faculty of Trinity College (in Singapore) has . . . decided to decrease the number of class-room hours in the interest of more time for individual work in the library and in the reading of reference material. It is my conviction that something like this will have to be done in most of the schools in Indonesia if they are to give more than simple indoctrination courses and attempt the real problem of education in the basic meaning of that word.

Oceania: The Secretary of the Anglican Mission in Melanesia writes as follows concerning the library at St. Peter's Theological College in Siota (Solomon Islands): "We have no funds for the purchasing of books for the students, apart from what can be allocated from the annual quota. We are anxious to raise this standard, so must find some funds from somewhere to do this."

The English Congregationalists report that "one serious need" of the Malua College in the Samoan Islands is the provision of "better library facilities"; and that the library of the Takamoa College at Rarotonga in the Cook Islands "is in serious need of improvement."

The Secretary of the Anglican Mission in New Guinea comments as follows concerning the library at Newton College in Dogura: "We have no special funds for the maintenance of Newton College, though the Principal keeps fowls and sells eggs and fowls for the upkeep of the College Library and the purchase of necessary new theological works."

Union Theological Seminary, Manila: The use of English as the medium of instruction in the Philippines affords a number of advantages, particularly with respect to the availability of textbooks and theological literature. The UTS "has a good library of some 9,500 volumes, almost all in English. . . . The budget item for the library in 1950–51 was US$2,125, or about $\frac{1}{10}$th of the whole Seminary budget. . . . The amount available for books and magazines is considerably larger than that available in the budgets of most of the theological schools of Southeast Asia."

By 1955 the UTS library reported a total of 11,233 books on hand. However, according to the report of the Sub-Committee on Evaluation of the Planning Committee of the Seminary's own Board of Trustees, the library as of May 31, 1956, had only 40 books relating to the Roman Catholic Church and 20 books relating to Protestant churches; in the fiscal year ended that date only $272 was spent for books and magazines; and in the library itself "there are only 24 chairs. . . . The library roof leaks very badly. Some books are in danger of getting wet. . . . More adequate space is needed. An average of 90 students use the library every day. . . . Important Roman Catholic books and literature must be acquired."

Silliman University College of Theology, Dumaguete: "The library of the College of Theology . . . has a good collection of some basic books for theological education but it badly needs to be brought up to date. There have not been many new accessions for some time."

Central Philippines University, College of Theology, Iloilo: The American Baptists report that this University's library "grew from nothing at the close of the war (no buildings, records or books) to a library of 32,000 bound volumes, of which 1,421 were added in 1955." Of the total number approximately 5,000 were classified as "religious."

Laoag College of Theology, Ilocos Province: This "library is part of the Northern Christian College library but the theological section is closed off and the door is usually locked. The Northern Christian College library is said to have a trained librarian in charge, and of its 9,000 books, 1,000 are said to be on theological subjects."

The Rotz report comments that the seminaries in the Philippines "need to . . . have their libraries housed more usefully, and the out-of-date and discarded books from the libraries of deceased and retired American pastors evaluated and replaced with more usable and up-to-date material. . . ." The author of that report also notes that a recent survey of approximately 335 Filipino ordained ministers disclosed the small number of books personally owned by them which would be of use professionally to them in their work. This information is summarized in Table 73.

These figures suggest the use which ordained ministers in the Philippines and elsewhere might (or should) make of the circulating departments of seminary libraries, provided the latter could be adequately stocked with suitable theological works. The Rotz report comments on this possibility as follows: "One of the most desolate conditions in the Philippine Church is the lack of books. Some will say this drives men to their Bibles—but actually it drives them into monotonous

TABLE 73.   SIZE OF PERSONAL LIBRARIES OF FILIPINO MINISTERS (1952)

Size of Personal Libraries		Purchases in Previous Year	
Number of Books	Percentage of Ministers	Number of Books	Percentage of Ministers
0	18	0	31
Less than 10	11	1	17
10–24	21	2	22
25–99	35	3 or more	30
100 or more	15		100
	100		

expression and the repetition of erroneous exegesis. . . . Loan libraries can never meet the problem of the lack of books, but they can help in the present situation."

5. East Asia

Japan: The supply of library books and texts is somewhat better in Japan than elsewhere, due largely to the comparatively widespread use of English and to the number of theological works which have been translated into Japanese.

The Union Theological Seminary in Tokyo has a comparatively large library of some 30,000 volumes, principally in English, German and Japanese, which was saved from the bombing and burning of World War II.

The Japan Lutheran Theological Seminary and the Central Theological College each have approximately 5,000 volumes in their libraries. A report of the latter seminary considers its collection is "far removed from the minimum of 35–40,000 volumes" which is required. "A gift we treasure greatly is the microfilming reader given by the Missionary Society of the General Theological Seminary in New York."

The library of the Doshisha University Theological School is said to be fairly strong, with about half of its books written in Japanese and the balance in various European languages. On the other hand, the Dean of the School reports as follows:

Doshisha is spread over campuses in three entirely different locations, miles apart. For the Graduate School, eight colleges and seven high schools there is one central library. . . . The School of Theology has its own library of 20,240 items. Previous to the war, during the conflict, and in postwar years the library acquisitions have fallen far behind the expected rate of increase, so that the overall coverage is entirely inadequate for present-day theological study, let alone scholarly research by the faculty. The library classification system is out of date and needs to be modernized. A trained librarian should be hired for a period of time in order to reclassify the entire stock, with the aid of a clerical staff.

At Kwansei Gakuin the university library "contains about 105,000 books (on all subjects), 40% of which are in English or other foreign languages." Thus this seminary probably has larger library resources on which to draw than does the UTS in Tokyo.

To the Kanto Gakuin University Library the American Baptists contributed $60,000 in 1956 for a new building. The University in its own newspaper states: "Our next effort must be directed toward collecting good books, especially religious ones because we lost more than 50,000 books, including very rare old books on Christianity in Japan, in the air raid" (i.e., May 29, 1945, on Yokohama).

The Southern Baptists report that the library of the Theological Department in Seinan Gakuin University in Fukuoka contains approximately 12,000 volumes and that this is "believed to be one of the best theological libraries in Japan."

Dr. Harold A. Bosley, whose comments on Japanese theological schools were cited earlier, reports the following: "The Library is easily and tragically the weakest point in the entire program of theological education in (Japan). . . ."

Korea: The Theological Seminary of the Presbyterian Church in Korea has requested the Presbyterians USA to contribute funds for the construction of a new library on its campus.

The Methodist Theological Seminary at Seoul reports a need for 20,000 books in order to meet the standards of an "accredited seminary" in Korea. This school also has plans for a new library. When it was visited in 1955 by Dr. Bosley, he reported: "*Inadequate Library.* Basic books are needed. . . . Translations are needed. . . . I am unaware of a recognition of either of these needs in the present allocation of funds to the Seminary in Seoul. . . ."

Formosa: The Taiwan Theological College (according to Dr. C. S. Smith) has a "library containing some good basic theological literature but it is certainly not up to date. It has about 1,000 books in English, two to three thousand in Japanese and about one hundred in Chinese. . . ."

At the Tainan Theological College "the library formerly contained some ten thousand volumes in prewar days but now only about 1,200 are left. Many of these are in Japanese. . . ."

Dr. C. Stanley Smith also comments that, since the writing of the Anderson-Smith report six years ago in 1952, there has been no significant improvement in the condition of the libraries of the seminaries in Southeast and East Asia.

6. *Latin America*

Union Theological Seminary, Matanzas: The library of this Seminary has a collection of about 13,000 books, the majority of which are not in Spanish. It is also said to be the only school in the Caribbean which has a full-time trained librarian.

Evangelical Seminary of Puerto Rico: The Stockwell report states:

The Librarian . . . stated that there are about 7,000 volumes in the library, although the serial numbers only run to 5,500. . . . Many of the volumes are antiquated and well-nigh worthless. The majority of the volumes are so badly injured by bookworms or mold that they are of little use. The reserve books which are most frequently called for, and the newer acquisitions, are kept in the personal office of the librarian but are accessible to the students during much of the day. The purchases of new books for 1953–54 amounted to less than $60.00. There were a few magazine subscriptions in addition. It is explained that few books are purchased because there is no satisfactory place to stack them without danger of bookworms. One professor says that he uses more or less personal funds to purchase needed magazines because there is no money for them in the regular budget. . . . A hasty examination of the card catalogue revealed manifest deficiencies, repetitions, etc., with no extensive use of subject headings, cross references, etc. Neither Professor Cardona nor the university student who helps him in the library has had any technical library training nor is familiar with the basic principles of library science.

In the little booklet by W. A. Rush, *Financing Church Schools, Colleges and Universities,* put out by the Department of Public Relations and Finance of the Board of Education of the Methodist Church, expenditures by function for colleges run: Instruction 53%, Administration 25%, Operation and Maintenance 17%, Library 4% and Misc. 1%. . . . The $20,000 budget of the (Evangelical) Seminary (of Puerto Rico) appears to give more than 65% to Instruction, (and) about five-tenths of a percent to Library (expenses). . . . *It is Recommended* that immediate physical care be given to the books to preserve them if possible (sic). It is recommended further that a skilled librarian be enlisted to counsel the Seminary until the entire classification of the books is brought into proper order.

With the improvement which took place in the condition of the Evangelical Seminary in 1957–58, provision was made for a librarian on sabbatical leave from the United States to visit this school's library and advise on the steps which should be taken to reorganize it. The Seminary's newly completed central administration building also contains adequate stack facilities, etc.

Moravian Theological School, Surinam: This School reports it has a total of 250 books in its library. "In addition, there is a Hindustani Mission Library (nearby, with) about 400 books and booklets in Dutch and Hindi."

Presbyterian Seminary of the North, Recife: In 1958 the Dean reported that a full-time librarian was endeavoring to "organize, classify, enlarge and modernize" the Seminary's collection of 5,000 volumes.

Presbyterian Theological Seminary of Campinas: The library of this school, according to Dean Shaull, contains a total of approximately 15,000 volumes, with up to 1,000 books having been added to it annually during the past few years. Approximately 25 theological periodicals are subscribed to. Recently the Campinas library has been endeavoring to obtain basic works in English in view of the paucity of available theological literature written in Portuguese. Writing in 1958, the President of the Seminary commented: "We have no full-time librarian and receive less than $100 annually from the National (Presbyterian) Church for the purchase of books, and an equal amount for maintenance. Most new books are received as gifts from authors and friends."

Independent Presbyterian Seminary of São Paulo: This Seminary's library is said to contain approximately 2,000 volumes, most of which are out of date.

Buenos Aires: The Union Theological Seminary has a library of approximately 18,000 volumes, thus making it the largest seminary library in Latin America. The quality of these books is said to be excellent. Included among them is the celebrated Lopez Collection of 700 volumes consisting essentially of first editions and reprints of works by 16th century Spanish reformers. The Seminary also issues two quarterly publications.

The Lutheran World Federation has set aside $15,000 for the books and furnishings at the new Lutheran Seminary in this City.

Finally, the International Baptist Seminary which the Southern Baptists recently opened in Buenos Aires is reported to have a collection of 8,000 volumes in its library.

7. Over-all

The libraries in the theological schools in the younger church areas are without doubt one of the weakest features of these seminaries. It would appear that the typical seminary overseas has between 2,000 and 3,000 volumes on its shelves. Assuming a rather generous average of 2,500 volumes per library, this would mean a total of 505,000 volumes for the collections of the 202 seminaries. The library of

TABLE 74. COMPARISON OF THEOLOGICAL SCHOOL LIBRARIES IN THE USA AND UNDERDEVELOPED COUNTRIES (1952–58)

	USA	Underdeveloped Countries
Total number of books in libraries	5,900,000	505,000
Average per seminary	55,000	2,500
Average per ordinand student	400	81

the Union Theological Seminary in New York City alone has 250,000 volumes (exclusive of 100,000 pamphlets and the 100,000 books and pamphlets of the Missionary Research Library). Table 74 presents a comparison of the typical seminary library overseas with its counterpart in the United States among the 108 accredited and associated members of the American Association of Theological Schools (as of 1952–53).

Thus the average seminary library in the United States has a collection which is 22 times the size of the collection in the typical seminary library in Africa, Asia and Latin America. If this comparison should seem unfair, it is of interest to note in Table 75 the number of volumes which (according to Father Paul Dezza, S.J.) are in the libraries of half-a-dozen Roman Catholic major seminaries and scholasticates in Africa, Asia and Latin America. These institutions probably have larger libraries than the typical Roman Catholic seminary in those areas has; but even after allowing for this factor, the comparison speaks for itself.

TABLE 75.   SIZE OF LIBRARIES IN SOME ROMAN CATHOLIC MAJOR SEMINARIES AND SCHOLASTICATES IN AFRICA, ASIA AND LATIN AMERICA (1957)

Name	Place	Country	Number of Volumes	Administration
Africa				
St. Peter's Regional Seminary	Tananarive	Madagascar	10,000[a]	Jesuits
Asia				
St. Mary's Theological College	Kurseong	India	50,000	Jesuits
Sacred Heart College	Shembaganur	India	50,000	Jesuits
Latin America				
Colégio Máximo[b]	São Leopoldo	Brazil	75,000	Jesuits
Saint Toribio	Lima	Peru	17,000	Holy Spirit Fathers[c]
Metropolitan Seminary	Buenos Aires	Argentina	25,000	Jesuits
St. Joseph's College	San Miguel	Argentina	60,000	Jesuits

NOTES: [a] As reported earlier in this chapter by the IMC.
[b] "Christ the King."
[c] Of Mexico.

The comments cited above on the libraries of Protestant theological schools relate almost entirely to the quantity of books in their collections and their physical condition. Very few of these appraisals relate to the quality of the libraries, i.e., the proportion of books that have recently been acquired, the adequacy of available encyclopaediae and reference works, and whether or not the collections are well balanced in the various theological fields. It seems likely that in the case of all but a handful of seminaries their libraries are even more deficient qualitatively than they are quantitatively.

B. The Need for Texts in the Vernaculars

The preceding section dealt with the quantitative and qualitative deficiencies of the seminary libraries. A further deficiency is the lack of texts written in the vernaculars which students in the underdeveloped countries can profitably use in their classroom studies. One of the greatest hindrances to the effective training of both ordinands and church workers in a number of countries is the necessity for conducting some or all of their courses in English or some other language which is foreign to them. The following comments made from different areas of the world illustrate this point.

Africa: At the Dager Biblical Seminary the Presbyterians USA are required to spend much time teaching students English solely so that they may read the theological literature. At the Pastors School at Kimpese in the Belgian Congo English is sometimes taught as a third language inasmuch as French is the official second language. If an adequate number of texts were available in French and

Portuguese, it would not be necessary to teach English to seminarians in Latin Africa. The Methodists report that because of language difficulties some seminarians from Portuguese East and West Africa are sent to the Theological Seminary of the Methodist Church at São Paulo in Brazil for their theological training.

In Madagascar the teaching at the seven theological schools is primarily in the local language of the island, Malagasy, and secondarily in French. However, because of the paucity of suitable theological texts written in either Malagasy or French, it has even been thought desirable that some students should be taught the English language as well. A better plan, in the view of others, would be to produce new theological texts in Malagasy or reprint those which have previously been written in that language.

Some indication of the potential which exists for reprinting theological texts already produced in Malagasy is mentioned by Dr. Fridtjov Birkeli:

> In the 1880s there was a real golden age in the production of theological literature in Malagasy. It is amazing to see what they were able to write in all the disciplines in that early period. On the other hand, it is discouraging to note how little has been accomplished along that line since then. One of the reasons is certainly that almost all the schools are understaffed: there has been no time for writing. The libraries are in general incomplete, though some of them contain valuable old books in Malagasy, such as Old and New Testament commentaries, church history, practical theology and even two large volumes of dogmatics. No country, I believe, in Africa or Asia has such a rich theological literature in the vernacular as had Madagascar.

At the Anglican College of Resurrection at Johannesburg virtually all of the instruction is first written on the blackboards and then laboriously copied by the students. Thus the lack of texts results in a mechanical, stereotyped teaching process.

A missionary of the Church of Sweden Mission at Masingo, Southern Rhodesia, writes: "If missions support the more or less exclusive use of a non-African language in this training, the consequence must be that the younger churches . . . will either be retarded in their growth, and will for a long time remain 'young,' or that they will remain foreign to the people concerned."

At the seminary which they recently established in Gwelo in Southern Rhodesia the Southern Baptists encountered a need for texts in the vernacular. They report: "Because some of the first students knew only the African language, the curriculum was divided into two groups: a three-year course with subjects based on text books and library study for the English-speaking students; and a two-year limited course in the vernacular for the others." It was anticipated that by 1958 all of the approximately 30 students would be enrolled in the three-year course taught in English.

Concerning the shortage in Southern Africa of suitable textbooks written in any language, the comment of Part III of the IMC African Survey was as follows: "We confine ourselves to repeating what has been said a hundred times before, namely, that the need for suitable theological text-books is desperate. . . . Despite the service which the International Committee on Christian Literature for Africa tries to render as a clearing-house, we were given the impression that there is very little interchange of information and experience between the Colleges regarding such text-books as are being used and their proved value or otherwise."

For the whole of Africa south of the Sahara there is a need for (1) simple theological texts in the vernaculars, and (2) more advanced texts in English and French which in their style and content will be both suitably oriented and free from Western preconceptions.

Southern Asia: In 1950 a prominent Indian, Mr. V. Jothipakiam of the Church of South India wrote: "The time has now come for provincial languages to take their proper place; and to carry forward education and theological training in them, every incentive should be offered so that all the subjects in theological colleges hitherto taught in English may be taught in the mother tongue. This does not mean that English is to be abandoned."

At the North India Union Theological College at Saharanpur, a visitor commented that the "most distressing" feature of the seminary was the lack of practically any theological literature in Urdu, which is the vernacular used there, and that this lack impressed him as "astonishing."

The United Theological College of Western India at Poona has been endeavoring to produce texts in Marathi, the language used in that area. At first the teachers had to dictate notes to the students as satisfactory texts were not available. But since 1948 the Principal, Dr. J. Reid Graham, has headed an effort to prepare mimeographed notes; now all the courses are so prepared. This has helped raise the level of discussion by giving adequate time for class discussion. It is planned to have these mimeographed notes printed and made available for more widespread use.

The Board of Directors of the Gujranwala Theological Seminary and the West Pakistan Christian Council sponsored a conference at Gujranwala on theological education in 1955, one of the findings of which was: "The Conference noted the great lack of suitable textbooks in Urdu." The Principal of Gujranwala Seminary writes that "in the absence of adequate text-book material, especially in Urdu, we have been mimeographing a considerable amount of material, but our present cheap machine is quite inadequate to meet the need. We ought to have a new Gestetner, but cannot get one out of our present budget."

The 1957 Harrison report, *After Ten Years* (previously cited), comments as follows on the losses in instruction time which occur as a result of the absence of suitable texts in the vernacular:

One reason which accounts for the serious overcrowding of the timetable in many institutions is the practice of using the lecture hours for the dictation of notes which are taken down by students word for word. This is a very time-consuming process, and there is every danger where it is employed that theological study will degenerate into the mere memorization of incompletely understood material. Doubtless the reason for this situation is that theological literature in the regional languages is insufficiently available and that many students can make only ineffective use of English books. Unfortunately, typewriters adapted to duplicating material in Indian scripts are rare, and the printing of notes is often regarded as too expensive.

In the case of a seminary whose students speak different local languages, e.g., Urdu and Hindi, the problem of obtaining suitable texts is even more acute. In 1957 a commission studying the Indian seminaries awarding L.Th. degrees commented as follows concerning their visit to the Union Theological Seminary at Bareilly:

Bareilly is listed as a "Hindi Area" Seminary, but only two of the five full-time members of the staff are fully competent in the Hindi language, and nearly half of the students have Urdu as their mother tongue and know little Hindi. There is thus a difficult problem both as to classroom procedure and as to use of textbooks. Teaching has to be done in "Hindustani" rather than in Hindi and textbooks in Hindi are of no use to nearly half the students. If full use were to be made of textbooks by the present student body, there would need to be identical texts in Hindi and in Urdu. It is probable that ten years hence, perhaps sooner, practically all students will be Hindi-speaking and this problem will then have disappeared. . . . There is a serious shortage of theological textbooks in Hindi, but we feel that maximum use is not being made of those that are available. . . . The statement was made to us that existing texts in Hindi are deficient in many respects: it seems to us better to use texts that may not be in every respect all that is desired than to go on dictating notes to students. . . .

Since India became independent in 1950 the use of English has been declining, thereby making the theological texts available in that language of less use than they were. In his 1956 report to the Theological Education Committee of the National Council of Churches in India, Dr. M. H. Harrison stated: "It was quite clear that in many cases the adequate use of English theological textbooks was beyond the competence of the majority of the students. . . . There is universal agreement that the standard of English in Indian schools and colleges is rapidly declining. . . . It is a problem for the L.Th. institutions, for . . . theological literature is mostly available only in English, and the reading of students is becoming more and more limited. Even with the best hopes from the Christian Students' Library and similar ventures, it is likely that this situation will be more or less permanent for I see no prospect in the foreseeable future that the Indian church will have the resources either in money or personnel to produce a body of theological literature comparable in variety or up-to-dateness with what is available in English. . . ."

Dr. Roland W. Scott of the DFM (and a missionary with long experience in India) comments that probably not one student in ten in the theological schools in India can really profit from a study of texts in English. Most of these students know some English, but the translation difficulties, when added to the studying process, results in a learning efficiency which has been characterized as "alarmingly low." He considers that of all the assistance which could be rendered to the seminaries in India, the most significant contribution would be the making available to them of an adequate number of texts suitable for their needs and written in or translated into the vernaculars. Included among the findings of the 1957 Harrison report *After Ten Years* was the following recommendation: "24. That urgent steps be taken in the provision of suitable theological literature in all the main language areas, and, in particular, that the writing, publication, and translation of the volumes of the Christian Students' Library be expedited as rapidly as possible."

Bishop Newbigin comments that in a number of the local languages in India there is a Hindu religious literature extending back some 2,500 years. In Tamil, for example, the vocabulary is as subtle and flexible as in Greek; and at present there is an important renaissance taking place in Tamil philosophical and poetical texts. However, as yet no significant number of Christian theological texts have been translated into that language.

These same language problems confront the Bible schools in India as well. At the Bible School Conference held in August 1956 under the auspices of the National Council of Churches of India, it was resolved that "(a) a list of suitable books now available (in Tamil and Kannada) be prepared and circulated to heads of Bible schools in the respective areas; (b) the special committees in Tamilnad and Karnataka responsible for the production of theological literature be asked to keep in mind the needs of Bible schools, and in particular to give priority to a Bible Concordance, Commentaries, and the subject of Christian worship. . . ."

Southeast Asia: Dr. F. Bruce Morgan, formerly a faculty member of a seminary in Thailand, wrote in 1952 that in some theological schools in that area the instruction is carried on entirely in English and in others entirely in the vernacular:

Perhaps most common is a compromise between the two, with English having a priority in reading and research . . . (and) the national language is used in the classroom and in "laboratory," (i.e., field) work, with a greater or smaller sprinkling of English thrown in, depending on the local situation. No one is quite happy about this use or non-use of English. . . . Most seminaries which use English are dissatisfied with the standard of English obtaining among their students, but most of those not using English contemplate its use at some later date, at least as a tool. . . . Since the truly bi-lingual student is very rare, at least at the time of his seminary training, work in English therefore must be so oversimplified and diluted that it loses much in effectiveness.

Dr. Morgan also pointed out the tendency on the part of some theological schools to open a "vernacular department" in the seminary where it will attempt to give these students "everything the others get except the ability to use English as a tool in theological study and the refreshment of the empty preacher and the worn pastor. This means that to be fair to these men, we must step up production of theological literature by several hundred percent, and that right soon."

In Indonesia it has already been noted that books in the seminary libraries there are written largely in Dutch and German. Since the Indonesian revolution resulted in the withdrawal of the Dutch, the study of that language by Indonesians has declined considerably. As a result Dutch and German are languages which are said to be becoming largely unknown to postrevolution students.

At the Conference on Theological Education in Southeast Asia which was held in Bangkok in 1956, it was concluded: "There is a great need for theological . . . textbooks written for Asians, by Asian theologians or by western theologians who have had experience in Asia. . . . Priority should be given to Asian Church History, Sermons and Sociology. . . . The theological institutions in Southeast Asia should exchange a bibliography of textbooks in various subjects as used in each of the institutions. . . ."

A similar recommendation, emphasizing the content of the texts which are needed, is contained in the Rotz report dealing with the schools in the Philippines:

The theological seminaries . . . must create text books with a Philippine frame of reference to replace their present text based upon American life and American concepts of theological training. Specifically they need new texts of the following types:
1. Treatises on Christian doctrine oriented to the actual present social conditions in the Philippines.
2. Short easily read pamphlets on single doctrines such as "The Sacraments," "The Resurrection," etc.
3. Philippine and general Church History.
4. Biographical materials on church leaders.
5. Simple Bible commentaries.

East Asia: In 1938 Bishop Henry St. George Tucker (who later became Presiding Bishop of the Protestant Episcopal Church) wrote as follows concerning his personal observation of the need in Japan for theological texts written in the language of that country: "We have done little to encourage literary activity. . . . The number of theological books adapted to the use of the clergy is woefully inadequate. Japanese are great readers, so that our failure to produce Christian literature means the loss of one of the most effective means of reaching them with our message. . . . This . . . means the expenditure of considerably more money than the Japanese Church can provide. It must look to us for help. The higher educational institutions would seem to form the natural center for literary activity. There should be a publishing department or university press, generously enough supplied with funds to enable it to remedy what is perhaps the greatest defect in our Christian propaganda."

In Japan the need for texts in the vernacular is alleviated somewhat by the fact that virtually all students at the college level have some reading and writing knowledge of English, so that the seminaries purchase some English texts for their libraries.

In Korea, theological education is particularly handicapped by the lack of suitable texts in the Korean language. Because this country was occupied by the Japanese during the first half of the 20th century, Japanese is the second language of the older generation of Koreans. However, the younger generation has not as yet adopted English or any other foreign tongue as a second language. Since most of the seminary faculty members in the country are Koreans conducting their courses in Korean, the absence of texts in that language serves to detract considerably from an already low standard of teaching.

When Dr. Harold Bosley returned from Korea in 1955, his principal recommendation was: *"A 'crash' program for translations is called for.* . . . Too few of the Korean students handle the English language well enough for it to be a useful tool in training. . . . Japanese is no longer taught in the public schools. . . . The field of language . . . is narrowing to the Korean language. . . . A regular committee to carry on this program of translations should be formed at once. . . . There seem to be enough scholars with bilingual and trilingual training to do the job in a most adequate manner."

Concerning the absence of books in Chinese in the library of the Taiwan Theological College on Formosa, the Anderson-Smith report states: "Many of the books . . . are in Japanese which only a rapidly decreasing number of students can read."

Latin America: In Latin America, where linguistic problems are simpler, the fact remains that few theological texts have been translated into Spanish or Portuguese. Dr. Gonzalo Baez-Camargo comments that in Mexico and Central America the foreign missionaries use English texts in their teaching work, and the local Protestant churches are content or obliged to use out-of-date material.

The Southern Baptists, as previously noted, have considerably expanded their missionary efforts in Latin America in the past decade. In the process they have found the language problem a stumbling block. Accordingly, at the International Baptist Seminary in Buenos Aires "a year of English is taught at the beginning of the bachelor of divinity course because many of the 8,000 volumes in the seminary library are in English."

In Mexico the same denomination reported in 1958: "The teachers in the Mexican seminary realize that their responsibility goes beyond classroom instruction to the making of whatever contribution they can to the production of much-needed religious literature in the native language. They have had published a total of 1,706 pages of translation and 253 pages of original works and two translations are being prepared. The school's library contains the largest percentage (71) of books in Spanish of any of the theological seminaries in Latin America which are related to Southern Baptist mission work."

The lack of a sufficient number of suitable theological texts written in Spanish was perhaps the decisive factor in leading to the Episcopalians' decision to establish a new seminary in Puerto Rico where the instruction would be carried on in English. According to Bishop Bentley, "the instruction will be in English, because all our Bishops from the Latin American fields agree that there is so little study material available in Spanish. Also, if a seminarian makes his studies in English, then when he returns to his mission or parish, we can send to him new books as they come out in English, whereas if he had made his studies in Spanish, these materials would not be immediately and readily available to him."

The absence of suitable theological texts in Portuguese is acute. The Dean of the Presbyterian Seminary of the North (which is located in Recife, Brazil) writes as follows: "The time has come for the Evangelical Church in Brazil to be supplied with high class religious literature in Portuguese, the country's language. Almost nothing has been done so far in this important department of Church life. It is probably the weakest point of Protestantism in Brazil. . . . The Brazilian Christian leaders who are able to produce this badly needed material are already overloaded with too many responsibilities. One of the best solutions to the problem, probably the most realistic one, is to enlarge the Seminary's faculty so that some of the most gifted professors may have time to write and to translate."

Dean Shaull comments that even though all the regular classes at the Presbyterian Seminary at Campinas are conducted in Portuguese it has nevertheless been necessary for this school to institute a special instructional course in the English language for students who have completed their second year at the Seminary: since there are no suitable texts at the advanced level in Portuguese it is necessary for the students to learn English in order to complete their course. The President of the same institution writes: "Theological text books in Portuguese practically do not exist. . . . Our present Greek professor . . . is preparing a fine Greek Grammar in Portuguese, but there is little likelihood of it being published due to lack of funds. Many other theological books could be written and others translated, but these things cannot be done without large sums of money."

In conclusion, it seems clear that translations are usually one of the last items taken up for action by the typical mission board operating in a younger church area. Furthermore, with so many of the outstanding personnel in the younger churches occupying administrative positions, this has resulted in a dearth of indigenous theologians and scholars, and, concomitantly, a greater need for suitable classroom texts in the vernacular. The less literate the ordinand student is in the foreign language of instruction at his seminary, the greater the need he has for texts written in his own local language.

Perhaps the simplest way of summarizing the point would be to present the situation in reverse. Specifically, one may ask the question: how many Americans would be likely to be converted to Hinduism by Indian missionaries in the United States if, in addition to being instructed in that religion they were also obliged to learn how to read and write Hindi or Sanskrit? Or how many Americans would be apt to be converted to Islam, if in addition they had to learn to read and write Arabic? Or to Buddhism, if they additionally were required to learn how to read and write Chinese or Pali?

C. THE LANGUAGES USED IN THE THEOLOGICAL SCHOOLS

Two questions arise: (1) What are the principal languages of instruction at the various seminaries? and (2) Are these languages suitable ones to use in the translation of English, French and German texts into the vernaculars?

The problems inherent in the choice of languages into which theological texts might best be translated relate to (1) the pattern of language distribution, and (2) the degree to which such languages are widely read. Were it not for these complexities, it is likely that the mission boards and agencies would by now have made further progress than they have to date in translating texts into the vernaculars.

In the case of some languages spoken by many millions of people there is little or no written literature (for example, Punjabi). Other languages have a wide literature but are not widely spoken (for example, Sanskrit, which is the classical language of the Hindu texts). Some languages are very similar in their spoken form (Hindi and Urdu) but are radically different in their written forms (Hindi being a Devanagari script and Urdu being written in a modified Arabic script). In the case of some major languages, the written characters are somewhat similar but the spoken language is radically different (Japanese and Chinese).

Inasmuch as there are over 2,000 different spoken and written languages and dialects in the world, the problem and cost of translating theological texts from English into the vernaculars necessitates a careful selection of only a small number of languages. The Bible societies, having only one text to translate, perforce translate the Scriptures into hundreds of languages. Similarly the literature and literacy programs of the American and European missionary agencies prepare and distribute simple religious tracts written in a great many languages. However, the cost of adapting and translating theological texts into the vernaculars is high, and into any given language many rather than a few texts need to be translated in order to make the effort worth while. Consequently the aim must be focused on selecting the smallest number of major languages for translation purposes which will enable as many ordinand students as possible to study theology in their local language.

There are at least seven factors to be taken into consideration in the choice of a language into which a theological text is to be translated. These are:

a. The number of persons speaking the language.
b. The extent to which the language is written.
c. The percentage of literacy and the degree of reading proficiency of the people using the language.
d. The adequacy of the number of translators who are both available for this task and capable of translating the words in that language to express Christian terms in the sense that other Christians use them.
e. The extent to which the language is or may be supplanted by a lingua franca.
f. The extent to which English theological texts have already been translated into that language.
g. The missionary opportunity and the number of seminaries located in the area in which the local language is used.

Curiously enough there are few statistics available which indicate the number of people who speak the major languages of the world; and no estimates seem to be publicly available which relate such statistics to the degree of literacy existing among such peoples in Africa, Asia and Latin America.

If a major language can be described as one spoken by at least 50,000,000 persons, then there are in existence in the world today only 14 such languages. These are listed in Table 76. The numbers of persons shown in that table as speaking each language are based on published estimates prepared by Professor Sidney Culbert.

TABLE 76.   LANGUAGES SPOKEN BY A MINIMUM OF
50,000,000 PERSONS (1958)

Language	Spoken as Primary Language (Millions of Persons)
Mandarin	432
English	275
Russian	153[a]
Hindi	146
Spanish	139
German	120
Japanese	95
Bengali	77[b]
Arabic	74
Portuguese	72
French	70
Malay[c]	69
Italian	57
Urdu	50[b]

NOTES: [a] Great Russian (excluding Ukrainian). [b] In India and Pakistan. [c] Including "Bahasa Indonesia."

However, (1) after removing from the list those languages which are not spoken in Africa, Asia and Latin America to any significant extent (i.e., Russian, German and Italian); (2) deducting those persons speaking Mandarin, English, Spanish, French and Portuguese who are not inhabitants of the non-Communist underdeveloped countries; and (3) allowing for the use of English and French as secondary tongues, the resulting list of ten languages then becomes as shown in Table 77.

TABLE 77.   SOME MAJOR LANGUAGES SPOKEN IN
AFRICA, ASIA AND LATIN AMERICA

Language	Spoken as Primary or Secondary Language (Millions of Persons)
Hindi	146
Spanish	115
Japanese	95
Bengali	77
Arabic	74
Malay[a]	69
Portuguese	61
Urdu	50
English[b]	30
French[c]	10

NOTES: [a] Including "Bahasa Indonesia." [b] Largely in South Africa, India, Philippines, Japan and Latin America. [c] Largely in North and Latin Africa, and in the Caribbean area.

After temporarily removing English from the list (since it is difficult to estimate how many people in each of the underdeveloped areas speak this language as a secondary tongue), there remain 21 other languages, each of which is spoken by more than 10,000,000 persons in Africa, Asia and Latin America. Adding these 21 languages to the nine previously listed results in the list of 30 languages shown in Table 78.

Of the 30 individual languages listed in Table 78 as being spoken by 10,000,000 or more persons, 13 are languages spoken by a total of 494,000,000 persons in India, Pakistan and Ceylon. From the point of view of over-all missionary strategy as it might be expressed in a translation program, the numerical preponderance of the speakers of the Indian languages presents a problem which is discussed later in this section.

The following may be noted concerning the major languages spoken in each of the areas listed in Table 78.

Africa: According to Rev. David Brown, in the Sudan

English and Arabic take the place of Hebrew and Greek in the curriculum at Bishop Gwynne College. English is taught regularly because it is the language of instruction at the college, and also because it is the language of theology. In most of the tribal languages only the New Testament has yet been translated and there is no vernacular literature to stimulate the pastor's reading. Arabic will in time supersede English and the vernacular languages in the Sudan, and thus it must be given a larger place in the curriculum, so

TABLE 78. THE LEADING 30 LANGUAGES SPOKEN IN AFRICA, ASIA AND
LATIN AMERICA[a]

Language	Spoken by Millions of Persons				
	Africa and Middle East	Southern Asia	Southeast Asia	East Asia	Latin America
Hindi		146			
Spanish					115
Japanese				95	
Bengali		77			
Arabic	74				
Malay[b]			69		
Portuguese	3				58
Urdu		50			
Javanese			42		
Telugu		38			
Tamil		34			
Korean				32	
Marathi		31			
Vietnamese			23		
Turkish	23				
Punjabi		23			
Persian	20				
Thai			19		
Chinese[c]			11	9	
Gujarati		20			
Kannada		19			
Malayalam		16			
Rajasthani		15			
Burmese			14		
Oriya		14			
Hausa	13				
Sundanese			13		
Pushtu		11			
Swahili	10				
French	10				
	153	494	191	136	173

NOTES: [a] Excluding Communist China and the English language. [b] Including "Bahasa Indonesia." [c] "Overseas Chinese" residing in Southeast Asia, Formosa and Hong-kong. These estimates include speakers of Cantonese, Hakka, Amoy and Mandarin which are distinctly different dialectical variants of spoken "Chinese."

that pastors may be able to preach and to witness in Arabic. . . . At Mundri itself on Sundays in company with the nearby training college students, class meetings are held in seven or more languages. Missions are conducted in towns such as Juba, Maridi, and Nzara as often as possible, although this again is hindered by transport and language difficulties.

Part II of the IMC survey points out: "At Libamba in the Cameroun, the secondary (secular) school conducted jointly by the Paris Society (French Evangelical Reformed Church) and by the American Presbyterian Mission (USA), recently counted representation among the students of twenty-seven tribes, with almost that many separate languages. Regular Sunday-school classes are conducted there in six languages."

In addition to Arabic in North Africa, there are only two other major indigenous languages spoken on the Continent of Africa. South of the Sahara there are over 600 different languages which have been classified into at least 21 major language groups (including Bantu, the Nilotic, Nilo-Hamitic, Cushitic, Bushman, etc.). However, it appears that only two of these tongues, Hausa and Swahili, are spoken by as many as 10,000,000 people.

Hausa is a Chado-Hamitic language which is spoken by about 13,000,000 persons, largely in the area of which northern Nigeria is the center. It has had a considerable vernacular literature since it was a literary language before the advent of Europeans. Swahili is a Bantu language with many of its words borrowed from Arabic. It has been used as a trade language along the East African coast and as the official language of Kenya and Tanganyika. However, as Lord Hailey points out in his African Survey, "the use of Swahili as a lingua franca has created some difficulty. In Kenya the Education Department Report of 1950 announced that its use would be gradually discontinued, a decision taken some years earlier in Uganda."

The same author discusses the thorny problems involved in trying to sort out or create a few additional major indigenous languages in Africa, and notes: "The standardization of language clusters has often been attempted, but seldom with success, and the attempt to unify dialects has as a rule also failed, the most notable example being the attempted union of Fante and Twi into a single Akau language of the Gold Coast. National jealousy and difficulties of orthography were in this case the main causes of the miscarriage of what appeared to be a feasible union of two not dissimilar dialects."

A comment along the same lines made in Part II of the IMC survey is also noteworthy: "Obviously, tribal and local language is the stronghold of particularism and conservatism. A language spoken by a comparatively small number of people . . . cannot hope to have an adequate literature for educational or for religious purposes, since the market for books, and the number of people who will write books, will be so narrowly limited."

Thus in British East Africa and in West Africa, it would appear that none of the native languages are eminently suitable for translation of theological texts and that ultimately English may become the lingua franca, either as a primary or a secondary tongue among the intellectual leaders. The Lutheran seminary at Makumira in Tanganyika carries on instruction in Swahili, but all or virtually all the others in British East and West Africa (including the new Lutheran postordination institute at Marangu) teach courses in English.

French colonial policy has been aimed at the development of French citizens within the empire. This policy has discouraged study of the vernacular and has concentrated on the study of the French language. The result is that in recent years many of the small secular schools using the vernacular have been replaced by French-speaking schools. In the French reformed seminary at Ndoungué in the Cameroons, the teaching was in the Douala language until 1947. In that year students from Togo and Gabon were admitted into the school, and it became necessary to conduct the courses in French. The extension of French as a primary and second-ary language continues steadily, and it may very well continue to be a lingua franca in Latin Africa, even after—as seems likely in the long run—the French and the Belgian colonial administrators have been withdrawn.

In the Belgian Congo and Ruanda-Urundi, according to Part II of the IMC sur-vey, "there are also several languages used, respectively, by hundreds of thousands of people over a wide area, such as: Tshiluba in the south central region, with nearly two million users; Kikongo in the lower basin, extending also into Angola on the one side and into French Equatorial on the other; Kingwana in the north-east, a variant of the Swahili so important in portions of British East Africa." However, it appears that the Kikongo language is not favored by Congolese speaking other lan-guages, as a result of which the Pastors' School of the American Baptists at Kim-pese (in the Kikongo area) teaches in French and English. The Anglican seminary in Ruanda teaches in the local vernacular (Kenyaruanda) but ultimately may adopt French for its medium of instruction as educational standards rise.

At the Emmanuel Theological Seminary at Dondi in Angola, Portuguese is used in the classroom work, except in the case of tutorial sessions where the vernacular is employed. A small number of its classroom texts in Portuguese are obtained from Brazil, rather than from Portugal.

In the countries south of Latin Africa, it would appear that English will become the lingua franca, either as a primary or secondary tongue. The one possible excep-tion, i.e., Afrikaans in the Union of South Africa, would not seem to be a promising candidate as a common tongue for the natives in that area.

The Middle East: The courses of instruction at the one Protestant seminary in this area, the Near East School of Theology in Beirut, are conducted orally in Lebanese Arabic and in English. As a secondary tongue in the Middle East, English has been rapidly displacing French during the past decade. English is said to be increasingly used by the educated classes as a lingua franca in business, science and education, even though it is far from having become the second language in all the countries in this area.

Southern Asia: As previously noted, of the 30 major languages spoken in Africa, Asia and Latin America as listed in Table 78, 13 are spoken in India, Pakistan and Ceylon. Of all the countries in the world, the language problems of India are per-haps the most complicated. They can be dealt with only briefly here.

At the Conference on American Books Abroad it was reported that

English still exists in all three countries (India, Pakistan and Ceylon) as the Government language and the language of the upper economic and social strata. India has a Constitu-tional provision that the official language of the nation will be Hindi within 15 years (1965) of the adoption of the Constitution (Articles 343, 348); Pakistan indicates that in 20 years Urdu will be the official language (it does not yet have a Constitution in which this is established); and Ceylon is slowly changing to Tamil and Sinhalese as official languages, but the exact time of final transfer of languages is indefinite. . . .

In India, it is likely that Hindi and English will continue side by side as the medium of communication between the scholars, intellectuals, and government servants of the various language areas. This is also even more probable in the State of Pakistan; and as long as Ceylon is a dominion with its close ties to England, she will find English an essential second language.

According to Professor M. H. Harrison's 1956 report to the National Council of Churches in India,

part of the difficulty in developing a definite and consistent policy in this matter (of the choice of a primary language) comes from our uncertainty as to the eventual decision of the Government about the language of ordinary education. Some would make Hindi the common medium throughout India. Others, and in the South they seem to have the majority, wish to extend the use of the regional language through the university stage. Some voices are heard for the retention of English for higher education, and it is significant that legal and medical colleges are generally expecting to retain English indefinitely. There can be no final decision in theological education until this question is more clearly answered.

In his 1957 report *After Ten Years,* Professor Harrison repeated these comments, adding: "In the South, at least, where the highest concentration of the Christian population is to be found, there has been distinct opposition to the introduction of Hindi. This has come about partly, although not solely, through the propaganda of the Dravida Kazhagam, which has endeavored to promote the interests of the Dravidian languages. In most parts of India the use of English as the medium of instruction at the high school level has been given up, although it is still taught as a subject."

At the Leonard Theological College, where English is the medium of instruction, Hindi was made a compulsory subject for all students in 1949 in view of the possibility of this language's becoming the medium of higher education in the foreseeable future.

In August, 1957, the Official Language Commission of the Indian Government expressed the view that it would be neither necessary nor possible for it to pronounce now whether a general change-over from English to Hindi would be found practicable by 1965.

Thus there appears to be a trend in India toward a growth in the use of Hindi and the regional languages, tempered only by a necessity to develop Hindi as the language of the Indian Government and to retain English as a secondary tongue among the intellectuals.

Southeast Asia: The Bangkok Conference Report notes that all of the 19 theological schools in Southeast and East Asia which answered its questionnaire replied that they "require and use English, either as a medium of instruction or as a second language. No other European languages are taught except German and Dutch."

In Malaya the dialects spoken by the Malayans are closely related to Bahasa Indonesia. A joint commission is attempting to resolve the few differences between the two tongues. Bahasa Indonesia is the official language of the Republic of Indonesia, although Javanese and Sundanese are spoken in many homes. The Government has also ruled that English is to be the second language after Bahasa.

In the Philippines, Tagalog is the official Government language. The number of people speaking it is estimated between 4,000,000 and 8,000,000 persons. However, English is the medium of instruction and is also spoken by at least 4,000,000 persons as a secondary language. Another 7,000,000 speak the various Visayan, Ilocano and other dialects which are quite separate and unrelated to each other.

East Asia: Within both Japan and Korea there is only one major language widely spoken in each country. However, there are considerable dialectical differences within those languages. In Japanese, for example, these dialects reflect the social and economic status of the speakers. Also in Japan students taking the college course are required to study English and German.

On Formosa the dialect difficulties are such that communications between Formosans and mainland Chinese are difficult. On the island, the Amoy dialect is the first language and Japanese the second among the Formosans, while the mainlanders speak Mandarin as their first language and often English as their second. Thus there are few means of communication between the groups, except when translated. Amoy dialect is used in private business and by three of the seminaries. Some observers believe that ultimately the seminaries will be obliged to switch from Amoy to Mandarin.

A recent report of the Lutheran Theological Seminary in Hongkong states that in that British colony "English is becoming a requisite, not only as a necessary medium for research, but also upon graduation and ordination when it becomes invaluable in public relations and in the daily administrative duties of the Church. The Cantonese language has also been added to the curriculum so that Mandarin-speaking Chinese may have more opportunity to serve among the Cantonese-speaking people in Hong Kong."

Latin America: In Latin America approximately 115,000,000 persons speak Spanish as their mother tongue. The next most important language is Portuguese which is spoken by approximately 58,000,000 persons in Brazil.

In addition there are about 15,000,000 Indians in the Andean area of South America and the mountainous regions of Mexico and Guatemala: however, they speak about 200 different languages or dialects. English, Dutch and French are also spoken as primary tongues by many of the inhabitants of the Caribbean area and in the

Guianas. Elsewhere in Latin America English is said to have become a minor secondary tongue among the intelligentsia in the large cities.

The third factor listed above among those to be taken into consideration in the choice of a language into which theological texts are to be translated, is the percentage of literacy and the degree of reading proficiency of the people using that language. For, one of the important by-products of a comprehensive translation program is that copies of the texts written in the vernaculars can be sold or made available through libraries to the intellectual leaders (Christian and non-Christian) who, in turn, influence the masses.

It appears that literacy statistics are also not widely available. The reason is that many different standards can be used in determining what distinguishes literacy from illiteracy, i.e., the minimum number of words which can be read, or the level of schooling which needs to be attained in order for a person to be classified as literate, etc. Different countries adopt different standards in measuring literacy, and

TABLE 79.   PERCENTAGE OF LITERACY IN SELECTED COUNTRIES (1957)

Africa	%	Southern Asia	%	East Asia	%
Union of South Africa	40–45	Ceylon	60–65	Japan	97–98
Belgian Congo	35–40	India	15–20	Hongkong	55–60
Madagascar	30–35	Pakistan	15–20	China	45–50
Uganda, Kenya	25–30			Korea	35–40
Egypt	20–25				
Ghana	20–25	Southeast Asia	%	Latin America	%
Northern & Southern Rhodesia	20–25				
Nigeria	10–15	Niue, Cook Island	90–95	Barbados	90–95
Sudan	5–10	Philippines	60–65	Argentina	85–90
Tanganyika	5–10	Burma	55–60	Bahamas, British Guiana	75–80
Cameroons	5–10	Thailand	50–55	Cuba, Surinam	75–80
Liberia, Sierra Leone	5–10	Singapore	45–50	Chile	75–80
Ruanda-Urundi	5–10	Malaya	35–40	Puerto Rico, Jamaica	70–75
Ethiopia	1–5	Indonesia	15–20	Mexico	60–65
French West Africa	1–5	Sarawak	15–20	Colombia	50–55
Angola, Mozambique	1–5	New Guinea	5–10	Brazil	45–50
				Bolivia	30–35
Middle East	%			Guatemala	25–30
				Haiti	10–15
Lebanon	45–50				
Turkey	30–35				
Jordan	15–20				

the tendency of some is to lower the standards in order to be able to report a higher percentage of literacy. Thus Japan may be 98% literate according to one standard, but it also appears that only about 50% of the Japanese are effectively literate in the sense that they can read a newspaper with ease. The statistics shown in Table 79 were assembled by UNESCO and are believed to be the most accurate available.

The following may be noted concerning the percentages of literacy prevailing in the countries listed in this table.

Africa: There is a very low level of literacy in Africa compared to the other underdeveloped areas. Professor Mario Pei has written: "Africa has by far the lowest literacy averages. Only Algeria, Kenya, Tunisia, Uganda and the Union of South Africa attain the maximum percentages of 10 to 30% literacy among their native populations. The percentage of literates is almost negligible in French Equatorial Africa, Gambia and Liberia. Despite this fact there are in Africa over 100 news-papers and periodicals published in native languages, with the Swahili of East Africa and the Zulu of South Africa in the lead. A single Nigerian weekly bears articles in English, Ga, Fanti, Ewe, Kru, Ibo, Yoruba, Hausa, Ijaw, Benin, Sobo, Jekri and Efik."

The inability of most Africans to read in their own vernaculars points to the value of English and French as written linguæ francæ.

Middle East: The estimated 20% literacy for the Egyptian population would seem to be a fairly generous one to use in connection with the literacy of the popu-lation of some of the other Arab countries in the Middle East. Possibly as low as 10% might be a more accurate figure. An exception is Lebanon where the literacy rate ranges close to 50%.

Written classical Arabic has one advantage, namely, that it is the one form of writing used by all the Arab people residing in the area stretching from Dakar to Baghdad. On the other hand, because of the importance of and need for technologi-cal texts in this area, it is believed by some that the number of readers of books in English in the Middle East may at least double and perhaps triple in the next decade.

Southern Asia: In India the variety of written languages cause difficulties. Those who speak Punjabi write in Urdu, the language of some 50,000,000 people, one-half in India and the other half in West Pakistan. Because of the complicated scripts of many of the Indian languages, it has been estimated that about $\frac{3}{4}$ of those who do not continue their education beyond elementary schools relapse into virtual illiteracy soon after they finish their studies.

The low level of literacy in India and Pakistan, 15–20%, detracts from the value of the vernaculars as languages into which theological texts might be translated. However, in Travancore with its large Christian community the literacy rate in some localities ranges as high as approximately 50%.

It was stated at the 1955 Conference on American Books Abroad that in India a serious book can probably be read more widely in English than in any single one of the Indian tongues:

Because of the mass of records and judicial decisions in English within these coun-tries, English will continue as an essential second language for generations, and although the literacy in English may decline, it will not disappear within our lifetimes. The neces-sity of English-language books will continue, and the majority of these will have to be imported, for the indigenous publishing industry itself will tend more and more to pub-lish in the national and regional languages.

. . . In South India translations into the Dravidian languages (Tamil, Telugu, Kannada and Malayalam) may be well distributed because of the greater literacy and the demand for reading materials, while in north India a translation program may be less effective. This is true not only of India but of Pakistan and Ceylon, where urban-rural distribution and differences in language literacy determine the effectiveness of a translation program to the same degree.

Southeast Asia: Bahasa Indonesia is said to be one of the most successful examples in history of an imposed lingua franca in its oral and written forms. With the withdrawal of the Dutch from the East Indies, the Indonesian Government selected Bahasa Indonesia as the official Government language. Its value as a medium into which theological texts might be translated is somewhat impaired by the very low level of literacy in that country, i.e., 15–20%. This figure, however, represents a considerable increase over the 8% literacy level which prevailed when the Republic of Indonesia was proclaimed in 1950.

In the Philippines the literacy rate of 60–65% is the highest of any nation in Asia, with the exception of Japan. This factor, coupled with the fact that English is the language of the texts used in the seminary classrooms, may account in part for the comparatively large size of the library at the Union Theological Seminary in Manila.

East Asia: With respect to the percentage of literacy, Japan at 98% is one of the most literate nations in the world. However, the degree of reading proficiency among the population is considerably lower than the literacy statistics would suggest. In other words, most Japanese can read a little, but probably only one-half are said to be able to read Japanese well.

Some Japanese students at the college level can read and write English fairly well, and possibly a majority of the texts used in the theological schools are in English. English is the second-most widely read and written language in Japan. The oral instruction in the seminaries is in Japanese.

In Korea two-thirds of the people cannot read their own language, and only a small percentage can read Japanese and/or English as a second language. The written form of the Korean language is considerably different from either Chinese or Japanese. There were reported to be only 12 libraries in the entire country in 1954. Of this number, four were libraries of the United States Information Service. The total holdings of these 12 libraries in 1954 were 8,314 volumes. But the attendance in them during that year totaled 991,320 visits.

Latin America: The variations in the literacy rates among the Latin American countries are quite wide. In Argentina a high proportion, 85–90%, read Spanish; but in the isolated and tropical countries of Central and South America the literacy levels sink to those prevailing in Africa.

Over-all: It is of interest to relate these literacy statistics to the 30 major languages spoken in Africa, Asia and Latin America (as previously listed) in order to gauge to

TABLE 80. NUMBER OF READERS IN 29 LEADING LANGUAGES

Language	Spoken by (Millions)	Literacy Percent	Read by (Millions of Persons)				
			Africa & Middle East	Southern Asia	Southeast Asia	East Asia	Latin America
Japanese	95	97				92	
Spanish	115	60					69
Portuguese	61	45					27
Hindi	146	15		22			
Bengali	77	15		12			
Arabic	74	15	11				
Korean	32	35				11	
Malay[a]	69	15			10		
Thai	19	50			10		
Chinese[b]	20	45			5	4	
Urdu	50	15		8			
Vietnamese	23	35			8		
Burmese	14	55			8		
Turkish	23	30	7				
French	10	70	7				
Javanese	42	15			6		
Telugu	38	15		6			
Tamil	34	15		5			
Marathi	31	15		5			
Malayalam	15	25		4			
Persian	20	15	3				
Gujarati	20	15		3			
Kannada	19	15		3			
Rajasthani	16	15		2			
Oriya	14	15		2			
Hausa	13	5	1				
Sundanese	13	10			1		
Pushtu	11	10	1				
Swahili	10	5	1				
	1,124		30	73	48	107	96

NOTES: [a] Including "Bahasa Indonesia."
[b] Overseas Chinese (as previously noted).

what extent the written forms of each of them are read by the people speaking them. Table 80 presents this data (with Punjabi having been eliminated from the list).

The data in Table 80 is only approximate and is intended to be indicative only. It discloses the importance of Japanese and Spanish as the two languages which are most widely read in the non-Communist countries in Africa, Asia and Latin America. Portuguese and Hindi might be placed in a second category of importance, with Bengali, Arabic, Korean, Malay (Bahasa Indonesia), Thai and Chinese in a third category. The remaining languages are more restricted in their importance as media for the translation of theological texts. Some of the regional languages of India may be supplanted by linguæ francæ (Hindi and/or English).

The fourth factor previously listed as one to be taken into consideration in connection with the selection of a foreign language into which theological texts might be translated was the adequacy of the number of translators who are both available for this task and capable of translating the words in that language to express Christian terms in the sense that other Christians use them. On this point, Dr. Eugene Nida comments as follows:

All languages have highly generic vocabulary for certain areas of life (the areas of abstraction depend entirely upon the cultural emphases). The problem for the translator is not whether a language has abstract vocabulary, but whether it has a "ready-made" vocabulary for translating theological concepts. But this is again not the real problem for if there is a "ready-made" vocabulary adapted to religious concepts, it is probably one which is already heavily loaded with non-Christian meanings, and hence the problem of the translator is at times even more difficult than if he has to construct generic terms "out of whole cloth." Many translators have been badly deceived by the presumed ease in finding corresponding terms, with the result that in the end they were actually not communicating the Christian message at all.

Thus the vocabulary factor is a complex problem, the solution to which depends upon the number of translators who are available for this work and who have both the requisite linguistic skills and an adequate understanding of the correct meaning of Christian theological terms.

The seventh factor previously listed as one to be taken into consideration is the missionary opportunity and the number of seminaries located in the area in which that language is spoken. On this basis, and in line with the comments expressed elsewhere in this Survey, one would eliminate eight languages from the list presented in Table 80. These are Arabic, Thai, Vietnamese, Burmese, Turkish, Persian, Hausa and Swahili. With the increasing use of Bahasa Indonesia one would also remove Javanese and Sundanese from the list.

The vernacular languages of India are spoken by vast numbers of people but

TABLE 81.   LANGUAGES USED ORALLY IN THE 29 THEOLOGICAL SCHOOLS IN INDIA AND PAKISTAN[a]

Tamil	Hindi	Urdu
Tamilnad Theological College*	Lutheran Theological College*	Union Theological Seminary,
Tamil Evangelical Lutheran	Union Theological College, Indore*	Bareilly*
Seminary	Allahabad Bible Seminary	North India United Theological
		College*
		Gujranwala Theological Seminary
		Theological Seminary of Pakistan
		Lutheran Church?
Telugu	Kannada	Malayalam
Luthergiri Theological Seminary*	Basel Mission Theological	Mar Thoma Theological Seminary*
Andhra Union Theological	Seminary*	Kerala United Theological
College*	Union Kanarese Seminary*	Seminary*
Baptist Theological Seminary,	Karnataka Bible Seminary	Concordia Seminary
Kakinada*		
Andhra Baptist Theological		
Seminary		
Marathi	Bengali	Gujerati
Union Theological College,	United Theological School,	Gujerat United School of
Poona*	Calcutta	Theology*
Union Biblical Seminary, Yeotmal	Nimasarai Bengali Divinity School	
Oriya	Assamese (various)	Santali
Theological Seminary, Kotapud	Cherta Theological College*	Santal Theological Seminary
Christian Training College,	Assam Baptist Theological	
Cuttack	Seminary	

NOTES: [a] Excluding the five theological colleges which teach in English.
* Affiliated with the Serampore Senate.

read by only comparatively few. The five theological colleges in that country use English as their medium of instruction because they draw students from all over India and very few theological works have been translated into the vernaculars. It would appear that these colleges will probably continue to use English, even if Hindi should become the official language of the country.

With respect to the remaining 29 theological schools in India and Pakistan, Table 81 presents the distribution of these seminaries in relation to the vernaculars they use as their oral media of instruction.

From Table 81 the importance to the theological schools of the Dravidian languages of South India is evident. This is in contrast with some of the major languages of the North (Bengali, Oriya, Gujerati, Santali, Assamese, etc.). The seven regional languages most widely used among theological seminaries in India are Marathi, Urdu, Telugu, Malayalam, Hindi, Tamil and Kannada in approximately that order. Of the 15 theological schools affiliated with the Serampore Senate, 13 use these seven languages as their medium of instruction and only two seminaries do not. Neither of the latter two schools are important. Although Bengali is spoken by an estimated 77,000,000 persons, in 1956 the United Theological School in Calcutta (one of the two schools using Bengali) had only two full-time members on its faculty, and no ordinand students were enrolled during that year. Thus one would eliminate Oriya, Bengali, Gujerati, Rajasthani, Pushtu, Santali and the various Assamese languages from the list of languages of major importance in India in connection with a theological texts translation program.

TABLE 82.   THE 14 FOREIGN LANGUAGES OF MAJOR IMPORTANCE TO SEMINARIES OVERSEAS

| | Seven "Foreign" Languages | | | | | Seven Indian Languages | | | |
| | (In Millions) | | Used by Number of | | | (In Millions) | | Used by Number of | |
Language	Read by	Spoken by	Seminaries	Students	Language	Read by	Spoken by	Seminaries	Students
Korean	11	32	9	1,346	Marathi	5	31	2	81
Japanese	92	95	12	590	Urdu	8	50	4	80
Spanish	69	115	16	276	Telugu	6	38	4	74
Indonesian	10	69	10	353	Malayalam	4	15	3	50
Portuguese	27	61	13	413	Hindi	22	146	3	49
Chinese[b]	9	20	9	321	Tamil	5	34	2	45
French[c]	7	10	12	171	Kannada	3	19	3	40
	225	402	81	3,470		53	333	21	419
Approx. %[a]	80	55	80	90		20	45	20	10

NOTES: [a] Percentage of combined totals of the seven foreign languages plus the seven Indian languages.
[b] Overseas Chinese.
[c] The data in this table relating to the seminaries and their students refers only to those instances where the language concerned is used as a primary language of instruction. Thus the extent to which French is used as a secondary language in Africa and elsewhere is not indicated.

After taking into consideration the seven factors previously listed, it appears that there are among the countries of Africa, Asia and Latin America (with the exception of India) some seven languages of crucial importance to the seminaries with respect to the translation of theological texts. The use made of these seven languages compared to the use made of the regional languages in India is shown in Table 82.

From the percentage figures included at the bottom of Table 82 it will be observed that the seven Indian languages, when taken together, have an aggregate importance to the seminaries which is about equal to one of the seven "foreign" languages listed in the column on the left-hand side of the table. Thus in chapter 17 a total of eight foreign languages is used as a basis for the cost estimates projected in connection with the translation program which is suggested therein.

Table 82 does not show the extent to which English is used orally as a primary language of instruction in the seminaries overseas. In addition English is also sometimes used as a secondary language in the French colonies in Latin Africa, is on a par with Afrikaans in parts of the Union of South Africa, and is reported to be frequently used as a secondary language in the classrooms of the theological schools in Lebanon, Burma, Thailand, Japan, Mexico, Puerto Rico and Argentina. Furthermore in Africa, Asia and Latin America as a whole there are more books in the seminary libraries written in English than in any other single language. Consequently, as previously mentioned, some of the schools which do not regularly use English in their classrooms nevertheless offer courses in the English language solely in order to enable their students to make a better use of their libraries.

TABLE 83. USE OF ORAL ENGLISH AS A PRIMARY LANGUAGE OF INSTRUCTION IN THEOLOGICAL SCHOOLS OVERSEAS

Area	Number of	
	Seminaries	Students
Africa		
East Africa	6	166
West Africa	9	269
Southern Africa	15	267
Southern Asia		
India	5	152
Southeast Asia		
Malaya	1	27
Oceania	6	128
Philippines	7	197
Latin America		
Caribbean Area	5	86
South America	1	5
	55	1,297

At this point English should be reincorporated into the list. Table 83 indicates the number of seminaries and the extent to which they use English orally as a primary language of instruction.

It appears that English, plus the seven foreign languages of major importance to the seminaries in the underdeveloped countries generally, plus the seven languages of regional importance to the seminaries in India, are the primary media of instruction in more than three out of four of the seminaries training 83% of the theological students in Africa, Asia and Latin America. This is shown in the column entitled "Users" in Table 84. Only 17% of the students (1,035) are being trained in seminaries (shown in the column entitled "Nonusers") which do not regularly employ these eight major or seven Indian languages in their classroom instruction.

TABLE 84. THE USE OF ENGLISH AND THE 14 FOREIGN LANGUAGES OF MAJOR IMPORTANCE TO THE SEMINARIES

Area	Users Number of		Nonusers Number of		Total Number of	
	Seminaries	Students	Seminaries	Students	Seminaries	Students
Africa						
North of the Sahara			1	25	1	25
East Africa	6	166	1	55	7	221
West Africa	9	269			9	269
Latin Africa	11	186	8[a]	202	19	388
Southern Africa	15	267	20[b]	504	35	771
Subtotal	41	888	30	786	71	1,674
Middle East			1	12	1	12
Southern Asia						
India, Pakistan and Ceylon	27	580	8	122	35	702
Southeast Asia						
Burma, Thailand and Malaya	1	27	5[c]	109	6	136
Indonesia	10	353			10	353
Oceania	8	148	1	6	9	154
Philippines	7	197			7	197
Subtotal	26	725	6	115	32	840
East Asia						
Japan	12	590			12	590
Korea	9	1,346			9	1,346
Formosa and Hongkong	7	282			7	282
Subtotal	28	2,218	—	—	28	2,218
Latin America						
Mexico and Central America	7	78			7	78
Caribbean Area	10	169			10	169
South America	18	501			18	501
Subtotal	35	748	—	—	35	748
Total	157	5,159	45	1,035	202	6,194
Percentage	78	83	22	17	100	100

NOTES: [a] Of which seven seminaries (having 192 students) are in Madagascar where Malagasy is the primary language of instruction.
[b] Principally seminaries of the various Dutch Reformed Churches, where English is sometimes used as a secondary language.
[c] Seminaries in Burma and Thailand (in Burma, most Christians read either Sgaw, Karen, Pwo Karen, Kachin, Chin and/or English—rather than Burmese).

The list of seven foreign languages of major importance to the seminaries outside of India, as set forth in Tables 82 and 84, is an arbitrary one. The purpose in constructing it is to point out the smallest common denominator of written languages serving the greatest common denominator of seminaries. On the basis of this list, or some similar list of less than 10 foreign languages, a program could be inaugurated which would envision the translation of many rather than a few theological texts into each of these local languages.

A criticism which can be made of this list is that it has been somewhat arbitrarily constructed. A case might be advanced for establishing two or three categories of languages having first, second and third priority. This might enable some languages to have a complete set of translations, some languages the majority of titles being translated, and the remainder a few titles. In the last-named category one might also include Arabic and Thai, for example. These two languages would not otherwise qualify on the basis of the seven criteria of language selection outlined above. However, in view of the fact that Arabic is the vernacular for many of the theological students in the seminaries of the Eastern Churches (Greek, Syrian, Coptic, etc.) in Egypt and the Middle East, the translation of some texts into Arabic might be of real use in an effort to strengthen those churches. In the case of Thai, this language is said to constitute an important point of contact with the Buddhist world.

The essential aim should be to keep the list of foreign languages down to an absolute minimum inasmuch as it would be a waste of funds to attempt to translate a few theological texts into a large number of foreign languages in the hope of providing a text or two for many foreign missionaries to use. As in so many aspects of Protestantism, what is needed is a concentration of effort; and the seminaries overseas need translations of theological texts which will be useful in all rather than a few of their courses, if a significant improvement in the level of their teaching is to be made.

CHAPTER 11

INTERBOARD AGENCIES ASSISTING THEOLOGICAL SCHOOLS

A. AGENCIES PRODUCING THEOLOGICAL TEXTS

There are a number of interboard agencies which have been engaged for some years in the production of religious literature. For the most part, these agencies of necessity supply the needs of the mission boards and younger churches with literature of all types, including sermons, devotional literature, Sunday school texts, religious plays, music items (hymnals, choir and sheet music), tracts, pictures and posters, language textbooks, books on health, religious diaries, readers, periodicals, audio-visual aids, as well as theological texts. In addition various individual mission boards maintain small printing establishments, "book rooms" and bookstores overseas. A few of these are fairly large, as, for example, the Lucknow Publishing House: this is the only Methodist concern of its type in Asia, and does most of the Methodist printing for all India and much of the printing for other denominations in north India as well.

It is not possible to formulate an easy definition of what constitutes a theological text, other than to say that it is a book used in the instruction provided for ordinands at a seminary. Since there is a fairly wide range in the academic levels of the seminaries overseas, such a definition is a broad one. Accordingly one cannot estimate with precision what part of the activities of most of the interboard agencies are devoted to the production of texts suitable for use in seminaries. Even though such a proportion in some instances amounts in all probability to not much more than 10%, some mention should be made of the accomplishments to date of those agencies which have ventured into this field.

1. *Africa*

The American and British missionary societies formerly coordinated their production of literature in English for use in Africa through the medium of the International Committee on Christian Literature for Africa (ICCLA). The Committee was founded in 1929 as a subcommittee of the IMC. The British section and executive office were located in the London headquarters of the IMC, and the North American section in the New York City offices of the Division of Foreign Missions (DFM). An affiliated group of the ICCLA in Paris is working on the production of literature for French-speaking Africa, and comparable efforts are being fostered for the Portuguese territories.

Comparatively little of the ICCLA's activities have been at the theological level.

In addition to the printing of religious texts of one sort or another, the Committee over the years granted small subsidies to missionary presses in the Belgian Congo. After World War II it was realized that a choice would have to be made between the radical expansion of a number of small and medium-sized presses scattered throughout the Congo and the "establishment of a central cooperative press capable of a relatively large volume of work. There was general agreement that the latter course was preferable." As a result La Librairie évangelique au Congo in Leopoldville was reorganized, and in 1946–48 a concrete building was erected for it on a site furnished by the Baptist Missionary Society. An up-to-date printing department was added to the already existing importing and distributing service. Since then, more than 75,000,000 pages of books and periodicals in 20 or more different languages have been produced by the Union Printing House and Book Store (as it is known in English). At this press "all stapling is done with brass wire as steel wire rusts rapidly in the hot, humid climate of Congo, allowing the books to fall to pieces."

The ICCLA also published four periodicals, *Books for Africa, Listen, The Daystar,* and *Comme des flambeaux.* The latter two are simple quarterlies for catechists and have not been notably successful. The ICCLA also sent parcels "of theological books to various Bible schools and theological colleges in British Africa." It was planned to extend this service in 1954 and 1955 to the French- and Portuguese-speaking areas of Africa.

The ICCLA received financial support from American, British and European missionary societies, Bible societies, religious publishing houses, etc., as well as from philanthropic foundations from time to time (e.g., the Phelps-Stokes Fund and the Carnegie Corporation). In 1956 the Committee's income amounted to $9,688 compared to expenditures of $11,074. Of the ICCLA income, $6,080 was contributed by the Africa Committee of the DFM and $2,290 by the Conference of Missionary Societies in Great Britain and Ireland.

In 1956 or thereabouts the Committee concluded that it would be advisable if its activities were transferred from London and New York to Africa itself, possibly through the establishment of regional offices under the auspices of the various national Christian councils in Africa. As of June 30, 1958, the ICCLA was merged into the Christian Literature Council of the Conference of Missionary Societies in Great Britain and Ireland. Under its new auspices it is hoped that work may be continued in London in support of the production in Africa of texts for use at all levels.

Mention should also be made of the series of books entitled "Simple Theology for East African Readers" which have been produced in Nairobi, Kenya, under the direction of Rev. E. K. Cole, Principal of St. Paul's United Theological College in Limuru. In 1958 three books on church history (all written by Dr. Cole) had been published, with two other volumes in preparation. It was hoped that it might prove possible at some point to publish an additional 14 titles by different authors relating to other important aspects of the church's work.

2. Southern Asia

In this area the one interboard activity of note with respect to the production and distribution of theological texts is the All-India Theological Textbook Program which is producing The Christian Students' Library (CSL). This program was commenced in 1948 under the auspices of the National Christian Council of India as an experiment in the production of vernacular theological literature based on texts in English.

Originally under the direction of Professor Marcus Ward of the United Theological College at Bangalore, the program is now being directed by Dr. J. Russell Chandran, Principal of that College. The Senate of Serampore University agreed to act as sponsor of the project. The Christian Literature Society undertook to publish the English texts, and the Indian Literature Fund provided approximately $200 for the initial expenses.

Professor Ward has written that it was decided to have the project commence by concentrating "on the preparation of manuscripts in English to serve as bases . . . for versions in the Indian languages. This is the origin of the term 'basic texts.' " The aim has been ultimately to produce about 60 volumes of theological texts at the rate of four books a year. "Within the list were degrees of urgency. Other sources of information suggested that provision should be made for about 12 Indian languages. . . . No one book on the required list was available in all the 12 languages and there were only a few suitable for the purpose in more than three. . . . Each completed basic text will be offered to the provincial literature committees. . . . They will be asked in consultation with the theological schools in the area to select Indian scholars to prepare the vernacular versions. . . . Much stress is laid on the intention that the vernacular books should be *versions* and not word-for-word translations."

In 1949, 16 titles were selected, the English texts of which were to be prepared by 16 scholars. These titles were aimed primarily to meet the needs of the L.Th.

syllabus and were considered to be the ones most urgently needed. However, the authors were "already engaged on (other) full-time work" and a number of them were "using or looking forward to the comparative leisure of furlough or sabbatical year to complete (their assignments). . . . The original intention that further lists of lower priorities should await the completion of the first 16 . . . had to be modified in view of the unequal rate of progress." In 1952 the Editorial Committee selected 16 additional titles and invited other scholars to prepare them as basic texts. Table 85 shows the progress made by the CSL project as of May 1957.

TABLE 85. STATUS OF CHRISTIAN STUDENTS' LIBRARY AS OF MAY 1957

	Titles
Already published	11
In press	3
Manuscripts under consideration or to be received	6
Other manuscripts in preparation	14
Additional titles accepted by authors	35
Titles not yet accepted	20
	89

The authors and titles of the works mentioned in Table 85 are listed in Appendix Al. Dr. Chandran commented in 1957 that

of the books published so far, one is on Church History, three on Doctrine, and all the others are commentaries. . . . We need to have a more even distribution of the subjects in the CSL selections. . . . I am sorry to report that, so far, no Indian author has completed his assignment for the Christian Students' Library. This, in a way, is discouraging because one of the purposes of the Basic Texts Scheme was to encourage Indian theological writers. In order to secure more Indian authors, I think, we should consider two things. First, some theological teachers in the Regional Colleges have expressed that they would rather write the books in their own language than English. It will certainly be good if they write in their own language and then translate it into English for the CSL series. Secondly, we should also consider the question of offering an honorarium. . . .

At the May 1957 meeting of the CSL Coordinating Committee it was announced with pleasure that Canon E. Sambayya had submitted a completed manuscript to the CSL, the first Indian to do so.

Dr. Chandran points out that to a Hindu the word "incarnation" in Hindi has a very different meaning than it does in English. Therefore, whenever this word appears in an English text it cannot be literally translated into Hindi, and the sense of the word must be conveyed by means of one or more idiomatic substitutes, depending upon its use. This points to one reason why the CSL translations must be prepared with care. Another reason accounting for delays is the fact that the CSL project has had no person serving full time in its activities. Furthermore, once a manuscript is completed and sent to the printer in India, as long as one year is occasionally required for the edition to be printed.

Some persons have asked why more use has not been made of existing English material for the production of Indian versions. Professor Ward has defended the practice of the CSL in concentrating on the preparation of new English texts as follows: "It is all a matter of what has been called 'unexpressed presuppositions.' The Indian Church needs the books which speak to her condition written by men who have the life of India in their blood. . . . We know of no single book (in English) which would fully answer the need which we are trying to meet in each of our titles, and we cannot afford more than one book on each theme."

In his 1957 report to the Theological Education Committee of the National Council of Churches in India, Dr. M. H. Harrison made the following remarks concerning the CSL: "A few (theological) institutions had hardly heard of this project, but most were already making use of the English volumes. In one institution there was considerable criticism of this series as being too Western in its approach and as suited to the needs of B.D. rather than L.Th. students. But most of those who had read the volumes were enthusiastic in their praise. Certain institutions were already using them as a basis for their teaching, and some progress in the translation of the volumes into the regional languages is being made."

At the end of 1955 several of the CSL books were being translated by regional theological literature committees into Bengali, Hindi, Kannada, Orya, Telugu, Tamil and Malayalam. Some have already come off the press and are in circulation. Permission has been granted to the Chinese Literature Society in Hongkong for the rendering of CSL books into Chinese. Several CSL books are also being translated into Thai, and the question has been raised whether it might be possible to have the CSL series expanded in scope so that it could be used by seminaries in other parts of Southeast Asia. Some of the CSL series of books have been sent by the American Board of Commissioners for Foreign Missions to Africa where they have been well received.

The report of the meeting of the CSL Coordinating Committee held on June 8, 1956, states: "In view of the increasing popularity of the CSL Book Club and the demand for the books in Southeast Asian countries, it was decided that from number 10 onwards, 3,000 copies of each book be printed. . . . It was decided to print 2,000 each of the first six numbers, all of which have been sold out." On the other hand, it appears that few of the CSL series are now being sold to non-Christians.

Because of the expenses involved in their production and the limited markets for them, most of the CSL books have to be subsidized. It was originally estimated that the sum of £5,000 (or $14,000) would be needed as a revolving fund to finance the publication of the basic texts in English and that other considerable sums would be needed for each of the 12 vernacular versions in India. The CSL Coordinating Committee once tried to estimate the ultimate total cost of the project and concluded that because there were so many variable factors involved it would not be feasible to try to arrive at a definite figure in this respect.

The project had spent approximately $5,000 up to 1958, but heavy translation and printing expenses are anticipated. Some of the funds of the CSL have been received from English and American mission boards, with the bulk ($4,000) having been contributed by the Board of Founders of the Nanking Theological Seminary. The Committee hopes to obtain support from the National Council of Churches in India. However, the total budget of the Council in 1955 amounted to approximately $60,000, so it is clear that the Council will not be in a position to assist the CSL to a significant extent.

3. Southeast Asia

The Christian Literature Society in Indonesia (Badan Penerbit Kristen) which was founded by Dutch missionaries, is carrying on some translations of theological texts into Indonesian. With its headquarters in Djakarta, the Society is a cooperative venture whose activities are headed by Professor Dr. J. Verkuyl, a Dutch minister who also teaches on the faculty of the Djakarta Theological College in that city. A small number of church histories, Greek and Hebrew grammars, Biblical commentaries and some theological texts have been translated into Indonesian (as well as evangelistic tracts, etc.). These have been of use primarily to the junior level seminaries in Indonesia rather than to the students at the Djakarta Theological College.

4. East Asia

Japan: The Japan Commission on Christian Literature (JCCL) was organized in 1949 to carry on the work of planning, editing, printing and distributing Christian literature under the management of its own Board of Commissioners formed by the representatives of the constituents of the National Christian Council of Japan. In addition, the JCCL receives the cooperation of the following churches and organizations:

> United Church of Christ in Japan (Kyodan)
> Japan Anglican Episcopal Church
> Evangelical Lutheran Church in Japan
> Japan Baptist Convention
> Japan Bible Society
> National Christian Education Association
> National Young Men's Christian Association
> Christian Kindergarten Union
> Japan Christian Literature Society (Kyo Bun Kwan).

A review of the *JCCL's Report of Christian Literature in 1955* discloses that the translation of theological texts into Japanese has proceeded somewhat farther than the CSL project in India, although the list is still fairly brief. The bulk of the Commission's output consists of tracts and texts designed for use at preseminary levels. In 1954 the Theological Committee of the National Christian Council was reported to be planning the publication of a series of the classics of theology, the study of which was felt to be urgently needed.

Korea: The major theological translation project in process in Korea in 1957 was the rendering of a Bible dictionary into Korean. There does not appear to be any central agency in Korea working in this field. The shortage of theological texts in the vernacular would appear to be greater in Korea than in almost any other country in Africa, Asia or Latin America.

Hongkong: The Council on Christian Literature for Overseas Chinese (CCLOC) was organized in Hongkong in 1952. Its activities are similar to those of the Japan Committee on Christian Literature. The CCLOC is supported in part by various American, British and Canadian mission boards which have an interest in Hongkong. In 1955 it had four staff members, plus nine experienced part-time translators. Approximately two-thirds of its sales were in areas outside of Hongkong, particularly in Formosa. It has published about a dozen theological texts, usually in printings of 1–2,000 copies.

The CCLOC received a grant from the United Society for Christian Literature to publish some of the titles in the *World Christian Books* series (see below). It has also published in Chinese four titles of the Christian Students' Library series (India) and has served as the publisher of *The Christian Classics Library* being produced by the Board of Founders of Nanking Theological Seminary.

In Hongkong the Lutheran Theological Seminary is said to have done some outstanding work in the translation and publication of theological literature into Chinese.

Board of Founders, Nanking Theological Seminary: During World War II the Nanking Theological Seminary (NTS) was obliged to move to West China. At this time some of the faculty members conceived the idea of translating into Chinese a series of the classics of Christian literature, as well as a number of substantial contemporary works having relevance to the problems confronting Chinese Christians inside and outside of China.

The choice of the titles to be translated proved to be something of a stumbling block. Accordingly the matter was referred to the Board of Founders of the NTS in New York City (see below). The Board organized a series of three conferences of leading theologians which took place in 1944–46. The result was the selection of a list of 54 titles under the name of *The Christian Classics Library*. Of the 54 titles, 20 are "classics of early Christianity," 26 are "classics of Protestant Christianity," and 8 are "modern works" (see Appendix A2 for the list). Most of the texts are basic reference works and in terms of their academic use their level is considerably above that of the texts comprising the *Christian Students' Library* list in India.

In 1946 Dr. Francis P. Jones (formerly on the NTS faculty and presently the head of the Board of Founders' literature program) returned to Nanking. A year later some translations were commenced. However, owing to the unsettled political and military conditions in China during those years, little progress was made. In 1949–51 the American members of the NTS faculty were obliged to return to the United States. In all, nine manuscripts in Chinese were left in Nanking where it is presumed they are safe and that they may some day be published there. All nine manuscripts are titles from the "classics of early Christianity" series.

In 1954 the Board of Founders decided to resume the literature project. Dr. Jones and a small staff of Chinese scholars were provided office facilities in the library of Drew Theological Seminary in Madison, N.J., where the work is being carried on. The number of Chinese assistants has ranged from between two and five full-time scholars, whose work is proofread by Dr. Jones. Subsequently the Founders purchased a house in Madison costing approximately $21,000 for the use of the project.

In the period 1947–50 the Roman Catholic Archbishop of Nanking, Most Rev. Paul Yu Ping, indicated that he might arrange to have some Dominican fathers translate five titles in the "classics of early Christianity" series (No. 6, 10 and 15–17 relating to the lives of various leading figures in the early church and the works of Augustine and Thomas Aquinas). This cooperation on the part of Roman Catholic scholars has never materialized, despite the fact that the expenses involved were to be underwritten by the Board of Founders.

TABLE 86.   STATUS OF THE CHRISTIAN
CLASSICS LIBRARY AS OF 1957

Translations not begun yet	21
Translation just begun	3
Manuscripts mostly or all in hand	16
Manuscripts in Nanking	9
Published	5
	54

With respect to the 54 titles selected over a decade ago, in 1946, Table 86 shows their status as of 1957.

It has not been possible to proceed with these translations as rapidly as had originally been hoped. Initially the expectation was that 5–6 volumes would be translated each year, but the current rate is 2–3 a year. It is not easy to obtain Chinese scholars having a good vocabulary in English. One of the most difficult problems is the need to refer back to the original texts which are written in Hebrew, Greek, Latin, French or German, and there are few scholars conversant with Chinese who also know these five other languages.

Originally the Board of Founders did not wish to subsidize the printing and production costs of the completed manuscripts. However, owing to the comparatively limited market for them, the Founders during the past two years have made small grants to the CCLOC (as noted above) for this purpose. The Founders pay the CCLOC the cost of printing the manuscript. Of the sales proceeds, the CCLOC retains 25% to cover its handling costs, and the remaining 75% reverts to the Founders. Of the four titles which have been published, 2,000 copies of each have been printed. Cloth-bound copies are sold in the United States for $1.50 and in Hongkong for about US$1. Paper copies are sold in the United States at $1 and in Hongkong for about US75¢. Information is not readily available as to how many copies of each of the four titles have so far been sold.

The Board of Founders has up to now been the sole financial supporter of this project (with the exception of a $1,000 contribution received some years ago from a Lutheran church in Baltimore, Md.). Some mission boards have expressed interest in this work, but not to the extent of granting subsidies to it.

In the four fiscal years 1954-57 the Founders appropriated out of current income a total of approximately $95,000 (or an average annual expenditure of $24,-000) to underwrite the on-going costs of the translation program. In the same period the project completed 21 manuscripts (consisting of four titles already published plus 17 which are "mostly or all in hand"). Thus these 21 titles cost $95,000 to produce, or $4,500 per title. Since three-fourths of them had not as yet been published in 1957, a conservative estimate would be that it will cost the Founders about $5,000 to publish each of the 17 manuscripts now awaiting publication.

Excluding the nine completed manuscripts in Nanking, there remain 21 manuscripts "not yet begun" plus three more which are "just begun," making a total of 24 in this general category. Assuming the cost of translating and publishing these 24 titles continues at the rate of $5,000 apiece, this would indicate that the Founders are confronted with a further expenditure of $120,000 for this project. If the current annual level of appropriations of approximately $25,000 is maintained (which amounts to about one-fourth of the total current annual income received by the Founders), this indicates the Founders might complete the financ-

TABLE 87. FINANCIAL OUTLOOK OF CHRISTIAN STUDENTS' LIBRARY PROJECT AS OF 1957

Appropriations	If Completed in 5 Years	If Completed in 10 Years
Voted 1954-57	$95,000	$95,000
Prospective	125,000	250,000
	$220,000	$345,000

ing of this project in five years. However, with the editing and translation of the texts now proceeding at the rate of two or three texts a year, it will require 8-12 years for the project to be completed (exclusive of the manuscripts still in Nanking). The over-all financial outlook of the project is summarized in Table 87.

Thus the Founders will have in all probability disbursed a minimum total of

$220,000 in the nine years 1954–62 to produce 45 titles at an average cost of approximately $5,000. If the rate of translation continues at the present level of 2–3 titles a year and thereby necessitates, say, an additional ten rather than five years to complete the translation of the remaining 24 titles, the result would be a prospective expenditure of $250,000, a total disbursement of $345,000, and an average cost of approximately $7,500 per title.

In May 1957 the Board of Founders voted to continue this project in 1958, with the suggestion being made that it should be reviewed with a view toward (1) reducing the number of books on the list, (2) setting up translation priorities for the remainder of the works, and (3) appending a time schedule for the next four years.

It would be less expensive if the Board were to transfer the operation of this project to a center such as Hongkong or Taiwan in Asia where university and seminary faculty members could serve as part-time translators. On the other hand, many of the important basic library resources on which the project is now relying at the Drew Seminary library are not to be found in Asia.

Whatever the verdict as to the location of this project in future years, it is clear that the Founders have made an important start in the task of translating basic scholarly texts into Chinese. Partly through circumstances beyond its control, the task has proved to be a lengthier and more costly one than was originally anticipated. It could, however, effectively serve as a nucleus for a more broadly based effort to translate into Chinese the theological texts which are suitable for daily use in the seminaries now enrolling overseas Chinese students.

5. *Latin America*

In 1938 the Union Theological Seminary in Buenos Aires commenced the publication in Spanish of a series of theological textbooks and manuals known as "La Biblioteca de cultura evangélica" and then consisting of eight titles, including translations of works by such American authors as Edgar Goodspeed, Shailer Matthews, etc.

Subsequently a number of national councils of churches in Latin America organized literacy and literature committees in their own countries. Later their activities were coordinated by the Committee on Cooperation in Latin America (CCLA) which grouped them into three regional committees. Dr. Gonzalo Baez-Camargo, professor of Christian literature and journalism at the Union Theological Seminary in Mexico City, has served as Secretary of the Literacy and Literature Committee of the CCLA and as a consultant to the two committees producing literature in Spanish.

The first regional committee serves the River Plate area, and its chairman is Dr. B. Foster Stockwell, President of the Union Theological Seminary in Buenos Aires. This committee produces religious literature of all sorts under the publishing name of "La Aurora" which is sent to all parts of South America. Most (i.e., about 20 in number) of the theological texts which have so far been translated into Spanish, and which are of use to seminaries and in the education of the ministry generally, have been produced under the auspices of this committee. Among its publications have been the Carnahan Lectures which are given each year at the Union Theological Seminary in Buenos Aires by prominent Protestant leaders from Europe, North America and elsewhere.

A second regional committee is located in Mexico City. It publishes texts and tracts under the trade name of "Casa unida de publicaciones." This committee has produced few theological texts in Spanish, having left this activity for the most part to the River Plate committee to undertake.

The third regional committee is located in Rio de Janeiro and translates books into Portuguese for the use of Protestants in Brazil. However, aside from a Bible Concordance issued some years ago, it has as yet published no text in Portuguese at the theological level.

In their operations, the two Spanish committees have resembled the Japan Commission on Christian Literature and the CCLOC in Hongkong in that their output has run the gamut from a few theological texts to large numbers of tracts, etc. On the other hand, the Portuguese committee has fallen considerably behind the two other committees in the extent of its output.

The Committee on Literacy and Literature of the CCLA has a budget of approximately $30,000 a year to devote to the work of its three regional committees. This $30,000 is usually not disbursed until, or only to the extent that, it has been matched dollar for dollar by the regional committees. Thus, in theory, a total of $60,000 a year could be available for the production of Protestant religious literature and literacy aids in Latin America. Since it would appear that no more than 10% of the activity of the regional committees is devoted to the production of theological texts, this would indicate that a maximum of $6,000 is being spent annually for this purpose in this area. The actual amount being spent each year is probably less than this.

Among the activities of the individual denominations producing texts in Latin America, mention should be made of the Committee on Spanish Publications which is supported by the United Lutheran Church (in the USA) and by Lutheran church bodies elsewhere. The Committee has published a small number (approximately half a dozen) of theological texts in Spanish which are being used by Lutheran seminaries in this area. Finally, note should also be made of the publication in the spring of 1958 by the Matanzas Seminary of *Lecciones de filosofía de la religion,* the first of what is planned to be a series of texts in this field.

6. *World Christian Books*

Bishop Stephen Neill is General Editor of the World Christian Books (WCB) series. After he completed the writing of Part I of the IMC African Survey,

Bishop Neill decided to devote his time to the preparation of a series of short
and simple religious texts which might be of use to ordinand students, pastors
and catechists in Africa and elsewhere. The aim has been to limit each book to
about 100 pages, or 25,000 words. "We work for those who, without having advanced technical qualifications, have a good general knowledge of the faith, and
want to build on it." Thus the level of the WCB series is somewhat below that
of the Christian Students' Library project in India.

The first title in the WCB series in English was published in Great Britain in
October 1954. Since then a total of 24 titles (listed in Appendix A3) have been
published at the rate of four to six per year in the period 1955–58. Title No. 25,
to be published in 1959, will inaugurate a second and similar series.

As of September 30, 1958, a total of 254,334 copies of the first 24 titles had
been sold in Great Britain. In England the books are published by the Lutterworth Press in London, and are sold at 2s 6d (35¢) per copy. The American edition is being published by the Association Press (National Board of the YMCA).
In the United States upward of 100,000 copies had been sold as of March 1957,
some through Book Club subscriptions.

About 60% of the WCB books in English now being sold are exported from
Great Britain. Some titles have been read in as many as 64 countries. Bishop Neill
reports: "It was gratifying to hear from a young American missionary in Indonesia
that he had used two of our books as the basis for lectures to theological students,
going through them almost sentence by sentence, and finding them satisfactory for
this purpose. . . . The most remarkable feature is the evenness of the sales of the
books. We have not yet produced an unsaleable book. . . . The first ten have all
had to be reprinted."

In 1958 the WCB inaugurated a system whereby prior to their being published
the basic English texts would be reviewed by faculties and students at 12 seminaries throughout Africa, Asia and Latin America. The purpose of this is to help
insure that as far as possible the texts of the books will be written in a proper
style, etc., and without Western preconceptions. Each seminary will receive four
typescripts a year for comment and criticism. The early results accruing from this
policy have been encouraging. One author, a missionary residing in Bengal, India,
received comments on her manuscript from reviewers in Japan, Samoa, Nigeria and
Buenos Aires.

From the start it was intended that these basic English texts should be translated
by local church councils and literature committees in Africa, Asia and Latin America into the vernacular languages used in their countries. Table 88 presents a list of
the 30 languages into which the first 20 titles of the series had been translated or
adapted as of April 30, 1958.

In this connection Bishop Neill writes: "Friends sometimes ask how we manage to control these translations, and to verify their accuracy. The answer, of course, is that we cannot. . . . In the matter of translation the agents and the authorities must be the Christian literature committees of the various National Councils. It is impossible for the central office either to direct or control these many translations. . . . In almost all these areas it is difficult to find competent translators."

As of April 30, 1958, three WCB titles had been translated into Malagasy, and one each into Setswana, Lushai and Khasi. At present the staffs of the Methodist Laymen's Training Institute in Western Nigeria and of Immanuel College, the seminary in Ibadan, are cooperating in preparing translations of eight WCB texts into Yoruba, the principal language of Western Nigeria which is spoken by nearly 8,000,000 people. A small number of titles are also being translated into the local languages of East Africa.

Owing to the large number of African vernaculars, most of the books in the WCB series used in Africa have been written in English. As previously noted, English is increasingly coming to be the lingua franca in many of these countries; nevertheless the style and vocabulary used in the WCB titles in English in some instances have proven to be too advanced for African theological students. Writing in September 1957, Bishop Neill cited a letter "from a good and valued friend in Nigeria" which contained "some of the severest criticism" the WCB project had as yet received:

After quoting from my report on theological education in Africa a list of requirements which I had laid down for theological text books for Africa (shorter than the ordinary English text book, in simple English style, avoidance of presuppositions which will be strange to the African mind, awareness of conditions of life in a younger Church), the writer continues:

"When World Christian Books was announced . . . we looked forward to being given the books which met these requirements. Our very deep disappointment in the series is due to the remarkable degree to which they fail to meet these requirements. When one hears on all sides complaints that the series is 'too hard' for nearly all those teachers and pastors for whom books are so urgently needed, the hardness can be analysed into (1) Style often involved (2) Vocabulary often too wide (3) Context very far removed from that in which the West African lives to-day, giving the impression that India was the context—or sometimes just England—in which the writer had written. . . . Everywhere I found disappointment at the series, and in most places this was coupled with a great hope that it may be possible to launch a simpler series. I do not know on whom the Editor relied for his information as to what Nigeria needed, but I did not meet anyone in any of the Churches whose opinion has been asked at any stage. If a new series can be launched, it is very greatly to be hoped that constant and widespread advice will be taken from those who are actually at work, both Africans and Europeans in Africa."

It is good that we should receive such criticism, and it is important that we should ask ourselves what we propose to do about it. Perhaps the first point to make is that nearly a quarter of the World Christian Books budget is spent in trying to keep in close touch with those actually engaged in the work, in Africa as elsewhere. But from the beginning we adopted the principle that we must accept the existing ecumenical structure of the Churches, and work in each country through the Christian Council and its Literature Committee. . . . Each manuscript is duplicated and sent out to our eight official advisers, one of whom is an African colleague in West Africa. . . . Information is constantly relayed to the Christian Councils and Literature Committees. Appeals have repeatedly been made for information as to the suitability of the books, both before and after publication, and also for guidance as to suitable writers from the younger Churches. If our friend in Nigeria knows how to get answers regularly out of these overworked and understaffed bodies, perhaps he will tell us. . . .

But even when we have done all that we ought to do, Africa remains our principal headache. In other fields, World Christian Books in English are not found too difficult by those for whom they are intended—those who have at least passed through high school, and can read an ordinary English newspaper. They are not found too difficult in translation by ordinary church members and village workers. But in Africa most Churches have decided, perhaps rightly, not to translate our books into the vernaculars, since over immense areas English and French are becoming the linguae francae. This means that in Africa those who use World Christian Books must use them, if they use them at all, in English or French; and in almost every case they find them too difficult for their needs. This is an overwhelming argument in favour of the production of the simpler series, which we have come to call the Third Level, and in favour of which we have so often argued. We have generally supposed that such a series would not be printed but only mimeographed in English, and sent out to the various areas for translation or adaptation. After studying the criticisms of our friend in Nigeria, we are convinced that the Third Level also ought to be printed in English, and that it would have a wide usefulness in that form in Africa, if not elsewhere.

Paradoxically, a short while after the Bishop wrote the comments quoted above, a "distinguished theological teacher" who had just spent two months in Nigeria reported to him that the WCB series "seem to be meeting a very real need in that country; this seems to be just the kind of material that the students in the Theological Colleges find that they can use." A few months later a letter from a theological school in the Orange Free State was received in which the author wrote: "The (WCB) books will not do as theological text-books for us, because they are too short. But if the World Christian Books are too brief for text-books, they have proved to be admirable as supplementary references or required reading for part of a course."

Thus it would appear that the WCB series meets a real need in sections of Africa or certain theological schools where the educational level is higher than in others; and that elsewhere a Third Level series might be found to be more useful. In response to the need for the latter type of books, in 1957 the United Society for Christian Literature in London commenced a project aimed at producing a series of a simpler type than the WCB books and which would be of use "often at a village level and for its evangelistic outreach."

Of the 189 WCB titles which had been translated or adapted into a foreign language as of April 30, 1958, as shown in Table 88, 153 were written in Asiatic languages. Japan was the first country to decide to translate the whole series.

TABLE 88. WORLD CHRISTIAN BOOKS LIST OF TRANSLATIONS OR ADAPTATIONS AS OF APRIL 30, 1958[a]

Language	1	2	3	4	5	6	7	8	9	10	11	12	13	14	15	16	17	18	19	20
Chinese	x	x	x	x	x	x	x	x	x	x	x	x	x	x	x	x	x	x	x	x
Telugu	x	x			x	x	x	x	x		x		x	x			x	x	x	x
Arabic	x	x		x		x	x	x	x	x	x	x	x	x						
Japanese	x	x	x	x	x	x	x	x	x	x	x	x								
Sinhalese	x	x		x	x	x	x	x	x		x		x							
Burmese	x	x		x	x	x	x	x				x								
Urdu	x	x		x		x	x		x	x			x	x						
Sgaw Karen	x	x			x	x	x	x	x			x								
Tamil	x	x		x	x	x	x			x			x							
German	x	x			x	x			x	x		x								
Persian	x				x	x							x	x						
Kachin	x	x			x	x			x			x								
Bengali		x		x		x		x	x				x	x						
Oriya		x	x		x	x	x	x												
Gujerati	x	x			x	x			x	x										
Spanish	x	x	x	x	x															
Kannada	x	x			x	x			x				x							
Chin		x			x	x			x			x								
Indonesian		x					x	x	x					x						
Marathi		x	x		x	x	x													
Hindi	x	x		x	x	x														
Pwo Karen	x	x			x	x														
Thai	x								x			x								
Portuguese	x	x		x																
Malagasy	x	x											x							
Malayalam	x			x																
French	x	x																		
Setswana		x																		
Lushai						x														
Khasi		x																		
	22	26	5	12	18	21	12	10	15	7	5	9	10	7	1	1	2	2	2	2

Total: 189

NOTE: [a] Projected, in preparation, and in circulation. Title No. 23 has been translated into Dutch. In addition, nine books have been transcribed into Braille.

Comparatively little progress has been made with WCB editions in the languages of Latin America, i.e., Spanish and Portuguese. Two books have been produced in Spanish in Mexico and two in Portuguese in São Paulo, Brazil. On the other hand Bishop Neill reports it is becoming evident that "the development of Christian literature in Spanish and Portuguese is not keeping pace with the astonishingly rapid growth of the Evangelical Churches in almost all the countries of Latin America." Some WCB books in English are being used as texts in Protestant seminaries in several Latin American countries.

According to Bishop Neill, "one of the gravest difficulties has been in effectively drawing in the younger churches in the whole process of writing, criticising and editing the book. . . . We cannot offer our authors commercial terms, and the small honorarium they are willing to accept is no more than the fee which would be offered for four short articles by any of the periodicals that remunerate writers at competitive rates. . . . Less constructive advice has been received from literature committees overseas than could be wished."

Despite the economies practiced in producing the WCB editions and the low sales prices charged per title, these books are reported to be still too expensive for many ministers in Africa, Asia and Latin America:

We keep our prices as low as we possibly can; yet there is no doubt that for some areas this price is still far too high. Clergy and teachers receive only a bare subsistence allowance, and have very little over for such purposes as the purchase of books. In certain areas, ministers and other regular Church workers are authorized to buy books from the Christian bookshops at half price up to a certain amount, the difference in price being borne by the Church authority. This means a certain amount of expense for the authorising authority, but it does bring books within the reach of many who would otherwise not be able to afford them; and on this system the Christian bookshops are not deprived of their legitimate profit—like any other business concern they must be able to pay their way. We wonder whether this system could not be much more widely extended. If we really believe in the importance of Christian literature, it should take a high place on the budget of all missions and Churches. We do not approve of a general free distribution of books; we do believe in an attempt being made by the Churches to relate the price of books to the amount that their servants can reasonably be expected to pay.

The 1957 expenditures of the WCB amounted to $8,837, against total receipts of $8,177, leaving an operating deficit of $660. Of the WCB's income, $1,500 was contributed by the Committee on World Literacy and Christian Literature of the DFM, and $2,240 was received in the form of royalties. The remainder of the WCB income was obtained largely in the form of small donations from various British and Canadian missionary societies.

In its early stages the WCB had some difficulty in raising the modest sums it needed for its operations. By 1958, however, it was able to report that through the contributions of mission boards and others its financial position was "stable and satisfactory." This comment was related to the first of the committee's two budgets, i.e., its own operating expenses. The second budget pertains to the cost of printing and publishing the individual WCB volumes. Here the prospect is unfavorable owing to the effects of inflation on book manufacturing costs in recent years. In order to maintain a selling price of 35 cents per volume to the public, the decision has regretfully been taken that the titles in the forthcoming second series will necessarily have to be somewhat shorter, and a reduced amount of royalties will be asked of the publishers.

In the light of the modest financial support it has received in comparison to other literature and translation projects, it would appear that the WCB has achieved truly impressive results.

Thus in almost all of the major areas a start has been made during the last few years in inaugurating the production of theological texts printed in the languages used in the seminaries overseas. Virtually all of the projects have been delayed by lack of funds and to some extent by an adherence to the most exacting of editing and translation standards. It would appear that the stage has been reached where a coordination, expansion and acceleration of the activities of these agencies might achieve an important "break through" during the next few years in the complicated task of making scholarly Christian texts available in all the vernaculars widely used in Africa, Asia and Latin America.

There have been a number of important efforts in recent years undertaken by nonmissionary American organizations for the purpose of making academic texts available to the libraries of secular educational institutions in the underdeveloped countries. These activities are summarized in *American Books in the Near East, Central Africa and Asia*—Report of the Second Conference on American Books Abroad, Sponsored by the National Book Committee, Arden House, Harriman, N.Y.—October 31–November 1, 1957, by Peter S. Jennison. It suffices to say that these efforts have met with a considerably greater success than have those which have been undertaken by the interboard missionary agencies in the theological field.

B. AGENCIES DISBURSING FUNDS TO SEMINARIES

Directly or indirectly the IMC and the majority of the Area and Functional Committees of the DFM have at one time or another been involved to a limited extent in activities related to seminaries in the underdeveloped countries. However, there are only two interboard agencies which disburse most or all of their funds in support of theological education overseas and which therefore call for comment here. The first is the Commission on Ministerial Training of the Africa Committee of the DFM, and the second is the Board of Founders of Nanking Theological Seminary. The record of these two agencies to date illustrates some of the problems which would confront the IMC in an attempt to assist overseas seminaries on a broad basis.

Africa Committee: The Africa Committee of the DFM, as mentioned in chapter 1 of this Survey, concerned itself for a number of years with social and political questions related to the African scene. The final recommendation in Part III of the *IMC's Survey of the Training of the Ministry in Africa* was that the IMC should "consider whether the time has not come for the formation of an International Committee on African Theological Education." Subsequently, in 1955, such a Committee was created by having the DFM Africa Committee form a Commission on Ministerial Training in Africa as the American segment of the International Committee. A similar commission was formed in London composed of representatives from the various British and continental missionary societies.

In 1955 the Division of World Missions of the Methodist Board of Foreign Missions contributed $50,000 to the Commission for the purpose of enabling it to "promote vigorously united advance in theological education in Africa." The minutes of the Commission's meetings disclose that in June 1955 the Commission expressed the hope that other boards "will as far as possible make at least token contributions to this common fund during 1955, and that substantial grants may be made available during 1956."

At the Commission's meeting held on November 8, 1955, "Dr. (M. Searle) Bates expressed the fear that the process of continued consultation in Africa might not speedily result in specific plans for action in respect to definite institutions. . . . Very few boards would be able to match the Methodist gift with proportionate contributions out of surpluses. In most cases substantial funds could only be allocated on the basis of detailed presentation of specific needs in areas and institutions in which those boards had reason to be directly interested. . . . The Commission recommended that North American Societies be asked to provide a budget of not less than $10,000 a year for three years for purposes of field consultation."

At the February 29, 1956, meeting "Dr. (George W.) Carpenter reported that we asked these boards for $10,000 a year for three years. We have definite commitments from two boards, in writing, for $1,500 a year." In 1955–56 the Disciples contributed $1,000 and the Congregational Church $500 to the Commission, and the Presbyterian Church US contributed and pledged $500 a year for three years. The Commission has not as yet engaged in a determined effort to raise funds over and above the aforesaid appeals to the mission boards. Thus for all practical purposes the only significant monetary response on the part of the boards to the recommendations made by the IMC African Survey was the $50,000 contributed by the Methodists to the Commission. Furthermore this $50,000 remains largely unspent. It is the Commission's policy as far as possible to utilize its resources primarily as "seed money" for launching projects and as funds to be matched by contributions from others for work in this field.

From a reading of the minutes of the meetings held by the Commission one gains the impression that so far it has not been able to accomplish a great deal, in part because of staffing difficulties and relationships abroad. Much of the discussion apparently has centered on the sending of individuals here and there, a proposal "to see what the responsibility of the African minister is to the urban situation—the relevance of the gospel to the urban society of Africa" and similar activities. In view of the purely advisory status of the Commission and the limited extent of its resources, it might not be reasonable to expect it to have achieved more than it has. Furthermore, the staff work of the Commission was added on to that of the African Committee as a whole which has increased in the past few years.

One of the more constructive accomplishments of the Commission, acting through the DFM Africa Committee, was the impetus it provided for the holding in July 1956 in Leopoldville, Belgian Congo, of the First Consultative Conference on the Training of the Ministry in Africa (previously cited). In general it may be said that the most important service rendered to date by the Commission has been keeping the subject of theological education in the forefront of the thinking of those mission boards which are concerned with Africa.

Board of Founders of Nanking Theological Seminary: The Board of Founders is the American organization which formerly supported the Nanking Theological Seminary in Nanking, China.

In 1932 the Methodist Board of Foreign Missions was the recipient of bequests from two wealthy, recluse sisters, Mrs. Rebecca A. D. Wendel Swope and Miss Ella V. von Echtzel Wendel. These bequests were designated for the work of the Nanking Seminary. In 1937 the Board of Founders was established, principally for the purpose of administering the income from these legacies. As of May 31, 1955, the book value of the Swope-Wendel Fund (which is maintained by the Division of World Missions of the Board of Missions of The Methodist Church for the benefit of the Board of Founders) amounted to $3,154,000. Of this sum, $2,561,000 was in the Permanent Fund, and $593,000 in the Unexpended Income Fund. The total income from the Swope-Wendel Fund amounts to approximately $100,000 a year.

When the Chinese Communists captured control of the mainland of China in 1949, it was no longer possible for the Board of Founders to transmit funds to the Nanking Seminary. For several years the income was allowed to accumulate in what is called the Unexpended Income Fund. In 1952, the Board obtained an order from the Surrogate's Court of New York County authorizing the use of its funds for activities in other parts of Asia, similar to the assistance which it had formerly contributed to the Seminary in Nanking.

The Chairman of the Board of Founders is Dr. Henry P. Van Dusen, the President of the Union Theological Seminary in New York City. The other officers and board members are mission board executives, etc., and the administration of the Founders' activities is headed by its Secretary-Treasurer, Dr. Frank T. Cartwright. In 1952 the Board appointed Dr. C. Stanley Smith as its field representative in Southeast Asia with offices in Singapore. Dr. Smith was a coauthor of the Anderson-Smith Report sponsored by the Board. Until the summer of 1956 he was also the Principal of the Trinity Theological College in Singapore. Dr. Smith retired in 1957 as the Board's field representative in this area and was succeeded in this capacity by Rev. John Fleming, formerly Secretary of the Malayan Christian Council in Singapore.

Since the inauguration in 1953 of its expanded program, the Board has made three types of grants:

1. small annual budgetary grants to 13 seminaries;
2. occasional capital grants to eight seminaries; and
3. appropriations for activities conducted directly by the Board itself.

Table 89 presents in a simplified form a list of the grants which the Board has made during the past six fiscal years.

A problem which has been a source of concern to the Board has been one confronting most grant-making organizations, namely, how far its grants should be scattered among recipient institutions. Consequently it is of interest to note the course which the Board of Founders has pursued in this respect during the past four years.

From a reading of the minutes of the directors' meetings held by the Board of Founders from 1952 to 1957, one gains the impression that much of the Board's time and money has been spent on matters such as traveling fellowships, scholarships and personnel arrangements. There is little set forth in the formal records concerning discussions on over-all strategy of theological education in Southeast Asia. At the 1953 annual meeting Dr. Eugene L. Smith raised the question whether in the long run the Board's funds could "best be invested in developing one top-flight school or in aiding a number of schools at various places in Asia."

An answer to this question was given at the 1954 annual meeting in which the Board resolved that "for the immediate future and until a suitable long-range policy can be evolved, grants-in-aid should normally be of a nonrecurring character . . . ," and that the Board should "endeavor to achieve a balanced program of translation, scholarship aid, operating help for institutions and funds for capital expenses." As for its long-range policy, the question whether "to develop one or more theological colleges of university grade" was to be studied in consultation with the IMC.

At the 1955 annual meeting, "the representative in Southeast Asia . . . referred to consideration which had been earlier given to the continuing policy of giving grants to the various institutions in Southeast Asia or a decision to concentrate on three or four institutions of strategic importance. The Founders recognize that no policy had been adopted with regard to this question, and it was voted that the consideration of a policy as between scattered appropriations or concentrated aid was to be deferred for later consideration."

In October 1955, "after long and sympathetic consideration . . . (the Board) expressed the conviction that in the interest of flexibility of program and effective use of its resources, the Board should make appropriations to qualified theological schools for their future service to the Christian Church without at present selecting any for special consideration."

The Founders did not wish in 1953 to start concentrating their support on one new institution because it was not then clear how soon it might be possible to resume contributions to seminaries on the mainland of China. If the Board were to become the major source of support for one or two institutions in Southeast Asia, this might make it difficult for the Founders to resume supporting the Nanking Seminary in a substantial way, assuming such action should once again become politically feasible.

TABLE 89. APPROPRIATIONS OF BOARD OF FOUNDERS OF THE NANKING THEOLOGICAL SEMINARY, 1953–58

	Appropriations for Fiscal Years Ending April 30 (in Thousands of Dollars)					
	1953	1954	1955	1956	1957	1958
For Current Work						
Burma Divinity School, Insein	4	2	2	2	2	2
McGilvary Theological Seminary, Chiengmai	2	2	2	1	1	1
Trinity Theological College, Singapore	3	3	6	5	6	6
Nommensen University Theological School						1
Djakarta Theological College	5	4	4	4	6	6
Theological School, Jogjakarta		2	1	3	3	4
Union Theological School, Makassar					1	3
Union Theological Seminary, Manila	3	4	3	3	5	6
College of Theology, Silliman University	2	1	2	2	3	2
College of Theology, Iloilo						1
Tainan Theological College	2	3	4	4	4	6
Taiwan Theological College, Taipeh	2	2	2	2	2	3
Lutheran Theological Seminary, Hongkong	1	1	1			
Subtotal	24	24	27	26	33	41
For Building Projects						
Burma Divinity School						2
McGilvary Theological Seminary						1
Tainan Theological College		1	27		23	12
Union Theological School, Makassar					14	
Trinity Theological College, Singapore	25		50	15		
Union Theological Seminary, Manila				80		
Djakarta Theological College		10	35			6
Ambon Theological School						10
Subtotal	25	11	112	95	37	31
For Board of Founders Activities						
Scholarships and Travel, etc.	4			4	2	7
Literature and Translation Projects		25	31	27	26	25
Singapore Office Expense		5	4	4	6	3
Missionary Support		14		14	14	14
Conferences on Theological Education		3		15		
Contingent Fund & Executive Secretary's Office		6	6	16	13	15
Subtotal	4	53	41	80	61	64
Total Appropriations	53	88	180	201	131	136

The Board believes it would be unwise for the Founders to select only one school in each country for support. The Board would prefer to support union seminaries, but if a denominational school serves a whole area and admits students from other denominations, the Board would also support such a seminary.

In the period 1953–58 the Board singled out five schools for exceptional support as shown in the tabulation of capital grants (of $10,000 or more) listed in Table 89. The funds for these capital grants were appropriated by the Board from its Unexpended Income Fund. This accounts for the fact that during the fiscal years 1955–58 the Board's total appropriations were larger than its current income of approximately $100,000 annually.

The Board will probably continue to adopt a flexible attitude toward the matter of how far it should concentrate its capital grants to a few seminaries. Meanwhile, writing from Indonesia in the summer of 1956, Dr. C. Stanley Smith stated: ". . . I am convinced . . . that the policy of the Board of Founders during the past four years of making comparatively small grants that would not impair the independence of the schools nor lessen the responsibilities of the school authorities and the churches for maintaining the general costs of the institutions has been very successful."

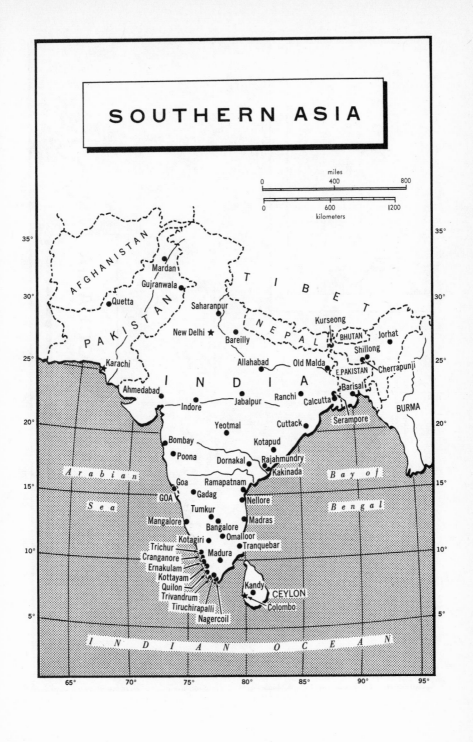

SOUTHERN ASIA

miles
0   400   800

0   600   1200
kilometers

AFGHANISTAN

Mardan

Gujranwala

Quetta

PAKISTAN

Saharanpur

New Delhi ★

Bareilly

Karachi

Ahmedabad

Indore

TIBET

NEPAL

Kurseong

BHUTAN

Jorhat

Shillong

Allahabad   Old Malda   Cherrapunji

E.PAKISTAN

Barisal

Jabalpur   Ranchi   Calcutta

BURMA

INDIA

Yeotmal   Cuttack

Serampore

Bombay   Kotapud

Poona   Dornakal   Rajahmundry

Goa   Ramapatnam   Kakinada   Bay of

GOA   Gadag   Nellore   Bengal

Tumkur

Mangalore   Bangalore   Madras

Kotagiri   Omalloor

Trichur   Tranquebar

Cranganore   Madura

Ernakulam

Kottayam   Kandy   CEYLON

Quilon

Trivandrum   Colombo

Tiruchirapalli

Nagercoil

Arabian   Sea

INDIAN   OCEAN

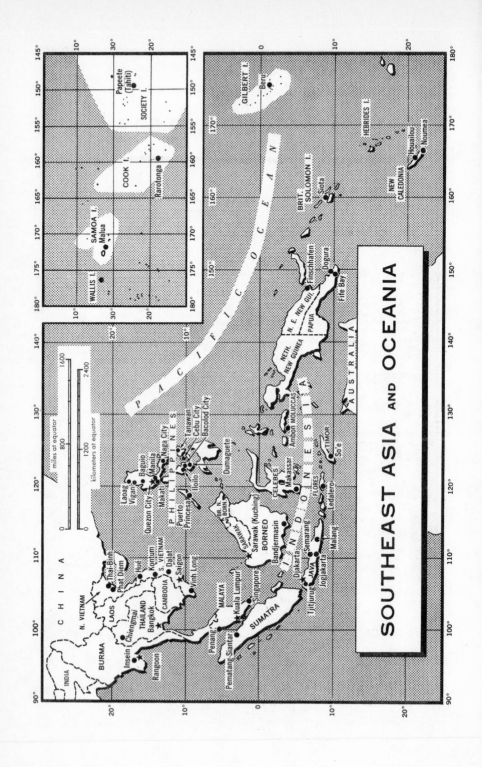

SOUTHEAST ASIA and OCEANIA

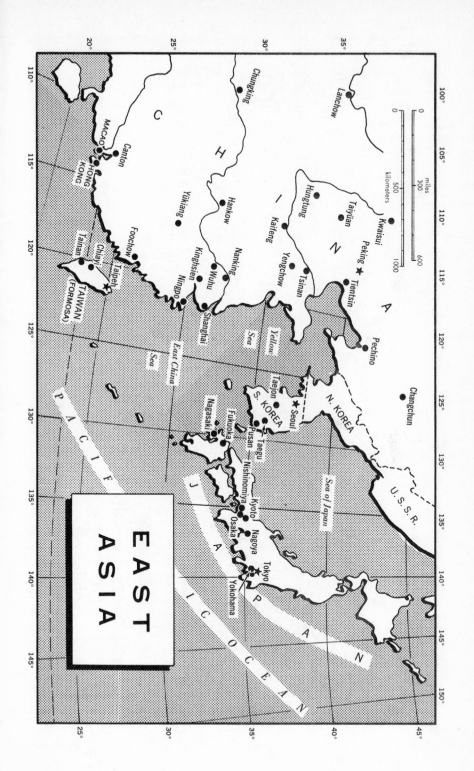

EAST ASIA

C H I N A

Lanchow
Chungking
Kwaisui
Taiyüan
Peking ★
Hungtung
Tsinan
Pechino
Tientsin
Kaifeng
Yengchow
Nanking
Hankow
Yükiang
Wuhu
Kinghsien
Canton
MACAO
HONG KONG
Foochow
Ningpo
Shanghai
Tainan
Chiayi
Taipei ★
TAIWAN (FORMOSA)

Yellow Sea
East China Sea

Changchun
N. KOREA
Seoul ★
S. KOREA
Taejon
Taegu
Pusan
Fukuoka
Nagasaki
Nishinomiya
Kyoto
Osaka
Nagoya
Yokohama
Tokyo

JAPAN

Sea of Japan
U.S.S.R.

PACIFIC OCEAN

miles
kilometers
0 300 600
0 500 1000

100° 105° 110° 115° 120° 125° 130° 135° 140° 145° 150°

20° 25° 30° 35° 40° 45°

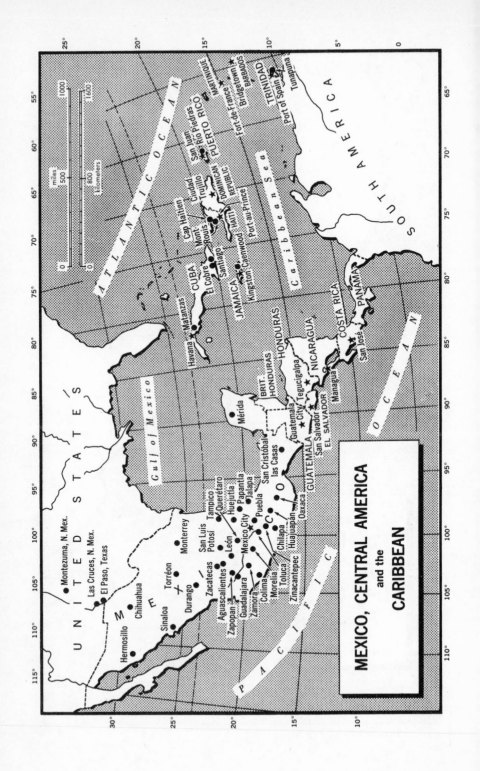

MEXICO, CENTRAL AMERICA
and the
CARIBBEAN

Part Two:

MAJOR SEMINARIES OF THE ROMAN CATHOLIC CHURCH

THE ADMINISTRATIVE STRUCTURE OF THE FOREIGN MISSIONS AND EASTERN RITES OF THE ROMAN CATHOLIC CHURCH

A. The Role of the Religious Orders and Communities of Priests in Furthering the Roman Catholic Foreign Missionary Enterprise

Although the conclusions and recommendations of this Survey are limited to the Protestant theological schools in the younger church areas, it is believed that a review at this point of the structure of the missionary enterprise and the seminaries of the Roman Catholic Church in these same areas would be appropriate. Indeed it appears that Protestants pay surprisingly little attention to the activities of the Roman Catholic Church, less than that paid by the Roman Catholic Church to the activities of Protestants.

The sheer magnitude of the Roman Catholic Church is such that it is not easy to grasp the full significance of some of the following statistics. Since the scope of this Survey is limited to Africa, Asia and Latin America, it is worth noting that the data below for the most part excludes the personnel of the Roman Catholic Church stationed in Europe and North America, the two areas where it is strongest.

With respect to the number of members of the Roman Catholic Church in Africa, Asia and Latin America, Table 90 lists those countries in which this Church has 1,000,000 or more baptized members. This table points to the comparatively small number of Roman Catholics in Africa and Asia as contrasted with Latin America. It also indicates the high proportion of Roman Catholics to the total population in the Latin American countries.

In chapter 1 of this Survey a brief summary was made relating to the growth in Protestant missionary personnel in recent decades. Table 91 presents this growth in comparison to the greater growth in the number of Roman Catholic foreign missionary personnel during the same period.

It will be noted that in the period 1925–50 there was an increase of approximately

TABLE 90.   COUNTRIES IN AFRICA, ASIA AND LATIN AMERICA HAVING A ROMAN CATHOLIC CHURCH MEMBERSHIP OF
1,000,000 PERSONS OR MORE (1957)[a]

| Number of Members (in Millions) | | | | Percentage of Roman Catholics to Total Population | |
Africa	Asia	Latin America	Country	65–100	1–64
		54	Brazil	93	
		30	Mexico	96	
		17	Argentina	89	
	17		Philippines	82	
		13	Colombia	97	
		8	Peru	95	
	5		India		1
		6	Chile	92	
		6	Cuba	91	
		5	Venezuela	95	
5			Belgian Congo (and Ruanda-Urundi)		32
		4	Ecuador	95	
		3	Bolivia	96	
		3	Guatemala	92	
		2	Haiti	72	
		2	Puerto Rico	92	
		2	Uruguay	79	
		2	Dominican Republic	95	
		2	El Salvador	99	
	1.7		Vietnam		7
		1.5	Honduras	99	
1.4			Uganda		27
		1.6	Paraguay	95	
		1.2	Nicaragua	94	
1.2			Angola		26
1.1			Tanganyika		12
1.1			Nigeria		4
	1		Indonesia		1

NOTE: [a] Source: adapted from C.S.M.C. World Mission map (Catholic Students' Mission Crusade). (The table excludes Communist China, having an estimated 3,000,000 Roman Catholics, or 0.5% of the total population.)

TABLE 91.   GROWTH IN NUMBER OF ROMAN CATHOLIC AND PROTESTANT FOREIGN MISSIONARY PERSONNEL (1925–56)

| | Roman Catholic | | Protestant | |
Year	USA	From All Countries[a]	From All Countries	North American
1925	[b]	22,477	29,188	14,043
1936	2,227	33,164	27,577	11,289
1950	4,377	44,227	[b]	15,039
1956	5,126	51,000[c]	34,692	23,432

NOTES: [a] Foreign priests, brothers and sisters under the authority of the Propaganda Congregation.

[b] Not available.
[c] Estimate.

100% in the number of Roman Catholic missionaries sent from all countries, whereas in all probability there was no significant increase in the number of Protestant missionaries sent out during the same period of time. It is quite likely that the total number of Roman Catholic missionaries in 1956 outnumbered the Protestant missionaries by a ratio of about 5:3, a significant reversal of the approximately 3:4 ratio which prevailed in 1925, early in the pontificate of Pope Pius XI. In the period 1936–56 this reversal was largely accounted for by the net decrease of 5,028 Protestant missionaries sent out from Europe when there was an estimated increase of 18,000 in the number of Roman Catholic missionaries sent overseas from Europe during the same period.

The significance of this shift in the balance between Protestant and Roman Catholic foreign missionary personnel in the field during the past three decades does not seem to have been widely appreciated in Protestant circles. In his encyclical letter *Evangelii praecones* (June 2, 1951), Pope Pius XII commented as follows on the growth in the Roman Catholic foreign missions effort during the years 1926–51: "The Catholic missionary movement both in Christian and pagan lands has gained such force and momentum and is of such proportions as perhaps was never witnessed before in the annals of Catholic missions."

In addition to the 44,227 foreign priests, brothers and sisters from all countries serving overseas in the Roman Catholic missionary enterprise in 1950, there were in the same year a total of 53,521 local priests, brothers and sisters serving in these same missionary areas, as shown in Table 92.

TABLE 92. PRIESTS, BROTHERS AND SISTERS SERVING IN MISSIONARY AREAS
(1950)

Area	Priests		Brothers		Sisters	
	Foreign	Local	Foreign	Local	Foreign	Local
Africa	6,366	1,096	2,140	801	9,876	4,202
Asia	5,841	6,751	1,057	2,258	6,723	18,968
Oceania*	2,067	2,113	852	1,342	4,037	11,688
Americas*	1,223	397	451	226	1,818	1,538
Europe	204	782	133	71	1,439	1,288
	15,701	11,139	4,633	4,698	23,893	37,684

NOTES: *a* Including Australia.
b Principally Latin America.

In the period immediately prior to World War I, approximately three-quarters of all the Roman Catholic foreign missionary personnel overseas were sent from France; and since then France has continued to send out more missionaries than any other country. Table 93 shows the trend in the period 1933–53 in the number of priests sent out from the 11 leading countries to missionary posts abroad. From this table it will be noted that in all but four countries there was an increase of 100% or more in the foreign missionary priests sent abroad from them during the period 1933–53. There was only a slight increase during the same period in the number of priests sent to missionary areas from France and Italy, and there was a decrease in the number of German and Spanish missionary priests. In the case of France and Germany, this may be accounted for by the adverse effects of World War II. In the case of Spain, the explanation is to be found in the effects of the Civil War which

TABLE 93. NUMBER OF MISSIONARY PRIESTS SENT ABROAD FROM LEADING COUNTRIES (1933–53)

	Number		Percentage	
Sending Country	1933	1953	Increase	Decrease
France	3,373	3,505	4	
Belgium	1,106	2,289	107	
Holland	941	2,229	137	
Italy	1,251	1,382	10	
Ireland	314	1,001	219	
Germany	954	847		11
USA	373	829	122	
Spain	860	779		9
Canada	285	709	149	
England	241	540	124	
Switzerland	159	362	128	

occurred in the years 1936–39 during which (according to the official *Guía de la Iglesia en España* for 1954–55) a total of 6,755 secular and religious priests lost their lives. Since a large number of Spanish missionary priests usually have been sent to Latin America each year, these losses in Spain tended to accentuate the shortage of priests in Central and South America.

Of the 5,126 American Roman Catholic missionary priests, brothers and sisters who were reported to be engaged in active service outside the United States as of January 1, 1956, 57% were men and 43% were women. By contrast, only 40% of the American Protestant missionaries overseas in the same year were men, and 60% were women. By September 1958 the total number of Americans serving as Roman Catholic missionaries abroad had risen to 6,124, an increase of about 1,000, or 20%, during the preceding two-year period.

TABLE 94. DISTRIBUTION AND GROWTH OF AMERICAN ROMAN CATHOLIC MISSIONARY PERSONNEL SERVING ABROAD (1940–58)

	1940		1958		Increase in Personnel 1958 over 1940	
Area	Number	% in Area	Number	% in Area	Number	%
Africa	108	4	617	10	509	471
Asia and Oceania	1,534	63	2,870	48	1,336	87
Latin America	489	21	2,127	34	1,638	335
Europe and North America	296	12	510	8	214	72
	2,427	100	6,124	100	3,697	152

The growth and geographic distribution of the Roman Catholics serving as foreign missionaries from the United States in the period 1940–58 is shown in Table 94. From this it will be noted that nine out of every ten Roman Catholic missionaries sent abroad from the United States are stationed in either Asia or Latin America, and one in ten is in Africa. Since 90% of all Roman Catholic missionaries are sent from Europe, and the great emphasis of Roman Catholic missionary activity in Africa is centered in the British, French, Belgian, Portuguese and Spanish colonies, this accounts for the comparatively small proportion of American Catholic missionaries being sent to Africa. Nevertheless, during the past two decades the percentage increase in their number has been sharp.

In the years 1940–58 the total number of American Roman Catholic foreign missionary personnel increased by 152%. During this period the most notable change in the distribution of such personnel serving abroad was in Latin America. On a world-wide basis in 1940, approximately 21% of all such personnel were stationed in Latin America. By 1958 this proportion had increased to 34%. The number of US Catholic personnel stationed in Latin America rose from 489 to 2,127 during this period, an increase of 1,638 persons, or 335%.

During the period 1925–56 the number of American Roman Catholic missionaries stationed overseas has consistently been only about 5–10% of the total number of Roman Catholic missionaries sent out from all countries. By contrast, during the same period at least one-third, and at present about two-thirds, of all Protestant missionaries overseas are Americans.

As mentioned in chapters 1 and 8 of this Survey, the ratio of the total number of Protestants to the total number of Roman Catholics in the United States is more than 2:1. This compares to the ratio indicated in Table 91, of approximately 4.5 American Protestant missionaries to each American Roman Catholic missionary stationed outside of the United States in 1956. Thus it would appear that as compared to the American Protestant missionary enterprise, the Roman Catholic Church in America sends proportionately fewer missionaries abroad. One of the reasons accounting for this is said to be the fact that in any originally non-Catholic country in the world it usually requires at least three generations of Roman Catholics before a large number of them are both willing and educationally qualified to serve as missionary priests outside of that country. In the case of the United States, many of its citizens whose forebears emigrated from predominantly Roman Catholic countries in Europe (Ireland, Italy and Poland) are members of families which have resided in this country for three generations or less.

Within the Roman Catholic Church there are two groups of priests, the secular and the regular clergy. Most of the secular clergy are attached to dioceses which are under the authority of bishops and archbishops, etc., with some others belonging to interdiocesan institutes. They derive their name from the fact that they live and work in the outside or "secular" world. The regular clergy are organized in a large number of orders and communities of men, and some of these priests lead secluded lives in monasteries. The members of the religious communities have comparatively fewer points of contact with episcopal authority (i.e., that of the bishops). The total number of members in the secular and religious clergy in 1955 is shown in Table 95.

TABLE 95.   Number of Roman Catholic Clergy (1955)

	World-Wide	Missionary Areas[a]	% of World-Wide Clergy in Missionary Areas
Secular (Diocesan)	257,763	11,279	4
Regular (Orders, etc.)	119,445	18,058	15
	377,208	29,537	7
Ratio of Secular to Regular	2:1	1:1.5	

NOTE: [a] Under the authority of the Propaganda Congregation.

Of the 6,124 American Roman Catholic missionaries in service abroad in 1958, almost half (47%) came from three states: Massachusetts, New York and Pennsylvania. Among them the priests and brothers were members of approximately 50 different religious orders and institutes, and the women belonged to 80 communities of sisters. A majority of these missionary priests and brothers belonged to the communities listed in Table 96.

TABLE 96.   Leading Religious Communities Sending Missionary Priests and Brothers from the United States (1958)

	Number
1. Jesuits	798
2. Maryknoll Fathers	532
3. Franciscans (O.F.M.)	209
4. Redemptorists	208
5. Divine Word Fathers	174
6. Oblates of Mary Immaculate	172
7. Marianists	136
8. Capuchins	104
9. Sacred Heart Congregation	97
10. Franciscans (Conventuals)	94

Since almost all of the priests engaged in the missionary activities of the Roman Catholic Church are members of its numerous religious orders and institutes, it is of interest to note in Table 97 the most important of these organizations of men, listed in accordance with the number of their members of all nationalities, which are engaged in missionary activities.

In addition to the religious orders and institutes of men listed in Table 97 there were 9,331 Roman Catholic brothers who were engaged in foreign missionary work in 1950. These nonordained men are employed full time as teachers, catechists, architects, carpenters, nurses' assistants, etc. The brotherhoods having a world-wide membership of 2,000 or more in 1950 were:

Christian Brothers	14,385
Minor Brothers of Mary	8,000
Christian Brothers of Ireland	2,226
Christian Brothers of Ploërmel	2,100

Table 97. The Principal Religious Orders and Communities of Priests Ranked According to Their Membership Engaged in Foreign Mission Activities (1950)

| Century Founded | Name | Membership | | % |
		Total[a]	Missionaries[b]	Missionaries
16th	Jesuits	28,426	3,978	14
19	White Fathers	2,538	1,797	72
13	Franciscans (Friars Minor)	24,614	1,774	7
19	Salesians (Society of St. John Bosco)	15,982	1,374	9
19	Oblates of Mary Immaculate	5,700	1,222	21
18	Holy Ghost Fathers	4,216	1,197	29
19	Divine Word Fathers	4,100	991	24
19	Scheut Fathers	1,512	865	57
16	Capuchins	14,095	825	6
17	Society of Foreign Missions of Paris	992	735	73
18	Redemptorists	7,120	695	10
13	Dominicans	8,000	664	8
6	Benedictines (five congregations)	11,200	637	6
19	Society of African Missions	1,308	585	5
19	Mill Hill Fathers	921	557	60
17	Lazarists (Vincentians)	5,300	521	9
19	Missionaries of the Sacred Heart of Jesus	2,520	470	15
19	African Missions of Verona	825	323	40
19	Foreign Missions of Milan	584	282	48
18	Montfortists	1,365	273	20
19	Marists	1,766	252	14
20	Mariannhill Fathers	?	247	—
20	Society of St. Columban for Chinese Missions	700	242	36
13	Augustinians (Hermits, Assumptionists and Recollects)	5,954	226	4
19	Priests of the Sacred Heart of Jesus	2,450	221	9
20	Consolata Fathers	800	209	25
20	Maryknoll Fathers	740	183	24
16	Carmelites (Discalced and Ancient Observance)	5,262	182	3
12	Premostratensians	1,555	159	10
19	Claretians	2,800	149	5
13	Franciscans (Conventuals)	3,415	136	4
18	Passionists	3,350	128	4
19	Pallottine Fathers	1,497	125	8
19	Congregation of the Holy Cross	2,135	114	6
19	Picpus Fathers	1,506	113	7
13	Order of the Holy Cross	375	105	28
19	Missionaries of St. Francis de Sales of Annecy	266	102	38
19	Xaverians (Foreign Missions of Parma)	314	82	26
13	Servites	1,511	77	5
19	Missionaries of Our Lady of "La Salette"	850	74	9

Notes: [a] May include lay brothers and scholastics.
[b] Personnel under the authority of the Congregation "de
Propaganda Fide."

Some of the older orders and congregations have brothers who are members of
their institutes. These brothers for the most part are also engaged as architects, carpenters, assistants, etc.

Finally, in 1950 there were also 61,577 foreign and local sisters engaged in foreign
missions work. These sisters were employed as catechists, hospital nurses, teachers,
helpers, etc. They were organized in a large number, approximately 1,390, of separate institutes and communities having an estimated world-wide membership of
nearly 1,000,000 women. Table 98 shows the total membership of *only* those communities, etc., which had 4,000 or more female members in 1950.

The lists of religious communities and Orders shown here do not indicate the number of provinces, chapters and other constituent units within each of these communities, etc. Some idea of their number and administrative complexity may be obtained by listing the individual Roman Catholic foreign missionary units stationed in one country alone. The large number of individual Protestant mission agencies now operating in the Belgian Congo and Ruanda-Urundi has already been

TABLE 98. PRINCIPAL RELIGIOUS COMMUNITIES OF WOMEN HAVING A TOTAL
MEMBERSHIP OF 4,000 OR MORE (1950)

Daughters of Charity of St. Vincent de Paul	41,925
Sisters of St. Joseph (all branches)	11,558
School Sisters of Notre Dame	10,582
Sisters of the Holy Cross (Third Order of St. Francis of Ingenbohl)	9,164
Sisters of Our Lady of Charity of the Good Shepherd	8,994
Daughters of Mary Help of Christians	7,979
Sisters of Charity of SS. B. Capitanio	7,404
Ursuline Nuns (Roman Union)	6,811
Society of the Sacred Heart of Jesus	6,519
Daughters of St. Anne	6,458
Sisters of Charity	6,064
Sisters of Mercy of St. Charles Borromeo (three branches)	5,826
Sisters of Mercy of the Union in the USA	5,504
Sisters of the Most Holy Savior	5,471
Little Sisters of the Poor	5,418
Daughters of Wisdom	4,752
Daughters of St. Francis de Sales	4,671
Daughters of the Heart of Mary	4,269
Sisters of the Holy Family	4,165
Sisters of Our Lady of Mercy	4,135
Poor Helpers of Jesus Christ	4,127
Institute of the Blessed Virgin Mary	4,127
Grey Sisters of St. Elizabeth	4,117
Sisters of the Third Order of St. Francis of Penance and Charity	4,093
Daughters of Charity of Canossa	4,079

noted earlier in this Survey. It is of interest, therefore, to list the even larger number (97) of individual Roman Catholic missionary orders and communities which in the period 1878–1949 sent missionaries to the same colony:

Congregations of Priests (26): White Fathers, Congregation of the Immaculate Heart of Mary (Scheut Fathers), Jesuit Fathers, Priests of the Sacred Heart, Premonstratensian Canons of Tongerloo, Redemptorist Fathers, Premonstratensian Canons of Postel (Retie), Mill Hill Fathers, Holy Ghost Fathers, Benedictine Fathers of Saint Andrew, Minor Capuchin Brothers, Salesian Fathers, Dominican Fathers, Minor Franciscan Brothers (of the Belgian Province of St. Joseph), Fathers of the Order of the Holy Cross, Sacred Heart Missionaries, Minor Franciscan Brothers (of the Belgian Province of Mary Mediatrix), Lazarist Fathers, Assumptionist Fathers, Josephite Fathers, Passionist Fathers, Oblate Fathers of Mary Immaculate, Fathers of the Sacred Hearts of Jesus and Mary (Picpus), Fathers of the Company of Mary (Montfortains), Canons Regular of Latran, Aumôniers du Travail.

Congregations of Teaching Brothers (6): Brothers of the Christian Schools, Brothers of Charity, Marist Brothers, Brothers of Saint Gabriel, Brothers of Our Lady of Lourdes, Xaverian Brothers.

Congregations of Nuns (65): Sisters of the Charity of Jesus and Mary, Sisters of Our

Lady of Namur, Missionary Sisters of Our Lady of Africa, Franciscan Missionaries of Mary, Sisters of the Precious Blood, Sisters of the Sacred Heart of Mary of Berlaar, Daughters of the Cross, Augustine Sisters, Missionary Canonesses of St. Augustine, Sisters of Charity of Namur, Benedictine Missionary Sisters, Franciscan Sisters of Herentals, Sisters of Saint Mary of Namur, Daughters of Mary of Pesches, Missionary Dominican Sisters of Our Lady of Fichermont, Daughters of Our Lady of the Sacred Heart, Dominican Sisters of "Val-des-Anges" of Bruges, Daughters of Charity, Daughters of Mary "Auxiliatrice," Franciscan Missionary Sisters (Saint Anthony of Padua), Sisters of the Infancy of Jesus, Sisters of the Union in the Sacred Heart, Sisters of Our Lady of Bunderen, Sisters of Mary of Pittem, Nuns of the Sacred Heart, Sisters of Maternal Charity, Canonesses of the Holy Sepulchre, Penitent Sisters of St. Francis of Assisi, Sisters of St. Francis de Sales of Leuze, Sisters of St. Vincent de Paul of Beveren-Waas, Sisters of Mary of Ingelmunster, Ladies of Mary, Sisters of St. Vincent de Paul of Gijzegem, Sisters of the Infant Jesus of Nivelles, Annunciation Nuns, Dominican Sisters of Lubbeek, Ursuline Sisters of Wavre-Notre-Dame, Sisters of St. Vincent de Paul of Saint-Denis-Westrem, Bernadine Ladies of Oudenaarde, Nuns of the Holy Family of Helmet, Ursuline Sisters of Overpelt, Sisters of St. Vincent de Paul of Wachtebeke, Sisters of St. Joseph, Nuns of St. Andrew, Sisters "de la Présentation Notre Dame," Sisters of the Visitation, Sisters of St. Vincent de Paul of Gits, Sisters of St. Vincent de Paul of Oostakker, Carmelites of Matagne-la-Petite, Missionary Passionist Sisters, "Filles de Sagesse," Oblate Sisters of the Assumption, Franciscan Sisters of the Reign of Jesus Christ, "Apostolines" Sisters, Sisters of Charity, Missionary Dominican Sisters of Namur, "Hospitalières" Sisters of St. Elizabeth, Sisters of the Sacred Heart of Mary of Nederbrakel, Canonesses Regular of St. Augustine of the Congregation of Our Lady, Carmelites of Rochfort, Sisters of the Holy Family of Bordeaux, Sisters of the Christian Doctrine, Sisters of St. Vincent de Paul of Termonde, Carmelites of Marche-les-Dames, Daughters of Mary Our Lady.

Since the administration and instruction given in the major seminaries is in the hands of the religious communities of priests, no further comment is required concerning the institutes of brothers and sisters.

The foreign missions of the Roman Catholic Church are conducted by the various religious communities under the supervision of the Propaganda Congregation. Furthermore, much of the Church's intellectual activities in mission and nonmission lands is furthered by members of the religious communities, particularly with respect to the administration of the major seminaries. Consequently it is of interest to note the structure and principal characteristics of the leading religious orders and institutes of priests.

The founding of the various ecclesiastical communities of men and the inauguration of their regulations (or "rules") require the approval of the Vatican. Their common purpose is to enable their members to work collectively toward the goals of the Church. The various orders and institutes may be divided into two general groups, those whose members take formal vows (the "religious orders and congregations") and those whose members make simple promises rather than vows. The latter usually are called "societies" or "secular institutes." The members of both types of communities lead a collective life. However, the priests in the religious orders and congregations bind themselves with public vows (perpetual or temporary) of poverty, chastity and obedience, whereas the promises subscribed to by the members of the societies and institutes, though along the same lines, tend to be less stringent.

The religious orders and societies have been developing ever since the fifth century, and historically there have been four main types as shown in Table 99.

TABLE 99.   MAIN TYPES OF RELIGIOUS COMMUNITIES

Types	Century Originated	Examples
Monastic	5th	Benedictines, Cistercians
Mendicant	13	Franciscans, Dominicans
Clerics Regular	16	Jesuits
Ecclesiastical Congregations and Institutes	17	Salesians, Lazarists, etc.

The monastic Orders were the first groups of laymen and priests who lived a common life. Owing to the lack of adequate communications during the Dark Ages, each monastery tended to be self-sufficient. Consequently there was initially no pressing need for centralized administrative structures within these Orders.

As the means of transportation improved and political conditions became somewhat less chaotic, the Mendicant Orders were founded early in the thirteenth century. These Orders maintained the system of a community life but their members were engaged in apostolic and missionary tasks outside the monasteries and priories, etc. This necessitated the organization of these Orders into provinces, and some administrative control was placed in the hands of a minister-general, or provincial, etc. The members of the Mendicant Orders are obligated to maintain a life of personal poverty and to spend several hours each day in liturgical exercises.

Prior to the 16th century the Clerics Regular were formed, of which the Society of Jesus is the most notable example. The principal differences between the Clerics Regular and the Mendicants is the reduction in the number of hours a day to be devoted by the former to saying Mass, etc. Thus, in theory a more varied type of mission could be assigned to its members, all of whom, however, subscribe to the three canonical vows.

Commencing with the end of the 17th and during the course of the next two centuries, there were formed a larger number of religious communities known as ecclesiastical "societies," "congregations," "institutes," etc. There is no need here to point out the technical differences which distinguish these communities one from another. The members of some take public vows, whereas others do not. In the case of the latter, it is simpler for their members to withdraw from their societies and institutes if they wish.

To those not familiar with the nomenclature of the various religious institutes, the similarity in their names is apt to cause some confusion. Thus, there are (to cite a few examples) communities named the Congregation of Jesus and Mary, Missionary Sons of the Immaculate Heart of Mary, Sons of the Sacred Heart for the Home and Foreign Missions, Missionaries of the Sacred Heart, Congregation of the Missionaries of the Holy Family, Missionary Priests of the Society of Mary, Missionaries of the Holy Spirit, Sons of the Sacred Heart of Jesus, Congregation of the Sacred Hearts, Society of the Priests of the Sacred Heart of Jesus, Sons of the Holy Family, the Company of Mary, the Fathers of the Sacred Hearts, the Congregation of the Immaculate Heart of Mary, and the Marian Fathers, etc.

Many of these groups or institutes have official Latin titles which occasionally differ from their official title in English. Two large congregations founded in France in the 19th century within a few years of each other have in English exactly the same name, the Society of Mary.

As a means of avoiding confusion, most communities of priests are known by short distinctive names. Thus the Order of Preachers is better known as the Dominicans. The Congregation of Jesus and Mary is known as the Eudists (named after their founder), and the Congregation of the Most Holy Redeemer as the Redemptorists, etc.

Some individual communities are known by several distinctive names. Thus, the members of the Congregation of the Mission are best known as Lazarists (a name derived from the house of St. Lazare in the suburbs of Paris where the congregation was founded). However, they are also widely known as Vincentians (after the name of their founder, St. Vincent de Paul) and as Paulists. The Divine Word Fathers are another example: this missionary society was originally founded by German priests in the Dutch village of Steyl. In Germany they are known as "Steyler" (or "Steyl Fathers") and in Italy as "Verbiti."

In view of this multiplicity in nomenclature, each community of priests has been assigned distinctive initials which follow their title. These initials are usually derived from their official Latin title. Thus the Divine Word Fathers' initial is "S.V.D." which is taken from its title "Societas verbi divini." Occasionally, however, different initials may be used to denote the same community. An example of this is the White Fathers, a French society, whose initials in French documents are usually written as "P.B." (Pères Blancs) but whose initials in English publications are often written as "W.F.," and elsewhere as "P.A."

In order to set forth more clearly the similarities and contrasts among the principal religious communities, it is of interest to consider in somewhat more detail their administrative structure and methods of operation. In this connection, the activities of four communities (the Benedictines, Dominicans, Franciscans and Jesuits) are briefly commented on below. Following this are some notes on a few of the characteristics of some of the more recently founded congregations and institutes which are active in the foreign mission field.

Benedictines: The Order of St. Benedict (O.S.B.) was founded at the monasteries of Subiaco and Monte Cassino in southern Italy by Benedict of Nursia in the year 529. During the Dark Ages (i.e., ca. 600–1200) the Benedictine monasteries served as the repositories and progenitors of Western culture. In the mediaeval period, as Father Martin Harney, S.J., notes, ". . . the Congregation of Cluny, to which for a long time numerous Benedictine monasteries belonged, so occupied itself with the solemn celebration of the liturgy as to preclude educational work. During the Middle Ages every reform in the Benedictine order involved the curtailment of teaching labors." In subsequent centuries the intellectual activities of this order have tended to center on research in the field of history and the liturgy rather than on contemporary social or polemical problems.

The great missionary age for the Benedictines also occurred during the Dark Ages. Most of their missions in that era were to convert the pagans in Northern Europe, and among the most famous Benedictine missionaries were St. Augustine of Canterbury (597), the Venerable Bede and Saints Anselm, Wilfrid Wilibrod and Boniface.

Various Benedictine congregations (American Cassinese, Primitive Observance, Congregation of St. Ottilia for Foreign Missions, Sylvestrines [S.O.S.B.]) now have missions in many parts of the world; but they are somewhat less active in Africa, Asia and Latin America than are the other larger communities of men.

It is estimated that over the centuries the Benedictines have had a total membership of 4,048,000 men. The high point among the Benedictine Orders was reached in the 12th century. Subsequently many of the Benedictine monasteries became so wealthy as a result of bequests received and through their own activities that they took less of an interest in spiritual matters. The Order suffered as a result of the Black Death and other epidemics, and particularly through the expropriation of its properties in England by Henry VIII and in France during the French Revolution. By 1815 the Benedictines were reduced to only about 30 monasteries with some 400 members. Yet by 1880 the Order had recovered to the point where it had 107 monasteries and a membership of 2,741; and in 1950 its five major congregations numbered 11,200 members, or four times the 1880 total.

The administrative structure of the Benedictines is comparatively simple. While the members of the Order in its early days tended to center their lives in one monastery independent of the other Benedictine communities, increasing mobility led to the need for reducing the autonomy of individual monasteries and centralizing the control of the communities comprising the Order. Thus the numerous Cluniac monasteries of the Benedictine Order placed themselves under the administration of the Abbott of the main monastery. On the other hand, as Theodore Maynard

points out, the Benedictines are unique in that to this day the Order has no provinces similar to those which have been set up by the Franciscans, etc. The individual
abbeys are relatively autonomous, and the abbotts are given wide discretionary
powers. In some instances Benedictine monasteries in one or more nations have
been grouped together into loosely organized "congregations," such as the English
and the Swiss-American Congregations. A centralization of authority among all of
the Benedictine communities has been attempted on several occasions (at Cluny,
Citeaux and Padua) but subsequently these headquarters either declined in power
or were separated into individual Benedictine congregations. Pope Leo XIII appointed a Benedictine as Abbott Primate with offices in Rome, but this official has
little real authority over the other Abbotts in the Order and serves principally as
ex-officio head of the Roman College of St. Anselm's.

Concerning the spirit of the Benedictines, it has been said that the word "stability" characterizes the essential basis of their life. A member of the Order (Dom
David Knowles) has written: "It is not a virtue for the monk, as it might be for the
missionary, to lack time in which to attend the office, read a certain amount and mix
with his community. And hence there should be in the Benedictine monk a certain
restfulness, a contentment, not in doing nothing but in doing the familiar, even the
monotonous and the ritual; an ability to remain physically unmoved and unexcited,
to produce, in fact, that stability which his Founder (St. Benedict) made a distinguishing and on occasion a unique religious vow."

The Franciscans: The founding of the Order of St. Francis in the year 1209 in Italy
by St. Francis of Assisi marked the beginning of the Mendicant Orders. These differ
from the Benedictine congregations in stressing a life of service in the world rather
than in a monastery. The members of the Mendicant Orders pledged themselves to
a life of utter poverty, modeled after that of St. Francis, and came to be known as
Mendicants in that they often begged for their daily bread. The life of St. Francis
has been retold countless times.

The Franciscan Order of Friars Minor (O.F.M.) is now the second-largest among
all the communities of priests. Formerly the Capuchins (O.F.M.Cap.) and the Conventuals (O.F.M.Conv.) were members of the O.F.M., but they are now completely
independent of each other. However, if one were to combine the membership of
these three Franciscan Orders, their total membership would exceed that of the
Jesuits by a wide margin. The activities of the Franciscans (O.F.M.) are most evident in Italy, but this Order conducts missions throughout the world. Since the
year 1342 it has been commissioned by the Vatican to be the custodian of the Holy
Land.

St. Francis was not only unlettered himself but originally was somewhat hostile
to scholars and books, believing that the mission of the Order could best be achieved
through works of charity. One of his successors, St. Bonaventure (who is known as

the "Seraphic Doctor"), did much to organize the administrative structure of the Order and to reorient some of its activities toward intellectual pursuits.

With its members carrying on their activities in many localities in the secular world, the Franciscans required a somewhat more centralized administrative structure than did the Benedictines. However, at present the administration of the O.F.M. is not as highly centralized as that of some other large orders. Where a Franciscan province is strong enough by itself to support a foreign mission, it does so. If not, several provinces cooperate—and usually these are provinces speaking the same language.

As in the case of the Benedictines, the Franciscans suffered grievous losses in their membership during the Black Death (124,000 members died, according to one account). During the French Revolution all of the O.F.M. provinces in France were broken up and (according to Piers Compton) in the 19th century Germany, Austria, Belgium, Italy, Spain, Russia and Poland each in turn suppressed the O.F.M. provinces, leaving the Order "in a state of absolute chaos."

Of all the religious communities of men, the Franciscans have suffered the most from fissionary tendencies. Among most Orders there are two groups of parties. The first are the conservatives who want their Order to adhere to past practices and conform exactly to the principles established by its founder. The second are the liberals or progressives who wish to modify or accommodate older customs to the changed conditions of modern times while still maintaining the essential principles of the founder. Often the disagreements between these two groups have related to the extent to which the Order and its members should be permitted to dispose of material wealth. In the 14th century many communities—especially the Mendicant Orders— had two parties known as the "observants" and the "conventuals." The former were the conservatives, and the latter were the liberals. The name conventual was originally merely the adjective of the noun "convent," the latter term designating either a community of men or the house of the collegiate chapter.

In 1517 the Conventuals (O.F.M.Conv.) split off from the Order of Friars Minor. Eleven years later the Capuchin Order (O.F.M.Cap.) was formed by two members of the Conventuals who believed the Conventuals were departing from the precepts of absolute poverty, etc. They also thought they had discovered the form of the original habit worn by St. Francis having a pointed "capuche" or hood. The Capuchins were dedicated principally to preaching and for a time were suspected of heresy when one of their leaders, Bernardino Ochino, became a Protestant. The Pope at that time considered suppressing them but did not do so, and today the Capuchins carry on numerous foreign missionary activities in Africa, Asia and Latin America, including the administration of a number of major seminaries.

The Franciscan historian, Herbert Holzapfel, O.F.M., has commented as follows on the difficulties involved in attempting to consolidate the various Franciscan Orders: "The divisions are caused and maintained not by the individual friars, who chanced to join the new societies, but by a few leaders who had gained commanding positions and feared, and that justly, that they would lose them if a union were consummated."

Concerning the charitable spirit of the Franciscan Orders, Alexandre Masseron has written:

The Franciscans have created great things, rendered the Church immense services, fulfilled a providential mission—but often in discord; it is the most curious feature of their genius. . . . The unity of a strong discipline has never been the essential character of the Order of Saint Francis; and the sons of the *Poverello* have maintained an old tradition of independence and of fantasy, of which one should never take the combative manifestations too tragically. . . . But the cheerfulness of mind, the fervour, the animation, the good humour, which are powerful arms against temptation; the joyous optimism, which is the fruit of a passionate confidence in the goodness of God; the freedom to soar. . . . The spirit of poverty and humility, of obedience and simplicity, of seraphic love and cheerfulness: (these are) the Franciscan spirit. . . .

The Dominicans: The Dominicans were founded four years after the establishment of the Franciscan Order. A Spaniard, Domingo de Guzmán, living in Toulouse in southern France established the Order of Preachers (O.P.) in that city in the year 1213. The Dominicans, according to a member of their Order, Raymund Devas, O.P., are "an Order wedded to truth and austerity—an Order of men whose minds should be devoted to prayer and study with a view to preaching, and whose bodies should be kept in subjection as far as possible by fasting, abstinence, and vigils."

A Roman Catholic editor in Germany, Walter Dirks, comments: "St. Dominic's first and most immediate tasks were decidedly ecclesiastical—within the Church, in the narrower sense of the word—the preaching of the word and the fight against heresy. The preaching brothers were theologically trained priests. The personal connection with the world of property and labor, with 'economics,' was quite given up. Whereas St. Francis rejected for his brotherhood only the Benedictine holding of property and in contrast regarded manual labor as the normal basis of life for the brothers, St. Dominic sacrificed manual labor as well. . . . The Order of Preachers is an intellectual order. . . ."

In order to be effective preachers, it was necessary for the Dominicans to be thoroughly trained in Roman Catholic doctrines. Those members who were not gifted with preaching ability were assigned to other tasks undertaken by the Order.

The change in the emphasis of the Dominicans from their primary role of preaching missions to heretical believers (such as the Albigenses in southern France) into a community of philosophers and theologians took place at a somewhat later date. This was the result of the teachings of two of their most noted members, St. Albert the Great and his celebrated pupil, St. Thomas Aquinas. The Dominicans soon focused their activities in the early university centers at Bologna, Paris and Oxford. As the clergy most interested in extirpating heresy, they also were the most active in furthering the Inquisition.

The early Dominicans encouraged the study of Greek and Oriental tongues. They promoted in their monasteries, particularly in Spain and Tunis, an interest in the Hebrew and Arabic languages and cultures so that the Church in general might have a better understanding of those peoples.

Over the centuries, the Jesuits and the Dominicans have been the most powerful influences in the intellectual life of the Roman Catholic Church. Their rivalry, e.g., on the explanation of the action of "divine grace," has sometimes been intense. In this instance, as Theodore Maynard points out, matters "reached such a pass that the Pope was obliged to intervene. Yet instead of delivering a definitive ruling, he issued merely a decision that each Order might hold to its own opinion but was not to accuse of heresy those who dissented."

The Dominicans' College in Rome, the "Angelicum" (named in honor of St. Thomas Aquinas, who is known as the "Angelic Doctor" of the Church) is rivalled in that city only by the Gregorian University administered by the Jesuits. Today the Dominican Order has approximately 8,000 professed friars or about one-fourth as many as are members of the Society of Jesus.

In their personal life, the Dominicans more closely follow Franciscan practices (as contrasted with the Jesuits) in that they devote several hours a day to recitation of the divine office in common. The combination of the contemplative with an active life in the world has produced some outstanding scholars and extraordinary mystics in this order over the years.

Unlike the Franciscans, the Order of Preachers has never been split up. Indeed the Dominicans have a system of provinces and election of officials which has been copied by other communities. This has been commented on by Bernard Wall as follows:

A regional group of convents forms a Province which is administered by a Provincial prior who himself is elected by the priors plus two delegates from each convent. The Master-General who resides in Rome is elected by the Provincial priors plus two delegates from each province called definitors. The government of the Order is carried on by the Chapter which meets every four years. The Chapter has a rotary form: one is composed of the Provincials only; the next—four years later—is composed only of delegates or representatives; and the next—four years later—is composed of both Provincials and delegates, and it is this Chapter which elects the General whose duration of office is thereby twelve years. . . .

Any specific piece of legislation or innovation has to go through all the Chapters and hence takes twelve years to pass. Secondly, the organization is unusually loose and is built from the bottom upwards by election, rather than from the top downwards, and therefore its whole tendency is the opposite to what has been happening in the Vatican itself during the last few hundred years. . . .

The Dominicans were suppressed in France and other European countries during the French Revolution and Napoleonic wars. As a result, the status of the Order in Europe reached such a low point that Cardinal Newman asked in a letter written in July 1846 whether the Order was not "a great idea extinct." Nevertheless a series of vigorous Master-Generals (e.g., Father Alexander Jandel, O.P., who guided the Order's affairs from 1850 to 1872) effected a recovery in its status. At present the Dominicans are active in the intellectual centers of the leading countries throughout the world and publish numerous reviews dealing with theology, philosophy and sacred art, etc.

The structure of the Order of Preachers permits a considerable diversity of opinion on nontheological matters to be developed on the part of its members in the different provinces. The French Dominicans are said by Wall to be the most important intellectually and by far the most outspoken and independent. The clash between the Vatican and the French Dominicans on the subject of the worker-priests in 1954 led to the Prefect of the Sacred Congregation of Religious, Cardinal Piazza, coming to France and closing down the seminary training the worker-priests and the imposition of a special censorship before books written by members of the Order could be published. As for the other Dominican provinces, Wall states: "The Belgian and Dutch Dominicans are chiefly concerned with missionary activities in India and Africa. The Spaniards have a high spiritual standard, a high standard of monastic observance and run first-class missions in Manila, Indo-China and the Philippines. In the English-speaking world the Dominicans are divided into two tendencies. The English, though few in numbers, are outstanding among priests for their intellectual achievements and their spirit of toleration—in this they take after the French. The Irish and Americans, though separated in administration, have remained on an extremely conservative tack. Neither, moreover, have any interesting or significant publications."

In August 1958, a few weeks before his death, Pope Pius XII urged the Third Order of the Dominicans to work as "missionaries" in Asia, Africa and Latin America to "counteract the advance of sects (i.e., Protestants) and the even more dangerous advance of Communism." The Third Order is the lay branch of the Dominicans and has about 50,000 members throughout the world.

The spirit of the Dominicans has been characterized by one of the members of this Order, John-Baptist Reeves, O.P., as follows:

Whereas the Franciscan genius has as usual been exuberantly inventive, often going like St. Francis to nature for its material and its inspiration, the Dominican tradition has been more conservative and restrained, holding for the most part to such time-honoured human and Christian institutions as holy water, beads and books—especially books. In its use of all such things it has stamped upon them very clearly its characteristic mark of mind informing matter. . . . There are few (Dominicans) who have not, from time to time, had reason to be thankful for wholesome reminders that theirs is not the only Order in the Church, but one of many raised up to help each other, as much by rivalry as by co-operation, under the pastoral care of an authority higher than them all. But since rivalry implies something resembling opposition, and since the Dominican Order has nothing to oppose to anybody but the truth and its high commission to teach this, the Dominican in controversy inevitably takes up the attitude of being the rightful teacher of all who oppose him, bowing to none but the highest authority in the Church. He will hear of no compromise on grounds of expedience, prudence or even charity, insisting that to satisfy without mitigation the strictest claims of Truth, whether Scriptural, traditional, metaphysical or logical, is the only sure way to satisfy every other claim that can legit-imately be urged.

The Jesuits: The Society of Jesus (S.J.) is the largest and perhaps the most re-markable of the various Roman Catholic communities of men. It has more than twice as many of its members engaged in foreign missions than has any other com-munity. Founded in 1540 by the Spaniard, Ignatius Loyola, the Society is one of the religious communities known as "Clerics Regular." This group of communities places somewhat less stress on the mendicant life and more emphasis on the indi-viduality of its members. Nevertheless, as a means of circumscribing the freedom of its members, the Society is noted for the thoroughness of the training it provides for applicants seeking admittance. On the one hand the intellectual individuality of its members is cultivated, while on the other their sense of discipline is explicitly developed. The Jesuits are dispensed from the long ceremonies of the liturgy which take much time in the daily lives of the Benedictines and Dominicans. Instead they are trained to follow the spiritual life in accordance with the precepts set forth by Loyola in his *Spiritual Exercises.*

The Jesuits have been referred to as the "shock troops" of the Roman Catholic Church. In contrast to the Benedictines they are trained to accept transfer orders at a moment's notice. The Society has been successful in creating among its members a comparative indifference to single places or occupations. This has been one of the factors accounting for the willingness of its members to engage in foreign mission-ary activity. Another factor is, of course, the inspiring example of Loyola's associate, Francis Xavier, and his illustrious successors in the foreign missionary enterprise. According to Bernard Wall, in 1948 the Jesuits controlled 24% of Catholic mission-ary schools and 62% of the universities in missionary lands.

In Europe the Society of Jesus experienced a spectacularly rapid growth in its early years. The Jesuits founded many institutions of higher learning and by 1675 had established in Austria alone some 55 colleges, six universities, and 28 seminaries. Pontifical seminaries were attached to some of the Jesuit colleges, especially in Germany, to provide for the training of priests where the bishops were slow to see the need for this. By 1700 the Jesuits were administering 769 establishments in Europe at the college and university level, in which as many as 200,000 students were enrolled. By 1773 the Society numbered almost 25,000 members.

The extraordinary growth of this Society was accompanied by mistakes on the part of a number of its members which created hostility toward it. Some Jesuits (especially in the missions) participated in commercial ventures; others engaged in various intellectual ventures and moral teachings which ultimately were disapproved; while still others devoted much of their time to political activities in the chancelleries of the European capitals. Thus reasons were available for use by the opposition to the Society which became such that the Jesuits were expelled from French, Spanish and Portuguese territories. Subsequently, in 1773 the Franciscan Pope Clement XIV, perhaps against his will, felt it necessary to suppress the Society. The Society's General in Rome was imprisoned, and some 2,000 Jesuits are said to have lost their lives in Portugal alone. Another 20,000 members passed from the public view or became members of the secular clergy, etc. A few Jesuits clandestinely continued their activities in Germany and Russia. At the time it was suppressed, the Society was staffing 670 colleges, 273 missions and 176 major and minor seminaries.

One of the effects of the Napoleonic wars was to cause the resentment against the Society to recede so that in 1814 the Benedictine Pope Pius VII approved its reestablishment. In the subsequent 100 years the Society has again become the largest and perhaps the most effective single religious community in furthering the intellectual activities of the Roman Catholic Church.

Having some 33,732 members in 1957 (with the largest single contingent of 8,156 members in the United States), the Society is now publishing 1,320 periodicals in 50 different languages, including the editing of the Vatican newspaper *L'Osservatore romano*. It is also currently administering 94 faculties, seminaries, colleges and universities throughout the world. Included in this number are the Gregorian Pontifical University, the Biblical Institute, and the Oriental Institute in Rome, and some 28 institutions of higher learning in the United States. The Jesuits are also the most active among the communities in publicizing their missionary activities, principally as a means of obtaining increased financial support therefor.

The Society is now organized in 58 provinces and 57 missions. These missions are supported by one or another of the provinces; and the provinces and vice-provinces are grouped into "assistancies" which are organized along more or less national lines. In 1958 there were nine such assistancies (Italian, German, French, Spanish,

English, North American, Slavic, Indian and East Asian, and Latin American). Each of these assistancies has from 1,000 to 5,000 members. Some have described the Society as an "ecclesia in ecclesia"—a church within the Church.

The chief legislative authority is vested in the General Congregation over which the Superior General presides. The Congregation consists of the provincials and two deputies from all the Jesuit provinces plus the General and his ten or so most important assistants. The Congregation always meets after the death of a General to elect his successor and his assistants.

The provincials are appointed by the General and usually hold office for three years, which is usually renewed for one more period of three years, following which they return to the ranks. Each provincial must make an annual visit to every house in his province and interview every member of the Society within his jurisdiction concerning his spiritual welfare. Each province is according to canon law considered to be a separate legal entity so far as its finances are concerned. The provincial is advised by a council of consultors or assistants. Some of the provincials' most important subordinates (provosts of professed houses, rectors of colleges, etc.) are also appointed by the General in Rome.

The General is elected for life. The title of his office has no military connotation since the Latin term *præpositus generalis* simply means Superior General, the *generalis* signifying "over-all." The form of the Society's government is officially described as "monarchical." But the General does not have absolute powers inasmuch as there is a balance between the powers of the Congregation, those of the General and those of the provincials. The General has approximately 100 Jesuits on his staff at the Central Curial House in Rome. At the Society's Extraordinary General Congregation held in Rome in September-November 1957 it was decided that the number of assistants to the General should be augmented by adding to it representatives for Africa, India and East Asia, and an assistant for South America.

The literature by and about the Jesuits is enormous. According to one list, since the Society's inception there have been more than 18,000 Jesuit authors whose works on a great variety of subjects have been published. Much has been written by them even on as seemingly abstruse a topic in the field of moral theology as "probabilism" versus "probabiliorism"—a controversy which caused considerable internal dissension in the ranks of the Society's membership (and elsewhere in the Roman Catholic Church) during the 17th century.

Anyone attempting to evaluate the many and important contributions made by the members of the Society of Jesus would be obliged to consult its numerous official publications, as well as the semiofficial, scholarly but not always completely objective accounts of its able historians (Harney and others). In addition there are the studies of its activities written by non-Jesuits (Fülöp-Miller, etc.) and the comparatively recent testimony of ex-Jesuits. Among the latter (to cite a few) are the mild comments of the former English Jesuit, Denis Meadows, the fervent letters of protest written by the Irish Jesuit, George Tyrrell, the encyclopedic attacks launched by a former member of the Society's German province, Count Paul Kajus von Hoensbroech, and the interesting but embittered polemics of the American, E. Boyd Barrett.

To a casual observer, however, it would appear that some of the success of the Society of Jesus may be attributed to (1) the spiritual exercises, established by Ignatius Loyola, which have been consistently observed by its members (and which have been followed in one form or another by other congregations as well), (2) the degree of vocational initiative and opportunity accorded by the Society to its members, and (3) the fact that in furthering its aims the Society utilizes carefully selected and trained individualists who are bound together in a highly disciplined community.

For the purpose of this Survey, there is no need to attempt to set forth in detail the histories of the many other large communities of priests which are active in foreign missions. Such accounts are available in the various religious encyclopediae and in the many individual histories recounting the founding and developing of the various orders and institutes. Many of these histories are fairly standardized, prosaic accounts of difficulties encountered and successes achieved. Since most communities have more points of similarity than dissimilarity, the following random comments are intended merely to provide a bird's eye view of the characteristics which distinguish one congregation from another. The communities are listed in alphabetical sequence.

Augustinians: The Augustinians' Rule dates back to St. Augustine of Hippo in the 4th century. They are a smaller order than the Benedictines and are divided into three main congregations, the Hermits (O.E.S.A.), Assumptionists (A.A.) and Recollects (O.R.S.A.). The Hermits were amalgamated in Italy in 1256 as a non-monastic group whose members preferred to lead an eremitical life. Later they became a preaching order, and the Recollects seceded from them in order to form their own communities. In the 16th century the main emphasis of the Spanish Augustinians' missionary activities were in Mexico, Peru and the Philippines. The Assumptionists were founded in France in 1850 and follow the Augustinian Rule. During the 19th century the various Augustinian congregations made a slower recovery from the effects of the French Revolutionary era than did the Franciscans and Dominicans: in 1910 the Augustinians had only one-tenth as many monasteries as they had maintained in previous centuries.

Carmelites: The Carmelites were founded in about the year 1210 when their Rule was approved by the Latin Patriarch of Jerusalem. The members of this Order prefer a contemplative life of seclusion and silence, sometimes as hermits. The Carmelites grew rapidly in number and then were all but extinguished by the advent of the Black Death in 1347–50. In England, where they have been known as the White Friars, they were active in the early days of Oxford and Cambridge. The Order was subsequently split between the Calced Carmelites (O.Carm.) and the Discalced Carmelites (O.C.D.). This division occurred as a result of a disagreement relating to the extent to which the detailed regulations of the Order's original Rule should be adhered to, and the founding of the Discalced Carmelites was largely the work of two Spanish mystics and reformers, Sts. Teresa of Avila and John of the Cross. The word "calced" means "shod": the two Carmelite Orders now both wear footgear, but of a slightly different design from each other.

Claretians: Founded in 1849 at Vich near Barcelona by the Blessed Anthony Mary Claret, the missionary activities of the Claretians (C.M.F.) are largely centered in Latin America.

Consolata Fathers: The Missions Institute of the Consolation of Turin (I.M.C.) was founded in the 19th century by the Reverend Giuseppe Allamano who was personally trained for this work by St. John Bosco. The Consolata Fathers conduct a number of missions in Africa.

Divine Word Fathers: During Bismarck's Kulturkampf in Germany, the times were not propitious for the founding of a new Roman Catholic society in that country. Accordingly in 1875 Rev. Arnold Janssen, S.V.D., established the Divine Word Fathers in the village of Steyl near Venlo in Holland, just across the border from Germany. In its initial phase, this society experienced considerable strife among its key personnel but subsequently came to be the leading predominantly German institute devoted almost exclusively to foreign missionary activity. Among its many accomplishments in Africa, Asia and Latin America was the administration of the Catholic "Fu Jen" University in Peking which the society took over from an American Benedictine congregation in 1933. Father Janssen understood clearly the value of his society of having its own printing facilities at Steyl. This enabled the Divine Word Fathers to print a widely circulated magazine which spread the news of its activities and contributed importantly to the increase in contributions it subsequently received from the laity. The Divine Word Fathers continued this practice in the field, establishing printing plants in South Shantung in China, in Togoland and in Buenos Aires. The Cardinal Archbishop of Peking, Thomas Tien, is a member of this society.

Many Divine Word Fathers lost their lives in World War II. The German provinces had 99 fathers, 605 scholastics and novices, plus 563 novice brothers and sisters called into the armed forces. Of this number 12 fathers, 153 scholastics and 106 brothers were killed while in service. Some were sent to concentration camps. Many of the Divine Word seminary buildings in Germany were commandeered, and some of them were badly damaged as a result of air raid attacks. In the East Indies a score or more of the society's members were imprisoned by the Japanese and a dozen perished when a Japanese transport vessel was torpedoed. After the War the society recovered, and in 1946–47 the newly founded College of St. Peter the Apostle in Rome (see below) was placed under its direction.

Escolapians: This is a comparatively small teaching institute founded in Spain. Because its members were almost entirely Spanish and its activities were largely in the educational field, this institute was not as severely attacked in Spain during the 19th century as were the Jesuits, etc.

Eudists: St. Jean Eudes joined the Oratorian Fathers in 1623 and was an active member of that institute for 20 years. He withdrew when its Superior General declined to permit him to found seminaries. Thereupon in 1643 he established the Congregation of Jesus and Mary (C.J.M.), a society of secular priests which has become better known as the Eudists. This was at approximately the same time as the establishment of the Lazarists and the Sulpicians, and all three of these communities have as one of their special aims the administration of seminaries at home and abroad. The Eudists are a comparatively small institute and the seminaries overseas administered by them are located in Colombia and in Venezuela.

Holy Cross Fathers: The Congregation of the Holy Cross (C.S.C.) has long been active in the dioceses of Dacca in Pakistan, and Santiago, Chile. The membership of this community is primarily American, and its major venture in the educational field to date is represented by the well-known Notre Dame University in Fort Wayne, Indiana. The University is of important assistance in gaining new recruits each year for the ranks of the Congregation.

Holy Ghost Fathers: The most notable person associated with the Holy Ghost Fathers (C.S.SP.) was one of its founders, the Venerable Franz Maria Libermann whose father was a French rabbi. Converted from Judaism, Father Libermann suffered from epilepsy for a number of years which impeded his entry into the priesthood. Nonetheless he came to be the guiding spirit and head of the Holy Ghost Fathers and was responsible for their pioneering missionary activities in the French colonies in Africa. In 1957, most of the 1,295 Holy Ghost Fathers in missionary work abroad were stationed in various parts of that continent.

Lazarists: The Lazarists (or Vincentians) have as their initial "C.M." which is derived from the community's title "Congregation of the Mission." Founded by St. Vincent de Paul in France during the 17th century, its original purpose was to engage in preaching and home missions to the poor. Subsequently it was recognized that, as in the case of the Dominicans, those who preach require special training. In this way, the Lazarists came to focus more of their activities on conducting seminaries in France. Although they were seriously affected by the French Revolution as were most other French congregations the Lazarists subsequently recovered and now are among the most active in conducting major and minor seminaries overseas.

Lyons Missionaries: The members of the Society of African Missionaries (S.M.A.)

are often called Lyons Missionaries in order to distinguish them from the members of the Society of Missionaries of Africa who are better known as the White Fathers. As the name of their society implies, the Lyons Missionaries were founded in France, and they have been active in French Colonial Africa. During World War II when it was difficult for French missionary agencies to continue supporting their missionaries in the field, a number of the areas in Africa within the missionary jurisdiction of the Lyons Missionaries were reassigned to other religious communities.

Mariannhill Fathers: The Mariannhill Mission Society (C.M.M.) was founded by some Trappist monks from Germany who established a mission in South Africa in 1882 and founded the congregation itself in 1914.

Marianists: The Marianists were founded in 1817 in Bordeaux by Very Rev. G. J. Chaminade for the purpose of engaging in educational work. The title of this community, the Society of Mary (S.M.) is exactly the same as that of the Marists. A somewhat higher proportion of its members are brothers than is the case of the Marist Fathers.

Marists: The Marists' Society of Mary (S.M.) was founded in 1836 in Lyons, France, by Very Rev. J. C. Colin. Father Colin wished to have his fellow priests engage in an active life in the world, particularly in education and foreign missions work. He believed, however, that the only way in which true modesty and humility could be achieved by the members of his institute would be through a combination of spiritual activity and the carrying out of their work in personal obscurity. This was known as *"la vie cachée"*—a life of humility which has no witness. Appropriately enough, this Society has concentrated much of its foreign missionary activities in the remote, scattered islands of Oceania.

Maryknoll Fathers: The legal title of the Maryknoll Fathers (M.M.) is the Catholic Foreign Mission Society of America. It was founded in 1911 by the hierarchy in the United States as a national movement to train young Americans for service as foreign missionaries. At present it is the only exclusively American society of secular priests engaged solely in this task.

Mill Hill Fathers: Founded in England in 1866 by Herbert Vaughan (who later became a Cardinal), this society is technically known as the Missionary Institute of St. Joseph of Mill Hill (M.H.F.). Its members are known as the Mill Hill Fathers, a name derived from a suburb of London where their original house was established. Many of its recruits came from Holland.

Missionaries of the Sacred Heart of Jesus (M.S.C.): Founded in France in 1864, the mother house of this congregation was formerly at Issoudun. It has sent missions to many parts of the world, particularly Indonesia, New Guinea and Oceania.

Oblate Fathers: The Oblates of Mary Immaculate (O.M.I.) were once described by Pope Pius XI as "specialists in the most difficult missions." The Oblates maintain activities in Ceylon, South Africa, etc., and are notable for the enthusiasm, zeal and energy with which they pursue their aims. The word "oblate" means "devoted" or "dedicated."

Oratorians: The Congregation of the Fathers of the Oratory of St. Philip Neri (C.O.) is one of the more flexible communities in that each of its members is said to be entitled whenever he wishes to withdraw from the institute with relatively little in the way of formalities. The Congregation is democratic in its organization. Its founder contended that religious priests in the world could aspire to be saints as well as those in the cloister. Some of its members (among them Antonio Talpa) once sought to introduce vows of stability and poverty for its members with a view toward making the society's discipline stricter. However, the founder's original conception of a free association of priests has been adhered to. Among its early members in France were St. John Eudes and Jean Jacques Olier who later withdrew in order to form societies of their own, the Eudists and the Sulpicians. The Oratorians' branch in Great Britain was founded by a well-known convert from the Church of England, John Henry Newman, whom Pope Leo XIII made a cardinal.

Pallottines: The title of this mendicant congregation is the Society of the Catholic Apostolate (S.A.C.). Its members are now called Pallottines after the name of their founder, the Venerable Vincenzo Pallotti, who established the Society in the 19th century. A pioneer in organizing the laity in the service of the church (a movement which is known today as Catholic Action), the Society also has been active in missionary work in Africa and Latin America.

Paris Foreign Missionary Society: This community (M.E.P.) is a society of priests which was formed in order to promote foreign missionary activity. Its Rule states: "All the evangelical work undertaken by the Society of Foreign Missions must therefore have as their principal aim, their chief obligation, to apply themselves to the formation of an indigenous clergy. . . ." The overseas activities of the Society have been concentrated in Asia, particularly in Viet Nam.

Passionists: The Congregation of the Passion (C.P.) was founded in Genoa in 1720 by St. Paul of the Cross. His aim for the community was to blend the solitary life adopted by the Carthusians and Trappists with the active life of the Jesuits or Lazarists, etc. The Passionists are a mendicant congregation which solved for itself the problem of accumulating wealth by prohibiting all of its houses from owning property except for a small amount of adjacent land.

Picpus Fathers: The Picpus Fathers (C.SS.CC.) commenced their foreign missionary activities in the Hawaiian Islands in 1825. In subsequent years, new missions were added from time to time in a westward direction—the Marquesas Islands, Tahiti and in Eastern Oceania. By the 20th century, the congregation had missions in all parts of the world. One of its most famous members was the Belgian Father Damien who administered to the lepers on the Island of Molokai in Hawaii. The special emphasis of the Picpus Fathers is on the adoration of the "Heart of Jesus."

They derive their name from the street in Paris on which their first house was founded by Father Coudrin in 1805.

Redemptorists: Established in 1732 by Alphonse Marie de Ligouri, the Congregation of the Most Holy Redeemer (C.SS.R.) helped to fill the gap caused by the shrinkage in the monastic orders in the 18th century and the dissolution of the provinces of the Society of Jesus in various European countries at that time (and its complete suppression in 1773). The Redemptorists themselves were suppressed and resurrected more than once, but ultimately obtained definitive approval from the Vatican. At first they deliberately avoided assuming the task of administering seminaries, preferring (like the Lazarists) to concentrate on preaching missions in rural areas and on works of charity and evangelization overseas. Later the Redemptorists broadened their scope to include seminary instruction.

Sacramentine Fathers: The Congregation of the Blessed Sacrament (S.S.S.) is engaged in encouraging the emphasis placed on the celebration of the Holy Eucharist by priests throughout the Church. Although it has over a thousand members, until comparatively recently it was not active in foreign missions work because its special type of work presupposes that Roman Catholic worship has already been fairly well established in a given area. The Congregation now maintains small missionary activities in Mozambique, Urundi and Ceylon, etc.

Salesians (St. John Bosco): This congregation was founded in 1841 by St. John Bosco in Turin, Italy, primarily for the purpose of caring for orphans and educating the youth. Its founder admired the work of St. Francis de Sales and named his congregation in honor of the latter. The new congregation grew considerably in size, with the result that its members are usually referred to as Salesians (Don Bosco) (S.D.B. or S.S.) in order to distinguish them from the members of the Oblates of St. Francis de Sales (O.S.F.S.) who are known as Salesians, and from the Missionaries of St. Francis de Sales of Annecy (M.S.F.S.). The Don Bosco Salesians commenced their foreign missionary work in Patagonia in 1880. They soon spread northward to Paraguay, Bolivia, Ecuador, Venezuela, Central America, and now have missions throughout the world.

Scheut Fathers: The members of the Missionaries of the Congregation of the Immaculate Heart of Mary (C.I.C.M.) are usually known as the Scheut Fathers. They are active in the Belgian Congo and derive their name from the suburb of Brussels (Scheutveld) in which the congregation was founded in 1863.

Sulpicians: The Sulpician Fathers (S.S. or P.S.S.) were founded by M. Olier in 1643 as a society of secular priests in France devoted exclusively to the training of men for service on seminary faculties at home and in missionary territories. They derive their name from the Church of St. Sulpice in Paris near which this institute was founded. Many bishops have graduated from the 35 seminaries the Sulpicians now administer in France.

Trappists: The Order of Cistercians of the Strict Observance (O.C.S.O.) was founded at La Trappe, France, in 1740. Their sole aim is to lead a contemplative life in silence, and in 1957 they had a membership of 3,612. This Order has not been active in mission areas, although in recent years they have established small monasteries overseas, including the Cameroons, the Belgian Congo, Indonesia and Japan. One of the difficulties encountered is the fact that a cloistered life in a monastery is said to be more difficult to pursue in a hot climate than in temperate areas. The Trappist Order is separate from the Cistercian Fathers (Cistercian Order of Common Observance, S.O.Cist.) and the similar Carthusian Fathers (O.Carth.).

Verona Fathers: The African Missions of Verona (Sons of the Sacred Heart of Jesus, F.S.C.J.) have been active in the Sudan.

White Fathers: The White Fathers (W.F.) were established in Algiers in the latter part of the 19th century by an extraordinarily able and energetic prelate, Cardinal Lavigerie. Their sole purpose is to convert the Muslims and pagans of Africa. They derive their name from the fact that the color of their vestments is white: Cardinal Lavigerie insisted that the members of this community should undergo the most rigorous physical training in preparation for their work, and he specified that their vestments should be similar to the clothing of those whom they were seeking to convert. The Cardinal required the fathers to speak, read and write in the local dialects, forbade them to teach the French language to the natives, and also distrusted "quick conversions." By 1957 the White Fathers had 1,599 of their members working in two parts of Africa—French Northwest and West Africa, and British East Africa, particularly in Uganda. The White Fathers have more missionaries in the field than any other community with the exception of the Jesuits. In order to maintain and increase the number of their personnel, it has been necessary for them to establish numerous major and minor seminaries throughout western Europe.

Space does not permit any comments to be included here on some other important congregations and institutes of the Latin Rite in the Roman Catholic Church which have conducted comparatively small (or in some instances no) foreign missionary activities. Among these are the Barnabites (C.R.S.P.), Bethlehem Missionaries (of Switzerland) (S.M.B.), Burgos Fathers (M.E.Burgos), Camillians (O.S. Cam.), Columban Fathers (S.S.C.), Crosier Fathers (O.S.C.), Holy Family Missionaries (M.S.F.), Josephites (S.S.J.), Josephites of Murialdo (Turin Society of St. Joseph, C.S.J.), "La Salette" Fathers (M.S.), Marian Fathers (M.I.C.), Milan Missionaries (P.I.M.E.), Monforains (S.M.M.), Paulines (O.S.P.), Paulists (C.S.P.), Paulists (S.S.P.), Premonstratensians or Norbertines (O.Praem.), Priests of the Sacred Heart of Jesus (S.C.J.), Piarists (S.P.), Salvatorians (S.D.S.), Sanguinists (C.PP.S.), Servites (O.S.M.), Stigmatines (C.P.S.), Theatines (C.R.), Trinitarians (O.SS.T.), Viatorians (C.S.V.), and Xaverians (Foreign Missions of Parma, S.X.).

The administration of a large community of priests requires considerable managerial ability and skill in personal relationships. Sometimes internal difficulties are encountered which threaten the very existence of a community. An example of this is to be seen in the case of the Sacramentine Fathers whose activities have already been briefly noted. This congregation was founded in 1856, and during its first three decades the community at no time had as many as 100 members. Subsequently it grew rapidly, so that by the end of 1955 its membership totaled 1,272. On the occasion of its centenary in 1956, the Superior General issued an address to the members of the Congregation in which among other things he stated:

> With the death (in 1868) of our founder (Father Eymard), the difficulties of the Order did not disappear. On the contrary they increased and menaced even the life of the young institute. The congregation experienced extremely critical moments, dissensions, defections, even treason to the ideas of the founder on the part of one or another of its sons. . . . To its internal difficulties, external difficulties were added: persecutions, the hate of those who wished to destroy the Religious Orders, to crush and suppress them. Expelled from the country of its origin, the congregation soon saw itself reduced to a single house in a foreign country. One must admire the superhuman courage of those who still continued the work of our Venerable Father. . . . (Later) the congregation knew still other perils. This was during the time when provinces were being established, when it would have been so easy to make a mistake, to allow itself to be too greatly influenced by diverse national sentiments. . . . The temptation is equally common to neglect the general extension of an institute in order to better consolidate the interest of its new provinces. But Providence watched over us. . . .

The supreme authority and administrative power over all religious congregations and institutes is vested in the Pope who can dissolve them or emend their Rules should the circumstances indicate the advisability of doing so. In mediaeval times some communities were suppressed (the Humiliati, the Beghards, etc.), principally because they supported doctrines considered to be heretical. In recent centuries there have been fewer instances of such action, with the notable exception of the dissolution of the Society of Jesus in 1773.

There is little doubt but that the large number of religious congregations of men tend to make it difficult for the Vatican to exercise a close supervision over their affairs. This is particularly true with respect to the 1,390 separate communities of women. It is stated that the Vatican does not seek to encourage the establishment of new religious communities, but rather prefers to effect consolidations among the already existing institutes and societies where this is feasible. In his Apostolic Exhortation, *Menti Nostræ,* of September 23, 1950, Pope Pius XII called in general terms for a modernizing of the organization and activities of the religious communities.

It is reported that some nuns who are members of convents of the contemplative Orders have been living in a state of want, occasionally bordering on starvation. In some of their large residence buildings in northern countries central heating and plumbing facilities are said to be lacking or are inadequate. This situation is reputed to be due in recent years in part to a reduction in the income of these cloistered orders, particularly in the number of bequests received.

In his Apostolic Constitution, *Sponsa Christ,* (November 21, 1950) Pope Pius XII suggested that it might be advisable for the members of various monastic Orders to join in federations, the purpose of which would be to improve the economic stability of their constituents. Such federations would respect the autonomy and independence of the individual monasteries, yet might better enable the monastic Orders as a group to survive adverse economic conditions.

Five days later, on November 26, 1950, a congress of representatives of the religious communities was opened in Rome by the Sacred Congregation of Religious. Convened after a year's preparation, its purpose was to strengthen the education and spiritual training provided by these communities to those seeking admission into them.

Early in April 1958 Pope Pius XII sent an Apostolic Letter to a Congress of the States of Perfection (i.e., religious communities) being held in Lisbon in which he urged their members "to adapt themselves to the needs of our era." It was recalled that Pius XII on several recent occasions had advocated that the communities conceive of their mission in a dynamic rather than in a contemplative way, and the Pontiff was reported to feel that there is still "an untapped manpower reserve in monasteries and convents."

It is not easy to amalgamate religious orders and societies, particularly when each of them has its own founder and to some extent its individual spiritual outlook. It also seems likely that one of the reasons why the Vatican neither suppresses the very small institutes, nor arbitrarily prohibits the creation of new ones, is due to the fact that within the Roman Catholic Church (or indeed in any large organization) some of its full-time members are apt to work far more effectively within small, semiautonomous groups than they would as members of large, disciplined congregations, etc. Furthermore, some priests who are endowed with the genius required to establish a new community might find membership in an older order less inspiring. For example, the official biographer of Father Arnold Janssen (the founder of the Divine Word Fathers) comments: "As at the beginning of the Steyl Foundation, so also later, many considered him (Father Janssen) unbalanced." Despite the fact that the Roman Catholic bishops in Germany felt the times were not propitious for the creation of a new society, Father Janssen persevered in his endeavor and ultimately achieved great success. Whether his talents would have been as fully employed if he had been a Benedictine or Lazarist Father in Germany is at least open to question.

The same point may be cited in connection with the founding of the Society of Jesus. When St. Ignatius Loyola was trying to obtain the approval of the Vatican for its establishment, some influential members of the Curia in Rome objected to the request. They maintained that from the point of view of administrative efficiency there were already (in 1540) too many Orders in the Church. Some officials even wanted to suppress all of the then existing Orders, except the three largest—the Benedictines, Franciscans and Dominicans. This view did not prevail, and the Jesuits were permitted to form their community, although originally they were limited to a maximum of 60 members.

The springing up of the many flourishing societies and institutes which were founded in France in the century following the French Revolution is another instance which might be cited by those who believe in the wisdom of permitting new communities to be freely established. Virtually all of these societies have been created and built up as a result of the efforts of their founders and members, rather than through the patronage of the Popes who have tended to remain aloof during their formative stages.

During the period 1940 through 1954 there was an average growth of about 25% in the over-all membership of the 40 leading orders and congregations of men. The most rapid percentage growth was experienced by some of the smaller congregations, such as the Holy Cross Fathers and the Priests of the Sacred Heart of Jesus, both of which had an increase of over 40%. By contrast, some of the larger communities, such as the Marists and Lazarists, had gains of less than 10%; while due to the effects of World War II the Divine Word Fathers suffered a slight loss in membership in the same period.

In connection with their recruitment of new members, the Jesuits, the Lazarists, the Holy Cross Fathers and some other communities are active in the education of the laity at the secondary and collegiate level. On the other hand, some smaller institutes are said to be occasionally pressed in their search for new members.

Some communities (especially among the female institutes) are stated to require entrants to present a dowry. In the case of the Oratorians it is reported that each aspirant for membership has been required to possess a private income sufficient for his maintenance while a member (except for lodgings which the Oratory provides). In other cases entrants must relinquish all their personal property, although occasionally the members of some communities are permitted to receive the income therefrom. The monastic orders are required to submit reports of their financial condition once every five years to the Vatican and more frequently to their local bishop. It is stated that no religious community may contract debts amounting to more than $6,000, except with the permission of the Pope.

Most of the larger communities have their headquarters (or "mother house") in Rome and provinces in the various countries in which they are active. The

"Master General" or "Superior General" is sometimes elected for life, but more often for a term of six years or so. In the latter instances, the office is sometimes rotated among members of the order or society from different countries. Thus the last seven previous Superior Generals (since 1832) of the Redemptorist congregation have been citizens of Spain, Corsica, Italy, Switzerland, Luxemburg, Ireland and Holland. Their present Superior General is an American.

The provinces of the various congregations usually include all or part of only one country, and these provinces often conduct missions of their own overseas. The provinces in European countries generally send missionaries to the present or former colonial territories of those countries. An example of this type of organization is that of the Dominican Order, as shown in Table 100. In 1949, 20 of the 33 provinces of that Order conducted foreign missions in Africa, Asia and Latin America. (Portugal is another country in which the Dominicans are active, but it is not listed in the table because their activities in that country are administered directly by the Order's headquarters in Rome.)

TABLE 100.   Organization of the Dominican Order (1949)[a]

	Provincia	Provincial Area	Provincial Missions in Africa, Asia & Latin America
1	Hispaniae	North-Central Spain	Latin America (several)
2	Tolosana	Southern France (Toulouse)	Brazil
3	Franciae	Northern France	Algeria, Iraq
4	Utrinsque Lombardae	Northeastern Italy	Brazil
5	Romana	Central Italy (Rome)	Pakistan, Ceylon
6	Regni	South Central Italy (Naples)	Chile
7	Hungariae	Hungary	
8	Teutoniae	Northern Germany	China
9	Angliae	British Isles	Granada (BWI); South Africa
10	Poloniae	Poland	China
11	Aragoniae	Eastern Spain	Argentina, Uruguay
12	Bohemiae	Czechoslovakia	
13	Dalmatiae	Yugoslavia	
14	Trinacriae	Southern Italy, Sicily	
15	Beticae	Southern Spain	Cuba, Mexico, Venezuela
16	Neerlandiae	Netherlands	Curaçao; South Africa
17	Hibernae	Eire	Australia, New Zealand
18	S. Jo. Bapt. de Peru	Peru	
19	S. Antonini de Columbia	Colombia	Venezuela
20	Immac. Concept. Lugdunensis	Central France (Lyons)	Vietnam
21	S. Catharinae V. et M. de Quito	Ecuador	
22	S. Laurentii Mart. de Chile	Chile	
23	SS. Rosarii Philippinarum	Philippine Islands	Hongkong, China, Japan
24	S. Petri Martyris	Northwestern Italy	Turkey, Lebanon
25	S. Rosae in Belgio	Belgium	Belgian Congo
26	S. Augustini Bonaërensis	Argentina	
27	S. Joseph in S.F.A.S.	Eastern USA	China
28	S. Pii V Melitensis	Malta	
29	S. Dominici in Canada	Canada	Japan
30	SS. Nominis Jesu in S.F.A.S.	Far West USA	
31	S. Marci et Sardiniae	Sardinia	
32	S. Alberti M. Germaniae Sup.	Bavaria, Austria	
33	S. Alberti Magni in S.F.A.S.	Western USA	

Note: [a] Source: Catologus generalis ordinis praedicatorum (1949).

Concerning the different missionary approaches adopted by the various communities a leading Roman Catholic missions expert, Father Joseph Schmidlin, has written:

. . . The whole organization and spirit of these Orders, their admirable system of division of labor and subordination, their community of goods and community life, their vows of poverty, chastity, and obedience . . . all these characteristics lend to the Catholic regular Orders advantages which make them appear especially fitted for the pagan missions. . . . We shall not attempt to decide the contest which is still being waged between the different religious institutes to prove which has rendered the greatest missionary services and which is best suited for the missions. . . . The older Orders have the advantage of possessing large organizations that are more firmly rooted in the general ecclesiastical life at home; while the modern bodies, on the other hand, are able to devote themselves more intensively and freely to missionary work. . . .

In view of the large number of religious orders and institutes, it is understandable that over the years competition and disagreements have arisen between different orders, within individual communities, and between the religious and secular clergy. The conflicts between the Franciscans and Dominicans in the 14th century concerning the theologies of Duns Scotus versus Thomas Aquinas, the strife concerning their Rule between the Observant and the Conventual groups within the Franciscan Order in the 16th century, the clash between the Jesuits and the secular clergy in the 17th century on the subject of Jansenism, the competition between the White Fathers and the Holy Ghost Fathers in Central and Western Africa in the 19th century—these are but a few examples.

In many ways the pluralist structure of Protestantism finds its counterpart in the multiplicity of religious communities in the Roman Catholic Church. In reviewing their activities it would be a mistake for any Christian to stress the errors occasionally committed in the past by some of the leaders of these organizations, and not to give credit to the selfless, devoted and sometimes heroic lives led by many of their members. When one reviews objectively the history and the present activities of the religious communities of the Roman Catholic Church, particularly in Africa, Asia and Latin America, one cannot fail to be impressed by the scope and diversity of their work. Also noteworthy is the system of checks and balances within their organization which combines a centrality of over-all direction and control in Rome with a relative degree of autonomy of action within the community and in the field.

With such a large number of missionary personnel stationed in so many localities throughout the world, the central administrative structure in Rome guiding these organizations in the field has understandably become somewhat complex. The authority of the Pope as sovereign Pontiff with supreme legislative, executive (and judicial) powers within the Roman Catholic Church is exercised through a number of bodies, principally the 11 Sacred Congregations whose jurisdictions are listed in Table 101. It is only in connection with the last five Congregations listed therein that detailed comment is called for in this Survey.

TABLE 101.   JURISDICTIONS OF THE SACRED CONGREGATIONS IN ROME (1958)

	Congregation	Jurisdiction
1	Holy Office	Matters of faith, morals and heresy; marriages between Catholics and non-Catholics; investigation of writings considered to be dangerous to faith or morals (The Index).
2	Consistorial	Creation of dioceses, provinces and chapters; the appointment of bishops and administrators apostolic in all areas not subject to the Propaganda or Oriental Congregations.
3	Sacraments	Discipline of the seven Sacraments; marital matters not reserved to other congregations; ordinations.
4	Council	Discipline of the secular clergy and the laity (including fasts, abstinence and tithes, etc.); property regulations.
5	Rites	Direction of the Latin Liturgy, Beatification and Canonization of Saints.
6	Ceremonies	Pontifical ceremonies; ecclesiastical protocol.
7	Religious	Formation and discipline of religious communities and their members.
8	Extraordinary Ecclesiastical Affairs	Matters connected with civil laws and concordats; supervises the Pontifical Commission for Russia, and such other matters as may be turned over to it.
9	Propagation of the Faith	Foreign missions in those areas in which the hierarchy is not fully constituted.
10	Oriental Church	All matters relating to persons, discipline and liturgy of the Eastern Rites.
11	Seminaries and Universities	Administration of all seminaries, excepting those administered by the Propaganda and Oriental Congregations. Also supervises the government and studies of all Roman Catholic universities and faculties wherever located.

The Congregation for the Propagation of the Faith is responsible for the direction of the foreign missionary activities of the Roman Catholic Church. From its Latin name, Congregatio de Propaganda Fide, it is often called either the Propaganda Congregation, or more simply the Propaganda. The common English word "propaganda" traces its origin to this source, although the word in ordinary parlance has subsequently acquired political overtones.

The Propaganda Congregation was canonically erected 336 years ago by Pope Gregory XV in accordance with the Bull *Inscrutabili* dated June 22, 1622. It was an outgrowth of a Commission of Cardinals previously created by Gregory XIII (1572–1585) for the purpose of trying to effect a reconciliation of the Eastern Churches with the Roman Catholic Church. In 1622 this Commission was transformed into a permanent Congregation whose aim was to spread the Roman Catholic faith in missionary territories. A second factor leading to its establishment was the need to coordinate the missionary activities of the numerous religious communities entering this field of work. A third and more immediate factor was the dispute between the Vatican on the one hand and the Kings of Spain and Portugal on the other, with respect to episcopal patronage, i.e., the power to nominate and appoint bishops.

Modern missions in a sense commenced with the discovery of America in 1492 by Christopher Columbus on behalf of the King of Spain, and the discovery in 1498 of the new route from Europe to India around the Cape of Good Hope by Vasco da Gama on behalf of the King of Portugal. With the opening of the new territories in Latin America and Asia to European trade and settlers, the Spanish and Portuguese Kings negotiated concordats with the Vatican by which these two monarchs obtained many rights and duties relating to the evangelization of the native populations. One of the privileges obtained from the Vatican was the right of patronage *(patronato-padroado)* permitting these Kings to present to the Pope the names of clerics to whom the Episcopal Sees in the new territories were to be entrusted by the Vatican. This privilege was granted irrevocably by the Popes and could not be legally removed except with the consent of the Kings. In return, as Father Carlos de Melo, S.J., points out, the Kings of Spain and Portugal were obliged "to build, support, restore or repair, according to need, all the churches, convents, oratories, that might be needed for the care of souls in the territory of the diocese; provide them with all that was needed for the maintenance of cult; support all the ministers of the Church attached to those Churches; defray all the expenses of the cult; build new churches or temples of worship as needs might arise and provide them in the manner mentioned above."

While the fortunes of the Spanish and Portuguese Empires were on the ascendant, the close relationship between the Hispanic Kings and the Vatican, as exemplified in the *padroado,* resulted in a vast extension of the influence of the Roman Catholic Church, particularly in Latin America. However, when the rise of the English and Dutch Empires, which were essentially Protestant, coincided in the early 17th century with the decline of the Hispanic Empires, the Kings of Spain and Portugal no longer supported the missionary efforts of the Roman Catholic Church to the same extent as previously. On the other hand, the Kings were unwilling to surrender the right of patronage. In fact they interpreted their ecclesiastical privileges so rigidly that at one point all foreign missionaries being sent to areas under their control—even those dispatched directly by the Vatican— were compelled to pass through Seville or Lisbon and receive the approval of the Kings before proceeding to their mission stations in Spanish and Portuguese colonies overseas. In addition, the territorial limits of a number of mission dioceses became confused. For example, the Bishop of Portuguese Goa in India at one point claimed jurisdiction over all the countries ranging from the Cape of Good Hope in Africa to the boundaries of China. Furthermore all the countries of Asia in the early 17th century were served by only seven Roman Catholic bishops. Despite this, the Portuguese Kings of this period not only refused to permit non-Portuguese missionaries to enter Portuguese colonies but they also even witheld nominations of bishops in a number of places where the Vatican considered them to be sorely needed.

After the situation had become intolerable from the point of view of the Vatican, the latter decided that the right of patronage must in some manner be circumvented without revoking the *padroado* or creating new dioceses. Accordingly, in 1622 the Propaganda Congregation composed of 12 Cardinals was established. At the same time the decision was taken to consecrate vicars apostolic who would have episcopal powers but with titles to extinct sees. These vicars were reponsible directly to the Pope through the Propaganda Congregation. Despite the opposition of the Hispanic Kings, vicars apostolic were installed by the Vatican in missionary areas without consulting Spain or Portugal who lacked the right either to appoint or legally to obstruct them. In the year 1637 the first missionary vicar apostolic was assigned to India by the Pope through the Propaganda. This was Mattheus de Castro, an Oratorian and a Brahman convert from Goa who had been educated in Rome. A year later an apostolic administrator was appointed in Japan. During the next decade others were sent by the Propaganda to China, Indochina and elsewhere.

The reaction of the Spanish and Portuguese Kings was vigorous. According to Father De Melo, the Viceroy of Goa received orders from the King of Portugal "to seize any bishop or missionary sent by Propaganda to India and dispatch him to Portugal. Censures and excommunications were liberally flung by either party on the missionaries of the other side. Complaints and protests were sent to Rome."

One of the earliest acts of the Propaganda was to investigate the conditions prevailing at that time among the Roman Catholic missions overseas. As Abbé Gérin notes, "the results of the inquiry in general revealed a truly deplorable state of affairs. There was distress among the missions, especially in the territories of the Portuguese *padroado* which was then decaying. Too large areas were assigned to dioceses; there was negligence on the part of pastors, even of prelates, in discharging their pastoral obligations, particularly with respect to the indigenous populations; misunderstandings between Bishops and regulars; . . . political intrigues among the missionaries (Spanish vs. Portuguese); conflicts between conventuals and seculars, between the religious of different Orders, between Europeans and natives. . . . A reorganization of the missionary effort was necessary."

The Propaganda took immediate steps to instill discipline and imbue a renewed zeal and missionary spirit among the personnel under its jurisdiction. On February 22, 1633, Pope Urban VIII solemnly forbade priests in Asia from engaging in commercial operations. When this measure failed to eradicate these practices, Pope Clement IX in his Constitution, *Sollicitudo pastoralis* dated June 17, 1669, not only confirmed the prohibition of Urban VIII but also provided that goods purchased by missionaries for speculative purposes would be confiscated and the proceeds distributed to the poor rather than to the priests of the Order concerned.

During this period the Propaganda served to coordinate the missionary efforts not only of the religious Orders but also those of the hierarchies in those European countries which were then establishing colonies overseas. Thus the Archbishop of Rouen in France at one point claimed ecclesiastical jurisdiction over "New France," i.e., Quebec. In order to avoid a repetition of the troubles previously experienced in connection with the *padroado,* the status and powers of the Propaganda Congregation were augmented from time to time.

When Portugal and Spain would not cooperate in the 17th century with the Propaganda Congregation (or transfer their colonial subjects to its jurisdiction), the Propaganda had to turn elsewhere in Europe for foreign missionary personnel. Accordingly the various religious congregations, particularly in France, were urged by it to undertake missionary activities overseas.

Today the jurisdiction of the Congregation for the Propagation of the Faith is limited to those regions where the hierarchy or secular clergy has not as yet been fully established and a mission state continues. All those individual members of religious Orders and institutes who are engaged in foreign mission work are subject to the authority of the Congregation, and the latter appoints the mission superiors. On the other hand, all matters relating to religious personnel simply as members, individually or collectively, of Orders and institutes are within the province of the Congregation of the Religious; and the generals or heads of the various communities appoint the local superiors to whom the missionaries are subordinate in personal matters.

There are, however, seven religious congregations and 15 missionary societies of priests which were originally established (according to Father de Reeper) for the sole purpose of engaging in foreign missionary work. Subsequently some of them assumed additional activities, but the affairs of these 22 organizations (listed in Table 102) still come entirely under the authority of the Propaganda Congregation rather than under the Sacred Congregation of the Religious.

Because of the importance of the Congregation de Propaganda Fide, its Cardinal Prefect is sometimes referred to as the "Red Pope" in the same manner that the Superior General of the Society of Jesus is sometimes referred to as the "Black Pope." The present Prefect of the Propaganda is Pietro Cardinal Fumasoni-Biondi, formerly Apostolic Delegate to India, Japan and the United States, successively.

TABLE 102. RELIGIOUS CONGREGATIONS AND MISSIONARY SOCIETIES DEPENDENT UPON THE PROPAGANDA CONGREGATION (1956)

Congregations	Societies
Scheut Fathers	Paris Foreign Missions Society
Divine Word Fathers (Steyl)	Milan Missionary Institute
Verona Fathers	African Missions Society (Lyons)
Xaverians (Parma)	Mill Hill Fathers (England)
Württemberg Fathers	White Fathers (France)
Turin (Consolata)	Bethlehem Fathers (Switzerland)
Xaverians (Goa, India)	Mission Society of Burgos (Spain)
	Maryknoll Fathers (USA)
	Maynooth Mission (Ireland)
	Mission Society of Scarboro (Canada)
	Foreign Missions Society of Province of Quebec
	Kiltegan Fathers (Ireland)
	Yarumal Seminary (Colombia)
	Society of Native Missionaries of St. Peter and St. Paul (India)
	Institute of Santa Maria de Guadelupe for Foreign Missions (Mexico)

Owing to Cardinal Biondi's advanced age, in June 1958 Pope Pius XII appointed Gregory Peter Cardinal Agagianian (Patriarch of Cilicia of the Armenian Rites of the Roman Catholic Church) to serve in the capacity of Proprefect of the Propaganda.

Under the Prefect are a Secretary and a number of subordinates, each specializing in activities relating to particular missionary areas throughout the world. Major decisions are submitted to the vote of all (approximately 25) of the Cardinals associated with the affairs of the Propaganda, with the most important decisions being subject also to the approval of the Pope.

As of July 1956 the various mission fields under the authority of the Propaganda were divided into 684 ecclesiastical circumscriptions (divisions) of various categories as shown in Table 103.

TABLE 103. ECCLESIASTICAL CIRCUMSCRIPTIONS UNDER THE PROPAGANDA CONGREGATION (1956)

Number	Type of Division	Title of Local Administrator
77	Archdiocese	Residential Archbishop
288	Diocese	Residential Bishop
6	Independent Abbacy	Independent Abbott
192	Apostolic Vicariate	Vicar Apostolic[a]
118	Apostolic Prefecture	Prefect Apostolic[b]
3	Independent Mission	Superior
684		

NOTES: [a] Ordinarily a Titular Bishop.   [b] Seldom a Bishop.

It would appear that the Propaganda has long pursued a policy of not assigning a large populous missionary area solely to the jurisdiction of a single religious institute. Rather, most large missionary areas in the world have a number of different communities working in them, with the result that no one institute or congregation can be said to have a paramount interest in that country—as, for example, the Jesuits once had in Japan and in Paraguay. This policy of intermixing the missionary units of the religious communities stationed overseas is followed even in those areas not technically considered to be missionary lands, as, for example, in Latin America. An instance of this can be seen in the Archdiocese of Belo Horizonte in Brazil, a typical circumscription (and by no means the largest) in that country. In addition to the units of the Jesuit, Barnabite, Lazarist, Carmelite, Dominican and Salesian communities stationed in this Archdiocese which are predominantly local in their membership, one finds these units geographically interspersed with units of the Redemptorists, Franciscans, Holy Cross and Picpus Fathers from Holland; Passionists, Capuchins and Orionites from Italy; Divine Word Fathers from Germany; and Claretians and Escolapians from Spain.

The geographical jurisdiction of the Propaganda Congregation has been considerably reduced during the past few decades. In 1908 the Roman Catholic Churches in England, Scotland, Ireland, Holland, Luxembourg, the United States, Canada and Newfoundland were detached from the Propaganda and elevated to a regular status under the Congregation of the Consistory and the other Sacred Congregations. In 1917 authority over church matters in the Middle East and a few other areas were assigned to the Congregation for the Eastern Church (see below).

Furthermore, among its variety of duties the Congregation for Extraordinary Ecclesiastical Affairs is responsible for the erection and division of dioceses, and the selection of Bishops for these dioceses, in those countries and places where such matters must be referred to the civil governments concerned in accordance with a concordat or some other special arrangement agreed to by the Vatican. At the present time this Congregation exercises this authority in Africa and Asia only in connection with the small number of colonies belonging to Portugal which still enjoy the privileges of the Portuguese *padroado*. In all other respects, the Portuguese colonies are subject to the other Congregations, including the Congregation of Seminaries and Universities. By the same token, these colonies do not come within the jurisdiction of the Propaganda.

Virtually all of Latin America and the Philippines are subject to the administrative jurisdiction of the Consistorial Congregation in matters relating to the creation of dioceses and the appointment of bishops, etc. The same Congregation has competence over Algeria and Tunis inasmuch as Algeria is still considered by the French to be politically a part of metropolitan France, as was Tunis prior to its having achieved its independence.

Thus there are four Sacred Congregations which have territorial jurisdictions in Africa, Asia and Latin America. These geographical jurisdictions are summarized in Table 104.

Because there are these four Congregations concerned with Roman Catholic activities in Africa, Asia and Latin America, it is difficult to compare—except in general terms—the over-all Roman Catholic missionary enterprise with that conducted by the large number of Protestant foreign mission boards and societies in these same areas.

TABLE 104.   Geographical Jurisdictions of Sacred Congregations (1958)

Area	Propaganda	Eastern Church	Extraordinary Ecclesiastical Affairs[a]	Consistorial
Africa	Remaining Areas	Egypt (& Sinai) Northern Ethiopia Eritrea	Angola Mozambique Portuguese Guinea Rio de Oro (Spanish)	Algeria Tunis
Middle East	Arabia Afghanistan	Remaining Areas		
Southern Asia	Remaining Areas		Goa	
Southeast Asia	Remaining Areas[b]		Timor	Philippines[c]
East Asia	Remaining Areas		Macao	
Latin America	A few vicariates[d]			Remaining Areas
North America	Alaska Northern Canada			Remaining Areas
Europe	Scandinavia[e] Switzerland Germany (part) Balkans (part)	Albania (part) Greece Cyprus Bulgaria	Russia	Remaining Areas

NOTES: [a] By virtue of the *padroado* accorded to Portuguese colonies and (in Africa) to Rio de Oro (a Spanish colony). Relations with the USSR are handled by a special commission for Russia, as directed by Pope Pius XI in 1930.

[b] Including Australia and New Zealand.
[c] With the exception of a few vicariates on outlying islands.
[d] Principally the Guianas and in tribal, mountainous or frontier areas.
[e] Including Iceland.

The Propaganda has authority over the major and minor seminaries within its territorial jurisdiction. It also has authority over those seminaries, wherever located, which have been founded exclusively for the purpose of educating missionary personnel for service abroad. The Congregation for the Eastern Church supervises the seminaries within its areas; and the seminaries which are located in the areas under the administrative jurisdiction of the Consistorial and the Extraordinary Ecclesiastical Affairs Congregations are supervised by the Seminaries Congregation.

In addition to its main function of providing the over-all direction of the missionary activities carried on within its areas, the Congregation for the Propagation of the Faith conducts a number of auxiliary activities.

First among these is The Pontifical College of Propaganda Fide which was canonically erected by Pope Urban VIII on August 1, 1627, five years after the creation of the Propaganda Congregation itself. Its initial enrollment was 12 students, which by 1798 had increased to 75. The advent of the French Revolution resulted in the closing of the institution in that year and it was not reopened until 19 years later, in 1817. For approximately 300 years the Urban College (as it is sometimes called in honor of its founder) was located within the Palace of the Propaganda. Then in 1931 it was transferred to a new structure (built largely with American funds) situated on the Janiculum Hill overlooking the Vatican. In 1957 there were about 240 students from countries all over the world studying at the College for missionary careers. In 1933 a Missiological Institute was added to it. The only other Roman Catholic missiological faculty in the world (as distinct from individual chairs of missiology) is that of the Gregorian University in Rome. In 1943 a Faculty of Canon Law was added to the Urban College, and in 1947 the College of St. Peter the Apostle was founded. At the latter College, ten years later there were 100 priests engaged in missionary studies at the postgraduate level. Of this number, 74 were from Asia, 14 from Africa, 11 from Oceania, and one from the United States.

The Propaganda Congregation also maintains large archives and a missionary library of approximately 250,000 volumes. This library is more than twice as large as the Missionary Research Library in New York City which has approximately 100,000 books and reports, etc. in its collection. Whenever books of missionary interest are published in any part of the world, it is the usual procedure for the Roman Catholic Church in that country to send a copy to the Propaganda's library. Pope Pius XI, much of whose early ecclesiastical career was spent directing the activities of the Ambrosian Library in Milan and subsequently the Vatican Library, strengthened the Propaganda's library and organized a large missionary exposition which was held in Rome in the jubilee year of 1925. The exhibits of the latter were subsequently transferred to a permanent Lateran Missions Museum.

As early as 1626 the *Tipografia poliglotta Vaticana* was established under the Propaganda for the purpose of printing books, catechisms and other materials in 50 different languages to be sent to foreign missionary personnel for their use. However, it has since been supplemented by other presses in Rome and in the field.

In 1927 the International Fides Service was created for the purpose of furnishing Roman Catholics throughout the world with news items of interest relating to foreign missionary activity. The Fides News Service is translated into Italian, French, German, English and Spanish and is distributed periodically in various forms to recipients throughout the world. Fides has also published a number of books relating to Roman Catholic missionary activity and has collaborated in the preparation of the *Guide to Catholic Missions* published every decade or so by the Propaganda. In addition, the Fides has a photographic section furnishing pictures of missionary activities to those interested in having them. In 1939 it also established a statistical office for maintaining current data on missionary personnel and their distribution, etc.

The Propaganda Congregation draws no revenue from the territories it administers. One source of its income, aside from that which it receives directly from the Vatican for the maintenance of its operations in Rome, is a monopoly granted by the Popes with respect to the dispensing of the Cardinals' rings. On the same day (June 22, 1622) that he created the Propaganda Congregation, Pope Gregory XV issued a Constitution, *Romanum decet,* concerning the Propaganda's finances which were to be augmented by a donation from the Cardinals known as "la tassa dell' annello." Each newly created Cardinal receives his ring from the Propaganda Congregation, and he in turn makes an offering of a generous sum of money to the Congregation. This offering amounted to 500 gold écus, a coin which later came to be known in France as a "Louis d'Or." However, Pope Pius VIII (1830) reduced this gift to 600 silver écus, owing to the financial difficulties experienced by the Roman Catholic Church following the French Revolution and the Napoleonic Wars.

The principal source of the income used by the Propaganda in support of its missions in the field is now furnished to it by four organizations.

The first and by far the most important is the Society for the Propagation of the Faith. This organization was founded in Lyons, France, in 1822 by a French lay woman named Pauline Jaricot. The Society does not send out missionary personnel but instead raises funds for the work of the Propaganda. On May 3, 1922, the centennial date of its founding, Pope Pius XI transferred the headquarters of the Society from Lyons to Rome where its activities could be more closely directed by the Propaganda Congregation. The Secretary of the Propaganda is customarily the President of the General Council of the Society. He is assisted by a Vice President who must be a Frenchman because of the fact that French Roman Catholics have traditionally been the most important supporters of the Society. The other members of the Council are the Presidents of the various national councils of the Society, as well as other ecclesiastical and lay members appointed for five-year terms by the Cardinal Prefect of the Propaganda. Since its transfer to Rome, one of the important achievements of the Society was its successful campaign instituting the observance in Catholic churches throughout the world of "Mission Sunday." In the United States the National Director of the Society since 1949 has been Most Rev. Fulton J. Sheen.

The second organization supporting the field activities of the Propaganda is the Pontifical Society of St. Peter the Apostle for Native Clergy. It was founded in Normandy, France, in 1899 as a result of the efforts of another French lay woman, Stephanie Bigard, and her daughter, Jeanne. They set out to interest their friends in sponsoring the education of a native seminarian in Nagasaki, Japan, as a result of an appeal they had received from Bishop Cousin of that diocese. The present purpose of the Society is to raise funds for the support of native students for the priesthood in mission lands and also for the creation of new seminaries in these same areas. In 1920 the Society was placed under the direct authority of the Propaganda Congregation. In the United States, Bishop Sheen is also National Director of this Society; and in this country every Diocesan Director of the Society for the Propagation of the Faith is at the same time Diocesan Director of the Pontifical Society of St. Peter. The members of the Society are classified as Founders, Benefactors, or Associates. In 1949, on the occasion of the 50th anniversary of its founding, the Bigard major regional seminary (named after Stephanie Bigard) was founded at Owerri in Nigeria. The Society has also issued a number of publications.

The third organization is the Holy Childhood Association which was founded in 1843, also in France, by Bishop Forbin-Janson. Originally its purpose was to ransom pagan children and provide Christian education for them. Later its scope was enlarged to include the establishment and support of orphan asylums. Only children up to 12 years of age can qualify as active members of the Association. Its headquarters are in Paris and it has a budget of approximately $2,000,000 a year. In some instances as a result of their participation in the Association's activities, the thoughts of its youthful members are said to have been directed toward choosing a future career in foreign missions.

The fourth organization is the Missionary Union of the Clergy. Unlike the three organizations mentioned above, it does not collect funds, nor is it a Pontifical society. Rather its purpose is to publicize among the clergy the missionary activities of the Roman Catholic Church. By this means it is hoped that the clergy will awaken the interest of the laity in missions and encourage them to contribute more liberally to the other three organizations. The Missionary Union was first established in 1916 as a diocesan organization in Parma, Italy. Subsequently, with the active support of Popes Pius XI and XII its activities were extended to many other countries. In the United States in the years 1943–50 it cooperated with the Society for the Propagation of the Faith in producing the Missionary Academia Course of Mission Studies for use in all the major Roman Catholic seminaries.

In the United States, the Society for the Propagation of the Faith has its national offices in New York City. It also serves at the present time the diocesan offices of the Society which are located throughout the country. In 1956 the General Fund income of the national office alone from all sources was $3,268,968, less expenses of $577,969, leaving a net income of $2,690,999. The sources of the net income of the national office included the publications "God Love You" (a syndicated column) and *Mission* (a bimonthly magazine recently renamed *Worldmission*) netting a total of $1,549,626. The television appearances of Bishop Sheen in that year brought in a total of $1,000,006, and the sale of rosaries, "God Love You" medals, etc., yielded an additional $141,367 in net income.

The operations of the General Fund for the Society in the United States as a whole in 1956 are set forth in Table 105.

TABLE 105.   OPERATIONS OF THE GENERAL FUND OF THE SOCIETY FOR THE PROPAGATION OF THE FAITH IN THE UNITED STATES (1956)

Collected by Diocesan Offices	$7,152,861
Collected by National Office	3,268,968
Total Collections	$10,421,829
Less National Office expenses[a]	577,969
Total sent to Propaganda Congregation in Rome	$9,843,860

NOTE: [a] Amounting to approximately 5.5% of total collections.

The growth in the contributions from various sources to the Society in the United States which were transmitted by it from its General Fund to the Propaganda Congregation in recent years is shown in Table 106.

TABLE 106.   NET AMOUNT OF THE GENERAL FUND OF THE SOCIETY FOR THE PROPAGATION OF THE FAITH SENT FROM THE UNITED STATES TO ROME (1945–56)

1945	$2,807,110
1946	2,949,511
1947	3,080,480
1948	3,108,469
1949	3,170,719
1950	3,557,089
1951	4,391,392
1952	5,683,809
1953	6,694,410
1954	7,259,681
1955	8,246,861
1956	9,843,860

Thus over the 12-year period the net amount sent annually from the Society's General Fund in the United States to Rome has been more than tripled, with the notable increases commencing in the year 1950.

In addition to the operations of its General Fund, the Society for the Propagation of the Faith also serves at the present time as a collection agency in the United States for the Pontifical Society of St. Peter the Apostle for Native Clergy, the Holy Childhood Association, the Missionary Union of the Clergy, and the Catholic Near East Welfare Association (see below). In addition the Society collects large sums for home missions in the United States. The annual report of the Society for the Propagation of the Faith for the year 1954 contained an analysis of its receipts as shown in Table 106A.

The Society reported that its total receipts in the United States rose from $24,-263,433 in 1954 (as shown in Table 106A) to $28,615,926 in 1956. Thus in 1954, and presumably again in 1956, the total receipts of the Worldmission Aid Society for the Propagation of the Faith (as the American unit has recently been named) which were designated for foreign missionary activity (i.e., excluding home mis-

sions) amounted to at least 65% more than the income received by the largest
individual Protestant foreign mission board in the United States (the Methodist) in those same years. On the other hand, the Society's receipts designated for
foreign mission activities amounted to only about one-sixth or one-seventh of the
total income received for this purpose by all the North American Protestant foreign mission agencies in the same years.

TABLE 106A. ANALYSIS OF RECEIPTS OBTAINED BY THE SOCIETY FOR THE
PROPAGATION OF THE FAITH (USA) DURING THE YEAR ENDED 12/31/54

General Fund			
Membership	$2,384,569		
Mission Sunday collection	1,902,928		
Schools	769,481		
Undesignated gifts	599,738		
Legacies	386,746		
Other income	1,870,458	$7,913,921	33%
Special Fund			
Designated gifts	$3,924,300		
Missionary Cooperation Plan	2,178,317		
Mass intentions	1,883,690		
Society of St. Peter the Apostle	393,351		
Leper Fund	79,208		
Missionary Union of the Clergy	10,734		
Other funds	904,794	9,374,394	39%
Holy Childhood Association		1,943,600	8%
Catholic Near East Welfare Association			
Mission Sunday Collection		335,811	1%
Total, Foreign Missions		$19,567,725	81%
Total, Home Missions		4,695,707	19%
Total Receipts		$24,263,433	100%

A number of reports state that the contributions of the Worldmission Aid Society in the United States to Rome in recent years have ranged between 60% and
70% of the total received by the Propaganda Congregation from sources throughout the world for the Roman Catholic foreign missionary enterprise. This is approximately the same percentage of financial support as is contributed by American
Protestants to the total cost of Protestant missionary activities in Africa, Asia
and Latin America.

The 1957 report of the Superior Council of the Society for the Propagation of
the Faith (according to the Fides Service) noted that on a world-wide basis, the
Society received 471 petitions for aid in 1957, of which 367 were granted and the
balance of 104 were not met. Of the 367 petitions to which the Society made an
affirmative response, only 35% of the total sums requested could be granted. In
1958, the Society had $15,760,000 available for grants, or approximately $760,000
more than it had in 1957 for this same purpose.

The Vatican does not publish the financial statements of the Propaganda Congregation as a whole. All Roman Catholic societies sending missionaries to the
field are directly responsible for raising the funds needed in connection with the
recruitment and formation (i.e., training) of their personnel, as well as the expenses involved in the personal care of these individuals while in the field. In addi-

tion, those religious communities which are in a position to do so, often defray the operating expenses of the mission station entrusted to their administration. Some communities raise funds independently and transfer the proceeds directly to their missions overseas rather than through the Propaganda.

According to Father Heston, C.S.C., the financial support of the Society for the Propagation of the Faith "on an average . . . covers about one-fifth of the normal expenses of the missions, not counting the special subsidies which may be voted in case of particularly urgent needs. That is why a religious or missionary community engaged in foreign missionary activity carries on its own campaign for funds to aid its own particular field."

While no figures are available concerning the total amount spent annually by all the agencies of the Roman Catholic Church in support of its foreign mission activities as a whole, experienced Roman Catholic students consider that such expenditures aggregate well over $100,000,000 a year. Because of the salaries factor it would not be accurate to try to compare the over-all financial aspects of Roman Catholic foreign missionary activities with those conducted by the Protestant Churches. Whereas most Protestant foreign missionary personnel receive annual compensation ranging ordinarily from $3,000 to $6,000 per capita (plus in many instances varying allowances for dependents), such compensation is not paid to Roman Catholic foreign missionaries.

Father Schmidlin has commented as follows on the use made in the field of missionary contributions: "A further but not insurmountable handicap is the financial. However inexpensive as compared with Europe may be the maintenance and education of clerics in the mission lands, and however strongly the Propaganda may urge the Vicars Apostolic to devote the major part of their missionary funds to seminaries (after deducting the sums necessary for the support of the missionaries), sufficient sums for this purpose are usually lacking because those received from abroad are needed for other purposes and the native Christians are as a rule too poor to defray the expenses of seminaries."

As for the support given to Roman Catholic seminaries by the Society of St. Peter the Apostle for Native Clergy, the International Fides Service reported on June 8, 1957, that in its fiscal year 1956–57 the Society raised $2,600,000 on a world-wide basis for a total of 386 major and minor seminaries. In addition the Society received $2,860,000 in grants from the Society for the Propagation of the Faith, making a total of $5,460,000 available to it for its purposes. The Society of St. Peter was seeking to raise an additional $1,000,000 in order "to take care of minimum needs."

In fiscal 1957–58 the Society of St. Peter reported that it had at its disposal $5,360,000 for grants compared to requests totaling $7,095,000 (or a shortage of $1,735,000). Most of the Society's income is obtained in the form of a large number of small gifts. Occasionally, however, it receives large contributions and bequests from individuals. For example, a Belgian Baron, Carton de Wyart, paid for the construction of the major seminary of "Mayidi" at Kisantu in the Belgian Congo.

The Society also reported that it recently made capital grants totaling $542,000 for the construction of the Pontifical Seminary of Poona, India; $375,000 for a regional seminary which is being built in Karachi, Pakistan; and $600,000 toward the estimated $700,000 cost of the new regional seminary being constructed in Nairobi, Kenya.

In addition to its capital grants, the Society of St. Peter contributes between $200 and $300 a year (depending upon the cost of living in the various countries) for each major seminarian being trained in seminaries under the jurisdiction of the Propaganda Congregation. It also contributes between $100 and $200 toward the support of each minor seminarian in those same missionary areas. Finally, the Society maintains the College of St. Peter the Apostle attached to the Urban College in Rome for approximately 100 priests at the postgraduate level, particularly with a view toward enabling them to serve on seminary faculties. Approximately two-thirds of the expenses of the College of St. Peter the Apostle are paid for by the Society and the remaining one-third is defrayed with the stipends received by its student-priests for celebrating Masses in various localities in Italy.

The total funds actually obtained by this Society cannot be compared with accuracy against the totals shown later in this Survey (chapter 16) as having been contributed by the leading Protestant foreign mission boards in the United States to theological education overseas. The Society of St. Peter helps to support 281 minor Roman Catholic seminaries (in addition to 105 major seminaries) whereas the Protestant figures cited do not include contributions to the estimated 325 Bible schools now operating in the younger church areas which in many instances might be considered as a Protestant counterpart to the minor Roman Catholic seminaries in missionary areas.

B. THE EASTERN RITES

The Congregation for the Eastern Church was established on January 6, 1862, by Pope Pius IX with his Apostolic Constitution entitled *Romani pontifices*. Although at first the Prefect of the Propaganda was also the prefect of the new Congregation, the staffs of the two organizations were separate. Pope Benedict XV in his motu proprio *Dei providentis* dated May 1, 1917, made the Oriental Congregation (as it is sometimes called) completely independent of the Propaganda and also increased its authority. At present the Congregation for the Eastern Church exercises over the dioceses, bishops, clergy, religious and faithful of the Oriental Rites all the powers of the other Sacred Congregations in Rome, except that of the Holy Office. The Pope is now always the Prefect of the Oriental Congregation. In accordance with his motu proprio *Sancta dei ecclesia* dated March 25, 1938, Pope Pius XI transferred to its jurisdiction authority over all Catholics of the Latin Rites living within the areas reserved to the Oriental Congregation.

At present the Congregation for the Eastern Church has exclusive jurisdiction over Roman Catholics of all rites residing in the following countries and geographical areas:

Africa: Egypt (and Sinai), Northern Ethiopia and Eritrea.
Middle East: Turkey, Syria, Lebanon, Israel, Jordan, Iraq and Iran.
Europe: Bulgaria, Southern Albania, Greece, the Dodecanese Islands and Cyprus.

Beyond these countries the Oriental Congregation retains jurisdiction over all dioceses, parishes, missions and persons of Eastern Rites anywhere in the world. In addition it is authorized to deal with problems arising from mixed relations of Catholics in the Latin Rites with those of the Eastern Rites. The present Secretary of the Congregation is Cardinal Eugene Tisserant, the Dean of the College of Cardinals. A special commission within the Oriental Congregation is charged with the responsibility of following the religious developments within the Russian Orthodox Church.

The reason why the Vatican has centralized so much authority in the Congregation for the Eastern Church during the past century is that previously there was a tendency on the part of some European religious communities to attempt to "Latinize" the Roman Catholics of the Eastern Rites. With respect to the missionaries of the Latin Rites who have been active in the Middle East, Very Rev. Andrew Rogosh, Assistant Secretary of the Catholic Near East Welfare Association, has written:

They have labored far and wide with great success. However, with great regret, but it must be said, disciplinary mistakes have been made. The desire of the Holy See has always been "that all men should be Catholics, but not that all should become Latins." The Supreme Pontiffs have exhorted, time and again, under threat of severe penalties, that missionary priests "shall not dare to persuade anyone . . . to pass from the Greek to the Latin rite, or even allow them to do so if they wish it, without having first consulted the Apostolic See." Some prelates and local superiors have acted against the expressed desires of the Supreme Pontiffs, either from ignorance or from prejudice.

Occasionally this process resulted in setbacks for the Roman Catholic Church. As the Catholic author Donald Attwater points out, it was the arbitrary actions of the Portuguese hierarchy in Goa, India, toward the native clergy in southern India which resulted in the conflict of almost the whole body of Syro-Indians with the Roman Catholic Church in 1653, leading to the formation of the Syrian Orthodox Church of Malabar in that country. There had been Christians on the Malabar coast of India since the 6th century. According to Father Rogosh,

Bishops were sent to them from Baghdad, the center of the Persian Church, and their original Rite is the rite of that Church commonly called Chaldean. The suspicion might arise that they also inherited from their Mother Church the Nestorian heresy, but that is a matter of dispute. . . . The Portuguese colonial authorities . . . looked askance at the dependence of the Malabar Christians on the Chaldean patriarch. Their scheme was to place them under the jurisdiction of their own Latin Archbishop of Goa. . . . The Portuguese clergy . . . began to latinize the Chaldean rite, under the pretense of trying to eliminate traces of the Nestorian heresy. Native bishops were terrorized by methods of the Inquisition. Rome tried to protect the natives. . . . The boiling point was reached in 1653 when a Catholic Chaldean bishop arrived in their parts from Baghdad and was immediately seized by the Portuguese. The rumor that he was drowned touched off the spark. The whole Chaldean Church in Malabar went into schism. . . .

In order to heal this breach, the Discalced Carmelites of St. Pancratius Seminary in Rome were sent to the Malabar area in 1656 and have worked there ever since. In part as a result of their efforts during the subsequent century, approximately one-half of the members of the Syrian Orthodox Church were converted to Rome. The latter now number about 632,000 persons of the Roman Catholic Malabar Rite and in 1896 their own hierarchy was reconstituted.

In 1930, two Syrian Orthodox bishops, Mar Ivanios and Mar Theophilos, joined the Roman Catholic Church and were accepted with special apostolic authorization. At the end of 1931, 35 secular priests and about 5,000 of the laity followed their example. Since then their number has grown to approximately 58,000 persons. They observe the Malankara Antiochean rite of the Roman Catholic Church and form an ecclesiastical province of their own.

It was in order to minimize the possibility of a repetition of the earlier setbacks that the Congregation for the Eastern Church was established. The aim of the Congregation is to help ensure that the contacts of the Vatican with the ancient Eastern Churches (including those which are in and out of communion with Rome) would be handled with a minimum of friction and a maximum of understanding. An example of the accommodation to local customs permitted by the Congregation is the fact that about one half of the Roman Catholic secular clergy in the Eastern Rites are married.

Table 107 presents a summary (adapted from Attwater and Rondot) of the most important of the Eastern Rites which are under the jurisdiction of the Oriental Congregation.

The schisms which separated the Eastern Churches from the Roman Catholic Church occurred at various times, notably at the Council of Chalcedon held in the year 451. The split with the Greek Orthodox Church was not made final un-

TABLE 107. THE EASTERN RITES OF THE ROMAN CATHOLIC CHURCH

Rite	Approximate Number of Roman Catholics	Approximate Schism from Rome	Date of Reunion with Rome	Language	
				Liturgical	Vernacular
Byzantine					
European					
Ukrainian[c]	5,471,000		1595	Church Slavonic	Ukrainian
Romanian	1,434,000	1054	1701	Romanian	Romanian
Other[a]	283,500	various	various	various	various
Middle East					
Melkite	173,000	1054	1709	Arabic	Arabic
Antiochean[d]					
Maronite[d]	391,000	650?	1182	Syriac	Arabic
Syrian	74,000	451	1662	Syriac	Arabic
Malankara[b]	58,000	1653	1930	Syriac	Malayalam
Armenian					
Armenian	100,000	525	1740	Armenian	Armenian
Alexandrian					
Coptic	63,000	451	1742	Coptic	Arabic
Ethiopian	30,000	550?	1839	Ge'ez	Amharic
Chaldean					
Malabar[b]	632,000	1653	1700?	Syriac	Malayalam
Chaldean	96,800	431	1552	Syriac	Arabic
	8,806,300				

NOTES: [a] Including Hungarian, Italo-Greek, Yugoslav, Russian, Bulgarian, Greek, etc.
[b] In addition to the Antiochean Malankara and Chaldean Malabar Catholics, there are over 500,000 Catholics of the Latin Rite in southern India organized in the Arch-diocese of Verapoly (with an indigenous archbishop, bishop, etc.) and the Diocese of Trivandrum.
[c] Including those of the Ruthenian Rite (Sub-Carpathia).
[d] The Maronites assert they have always been in communion with Rome.

til after 1350. Space does not permit the recounting of how each of the Eastern Rites of the Roman Catholic Church came to be established. It is sufficient to point out that all but one of these Rites within the Middle East and Africa is a counterpart of an Eastern Church as shown in Table 108.

TABLE 108. ROMAN CATHOLIC EASTERN RITES AND THEIR EASTERN CHURCH COUNTERPARTS IN AFRICA, ASIA AND LATIN AMERICA

Eastern Rite	Eastern Church
Melkite	Greek Orthodox
Maronite	
Syrian	Syrian Orthodox
Malankara	Syrian Orthodox Church of Malabar
Armenian	Armenian Orthodox
Coptic	Coptic Orthodox
Ethiopian	Ethiopian Orthodox
Malabar	Syrian Orthodox Church of Malabar
Chaldean	Church of the East (Assyrian)

The Maronites, who constitute the leading Roman Catholic Rite in Lebanon, joined the Church in large numbers in 1516. The members of the Melkite, Syrian, Armenian, Coptic, Ethiopian and Chaldean Rites are the descendants of those who were won over at various dates from their membership in the counterpart Eastern Churches. The members of the Chaldean Rite (principally in Iraq, Iran and Syria) are descendants of Nestorian Christians who joined the Roman Catholic Church in the 16th century, and today they actually outnumber the remaining Nestorians.

The Council of Florence held in the years 1438–39 represented the high point in the efforts of the Roman Catholic Church to bring about a reunion with Rome of elements within the Eastern Churches: many of the members of the Armenian Rite joined the Roman Catholic Church at this time, as did small numbers of persons of the Greek Rite. Some of the members of the Eastern Rites were subsequently won over as a result of the missionary activities of the Western religious Orders commencing in the 16th century. The Jesuits were active in Armenia, the Dominicans in Persia, the Capuchins in Turkey and the Franciscans in the Holy Land. However, due to various factors, their successes in terms of the number of converts gained was limited.

In a number of major cities more than one of the Eastern Rites of the Roman Catholic Church are observed. For example, in Alexandria one may find Catholics of six Rites besides the Coptic. These would be the Latin, Melkite, Armenian, Syrian, Maronite and Chaldean Rites. In addition, there have been in the recent past three Roman Catholic Patriarchs of Alexandria—one for the Coptic Catholics, the Melkite Patriarch of Antioch who also retains the title of Alexandria, and a titular Latin Patriarch of Alexandria (who resides in Rome).

There are now reported to be about 28 religious Orders or congregations of Eastern Rites for men, and approximately 41 for women. Some of these were originally Eastern Orders, some are branches of Western communities, and about one half of them are foundations at present modeled after Western Orders. The growth in the number of Orders in the Eastern Rites during the past four centuries has not matched the growth in the communities of the Latin Rite in the West. Recent membership figures are not available for a number of Orders and congregations of the Eastern Rites. Table 109 lists the principal communities of priests and indicates their comparatively small size.

Of the communities listed in Table 109, perhaps the most interesting are the Mechitarists. One of the by-products of the activities of the Oriental Congregation, and of the members of those congregations which are concerned with its work, is assisting in the preservation of the cultural heritage of those minority peoples of the Middle East who in the last few centuries have been widely dispersed. The Mechitarist Order serves in this capacity. They were founded in 1701 in Constantinople by an Armenian named Peter Manuk who came to have the surname Mechitar ("Comforter") of Sebaste. The Order follows the Benedictine rule, and at one time or another it has maintained schools and colleges in Cairo, Beirut, Constantinople and in Bulgaria. The Mechitarists have had as one of their functions the double task of introducing important Western ideas to Armenians and at the same time helping to preserve the Armenian cultural heritage. The Order has a reputation for a high level of learning and has translated a number of theological texts into Armenian. The Mechitarists are split into two sections which are completely independent of each other. The first with 47 professed members transferred its chapter house to the island of San Lazzaro near Venice in 1717; and the second with 32 members split off from the first and located its house in Vienna in 1811. Each

TABLE 109. Principal Religious Communities of Priests of the Eastern Rites

Name	Rite	Location	Number of Priests in 1957
Antonians			
Baladites	Maronite	Lebanon	450
St. Isaiah	Maronite	Lebanon	100
Aleppines	Maronite	Lebanon, Egypt	100
Missionary Congregation (Kraim)	Maronite	Lebanon	70
St. Hormside	Chaldean	Iraq	75
Basilians			
Salvatorians	Melkite	Lebanon, Israel	131[b]
Shuwairites[c]	Melkite	Lebanon, Syria	63[b]
Aleppines	Melkite	Lebanon, Egypt	50[b]
Missionary Society of St. Paul[e]	Melkite	Lebanon	[d]
Josaphats	Ukrainian-Ruthenian	Poland, USA	127[a]
Italians	Italo-Greek	Italy	50
Mechitarists			
Venetians	Armenian	Italy	47
Viennese	Armenian	Austria	32
Carmelites			
Third Order	Malabar	India	135[a]

NOTES: [a] As of 1932.
[b] As of 1946.
[c] Order of St. John the Baptist.
[d] Not available.

[e] Founded in 1903, with its headquarters in Harissa, the members of this institute are known as Paulists, but are a separate community from the American society whose members are also known as Paulists.

section is headed by a Superior General having the rank of Archbishop. In some ways the Mechitarists function on behalf of Roman Catholic Armenians in the same manner that the Benedictine monasteries functioned on behalf of learning and culture in Western Europe during the Dark Ages.

When elements of the Eastern Churches have transferred their allegiance to the Roman Catholic Church at different times during the past two centuries, it has been apparent that there was a shortage of clergy among these "Uniate" groups, and that their priests were seriously deficient in the level of their theological education. In order to meet this need, the Vatican sent representatives of Western congregations and Orders to work among them as teachers. Pope Pius XI encouraged Latin Orders and congregations to form branches using the Eastern Rites, and the Benedictines, Carmelites, Franciscans, Dominicans, Augustinians, Redemptorists and Jesuits are among those who have done so.

The Assumptionists (Augustinians of the Assumption, an Order founded in France in 1845) have been particularly active, carrying out missions in Eastern Europe and the Middle East (Turkey, Bulgaria, Roumania, and Yugoslavia), in promoting studies of the various Eastern Churches, and in seeking to reconcile them to Rome. However, the disruptions caused by World Wars I and II and their aftermaths set back the activities of this Order. Another community, the Resurrectionists, specializes in similar missions to "schismatic Slavs," particularly non-Roman Catholics of Polish extraction residing in France, Czechoslovakia and the United States. Some members of the Redemptorist congregation have passed over from the Latin to the Eastern Rites in order to help the Ruthenian and Ukrainian clergy in Europe and the United States. The Sionists (Fathers of Sion) were founded in Palestine by a Jewish convert, and they have as one of their aims the conversion of the Jews to the Roman Catholic Church.

As an additional effort toward promoting the unity of the Roman Catholic and the Eastern Churches, Pope Pius XI addressed a letter in 1924 to the Abbot Primate of the Benedictines pointing out the special qualifications of this Order for conducting such reunion work. The Pope requested that one Abbey in each Benedictine congregation should concern itself with Eastern Rite affairs. Subsequently the Benedictine Priory of Amay-sur-Meuse in Belgium (later transferred to Chevetogne) established two sections, one for the Latin and one for the Byzantine Rites. This Priory specializes in following the activities of the non-Roman Catholic Churches in the Middle East, and in this connection it publishes a leading quarterly (in French) entitled *Irénikon* which summarizes these developments.

The major seminaries and the scholasticates of the religious communities of the Eastern Rites are under the jurisdiction of the Oriental Congregation in the same manner as the Propaganda has authority over similar institutions in the missionary areas of the Roman Catholic Church. The seminaries and scholasticates preparing men for service as priests in the Eastern Rites are listed in the next chapter. In addition to these institutions, the Oriental Congregation has authority over seven colleges of Eastern Rites in the City of Rome itself, as shown in Table 110.

TABLE 110.   MAJOR SEMINARIES IN ROME OF THE EASTERN RITES

College	Founded	Approx. Number of Students	Administration
Greek	1577	38	Benedictines
Maronite	1584	?	Secular
Armenian	1883	12	Sulpicians
Ukrainian-Ruthenian	1897	14	Ukrainian Basilians
Ethiopian	1919	7	Capuchins
Russian	1929	9	Jesuits
Romanian	1930	none	

These institutions are not "colleges" in the American sense of the word. Rather they resemble the colleges to be found in European universities in that they provide only separate dormitory and refectory accommodations. Most of the students of these colleges receive the major part of their instruction at the Pontifical Gregorian

University which offers courses to students of all rites from all over the world. At the individual Eastern Rite colleges, separate worship services according to the liturgy of that Rite are held. Their students receive instruction in their own liturgy, as directed by Pope Leo XIII who commented in *Orientalium dignitas* (1894): "There is more importance in the conservation of the Eastern rites than might appear at first sight."

The Oriental Congregation has jurisdiction over six other educational institutions outside of the Middle East for training priests of the Eastern Rites, as listed in Table 111.

TABLE 111. Major Seminaries in Europe and the United States under the Jurisdiction of the Oriental Congregation

Institution	Location	Approx. Number of Students	Rite
College of St. Basil the Great	Rome	?	Italo-Greek
Scholasticate of Basilian Order of St. Josaphat	Rome	6	Ukrainian-Ruthenian
Scholasticate of the Cistercian Order[a]	Casamari, Italy	6	Ethiopian
St. Cyril and Methodius Seminary	Pittsburgh, Pa.	62	Ruthenian
St. Josaphat Seminary	Washington, D.C.	23	Ukrainian-Ruthenian
St. Basil's Seminary	Methuen, Mass.	?	Melkite

NOTE: [a] A Latin Rite seminary with a few Eastern Rite students (as shown).

In the same year (1917) in which the Oriental Congregation was established on an independent basis by Pope Benedict XV, the Pontifical Oriental Institute was also founded by him and placed under the jurisdiction of the new Congregation for the Eastern Church. The Institute has been under the direction of first the White Fathers, later the Benedictines, and now the Jesuits. Its three-year course includes Catholic theology, the doctrines of the Eastern Rites and of the Eastern and Orthodox Churches, the forms of Eastern worship, Eastern canon law, patristics, archaeology, ascetics, languages and other cultural studies related to these Churches. Non-Roman Catholic students may also attend its courses, the purpose being to enable members of the Eastern and Orthodox Churches to study the history and rites of all the churches in the Middle East and thereby serve to eliminate mutual prejudices. In 1956 the Institute had 26 professors and 84 students.

The Oriental Institute, together with the Pontifical Biblical Institute, at present form parts of the Gregorian University. The library of the Oriental Institute has been built up, and in 1956 it had 70,000 volumes relating to its particular field of interest. The Institute publishes two periodicals, *Orientalia Christiana periodica* (a quarterly review) and *Orientalia Christiana analecta* (an annual, first published in 1923, containing longer studies).

In his encyclical, *Rerum orientalium,* dated September 8, 1928, Pope Pius XI recommended that increased emphasis be placed by seminary students on the study of the activities of the Oriental Rites: "Indeed it should not be too difficult for each theological seminary to have one professor who, together with the study of history or liturgy or canon law, may at the same time explain at least the elements of those things which concern the Near East." It is the aim of the Oriental Institute to spread such knowledge, and it has been the hope that one student from every Roman Catholic diocese might specialize in Oriental matters. The Vatican and (since its establishment) the Oriental Congregation have during the past two centuries published a full set of books in Greek for the Byzantine Rite and another set has been issued for the Coptic Rite. In 1930, Pope Pius XI established a Liturgical Commission within the Oriental Congregation which subsequently has published new works, including a Greek *Horologium* (a book of the office for canonical hours) and a revised *Pontifical* of the Chaldean Rite, etc.

Finally, the Vatican has taken a number of measures in recent years to raise funds for Roman Catholic activities in the Middle East. In 1926 Pope Pius XI founded the Mission Aid for the Near and Middle East. Five years later he reorganized the Catholic Near East Welfare Association which had originally been established in the United States shortly after World War I to send funds and supplies for the relief of the suffering peoples in the Middle East. The new purpose of the Association was to serve the Oriental Congregation in the same manner as the Society for the Propagation of the Faith is active in the United States on behalf of the Propaganda Congregation—specifically, collecting funds and promoting a greater interest in and knowledge of the activities of the Roman Catholic Church in the Middle East. Pius XI also ordered that the Association should receive 9% of the collections received in churches throughout the United States on Mission Sunday. At present the Association is by far the largest single source of financial support for the Oriental Congregation. Since World War II the Association has stepped up its efforts through the publication of an additional number of pamphlets and articles dealing with the Middle East, more lectures given by its staff, and the sponsoring of "Oriental Days" when priests of the Eastern Rites offer the various liturgies in colleges and seminaries.

It is along these lines that the Vatican is conducting its efforts in the Middle East, both in strengthening the training of the clergy of the Eastern Rites in communion with Rome and ultimately with the hope of persuading the Eastern Churches, which it considers to be dissident and schismatic, to join the Roman Catholic Church.

CHAPTER 13

THE DEVELOPMENT AND ADMINISTRATION OF THE ROMAN CATHOLIC MAJOR SEMINARIES AND SCHOLASTICATES

A. The Historical Development of the Seminaries

The development of the major and minor seminaries training the secular clergy, and of the scholasticates maintained by the religious communities, was an evolutionary process. They had their origin in the catechist schools which were established in the eastern provinces of the Roman Empire during the first three centuries of the Christian era (and which are discussed in chapter 15 of this Survey).

In the West, St. Augustine (354–430) established a "clergy house" at his home near the principal church of Hippo Regius (a port in North Africa, some 200 miles west of Carthage) where men were educated for the priesthood. This was essentially a training class inasmuch as it had no full-time faculty. The students lived together under St. Augustine's supervision, dressed alike and performed their spiritual devotions in common. This school might be considered as a forerunner of the later scholasticates since each student was bound by a vow of poverty and only clerics above the rank of subdeacon were admitted to it. Many of its students were already officiating in churches. The class furnished at least ten bishops to the Church in Africa. As a result of its success, bishops in other dioceses in North Africa followed St. Augustine's example and established what later came to be known as episcopal or cathedral schools. After the Vandal invasions similar institutions were founded in the 5th and 6th centuries in Spain and Southern Gaul (e.g., at Arles). As the barbarian intrusions increased, and the secular schools could no longer be maintained by the governments in the Mediterranean area, the number of episcopal schools increased. In Rome the Pope's school at this time is reputed to have devoted its attention principally to the training of the clergy in the creed, canon law, and the liturgy.

Owing to their rudimentary curricula, etc., none of these schools could be called seminaries in the sense that this word is used today. One of the reasons for the neglect of theological education in the early life of the Church was the confident belief then prevalent that the men devoting their lives to the work of the ministry were selected for these careers as a result of divine choice.

Concerning the differences between the training provided for the clergy during the first five centuries in the East as compared to the West, Dr. C. Stanley Smith has written: ". . . In the Eastern Church, the clergy were educated in the catechetical schools and trained in the various grades of ecclesiastical orders which preceded ordination to the priesthood; while in the West, they were educated in the episcopal schools conducted by the bishops and trained in the various successive offices from reader to bishop. This might also be said, that in the East there was more emphasis on the education and less on the training in office, while in the West it was just the opposite."

The Monastic Age, which followed next, might be said to comprise the years 500–1200. At first the monasteries did not commence as centers of learning, but rather as houses where laymen could seek a life of contemplation and prayer. Occasionally discipline was lax. However, with the founding of the Benedictine Order in the year 529, many previously established monasteries in the West instituted reforms. Schools were founded at a number of monasteries for the purpose of training men for membership and careers in those Orders. Books were written and copied by the monks, and libraries were accumulated. Soon a proverb arose among the Benedictines: "Monasterium sine armario quasi castrum sine armamentario" (a monastery without a library is like an armed camp without an arsenal).

Among other places, the Benedictines established a well-known school at St. Gall, Switzerland, and this Order attracted some of the ablest men of the times. The Augustinians in Gaul also maintained cloister schools but later devoted their attention to staffing the episcopal schools. During this period the clergy were virtually the only men receiving education at a secondary level.

In this educational endeavor the monastic schools tended to outstrip the cathedral schools in importance at this time. Father Joseph Cox points out:

There were two classes of monastic schools: (1) The interior or conventual school, in which aspirants to the monastic state were educated. They were also called Claustral schools, and the pupils were styled oblati. (2) The exterior or secular school, in which candidates for the secular priesthood, together with lay students, were taught. The pupils were called nutriti.

After the general adoption of the Benedictine rule, a further division into major and minor schools existed in most monasteries. In the latter were taught the fundamentals of Christian doctrine, chant, arithmetic, grammar, etc.; in the former, theology and Sacred Scripture. This presents a striking analogy to the present system of major and minor seminaries.

Pope Gregory the Great (590–604) had a deep interest in clerical education and founded a school in Rome which was somewhat similar to that of St. Augustine's and has been described as the First Pontifical Seminary. It was attached to the Cathedral Church of St. John Lateran. In Spain, sessions of the Council of Toledo which were held in 531 and 633 decreed that students destined for the priesthood should be trained in episcopal schools under the oversight of an experienced cleric of higher rank.

The first cathedral or episcopal schools which had a systematic curriculum were established by the Roman Catholic Church in England. A graduate of one of these schools was the celebrated missionary to the pagans in Germany, St. Boniface (680–755). In 744 he founded the monastery at Fulda in Germany whose reputation as a training school for the clergy spread rapidly throughout Western Europe. At one point it had as many as 22 affiliated institutions.

The Emperor Charlemagne brought about some order in the chaotic political conditions which existed at the time. One of Charlemagne's predecessors established a palace school for the secular and religious training of princes and nobles. It moved about with the monarch from place to place, and Charlemagne himself received his education there. After coming to the throne in 768, he appointed Alcuin as its superintendent; and in 789 he issued a capitulary directing that episcopal and monastic schools organized along somewhat similar lines should be established within each bishopric and monastery. The Emperor also issued an edict to Bangulf, Abbot of Fulda, in which he wrote in part: "During past years we have often received letters from different monasteries informing us that at their sacred services the brethren offered up prayers on our behalf; and we have observed that the thoughts contained in these letters, though in themselves most just, were expressed in uncouth language, and while pious devotion dictated the sentiments, the unlettered tongue was unable to express aright. Let there, therefore, be chosen for this work men who are both able and willing to learn, and also desirous of instructing others; and let them apply themselves to the work with a zeal equalling the earnestness with which we recommend it to them."

The episcopal and monastic schools were so few in number that they were unable to provide even rudimentary training for many of the clergy, including those residing in some of the larger towns and cities. Accordingly, during this era, there were established in rural parishes a number of "rectory schools" where students for the priesthood were instructed by the local pastor. The courses of instruction at these training classes varied greatly in the length of time required and in accordance with the educational competence of the priest in charge. Sometimes their graduates subsequently attended episcopal schools.

Father Sackett notes: "Where churches and monasteries were sacked and destroyed by Normans, Magyars or Saracens, the schools flourished only if the bishop or abbot chanced to foster them." Throughout the Dark Ages, instruction at most of these institutions was at a low level, centered largely on the writings in the Bible and those of the early Church Fathers. There was little in the way of systematic theology taught, and few cathedral schools (with the exception of those at Rheims, Paris and Chartres) were notable for the quality of their instruction.

The vigorous Pope Gregory VII (1073–1085) strengthened the cathedral schools and allocated various prebends and benefices for the support of their faculty members. This and other factors tended to raise the episcopal schools in stature as compared to the monastic schools of the times. However, this was short-lived inasmuch as the subsequent steep decline in the fortunes of the Papacy resulted in a corresponding decline in the importance of the cathedral schools as educational institutions. The third and the fourth Lateran Councils (in 1179 and 1215) attempted to improve their caliber; and once again it was decreed that to every cathedral there should be attached a school for training the clergy. The three principal subjects taught in these schools were medicine, law and theology; and these institutions began to lose their exclusively clerical character.

Founded in the year 1213, the Dominicans were the first religious Order to adopt definite, formal rules of study for their members. Students commenced their studies in a local "conventual" school. After completing an arts course there, the students entered a course in philosophy and theology offered by the provincial schools. The most promising candidates were then sent to a "studium generale" which was usually attached to a university. The first studium generale was located in Paris, but by 1248 four others had been established and attached to the universities in Cologne, Oxford, Montpellier and Bologna. The fame of the Dominican teachers of theology increased to the point where some of the older religious Orders (such as the Cistercians) employed Dominican Masters of Theology on the faculties of their monastic schools.

The rise of the great universities marked the beginning of another phase in the training of the clergy. The University of Paris grew out of a cathedral school and was originally a scholastic "guild" of students and teachers. It soon came to be called the "Mother of Theological Faculties." The University of Bologna rose to prominence at about this time, but the teaching of law was its specialty. Shortly thereafter, Oxford University was established, possibly as a result of students and professors migrating from Paris. The founding of Cambridge University soon followed as an outgrowth of Oxford.

Theological education was centered in Paris and the English universities until late in the 14th century. At first, according to J. E. Roscoe, "it was the policy of the Popes to concentrate theological instruction at certain centres, notably at Paris, which for a long time retained the monopoly of granting theological degrees, but in due course this privilege was extended to other universities, e.g., Rome, Perugia,

Padua, Salamanca, Montpellier, Toulouse, Vienna and Prague. None of these later foundations, however, could compete in importance with Paris, which throughout the Middle Ages remained the great centre of theological study."

Many of the chairs at the University of Paris, especially in theology, were filled by leading Dominicans and Franciscans. Outside the walls of Oxford there were colleges maintained by the Dominicans, Franciscans, Carmelites and Augustinians. At Dublin, the Dominicans opened a training school in 1248 and seven years later, in 1255, they founded the Minerva College in Rome.

In the 13th century, a student could qualify at Paris for the degree of Master of Arts at the age of 21, but he could not obtain a doctorate in theology until he was aged 35. As Professor Lewis J. Sherrill points out,

this "Master of Arts" was the academic equivalent of our Ph.D., and signified that one was "a professor" in the Arts Faculty. . . . Upon becoming a theological student, he spent his first six years as an *auditor*. For the first four years of this period, he attended lectures on the Bible; and for the next two years, he heard lectures in what we should now call systematic theology. If by that time, he had attained the age of 26, he might, after certain formalities, enter upon his Baccalaureate. . . . Upon becoming a "Bachelor of Divinity" a man embarked upon his own lectures . . . on some book of the Bible. . . . This much would occupy him for eight years as a theological student. . . . Rounding out his tenth year after he had become a Master of Arts, he was now supposed to reside in Paris for three or four years longer . . . partaking in disputations. Finally, at the expiration of 14 years or more after he had already become a Master of Arts, he received his license to teach, becoming a "Doctor of Divinity". . . . After the Reform of 1366, a total of as much as 15 or even 16 years were necessary after earning the Master of Arts to advance to the Doctorate in Theology.

Most of the instruction at the early universities consisted at first of courses in theology, canon law, logic and philosophy. The faculties of theology tended to emphasize the intellectual training of men for a professional career rather than their spiritual development as pastors. As Dean Rashdall points out, "the professional work of the higher clergy consisted almost entirely in ecclesiastical administration, for which the study of canon law was considered the most important qualification."

Clerical students at these universities came into close contact with secular students, both in class and in their boarding houses. The religious discipline and even the morality of the ordinand students were relaxed. Furthermore, it is likely that less than 5% of the clergy obtained university training during the Middle Ages, so that the overwhelming majority of the priests and bishops of those times were men who had received no formal higher education at all.

The new universities attracted the most promising teachers and scholars away from the cathedral and monastic schools. As a result, the academic level of the latter declined to the point where some became very elementary theological schools and others little more than grammar schools. Father Sackett notes: "The episcopal palace which housed the cathedral school was too often crowded with other officials, was full of distractions, and evidently not the best place for quiet, serious study. On the other hand, the existing colleges with their relaxed discipline and mixed student body of clerics and lay students were not an ideal place to train future priests in sanctity."

The turning point in the effort of the Roman Catholic Church to provide comprehensive systematic theological training for the bulk of its clergy occurred in the 16th century as one of the consequences of the Reformation. When the defection of Roman Catholics to Protestantism in Germany and elsewhere in Europe reached considerable proportions, Pope Paul III created six able men as Cardinals in 1536–42 and set them to work on a plan for the reform of the Roman Catholic Church. This plan was published in 1538 under the title of *Consilium delectorum cardinalium de emandanda ecclesia.* It called for reforms in the Church along many different lines. The first recommendation was: ". . . and first such as concerns the choice of the clergy (1) greater care should be taken in the selection of ordinands." It was widely believed that any attempt at a general reform in the Church would be condemned to failure as long as the evils prevalent among the clergy were permitted to endure.

This plan ultimately bore fruit at the long Council of Trent held in 1545–63 for the purpose of implementing the suggested reforms. As Father De Melo has noted, at its fifth session on June 17, 1546, the Council decreed that there should be "in the metropolitan or cathedral churches of important or populous cities as well as in the collegiate churches provided with a sufficiently numerous clergy, the course of Arts (Logic and Philosophy), of Canon Law, at least for three years, and all must be men of good reputation. In every capital of a province the Bishop and the rulers should establish a college for clerical students. . . . A long interval of over thirteen years followed, before the sessions could be resumed. The decree on the creation of Seminaries was promulgated only in 1563, but two documents written during the interval had a decisive influence on that important decree."

One of these documents was the 11th decree of Cardinal Henry Reginald Pole's celebrated *Decrees of Ecclesiastical Reform* in England. Cardinal Pole, a Papal Legate to the country of his birth, suggested that the best means of remedying the lack of priests in England would be to gather together promising young men and educate them in a special college. Since funds for this purpose were lacking, he advocated that each bishop should contribute $\frac{1}{40}$ of the net income he obtained from his benefice, and that the same $2\frac{1}{2}\%$ tax should be imposed on every ecclesiastic whose benefice netted him an income of £120 or more a year. Cardinal Pole's suggestions were not put into effect in England because of his untimely death in

1557. Furthermore, the death of Queen Mary Tudor in 1558 and the accession of Queen Elizabeth I resulted in a renewal of the Protestant persecution of Roman Catholics in that country. Consequently British and Irish candidates for the priesthood were obliged to journey to the Continent to obtain their seminary training, particularly in the College at Douai, 50 miles southeast of Calais in France.

The second document influencing the Council of Trent was written in 1551 by the Blessed Juan d'Avila, a friend of Ignatius Loyola and one of the early Spanish Jesuits. It was composed at the request of the Archbishop of Granada in Spain for his use at the Council sessions. According to Father De Melo,

the general theme of the memorial is the "Reform of the ecclesiastical state." The author begins by stating that the framing of wise laws is not enough to bring about the reform of customs if the persons who have to observe those laws are not themselves reformed. If, therefore, the Council wished its laws to be obeyed . . . the chief care of the Council should . . . be to devise means of recruiting and training good clerics. A few remedies are then suggested. First of all, comes a general remedy, namely, to make admission to the clerical state more difficult. The clerical life should be so regulated that only the virtuous would be able to conform themselves with it. A selection would then come by itself. The number of the clerics will become smaller but the quality will be better. . . ."

The Council of Trent reopened in 1562, and on July 15, 1563, proclaimed a series of decrees, arranged in 18 chapters, with the last chapter relating to the founding of seminaries. The following are the important sections of this chapter:

Whereas the age of youth, unless it be rightly trained, is prone to pursue the pleasures of the world; and, unless it be formed, from its tender years, unto piety and religion, before habits of vice have wholly taken possession of men, it never will perfectly, and without the greatest and almost singular help of Almighty God persevere in ecclesiastical discipline; the holy synod ordains that all cathedrals, Metropolitan, and other churches greater than these, shall be bound, each according to the measure of its means and the extent of the diocese, to maintain, to educate religiously, and to instruct a certain number of youths of their city and diocese, or, if (that number) cannot there be found, of that province, in a college to be chosen by the bishop for this purpose near the said churches or in some other convenient place. And into this college shall be received such as are at least twelve years old, born in lawful wedlock, and who know how to read and write competently, and whose disposition and inclination afford a hope that they will always serve in the ecclesiastical ministries. And it wishes that the children of the poor be principally selected; though it does not, however, exclude those of the more wealthy, providing they be maintained at their own expense, and carry before them a desire of serving God and the Church.

The Bishop, having divided these youths into as many classes as seem fit to him, according to their number, age, and progress in ecclesiastical discipline, shall, when it seems convenient to him, assign some of them to the ministry of the Churches (and) keep the others in the college to be instructed; and shall supply the place of those who have been withdrawn by others; that so this college may be a perpetual seminary of ministers of God.

And to the end that the youths may be the more conveniently trained in the aforesaid ecclesiastical discipline, they shall always at once wear the tonsure and the clerical dress; they shall learn grammar, singing, ecclesiastical computation and other liberal arts; they shall be instructed in sacred Scripture; ecclesiastical books; the homilies of the saints; the manner of administering the sacraments, especially those things which shall seem suited unto hearing confessions; and the forms of the rites and ceremonies.

The Bishop shall take care that they be every day present at the sacrifice of the Mass, and that they confess their sins at least once a month; and receive the body of our Lord Jesus Christ, according to the judgment of their Confessor; and, on festivals, serve in the cathedral and other churches of the place. All which, and other things advantageous and needful unto this object, all bishops shall ordain, with the advice of two of the senior and most discreet canons whom themselves have chosen, as the Holy Spirit shall have suggested; and shall make it their care, by frequent visitation, that the same be always observed. The forward and incorrigible and disseminators of evil morals, they shall punish sharply, even if necessary by expulsion; and removing all hindrances, they shall carefully attend to whatsoever things appear to tend to preserve and advance so pious and holy an institution.

The Cardinals participating in the Council realized the futility of drawing up plans for the founding of educational institutions without providing for ways and means to meet their cost. The following paragraphs from this same chapter specify how the funds for the proposed seminaries should be raised and indicate explicitly the priority in importance assigned by the Cardinals to this project:

And forasmuch as some certain revenues will be necessary for raising the building of the college, for paying their salaries to the teachers and servants, for the maintenance of the youths, and for other expenses; . . . the bishops . . . shall take a certain part or portion out of the entire fruits of the episcopal revenue, and of the chapter, and of all dignities whatsoever, personates, offices, prebends, portions, abbies, and priories of whatsoever order, even though Regular, or of whatsoever quality; or condition they may be . . . and of all benefices whatsoever . . . even those which are under any right of patronage, even those that are exempted, that are of no diocese, or are annexed to other churches, monasteries, hospitals, or to any other pious places. . . . The bishop of the place shall, by ecclesiastical censures, and other legal means . . . compel the possessors of benefices . . . to pay this portion not merely on their own account, but also on account of whatsoever pensions they may happen to have to pay to others, out of the said revenues. . . .

But if the prelates of cathedrals, and of the other greater churches should be negligent in erecting the said seminary and in preserving the same, and refuse to pay their share; it will be the duty of the archbishop sharply to reprove the bishop, and to compel him to comply with all the matters aforesaid, and of the provincial Synod to reprove and to compel in like manner the archbishop, and sedulously to provide that this holy and pious work be as soon as possible proceeded with, wherever it is possible. . . .

In order to help ensure that (1) competent men would serve on the faculties of the new seminaries, and (2) the cost of operating these institutions would not be too great, the Council decreed :

Furthermore in order that the teaching in schools of this nature may be provided for at less expense, the holy Synod ordains that bishops, archbishops, primates and other Ordinaries of places, shall constrain and compel, even by the substraction of their fruits, those who possess any dignities as professors of theology, and all others to whom is attached the office of lecturing, or of teaching, to teach those who are to be educated in the said schools. . . . And the aforesaid masters shall teach those things which the bishop shall judge expedient. And, henceforth, those offices or dignities, which are called professorships of theology shall not be conferred on any but doctors, or masters, or licentiates in divinity, or canon law, or on other competent persons, and such as can personally discharge that office; and any provision made otherwise shall be null and void: all privileges and customs whatsoever, even though immemorial, notwithstanding.

But if the churches in any province labour under so great poverty, as that a college cannot be established in certain (churches) thereof; the provincial Synod, or the metropolitan shall take care to establish one or more colleges, as shall be judged expedient, in the metropolitan, or in some other more convenient church of the province, out of the revenues of two or more churches, in which singly a college cannot conveniently be established, and there shall the youths of those churches be educated. . . .

This famous decree became the law of the Roman Catholic Church through the Bull *Benedictus Deus et pater* issued by Pope Pius IV on January 26, 1564, which confirmed all the decrees of the Council. To this day it has remained the fundamental directive of the Church concerning the education of candidates for the priesthood.

While the Council of Trent was concerned with many other matters related to the reformation within the Roman Catholic Church, an historian, Cardinal Pallavicini, declared that the institution of the seminaries was the most important reform executed by the Council. Several other members of the Council declared that had no other business been conducted by it, this decree alone would have justified their efforts during the 18-year life of the Council. A Protestant historian of the Catholic reformation, Dr. B. J. Kidd, has concluded that the creation of the seminaries by the Council did "more than all the other decrees and canons of Trent put together for the revival of the Catholic Church."

The revival of the old diocesan seminaries (cathedral schools) by the action of the Council of Trent did not result in either the disappearance of the small monastic schools or the removal of the study of theology and philosophy from the universities' curricula. But the major seminaries became the chief means for training priests after the Reformation; and the universities continued to offer courses in theology, canon law, etc., for the postgraduate education of priests and laymen. Thus, using rather arbitrary dates and periods, one might summarize the historical development of the seminaries in the West as shown in Table 112.

TABLE 112.   THE DEVELOPMENT OF THE SEMINARIES

Institution	180–500	500–1200	1200–1563	1563 to date
Clergy Training				
Classes	x			
Rectory Schools		x		
Cathedral Schools		x	x	Seminaries
Monastic Schools		x	x	Scholasticates
Universities			x	Faculties of Philosophy and Theology

Pursuant to the decision of the Council of Trent, Pope Pius IV founded the Roman Seminary in the year 1565 in Rome, the administration of which was entrusted to the Jesuits. Later Pope Gregory XIII (1572–85) endowed this institution with a stable income, and from that time on, it came to be known as the Gregorian University.

Within the year following the publication of the recommendations of the Council of Trent, the Cardinal Archbishop of Milan, St. Charles Borromeo, founded three seminaries in that city (and three more elsewhere) for the secular clergy in accordance with the Tridentine decree. In Milan the most promising students were sent to the seminary attached to the cathedral. Less promising students were sent to a second school, and the third offered refresher courses for priests in need of training. He frequently visited these institutions, sometimes spending one or two weeks in each at a time.

Borromeo placed the faculty of the cathedral seminary in the hands of the Jesuits and introduced devotional practices in the priestly life which were based on Loyola's *Spiritual Exercises.* The Jesuits efficiently administered this and five other seminaries later established by Borromeo in Milan and the Piedmont area. However, as the Cardinal's biographer, Most Rev. Cesare Orsenigo, points out, "the only drawback was that the best seminarians, attracted inevitably by their superiors, entered into the Society of Jesus, thus depriving the Bishop of their services. And this fact was one of the reasons why the direction of the seminaries was taken away from the Jesuits and later given to the Oblates." The Oblates of St. Ambrose was a congregation of diocesan priests founded by Borromeo expressly for this purpose.

Borromeo, who was one of the noblest figures in the entire history of the Roman Catholic Church, also established a seminary in Milan for Swiss priests whom he felt needed special training in apologetics because of their proximity at home to cantons in Switzerland which had adopted Protestantism.

The Tridentine decree did not include provisions for the internal administration and discipline of the seminaries. Accordingly Borromeo formulated the *Institutiones seminarii* as a constitution for their management, and its provisions are now largely embodied in the canon law of the Church. Because of his work in advancing the establishment of the seminaries within the Church, many of these institutions have subsequently been named "St. Charles Borromeo."

Subsequently other bishops in Italy, France, Germany and elsewhere established diocesan seminaries. In Germany the Bartholomites (a congregation founded by Fr. Holzhauser, 1613–1658) was placed in charge of a number of seminaries, and this society extended its activities to Spain, Sicily and Poland.

However, during the first fifty years following the Council of Trent there were numerous difficulties encountered by the diocesan authorities in setting up the seminaries. In the first place it was found that many dioceses had insufficient trained personnel and financial resources with which to establish and operate these institutions. In Germany, where Protestantism was strong, it was necessary to make a compromise: in some German universities there were established separate Protestant and Roman Catholic theological faculties side by side. In France a number of newly established seminaries failed or were later changed into secular colleges. The Cardinal Archbishops of Lorraine, Rheims, Rouen and Bordeaux all saw their seminaries fail after the first decade or so of their existence.

It was not until the middle of the 17th century that the system of major seminaries envisioned by the Council of Trent came to be established. This first took place in France and was made possible by a departure from the Borromean tradition of taking boys at an early age and training them in only one institution until their ordainment as priests.

In the year 1635, St. Vincent de Paul established a seminary, Le Collège des bons enfants, in Paris. This institution and a second one founded by him for the training of priests both failed. The conclusion was reached that the failure had been caused by the fact that the students were being trained at both the major and the minor seminary level in the same institution without a sufficient distinction being made between their classroom work and institutional life as students. Accordingly separate major seminaries were established, and St. Vincent de Paul founded the Congregation of the Mission (Lazarists) whose members would serve on their faculties.

During the same period two other congregations of priests were formed in France for the same purpose. An associate of St. Vincent de Paul, M. Olier, established a seminary at St. Sulpice in Paris in 1642 and founded the Sulpician Society which devotes a greater proportion of its efforts to the administration of seminaries than does any other religious community. The Sulpician regulations were adopted by other seminaries and stressed the need for developing the spiritual as well as the intellectual aspects of a priest's training.

The Eudists were a third society established at this time in France for a similar purpose. St. Jean Eudes, along with St. Vincent de Paul and M. Olier, realized that one of the most important factors in attracting able students to enroll in a seminary is the character and personality of the directors assigned to administer those institutions. By 1789, the time of the French Revolution, the Eudists (according to Father Sackett) were conducting 14, the Sulpicians 30, and the Lazarists 40 seminaries in France.

Elsewhere in Europe, particularly in Italy, the Borromean tradition persisted until the 20th century. In Germany, as Father Manning notes, the development of the major seminaries was hampered by the attitude of the government which often led, instead, to the establishment of Faculties of Theology at the various State Universities. In Ireland the seminaries were distinguished for the number of their graduates who were sent to missionary countries overseas. In the United States and Canada, the founding of the major seminaries was pioneered by Sulpician fathers who came to America from France during and after the time of the French Revolution.

B. THE ADMINISTRATION OF THE SEMINARIES

Initially the Sacred Congregation of the Consistory was charged with the authority of overseeing the training of the secular clergy in the diocesan seminaries. The reason for this was that the Consistorial Congregation has the responsibility of creating dioceses and appointing bishops, and it is the latter who have the duty to establish seminaries. It was not until 1915 that Pope Benedict XV (in accordance with his motu proprio *Seminaria clericorum* dated November 4, 1915) transferred the supervision of the major and minor seminaries to the Congregation of Studies, and he gave to this Congregation its present title, "S. Congregatio de Seminariis et Universitatibus studiorum."

The activities of the Sacred Congregation of Seminaries and Universities in the field of secular education were originally under the jurisdiction of the former Congregation of the Roman University created by Pope Sixtus V in his apostolic constitution, *Immensa Aeterni,* dated January 28, 1588. The Congregation of the Roman University was initially established for the purpose of supervising education in the Papal States in Italy. In time the functions of this Congregation diminished in importance. It was re-established by Pope Leo XII as the Congregation of Studies in his apostolic constitution, *Quod Divina Sapientia,* dated August 21, 1824. However, with the loss to the Italian Government of the Papal States in 1860 (and the City of Rome in 1870), the authority of the Congregation of Studies was reduced to the supervision of higher Catholic education in all countries of the world, with the exception of the mission areas under the Propaganda Congregation (and, after 1917, the territories under the authority of the Oriental Congregation).

Because of the importance he ascribed to the work of the Congregation of Seminaries and Universities, Pope Pius XI (who at one time was Rector of the major seminary in Milan) was serving as the Prefect of this Congregation at the time of his death in 1939. The present Prefect is Cardinal Giuseppe Pizzardo. The Prefect is assisted by a Secretary and several Undersecretaries.

The Seminaries Congregation has four principal bureaus, each of which is staffed by two or three officials. The jurisdictions of these bureaus comprise:

1. Seminary and Ecclesiastical Colleges.
2. The Regional Seminaries in Italy.
3. Universities and Faculties.
4. Cultural and Scholastic Activities.

The activities of the Seminaries Congregation are supervised by a committee of 28 Cardinals and 26 Consultors. Of the latter, 13 represent the secular clergy, and 13 are representatives of the religious communities. Among the latter, in 1957, were three Jesuits and three Benedictine fathers of various congregations, plus one representative each from the Franciscans (O.F.M.), Dominicans, Capuchins, Oblates of Mary Immaculate, Sulpicians, Holy Ghost and Redemptorist Fathers. In addition, the Seminaries Congregation is served by 22 counsellors.

Attached to the Congregation of Seminaries is a Central Education Office which supervises the religious and secular education in boys' and girls' schools of all types and grades, including those administered by religious communities or in any way depending upon ecclesiastical authority. Within the headquarters of the Congregation there are also departments dealing with administrative matters, legal counsel, archives and protocol, and a secretariat. In addition, the Congregation conducts two research organizations, the Biblical Institute and the Institute of Ecclesiastical History (the latter founded by Pope Leo XIII).

The function of the major seminaries is to prepare candidates for the priesthood. The level of their scholastic work is generally considered to be of a college undergraduate character. The purpose of the major seminary is not to turn out scholars or research students, but rather to produce good parish priests, preachers and confessors.

The minor seminaries offer courses in arts and sciences at the high school, precollegiate level, preparing men for the major seminaries. Among every half-dozen or so students enrolled in a minor seminary, on the average only one or two enter a major seminary. It is not uncommon to find that among every 50 students entering a minor seminary only two or three are eventually ordained.

In the Roman Catholic directories for a number of countries there are listed (in addition to the major and minor seminaries) some institutions which are described as either "apostolic," "catechetical," "conciliar," "diocesan" or "seraphic" seminaries, or as "seminary-colleges." The term "conciliar" refers to the Council of Trent, and these institutions are often at the major seminary level and sometimes serve as regional seminaries. On the other hand, a number of conciliar seminaries in Latin America are at the minor level. A diocesan seminary (particularly in Latin America) more often than not is at the minor seminary level, as are the apostolic and the seraphic seminaries. The seraphic seminaries are under Franciscan administration.

The catechetical seminaries are for the instruction of the laity. Some religious communities (for example, the Holy Ghost Fathers in Haiti, Guadeloupe and Martinique in the Caribbean, and on the Island of Réunion in the Indian Ocean) maintain seminary-colleges. These are "mixed" institutions for the instruction of lay and clerical students, but the "college" is at the high school-junior college level, and the "seminary" is at the minor seminary level.

The term "seminario" alone is not infrequently used in Spanish (as the word "seminary" formerly was used in English a century ago) to refer to a secular school. Thus an institution listed in a secular directory in a Latin American country simply as a "seminary" may not have any connection with the Roman Catholic Church at all.

Some individual Roman Catholic seminaries offer courses at both the major and minor levels. In these institutions, the teaching of the minor and major seminary students is carried on in separate departments. Formerly there were so-called "mixed" seminaries which differed from the seminary-colleges mentioned above in that the clerical and lay students were enrolled together in courses at the major seminary-collegiate level. These mixed seminaries were explicitly forbidden by Pope Leo XIII in a letter (*Paternæ providæque,* dated September 18, 1899) addressed to the Brazilian hierarchy. In the same letter, the Pope recommended that, in order to avoid worldly distractions, major seminaries should be located in rural rather than in urban areas.

A diocesan major seminary is under the authority of one bishop, an interdiocesan seminary is under the authority of several bishops, and a provincial (or central, or national) seminary comes under the authority of all the bishops of that province, district or nation.

The regional seminaries in missionary areas are directly under the authority of the Propaganda in Rome, as stipulated in the decree of that Congregation dated April 27, 1934. The Propaganda appoints the rector and the professors who are nominated by the Superior General of the religious community administering the regional seminary. The advantages of regional seminaries are the savings in money and personnel which they afford, and their greater uniformity in curricula. Furthermore they provide a more secure tenure for their faculty members who cannot be easily transferred to nonteaching tasks elsewhere by the religious communities of which they are members. Other advantages are said to be in a broader outlook imparted to the students, which is important in the case of those whose viewpoints have previously been limited by their tribal or village life.

A pontifical seminary (which is not located in a mission area) comes under the supervision of the Congregation of Seminaries and Universities. In his apostolic constitution *Deus scientiarum dominus* of May 24, 1931, Pope Pius XI provided for the organization of pontifical seminaries which would be attached to pontifical universities and would offer advanced courses in philosophy and theology. A special emphasis in these courses is placed on questions of science which have a bearing on religious matters. All regional seminaries in nonmissionary lands are considered to be pontifical seminaries, and these institutions have the authority to confer graduate degrees in philosophy and theology. Thus, to some extent, a pontifical seminary is by definition more nearly akin than is a major seminary to a Protestant "theological college" (as defined in this Survey) or to a fully accredited divinity school (as this term is used in the United States). A pontifical university offering courses in sacred theology and scholastic philosophy leading to graduate degrees might be compared to the graduate department of religion in a private non-Roman Catholic university in the United States.

Some major seminaries are called "colleges" although all their courses are at the philosophical and theological level. Some Roman Catholic theological colleges themselves offer no courses but are essentially residential halls connected with a university. The latter colleges are mostly in Rome, and, as previously noted, seven of them are limited to housing students being trained as priests in one or another of the individual rites under the authority of the Oriental Congregation. In addition there are approximately 24 similar residential "national colleges" for Latin rite students living in Rome who come principally from Europe and North America. Among them are two national colleges for Latin American students. These are the South American College (Pio Latino Americano) founded in 1858, and the Brazilian College which was founded in 1934.

There are 18 Roman Catholic institutions located in Rome at which instruction at the postgraduate level is carried on. These are listed in Table 113. Again, it should be noted that most of the 5,562 students who were enrolled in the various departments of these institutions in 1956 came from Europe and North America. In some instances the most promising students in the major seminaries in Africa, Asia and Latin America are subsequently sent to Rome for graduate study. This affords them the opportunity to learn some of the aspects of the world-wide activities of the Roman Catholic Church. It also enables the authorities in Rome to evaluate the personal qualities of these students and their worthiness for promotion in later years to higher offices within the Church.

The Congregation of Seminaries and Universities supervises the faculties of

philosophy and theology at Roman Catholic universities which have been canonically erected (i.e., fully accredited by the Congregation) and which have received
authority from the Congregation to award degrees in recognized fields of study.
All major seminaries (by definition) have been canonically raised, but there are

TABLE 113.   ROMAN CATHOLIC INSTITUTIONS OF HIGHER LEARNING AND GRADUATE STUDIES LOCATED IN ROME, 1956[a]

| | | | Approx. Number of | |
| | | | | |
Name	Prof.	Stud.[b]	Books in Library	Administration
Gregorian University	97[c]	2,543	306,000	Jesuits
Biblical Institute	24	176	100,000	Jesuits
Institute of Oriental Studies	26	84	70,000	Jesuits
Lateran International Institute[k]	14[c]	585	155,000	Vicariate of Rome
Urban International Institute[d]	20[c]	378	130,000	Propaganda Congregation
"Angelicum" International Institute	40[c]	731	130,000	Dominicans
St. Anselm International Institute	28	180	37,250	Benedictines
"Antonianum" International Institute	36[c]	94	215,000	Franciscans
St. Bonaventure Theological Faculty	15	79	35,000	O.F.M. Conventuals
Theological Faculty[e]	19	82	55,000	Discalced Carmelites
"Marianum" Theological Faculty	19	63	50,000	Servites
Institute of Sacred Music	12	62	7,000	Seminaries & Universities Congregation
Institute of Christian Archeology	7	15	23,000	Seminaries & Universities Congregation
University Institute for Teacher Training[f]	27	200	[g]	Vicariate of Rome
Institute "Queen of the World"	35	212[h]	[g]	Congregation of Religious
Commission for Biblical Studies	[g]	[g]	[g]	Commission of Cardinals
Vatican Library School	5	43	[g]	Vatican Library
Vatican School of Paleography, Document Reading and Archives	2	35	1,000[j]	Vatican Secret Archives
	426	5,562	1,314,250	

NOTES: [a] The data relating to a few of these institutions
are as of 1955 or 1957.
[b] In all faculties, departments, etc.
[c] Plus part-time or special instructors, etc.
[d] "De Propaganda Fide" (Urban College).
[e] Sts. Theresa of Jesus and John of the Cross (International

College of the Discalced Carmelites).
[f] "Mary of the Most Holy Assumption."
[g] Not available.
[h] Religious priests.
[j] Plus the use of the Vatican Library.
[k] Of the Roman Seminary.

a number of Roman Catholic universities and colleges whose faculties have not
been canonically erected. Table 114 lists the Roman Catholic universities in Africa,
Asia and Latin America with faculties of philosophy and/or theology attached to
them which have been canonically erected.

The faculty of theology in a university does not constitute a seminary inasmuch as such a faculty is concerned with only the intellectual but not the spiritual
training of its students. By contrast, a major Roman Catholic seminary might be
described as an educational and residential institution offering courses in the fields
of philosophy and theology at the collegiate level and providing for the spiritual
training of its students.

The seminaries within the missionary areas and those areas under the authority
of the Oriental Congregation are supervised by the Propaganda Congregation and
the Congregation for the Eastern Church, respectively. However, the Congregation of Seminaries and Universities has authority over all Roman Catholic uni-

versities and their various faculties, wherever they are located. Since virtually all the seminaries and all of the scholasticates in Africa, Asia and Latin America are conducted locally by one or another of the religious communities, the authority of the Propaganda and Oriental Congregations over the training of men for the

TABLE 114. CANONICALLY ERECTED ROMAN CATHOLIC UNIVERSITIES IN AFRICA, ASIA AND LATIN AMERICA HAVING FACULTIES OF PHILOSOPHY AND /OR THEOLOGY (1956)

Name	City	Country	Date Canonically Erected	Administration
Africa				
None				
Asia				
St. Joseph University	Beirut	Lebanon	1881	Jesuits
Pontifical Athenaeum[a]	Poona	India	1926	Jesuits
St. Thomas University	Manila	Philippines	1645	Dominicans
Sophia University	Tokyo	Japan	1913	Jesuits
Latin America				
Pontifical Catholic Xaverian University	Bogotá	Colombia	1937	Jesuits
Pontifical Catholic University	São Paolo	Brazil	1947	Secular
Catholic University of Ecuador	Quito	Ecuador	1954	Secular
University of San Marcos[b]	Lima	Peru	1551	Secular
Theological Faculty of the Immaculate Conception[c]	Buenos Aires	Argentina	1944	Jesuits
Pontifical University of Chile	Santiago	Chile	1930	Secular

NOTES: [a] An independent Faculty of Ecclesiastical Studies which in 1956 had a faculty of 22, and 430 students. [b] A state university. [c] A Faculty of Ecclesiastical Studies attached to the Pontifical Metropolitan Seminary in Buenos Aires.

priesthood in those areas is limited largely to over-all direction, with the administrative details being left to the competence of the individual religious institute concerned. It would appear that much of the time of the Seminaries Congregation is devoted to the supervision of the Roman Catholic educational institutions in Rome and with the many major and minor seminaries located throughout Italy. Another function of the Congregation is to administer the Pontifical Work for Vocations to the Priesthood which was entrusted to its care by Pope Pius XII in accordance with his motu proprio *Cum nobis* dated November 4, 1941.

The Congregation of Seminaries and Universities is responsible for the supervision of the curricula in the major and minor seminaries which come under its authority. Once every three years all bishops are required to return a questionnaire submitted to them by the Congregation of the Consistory. A section of this questionnaire relates to the condition of the seminaries within their care, and the answers in this section which are supplied by the bishops are referred by the Consistorial Congregation to the Congregation of Seminaries and Universities. The triennial questionnaire which is "divided into seven articles, requires particulars regarding the personnel of seminaries, their buildings, financial situation, piety and discipline, studies, ordination and the personal relations of the bishops with the seminaries, as well as what has been done in the matter of recruiting new priests."

If a seminary adopts a new manual of theology (or philosophy, or canon law, or Holy Scripture), the local bishop must report this fact immediately to the Congregation of Seminaries and Universities. Seminary professors are required to report to their local bishop the names of the textbooks which are used in their classes, and such reports often are included in the annual report submitted by the rector to his diocesan authorities.

Any diocesan bishop can establish a seminary within the area of his jurisdiction without the permission of the Congregation of Seminaries and Universities. Sometimes this leads to a multiplicity of institutions in relation to the number of available students. However, the regulations of the Seminaries Congregation issued on May 24, 1931, outline in general terms the requirements to be met in order for a seminary or university faculty to be canonically erected. These regulations specify the number and the qualifications of the rector and professors on the faculty, details relating to the size and facilities of classrooms, the minimum amount of funds to be on hand, the major and secondary courses of study, and the discipline of students, etc. It is also specified that the institutions must have at their disposal adequate funds for the upkeep of their libraries, including the purchase of recently published books and subscriptions for periodicals.

In the *Codex juris canonici,* title 21, "De Seminariis," contains 20 canons (Nos. 1352–1371) relating to the administration and operation of the seminaries. In every diocese the bishop is charged with the responsibility of establishing a seminary. If there are insufficient revenues available for the building and maintenance of the seminary, the bishop is empowered to order pastors of churches to take up at stated times a collection for that purpose. Alternatively he can impose a seminary tax or annex some simple benefice to the seminary. In accordance with the Tridentine decree, such a tax or assessment must be paid by all parishes, etc., even though exempt from other taxes. The annual tax cannot exceed 5% of the taxable (net) income of the church or institution, and it is to be lowered as the revenue of the seminary increases. The bishop is directed to visit the seminary frequently and to take a direct personal interest in its welfare.

While the Congregation of Seminaries passes on the basic curricula taught in the seminaries within its jurisdiction, there have been few changes in the study emphases of major seminaries in recent decades. Occasionally the Congregation issues directives suggesting, for example, that more emphasis in the seminaries might be placed on one course or another, etc. Thus, on April 26, 1920, the Congregation issued a lengthy decree entitled *Ordinamento dei seminari* to the Italian hierarchy summarizing in very general terms the Congregation's views relating to desirable teaching methods to be used in the seminaries, the choice of texts, and the program of studies for philosophy and theology students.

Father Markham mentions some additional directives which were subsequently

issued by the Congregation of Seminaries relating to seminary courses in catechetical instruction (1929), the establishment within their philosophy courses of a
theoretical-practical course (one hour a week for two year) in pedagogy and di-
dactics (1944), the prescription of certain courses in sacred music (1949), etc. He
then continues: "Many other documents, some private, some of canonical interest only to certain groups, have appeared in the name of the Congregation of the
Seminaries and Universities since the Code. . . . Most of these documents one can
find by checking the annual indices of the *Acta apostolicae sedis,* while certain others
remain unavailable to the general reader."

The Seminaries Congregation does not itself issue the texts to be utilized in
the seminaries, nor does it usually decree which books must be used for this purpose. These texts have been written and developed by individual Roman Catholic scholars over the years and are said to have become fairly standardized. The
selection among the approved texts to be used is exercised by the individual seminary faculties. New texts become known to faculty members through the reviews
of them appearing in Roman Catholic theological journals.

In cases where the doctrine expressed in such texts is considered erroneous,
this would be a matter to be dealt with by the Supreme Sacred Congregation of
the Holy Office, one of whose functions is to keep up to date the Index, a list of
books condemned as being injurious to faith or morals. Ordinarily, however, it
would be the function of the Seminaries Congregation to ban such a text from
use in seminaries, based, if necessary, on an interpretation or ruling handed down
by the Holy Office.

Two recent instances of such action were cited by Paul Hofmann. In 1957 the
Seminaries Congregation ordered the Sulpicians to "withdraw a new French cate-
chism purporting to teach the tenets of the Catholic faith to children in a 'modern way' including the use of illustrations." In 1958 the Seminaries Congregation
banned an 880-page textbook entitled *Introduction to the Bible, Vol. I,* which had
been prepared by the Society of St. Sulpice "with a Jesuit father and several lay
scholars." The text was considered to contain a "corrosive" treatment minimizing
the "divinely inspired" role of Moses as set forth in the Pentateuch (the first five
books of the Old Testament): "The Vatican theologians who examined the text-
book objected to its method of introducing into biblical studies modern theories
they felt were at best questionable. The work's stress on social conditions prevailing in the era of Moses appears to have been a main reason for its condemna-
tion. The textbook bears the imprimatur, or ecclesiastical printing license,
personally granted by Maurice Cardinal Feltin, Archbishop of Paris. It has a preface by the Most Rev. Julien Weber, Bishop of Strasbourg. The preface suggested
that Catholic biblical science was in danger of becoming obsolete."

The Congregation of Seminaries does not issue the examinations which seminarians are required to take at the end of their courses. These tests are prepared by the individual seminary faculties. The latter report to the Congregation of Seminaries (or if in a missionary or Middle Eastern area to the Propaganda or Oriental Congregations, respectively) the subject matter or propositions in philosophy and theology to be dealt with in such examinations (e.g., "God is triune," etc.). In this way the Congregation is informed of the type of questions being asked and the topics covered. However, it is not informed concerning the students' answers to these questions, or (except in a general sort of way) concerning the relative academic standing of one seminary as against another.

The Congregation of Seminaries is not frequently in contact with individual major seminaries. The latter look more to the local bishop for guidance, and the Congregation relies largely on the bishop's triennial reports for its information. The Seminaries Congregation does not usually send out inspectors from its own staff to visit the institutions within its jurisdiction. Occasionally it relies on the reports of apostolic visitors for the investigation of the activities of seminaries where changes are thought to be needed.

While the Congregation of Seminaries has the right to suppress a seminary which has not maintained minimum standards, in actual practice it rarely takes such direct action. Even in instances where the consolidation of a number of institutions into a regional seminary appears to be clearly desirable, it is said that the Congregation nevertheless tends to rely on methods of persuasion rather than fiat in order to attain its objectives.

Thus it would appear that the role of the Congregation of Seminaries in relation to the major seminaries tends to be passive rather than active, i.e., primarily to help ensure that certain minimum standards are met, and only secondarily to promote and develop new courses and new training techniques, etc. This role is understandable when it is appreciated that the major seminaries' curricula have become fairly well standardized, with the content of the core subjects in philosophy and theology changing very little over the years. It would also appear that, with respect to the major seminaries in the underdeveloped countries, the chief function of the Seminaries Congregation is that of an accrediting and disciplinary agency, helping to ensure that these institutions adhere to the approved norms; and the essential, basic content of the major seminaries' curricula might be described as being in the nature of a prescribed constant.

In countries where the cultural level is already fairly high, the basis for a further improvement in the teaching standards of the major seminaries would appear to involve an improvement in the caliber of the personnel serving on their faculties and in their instructional methods, etc. It is along the latter lines that the Seminaries Congregation does not appear to be very active. A part of the reason for this is that throughout the world there are more than 1,000 Roman Catholic seminaries and scholasticates at the major seminary level, and the selection and administrative supervision of their faculty personnel is perforce left in the hands of the diocesan bishops and the superiors of the religious communities concerned.

None of the seminaries under the administrative jurisdiction of any of the Congregations of the Roman Catholic Church are accorded any latitude with respect to the development of theological doctrine or in matters relating to the definition of the Faith. This function is reserved exclusively to the Supreme Sacred Congregation of the Holy Office of which the Pope is always the Prefect. This point was made explicitly clear by Pope Pius XII in his encyclical *Humani generis* dated August 12, 1950:

> . . . It is true, of course, that the Popes generally allow freedom to theologians in matters which are disputed between scholars of repute; but history shows that many things which had formerly been left free for discussion can no longer be treated as open to discussion. . . . Theology, even positive theology, cannot be likened to a mere historical science. For God has given his Church . . . the living authority, also to illustrate and develop those truths which are contained only obscurely and, as it were, implicitly in the deposit of the faith. And the divine Redeemer did not entrust this deposit, for authentic interpretation, either to the individual believer or to the theologians themselves, but only to the authority of the Church. . . . Teachers of ecclesiastical institutes should know that they cannot, with a safe conscience, exercise the office of teaching that has been entrusted to them unless they accept religiously the rules We have set up, and observe them exactly in the teaching of their subjects. . . .

Six years later, Pope Pius XII reiterated this point even more explicitly in his apostolic constitution, *Sedes sapientiae,* dated May 31, 1956, as follows:

> Since the deposit of Revelation has been entrusted to the Church alone for its authentic interpretation, this deposit of faith must be expounded not by merely human reason and private judgment, but in complete fidelity to the meaning accepted by the Church and in accordance with the mind of the Church. The professors of philosophy and theology, therefore, must be fully aware that they do not carry on their work in their own right and person, but exclusively in the name and authority of the Supreme Magisterium, and that they perform this ministry under the watchful eye and guidance of this same Magisterium. . . . With the exception of open questions in which there is still a legitimate freedom of opinion, they are to remember that they have been given their teaching positions, not to impart their private opinions to their students, but rather to communicate to them the approved teachings of the Church.

Outside the realm of matters of faith and morals which have been defined or prescribed by the Vatican, or which are recognized as the common teaching of the Church, the theologians of the Roman Catholic Church are said occasionally to differ quite vigorously among themselves. Thus Roman Catholic doctrine might be described as a statement of faith whose further elaboration and development must be within the limits prescribed by Rome. The Supreme Sacred Congregation of the Holy Office is entrusted with the task of seeing that these limits are not exceeded.

The basis of the Roman Catholic system of theology and metaphysics is the system evolved by Thomas Aquinas. Early in his pontificate, Pope Leo XIII issued an encyclical (*Aeterni Patri,* dated August 4, 1879) in which he stated that from henceforth the philosophy and theology courses in seminaries should be based primarily on the teachings of "The Angelic Doctor," and subsequent Popes have repeated this directive.

Pope Pius XII continued to emphasize the primacy of the Thomist system as the foundation of Roman Catholic theological doctrine. But in a discourse which he delivered on October 17, 1953, to the professors and students of the Gregorian University in Rome he was also careful to point out that "not even the holiest or most eminent Doctor has ever in the past been appealed to by the Church as the primary source of the truth, nor does she do so now. The Church regards Thomas and Augustine as great Doctors and bestows upon them the highest tributes of praise, but it is only to the divinely inspired authors of the Sacred Scriptures that she attributes inerrancy. The Church, which by God's command is the interpreter and guardian of the Sacred Scriptures and the repository of living sacred tradition, is the door through which one reaches salvation; and under the protection and guidance of the Holy Spirit, she is for herself the source of the truth."

From the doctrinal point of view the Supreme Sacred Congregation of the Holy Office might be described as the capstone in the administrative arch of the Church's structure. The Pope always presides over this Congregation and in some respects it interprets the Church's approved doctrine much as the constitution of the United States is interpreted by the United States Supreme Court. Like the Court, its decisions are made by a small number of elderly men. These are assisted by a staff of theologians and canonists. Some of the latter are usually Dominicans, in accordance with a tradition which has been maintained since the days when the members of the Order of Preachers were the leaders in promoting the Inquisition.

Unlike the Supreme Court, the Holy Office seeks to regulate not only the actions of men but also their beliefs. It is in the latter, intangible realm where additional difficulties arise, and the tendency would appear to be to modify the formulation of accepted doctrine as little as possible. Nevertheless, by means of this ability to regulate to some extent the religious beliefs of hundreds of millions of Roman Catholics throughout the world, the Vatican is in a position to decentralize in some degree the Church's administrative and fiscal controls without impairing the sovereignty of the Pope within the organization and the Church's essential unity of action as a whole.

The crux of the problem confronting the Supreme Sacred Congregation of the

Holy Office is the degree to which it is successful in relating approved doctrine to changing conditions as they evolve. This is implicit in the statement made by Pope Leo XIII in his encyclical *Fin dal principio* dated December 8, 1902: "If, then, it is reasonable and just, that, within lawful limits, the clergy should accommodate themselves to the needs of the present age, it is similarly just and necessary, that, far from yielding to the dangerous current of the time, they should resist it with vigor."

Throughout the pontificate of Leo XIII there was an increasing trend among Roman Catholic theologians to favor "modernism." The latter was a movement to adapt Roman Catholic doctrine in the light of intellectual, social and moral trends, at times without what was considered by some experts to be sufficient regard for the evidence. A small minority of able European scholars (Renan, Schell, Loisy, von Hügel, Tyrrell, etc.) attempted to apply current methods of historical criticism to the study of the Bible and the history of the Roman Catholic Church.

Leo XIII opposed this development, recognizing the difficulty which would confront seminary professors if they were to apply rigorous standards of objective truth in their teachings concerning the history of the Roman Catholic Church. In his encyclical *Depuis le jour* (September 8, 1899), the Pope commented as follows:

The history of the Church is like a mirror which reflects the life of the Church through the ages . . . they who study it must never lose sight of the fact that it contains a body of dogmatic facts which none may call in question. That ruling, supernatural idea which presides over the destines of the Church is at the same time the torch whose light illumines her history. Still, inasmuch as the Church . . . is composed of a divine and a human element, this latter must be expounded by teachers and studied by disciples with great probity. "God has no need of our lies," we are told in the Book of Job (Job XIII: 77). The Church historian will be all the better equipped to bring out her divine origin, superior as this is to all conceptions of a merely terrestrial and natural order, the more loyal he is in naught extenuating of the trials which the faults of her children, and at times even of her ministers, have brought upon the Spouse of Christ during the course of centuries.

The next Pope, St. Pius X (1903–14) prosecuted "modernism" with vigor. In an allocution he delivered on December 12, 1904, to the bishops assembled in Rome for the 50th anniversary of the proclamation of the Dogma of the Immaculate Conception, he stated: "As you yourselves know, an air of independence which is fatal for souls is widely diffused in the world, and has found its way even within the sanctuary; it shows itself not only in relation to authority but also in regard to doctrine. Because of it, some of our young clerics, animated by that spirit of unbridled criticism which holds sway at the present day, have come to lose all respect for the learning which comes from our great teachers, the Fathers and Doctors of the Church, the interpreters of revealed doctrine. If ever you have in your seminary one of these new-style *savants,* get rid of him without delay; on no account impose hands upon him. You will always regret having ordained even one such person: never will you regret having excluded him."

Two months later (February 23, 1905) in an allocution given to the French Seminary in Rome, Pope Pius X stated: "If you are to be genuinely the salt of the earth, you must not seek to press learning beyond that which the Church asks. . . . Do you believe that God wishes you to know more than the Fathers and Doctors of the Church, the pillars of this mystical temple, or more than the saints who were favoured with special illumination and raised up by God's design to teach the truths bequeathed to us by Jesus Christ? Take care that you are not led astray by the demon of learning, I mean, of course, false learning; you might easily have cause to regret it, and imperceptibly you might be led to complete disaster."

In his decree *Lamentabili* (July 3, 1907) and its related encyclical *Pascendi dominici gregis* (September 8, 1907), Pius X ordered the bishops to "purge their clergy of modernistic infection" and specified that the administrators of Roman Catholic universities and seminaries must be careful to eliminate "modernist" texts from use in their institutions.

Three years later, in his *motu proprio, Sacrorum antistitum,* dated September 1, 1910, Pope Pius X prescribed a lengthy antimodernist oath and ordered every Roman Catholic priest from henceforth to swear to it. In the same *motu proprio* the Pope stated: ". . . Whenever there is question of choosing directors and professors for seminaries and Catholic universities, anybody who in any way is found to be imbued with modernism is to be excluded without compunction from these offices and those who already occupy them are to be removed. . . . In all this question of studies, Venerable Brothers, you cannot be too watchful or too constant, but most of all in the choice of professors, for as a rule the students are modeled after the pattern of their masters. . . . Equal diligence and severity are to be used in examining and selecting candidates for Holy Orders. Far, far from the clergy be the love of novelty! . . ." Extensive measures were undertaken so that the Church would be in a position to ascertain the identity of priests subscribing to "modernist" tendencies.

Early in his pontificate (i.e., in 1922) Pope Pius XI issued an encyclical *Ubi arcano* in which he condemned the attitude of those Roman Catholics who, while appearing to accept the teachings of the Church in social and juridical matters "act exactly as if the doctrine and precepts promulgated on so many occasions by the sovereign pontiffs, notably Leo XIII, Pius X and Benedict XV, had become completely obsolete, or had lost their original force. This fact reveals some sort of moral, juridical and social modernism. We condemn it as vigorously as we do dogmatic modernism."

A few months after he became Pope, Pius XII commented on the above statement of his predecessor. In a discourse he gave on June 16, 1939, to a group of priests, principally from South America, who were attending a course in the Pontifical Latin American College in Rome, he described this type of modernism as "a form of Relativism which . . . no longer recognizes the unchangeable laws of justice and right as the supreme norm of true and false, of good and bad, but claims to establish, as a principle, the everchanging utility of individuals or classes or State or race. This modernism, as becomes preachers of the Gospel, you must courageously oppose with the perfect and absolute truths which have their origin in God. . . ."

Seven years later (on September 17, 1946) Pope Pius XII addressed the Jesuit Fathers who were attending their Society's 29th General Congregation in Rome. He pointed out his belief that "there has been too much talk, with too little investigation of a 'new theology,' which, with everything constantly evolving, must also evolve and be always progressing and never reach finality. If such an opinion were to be accepted, what would become of the unchanging dogmas of the Catholic Church, and of the unity and stability of the faith? . . . Whatever sounds completely new in Catholic theology ought to be examined with vigilance and caution, and what is certain and sure must be distinguished from what is put forward as conjecture."

In his apostolic exhortation, *Menti nostræ,* dated September 23, 1950, Pope Pius XII stated: "In the intellectual training of young seminarians . . . the greatest importance must be given to philosophical and theological teaching according to the method of the Angelic Doctor brought up to date and adapted to meet modern errors."

The task of how best to (1) "bring up to date" and "adapt to meet modern errors" the theological system elaborated in detail by St. Thomas Aquinas in the 13th century, and (2) at the same time formulate definitive directives dealing successfully with changing social relationships and moral concepts as they evolve in the 20th century—this perhaps is the central philosophical problem confronting the Roman Catholic Church today.

All of the recent Popes have taken a considerable interest in furthering the welfare of the major seminaries. During his long pontificate (1878–1903), Pope Leo XIII interested himself particularly in the intellectual activities of the Roman Catholic Church. The excerpts, quoted above, from his many encyclicals indicate the concern which he had for the proper functioning of the seminaries.

His successor, Pius X (1903–14) issued an encyclical entitled *E Supremi* dated October 4, 1903, upon the occasion of his becoming Pope. In this letter, Pius X stressed the importance of the major seminaries in the life of the Church as follows: "Now that We are about to address you for the first time. . . . Let this be the first of Our cares, to form Christ in those who are destined for the duty of forming Christ in others. . . . Wherefore the chief part of your cares must be the right ordering and ruling of the sacred Seminaries. . . . Let each one of you make the Seminary the delight of his heart, omitting nothing whatsoever that the Council of Trent has prudently appointed for its profit. . . ."

During his reign, Pius X instituted a number of reforms and suppressed approximately 200 seminaries in Italy in order to merge them with others for the sake of concentrating the training of the clergy in that country in a smaller number of institutions of higher quality. When he commenced this program, it is estimated there were nearly 300 seminaries in Italy.

At the beginning of his reign, Pope Pius XI (1922–39) issued an apostolic letter *Officiorum omnium* dated August 1, 1922, in which he expressed his concern over the short supply of priests in several countries immediately after World War I. In it he commented: "Of all the sacred duties which the supreme pontificate includes, there is none more important or of more far-reaching significance than the responsibility of ensuring that the Church has a sufficient number of worthy ministers to enable her to discharge her divine mission."

Pope Pius XI established a number of regional seminaries in Italy. Because some bishops enjoyed and exercised vested rights in these regional institutions, Pius XI withdrew these seminaries from the jurisdiction of the bishops in whose dioceses they were located and placed them instead under the direct authority of the Seminaries Congregation.

On December 20, 1935, Pope Pius XI issued a lengthy encyclical entitled *Ad Catholici sacerdotii* on the subject of the Catholic priesthood. While its scope was not limited solely to the training for the priesthood, nevertheless the following portion of this encyclical clearly illustrates the importance attached by him to the work of the seminaries, and more particularly to the need for consolidating them into regional seminaries serving large areas:

. . . The seminary is and should be the apple of your eye, Venerable Brethren . . . ; it is and should be the chief object of your solicitude. . . . Give the best of your clergy to your seminaries; do not fear to take them from other positions. These positions may seem of greater moment, but in reality their importance is not to be compared with that of the seminaries, which is capital and indispensable. . . . There are some regions where the dioceses are small, or students unhappily few, or where there is a shortage of means and suitable men. Hence it is impossible for every diocese to have its own seminary. . . . Where this happens, it is most proper that the bishops of the district should help one another in brotherly charity, should concentrate and unite their forces in a common seminary, fully worthy of its high purpose. The great advantages of such concentration amply repay the sacrifices entailed in obtaining it. It is indeed a sacrifice, grievous to the fatherly heart of a bishop to see his clerics, even for a time, taken away from their shepherd. . . . But these sacrifices will all be repaid with interest when these clerics return as priests. . . . We have Ourselves, as is well known, erected or improved or enlarged such regional seminaries, not without heavy expense and trouble; and We will continue in the future to apply Ourselves with all zeal to this work; for We hold it to be most conducive to the good of the Church. . . .

In the same encyclical Pius XI warned that in the recruitment of candidates for the priesthood the quality of the seminarians was more important than their mere number. In support of this thesis, he cited St. Thomas Aquinas' "pertinent remark in words taken almost verbatim from the fourth Lateran Council: 'If it should ever become impossible to preserve the present number of priests, it is better to have a few good ones than a multitude of bad ones.' . . . We (have) said that beyond any doubt one priest who was thoroughly trained for his sacred office was worth more than a great number if they had received little or no priestly formation. . . ."

C. The Formation of Priests

In an allocution delivered on September 24, 1903, on the occasion of the 50th anniversary of the French seminary in Rome, Pope Pius X commented as follows on the type of seminary training candidates for the priesthood should receive: ". . . clerics should be trained by serving a long apprenticeship in study and religious training in the seminary, which may be compared to a workshop where weapons for battle are forged."

The modern seminary on the Tridentine model places a primary emphasis on the spiritual development of priests. According to the *Maryknoll Spiritual Directory,* the most important purpose of a major seminary is "the sanctification of the sacerdotal candidates. All other ends must be subordinate to this one. . . . Secondary purposes are the mental and physical preparation of the priestly aspirants for their divine vocation." Thus the training of a priest is considered to be primarily a process of forming his character and spiritual powers, and only secondarily the education of his intellect. This is the origin of the phrase, "the formation of priests."

This priority in emphasis was stressed by the English Cardinal, Francis Bourne (1861-1935), when he wrote:

A seminary is not primarily a place of study. When the holy Council of Trent passed its famous decree for seminaries, the Fathers of the Council were not thinking principally of the need of study for the clergy, they were concerned chiefly about their sanctification. . . . The great founders (of seminaries)—namely, Jean Jacques Olier and St. Vincent de Paul—had no thought of setting up new houses of study. . . . A seminary is a place the only essential object of which is to train (priests) to a truly spiritual and supernatural life. . . . There may be other ends and aims, but they must be wholly subsidiary to these. . . . It is true that since the 16th century seminaries have become more and more places of study. . . . But this important change is in no way incompatible with the primary and essential object of the seminary, provided it be not allowed to obliterate or even to obscure it. There is a real danger that it may be allowed to do so.

With respect to the intellectual aspects of seminary training, the Venerable Olier, founder of the Sulpician Society, recommended (according to Monval) to his disciples that they inculcate in seminarians: "Not a science which is glittering and showy but rather a knowledge which is more solid than brilliant, more profound than vast, more practical than theoretical."

The Seminaries Congregation has established the minimum requirements to be met when a major seminary is to be canonically erected, i.e., officially accredited by the Church. According to canon law, the faculty of a seminary is to consist of a rector and an unspecified number of professors. In addition, there is to be an "economus," distinct from the rector, who is to be in charge of the business affairs of the institution; and, finally, at least two ordinary confessors and a spiritual director. It is also prescribed that two boards shall be appointed for each seminary, one for discipline and the other for the administration of its business affairs. Each board is to consist of two priests, selected by the bishop. The professors of Sacred Scripture, Dogmatic Theology, Moral Theology and Church History are to be distinct, i.e., four different individuals. This implies that the minimum number of teachers serving on a seminary faculty is to be four professors, some of whom presumably may in some instances be serving in other capacities as well.

Canon law prescribes that the curricula of major seminaries shall cover a period of at least six years, two years spent in the study of philosophy and four years in the study of theology. This six-year minimum is required of all candidates for the priesthood although an exception can be made in the case of an older man entering seminary who has previously had graduate training in related subjects. (In exceptional cases widowers and men up to the age of 60 are admitted as students in the seminaries.) On the other hand, the six-year minimum curriculum is often exceeded. In Africa a number of major seminaries require their students to spend three years in the study of philosophy and six in the study of theology, resulting in their courses lasting a total of nine years. The White Fathers often require their students to spend "two by two" an additional probationary year engaged in field work at a mission station.

Instruction at the major seminaries usually is given for 10 or 11 months each year, with an annual vacation of one or two months for the students. The timing of the vacation depends upon the climate belt in which the seminary is located.

Table 115 indicates the number of hours which are spent in class each week by the student during the six years in which he is enrolled at a typical major seminary.

The study of philosophy, the subject which heads the list, includes logic, cosmology ("the study of the world"), psychology, criteriology ("the study of what we know and how we know it is true"), ontology ("the study of being, of essence

TABLE 115. Number of Class Hours per Week Spent in Major Seminary Courses

		Course					
		Philosophy		Theology			
Subject	Year:	1	2	1	2	3	4
Philosophy		8	8				
History of Philosophy			3				
Science		3	3				
Religion		2	2				
Indigenous Language		3	3				
Foreign Language		2	2				
Apologetics and Dogmatic Theology				5	5	5	5
Moral Theology				5	5	5	5
Sacred Scripture				3	3	3	3
History of the Church				2	2	2	2
Canon Law				3	2	2	2
Liturgy				1	1	1	1
Sacred Eloquence (Homiletics)					1	1	1
Pastoral Theology							2
Ascetic Theology							1
Chant		1	1	1	1	1	1
Total Number of Class Hours per Week		19	22	20	20	20	23

and existence"), and theodicy ("the study of God by the light of reason alone, unaided by faith"). These are not necessarily the only courses taught in the philosophy curriculum. The latter may in some instances include a few literature, history and natural science courses. It is stated that the Seminaries Congregation favors the introduction of such courses in the major seminaries so that their curricula may be more on a par with comparable colleges.

In some instances, there is considerable variation in the length of time devoted to one or another of the courses listed in Table 115. The reason is that canon law prescribes only the general principles on which seminaries' curricula are to be based and leaves wide discretion to the bishops and seminary rectors as to the number of hours to be spent on each subject. Father Theodore Heck reports that a survey made in 1933-34 in the United States disclosed that the highest number of courses taught in any one seminary was 26, and the lowest, 13. "The wide range in textbooks reveals the extensive nature of such a course (in philosophy). Some professors employed different authors for each major division; others use a standard manual. . . . Seminary professors are not in accord in the order of treating the seven major fields of philosophy. . . ." If such a variation exists among the major seminaries in the United States, it would seem likely that a similar or greater variation exists among those in Africa, Asia and Latin America.

A distinguishing feature of Roman Catholic seminaries is the fact that their courses in scholastic philosophy as well as sacred scripture, dogmatic and moral theology, and in canon and Roman law, are taught in the Latin language. The remaining courses may be conducted in the vernacular. Latin serves not only as the language of Roman Catholic liturgy in the Latin rite but also as a lingua franca of the Church. In his apostolic letter, *Officiorum omnium* (August 1, 1922) addressed to the Cardinal Prefect of the Seminaries Congregation, Pope Pius XI stressed the importance of Latin being taught as a universal administrative language of the Church and as an important element in contributing to the unity of its diverse organizations throughout the world.

The same point was stressed again in a letter entitled *The Sacred Congregation* dated May 26, 1928, which was sent to the American bishops by the Apostolic Delegate to the United States. Acting in the name and under the authority of the Sacred Congregation of Seminaries and Universities, the Delegate wrote: ". . . In the literary courses of the (minor) Seminary the Latin language (must) be regarded as the most important element and . . . it (must) have precedence over every other subject. Moreover the course in Latin must not be purely theoretical. By oral and written exercises, by competitions and like practical means the aim of such (a) course should be . . . that both a knowledge of and a proficiency in the language is gained. Students must not be admitted to the study of philosophy and theology who do not possess a sufficient mastery of the Latin language. . . ."

During the pontificate of Pius XI, the Seminaries Congregation issued a letter to the Italian bishops dated May 5, 1934, entitled *E Certamente noto* relating to the importance of instructing seminarians concerning Protestantism. The following passage appears in that letter:

Considering that the most effective means for making obstacles for the Protestants' propaganda and hindering their proselyting is to have the priests forewarn and instruct the faithful, this Sacred Congregation has decided to order that adequate teaching for this purpose be given in the Seminary. Let Your Excellency provide, therefore, if you have not already done so, that the pupils of this Seminary, in the Pastoral Theology course or by means of a special yearly cycle of conferences, learn the historical origin, the fundamental errors and the controversies of Protestantism, *in particular* the various forms which it presently takes and the subtle methods it uses to insinuate into people's minds and hearts the tried maxims of heresy, profiting by the vulnerable tenderness of age, the insufficiency of culture, the simplicity of mind and above all the sad economic conditions of many.

The academic examinations which seminary students are required to take are often in oral form. Occasionally, supervisors from other seminaries are invited to question the students, and in these instances, the interrogators report to their superiors concerning the progress being made by the students. The questions asked, whether in oral or written form, tend to be factual and call for answers along approved lines. The following are typical questions asked in examinations in major seminary courses:

Philosophy: Thesis to be defended:
                (a) "The power of God is infinite."
                (b) "God is immutable."

Church History: "What are Jansenism, Febronianism and Josephism? Give the history of each."

Canon Law: "What is a canonical election? An exemption? The function of a consultor?"

Dogmatic Theology: "List the acts of contrition involved in penance."

The spiritual director is one of the most important officials in a seminary and is principally responsible for the spiritual formation of priests. It is his duty to know the life and character of each student in order to be able to advise them concerning their vocation and to weed out those who are not spiritually qualified to make good priests. The director hears students' confessions and advises them in the practice of prayer, either by assigning to them a short devotional reading, or an exposition of a subject for meditation, or by indicating the most appropriate book the student should study. As Father Sackett points out, in order to guide the students properly, the director must know their past life, habitual faults and their efforts to correct them. In view of the delicacy of his work, a sensitive and perceptive priest is needed for this position. The Borromean tradition is to have only one spiritual director in a seminary, whereas the French tradition is to have several directors, thereby enabling the students to make a choice among them.

The spiritual formation of major seminary students is also developed by means of annual retreats lasting approximately five days or more. Those who attend these retreats conduct examinations of conscience and engage in readings on spiritual subjects, etc.

A feature of the daily seminary routine is the observance of silence on the part of the students, not only in the library, common rooms, etc., but elsewhere whenever this is appropriate. A Marist seminary professor, Father Thomas Dubay, S.M., comments: "The seminary rule of silence, therefore does not have as its purpose the creation of a mere vacuum. It aims at an emptiness of noise and a consequent fullness of God. . . . Where seminarians have private rooms they should never talk at one another's door without permission; nor should they ask for such a permission except when the business at hand cannot be transacted at any other time. . . . Somebody has well said of religious houses, 'Tell me how silence is kept, and I'll tell you how fervent the house is.' The implication is true."

Discipline is also an important element in seminary life. In his apostolic exhortation *Menti nostræ* dated September 23, 1950, Pope Pius XII declared: "At all costs the young students must acquire the spirit of obedience, so that they will become accustomed to submitting their wills sincerely to the will of God, of whom the directors of the seminary are to be regarded as interpreters. . . . Young students in seminaries should learn, from their first years there, to obey their superiors sincerely with the devotion of sons to fathers, so that later on they will accept the will of their bishops meekly. . . ."

On the subject of discipline the *Maryknoll Spiritual Directory* states:

The basic method used in ecclesiastical training houses to attain their purposes is the simple one of habit-forming practice : *we learn by doing*. Discipline, therefore, is imposed for only one reason: to enable the candidate to advance in acquiring, as an habitual possession, a degree of that personal sanctification without which one may not properly enter the priesthood. . . . This training is chiefly an intensive repetition of certain acts— inspired by supernatural motives—so that: (1) they are recognized by the individual as the correct acts in given circumstances . . . ; (2) they become easy to do when the circumstances arise in which they should be evoked; (3) they become almost automatic, second-nature or habitual, as a result of both conviction and practice. Virtue is a *habit* of performing that which is morally right. Hence, the Rule is not meant to deprive anyone of his freedom, or to be repressive; it is meant as a guide to right action. . . .

A number of Roman Catholic priests, including Father John Talbot Smith, have advocated that the major seminaries in America should pattern many of their routine daily activities along the lines pursued at the United States Military Academy at West Point, New York.

The daily life of a major seminarian is a crowded one with few free moments provided in his schedule. Table 116 lists the typical weekday activities of a major seminary student. Some seminaries might not place as much stress on recreation periods or manual labor. On Sundays and feast days, classes are suspended and more time is spent in chapel. In addition to those duties listed in Table 116 there are a number of self-help tasks of a housekeeping nature (cleaning, painting, etc.) for which the students are often held responsible.

The effort is made to have the priests serving on seminary faculties to be as close to their students as possible in order that the student will not feel he is leading an isolated life. Occasionally when seminarians are obliged to live outside the institution for any reason, the bishop is required by canon law to appoint a priest in the neighborhood who is responsible for their conduct. During summer vacations seminary students may reside with their families. In these instances the priest in charge of that parish will be called upon to give a general report concerning the student's conduct.

It has been said that among the many institutions of the Roman Catholic Church throughout the world, its major seminaries are more closely similar in organization and operation to each other than are any other Roman Catholic organizations. In addition to Micheletti's summary published in 1919, two operating manuals prepared by different religious communities illustrate this point and provide an insight into some of the aspects of the problems involved in seminary administration.

The first, the *Directoire des grand séminaires confiés aux prêtres de la mission,* was originally prepared by the Lazarists in France in 1895 (and reprinted in 1942). With the exception of the Jesuits, the Lazarists administer more major seminaries in Africa,

TABLE 116. TYPICAL WEEKDAY SCHEDULE OF A
MAJOR SEMINARY STUDENT

5:30	Rise
5:55	Morning Prayers, Meditation
6:25	Mass
7:10	Breakfast
7:30	Morning Duties
7:50	Tidy Rooms, Study
9:10	Class or Study
10:00	Recreation
10:10	Class or Study
11:00	Recreation
11:10	Class or Study
12:00	Remission
12:20	Part. Examen, Hymn—Angelus
12:30	Dinner
1:10	Manual Labor
2:10	Recreation
3:10	End of Recreation
3:30	Class or Study
4:20	Recreation
4:25	Class or Study
5:15	Rosary
5:30	Spiritual Reading
6:00	Supper, Free Time
7:15	Study
9:00	Night Prayers
10:00	Lights Out

Asia and Latin America than any other religious community. The *Directoire* is concerned primarily with outlining (1) the duties of the administrative officials and faculty of a major seminary, and (2) the rules of conduct to be followed by the students. The observations and suggestions listed in the *Directoire* cover many points, including the following:

1. *Duties of Seminary Officials and Faculty Members:* The prayers to be recited by them throughout the day and the number and types of retreats they should attend throughout the year; the best methods of rendering advice to seminarians; the importance of not permitting students to talk during mealtimes except on rare occasions; the advisability of inspecting students' rooms to insure that all superfluous or luxurious furnishings are avoided; the types of reports to be sent in a spirit of "perfect submission" by the seminary officials to the superior general of the congregation, the local superior and to the diocesan authorities; the need to avoid (a) expressing complaints and criticisms, or (b) forming groups of contrary schools of thought within the seminary administration; the advisability for young professors not to read a large number of authors in the field in which they are giving courses: since this is said ordinarily to lead "only to a considerable waste of time and to a burdening of one's memory with a multitude of vague and incoherent ideas,

let them choose with the aid of the Superior and his most experienced associates four or five of the best authors who have investigated and clarified these questions. . . ."

2. *Conduct of Students:* Suggested precautions against holding discussions within the seminary which are contrary to the faith; bringing in or keeping prohibited books (or food or beverages) in their rooms; maintaining unauthorized correspondence with persons outside of the seminary; indulging in excesses of any sort; visiting the room of another student or leaving the seminary grounds without permission.

The second operating manual for seminary administrators was published in Dallas, Texas, in 1949 under the title of *Directorium seminariorum (in Sinis).* The preparation of this guide was commenced in 1944 by a number of missionary priests of the Scheut Fathers who were then stationed in China, but who were subsequently obliged to leave that country with the advent of the Communist Government. In the compiling of this book, the authors consulted members of other religious communities then stationed in China (e.g., the Lazarists, Divine Word Fathers, Jesuits, Franciscans, etc.). The purpose of the *Directorium* is to advise any bishop, superior of a religious institute, or priest concerning (1) the steps which are required in order to establish a seminary, and (2) the methods of operating a seminary successfully. The following are a few points, selected at random, which are discussed in this guide:

1. *Concerning the Construction of a Seminary:* The location of a suitable site; protection against floods; proper types of building materials; approved architectural styles and ornamentation; the most favorable location of rooms within the seminary building; a suggested range of interior temperatures (when artificial heating is used); the proper use of fire extinguishers; the recommended range in the height of students' desks and benches; drawings of model closets and bureau drawers; desirable floor plans for laboratories, libraries, chapels, kitchens and lavatories; the various types of disinfectants which are most suitable for sewage treatment, etc.

2. *Concerning the Operation of a Seminary:* Sample questionnaire to be filled out relating to each entering student, detailing his family background and means; a list of approved vestments, and diagrams illustrating the most suitable order in which to hang them in a closet; the proper feeding of minor and major seminarians (suggested daily minimum caloric intake requirements: 1408 calories for boys weighing 100 pounds and 1858 calories for men weighing 160 pounds); instructions concerning the personal hygiene of minor seminarians; the number of times the rosary should be said each day or week; ways and means of educating seminarians to achieve perfect chastity; types of recreation permitted —the relative merits of football, volleyball and basketball as sports for seminarians; the proper number of hours of sleep for students (a minimum of seven and a maximum of nine); types of vaccinations required; a sample letter which a bishop may use in admonishing a priest concerning the conduct of a seminarian while on vacation in his parish; the need for a seminarian to be withdrawn from the world, and the uses of silence; the

frequency with which students should take confession and attend Mass; sample testimonial letters concerning candidates for Holy Orders.

In the Belgian Congo and Ruanda Urundi, a total of 239 major seminary students replied in a recent year to a series of questions asked of them concerning their reactions to seminary life. As reported in 1957 by Father Masson, one of the questions was: "What has caused you the most difficulty in seminary?" The students replied as follows:

	Number
Keeping up scholastically	67
Common student life	47
Self-denial, discipline, obedience	40
Perfect chastity	37
Health deficiencies	19
Separation from family	18
Miscellaneous	11
	239

No educational institution of any sort is able to provide its students with all of the skills they will require in later life. This fact is equally true in the case of the major seminaries and was commented on at the Lima Methods Conference held by the Maryknoll Fathers in Lima, Peru, in 1954. On that occasion Father James E. Walsh, M.M., commented: "We cannot hope to equip a man for everything that's going to confront him in life. We cannot expect that every man who comes out of Maryknoll is going to be able to deal with every problem that arises in a parish. One of the important things that a seminary has to do is to open up a man's mind and keep it open. When he is confronted with a problem in the field, he should not say to himself 'I should have the answer to that already—it should have been given to me—but I have not got it.' He should be so equipped that he knows where to turn quickly and confidently and find his answers." To this Father John J. Considine, M.M., added: "That is the definition of an educated man—the man who knows where to find things."

In any educational institution the students "find things" (i.e., written facts) principally in its library. The libraries of the major seminaries have been the object of the Vatican's concern for many years. During the pontificate of Pope Leo XIII, his Secretariate of State issued a lengthy circular letter entitled *Le Cure delle religiose* (September 30, 1902) addressed to the bishops in Italy. This letter points out the need for carefully preserving the books and manuscripts in Roman Catholic libraries, for setting up an adequate catalogue system (listing the details to be included on the catalogue cards to be used) and for establishing suitable rules concerning the use of library books by students and the general public (including a suggested set of 19 model regulations to be adopted by the libraries).

The next Pope, St. Pius X, was particularly concerned with "modernism," as previously noted, and issued a number of explicit directives to ensure that no modernist literature should be permitted in seminary libraries. In his encyclical letter *Pieni l'animo* dated July 28, 1906, Pius X declared that "frequentation of the universities is not to be permitted to young clerics except for very grave reasons and with the greatest precautions on the part of the bishops. Seminarians must not be allowed to take part in secular polemics, and therefore We forbid them the reading of newspapers and periodicals, with the exception in a particular case of some periodicals of solid principle which the bishop may think useful for the student."

This prohibition was renewed in the *motu proprio, Sacrorum antistitum,* issued by Pius X on September 1, 1910, in which the reading of most periodicals was prohibited on the grounds that such reading tends to take the time of the seminarians away from their studies. During this Pope's reign the Sacred Congregation of the Consistory issued a circular letter, *Con circolare,* dated October 17, 1913, to the ordinaries (bishops) in Italy listing specific scholarly works which should be eliminated from seminary libraries as being contrary to approved Roman Catholic doctrine.

In subsequent years these restrictions have been relaxed somewhat but not to the point of permitting seminary students to read books or periodicals which might be an obstacle or impediment to their studies or which might prove to be a danger to their faith or morals. The Consistorial Congregation (according to Father Bolduc in a dissertation published in 1942), has classified periodicals into two groups: (1) those dealing with political or controversial matters, either scientific or theological, and (2) those which contain documents issued by the Vatican or bishops, or which contain only those articles which are useful in propagating Roman Catholic doctrine along approved lines. The first category must be treated with great circumspection. Leading theologians in the Church, such as Vermeersch and others, have considered the problem of which Roman Catholic periodicals might be included in the second category and would therefore be eligible for seminary libraries.

The present Pope, Pius XII, has pointed to the need for acquainting seminary students with world developments. In his encyclical *Menti nostræ* dated September 23, 1950, he stated: "Let directors have no fear in keeping them in contact with the events of the day. . . . We urge that the literary and scientific education of future priests be at least not inferior to that of laymen who take similar courses."

Nothing is said in *Menti nostræ* concerning specific books and periodicals to be admitted in seminary libraries. However, it is interesting to note that in the same encyclical Pius XII makes the following recommendation concerning the libraries in Roman Catholic *university* libraries which can be used by priests after they have been ordained: "These libraries must not be neglected receptacles for books but living structures with a room for reference and reading. Above all, however, let them be up to date and enriched with works of every kind, especially those relating to the religious and social questions of our times, so that teachers, parish priests, and particularly young priests may find there the doctrine necessary for diffusing the truth of the Gospel and for fighting error."

Thus, by inference, a distinction is made between the function of a university library and the more limited scope of a seminary library. To the extent that this distinction has been institutionalized it would appear to have served to limit the intellectual scope of the training afforded in the seminary.

In his conferences with seminarians, Cardinal Mercier of Belgium customarily stressed that "a soul called to the priesthood seeks retirement from the world." Yet the practice of imposing virtually a semimonastic regime upon Roman Catholic major seminarians, including those destined for the secular priesthood during their period of training, reportedly tends to disorient some of the students in Africa, Asia and Latin America unduly from the practical day-to-day living problems of their own peoples. Father Schmidlin commented on this point as follows: "Whether this difficulty can be solved by removing completely from their environment unspoiled youths of the most tender years, enclosing them hermetically in seminaries for 'long, long years' (as the Propaganda prescribes), and then sending them back to the milieu from which they have grown entirely estranged and which is perhaps rendered thereby more perilous, we may leave the future to decide."

This problem was recognized by Pope Pius XII in *Menti nostræ* in which he stated: "If young men—especially those who have entered the seminary at a tender age—are educated in an environment too isolated from the world, they may, on leaving the seminary, find serious difficulty in their relations with either the ordinary people or the educated laity, and it may happen that they either adopt a misguided and false attitude toward the faithful or that they consider their training in an unfavorable light. For this reason, it is necessary that the students come in closer contact, gradually and prudently, with the judgments and tastes of the people in order that when they receive Holy Orders and begin their ministry they will not feel themselves disorientated—a thing that would not only be harmful to their souls but also injure the efficacy of their work."

In line with this precept, some major seminaries have been adding courses in sociology, economics, etc., in recent years. In India, the Roman Catholic bishops have taken steps to relate the courses in the major seminaries to Indian culture. Similarly, in 1950 the Pontifical Latin American College in Rome instituted courses in social studies.

In addition Pope Pius XII advocated in *Menti nostræ* that after they had graduated from the seminary, young priests should be given field work instruction in groups. The Pope wrote:

The passage from the sheltered and tranquil life of the seminary to the active ministry may be dangerous for the priest who enters the open field of the apostolate if he has not been prudently prepared for the new life. You should realize that the many hopes placed in young priests may fail if they are not gradually introduced to the work, wisely watched, and paternally guided in the first steps of their ministry. We approve, therefore, the gathering of young priests when possible for some years in special institutions where, under the guidance of experienced superiors, they can develop their piety and perfect themselves in sacred studies and be put on the path toward that form of the ministry more closely corresponding to their temperaments and aptitudes. For this reason We would like to see institutions of this nature established in every diocese or, according to circumstances, for a number of dioceses together. In Our own Beloved City, We Ourselves did this when, on the 50th anniversary of Our priesthood, We erected the St. Eugene Institute for young priests.

D. THE SCHOLASTICATES

The scholasticates are the major seminaries conducted by the religious communities for the purpose of training aspirants for membership in those Orders, institutes, etc. They are an outgrowth of the monastic schools described earlier in this chapter. As such, they were not as directly affected by the decree of the Council of Trent, nor does it appear that in the past they have usually received as close supervision from the Vatican. The diocesan bishops are not ordinarily concerned with their management inasmuch as this is within the purview of the superior of the religious community concerned.

Canon law sections 587–589 provide that in nonmissionary areas the scholasticates come under the supervision of the Sacred Congregation of the Religious rather than under the Seminaries Congregation. However, since the curricula of the major seminaries and the scholasticates are essentially the same, the Congregation of the Religious tends to be guided in educational matters by those directives of the Seminaries Congregation which relate to the training of candidates for the priesthood. This is reflected in the *Enchiridions* (collections of abstracts of important documents relating to the administrative procedures of a Sacred Congregation) which are published by the Seminaries and the Religious Congregations.

The courses of study offered by the scholasticates are usually not open to students aspiring to become members of the secular clergy. The scholasticates receive students who have graduated from novitiates and juniorates, which are preparatory institutions comparable to the minor seminaries.

Scholasticates are called by various names. For example, in the Order of Preachers (Dominicans) they are called houses of studies ("domus studentatus"), whereas in the Franciscan (O.F.M.) Order they are known as houses of formation for the regular clergy ("domus formationis regularis ordinis"), or as a "studium philosophicum," etc.

A number of religious communities (notably the Jesuits, Dominicans, Salesians, Capuchins, Divine Word Fathers and the Franciscans) utilize scholasticates overseas for the training of indigenous students for the priesthood and membership in their own congregations and institutes. The number of students enrolled in the typical scholasticate in Africa, Asia and Latin America is usually smaller than the enrollment in a typical major seminary in those same areas.

In a few instances (for example, in the Philippines and in Japan) the Jesuits operate institutions called "colleges" which in effect are comparatively large scholasticates having either faculties of philosophy or theology, but not both. Often such a college is located in close proximity to another college having the complementary faculty, thereby enabling the student completing the courses at the two institutions to fulfill the academic requirements for admission to the priesthood. More frequently these institutions are called by the various religious communities their "philosophates" or "theologates," and these are not uncommon throughout Africa, Asia and Latin America.

The published data and statistics relating to the scholasticates, particularly those in areas not under the authority of the Propaganda, are comparatively meagre. One reason for this is that of all the Sacred Congregations, the Propaganda publishes the most information concerning its current activities: the Propaganda relies on supplementary contributions from the laity for a very large proportion of its income, whereas the Seminaries Congregation and the Congregation of the Religious do not.

It appears that the quality of the instruction in the scholasticates varies among the religious communities and sometimes from province to province within one congregation, depending upon the caliber and availability of the priests chosen to serve on their faculties. The life of the students in the scholasticates, as in the case of the major seminaries, is continuously occupied, under constant supervision, and relatively little free time is afforded them.

Some of the variations which exist among the scholasticates are the product of the special characteristics of a religious community. For example, in some congregations a student pursues all of his studies in philosophy and theology at only one scholasticate. On the other hand, in the case of the Franciscans it is unusual for a student to pursue his entire course of studies at only one monastery; and the Swiss Capuchins deliberately rotate their students every one or two years among their houses of study.

In April 1951 (shortly after the congress of representatives of religious communities which was held in Rome in November and December 1950) the Franciscans (O.F.M.) issued a small hand book (*Normæ de seraphica . . .*) for the use of the administrators of their scholasticates. The book is concerned with methods of promoting the spiritual formation of candidates for membership in the Order of Friars Minor, with especial emphasis on those aspects of the Franciscan life and viewpoint which are to be taught to these scholastics. Thus, in addition to their core courses during their seven-year period of study at the major seminary level, Franciscans are to be instructed among other things concerning:

Philosophy

1st year The life of St. Francis of Assisi, his personal characteristics and accomplishments; the founding and development of the Order of St. Francis.

2nd year Characteristics of Franciscans: evangelical life, love of God, humility, poverty, prayer, etc.

3rd year Franciscan practices: reception into the Order, types of daily work, the functions of superiors, visitations, the hearing of confessions, etc.

Theology

1st year The sacerdotal life and acts of Christ.

2nd year The sacerdotal life and acts of Franciscans.

3rd year The life of famous Franciscans and the Franciscan mission in the educational field.

4th year The Franciscan sacerdotal life, the grades of ordination and the celebration of the liturgy.

The distinguishing characteristics of Jesuit scholasticates are the length of their training, the standardization of their curricula, and the excellence of their faculties.

According to Father William J. McGucken, S.J., it was never the original intention of Ignatius Loyola that the Society of Jesus should be engaged in educational work. "He had not visualized a vast organization, but rather a small group of men, gifted, trained university men bound by no petty parochial cares, much less by the daily routine of the classroom. . . ." However, when large numbers of men sought to be admitted to the new Society, they were at first dispatched in small groups to the universities in Paris and elsewhere for training. When this proved to be unsatisfactory, it was then that the Jesuits decided to enter the educational field themselves and "that neither pains nor expense should be spared in the formation of the Jesuit master."

The basis of the Jesuit educational effort was, and continues to be, the "ratio studiorum," a formal, graded program of studies based upon the ancient classics. "Rigidity and unity characterized the ratio . . . and thereby efficiency was gained." The education of a Jesuit usually commences at the age of 18 and is not completed until the age of 33 or so. Table 117 lists the academic training program involved.

During the novitiate, in which the course of study is at the minor seminary level, the novice is perfectly free to withdraw from the Society at any time if he finds the life or work of a Jesuit is not congenial. During the first year of the novitiate, according to Father McGucken,

all the novices make the 30-day retreat, the most influential single factor in the formation of the Jesuit. This consists of an entire month of silence and absolute retirement, devoted to the *exercitia spiritualia* (spiritual exercises), St. Ignatius Loyola's great con-

tribution to Christian asceticism, consisting of basic meditations on the relations between God and man, enforced and vivified by the study of the life of Christ as presented
in the Gospels.

The Jesuit is expected to be an efficient educator of youth, an able priest, and at the
same time a cultivated man of the world . . . (Jesuits) are forbidden by rule to induce
youths to enter the Society. One of the questions asked of the candidate for the Society is whether he has been influenced by a Jesuit "to choose this manner of life." If
so, this constitutes an impediment to his entry. Nevertheless, it is undoubtedly true
that the attraction of Jesuit life, with its opportunities for intellectual advancement,
serves as a powerful inducement to promising youths in their colleges.

TABLE 117. THE TRAINING OF A JESUIT PRIEST

Phase	Number of Years	Average Age of Student at Close
Novitiate[a]	2	20
Juniorate[b]	2	22
Philosophy	3	25
Teaching[c]	3	28
Theology	4	32
Tertianship[d]	1	33

NOTES: [a] Minimum en-
try requirements in USA:
completion of fourth
year high school; aver-
age age of entrant: 18
years.
[b] Courses include classics,
literature and history at
the undergraduate level.
[c] Or practical field work
experience.
[d] A postordination course
concerned with the spir-
itual development of the
student.

Another characteristic of the Jesuit scholasticate is the emphasis placed upon
disputations, particularly in moral theology. These are held one or more times
each week and are generally of one hour's duration. Several times a year public
disputations are held in the presence of the entire body of scholastics and the faculty. At these disputations, the defender announces a thesis (e.g., "the inconsist-
ency of absolute skepticism"), and explains what the thesis does and does not
assert. Then he states the argument, for the sake of correctness, in syllogistic form.
Thereupon an oral dispute commences between the defender and those who oppose
him. It continues until the defender either succeeds in solving the difficulties raised
by his opponents or else fails in his attempt to do so.

These problems are discussed in the Latin language in a highly formal manner
and are often resolved on the basis of subtle scholastic distinctions in the terminology employed. A former Jesuit, Denis Meadows, describes the process as follows:
"The most skill was shown in finding a distinction that split your opponent's propo-
sition in half. You conceded one part, but denied the other, or, better still, subdis-
tinguished again on the second part. Thereby, very often, you anticipated what he
was going to propose and so cut the ground from under his feet. . . . When you
have learned to enjoy the mental rapier work, you can easily understand why it

was popular in medieval Paris, Oxford, Bologna, and the other centers where the intellectuals of those days assembled." Another former Jesuit, George Tyrrell, reaches a somewhat adverse conclusion: "In the disputations there is, no doubt, a great display of intellectual freedom and fearless dialectic, but it is all subject to foregone conclusions, which must come out triumphant over every sham assault. Only within the very narrowest limits is there room for any real, as opposed to merely methodic, difference of opinion."

Alternatively a weekly seminar is sometimes held on a topic dealing with a doctrinal or pastoral subject such as "hearing confessions." In this instance a lector reads to the group the details of an individual case history involving moral principles and then describes the statements made by an imaginary penitent confessing his sin. Thereupon a student chosen by lot is called upon to discuss the principles involved. The other students in the room then criticize his discussion. Following this the professors conclude the discussion by bringing up fine points which might have previously been overlooked, or by noting relevant decisions recently handed down by the Curia in Rome.

Another feature of Jesuit scholasticates is their uniformity. This enables the Society to transfer its scholastics from one country to another while continuing their studies and without any loss of academic time on the part of the student. Thus European and American scholastics can take a year or more of their education in the country in Africa, Asia, or Latin America in which they later plan to serve as foreign missionaries. This helps to solve the students' foreign language problems and also enables them to adjust themselves to foreign customs and cultures while they are at an early and more pliable age. Furthermore there is an attempt to make the student bodies and faculties of the Jesuit scholasticates multinational in composition. This is made possible as a result of the uniformity of their curricula and the use of Latin as the lingua franca employed in the core courses.

The Jesuit system of training has had many critics. Among them was the English historian, Lord Macaulay, who commented that the Jesuits appeared to have discovered the precise point to which intellectual culture can be carried without risk of intellectual emancipation. However one may choose to evaluate this verdict, it would appear that the graduates of the Jesuit scholasticates tend to be more highly trained individuals than are the graduates of the scholasticates maintained by many of the other religious communities which are not as well organized.

Some indication of this is implicit in the apostolic constitution *Sedes sapientae* issued by Pope Pius XII on May 31, 1956, in which he stated:

Now it is obvious to everyone that if the religious clergy are to realize fully their twofold purpose, wise rules are needed which will direct and promote their education and formation as religious, and as apostolic clerics. . . . This need has hitherto been met satisfactorily by the Constitutions of the individual communities or statutes which regulate the education of their younger members and their program of studies. On this subject there has also been no dearth of directives and recommendations of the Holy See. Nevertheless, there has been a long-felt want of general directions, properly coordinated and more complete, which would be supported by Our Apostolic Authority and obligatory on all everywhere.

Previously, in 1945, Pope Pius XII had commissioned the Sacred Congregation of Religious to appoint a special commission of competent persons to handle all questions relating to the clerical training of men seeking admission to religious communities. This group had framed a comprehensive program by the time when the congress of representatives of religious Orders and congregations was held in Rome in 1950. The discussions at that congress led to a revision in some of their recommendations. Finally, with the publication of *Sedes sapientae* six years later, there were also promulgated by the Sacred Congregation of Religious a series of general statutes dated July 7, 1956, based on the general principles and norms as set forth in *Sedes sapientae*. In general, these resemble the principles adhered to in the administration of the major seminaries.

In any large organization, no matter how explicitly the directives from the central administrative headquarters may be phrased, problems arise in connection with their implementation. In the case of the Roman Catholic major seminaries and scholasticates, the Vatican may prescribe constantly higher minimum curriculum standards to be met. Beyond a point, however, the improvement in the quality of these institutions depends increasingly on improving the caliber of their student bodies, and particularly their faculties. Alert Japanese seminarians are doubtless capable of better work than their counterparts, for example, in some of the smaller countries in Central America. Likewise, the *Summa* of Thomas Aquinas when studied under an inspiring teacher will mean far more to the seminarians than if its principles are expounded to them by a pedant concerned with rote rather than reason.

In the case of the seminary students and scholastics in Africa, Asia and Latin America, an over-all improvement in their caliber as a whole is dependent upon the cultural level and the efficiency of the general educational system within the individual country concerned; and these are factors which are beyond the competence of any single church to change significantly—except over a period of many generations. On the other hand, the staffing of seminary faculties is a simpler matter, at least in terms of the number of persons involved.

But here a problem arises. The purpose of a seminary as commonly understood and expressed is primarily the pastoral and spiritual formation of priests, and only secondarily their intellectual education. Added to this is the fact that in the case of the seminaries the manner in which supervision is exercised over the selection of their textbooks and the development of doctrinal formulations would appear to be such as to discourage rather than foster creative theological research on the part of their faculty members. While the seminaries and scholasticates undoubtedly have sincere and devoted men serving on their faculties, nevertheless such an intellectual atmosphere is not calculated to attract to them teachers who will be intellectually inspiring as well as creatively learned, or who will be successful in inculcating in their students a life-long curiosity and quest for the truth, even within areas not restricted by the Supreme Sacred Congregation of the Holy Office.

A well-known Archbishop of Baltimore, the late John Lancaster Spalding, was one of the early leaders in the effort to establish the Catholic University of America. In this connection he preached a sermon at the Third Plenary Council of Baltimore in November 1884 in which he stated:

the education of the priest must be more than a professional education; and he must be sent to a school higher and broader than the ecclesiastical seminary, which is simply a training college for the practical work of the ministry. The purpose for which it was instituted is to prepare young men for the worthy exercise of the general functions of the priestly office, and the good it has done is too great and too manifest to need commendation. But the ecclesiastical seminary is not a school of intellectual culture, either here in America or elsewhere, and to imagine that it can become the instrument of intellectual culture is to cherish a delusion. It must impart a certain amount of professional knowledge, fit its students to become more or less expert catechists, rubricists, and casuists, and its aim is to do this; and whatever mental improvement, if any, thence results, is accidental. Hence its methods are not such as one would choose who desires to open the mind, to give it breadth, flexibility, strength, refinement and grace. Its textbooks are written often in a barbarous style, the subjects are discussed in a dry and mechanical way, and the professor, wholly intent upon giving instruction, is frequently indifferent as to the manner in which it is imparted; or else not possessing himself a really cultivated intellect he holds in slight esteem expansion and refinement of mind, looking upon it as at the best a mere ornament. I am not offering a criticism upon the ecclesiastical seminary, but am simply pointing to the fact that it is not a school of intellectual culture, and consequently, if its course were lengthened to five, to six, to eight, to ten years, its students would go forth to their work with a more thorough professional training but not with more really cultivated minds. . . . Hence it is not surprising that priests who are zealous, earnest, self-sacrificing, who to piety join discretion and good sense, rarely possess the intellectual culture of which I am speaking, for the simple reason that a university and not a seminary is the school in which this kind of education is received. . . .

Seventy-two years later (in 1956) a distinguished Professor of Church History at the Catholic University of America, Msgr. John Tracy Ellis, commented as follows on the third sentence of Archbishop Spalding's remarks quoted above:

Spalding rightly maintained that the seminary was, and must necessarily be, a training school for a profession, albeit a profession that might be expected to have more
than an ordinary kinship for intellectual pursuits. But I wonder very much if the seminaries and scholasticates of our religious orders have made the most of their opportunities for intellectual stimulation and the cultivation of serious reading habits in their
students that they should have. Speaking of the failure of the American priest to be
more intellectually alive, John Talbot Smith, a respected New York priest, said nearly
sixty years ago something which prompts one to ask if it is not still substantially true.
He wrote:

"The habits of the intellectual life in the seminary have dwarfed him. The curriculum rarely recognizes anything but theology and philosophy, and these often isolated
from present conditions and without practical knowledge . . . (and) . . . history is taught
in random, unscientific fashion, to judge the method by the results. . . . It is not then
a cause for wonder that the young priest should graduate so rude and unfinished. The
wonder is that he should at all be able to hold his own in the sneering world, so skilled
in knowledge of its times, so devoted to science and history. . . ."

Smith placed a good deal of responsibility on the hierarchy for the low state of intellectual endeavor among the priests of his generation. . . . Furthermore, he made it
quite clear that he had in mind the religious orders as well as the diocesan priests, for
with the religious superiors, too, he felt that only the bishops could bring about a
change.

The comments of a Jesuit educator at the Annual Meeting of the Jesuit Educational Association held in April 1957 at Marquette University are of interest:

The post-Tridentine seminary, at least as found in the United States rather generally,
has with Kempis sought out the cloister and the mountain top, and run away from
the university city. It has even been implied, quite erroneously, that spiritual matura-
tion and intensive intellectual activity are in conflict, and that the seminary must not
run the risk of promoting the latter at the expense of the former. In effect, this trend
of thinking has brought it to pass that the better-trained philosophical and theological
minds live in places of solitude which may foster contemplation but hardly intellectual
communication. . . .

Is it too much to hope that the day will come when members of the clergy who
show scholarly instincts and academic interests can have the opportunity, while still
young, to develop similar competence and to secure the necessary training and degrees!
As things now stand, in the average seminary such early preparation of scholars would
be quite difficult if not impossible. Here is a major reason why clerical scholars are
lacking in this country or are unduly late in developing. . . .

With respect to the development of the core segments of Roman Catholic theology, the function of the Supreme Sacred Congregation of the Holy Office is
two-fold: first, to guard against and eliminate deviations from accepted doctrine;

and second, to assist in the reformulation of doctrine in the light of new problems as they arise. The emphasis placed by the Holy Office on the first of these functions is well known. To some extent, at least, it would appear that within the Office itself study and research is undertaken. One might cite as a fairly recent major example the Office's deliberations which led to the promulgation by Pope Pius XII in his Apostolic Constitution *Munificentissimus Deus* (November 1, 1950) of the Dogma of the Assumption of the Blessed Virgin Mary. Some of the theological consultants of the Office have themselves been noted as scholars making original contributions to theological literature.

Within the limits indicated, then, the theologians serving on the faculties of the Roman Catholic universities in Europe and America are in a position to engage in research, and in this connection the members of the religious communities have an important role. Within the Roman Catholic Church the possibility of departing from accepted doctrine is one which must be carefully guarded against by priest and prelate alike, particularly those seeking personal promotion within the organization. A consequence of this is the tendency among many of the more energetic members of the secular clergy to focus their attention on the external activities of the Church rather than on extending the frontiers of its thinking in theological matters. The individual members of the religious communities, on the other hand, are usually not so personally concerned with questions of rank and ecclesiastical circumscriptions, etc. Therefore in principle they are in a better position to address themselves to the all-important problem of helping to insure that the basic doctrine of the Church is considered and handed on in a dynamic rather than a static manner.

CHAPTER 14

THE EFFORTS OF THE ROMAN CATHOLIC CHURCH TO CREATE AND TRAIN A LOCAL CLERGY IN AFRICA, ASIA AND LATIN AMERICA

A. As Directed by the Vatican

In the year 1626—four years after its establishment—the Congregation for the Propagation of the Faith admonished the Bishop of Japan to ordain young Japanese seminarians to the priesthood, because the native Roman Catholic Church and missions in that country were in dire jeopardy owing to the persecution of Christians by the Shoguns. In 1628 the first Secretary of the Propaganda sent a long memorandum to the Cardinals associated with this Congregation recommending the necessity of fostering a local priesthood: the arguments presented in this document were repeated some three hundred years later by Pope Pius XI in his encyclical, *Rerum ecclesiae* (1926). The conclusions of this early letter were published soon afterwards and were sent by the Propaganda in a letter dated November 28, 1630, to the first two vicars apostolic of China and Indochina. In 1633 the Propaganda recommended, without success, the establishment of a hierarchy for Japan, China, Tonkin and Siam.

In 1659 Pope Alexander VII reminded the first vicars apostolic being sent out by the Paris Foreign Missions Society to the Kingdoms of Tonkin and Cochin-China that "the principal reason which causes the Sacred Congregation (*de Propaganda Fide*) to send you to the missions with the rank of bishop is to enable you by every means possible to instruct the young men in order to make them capable of being raised to the priesthood." In 1663 the Propaganda issued a general order for the establishment of native colleges to train "national priests." In the next few decades similar admonitions and apostolic letters were dispatched by Popes Clement IX (1667–69) and Clement X (1670–76).

In an apostolic letter dated April 1, 1680 (*Onerosa pastoralis*), Pope Innocent XI (1676–89) ordered the number of vicars apostolic in China increased "so that . . . each of the Vicars might, above all else, aim at the formation and ordination of native priests." In order to ensure that his wishes would be carried out, this Pope went so far as to confer upon his legates (Bishop Pallu of Heliopolis and Bishop de la Mothe-Lambert of Berito) the "power of forcing the Vicars Apostolic, with penalties inflicted by the Sacred Canons, to train and ordain native or indigenous clerics and priests so that the way might gradually be prepared also for the erection of a native hierarchy." It is reported that Innocent XI told Bishop Pallu "that a single native priest is worth more than 50,000 pagan conversions."

Similar letters and decrees were sent out by succeeding Popes as follows:

Pope	Pontificate	Title	Date
Clement XI	1700–21	*Dudum felicis*	December 7, 1703
Clement XII	1730–40	decree	April 16, 1736
Benedict XIV	1740–58	several decrees	various
Pius VI	1775–99	encyclical	May 10, 1775

One of the results of the French Revolution and the ensuing Napoleonic wars was the reduction in the number of Roman Catholic foreign missionaries serving abroad to approximately one-third the number which had been stationed overseas before the Revolution. Indeed, it is stated by Msgr. Freri that the activities of the Roman Catholic Church in East Asia were largely sustained during this turbulent era as a result of the work of approximately 300 native priests.

At the time of his election as Pope, Gregory XVI had been serving as Cardinal Prefect of the Propaganda Congregation. During the 15 years of his pontificate (1831–46) he did much to rebuild Catholic missionary activities. Under his direction the Propaganda issued an instruction dated November 23, 1845, entitled *De Clero indigena* and addressed to all the vicars apostolic of East Asia. It recommended with especial urgency the training and ordination of an indigenous clergy, summarizing the Vatican's previous directives on this subject. The following is a portion of that letter:

there also hover before the mind's eye the extremely pitiable inhabitants of so many regions from the most distant reaches of the earth. . . . Among these the vineyard of the Lord was planted long ago with great labor; nevertheless, due to a lack of husbandmen, certainly ascribable to the failure to form a native clergy, that vineyard finds itself almost at the point of drying up. . . . Wherefore . . . (the Propaganda has) decided to decree definitively and to command. . . . First, that all the heads of missions without exception, by whatever title they may hold their office, actively assist in the promotion and consolidation of the Catholic religion in such a way that, where there is still a lack of bishops, they may be appointed as soon as possible. . . .

The instruction declared it was necessary for seminaries to be founded where ordinands "should receive a good and extensive training."

In a Rescript for Ceylon issued by the Propaganda in 1852, the Congregation directed that the seminary there should be open to all qualified applicants, including men from the lower castes.

The Propaganda's instruction dated June 7, 1853, stated: "Native priests should be raised out of that condition of quasi-servitude, abjection and contempt in which they have been held before this; and, little by little, through solid and careful training in knowledge and piety, they should be gradually made fit to perform even the principal duties in the missions; so that, eventually, rectors, shepherds and pastors from among these indigenous priests can be placed in charge of these missions, sufficiently supplied with a native clergy to no longer require foreign reserves, that is, the support, and service of European missionaries. . . ."

Additional instructions along these lines were issued by the Propaganda on September 8, 1869, to the vicars apostolic in the East Indies and on October 18, 1883, to those in China. In the latter instruction (*Quæ a præsulibus*), the Propaganda among other things cautioned against shortening the period of training provided for seminarians in China and urged the vicars apostolic to establish central or regional seminaries within the areas under their jurisdiction.

The two long pontificates of Pius IX (1846–78) and Leo XIII (1878–1903) covered over half a century. In the main these two Popes continued the work of Gregory XVI in extending the outreach of Roman Catholic foreign missions, particularly in areas to which Roman Catholic missionaries had not as yet been sent in any large number. These regions included Central Africa, North India, Central China and the islands of Oceania.

Toward the close of the pontificate of Pius IX (i.e., on June 1, 1877) the Propaganda issued a circular letter asking the missionary bishops and vicars apostolic to reply periodically to a list of 63 questions, of which three (Nos. 7–9) related to the local clergy: "What is the situation with respect to the training and development of a native clergy? Is there a seminary in existence in which the (ordinand) students are separated from the secular students? What is the course of study? Are the regulations stipulated by the Council of Trent being entirely or only partially observed? In the case where there is still no seminary, is there any prospect of somehow making up for this lack?" Other questions called for answers concerning the position occupied by indigenous priests and whether they had been considered for appointment to positions still occupied by European priests. (Similar questions are now required by Canon Law to be answered by mission superiors in their reports sent every five years to the Propaganda.)

In an instruction issued in 1883 to the mission superiors in China, the Propaganda recommended the establishment of central seminaries to train students coming from several vicariates, with the directors of such seminaries to be relieved of all other functions. Furthermore it directed that the surplus of mission income remaining after providing for the support of missionary personnel should be applied first to the seminaries.

In 1893 Pope Leo XIII founded a Papal seminary in Kandy, Ceylon, to be administered by the Jesuits. In order to draw attention to the importance of this occasion, the Pope issued an encyclical letter on June 24 of that year entitled *Ad Extremas orientis*. The following is a portion of that letter:

The Catholic faith in the Indies will not have a certain future, its propagation will not be assured as long as there does not exist an indigenous clergy prepared to carry out the functions of the priesthood and who are capable, not only of helping the missionaries, but of fulfilling pastoral charges themselves. . . . Again, it is to be noted that the missionaries who come from abroad are too few in number to administer the Christian communities which are spread throughout these countries today. This lack becomes evident from an examination of the statistics of the missions and the requests which they make incessantly to the Propaganda to obtain missionaries which they ask for in greater and greater numbers. . . . And it is well known one cannot hope that Europe will supply a number of missionaries proportionate to these needs. This is why, if one wishes to provide for the welfare of the Indies and to establish Christianity in these regions in a way that will endure, it is necessary at all costs to create among the natives priests capable, after a serious preparation, of fulfilling all the priestly and ministerial functions.

This encyclical was issued during a relatively peaceful era. Nevertheless Leo XIII went on in the same encyclical to point out with considerable foresight what might happen in the future to Roman Catholic missions in the event a local clergy were not established:

. . . One must not forget, which is most unlikely, but which nevertheless could take place, that a time may come in Europe or in Asia when the foreign clergy will be obliged, through necessity or by force, to abandon the Indies. Then, if a native clergy is lacking, who will be able to safeguard the religion, since there would not be a single minister at the altar or a single preacher? The history of China, Japan and of Ethiopia provides a clear lesson on this point. Very often, among the Ethiopians and the Chinese, as a consequence of hatreds and wars against the Christian name, the enemy has massacred or exiled the foreign priests, sparing the native priests. Knowing the language and customs of their country perfectly . . . the latter have been able to remain in their country not only without fear but also to carry on their sacred ministry there. . . . On the contrary, in Ethiopia where the Christians had already reached 200,000 in number, the missionaries were massacred or exiled, and as there was not a single native priest, the fruit of their long hard work was completely destroyed by the persecution.

. . . For this reason, and in obedience to the advice and exhortations of the Holy See, the prefects of the missions of India have founded seminaries everywhere they were permitted to do so. Besides, at the synods of Colombo, Bangalore and Allahabad it was decided in the year 1887 that each diocese would have a seminary for the training of the native clergy, and if some suffragan bishops were prevented from doing so by reason of poverty, they were to send their scholars to the metropolitan seminary and pay their expenses there. Now, the bishops endeavored as far as they could to carry out these decrees; but their good will was impeded by the poorness of the families and by the penury of the priests qualified for instruction and wise guidance. That is why it is possible to say that there still does not exist a single seminary where the education of the students is perfect, and that (continues to be true) in an epoch when the civil governors and the numerous Protestants of these countries spare neither money nor effort to provide an unwholesome education for the youth.

Toward the end of his pontificate, Leo XIII wrote a letter entitled *The Church in the Philippines* which was issued at a time when approximately one thousand Spanish missionary friars were being withdrawn against their desire from the Islands. The following are excerpts from that letter:

Since it is proved by experience that a native clergy is most useful everywhere, the bishops must make it their care to increase the number of native priests. . . . Above all things the clergy should hold to the rule that they are not to allow themselves to be mixed up in party strifes. . . . We deem it necessary that men in Holy Orders in the present condition of affairs in the Philippine Islands should avoid this in a special manner. . . . The bishops . . . are not to leave those who go out from the seminary entirely to themselves; but to keep them from idleness and from abandoning the study of the sacred sciences, it is an excellent thing to have them every year for at least five years after ordination submit to an examination in dogmatic and moral theology before men of learning and authority. Since the halls of Rome also are open to young students from the Philippines who may wish to pursue the higher studies, it will afford Us much pleasure if the bishops send hither from time to time young men who may one day communicate to their fellow citizens the knowledge of religion acquired in this very centre of truth. This Holy See will do its share in the most effective way to advance the secular clergy in higher learning and better ecclesiastical training, so that in good time it may be worthy to assume the pastoral charges now administered by the regular priests.

Pope Leo XIII issued a bull (*Quæ, mari sinico*) on September 17, 1902, on the same subject relating to the Church in the Philippines. He also addressed letters on this subject to the hierarchy in Peru in 1894 and in the years 1892, 1894 and 1899 to the hierarchy in Brazil. In his letter, *Inter graves,* dated May 1, 1894, addressed to the Peruvian bishops, Pope Leo advised them to make sure that the students in the seminaries under their jurisdiction applied themselves industriously to their studies.

The long pontificate of Leo XIII was succeeded by the comparatively short one of Pius X (1903–14). Pope Pius X was not as directly concerned with missionary activities as was his predecessor. The next Pope, Benedict XV, reigned only eight years (1914–22), and most of his activities consisted of attempts to bring World

War I to an end and to promote peace among the nations during the postwar era. Nevertheless on November 30, 1919, Benedict XV issued an encyclical entitled *Maximum illud* which states clearly the need for fostering a native clergy. The following paragraphs appear in that encyclical:

. . . Finally, the point on which all those who rule over Missions must fix their principal attention, is to educate and instruct members of the sacred ministry from among the people with whom they live, for in this is contained the principal hope of new Churches. For the native priest, inasmuch as he is one with his countrymen in birth, in character, in feelings, in interests, has a peculiar power of introducing the faith into their minds; for he knows far better than any other the right way to persuade them of any point. And thus it often happens that he can easily enter where a foreign priest may not set his foot.

But a Native Clergy, in order that it may bear the desired fruit, must necessarily be well formed and trained. For this end, a partial and hasty instruction, sufficient to make the candidate fit for the priesthood, will be by no means enough, but it must be thorough and complete, covering all the ground, just as for the priests of civilized nations; for the Native Clergy is not to be trained in order to assist the foreign missionaries in humbler offices, but in order that it may be equal to the accomplishment of its divine task and in course of time duly assume the government of its own people. . . . Hence where there exists a sufficient number of indigenous Clergy, well instructed and worthy of their holy vocation, it may justly be said that the missionaries have successfully completed their work, and that the Church has been thoroughly well founded. And even if a storm of persecution should arise to ruin it, there need be no fear that with such a foundation and such roots it will fail to withstand the attacks of its enemies.

The Apostolic See has always persisted in impressing upon the heads of Missions the importance of estimating at its true value and diligently executing this grave duty of their office, and its desires have been clearly indicated by the existence of Colleges, both of ancient and of recent erection in this City, for the education of the clerics of various nations, especially of the Oriental rites. Yet in spite of this urging on the part of the Pontiffs, it is to be deplored that there are regions in which the Catholic faith has been introduced for centuries, without any indigenous clergy being as yet to be found there, except of a lower class; and that there are certain nations which have long been illuminated by the light of the faith, and have emerged from a savage state to such a degree of civilization that they possess men who excel in all the varieties of the civil arts, yet, after many centuries of the influence of the gospel and of the Church, can show no bishops to govern nor priests to teach their own countrymen. It is clear, therefore, that there has been something wanting and unsuitable in the method up till now employed in some places for the education of clergy for the Missions, and, for the removal of this unfortunate state of things, We order the Sacred Congregation for the Propagation of the Faith to decree what is proper for the various regions, and to see to the foundation and good government of Seminaries, which shall serve for each region and for several dioceses at once; and especially We wish the Sacred Congregation to be solicitous with regard to the formation of the new clergy in Vicariates and other missionary parts. . . .

In 1923 the Propaganda Congregation sent a letter to all religious communities concerned with missionary activities making certain recommendations. With respect to the formation of the local clergy, the latter stated: "The Mission is not to be considered as a property of the institute. . . . It is of the highest importance that superiors watch carefully that in the Missions entrusted to their institutes attention be paid to the formation of native clergy. And indeed that is necessary, since the various territories were committed to them precisely for the purpose of founding and establishing the Church there. . . ."

Pope Pius XI whose pontificate lasted from 1922 to 1939 has frequently been called the "Pope of the Missions." On February 28, 1926, he issued an encyclical entitled *Rerum ecclesiæ* which states as clearly as any single document could the need for training an indigenous ministry. The following paragraphs appear in that encyclical:

Before anything else, We call your attention to the importance of building up a native clergy. If you do not work with all your might to attain this purpose, We assert that not only will your apostolate be crippled, but it will become an obstacle and an impediment to the establishment and organization of the Church in those countries. We gladly recognize and acknowledge the fact that in some places steps have already been taken to provide for these needs by the erection of seminaries in which native youths of promise are well educated and prepared to receive the dignity of the priesthood, and are trained to instruct in the Christian Faith members of their own race. But in spite of all this work, we are still a great distance from the goal which we have set for ourselves.

. . . From a study of the earliest monuments of Christian antiquity it is clearly evident that the clergy placed in charge of the faithful in each new community by the Apostles were not men brought in from the outside but were chosen from the natives of that locality. . . . You ought not to conclude that the role of the native clergy is merely one of assisting the missionaries in minor matters, of merely following up and completing their work. . . . How can the Church among the heathens be developed today unless it be built of those very elements out of which our own churches were built; that is to say, unless it be made up of people, clergy, and religious orders of men and women recruited from the native populations of the several regions? . . . In order to enable you to progress in winning from heathenism new converts to Christ, would it not be of great assistance if you would entrust to the native clergy the people already converted so that they could minister to them and preserve their faith? As a matter of fact, the native clergy will prove to be most useful (more useful than some people imagine) in extending the Kingdom of Christ. . . .

Moreover, the foreign missionary, because of his imperfect knowledge of the language often finds himself embarrassed when he attempts to express his thoughts with the result that the force and efficacy of his preaching are thereby greatly weakened. In addition to the aforementioned difficulties there are others. . . . Let us suppose, for example, that either because of the fortunes of war, or because of certain political happenings in a mission field, the ruling government is changed in that territory and that the new government decrees or requests that the missionaries of a certain nationality be expelled; or let us suppose—something which rarely, if ever, occurs—that the inhabitants of a particular territory, having reached a fairly high degree of civilization and at the same time a corresponding development in civic and social life, and desiring to become free and independent, should drive away from their country the governor, the soldiers, the missionaries of the foreign nation to whose rule they are subject. All this, of course, cannot be done without violence. Everyone can see what great harm would accrue to the Church in that land in the circumstances, unless a native clergy had been spread beforehand throughout the country like a network and were, by consequence, in a position to provide adequately for the population which had been converted to Christ. . . .

Pius XI then goes on to point out that the financial difficulties involved in establishing new seminaries in missionary areas must be faced by the religious congregations concerned, and shall be overcome:

In some places, as We have already pointed out, seminaries for the native clergy have been opened. These seminaries are being erected in points central to the nearby missions and entrusted, as a rule, to the same religious order or congregation which has charge of the missions. At these central institutions the Vicars and Prefects send their chosen men and pay for them while they are being trained, to receive them back one day ordained priests ready for the sacred ministry. This policy, which has been followed in some places, We sincerely wish, nay, We command, shall be followed likewise by the Superiors of all missions, so that it cannot be said that any native youth has ever been kept out of the priesthood and the apostolate, provided, of course, he exhibits the mark of a true vocation and is a young man of genuine promise. . . .

It need scarcely be added that the greater the number of students you select for this training (there is need of greater numbers) the greater will be the expense. Do not lose heart because of this fact, but have confidence in the most loving Savior of men to whose Providence We must look to find ways and means whereby the generosity of Catholics shall be stimulated so that there may come to the Holy See the increased funds required to aid more adequately such worthy enterprises. . . .

The Pope warned against assuming that native students have inferior intellectual capacities:

It is also important that simultaneously with this priestly formation these seminarians receive a scientific education both in the sacred and profane sciences. This education should follow the most approved methods. The course of study should not be unduly shortened or curtailed in any of its important features. The students as a matter of fact should follow the general accepted course of studies. . . .

Anyone who looks upon these natives as members of an inferior race or as men of low mentality makes a grievous mistake. Experience over a long period of time has proven that the inhabitants of those remote regions of the East and of the South frequently are not inferior to us at all, and are capable of holding their own with us, even in mental ability. If one discovers an extreme lack of the ability to understand among those who live in the very heart of certain barbarous countries, this is largely due to the conditions under which they exist, for since their daily needs are so limited, they are not often called upon to make use of their intellects. . . . We have here under Our very eyes the example of certain native students attending the colleges of Rome who not only are equal to the other students in ability and in the results they obtain in their studies, but frequently even surpass them. Certainly you should not allow the native clergy to be looked upon as if they were a lower grade of priests, to be employed only in the most humble offices of the ministry. These priests have been admitted to the same priesthood that the missionaries possess, they are members of the selfsame apostolate. On the contrary, you should prefer the native priests to all others, for it is they who will one day govern the churches and Catholic communities founded by your sweat and labor. Therefore, there should exist no discrimination of any kind between priests, be they European missionaries or natives, there must be no line of demarcation marking one off from the other. Let all priests, missionaries and natives be united with one another in the bonds of mutual respect and love. . . .

To return to a subject which We discussed above. If it is necessary, Venerable Brothers and Beloved Sons, in the cities where you have your residences and in other more-important centers, to erect large churches and other mission buildings, you must, however, avoid building churches or edifices that are too sumptuous and costly as if you were erecting cathedrals and episcopal palaces for future dioceses. This type of structure will come in due time and when the need really exists. . . . We also exhort you not to neglect in this work of education the better classes, especially the rulers of the locality and their children. It is beyond question that the word of God and its ministers are received more readily by the poor and humble than by the proud and rich . . . (yet) both history and experience teach that when once the rulers of a people have been converted to Christianity, the common people follow closely in the footsteps of their leaders. . . .

In the final portion of this encyclical, Pope Pius XI issued a flat warning to any religious Order or institute which might fail to heed his admonitions:

Finally, Venerable Brothers and Beloved Sons, receive, in the well-known spirit of zeal for religion and the salvation of souls which consumes you, with docile minds and with the will to obey promptly, this, Our last but most important recommendation of all. The districts confided by the Holy See to your care and labors in order that they too may be added to the Kingdom of Christ the Lord, are for the most part vast in extent. It may thus happen that the number of missionaries belonging to your particular Institute is much smaller than your actual needs require. In this case, just as in well established dioceses members of different religious families, priests, laymen, and nuns of many different Congregations, are accustomed to come to the aid of the bishop, so you also, where there is question of spreading the Faith, of educating the native youth or other similar undertakings, ought not to hesitate to invite and to receive as companions of your labors religious missionaries, even though they be of a different Institute than your own, and also priests or others though they are members of lay Institutes. The Orders and Religious

Congregations may well be proud of the missions given them among the heathen and of the conquests made up to the present hour for the Kingdom of Christ. Let them remember, however, that they do not possess the mission fields by a peculiar and perpetual right, but that they hold them solely at the discretion and pleasure of the Holy See which has both the duty and the right to see to it that these missions are well and adequately taken care of. The Roman Pontiff would not be doing his full Apostolic duty if he limited his interest solely to the distribution of missions of greater or lesser extent to one or another Institute. What is of much more importance is that he must always, and with great care, see to it that these different Institutes are sending into the regions confided to them as many qualified missionaries as are needed to carry on in a thorough manner the task of diffusing the light of the truth over the whole extent of these countries.

Therefore, since the Divine Pastor shall demand of Us an accounting of His Flock, We, without hesitation and whenever it shall appear to be either necessary, more opportune, or useful for the larger growth of the Catholic Church, shall transfer the mission territory of one Institute to another Institute; We shall also divide and subdivide a mission territory and shall confide it to the care of native priests or shall assign new Vicariates and new Apostolic Prefectures to other religious Congregations than those occupying the original territory. . . .

The next Pope, Pius XII, according to Cardinal McGuigan of Toronto, may in time become known as the "Pope of the Liturgy." He continued the work of his predecessor in furthering Roman Catholic foreign missions, although the advent of World War II at the outset of his pontificate made this task more difficult. On June 13, 1940, he addressed an encyclical entitled *Sæculo exeunte* to the Patriarch of Lisbon and the archbishops and bishops of Portugal. In it the Pope urged them (as the religious leaders of a Roman Catholic country not at war) to stress in Portugal the need for sending more missionaries overseas. He also wrote: ". . . We have one thing especially at heart. In the Archdiocese of Goa, native priests and native religious abound. We desire that in the ecclesiastical territories of other Portuguese dominions, also, a generous beginning should be made to have as soon as possible a flourishing and exemplary native priesthood. . . . One of the most fervent dreams of the Church in recent times (has been) the formation of an indigenous clergy. . . ."

Twenty-five years after the encyclical *Rerum ecclesiæ* by Pope Pius XI, his successor Pius XII issued an encyclical commemorating it. Dated June 2, 1951, this encyclical was entitled *Evangelii præcones*. In it the Pope commented on the development of various aspects of Roman Catholic foreign missionary activity during the previous quarter century and the need for training a native clergy. Finally, on November 28, 1959 (the 40th Anniversary of "Maximum Illud") Pope John XXIII issued his first encyclical on foreign missions, entitled "Princeps Pastorum,"devoted almost entirely to stressing the importance of this same need.

B. As Carried Out in the Field

The Papal encyclicals and the directives of the Congregation for the Propagation of the Faith, as noted above, have been quite explicit in pointing to the necessity for the formation of a local clergy. Some of the early setbacks sustained by the Vatican in its attempts to establish major seminaries in Africa, Asia and Latin America, as noted below, were caused by measures taken by the colonial European powers for imperialist rather than religious purposes. Thus as far back as 1633 the recommendation of the Propaganda for the establishment of a hierarchy in Japan, China, Tonkin and Siam was blocked by the Portuguese who were jealous of the rising influence of the French in these areas and who claimed the right to appoint all the clergy in Southeast and East Asia.

A review of the evidence (drawn almost entirely from Roman Catholic sources) also suggests that to some extent the same general types of differences of opinion as have existed between Protestant mission boards and their missionaries in the field have arisen from time to time between the Vatican and the members of the religious communities serving as missionaries in the underdeveloped countries. As Father Schmidlin points out, as early as 1677 the Vicar Apostolic Pallu submitted to the Vatican a plan calling for the immediate appointment of 13 native bishops whose position would correspond at first to that of coadjutor bishop and would be under European supervision. However, in the subsequent discussion and consideration this plan was reduced to the nomination of one Chinese bishop. Furthermore, during the 17th century a few East Indian bishops were appointed with such unfortunate results that similar attempts were discouraged for an extended period. Finally, in the 19th century Gregory XVI appointed two native-born Oratorians as Vicars Apostolic of Ceylon.

With respect to the directive of the Propaganda dated November 23, 1845 (noted above), Rev. Edward Goulet, S.J., commented "the letter bore no immediate fruit but it did furnish ample testimony to the attitude of the Holy See." Some of the difficulties encountered during the 19th century in raising the local clergy to governing positions in the Church were the result of the policy of the Propaganda of not placing natives over Europeans but rather of appointing them to supervise mission districts in which there were indigenous priests alone.

In 1907, at the high tide of the pre-World War I imperialist era, a book entitled *Le Christianisme et l'extrême Orient* by Canon Léon Joly of Paris was published. In it Father Joly forecast with an almost uncanny accuracy the likelihood that Europeans would at some point be ejected from China, Japan and the other countries in the Orient. He also commented that the political role played by foreign missionaries in colonial areas had brought discredit to the Roman Catholic Church. His main theme was the urgent necessity of forming an indigenous clergy, a need which he said the Roman Catholic missionaries in the Far East were failing to meet. His criticisms of the Jesuits in this respect were sharp, although he also commented adversely on the missionaries of the Paris Foreign Mission Society, as well as those of the Franciscan, Dominican, and Lazarist Fathers, on the same score. Canon Joly wrote that owing to their failure to stress sufficiently the training and formation of a local clergy, the Jesuits in the 17th and 18th centuries "saw their foreign missions in Japan, the Indies, China, Paraguay and the entire world collapse. . . . It can be said of the Jesuit Fathers, without being their enemy, that they think too much of their own Order when they should be occupying themselves exclusively with the work to which the Church directs them. . . . The Jesuits have not seriously tried to form a native clergy in their missions. . . ."

According to Father Joseph Schmidlin, S.V.D., Canon Joly was joined in his attacks by "Luguet, Bertrand, Cahours and others . . . (who went) much too far in their generalizations and deductions, although it cannot be denied that the regular Orders might have done very much more than was done in this direction."

Replies to Canon Joly were issued by Fathers Brou, Damerval and Huonder, all members of the Society of Jesus. The last named, Father Anton Huonder, a Swiss, published a fundamental monograph in 1909 entitled *Der einheimische Klerus in den Heidenländern.* In it he discussed, area by area as of that date, the efforts which had been made by the Propaganda and by the Jesuits and other religious communities to create and train a local clergy. He also outlined the difficulties encountered in this endeavor, and the successes and failures experienced. His study became a source book for subsequent writers and tended to allay the controversy for a while.

Right Rev. Msgr. Joseph Freri wrote in 1917: "Have the instructions of the Propaganda been faithfully obeyed? It is not our purpose to discuss this point. We may say in passing that certain superiors seem more anxious to recruit members for their congregations than for the secular clergy on whom nevertheless rests the real organization of a diocese."

A contrary opinion was advanced in 1919 by Very Rev. Wlodimir Ledochowski, who was then Superior General of the Society of Jesus. In a letter he wrote to the Superior of the Jesuit Mission of Kiang-Nan, China, Father Ledochowski pointed to the difficulty experienced by the Jesuits in finding capable students who would be worthy of the rigorous training prescribed by the Society:

It may be that, now and then, there has been hesitation due to excessive caution, or individual errors, but to reproach the Society, as some have done at times, with having on this point proved false to the wishes of the Church, is to betray ignorance of her history. The Church knows that she can reckon upon the docility of the sons of St. Ignatius, and she has shown it again and again. . . . Priests of inferior quality, how numerous soever they may be, would be powerless to stimulate vast movements towards the Church, or even to keep the faith alive in a country. History shows us alas! too many churches which a fully organized native clergy was unable to save from stagnation, schism, heresy, and utter ruin. A serious formation counts for more in the priestly body, than numerical expansion. . . . We have heard religious of another Order and of other countries ask themselves in dismay: "Is it not better to get on without native priests, despite the immense services they are called to render, than to run the risk of seeing the priesthood degraded?" To be sure it is, and hence the strictest precautions become obligatory upon us before definitely enrolling natives in the sacred militia. We have been taught so already by the mouth of the Pastors of the Church: rather a *pusillus grex* ("tiny flock") composed of priests of irreproachable lives, and altogether reliable, than a host of mediocrities ill equipped for the fray, and exposed to pitiable falls. . . . The Church exhorts us to take account of concrete possibilities. Lay hands, she says, "on tried men," who "little by little . . . at the opportune moment . . . when it can be done prudently" shall be invested with the highest functions and dignities. . . .

In closing the letter, Father Ledochowski makes one other comment of interest: "Had the work (of training a native clergy) been undertaken fifty years ago, and on a big enough scale, the efforts would not have cost more than it has actually cost, and would probably have led to the creation of a new and thriving province. . . ."

In 1950, Professor Anton Freitag noted that after the publication of the encyclical *Maximum illud* by Pope Benedict XV in 1919, the controversy on this subject continued during the 1920s: "They grouped themselves for and against the two spokesmen for a native clergy and an episcopate in China, P. Lebbe, C.M., and in India, P. Gille, S.J. They opposed each other with an ardent vehemence which often made them literally blind and unfair toward the viewpoints of others. . . . They evoked just as emphatic and fiery spokesmen in the opposition who went overboard in their contentions, as did Garnier in China and Huismans and others in India. For the most part the Belgian missionaries tended to be active promoters of their cause, while the French were more inclined to emphasize a slow procedure. . . . Rome kept itself outside the entire conflict"—until Pope Pius XI issued his encyclical *Rerum ecclesiæ* in 1926.

Father Schmidlin summarizes the significance of this controversy as follows:

. . . There are mistakes and blunders, which have been made especially in the modern missions and are repeated even to this day—mistakes arising from the neglect and lack of understanding of many missionaries and, more pointedly of their particular Orders. Through short-sightedness, timidity, indolence, egotism, ambition, or some other reason, these do not desire a native secular clergy, or devote insufficient attention to its training. To saddle the sending church with the responsibility for these undeniable "errors of the system," as Huonder does, is just as "monstrous" as the accusation leveled by Joly and Luguet at the Society of Jesus. We gladly concede that other causes have aggravated the problem in modern times, and hampered its solution. Huonder himself admits that "the missionary Orders, including a certain tendency in the Jesuit Order," are not always mindful of the importance of this need and are partly responsible for the slow development, but holds that the newer Orders, comparable to the flying columns of an invading army, are more easily adapted to native recruiting than the old, strictly monastic, societies which, owing to their principle of stability, must aim at recruiting their monasteries from their vicinity. Again, the dependence of certain modern missions on the Hispano-Portuguese and later on the French state authorities, which believed their political purposes better served by a foreign than a native mission personnel, was largely to be blamed for the repression of the natives; and many missionaries, instead of accepting the natives as they were and accommodating themselves to them, demanded the renunciation of their national characteristics, offered them Christianity in an exclusively European form, and thought that they ought to Europeanize or Latinize them in order to overcome them. Moreover, native priests were often systematically neglected by and in favor of Europeans, and the European clergy often claimed a positive superiority over natives and reduced them to the status of an auxiliary clergy because the former received their faculties from Rome and the latter only from the Vicars Apostolic. . . .

Up to the 20th century it was believed by some that the best results would be obtained if promising minor seminarians from mission lands were sent to pursue their studies at the major seminary level in Rome or elsewhere in Europe. The activities of the Pontifical Urban College of the Propaganda Fide and its associated educational institutions in Rome have already been noted as well as those of the seven small national colleges maintained in Rome by the Oriental Congregation for the training of students of the Eastern Rites.

As far back as 1723 an Italian secular missionary priest in China, Matteo Ripa, sought without success to establish a seminary in Peking and then took six of his students to Naples, in which city he founded the College of the Holy Family for China. This seminary trained 106 Chinese priests until it was closed in the 19th century. Father Schmidlin has listed a number of seminaries established in Europe especially for African students, none of which had much success. Among them were "the Della Palma College for Negroes in Naples, the Mazza Institute for Negroes in Verona, the St. Barnabas Mission College founded by Cardinal Massaja in Naples, Comboni's undertaking in Egypt, and the experiments of the Fathers of the Holy Ghost. However, the tragic collapse of the vast majority of these attempts demonstrated that such a transplantation of exotic plants into an entirely strange soil is, as a rule, doomed to failure, primarily because of the hygienic dangers of the climate, but also because the students are all too liable to suffer serious spiritual harm as the result of artificial Europeanization. . . ."

Accordingly, during the past 50 years the chief emphasis of the Roman Catholic Church in fostering the formation of an indigenous clergy has been in establishing major seminaries in the underdeveloped countries themselves, with only the more brilliant students being sent to Rome for advanced training in specialized fields. A few of the religious communities continue to send their most able scholastics to Europe for their major seminary training: the Holy Ghost Fathers, for example, maintain a scholasticate at Croix-Valmer (near Marseilles) expressly for students (35 in 1956) coming from underdeveloped countries and preparing for admission to that congregation.

Within the major areas of the world the progress of the Roman Catholic Church in fostering a local clergy has in some respects been uneven, partly owing to the different emphases placed on this type of activity by the various religious communities and partly owing to the missionary situation in the individual underdeveloped countries. Over-all, it would appear that the great majority of the native candidates for the priesthood in missionary areas who are studying philosophy and theology are enrolled in major seminaries rather than in scholasticates. Thus in 1950 there were reported to be 4,291 major seminarians under the authority of the Propaganda, compared to only 522 scholastics, or a ratio of approximately 8:1. (The number of scholastics listed in that report was incomplete, so the ratio that year was actually lower than this.) Professor Freitag points out in his recent (1953) book, *Die neue Missionsära,* that the tendency persists in the underdeveloped countries for some native candidates for the priesthood to choose vocations in religious communities rather than in the secular clergy. This is because (as reported by Dutch Jesuit missionaries in Indonesia) the native priest in a religious institute has a life free from want, is on an equal basis with the other members of his community, and to some extent is protected from the dangers of the world; whereas the indigenous secular priest must depend more on his own efforts and upon the willingness of the foreign missionary priests stationed in his locality to cooperate with him.

The following discussion of the major seminaries now training students in Africa, Asia and Latin America is largely a sketch of the development of a local Roman Catholic clergy, rather than a summary of the characteristics which distinguish the individual seminaries and scholasticates from one another. The activities of the Roman Catholic major seminaries are highly standardized as compared to those of the theological schools and seminaries of the Protestant and Eastern Churches.

Neither the Oriental Congregation nor the Congregation of Seminaries and Universities has published a recent list of the major seminaries under their jurisdictions. Furthermore the latest comprehensive list of seminaries in missionary areas was published by the Propaganda Congregation in 1950 (*Le Missione cattoliche*). Consequently, in compiling the following lists of seminaries a number of different sources of information have been used, as noted in the bibliography. It seems likely that a few major seminaries and scholasticates which have recently come into existence may not be listed herein; and a few which have been listed may no longer be in existence. Furthermore a source of confusion in the literature arises from the fact that when presenting statistics some Protestant and Roman Catholic writers—and even some official Catholic directories—fail to distinguish between the major and minor seminaries, or group the students at major and minor seminaries together under the general heading "seminarists." The effort has been made to make the lists presented below as complete and as accurate as is possible at this time.

C. AFRICA

The Continent of Africa was the last major area in which the Roman Catholic Church established an indigenous hierarchy. It is also the area where perhaps the greatest difficulties have been encountered in training a local clergy.

Over 450 years ago, i.e., in 1491, King Alfonso of Congo (an area in Angola, south of what is now the Belgian Congo) and many of his subjects became Roman Catholics. In 1506 his son, Prince Henry, was sent by the King to Portugal in order to receive his education from the members of a religious Order, the Canons of St. John the Evangelist. In 1518, at the request of the King of Portugal, Pope Leo X reluctantly nominated Henry a bishop. The Pope's hesitation was due to the fact that the Prince was only 23 years old and not yet a priest, whereas canon law specified a bishop must be at least 30 years old: however, in view of the special factors involved, an exception was permitted in this case. In the same year Prince Henry was nominated auxiliary Bishop to the Bishop of Funchal in Madeira whose diocese at that time included all Portuguese territory in Africa. However, the young Bishop died shortly thereafter, and he appears to have been the first and last Negro priest of that period. This was due to the reactions of the natives to the poor example set by the Portuguese secular clergy in the early days in Africa and to the brutalities committed by the Portuguese slave traders; and when the Congo was subsequently placed by Rome under the jurisdiction of a later bishop of St. Thomas, the Congo clergy are said to have revolted.

During the next 350 years the major missionary emphasis of the Propaganda was directed toward the Orient rather than Africa. The unhealthy climate of most African areas retarded the development of missionary activities. Perhaps the greatest obstacle was the low level of education and culture among the native Africans encountered. Furthermore the requirement that native priests must remain celibate made a career in the Church seem less attractive to many African candidates. The necessity of learning Latin also caused difficulties. Many missionaries are said to have believed that it would be necessary to wait until the second or third generation of African Roman Catholics in order to obtain an adequate number of candidates for the priesthood.

As was noted in chapter 2, the main areas of Roman Catholic missionary efforts in Africa have for the most part been in the colonies belonging to countries in Europe (France, Belgium, Spain and Portugal) where the Roman Catholic Church predominates. With the friendly backing of the governmental administrations in these colonies, Roman Catholic missionaries have had a more favorable situation in which to carry on their activities. The Belgian Congo has been the most important single mission country in Africa. Uganda, Tanganyika and Nigeria are the only areas on the Continent not administered by a Roman Catholic colonial power in which this Church has had an outstanding missionary success.

The three religious communities having the largest number of missionary priests in Africa are the White Fathers, Holy Ghost Fathers, and the Lyons Missionaries (Society of African Missions, S.M.A.). All of these societies were founded by French priests, and most of their missionaries in Africa continue to be sent from France.

The recent increase in the importance of Africa in the post-World War II era was reflected in the encyclical *Donum fidei* issued by Pope Pius XII on April 21, 1957. In it the Pope made a vigorous appeal for support for Roman Catholic missions in all the underdeveloped countries, but particularly those in Africa, as follows:

In the social and political crisis which Africa is undergoing, it is necessary quickly to form a select group of Christians in the midst of a still neophyte people. . . . Colleges must be founded and Christian teachings in various degrees must be propagated. . . . You know, Venerable Brethren, that the number of priests compared to that of the faithful is decreasing in Africa. The African clergy is undoubtedly growing, but it will not be able to take complete charge of the management of its own dioceses for many more years, even with the help of the missionaries who bring the faith there. . . . These conditions of the apostolate . . . clearly show . . . that the problems of Africa are no longer a limited and local matter which can be removed at leisure, little by little. . . . The repercussions of the Catholic situation in Africa go greatly beyond the frontiers of that continent and it is necessary that . . . the fraternal response to so many needs should come from the entire Church. . . .

Some indication of the success (in terms of the number of converts) of the Roman Catholic Church in concentrating on Africa as a missionary territory is seen in the statistics (cited by Abbé Bouffard) shown in Table 118.

TABLE 118. PERCENTAGE INCREASES IN ROMAN CATHOLICS BY AREAS (1883–1956)

	Population	Roman Catholics
Africa	118%	707%
Asia	79%	255%
America*a*	243%	278%
Europe	89%	49%

NOTE: *a* Including North and Latin America.

TABLE 119. NUMBER OF CONVERTS PER PRIEST IN 1956

Ruanda-Urundi	102
Nigeria	94
Kenya	75
Belgian Congo	51
Ghana	47
Cameroons	36
Tanganyika	25
Union of South Africa	19
Madagascar	17

Within Africa, the Fides Service reported that the number of baptisms of adults (i.e., converts) per priest in the year ended June 1956 was as shown in Table 119. By contrast, in Asia the number of converts per priest in the same 12-month period was: Japan, 10; India, 7; and Siam, 3.

Among the approximately 226,000,000 persons in Africa in 1957, about 20,000,-

000 were members of the Roman Catholic Church, or 8%. Among the Roman Catholics, in round figures 16,600,000 reside in areas which are under the authority of the Propaganda, 1,800,000 in areas (Angola, Mozambique and a few other smaller Portuguese colonies) which are under the authority of the Sacred Congregation for Extraordinary Ecclesiastical Affairs, 1,300,000 in areas (Tunis, Algeria, the Azores and Canary Islands) which come under the authority of the Consistorial Congregation, and about 300,000 persons in Egypt and Northeast Africa which come under the Sacred Congregation for the Oriental Church.

Table 120 lists the major Roman Catholic seminaries in Northeast Africa. Within Africa the training of a local clergy has proceeded at varying rates of speed. In Africa north of the Sahara the strength of Islam has been such that the Roman Catholic missionary efforts have encountered difficulties similar to those experienced by the Protestant and Eastern Churches.

TABLE 120.   MAJOR SEMINARIES IN NORTHEAST AFRICA (1957)

Name	Location	Approx. Number of Major Seminary Students	Rite	Administration
Egypt				
Catholic Seminary of St. Leo	Maadi	31	Coptic	Secular
Oriental Seminary of St. Cyril	Ghiza	14	Coptic	Franciscans
Sudan				
Major Seminary[a]	Tore River (Yei)	23	Latin	African Missions of Verona
Ethiopia				
Catholic Seminary	Adigrat	12	Ethiopian	Secular
Eritrea				
Seraphic Seminary of Gaggiret	Asmara	15	Ethiopian	Capuchins
Total: 5		95		

NOTE: [a] Under the Propaganda Congregation.

From this table it will be noted that all of the major seminaries of the Roman Catholic Church in Northeast Africa are fairly small and all but one are under the authority of the Oriental Congregation, rather than under the Propaganda Fide.

In Egypt the only Christian Church of any large size is the Coptic Orthodox Church, whereas the membership of the Greek Orthodox Patriarchate of Alexandria, and of the Evangelical Church in Egypt (Protestant), and the adherents of the Coptic Rite of the Roman Catholic Church in Egypt are all small in number. Of the 227,000 Roman Catholics of all rites in Egypt in 1946, 116,000 (or one-half) were members of the Latin Rite, 63,000 were members of the Coptic Rite, 25,000 were Melkites and the remainder of 23,000 were distributed among the Maronite, Armenian, Syrian and Chaldean Rites.

In 1957 there were only 20 foreign Franciscans plus a handful of other missionary priests of various religious communities stationed in Egypt, together with about

100 native Egyptian Roman Catholic priests serving in 94 parishes. The interest of the Franciscans in Egypt is an outgrowth of the brief missionary activity of St. Francis of Assisi in that country in the year 1219. This Order now maintains a Center of Oriental Studies in Cairo and a score or more of primary and secondary schools in upper Egypt.

Until the last few decades it was comparatively difficult for the Vatican to obtain African priests who would be capable in its opinion of serving effectively as bishops. Thus in 1895 the Coptic Patriarchate of Alexandria for the Roman Catholic Copts was re-established in Egypt, but for lack of suitable candidates the office remained unfilled for several years. In 1899 an Egyptian priest, Amba Cyril II Makarios, was proclaimed Patriarch, but he proved unsatisfactory, and after his removal in 1908 the office again remained vacant until the nomination of Patriarch Mark Khouzam in 1947.

Although the members of the Coptic Rite in Egypt are not numerous, nevertheless it is reported to be the fastest growing of all the seven Roman Catholic Rites in that country. Most of its 2,000 converts each year are reported to come from the Coptic Orthodox Church rather than from Islam.

In 1880 the Jesuits established a seminary in Cairo for the purpose of training priests for the Coptic Rite. Progress was slow, and the institution was closed in 1907. Subsequently major seminarians in this Rite were sent to study for their courses in philosophy and theology at the Interritual Oriental Seminary of St. Francis Xavier maintained by the Jesuits in Beirut, Lebanon.

Meanwhile, in 1899 Pope Leo XIII established the Coptic Catholic Seminary of St. Leo the Great in Tahta, Egypt, also for the purpose of training Coptic Rite priests. Its administration was placed in the hands of the secular clergy. However, for various reasons—especially the lack of suitable teaching and administrative personnel—this Seminary was not very successful. In 1917, owing to the need for Coptic Rite priests, its courses in philosophy and theology were shortened, and the best students were sent either to Beirut or to the Ethiopian College in Rome which was founded by Pope Benedict XV in 1919. In 1927 the minor seminary was detached from the St. Leo Seminary and was transferred to Cairo. After World War II, the major seminary was also transferred and installed in an imposing modern building at Maadi, 20 miles from Cairo, and was reopened by Cardinal Tisserant, the Secretary of the Oriental Congregation, in 1953. This institution can house 130 major and minor seminarians and thus is larger than the Oriental Seminary of St. Cyril which is maintained by the Franciscans at Ghiza for the training of Coptic Rite priests.

Finally mention should be made of the Institute for Oriental Studies which the Dominicans have maintained in Cairo during the past two decades. The purpose of this study center is to gain a better understanding of the various phases of Islam by means of collecting, carefully appraising and editing Muslim theological texts, and through cooperating with the professors at El Azhar University. In this way it is hoped that a more successful Roman Catholic missionary approach to Muslim countries may eventually be evolved.

For a number of reasons mentioned in chapter 15, the pressure of Islam over the centuries has not been as effective in Ethiopia as it has been in Egypt. The history of the early Roman Catholic missions in Ethiopia has been summarized by Father Andrew Rogosh as follows:

The Dominicans had once tried to enter Ethiopia, but with very little success. With the arrival of Portuguese military missions, Portuguese Jesuits entered the country and had considerable influence. In a turmoil of civil wars and revolts, it was no easy task to make the necessary reforms in order to raise the moral level of the population. Negus Susneyos (1607–1632) became Catholic, one of the Jesuit priests was made "patriarch"— a dignity that never existed in Ethiopia. To enforce the reforms, there was need to have the help of the rulers, and the Negus cooperated with the missionaries to the fullest extent. But unfortunately the methods of enforcement were of gross cruelty. The late Cardinal Hinsley writing in the *Dublin Review* of October 1935 described the coercive measures as "inexcusable in the eyes of the Church and before the court of Christian civilization." Adding to this the enforcement of wholly unnecessary alterations in the Ethiopian rite to conform with Roman usages, a violent reaction set in which banished all Catholic priests and ruined the cause of church-union for a long time. When in 1637 a new mission of Capuchins was sent to Ethiopia, its members suffered immediate martyrdom.

As a result of this episode, Ethiopia subsequently remained closed to all Roman Catholic missionary priests for a period of more than 200 years. When the country was reopened to missionaries in the middle of the 19th century, the Capuchins again entered Ethiopia under the leadership of their celebrated missionary, and later Cardinal, William Massaja (who personally baptised 36,000 converts, mostly from Islam). Throughout this period the attempt was made to found a local clergy in this country. As far as possible the Ethiopian liturgy was retained, with insistence being placed only upon the observance of Roman Catholic canon law and dogma. In 1890 Msgr. Crouzet, Apostolic Vicar of Abyssinia, stated that "the development of a trustworthy native clergy is the main point of emphasis of our mission. The salvation of this unhappy land depends on this."

Nevertheless the major seminaries in Ethiopia and Eritrea have been small, with the better students being sent to the Ethiopian College in Rome for their training. In 1930 Pope Pius XI named Msgr. Chidanè-Maryam Cassá as the first indigenous Bishop of the Coptic Rite for Ethiopia and Eritrea. He was, in fact, the first African bishop appointed in modern times.

During World War II the Roman Catholic Church in Ethiopia was badly dis-

rupted as a result of the internment by the Ethiopian Government of all missionaries of Italian origin, a number of whom had entered the country following Musso-
lini's invasion in 1936. After the termination of hostilities, the Emperor realized
that Ethiopia's educational system needed improvement. In 1945 the Canadian
Jesuits were invited to re-enter the country as educators in civilian clothes. As
part of the reconstruction effort, the University College of Addis Ababa was founded
a few years later and the Jesuits assumed direction of it. Thus the experience of this
religious community in Ethiopia demonstrates its vitality and persistence over the
centuries.

Table 121 lists the major seminaries in Northwest Africa (Tunisia, Algeria and
Morocco).

Since Algeria is still considered administratively as a part of metropolitan France,
the Archdiocese of Algiers and the Dioceses of Oran and Constantine are under the
authority of the Consistorial Congregation. Accordingly the three major seminaries
in Algeria come under the authority of the Seminaries Congregation. Although
Tunis is now independent, it was once part of metropolitan France and the Archdiocese of Carthage still remains under the authority of the Consistorial Congregation. On the other hand, French Morocco has been under the authority of the
Propaganda: formerly an apostolic vicariate, in 1955 the Archdiocese of Rabat was
created.

According to Robert Cunningham, "the Catholic clergy of North Africa has been
split until quite recently into two specialized groups. One, known as the 'established church' has been concerned almost exclusively with the European community. The other, known as the 'missionary church' has sought to bring the
warm message of Christian love to the world of Islam. . . ." The outstanding
leader in the missionary church was Cardinal Charles Lavigerie who was once a
professor at the Sorbonne and became Bishop of Algiers in 1867. In 1874 he
founded the White Fathers, a religious society whose activities and success were
commented on in chapter 12. The headquarters of the White Fathers is at the

TABLE 121.   Major Seminaries in Northwest Africa (1956)

Name	Location	Approx. Number of Major Seminary Students	Administration
Tunisia			
Grand Séminaire de Carthage	Mutuelleville	16	Lazarists
Algeria			
St. Eugène	Kouba	28	Lazarists
St. Augustine	Constantine	10	Lazarists
Grand Séminaire	Oran	34	Lazarists
Morocco			
Grand Séminaire	Souissi, Rabat	15	Claretians
Total: 5		103	

Maison Carrée which is located in a suburb of Algiers. It is of interest to note that the White Fathers "are instructed to avoid any official connection with the colonial administration and, in Moslem North Africa, they have not preached the Gospel openly since this would rouse religious fanaticism."

All of the four major seminaries in Tunisia and Algeria are administered by the Lazarists. The interest of this congregation in Northwest Africa arises from the fact that St. Vincent de Paul while still a young priest was captured by Muslim pirates on the Barbary Coast and was sold into slavery there, from which he later escaped back to France. Progress in training a local clergy in Algeria, Tunis and Morocco has been slow in view of the strength of Islam and (in recent years) the unsettled political conditions which have prevailed.

Table 122 lists the major seminaries in East Africa and West Africa, all of which are under the authority of the Propaganda.

In Uganda, political unrest delayed the founding of major seminaries in that area in the 19th century. The White Fathers commenced their educational work here with Latin instruction in 1885. The first regular seminary was organized in 1893, and during the first decade it encountered many difficulties. The first of its graduates to be made a priest was not ordained until 1913. According to Father Johannes

TABLE 122.   Major Seminaries in East Africa and West Africa (1956)

Name	Location	Approx. Number of Major Seminary Students	Administration
East Africa			
Kenya			
St. Joseph	Kakamega	9	Mill Hill Fathers
St. Paul	Nyeri	15	Consolata Fathers
Uganda			
Sacred Heart	Gulu	27	African Missions of Verona
St. Mary	Ggaba, Kampala	30	Mill Hill Fathers
St. Thomas	Katigondo, Masaka	77	White Fathers
Tanganyika			
St. Thomas	Morogoro	24	Holy Ghost Fathers
Our Lady of the Angels	Kibosho, Moshi	35	Holy Ghost Fathers
St. Augustine	Peramiho	32	Benedictines (St. Ottilia)
St. Paul	Kipalapala, Tabora	44	White Fathers
Major Seminary	Tosamaganga, Iringa	8	Consolata Fathers
Subtotal: 10		301	
West Africa			
Nigeria[a]			
St. Peter and St. Paul	Ibadan	46	Lyons Missionaries
Bigard Memorial	Enugu	90	Holy Ghost Fathers
Ghana			
St. Theresa	Amisano, Cape Coast	31	Lyons Missionaries
Major Seminary	Wiaga, Tamale	8	White Fathers
Subtotal: 4		175	
TOTAL: 14		476	

Note: [a] As of 1958.

Beckmann, S.M.B., "in the 20 years of the existence of the minor seminary, 650 seminarians were admitted into it, of whom 94 were permitted to enter the major seminary, of whom 36 finally reached their goal. Three hundred of the candidates belonged to the first period of this seminary (1893–1903), three of whom became priests." These numbers point to the difficulties involved. This seminary is now known as the St. Thomas Seminary, at Katigondo, Masaka.

The Roman Catholic Church has made greater progress in establishing a native clergy in British East Africa than it has in Nigeria or Ghana. This has been true even though East Africa in general came under European influence at a later date than did West Africa. The Roman Catholic missionary accomplishments in East Africa in large part have been due to the successes achieved there by the White Fathers. This religious community administers both of the two largest seminaries in these areas—St. Thomas, as noted above, and St. Paul's at Kipalapala, Tabora in Tanganyika. Father Bouniol, a member of this institute, wrote in 1929 that "at Rome, someone remarked to the Bishop of Uganda that of all the undertakings in his mission, the work of the native seminary was the most sublime. 'I do not know,' replied the Bishop, 'if it is the highest; of that God alone is the Judge. But I do know that it has involved harder work and more continual sacrifices than any other undertaking, and that, as we look forward into the future, it causes us by far the most anxiety'."

As a result of the growth in the number of local priests in British East Africa, Pope Pius XII in 1939 consecrated the first indigenous Bishop of Uganda, Msgr. Joseph Kiwanuka, who was assigned to administer a new vicariate at Masaka. Subsequently he was elevated to the rank of Archbishop, and it has been speculated in the press that he would be one of a number of African prelates who might logically be considered for the honor of becoming the first Negro Cardinal. In 1949–50 he made a five-month tour of the United States seeking funds for the construction of a seminary in his diocese.

In May 1958 the Fides Service announced that a new regional seminary would soon be completed in Nairobi in Kenya. It will train priests for seven dioceses and its cost was estimated at $700,000. Of this sum, $600,000 was contributed by the Society for St. Peter the Apostle.

In Nigeria, the Holy Ghost Fathers have been active, and one of them (Rev. J. Whelan) commented in 1945 on the difficulties these missionaries have faced: "The Mission of Southern Nigeria . . . had the unenviable reputation of being the most hopeless of missions, a place where men of self-sacrifice might toil in vain. . . . Although the mission was founded in 1885, yet in 1944 after 59 years of incessant work there were only four native priests. . . ." During the next 14 years (i.e., by 1958) the number of local priests in this circumscription was 17. However, the number of major seminarians studying at the Holy Ghost Fathers'

Bigard Memorial Seminary at Enugu in Eastern Nigeria had risen to 90. This Seminary is named after the founder, Stephanie Bigard, of the Society of St. Peter the Apostle for Native Clergy. It was opened in 1951 and offers a seven-year course. The first three are spent in philosophy and the last four in theology. In between these courses the students interrupt their studies and spend a year gaining practical experience in the field, living with an experienced missionary and doing catechetical work, etc.

In 1957 the Lyons Missionaries moved the St. Peter and St. Paul Seminary from Benin City (in the eastern portion of Western Nigeria) to Ibadan, the largest city and the capital of this region. According to a release (July 12, 1958) of the International Fides Service, "the seminary occupies a commanding position on the side of a valley opposite the wide-flung buildings of the Regional Government Headquarters. Its main entrance opens to a passage that runs through a newly planted grove of citrus trees. The buildings that will eventually make up the seminary are far from complete. At the present moment only two buildings are in existence: one a residential block for students and the other a staff building. . . . It is expected that the number of students will increase quite rapidly and with that increase it will be imperative to provide a suitable chapel, a library, lecture rooms, recreation rooms, a dining room, and additional students' rooms. Today the students' building and the staff building are partitioned to meet these requirements. (There is) a decided increase in enrollment in (the) minor seminaries in Nigeria. . . ."

In 1957 it was reported that of the 265 Roman Catholic priests in Ghana, only 39 were native Africans. The major seminaries listed in Ghana in Table 122 were as of June 30, 1956. In January 1958 the Fides Service reported that a National Seminary of St. Peter had recently been founded in Ghana with a capacity of 48 students, and that plans were being made to enlarge it.

Table 123 lists the major seminaries in French Colonial Africa, all of which are under the authority of the Propaganda.

The long "lead time" needed to establish a major seminary during the 19th century in Africa south of the Sahara is perhaps best illustrated by the history of the founding of a number of these institutions located in the French colonies.

One of the leaders in the effort to create a local clergy was the Venerable Francis Mary Paul Libermann (1802–52), a cofounder of the Holy Ghost Fathers. As early as 1844 he wrote to the Vicar Apostolic of the Two Guineas: "I believe it is absolutely necessary for us to obtain an indigenous clergy. Once there are several Negro priests, this will lead to others and their number will augment." Accordingly, in the provisional rule for his Society, an entire chapter is devoted to the necessity of forming a local clergy in Africa. The Venerable Libermann did not wish his own congregation to commission other societies and Orders with the administration of

Table 123. Major Seminaries in French Colonial Africa (1956)

Name	Location	Approx. Number of Major Seminary Students	Administration
Senegal			
Libermann	Sebikhotane, Dakar	12	Holy Ghost Fathers
Upper Volta			
St. Peter Claver Regional	Koumi, Bobo Dioulasso	25	White Fathers
Dahomey			
St. Gall Regional	Ouidah	65	Sulpicians
Cameroons[a]			
St. Lawrence	Otélé	64	Benedictines
French Congo			
Libermann	Brazzaville	25	Holy Ghost Fathers
Madagascar			
St. Peter's Regional	Ambatoroka, Tananarive	47	Jesuits
Réunion Island			
Major Seminary[b]	St. Denis	7	Holy Ghost Fathers
Total: 7		245	

Notes: [a] As of 1958.
[b] As of 1950.

seminaries located in missionary territories assigned to the Holy Ghost Fathers. He once wrote to the Cardinal Prefect of the Propaganda: "If the Negro priests are formed by us, our missionaries will have an influence over them which is absolutely necessary for they will need to be supported. If, on the contrary, they are formed by others than ourselves, instead of having confidence in our missionaries, they will rather be inclined to be jealous and this will place a major obstacle in the good which they would wish to do."

Although Father Libermann never personally visited Africa, it is evident from the long memorandum he sent in 1846 to the Propaganda Congregation that he had an acute and accurate insight into African mentality and the future missionary needs of the Roman Catholic Church.

In Senegal the Holy Ghost Fathers established what was initially a minor seminary at Dakar in 1847. However, it was not until 1864 that the first of the graduates from the Dakar seminary was ordained. By 1924, 77 years after its establishment, the seminary could still point to only 11 priests among its graduates. The principal difficulties which were encountered then were the Church's insistence on celibacy, the indolent character of some of the students, the opposition of many of their parents, and the fact that they could earn a higher income outside of the Church. In subsequent years the output of priests at the Dakar seminary increased; however, at its centennial anniversary in 1957 it was reported that less than 40 of its graduates during this 100-year period had been ordained.

The opening of the University of Dakar in September 1957 will undoubtedly serve in the long run to raise the intellectual level of the residents of all French West Africa. By May 1958, the end of its first academic year, some 1,000 students were enrolled in this institution. This is in sharp contrast to the enrollment of only 12 major seminary students in the Dakar (Libermann) seminary which is now located in the village of Sebikhotane, two kilometers outside of Dakar.

In 1939 a Senegalese, Msgr. Joseph Faye, was named Apostolic Prefect in Senegal by Pope Pius XII. In 1947 he resigned from this office in order to become a Trappist monk at Aiguebelle in France.

In the French Congo the Apostolic Vicar from 1886 to 1904 was Msgr. Carrie who wrote in a letter: "Two native priests are worth more than the conversion of 40,000 heathen." In 1886 he had 11 students in his newly organized seminary in that area, and in 1892 the first two local priests were ordained. In a letter to his bishop, Msgr. Carrie wrote: "These are the costly fruit of 15 years of work and patience."

In Gabon (a district in the French Congo) instruction in Latin was undertaken in 1857 with two native youths, and in 1861 a regular seminary was established. Nevertheless, as a result of the many difficulties encountered, it was not until 1899—after 42 years of effort—that a graduate from this seminary was ordained.

The Regional Seminary of St. Gall, located at Ouidah in Dahomey, was founded in 1930 and is named after the Roman Catholic diocese in Switzerland which contributed the funds for the construction of its large concrete building. Originally the Lyons Missionaries administered the Seminary, but in 1955, the Sulpicians took over this task. It now trains students from Dahomey, the Ivory Coast and Togo.

The St. Lawrence Seminary at Otélé in the Cameroons has been staffed since 1932 by Swiss monks from the Benedictine Abbey of Engelberg in Switzerland. Founded by the Holy Ghost Fathers in 1927, this institution serves as the major seminary of the Archdiocese of Yaoundé, the capital of the Cameroons. Up until 1958 its students were trained in two sections, one at Yaoundé and the other at Otélé which is 60 miles' distance away. In the latter year the two sections were united at Otélé where the Benedictines have a monastery.

In the French Congo, the Holy Ghost Fathers administer another seminary named after their founder, the Venerable Libermann. In earlier years the members of this religious community opened a special school in this area which was reserved exclusively for the sons of kings, princes, and the higher-ranking tribal chiefs.

The Jesuit Seminary of St. Peter in Ambatoroka, near Tananarive, the capital of Madagascar, was visited in the fall of 1956 by three leading Protestant missionaries who were making a survey of the Protestant theological schools on the Island on behalf of the International Missionary Council. Their report comments on the over-all superiority of St. Peter's Seminary to any of the seven small Protestant theological schools on the Island. The grounds of St. Peter's were said to be extensive, surrounding an impressive building kept in excellent repair. The Seminary had 11 full-time professors plus a number of other instructors, all Jesuits.

There were about 58 students enrolled. They had been drawn from all over Madagascar and were recruited principally from the minor seminaries. As the one main Roman Catholic center on the island for the education of candidates for the priesthood, St. Peter's was offering a more thorough training than that provided by the Protestant schools for their ordinands. A selected number of the students at St. Peter's were being trained for membership in the Society of Jesus. While the curriculum seemed to the visitors to be somewhat narrow by Protestant standards, nevertheless its students were required to undergo a "formidable" discipline. They

follow a time-table which covers in minute detail every moment of the day. Teaching is carried on almost exclusively in Latin and French. . . . Moreover, Biblical study also entails learning Greek and Hebrew. . . . The intellectual, moral and spiritual discipline of the students is set down in a detailed code of rules covering every aspect of their daily existence. . . . Even if their outlook on theological education differs from ours, and practical problems do not occur in the same form (e.g., the celibacy of the Roman priesthood does away with the problem of housing and supporting students' families), it must be admitted that the Roman Catholic Grand Séminaire, with its excellent teaching staff, is a centre of theological study which is doing very sound work.

In 1875 there was only one Malagasy Roman Catholic priest in Madagascar. By 1925 there were still only five. However, by 1950 the number had reached 150. In 1939 a Malagasy, Msgr. Ramarosandratana, was named Apostolic Prefect of the newly created district of Miarinarivo.

Although Réunion Island is situated in the Indian Ocean some 500 miles east of Madagascar, its inhabitants are partly of African descent, and this colony is considered to be related to that Continent. The major seminary at Réunion's capital, St. Denis, was opened in November 1947 by the Holy Ghost Fathers to provide the last two years in the course in theology for local seminarians. A number of other major seminary students from Réunion continue to be sent to the Colonial Major Seminary in Paris for their training.

Table 124 lists the major seminaries and scholasticates training students in the Belgian Congo and Ruanda-Urundi.

In the Belgian Congo, the Jesuits began their work in 1893. They established a minor seminary there in 1896. However, the death in 1899 of the founder of the seminary and the devastating effect of sleeping sickness in the area destroyed the initial work and hindered an early renewal of it. Finally in 1922 a new minor seminary was opened in Limfu. The historian of the mission reported on the difficulties involved as follows: "The first years were hard. Inexperience, experimentation, and lack of discipline organizationally resulted in the depopulation of the student body. Despite everything the first three priests from this school were ordained in 1937 with 12 more being ordained in the next three years."

At another seminary in the upper Belgian Congo, 13 students were selected in

1898 for training for the priesthood, and only one completed the course. In the following years the same process was continued. Of about 200 students who commenced such studies, only ten completed them. The difficulties encountered were often discouraging in the extreme. As Msgr. V. Roelens noted at the first conference of the bishops of the Belgian Congo held in Leopoldville in 1932: "Formerly the blacks of these areas were themselves convinced that it would be impossible for them to become priests or to lead a priestly life."

TABLE 124.   MAJOR SEMINARIES AND SCHOLASTICATES IN THE BELGIAN CONGO AND RUANDA-URUNDI (1956)

Name	Location	Approx. Number of Major Seminary Students	Administration
Belgian Congo			
St. Thomas Aquinas	Baudoinville	123	White Fathers
St. Robert Beliarmine	Mayidi, Kisantu	76	Jesuits
St. Peter Canisius	Kimwenza	12[a]	Jesuits
Christ the King	Kabwe, Luluabourg	71	Scheut Fathers
St. Albert the Great	Niangara	67	Dominicans
Ruanda-Urundi			
Major Seminary	Burasira, Ngozi	68	White Fathers
Major Seminary	Nyakibanda, Kabgayi	69	White Fathers
Total: 7		486	

NOTE: [a] Scholastics.

Father Van Hemelryck, C.I.C.M., has commented on the problems faced by the members of his congregation, the Scheut Fathers, in administering the major seminary which they founded in 1928 at Kabwe near Luluabourg in the Belgian Congo. This seminary receives graduates from the minor seminary at Kasai: at the latter institution, of the first 60 or 70 boys who were admitted, only six or seven were graduated. At Kabwe, approximately half of the students admitted each year eventually graduate. In answer to a question concerning the intelligence of the students, Father Van Hemelryck writes: "As a general rule we don't meet among them the sharp and subtle minds that we find among the best students of Europe and the United States, but they assimilate in a satisfactory way the knowledge necessary to make good priests. . . . The main difficulty is to complete their general knowledge. They were reared in the primitive villages of the Congo bush. . . ."

It would appear that a significant improvement in this situation occurred during the pontificate of Pius XI, and largely as a result of his efforts. At the Fordham University Conference of mission specialists in 1954, Professor Jean Comhaire of Seton Hall University commented as follows on the difficulty of persuading missionaries in the field concerning the importance of training a local clergy: "Because of its outstanding success, Belgian missionary policy is worth special mention. . . . If there are today 350 Congolese priests in Belgian Africa, it is because in 1930, when there were only a handful of them, and no large-scale increase was contemplated, an Apostolic Delegate was appointed, who insisted that the Holy Father wanted a native clergy at all costs, even if this entailed grave risks. The experiment was conducted by the Belgian missionaries with perfect loyalty but also with great misgivings. Their triumph today is a tribute to their faith rather than to their judgment."

Professor Freitag points out that in 1923 there were only three local priests in the upper Congo and five in Ruanda, whereas in 1949 the total for the area amounted to 264. Father Beckmann states that in 1926 the White Fathers had 52 local priests in their missions in the Belgian Congo. By 1942 the number had grown to 235. According to the Fides Service, the number of Roman Catholic priests in the Belgian Congo and Ruanda-Urundi as of July 1, 1956, totaled 2,486, of whom 466 were Africans. While this proportion of local priests is less than 15% of the total, nevertheless the fact that there are now as many as approximately 500 local priests serving in this area represents an important achievement. On the other hand, of the 26 Roman Catholic bishops in the Congo in 1957, only one was a Negro (with a second Negro bishop serving in Ruanda).

The bulk of the Roman Catholic missionary priests sent out from Belgium serve in the Congo and are members of the Jesuit and Scheut Fathers. As was previously noted in chapter 2, in 1954 there were a total of about 4,800 European priests, brothers and sisters in the Belgian Congo, or four times the number of Protestant missionaries stationed in that colony. This policy of concentrating missionary forces in a promising area has achieved considerable success in terms of the mass movements to the Roman Catholic Church which have been generated and the number of Roman Catholic converts obtained. For example, the number of baptized Catholics in the Belgian Congo and Ruanda-Urundi is reported to have increased by 400,-000 in the year 1956 alone.

Lovanium University was founded in Kimwenza, eight miles south of Leopoldville in 1925. At first most of its courses were in the medical field. It is affiliated with the University of Louvain in Belgium and now offers courses in a fairly wide range of technical subjects. At the end of 1957 (in which year it became a full-fledged university) 249 students (two-thirds Africans and one-third Europeans) were enrolled in courses taught by 56 full-time professors and lecturers. Among the students only seven were reading in theology. The University also lists a Higher Institute of Religious Sciences in its catalogue.

Ruanda-Urundi is stated to have the highest density of population (184 persons per square mile) of any area in Africa. The White Fathers have been active there for about 50 years. In the period 1920–53 about 45% of the 4,000,000 population of Ruanda-Urundi became Christians, and almost all of them Roman Catholics. One of the missionary principles followed was devoting special attention at an early age to the sons of chiefs who would later be the future chiefs according to the customs of the tribes. Thus, against the wishes of his father, Matara II Charles Leon Pierre Rudahigwa became a catechumen in 1930 at the age of 19. He succeeded his father as Mwami, or King, in 1931 and was baptised a Roman Catholic in 1943. Three years later, on October 26, 1946, he is reported to have "solemnly consecrated his kingdom and its 2,000,000 inhabitants to 'Christ the King' and the Roman Catholic faith." According to Michael Williams "in Urundi, Catholics constitute 49% of the total population, and here the Pope has been forced to ask the missionaries to slow up baptisms in order not to repeat the dilemma of the priestless areas in Latin America and the Philippines."

Table 125 presents a list of the major seminaries in the Spanish and Portuguese colonies in Africa.

Although the Azores and the Madeira Islands are Portuguese colonies situated in the Atlantic Ocean (the latter off the northwest coast of Africa) their ecclesiastical affairs are administered directly by the Patriarch of Lisbon. There are 316,000 Roman Catholic inhabitants in the Azores and 247,000 in Madeira: this explains the fact that there are over 100 major seminary students being trained in the two major seminaries located in these colonies.

TABLE 125. MAJOR SEMINARIES IN SPANISH AND PORTUGUESE COLONIES IN AFRICA (1956)

Name	Location	Approx. Number of Major Seminary Students	Administration
Azores (Portuguese)[a]			
Episcopal Seminary	Angra do Heroismo, Terceira	70	Secular
Madeira (Portuguese)[a]			
Our Lady of the Incarnation	Funchal	34	Secular
Canary Islands (Spanish)[b]			
Immaculate Conception	Las Palmas, Gran Canaria	46	Secular
Conciliar Seminary	La Laguna, Tenerife	40	Secular
Spanish Guinea			
Our Lady of the Pillar	San Fernando Po	3	Claretians
Angola (Portuguese)			
Archdiocesan Seminary	Luanda	22	Holy Ghost Fathers
Christ the King	Nova Lisboa	84	Holy Ghost Fathers
Mozambique (Portuguese)			
Christ the King	Lourenço Marques	13	Congregation of the Most
Total: 8		312	Holy Sacrament

NOTES: [a] Under the authority of the Patriarchate of Lisbon.
[b] Under the authority of Diocese of Seville.

Similarly, in the Canary Islands, which are a Spanish colony situated just off the coast of Spanish Morocco (Rio de Oro) in Africa, there are 700,000 Roman Catholic inhabitants who come under the authority of the Diocese of Seville. There are two major seminaries in the Canary Islands having a total of 86 students. In addition, a few other seminarians are sent for their training to the University of Salamanca in Spain and to Rome.

The Claretians operate a small major seminary in San Fernando Po, the capital of

Spanish Guinea. This religious community administered virtually all of the secular educational institutions in this colony without receiving a governmental subsidy therefor until the end of 1930.

In Portuguese Angola, the Holy Ghost Fathers took over a diocesan seminary which had already been in existence in Luanda. The first priest to be graduated from this seminary was consecrated in 1895, followed by only four more in the period up to 1907 although, according to Father Beckmann, "the seminary from time to time counted up to 100 candidates enrolled in the minor and major seminary there." Luanda is today the political and ecclesiastical capital of Angola, but the Arch-diocesan Seminary is smaller than it was formerly. At one point, Nova Lisboa was intended to be the capital, and the major seminary there is considerably larger than the one at Luanda.

The Portuguese colony of Mozambique on the southeast coast of Africa has one small major seminary. It also has a resident Portuguese Cardinal, Teodosio C. de Gouveia, serving as Archbishop of Lourenço Marques, the capital. The number of Roman Catholics has increased from 40,000 in 1927 to approximately 300,000 in 1952.

Table 126 lists the seminaries and scholasticates in Southern Africa.

For more than 150 years after the original European settlement in South Africa, the Dutch government authorities (who were Calvinists) forbade any immigration by Roman Catholics and officially prohibited public demonstrations of the Roman Catholic religion in the colony. Full religious tolerance was not granted until 1804 at which time three priests came from Holland to commence missionary work. For this reason the number of men being trained for the priesthood in Southern Africa has been comparatively small. Another factor has been the concentration of Roman Catholic missionary forces in other areas of Africa. During World War II it was difficult to send missionaries from Europe to Africa, and in some instances the supply of candidates for admission to seminaries in Southern Africa dwindled.

Basutoland is not a part of the Union of South Africa, and there are a number of restrictions against the immigration and property rights available for white settlers in this British protectorate. As a result, the white population is small in number and the racial discrimination laws prevailing in the Union do not apply in Basutoland. In 1924 the Oblates of Mary Immaculate established a seminary at Roma near Maseru in Basutoland. In its first 25 years (1924–49), the Seminary graduated 24 priests, of whom 21 were Africans. St. Augustine's serves both as a major seminary and as a scholasticate for the Oblates. Also located in Roma is the Pius XII University College for Negro students which was founded in 1945 and whose faculty is staffed largely with Oblates drawn from the Catholic University of Ottawa in Canada. In 1956 the University had a faculty of 21, and 60 students. In addition there

Table 126.   Major Seminaries and Scholasticates in Southern Africa (1956)

Name	Location	Approx. Number of Major Seminary Students	Administration
Cape Province			
St. Nicholas Priory	Stellenbosch	3[a]	Dominicans
Basutoland			
St. Augustine	Roma	31[b]	Oblates of Mary Immaculate
Natal			
St. Peter's Regional	Pevensey, Mariannhill	15	Mariannhill Fathers
St. Joseph's Scholasticate	Cedara	29	Oblates of Mary Immaculate
Transvaal			
National Seminary of St. John Vianney	Waterkloof, Pretoria	29[c]	Franciscans
Southern Rhodesia			
Sts. John Fisher and Thomas More	Salisbury	29	Jesuits
Nyasaland			
St. Anthony	Kachebere, Zikuni	54	White Fathers
Total: 7		190	

Notes: [a] As of 1949.
[b] Including 19 Oblate Scholastics.
[c] Trains only white students.

are Roman Catholic high schools for boys and girls and a number of other educational institutions operated in this protectorate under Church auspices, thus making it a center of Roman Catholic influence in Southern Africa.

In Natal (which is part of the Union) a group of Trappist Monks arrived in 1882 from Austria and Hungary. They purchased a valley which was some seven miles long located 15 miles outside of the city of Durban. There they founded an abbey which they called Mariannhill. Their aim was to combine the Trappist monastic life with missionary activities in a remote, primitive land. The region is occupied by the Zulu people, and at first it was difficult to make missionary progress among them. In 1909, the monks were authorized to dissolve their connection with the Trappist Order, and in 1914 they founded their own community, the Religious Missionaries of Mariannhill. In 1925 they established a major seminary, St. Peter's, at Pevensey (Donnybrook). In 1951 this institution was elevated into a regional seminary, the first in Africa. The number of students enrolled at St. Peter's continues, however, to be small: only ten of its graduates were ordained during the years 1951–57, an average of less than two a year.

According to the Fides Service (July 12, 1958),

St. Peter's Regional Seminary . . . serves an area in which 7 African and 2 European languages are used. In the industrial areas, up to 35 African languages from neighbouring territories may be encountered by a priest in his pastoral work. "It is clear, therefore," writes the Rector, Very Rev. Fr. Oswin Magrath, O.P., in a newsletter, "that the seminary should prepare its students accordingly." Among the 21 students present, there are 10 whose home language is Zulu, 3 speaking Xhosa, 2 Iswana, one Pedi, one Ronga, 3 southern Sotha and one Afrikaans. The only South African languages unrepresented are Venda and English. "In stocking the library, special attention is given to grammars, dictionaries and literature in these languages," the newsletter says. . . . Fr. Finbar Synnott, O.P., holds regular academies of languages at which some particular range of terminology for theology, philosophy, or religion is discussed. It is planned to produce multilingual word-lists of Catholic terms for criticism by more expert linguists. Classes are given in elementary Afrikaans for some of those who do not know it. English is in daily use. In these and other ways it is hoped to develop a workable and profitable multilingualism among the students.

The Oblates of Mary Immaculate established St. Joseph's Scholasticate in Prestbury in 1943. It was moved to Cleland in 1947 and to Cedara in 1952. The latter two localities are near the city of Pietermaritzburg which is 40 miles northwest of Durban. In addition to the African scholastics studying at St. Joseph's, a number of Oblates from this community's Australian province are also being trained at Cedara.

In the Transvaal, the seminary at Pretoria was formerly located in Queenstown where it was opened in 1948 under the administration of the Franciscans (of the Irish province). In 1950, the foundation stone for the new National Seminary of St. John Vianney for the Transvaal was laid, and it was estimated that the cost of the new building would amount to £100,000. This institution trains only white students, and in 1956 there were 29 seminarians enrolled in its philosophy and theology courses.

The seminary of Saints John Fisher and Thomas More at Salisbury is sometimes known as the Chishawasha Seminary. It is administered by English Jesuits.

In South Africa there were only four local priests in 1923. However, by 1948 this number had risen to 103.

At the Conference of Mission Specialists held at Fordham University in 1954, the following summary was presented concerning the points of superiority and inferiority of African priests as contrasted with white priests:

Superior Abilities
1. Better knowledge of local languages, customs and mentality.
2. More acceptable to natives.

Inferior Abilities
1. Lack of sufficient general educational background.
2.   "   " initiative and sense of responsibility.
3.   "   " energy and love of work.
4.   "   " practical skills and interest in manual work.
5.   "   " organizational capacity, particularly regarding finance.
6.   "   " profound religious convictions unless well trained.
7.   "   " sufficient contact with own people.
8. Tendency toward a narrow nationalistic outlook.

Throughout Africa, Roman Catholic seminaries in earlier decades experienced a shortage of suitable textbooks. In Uganda a number of texts were created by compiling the notes used by previous professors at the seminaries there. Professor Dr. Franz S. Schäppi, O.F.M.Cap., notes that at present there is a lack of suitable reference books which are adapted to the level of education and mental ability of the Negro seminarians. Even a simple volume which was published in Hongkong for Chinese seminarians proved to be too difficult and insufficiently clear to the African students. Another difficult point is the choice of Latin classics which are to be placed in the hands of the Negro seminarians for study.

A problem related to the religious communities' activities in missionary work in Africa has been the admission of Negroes as full members of their congregations or societies. With the decline in colonialism, the institutes have become increasingly multinational in their composition, particularly in the Belgian Congo.

According to Father Beckmann, up to 20 years ago Negro priests were trained in the seminary maintained in their own missionary district. Then with increasing frequency some of the seminaries were consolidated into central or regional seminaries, or new seminaries were founded to serve a group of mission districts. In one instance four bishops of the White Fathers joined together in order to found a single seminary for their four districts in central Africa to replace the small individual vicariate seminaries previously in existence.

According to the Fides Service, the 33 major seminaries administered by the Propaganda Congregation in Africa had a total of 1,353 students enrolled in them in June 1956. In addition, the Propaganda reported 72 additional students at the major seminary level enrolled in institutions outside of Africa. In the Propaganda's areas of Africa there were 95 priests ordained during the academic year 1955–56: this number constituted about one-third of the number of students who commenced their major seminary training at the same time as did these priests. Thus at the present time an average of two out of every three major seminarians in Africa still fail to reach their ultimate goal of becoming ordained priests.

Table 127 indicates the increase which has occurred in the number of the local

TABLE 127. LOCAL ROMAN CATHOLIC
CLERGY IN AFRICA (1913–57)[a]

Year	Number of Priests	Number of Bishops
1913	25	
1933	281	
1948	958	1
1951	1,254	3
1957	1,690	20

NOTE: [a] In areas under the authority of the Propaganda Congregation.

Roman Catholic clergy in the areas in Africa that are under the jurisdiction of the Propaganda.

Of the 20 indigenous Roman Catholic bishops of the Latin rite serving in Africa in July 1957, 12 were consecrated in the period 1955–57. Half of these 20 bishops were serving in an auxiliary capacity. As Table 128 indicates, the 20 prelates were evenly distributed among 15 different countries and colonies.

TABLE 128.   DISTRIBUTION OF NEGRO BISHOPS IN AFRICA (1957)[a]

East and West Africa (10)	Latin Africa (7)	Southern Africa (3)
Sudan	Upper Volta	Union of South Africa
Kenya	Dahomey	Basutoland
Uganda	Cameroons (2)	Nyasaland
Tanganyika (2)	Belgian Congo	
Nigeria (3)	Ruanda	
Ghana (2)	Madagascar	

NOTE: [a] In areas under the authority of the Propaganda Congregation.

It appears that the majority of the recently appointed African bishops were selected in accordance with a fairly standardized procedure. Usually a Negro priest first attracts attention as a result of his record while enrolled in the local major seminary in his diocese or region. After graduation, such a priest spends a year or more in active work in his home area where his activities are under observation. If he achieves success in the field, he is sent to Rome for advanced studies at the Propaganda's Urban College or at the Gregorian University. He may spend one year or so in Rome at the end of which he obtains a licentiate in theology, or three or four years at the end of which he obtains a doctorate in canon law or theology, often the former. One of the by-products of his years in Rome is that he is enabled to take courses with students from many other countries throughout the world and thereby gains a cosmopolitan viewpoint which it would be difficult for him to obtain at a Roman Catholic university in Africa. Also, during these years his abilities are observed by the Vatican authorities. Then the priest returns to Africa and serves for one or more years in his home area. Those few who obtained their doctorates in Rome and subsequently passed the final scrutiny of their own diocesan authorities are then raised to episcopal rank and appointed as auxiliary bishops. In one or two instances Negro bishops in Africa have been appointed to posts where they supervise the activities of white bishops.

According to Professor Freitag, the Roman Catholic Church by 1948 had achieved "a complete break-through and victory" in the formation of a local clergy. Yet it is of interest to note that *since* 1948 the number of local priests has risen by about 70%, a very creditable achievement. Furthermore it is reported that up to 200 African priests are now being ordained annually. Despite this, owing to the large number of converts obtained each year in some areas in Central Africa, the Roman

Catholic Church has experienced difficulties in maintaining a satisfactory ratio between ordained priests and the laity.

D. MIDDLE EAST

Table 129 lists the major seminaries and scholasticates in the Middle Eastern countries.

In the Middle East the Franciscans were entrusted by the Vatican as far back as 1333 to represent the Roman Catholic Church in the custody of the Holy Sepulchre in Jerusalem. Later this Order was given additional responsibilities in the Holy Land. When Ignatius Loyola visited this area prior to founding the Society of Jesus in 1540, he was advised by the Franciscans not to undertake missionary work in the Holy Land inasmuch as all the Christian Churches in the area were operating only on the sufferance of the Muslim authorities.

For many years prior to World War I the Jesuits undertook a number of missions among the Armenians, and the Dominicans have been active in Persia.

From Table 129 it will be noted that with but one exception the student enrollment at these seminaries is comparatively small. The reason for this has been the policy in the past of enabling the clergy of each of the various Eastern Rites to maintain seminaries and scholasticates of their own. Because of the delicate

TABLE 129.   MAJOR SEMINARIES AND SCHOLASTICATES IN THE MIDDLE EAST (1957)

Name	Location	Approx. Number of Major Seminary Students	Rite	Administration
Lebanon				
Oriental Seminary of St. Francis Xavier (University of St. Joseph)	Beirut	50	Interritual	Jesuits
Maronite Patriarchal Seminary	Mar-Abda	26	Maronite	Secular
Seminary of St. Anthony	Karmsadde, Tripoli	14	Maronite	Baladites (Antonian)
Scholasticate of the Antonian Order of Aleppo	Beirut	10?	Maronite	Aleppines (Antonian)
Scholasticate of the Missionaries of St. Paul	Harissa	10	Melkite	Missionaries of St. Paul
Scholasticate of the Basilian Order of Shuwayr	Khonchara	10?	Melkite	Shuwairites (Basilian)
Scholasticate of the Basilian Order of the Saviour	Saida	3	Melkite	Salvatorians (Basilian)
Syrian Patriarchal Seminary in Sharfeh	Daroun-Harissa	14	Syrian	Secular
Carmelite Mission Seminary	Tripoli	10?	?	Carmelites
Jordan				
Seminary of St. Anne	Jerusalem	14	Melkite	White Fathers
Theologate (Scholasticate)	Jerusalem	15?	Latin?	Franciscans
Latin Patriarchal Seminary	Beit-Jala, Bethlehem	15	Latin	Picpus Fathers
Iraq				
Syrian Seminary of St. John	Mosul	21	Syrian	Dominicans
St. Peter's Patriarchal Seminary	Mosul	13	Chaldean	Secular
Total: 14		225		

problems involved, it would appear that the Oriental Congregation is not in as strong a position to encourage the consolidation of seminaries as is the Propaganda with respect to seminaries in missionary areas. Furthermore the strength of Islam in the Middle East, as well as the activities of the various Eastern Churches, have a bearing on the scope of Roman Catholic activities. Finally, in the Maronite Rite, for example, there is currently a shortage of priests available for service in rural areas. In order to remedy this situation, Msgr. Etteldorf (an official in the Oriental Congregation) has noted that married men from the villages who are of a suitable age and have sufficient ability and piety are requested to volunteer for the priesthood. They are ordained after a course of studies in a special seminary. "This practice is regarded as a temporary but necessary measure."

The largest of the major seminaries in the Middle East is the Oriental Seminary of St. Francis Xavier which is part of the University of St. Joseph in Beirut. It was founded in 1846 in Ghazir (Lebanon) and was transferred in 1875 to Beirut in order that it might be more centrally located. In 1881 Pope Leo XIII elevated it to the rank of a faculty of philosophy and theology of a Papal university. This faculty and the Oriental Seminary of St. Francis Xavier were for administrative purposes subsequently separated, with the former granting advanced degrees and the latter training priests. Both are part of St. Joseph's University which in 1958 had a total enrollment of 1,556 students from all parts of the Middle East.

During World War I St. Joseph's was closed and its buildings were damaged. Subsequently it was reopened, and the St. Francis Xavier Seminary has since become the leading Roman Catholic interritual institution training Roman Catholic priests in the Middle East. During World War II some Jesuit and Lazarist scholastics were trained here, as well as a group of 18 Polish seminarians who pursued their theological studies in this institution from 1942 to 1946. Administered by the Jesuits, this Seminary is said to provide a thorough training for its students. It has a library of 8,000 volumes, and is separate from the Oriental Library at St. Joseph's which has a collection of 30,000 volumes and 2,000 manuscripts.

While the instruction at St. Francis Xavier is carried on in Latin, the celebration of the sacraments according to the Latin rite is not required and seldom is practiced. Each Eastern rite maintains its own "college" at the Seminary. However, according to Father Beckmann, one important factor accounting for its success is that the major seminarians of different rites are brought together at this institution where they may pursue their studies in common. This helps to overcome the differences which separate the peoples of the small nations in the Middle East who, as he points out, often place an exaggerated emphasis on their own chauvinist aspirations. The majority of the students at St. Francis Xavier are Maronites, with the next largest group being Melkites. At this Seminary "Maronites and Chaldeans, Syrians, Copts, Greeks and Armenians come to know one another and . . . overcome their nationalistic prejudices to the greater advantage of their future pastoral and cooperative activities." Father Arens points out that in the period 1919–42 the graduates of this Seminary included three patriarchs, seven archbishops and 290 secular and religious priests.

The second outstanding Roman Catholic institution in the Middle East is the Seminary of St. Anne in Jerusalem. In the year 1878 the ownership of the sanctuary of St. Anne in Jerusalem was transferred by the Turkish to the French Government, and the latter placed the sanctuary under the supervision of the White Fathers. In 1881 the Greek-Melkite Patriarch suggested that the White Fathers might engage in educational work. The French Government approved the plan for establishing a seminary there and made a substantial grant toward the building costs involved. In 1882 an apostolic school was opened with an enrollment of 16 students of the Melkite Rite. In 1886 the major seminary was opened, and the first priest among its graduates was consecrated in 1890. Cardinal Lavigerie, the head of the White Fathers, was largely responsible for the establishment of this institution and took a particular interest in it, even though most of the activities of this congregation have always been concentrated in Africa. He told the White Fathers administering St. Anne: "The Latinizing of Orientals is one of the deplorable errors of Latin missionaries working in the Orient. . . . By contrast you must apply yourself to becoming, as far as possible, Orientals in the Orient. . . ." From the start, the St. Anne Seminary is said to have exhibited an essentially Oriental character, with only the Melkite Rite being celebrated by it. Cardinal Lavigerie also insisted that the Seminary should be open to aspirants for membership in all the Melkite Orders—Basilian Shuwairites and Salvatorians, etc. On the other hand, none of the Eastern rites, except the Melkites, send their students to St. Anne since the White Fathers have felt that interritual institutions present administrative difficulties. Among the graduates of St. Anne during the years 1890–1940 were eight bishops and 126 priests of the Melkite Rite, and it is generally recognized that this seminary has been largely responsible for the improvement over the years in the quality of the Melkite priests.

A third seminary of note is the Syrian Patriarchal Seminary in Sharfeh near Beirut which trains priests in the Syrian Rite. In the spring of 1951 there appeared an interesting letter in the *Eastern Churches Quarterly* written by Dom Bruno Fehrenbacher, O.S.B., the Abbot of Buckfast, England. In this letter the Abbot summarized as follows, the history of the Seminary which was founded in 1903 and on whose faculty he had taught during the years 1937–39:

. . . In the early years of this century the Benedictines of the French province of the Cassinese Congregation P.O. were entrusted by the Holy See with the training of the

Catholic Syrian clergy. The seminary was established on the slopes of Mount Olivet overlooking the holy City of Jerusalem. With the increase of students, the higher seminary was transferred (in 1930) to Sharfeh, the patriarch's summer residence near Beirut. The professors at both seminaries were partly Benedictines, partly Syrian priests. The Benedictines, however, had the training of the students in the humanities and the higher ecclesiastical studies such as philosophy, theology, etc., the Syrians taking particularly the oriental languages and liturgy. For nearly fifty years the Syrians and Benedictines worked fruitfully together. Nearly half the Catholic Syrian clergy of to-day have come from the seminary. . . . It is, therefore, with great regret that we learned that . . . the French Benedictine province . . . has recently decided to withdraw its members from the Syrian seminary. It is difficult to understand this action. . . . The work done in Jerusalem and Sharfeh has been an undisputed success. . . . And when we realize that the French monasteries have no lack of vocations, especially during the last ten years, the decision to block such a wonderful outlet for truly monastic and Benedictine activity, is well-nigh unintelligible. . . . May it be given to the Assumptionist Fathers of the Dutch Province, who are now succeeding to the work of the Benedictines at Sharfeh and Jerusalem, to consolidate that work for the Catholic Syrian clergy!

There are no seminaries in the Middle East serving only Roman Catholic ordinands for the Armenian Rites. An Armenian patriarchal seminary was operated at Bzommar near Beirut in the 1920s, but at present all of the major seminary students of this Rite are being trained either at the Interritual Oriental Seminary in Beirut, or at the Armenian College in Rome.

For the training of priests in the Chaldean Rite, St. Peter's Patriarchal Seminary was established at Mosul in Iraq in 1866. Eleven years later, French Dominicans established the Syrian Rite Seminary of St. John in the same city. It is reported that some members of the Nestorian churches in the Mosul area in recent years have sought to be admitted to the Roman Catholic Church but have had to be turned away owing in part to the shortage of Catholic priests in the Chaldean Rite.

The Capuchins founded an interritual seminary (The Oriental Seminary of St. Louis) in Constantinople in 1882. However, this institution was closed at the outbreak of World War I when its buildings were occupied by troops. It was reopened after 1918 but subsequently was closed again owing to the fact that the dispersion of the Armenian peoples had reduced the number of students applying for admission. It is stated that the strength of Islam is such that during the past five years only two Turkish Muslims in the country's entire 25,000,000 population have become Roman Catholics. As a means of helping to ensure this Church's future in Turkey, the Capuchins are now instructing a handful of students at a minor seminary level in the Seminary of St. Louis which is located in an old wooden building on the grounds of the French Embassy in Istanbul.

There are no major Roman Catholic seminaries located in Israel or Iran. A seminary for the training of the Chaldean Rite clergy in Persia was opened by the Lazarists in 1845 at Khosrova. It was later closed and subsequently reconstituted in 1923 at Urmia (Rezayyeh). However, this institution remained open for only a few more years; and today there is only a minor seminary of the Chaldean Rite in Iran which is located at Teheran.

E. SOUTHERN ASIA

The major seminaries in India are listed in Table 130. In addition to the 1,321 major seminarians enrolled in 12 major seminaries in India in 1956, there were also approximately 659 scholastics enrolled in 14 scholasticates in the same year, as shown in Table 131.

TABLE 130.   MAJOR SEMINARIES IN INDIA (1956)

Name	Location	Approx. Number of Major Seminary Students	Administration
St. Joseph	Allahabad	67	Jesuits
St. Peter's Regional	Bangalore	100	Foreign Missions of Paris
Diocesan Seminary	Bombay	95	Jesuits
St. Joseph's Apostolic[a]	Ernakulam (Alwaye)	350	Discalced Carmelites
Patriarchal Seminary of Rachol	Rachol, Goa	58	Secular
Missionary Seminary of St. Francis Xavier	Pilar, Goa	21	Missionary Society of St. Francis Xavier
Sacred Heart	Madras	91	Salesians (St. John Bosco)
St. Joseph[a]	Mangalore	117	Jesuits
St. John	Nellore	68	Mill Hill Fathers
Papal Seminary[a]	Poona[b]	145	Jesuits
St. Paul[a]	Tiruchirapalli	115	Jesuits
St. Albert	Ranchi	94	Jesuits
Total: 12		1,321	

NOTES: [a] Interritual (Latin and Eastern Rites).
[b] This seminary was transferred from Kandy, Ceylon, to Poona in 1956.

Most of the seminaries and scholasticates listed in Tables 130 and 131 come under the authority of the Propaganda. The four interritual institutions where students of both the Latin and the Eastern Rites are trained come under the joint authority of the Propaganda and the Oriental Congregations. The Patriarchal Seminary in Goa is under the jurisdiction of the Congregation of Seminaries.

It will be noted that a large number (1,980) of students are now enrolled in the major seminaries and scholasticates in India. The comparable institutions in all of Africa have a slightly smaller total enrollment of 1,907 students. The comparatively large number of students in India results in part from the much longer period of time in which Roman Catholic missionaries have been active there. Also, the population of India at 381,000,000 persons exceeded by 68% the 226,000,000 population of the Continent of Africa in 1957. Only two other countries (Brazil and Mexico) in Africa, Asia and Latin America exceed India in the number of their major seminarians and scholastics.

The initial Roman Catholic seminary was founded at Cranganore as early as 1540, two years before St. Francis Xavier first landed in India, and 13 years before the publication of the decrees of the Council of Trent. It was established by the

TABLE 131. SCHOLASTICATES IN INDIA (1956)

Name	Location	Approx. Number of Scholastics	Administration
Sacred Heart Theologate	Mawlai, Shillong	42	Salesians (St. John Bosco)
St. Mary's Theological College	Kurseong	110	Jesuits
Scholasticate	Bangalore	32	Redemptorists
St. Anthony's Friary	Bangalore	35	Franciscans
Sacred Heart College[d]	Shembaganur, Madura	107[e]	Jesuits
Scholasticate	Ernakulam (Alwaye)	15[a]	Discalced Carmelites
Scholasticate	Madras	12[a]	Salesians (St. John Bosco)
De Nobili College	Poona	215	Jesuits
Scholasticate	Poona	18	Fransalians[b]
Scholasticate	Poona	22	Order of the Imitation of Christ
St. John de Britto	Poona	25	Divine Word Fathers
Scholasticate	Poona	6	Carmelites[c]
Philosophate	Quilon	10?	Capuchins
Theologate	Kotagiri	10?	Capuchins
Total: 14		659	

NOTES: [a] As of 1953.   [d] Faculty of Philosophy.
[b] Missionaries of St. Francis de Sales d'Annecy (M.S.F.S.)   [e] Plus students at a lower level of training.
[c] Third Order, Discalced Carmelites.

Franciscans for the purpose of training priests for the Chaldean (Malabar) Rites in India, whose members consisted of converts from the so-called "St. Thomas Christians." Francis Xavier wrote a number of enthusiastic letters to Ignatius Loyola about the institution, and by 1547 it had a total of 70 students. Apparently about a half century later it went out of existence.

One year after the founding of the Cranganore seminary, the Jesuits established the Santa Fé college and seminary in Goa with 60 students. It was intended to serve as the principal seminary for the training of an indigenous clergy not only for India but also for the other Portuguese colonies in Asia. From this college, Francis Xavier obtained a number of local priests who accompanied him on his missionary journeys elsewhere in Asia. In his letters concerning Santa Fé, Francis Xavier commented on the prevailing lack of an adequate number of Indian clergy in relation to the needs of those times.

Shortly thereafter (in 1555), the Franciscans founded a seminary near Goa, and during the 16th century the Jesuits administered another seminary at Vaipcotta for the priests of the Malabar Rites. The Franciscans also established a seminary near Bombay with the help of the Portuguese King, Dom João III, the administration of which was subsequently transferred to the Jesuits in 1551.

Despite the founding of these and other seminaries in the 16th century, according to Father De Melo, "the first attempts in the formation of a native clergy had not been, it would seem, precisely a brilliant success. Considering all this, it was natural for the Fathers of the Council (i.e., the missionary leaders) to think that nothing better could, for the time being at least, be obtained from the natives. . . . It was a different story with the Syrian Christians at Malabar. The clergy there was entirely native, except for the Archbishops who were mostly sent from Persia."

It would appear that the intellectual standards of these early seminaries were not sufficiently rigorous; and the fact that the students could be sent to them at little or no cost to their parents attracted less capable candidates to the priesthood than was desirable. For example, on December 24, 1631, the Viceroy of India wrote to the King of Portugal concerning the inconvenience of having so many schools and colleges in India: according to him they induced "everybody" to send their sons to them, in part as a means of reducing expenses at home!

Two decades later, in 1653, occurred a major setback in the Roman Catholic missionary effort in India, namely, the conflict with the St. Thomas Christians who later joined the Syrian Orthodox Church of Malabar, which has already been commented on in chapter 12.

A second setback occurred a century later when the Society of Jesus was expelled from Portugal by Pombal in 1759 and was obliged to withdraw its missionaries from Portuguese India as well. This resulted in a diminution in the momentum of Roman Catholic missionary efforts in this country. For example, the Santa Fé college was closed, and its seminary was eventually transferred to the jurisdiction of the secular clergy. Many of the Jesuit stations were handed over to the Paris Foreign Mission Society, but the efforts of the latter to train a local clergy achieved results which have been described as "meager and extremely slow."

Another setback of a different sort was sustained in Goa in the 19th century. With a view toward encouraging Roman Catholic missionary activities in Southern and Southeast Asia, Gregory XVI detached various ecclesiastical areas from the authority of the Patriarch of Goa and converted them to apostolic vicariates which were entrusted to a number of missionary congregations. Then followed what Canon Joly describes as "the deplorable scandal of 1844 . . . Portugal, feigning to agree with the views of Rome, had proposed Joseph de Sylva y Torrés for the archdiocese of Goa. The future archbishop swore . . . to obey all the prescriptions of the bull *Multa praeclare*. . . . Then, having arrived at Goa, he forgot his oath, claimed jurisdiction over all India and ordained in one fell swoop 800 priests chosen in large part from among the coolies of the port of Goa." Archbishop de Sylva's example was soon followed by the Portuguese Bishop of Macao, Hierononymous Joseph da Matta, who within eight days ordained 536 men to the priesthood.

These mass ordainments damaged the prestige of the Roman Catholic Church in Southern and East Asia, and proved to be futile attempts on the part of these dissident prelates to extend Portuguese influence and direction over Roman Catholic missions in these areas. In 1857 Pope Pius IX vainly proposed a new concordat with Portugal concerning the *padroado*. But it was not until 1886 that Pope Leo XIII was able to bring about a substantial improvement in this matter through an agreement he negotiated with the Portuguese.

A significant development in the formation of a local clergy in India occurred as a result of a visitation to this country in the years 1859–62 by two French clerics, Msgrs. Bonnand and Charbonneaux, on behalf of the Propaganda. They reported (according to De Melo) that seven of the 18 vicariates in India at that time did not have a single local priest serving within their jurisdictions. The visitors noted with regret that the ordinaries (i.e., prelates in higher administrative positions) were not paying sufficient attention to the promotion of a local clergy. "Some, like the Carmelites, the Jesuits, the Oblates of Mary Immaculate, (and) the Salesians of Annecy were rather inclined to promote vocations to their own Orders than to foster native secular clergy. 'Monachi monachos gignunt' (monks beget monks) says Mons. Bonnand. In general it could be said that the vicars did not show diligence enough in the fulfilment of their duty in that matter. Some were even decidedly opposed to the establishment of Seminaries in the territories and to the formation of native priests, at least of native secular priests. One such was Mons. Bravi, O.S.B., the late Vicar Apostolic of Colombo, who had gone so far as to say: 'As long as Bravi is Bishop his hands will never ordain a colored priest'. . . ."

At the time of their visitation, Pondicherry was the only vicariate which had seminaries at which courses were offered at two distinctly different levels, i.e., had separate major and minor seminaries. Both of the visitors were dissatisfied with the quality of the education provided at the Latin and Syrian Rite seminaries. They reported that the Government of India and the Protestants were providing the leadership in educational matters, offering up-to-date courses for their students. Accordingly the visitors made a number of recommendations. They suggested that classes no longer should be conducted in Portuguese since that language had lost its importance in that part of India as compared to Malayalam and English. They also noted that the local priests were "good and pious, but on the whole mediocre, ignorant, weak and devoid of ardour and of a great zeal for souls. . . ."

One of the questions raised at this time was the possibility of establishing a central major seminary for all India. The immediate reaction was adverse on the grounds that if the numerous local teaching institutions of the Roman Catholic Church were destroyed, this would tend to impair the movement toward training a national clergy. Two decades later, in 1884, Pope Leo XIII sent the first Apostolic Delegate to India accompanied by a Polish Monsignor as his secretary, Rev. Ladislas M. Zaleski. The latter was confidentially commissioned by the Vatican to study the possibilities of establishing a general seminary for India. In his report Msgr. Zaleski commented that he had visited most of the leading Catholic seminaries in Europe, and he believed that if the European type of training could be offered in Indian institutions to Indian students, the latter in his opinion would fully measure up to European standards for the clergy. He also commented: "Wherever a native clergy is in office, the people support their pastors and often build the churches, too. On the other hand, in the missions founded by Europeans, the people depend upon the missionary, and expect from him almost every penny."

The result of Msgr. Zaleski's report was the founding, in spite of opposition and difficulties, of the Papal Seminary at Kandy, Ceylon, in 1893 by order of Leo XIII. It was opened with an enrollment of 23 students, of whom five were Benedictine scholastics. The administration of the seminary was placed in the hands of the Belgian Jesuits who continue to staff its faculty. The philosophical and theological courses are modeled on the Jesuits' *ratio studiorum*. Many doubted that it would be possible for the seminary to gather students from all parts of India and Ceylon, but eventually it did.

In 1950 there were 138 Latin Rite students enrolled in the Papal Seminary, plus a number of Eastern Rite students. When India and Ceylon became independent in the 1948–50 period, it was no longer feasible to have a Papal Seminary located in Ceylon whose aim was to train as many as possible of the Indian major seminarians. Accordingly in June 1955 the institution was transferred from Kandy to Poona, the latter being 150 miles southeast of Bombay.

Toward the cost of the new buildings at Poona, the Society of St. Peter the Apostle contributed $542,000. The Pontifical Seminary now has a large number of Jesuits on its faculty, and associated with it are scholasticates of the Society of Jesus (De Nobili College), the Order of the Imitation of Christ, the Third Order of the Discalced Carmelites, the Salesians (St. John Bosco), the Divine Word Fathers and the Fransalians. A total of 431 major seminarians and scholastics were studying at Poona in 1956, thus making it the second largest center in India training men for the Roman Catholic clergy. In addition, the Pontifical Athenaeum of Poona (which is a faculty of higher ecclesiastical studies related to the Seminary but not to any university) is also staffed by the Jesuits, thereby serving to broaden the resources in theological faculty personnel located in this city.

Meanwhile the ancient Patriarchal Seminary of Rachol in Goa has continued to graduate major seminarians, some of whom have been sent as missionary priests in recent years to Portuguese colonies in Africa. In 1956 the Rector of the Seminary was consecrated a bishop and was also sent to Africa, joining another bishop of Goan origin serving there.

With respect to the training provided over the years to the major seminarians in the Eastern Rites in India, the Secretary of the Oriental Congregation, Cardinal Eugene Tisserant, recently wrote:

In bygone days several seminaries at Cranganore, Vaipicotta and Ambazhakat had trained excellent priests (of the Eastern Rites) and more recently Verapoly had done the same. However, these seminaries had never educated more than a very small portion of the clergy. Most priests were given orders after going through a very jejune and elementary training with a priest. . . . Msgr. Baccinelli had the courage to close some twenty local seminaries (note: presumably at the minor seminary level) where up to then the Syro-Malabar clerics had been initiated to the priesthood. He replaced them by five seminaries. . . . In 1866 the Seminary of Puthenpally became the central seminary for all the Syrian Catholics and also for the local Latin clergy of the dioceses of Verapoly, Quilon and Mangalore. In 1922 it contained more than 120 students. Brought over to Alwaye (Ernakulam) in 1933, it is large enough to house more than 500 seminarists, the majority of whom now belong to the Eastern rite. It is also subject to the jurisdiction of the Sacred Congregation for the Oriental Church. At Trichur, a seminary was started in 1927 for the clerics of this important Syro-Malabar diocese; but for some reason, possibly the problems of a suitable staff and finances, the project was abandoned on the eve of World War II.

A member of the Third Order of Discalced Carmelites, Father P. Placid, recently made some interesting comments on the training of the Syro-Malabar clergy, as follows:

The Syro-Malabarians have never had a dearth of vocations. At present (1955) they have about 1200 priests and more than 800 seminarians. Every year more than 300 young men apply for admission to the seminary. But the bishops have to limit the number due to lack of material means. The bulk of the clergy is trained in the Apostolic Seminary of Alwaye (Malabar) under Spanish Carmelites. Some are at the Propaganda College, Rome, at the Papal Seminary, Poona, and at other Latin seminaries in India. . . . The standard of the clergy is high. But it is to be pitied that their educations in matters liturgical and historical is not at all satisfactory. They come out of the seminaries Latinized in mind and also cut off from all traditional moorings.

St. Joseph's Apostolic Seminary at Alwaye, mentioned by Cardinal Tisserant and Father Placid, is now the largest individual Roman Catholic seminary in India, though in 1956 it was smaller than the complex of institutions at Poona. St. Joseph's trains priests for both the Latin and Eastern Rites, mostly the latter. Located in the Malabar region, the Seminary has been confronted with the rising tide of Communism in India, particularly in the state of Kerala. Recently, St. Joseph's instituted training courses for labor leaders and the Catholic laity, setting forth the Roman Catholic approach to social and economic affairs. In 1958 the Fides Service reported that 650 students were enrolled at Alwaye—300 in theology and 350 in philosophy.

The difficulties of recruiting a local clergy of requisite quality in India were discussed at the 1954 Fordham Conference of Mission Specialists as follows: "Low-qualified (Roman Catholic) seminarians will, after ordination, prove, often enough, to be but mediocre leaders in the Indian Catholic communities. Either because they are wanting in intellectual equipment, or because they lack the prestige that in India attaches to a college education, a number of priests of this kind have shown a tendency to be too timid and too self-conscious in their dealings with the better educated classes. . . ."

Table 132 shows the growth of the Roman Catholic clergy of the Latin and Eastern Rites in India since 1900 as reported by Archbishop Thomas Pothacamury of Bangalore.

TABLE 132. GROWTH OF THE ROMAN CATHOLIC
CLERGY IN INDIA (1900–1955)

	Priests			
Year	Indian	Foreign	Total	% of Indian to Total
1900	1,580	826	2,406	66
1920	1,945	1,056	3,002	65
1955	3,500	2,335	5,835	60

From this table it will be noted that since 1900 the Indian Roman Catholic clergy has doubled in number and that it has consistently outnumbered the foreign priests. At the same time, there has been a proportionately larger increase in the number of foreign clergy in India so that the ratio of national to foreign priests has fallen. However, as vacancies in the hierarchy have occurred, these for the most part have been filled with Indians. Thus in 1955, 12 of the 15 archbishops and 30 of the 51 bishops were nationals rather than foreigners.

The sizeable Roman Catholic seminaries in Southern Asia are all located in India, either in the predominantly Hindu areas or on the Malabar Coast. There are comparatively few Roman Catholic institutions training priests in Pakistan and Ceylon, and these institutions are all small. The reason for this is the difficulties encountered by all Christian missionaries in competing with Islam in Pakistan and Buddhism in Ceylon. Of the 338 Roman Catholic priests serving in Pakistan in November 1957, 64 were nationals and 274 were foreigners. Table 133 presents a list of the institutions training men for the priesthood in Pakistan and Ceylon.

The Franciscans founded a scholasticate in Karachi in 1940. Following the separation of Pakistan from India in 1950, the Archdiocese of Karachi opened a diocesan seminary, named after Saint Pius X, at Quetta in October, 1952. During the ensuing year, discussions were held among the missionaries in Pakistan of the Franciscan and Mill Hill Fathers from Holland, the Capuchins from Belgium and Dominicans from Italy, looking toward the establishment of a major regional seminary to be constructed in West Pakistan as a joint effort on the part of these religious communities. In May 1958 the Fides Service announced that the Society of St. Peter the Apostle had contributed $375,000 for this purpose and that the seminary building was in process of being constructed.

The largest number of missionary districts in Ceylon have been under the administration of the Oblates of Mary Immaculate. The Jesuits and the Benedictines of the Congregation of St. Silvester have also been active on the island. The Oblates

TABLE 133.   MAJOR SEMINARIES AND SCHOLASTICATES IN PAKISTAN AND CEYLON (1956)

Name	Location	Approx. Number of Major Seminary Students	Administration
Pakistan			
St. Pius X Diocesan Seminary	Quetta	14	Secular
Portiuncula Friary	Karachi	12	Franciscans
Sacred Heart Scholasticate	Barisal (East Pakistan)	10	Holy Cross Fathers
Ceylon			
St. Bernard	Colombo	21	Oblates of Mary Immaculate
National Seminary	Kandy	26?	Oblates of Mary Immaculate
Our Lady of Lanka (Scholasticate)	Kandy	7	Oblates of Mary Immaculate
Scholasticate	Kandy	10?	Benedictines (Silvestrine)
Total: 7		100	

administer the St. Bernard Seminary in Colombo which trains men for the secular clergy. Formerly they also had a scholasticate in Colombo. However, when the Papal Seminary at Kandy was moved to Poona, India, in 1956, its campus at Kandy was taken over by the new National Seminary for the secular clergy in Ceylon, whose faculty is staffed by the Oblates. In line with this move, the Oblate scholasticate in Colombo was transferred to Kandy where their scholastics now study at the National Seminary as do the scholastics of the Silvestrine Benedictines.

F. SOUTHEAST ASIA

There are no major Roman Catholic seminaries in either Burma or Thailand, although a number of students are being trained there at the minor seminary level. As in the case of Protestant missions in these two countries, the Roman Catholic Church has encountered extraordinary difficulties, not only because of the strength of Buddhism, but also in the case of Burma by the post-World War II unrest and civil wars. Professor Freitag notes that in Burma there were 33 local priests and 41 major seminarians in 1923. By 1956 there were 86 local priests, mostly concentrated in the Vicariate of Rangoon, but only 31 major seminarians. Between 1945 and 1950 only five local priests were ordained in Thailand, and in 1952, 77 of the 171 priests were indigenous. In 1956 there were 38 major seminarians in Thailand and 14 in Malaya. Virtually all of the seminarians from these three countries were being sent to Penang in Malaya for their training.

Table 134 presents a list of the major seminaries and scholasticates in Malaya, Indonesia and Oceania.

Of the institutions listed in this table, the General College at Penang in Malaya has had the most interesting history and is an example of the vicissitudes encountered by a number of seminaries in the Orient during the past three centuries.

A celebrated Jesuit Father, Alexander de Rhodes, S.J., born in 1591, spent his entire career (until his death in Ispahan, Persia, in 1660) serving in various Roman Catholic missions in India, the Molucca Islands (East Indies) and in Indochina.

TABLE 134.   MAJOR SEMINARIES AND SCHOLASTICATES IN MALAYA, INDONESIA AND OCEANIA (1955)

Name	Location	Approx. Number of Major Seminary Students	Administration
Malaya			
General College	Penang	75[a]	Paris Foreign Missions Society
Indonesia			
St. Paul Regional Seminary	Jogjakarta	19[a]	Jesuits
Ignatius College[b]	Jogjakarta	17[a]	Jesuits
Scholasticate	Batu, Malang	10[a]	Carmelites (Ancient Observance)
Padua Seminary	Tjitjurug, Java	10?	Franciscans
St. Paul[b]	Ledalero, Flores, Lesser Sunda Islands	18[c]	Divine Word Fathers
Oceania			
Lano Seminary	Wallis Islands	4[a]	Marists
St. Leone	Nouméa, New Caledonia	11[a]	Marists
Total: 8		164	

NOTES: [a] As of 1950.
[b] Scholasticate.
[c] As of 1958.

Condemned and banished three times from Tonkin, he finally returned to Europe in 1646 to plead for the formation of a local clergy and the appointment of an indigenous hierarchy in Asia. Largely as a result of his efforts (and those of François Pallu, Bishop of Heliopolis, François de Montmorency-Laval and Bernard Piques), the Paris Foreign Missions Society was founded in 1658 for the purpose of training secular priests for missionary work. Five years later, in 1663, its seminary was established in Paris. The instructions given to Fathers Pallu and Laval upon the occasion of their consecration as vicars apostolic to the Far East were as follows: "Your main duty in the missions will be to form a good and zealous native clergy, capable not merely of administering a poor mission station or parish but even of governing large dioceses." Shortly after their arrival in the Orient, the vicars founded a seminary in Siam at Mahapram, a suburb of the capital, Juthia, in 1664 (some 124 years after the founding of the first seminary in India). Siam was selected as the best location because during the 18th century some freedom of religion was accorded by the Government of Siam—in contrast to the persecution being suffered at that time by Roman Catholic missionaries in Indochina. In fact, King Phra-Narai of Siam donated the land upon which the seminary was located. Furthermore Juthia (like modern Bangkok) was comparatively easily accessible for students and travelers coming from the other countries in Southeast Asia.

During its first century the seminary had a considerable success. By 1700 its enrollment had risen to about 60 students, and the institution was divided into a major and minor seminary. However, the invasion of Siam by the Burmese army in 1769 resulted in the destruction of the school. Accordingly in that year it was transferred to Virampatnam in the French colony of Pondicherry on the eastern coast of the peninsula of India. It continued to train priests here until 1805 when it was forced to close owing to a lack of support in funds and personnel coming from Europe: this was the result of the temporary ruin of the Foreign Missions Society of Paris occasioned by the French Revolution.

After the Revolution an attempt was made to reopen the seminary first at Macao and later in Manila, but without success. Finally in 1808 a house was obtained on Penang, an island in the Straits of Malacca off the west coast of Malaya, some 600 miles northwest of Singapore. Penang had been a British colony since 1786, and here the seminary was reopened. Four years later its building was burnt down (1812) and in 1816 it was rebuilt. The number of its students increased from 25 in 1822 to 126 in 1850, and it became the leading seminary for training priests for Southeast Asia. Among its students were Chinese, Japanese, Burmese, Koreans, Siamese, Laotians, Annamese and even some Hindus. Latin was the lingua franca, and the students are said to have benefited from being mixed with seminarians from other nations. In addition to the usual subjects of philosophy and theology, they were also taught printing, bookbinding and carpentry.

In 1872 the Penang Seminary had 132 students, but by 1890 the number had dropped to about 15. This was the result of the founding of major seminaries elsewhere in Southeast Asia and the fact that the climate at Penang is hot and uncomfortable. In 1950 the institution was training 75 students coming from Burma, Siam and Malaya. Of its approximately 700 graduates during the past 150 years, 92 were martyred and 25 were subsequently canonized.

Indonesia. According to Professor Freitag, Roman Catholic missionary efforts in the East Indies were impeded during the past century by the unfriendly policies of the Dutch colonial administration. The Jesuits have been active on the Island of Java, with other congregations concentrating in the various island groups forming the Indonesian archipelago. The Jesuits founded a small minor seminary at Moentilan in 1911 which eventually was transformed into the St. Paul Major Seminary at Jogjakarta. It survived World War II and the postwar period of unrest to become the regional seminary for Java.

During World War II the Japanese occupation authorities interned most of the Dutch, French and German missionaries in Indonesia and Oceania. A substantial number of them lost their lives. Four Japanese priests were sent by the Bishop of Nagasaki to help maintain Roman Catholic missionary activities in Indonesia during this period. The Seminary of the Divine Word Fathers at Ledalero (Flores, Little Sunda Islands) was permitted by the Japanese army to operate throughout the war, though for a time it was transferred to Lela.

Oceania. Roman Catholic missionaries in Oceania have faced formidable obstacles, among them the backwardness of the natives, cannibalism, the remoteness of the individual island groups and the difficult climate and living conditions in some areas. During the past century the Picpus Fathers (Congregation of the Sacred Heart) have been active in the eastern portion of Polynesia, the Marists in Central Oceania, and the Steyl Fathers (Divine Word) in the western area. Their combined efforts had resulted in 1948 in the training of only 27 ordained local priests.

Both of the major seminaries in Oceania are small and under the direction of the Australian Province of the Marists. Their seminary in the Wallis Islands was originally founded in 1845 as a minor seminary and now has both a major and a minor department. It is located at Lano, an independent station on Hihifo territory on the island of Uvea, where the Marists are also maintaining a novitiate for local sisters and brothers. In the past this religious community also maintained minor seminaries at Torokina and Chabai in the Solomon Islands. The former is reported to have offered courses at the major seminary level in 1950.

In earlier years some students were sent to seminaries in Australia and New Zealand for their training. When this did not prove to be successful, others were sent to Madagascar and Manila. Here again the results were minimal. Later it was planned to establish a large central seminary for the entire region of Oceania. However, this plan also came to naught, according to Fathers Freitag and Beckmann, because of the great distances involved, differences in language and culture, the lead already obtained in some areas by Protestant missionaries, and the varying political conditions (i.e., the colonies in Oceania were divided among the Dutch, English, French, Australians and Japanese).

Vietnam: Table 135 lists the major seminaries and scholasticates in Vietnam.

TABLE 135.   MAJOR SEMINARIES AND SCHOLASTICATES IN VIETNAM (1950)

Name[a]	Location	Approx. Number of Major Seminary Students	Administration
Major Seminary	Buichy	83	Secular
St. Sulpician	Vinh Long[b]	46	Sulpicians
St. Peter Canisius	Hué	24	Secular
Major Seminary	Kontum	8	Paris Foreign Missions Society
Major Seminary	Phat Diem	78	Secular
Major Seminary	Saigon	74	Paris Foreign Missions Society
Scholasticate	Saigon?	16	Franciscans
Scholasticate	Dalat	39[b]	Redemptorists
Cat-Dam Priory	Thai-Binh	10	Dominicans
Total: 9		378	

NOTES: [a] Excluding the Dominican Seminary (St. Albert   [b] As of 1957.
the Great) which in 1950 was located at Buichy-Nam
Dinh (see text).

In all the countries of Africa, Asia and Latin America, the Roman Catholic Church achieved in Indochina (Vietnam) one of its greatest successes in creating a trained local clergy. The baleful effects of the Portuguese *padroado* were overcome at an early date through the activities of apostolic vicars dispatched from Rome. In addition the missionary leaders in Indochina during the past century, French Jesuits and particularly the members of the Paris Foreign Mission Society, displayed far-sighted leadership against considerable odds. For example, during the first 150 years following 1664 it was necessary for the Society's missionaries to be constantly on the move in order to escape persecution. Accordingly they created "portable" seminaries whose faculties and student bodies were often transferred from place to place. Occasionally the seminaries were conducted on river boats. Only in the 19th century did the persecution of missionaries in Indochina cease. However, even under the French administration, according to Professor Freitag, Roman Catholic missionaries encountered almost insuperable difficulties. The first local Bishop, Msgr. Tong, was consecrated at St. Peter's in Rome by Pope Pius XI in 1933.

The growth of the local Roman Catholic clergy in Indochina in the period 1819–1948 is shown in Table 136.

TABLE 136. GROWTH OF THE ROMAN CATHOLIC CLERGY IN INDOCHINA (1819–1948)

		Priests			Major Seminaries	
Year	Approx. Number of Catholics	Native	Foreign	Ratio of Native to Foreign	No.	Students
1819	400,000	175	25	7.0		
1910	1,000,000	603	443	1.5		
1923	1,175,000	713	402	1.7	11	425
1933	1,387,000	1,223	383	3.2	9	523
1948	1,534,000	1,469	402	3.6	8	516

At the Fordham Conference in 1954 Rev. John J. Considine, M.M., pointed out that in Vietnam (where there is comparatively little Protestant missionary activity) out of a population of 24,000,000 persons (prior to the partition of the country in 1954 into North and South Vietnam) there were approximately 1,500,000 "Catholics with a tradition of persecution and a sense of mission that makes them one of the few important units of Catholicity in Asia. Of the 15 ecclesiastical territories, half a dozen are headed by Vietnamese bishops, while of the 1,766 clergy, 1,430 or 81% are Vietnamese, a percentual record for the entire mission world. Of the 4,527 sisters, 94% are Vietnamese."

In this connection Rev. Gerard Marinan, S.S.C., wrote in 1948: "This high proportion of native priests has always been the outstanding mark of the Church in Indochina. In fully Catholic countries there is, on an average, one priest to every thousand Catholics; this average has been reached in . . . (Indochina) . . . and indeed the seminaries cannot accommodate all the boys who wish to study for the priesthood. . . ."

As noted above, in the period 1923–48 the number of major seminaries in Indochina was reduced from 11 to 8 in line with the policy of establishing regional seminaries. These eight institutions had an average of 64 major seminarians, an unusually high average enrollment in mission lands. Of the eight seminaries listed in the Propaganda's 1950 Guide, three were being administered by the secular clergy. Of these three, two had the largest individual enrollments of all of the major seminaries in the country.

In 1954 the previously French provinces comprising Indochina were split into North and South Vietnam, the former having a population of about 12,000,000 and the latter about 10,000,000. Much of the indigenous leadership under which the evacuation of large numbers of non-Communists from North to South Vietnam took place in 1954–55 was provided by the Roman Catholic clergy. Some of the seminaries which in 1950 were located in North Vietnam were subsequently relocated in South Vietnam in order to avoid being under Communist rule. An example of this is the St. Sulpician Seminary which was transferred from Hanoi to Vinh Long. Their former large building in Hanoi is now being used as an army barracks. In 1954 the Dominican seminary St. Albert Magnus (which in 1950 was located at Buichy-Nam Dinh) was transferred to Hongkong.

Philippines. The contrast between the progress made by the Roman Catholic Church in developing a local clergy in the Philippines when compared to Vietnam is of interest. While there are many more members of the Roman Catholic Church in the Philippines than in Vietnam, this is largely due to the fact that the missionary work in the former country commenced a century earlier. More particularly, most of the Filipinos at that time were animists rather than believers in a comparatively strong and sophisticated religion such as Buddhism in Vietnam. It is also stated by some Protestant sources that many of the Roman Catholics in the Philippines are only nominal Christians. The contrast between the two countries as of 1948 is shown in Table 137.

TABLE 137. DEVELOPMENT OF THE LOCAL CLERGY IN THE PHILIPPINES AND
INDOCHINA (1948)

	Philippines	Indochina
Population (1955)	22,614,000	21,849,000
Number of Roman Catholics	13,760,000	1,534,000
Priests		
Local	1,046	1,469
Foreign	1,007	402
Total	2,053	1,871
Foreign Priests (% of Total)	50%	20%
Number of Catholics per priest	6,700	820
Number of Catholics per local priest	13,150	1,045

The reasons for the lag in the development of a local clergy in the Philippines are in part historical. The first Roman Catholic missionary work in the islands commenced in 1565, and Manila was created a diocese as early as 1571, and an archdiocese in 1578. However, no effort was made for more than a century to ordain Filipino priests. For a long while the missions in the Philippines were exclusively in the hands of missionary priests sent from Spain by the major religious communities, i.e., the Augustinians, Franciscans, Dominicans and Jesuits. Although the Dominicans founded the University of St. Thomas in Manila in 1611, nevertheless a year later the Archbishop of Manila wrote to King Philip II of Spain reporting that among the orders and congregations only the Jesuits interested themselves in educational matters.

The record shows that not only the Vatican but also even the Kings of Spain had their difficulties during colonial times in attempting to establish a local clergy on the islands.

Rev. Peter Weyland, S.V.D., has commented as follows: ". . . A Spanish royal decree of August 22, 1677 ordered that: first, the Archbishop (of Manila) should make all efforts that he possibly could to maintain at their studies such natives of the Islands, of Filipino blood, who were inclined to that pursuit; second, when he found them properly instructed, he should, in due time, promote them to Holy Orders. . . . The Archbishop, who was the recipient of this decree, thought otherwise, and suggested that what should be done was to send from Spain those religious who were most zealous for the conversion of souls. The King had expressed the mind of the Church; the Archbishop was simply expressing the mind of the Archbishop. . . ."

In 1702 the Spanish King decreed that a seminary should be established in Manila for the instruction of eight Filipino seminarians. Archbishop Camacho established this seminary in 1703, and it was the first to accept native Filipinos. However, against the wishes of the King, the seminary was subsequently diverted from its original purpose, and other students besides those of Filipino blood were admitted. In 1710 the King ordered that all foreign seminarians should immediately be removed from the institution, and soon thereafter the first Filipino students were ordained as priests.

Rev. H. de la Costa, S.J., has written that under Spanish rule "Filipino priests were given the training of a second-rate clergy because they were not expected to be anything else; and because of the kind of training they were given they did not, as a matter of fact, become anything else. . . . Soon after Spain's cession of the Philippines to the US in 1899, the religious Orders withdrew almost two-thirds of their personnel from the Islands. . . . Responsibility for the parishes devolved on a native clergy that had been sedulously shielded from responsibility."

Father Regan comments that at the height of the ecclesiastical crisis caused by the Spanish-American War, some of the Spanish bishops in the Philippines "seeing the great need of priests in the provinces, tried to remedy the situation. In the haste to catch up with the desperate lack of priests, candidates were ordained who lacked the proper training for the priesthood. There was a saying in Manila at one time, 'There are no longer any boatmen for the barges because the Archbishop has ordained them all.' "

The schism of the Aglipayan Church from the Roman Catholic Church at the same time originated in part as a result of the unwillingness of the Spanish hierarchy in the Philippines to elevate Father Aglipay to the episcopacy. Coincident with the departure from the Philippines during these years of between 750 and 1,000 Spanish priests and monks, the first Filipino Bishop, Jorge Barlin, was consecrated Bishop of Nueva Ceres in 1905. Several other Filipino priests were created bishops in the next few years. As the Spanish bishops died or resigned, the Vatican replaced them with bishops from the United States; and the Spanish friars were replaced with Sacred Heart Fathers from Belgium, Divine Word Fathers from Germany, Mill Hill missionaries from England and Redemptorists from Ireland and Australia. In addition some of the irritation against the landlordism of the friars was abated through the purchase by the Philippine Government of over 400,000 acres of land which had been owned by the religious communities.

There was a local clergy which prevented the total collapse of the Roman Catholic Church in the Philippines, but it was not strong enough to prevent considerable harm being done to the Church. In order to provide training for Filipino seminarians during the period of the Spanish withdrawal from the Philippines, the American Archbishops of Philadelphia, New York, Cincinnati and St. Louis, as well as the Bishops of Trenton, North Carolina and elsewhere, made it financially possible for a total of 60 Filipino students to study in their diocesan seminaries in the United States.

Since then a considerable amount of effort has gone into the establishment of major seminaries and scholasticates in the Philippines. At first the process was slow because, with the departure of the Spanish priests, many of the seminaries were disbanded. Thus, after 27 years of American occupation, by 1926 only one Filipino priest had been ordained in the Archdiocese of Manila.

Table 138 lists the major seminaries and scholasticates now training students in the Philippines.

Most of the seminaries in the Philippines are under the jurisdiction of the Congregation of Seminaries. A few which are located in the outlying missionary vicariates and prefectures, e.g., Montosa (which has been administered by a Belgian Scheut Father), Mindoro (headed by an Argentine Divine Word Father), and Palawan (headed by a Spanish Augustinian) come under the authority of the Propaganda.

The leading seminary in the Philippines, as well as being one of the oldest, is the St. Thomas Central Seminary which is administered by the Dominicans. It is a part of the Royal and Pontifical University of St. Thomas in Manila which also has faculties of philosophy and theology for advanced studies in this field.

The Jesuits' San José seminary in Quezon City has the largest number of students (138), and it was also once part of St. Thomas University. However, with the expulsion of the Society of Jesus from the Philippines in 1768, its administration was placed in the hands of its alumni priests, and its affairs soon languished. At one point the University used its buildings for its School of Medicine and Pharmacy. In 1910 the Society of Jesus resumed control of San José, but it was not until after World War II that the institution commenced to flourish. In 1951 it occupied a new building located in Quezon City. The history of San José is an interesting example of success achieved by the Jesuits where others have failed.

With the Communist capture of the mainland of China in 1950, the bulk of the Chinese major seminarians who were able to emigrate were transferred to Hongkong and the Philippines, particularly the latter. Thus of the 916 major seminary students enrolled in the Philippines in 1956, 102 were Chinese seminarians and scholastics in exile.

In 1956, of the 37 bishops and archbishops in the country, 24 (including the Archbishop of Manila) were Filipinos. Nevertheless the situation with respect to

TABLE 138.　Major Seminaries and Scholasticates in the Philippine Islands (1956)

Name	Location	Approx. Number of		Administration
		Faculty	Students[d]	
St. Thomas Central	Manila	36	96[a]	Dominicans
St. Joseph's Regional	Manila	11	25[b] [e]	Jesuits
Chabanel Hall	Manila	17	27[c] [e]	Jesuits
Christ the King	Manila	28	30[b]	Divine Word Fathers
San Jose	Quezon City	23	138[b]	Jesuits
Our Lady of the Assumption	Baesa, Quezon City	?	3[b]	Oblates of Mary Immaculate
Immaculate Heart[f]	Baguio City	6	3[b] [c]	Scheut Fathers
St. Robert Bellarmine College[g]	Baguio City	14	50[c] [e]	Jesuits
Immaculate Conception[f]	Vigan	11	66[b]	Divine Word Fathers
Our Lady of the Most Holy Rosary	Naga City	12	62[b]	Lazarists
Sacred Heart Seminary	Bacolod City	7	11[b]	Lazarists
Berchman's College[h]	Cebu City	7	59[c]	Jesuits
Archdiocesan Seminary of St. Charles	Cebu City	8	111	Lazarists
St. Charles	Makati, Rizal	15	113[b]	Scheut Fathers
Sacred Heart Mission Seminary	Talisay, Cebu	8	15[b]	Missioners of Sacred Heart of Jesus
Sacred Heart Metropolitan Seminary of St. Vincent Ferrer	Tanawan (Palo), Leyte	9	28[b]	Divine Word Fathers
	Iloilo City	15	70[b]	Lazarists
St. Joseph	Puerto Princesa, Palawan	4	9[b]	Augustinians (Recollects)
Total: 18		231	916	

NOTES:　[a] Plus 18 postgraduate students.　　[e] Mostly Chinese students in exile.
[b] Plus students at minor seminary or novitiate level.　[f] Interdiocesan.
[c] Scholastics only.　　[g] Faculty of Theology only.
[d] At the major seminary level.　　[h] Faculty of Philosophy and Science.

the faith of the laity and the formation of a local clergy, according to Father Regan, still leaves much to be desired:

Many Filipinos go to church only three times in their lives: to be baptized, to be married, and to be buried. Twice in these three times, they have to be carried in. . . .

Today Filipino priests are far more numerous than in the days of the Spaniards. They are in charge of most of the large parishes; they are better trained than native priests were in the old days; and many hold high positions in the Church. But vocations to the priesthood are still too few. One difficulty is the lack of funds. Many poor boys cannot afford to pay their way through the seminary, and the bishops cannot supply free tuition money to all the deserving young men. If burses were established in the seminaries for the education of Filipino priests, that arrangement would be a great boon to vocations. . . .

With but one priest for every 8,359 Catholics, the Philippine Islands have a crying need for more priests. (By way of contrast—the United States has a priest for every 640 Catholics.) And of the 2,938 priests in the Philippines, more than one third are located in the Manila area, where many of them teach in schools. . . .

At the 1954 Fordham Conference, Father Considine commented on the Roman Catholic leadership in the Philippines as "pitifully inadequate. . . . They are served . . . by fewer local clergy than are found among the million and a half Vietnamese Catholics across the China Sea. Here is one of the major weak spots of the Church in all Asia."

While the comments of Fathers Regan and Considine relating to the number of Filipino priests may be true, it would also appear that the 129% increase in the number of Filipino students at the major seminary level (from approximately 400 to 916) during the period 1947–56 is indicative of the effort which is now being made by the Roman Catholic Church to bring about an improvement in this situation.

G. EAST ASIA

Table 139 lists the major seminaries and scholasticates in Japan.

Japan is an example of a country where the Roman Catholic Church was driven underground and survived, after a fashion, for two centuries without having any clergy at all, foreign or local.

St. Francis Xavier brought the Roman Catholic faith to Japan when he landed at Kagoshima on the southern extremity of Kyushu on August 15, 1549. The Japanese Province of the Society of Jesus was founded in the same year. It depended upon Macao, Malacca and Goa for its financial support. At first, the Jesuits made good progress in Japan, since there were some points of similarity between the thoroughness and austerity of Jesuit training and the Spartan type of living favored by the Japanese Samurai class upon whom the Jesuits focused their missionary efforts. It was hoped at the time that the conversion of Japan might in part counterbalance

TABLE 139.   Major Seminaries and Scholasticates in Japan (1958)

Name	Location	Approx. Number of Major Seminary Students	Administration
Seminaries			
Interdiocesan Seminary	Tokyo	150	Jesuits
St. Sulpician Regional	Fukuoka	65	Sulpicians
Scholasticates			
St. John Bosco Seminary	Tokyo	33	Salesians (St. John Bosco)
St. Mary's College	Tokyo	61	Jesuits
St. Anthony	Tokyo	14	Franciscans
St. Bonaventure	Tokyo	36	Conventuals (O.F.M.Conv.)
Scholasticate	Nagoya	7	Divine Word Fathers
Total: 7		366	

the loss, to the Roman Catholic Church, of England which under Henry VIII had just transferred its religious allegiance to Protestantism.

In the year 1579—30 years after Xavier's arrival in Japan—an apostolic visitor, Father Alexander Valignano, S.J., raised the question whether a local clergy was being created and whether Japanese scholastics would be admitted into the Society of Jesus. Father Valignano resided in Japan from 1579 to 1603 during which time the Japanese scholastics in the Society of Jesus complained of the long delays before they were being ordained. One of the reasons for this was the difficulty the students had in acquiring a fluency in Latin.

At about this time seminary colleges were being operated in Arima and Macao serving both Japanese and Chinese students. A Seminary of the Nobles was also established at Azuki in Japan and later transferred to Osaka. Other institutions, all of them at the minor seminary level, were established in 1589, 1599 and 1604, the last at Nagasaki. None of these survived the later persecutions.

By virtue of the bull *Ex Pastorali officio* dated January 28, 1585, Pope Gregory XIII assigned the Roman Catholic mission in Japan exclusively to the Society of Jesus. During the latter half of the 16th century, according to Fülöp-Miller, "the Jesuits established schools, instituted courses of debates, and had a printing press sent from Europe with which they produced books in Japanese: grammars, dictionaries, literary works, theological treaties, Aesop's Fables translated into Japanese, as well as extracts from the Chinese classics, particularly from the works of Confucius. Produced in many thousands of copies, these cheap books found their way throughout the whole of Japan."

Table 140 indicates the progress made toward establishing a local clergy in Japan during a single decade in the early years.

Toward the end of the 16th century, Spanish Franciscans from Manila commenced engaging in missionary work in Japan, contending that a letter of Pope Sixtus V had granted freedom to the Franciscans in the Philippines to preach throughout East Asia. The zeal of the Franciscans caused concern to the Jesuits who were mostly Portuguese and were endeavoring to work inconspicuously in order to avoid antagonizing the Shogun Hideyoshi. Whereas the Jesuit missionary approach was directed toward the upper classes, the efforts of the Franciscans were oriented toward the poor. Furthermore, the Jesuits sought to retain as much of Japanese culture as possible in developing the Roman Catholic Church, whereas the Franciscans wished to make a clean sweep of it and create an entirely new culture as well as re-

TABLE 140.   GROWTH OF JAPANESE CLERGY (1583–93)

Year	Priests		Scholastics, Brothers & Novices	
	European	Japanese	European	Japanese
1583	29		33	27
1593	56		11	92

ligion for the Japanese. The efforts of the Jesuits to restrict the entrance of the Franciscans into Japan were not successful. It is difficult to say whether the Church (even in the absence of the subsequent persecutions) would have fared better had only one rather than both of these missionary approaches been pursued.

In 1597 Hideyoshi commenced a systematic, ruthless suppression of the Roman Catholics in Japan, in part because of his belief that foreign missionaries might prove to be the forerunners of colonial powers. By 1614 the Roman Catholic Church was forbidden to appoint bishops in the country. Around the year 1628, approximately 80 Japanese sent a letter to the General of the Dominican Order requesting him to suggest to the Pope the advisability of ordaining Japanese in order to make up for the scarcity of foreign missionaries. A short while later, 73 Japanese men and 43 women signed a letter and sent it directly to the Pope asking him to establish a seminary in Japan for the training of their sons for the priesthood. A few Japanese Dominican seminarians were occasionally sent to Manila for their studies; after being ordained there, they returned to Japan. However, by 1638 all of these men had been captured and martyred, and the Dominican mission in Japan came to an end.

The persecution of the Roman Catholic Church continued with even greater severity, and by 1650 contacts with the West were entirely cut off. During the next 200 years all foreign trade with Japan was limited to commerce with the Dutch who were permitted to land only on an island in the harbor of Nagasaki on Kyushu, the southernmost of the five main Japanese islands.

Commenting in 1907 on this setback to the missionary effort, Canon Joly declares that the early missionaries had the means of training a local clergy but failed to utilize them sufficiently: "The missionaries did not want to do so, did not know how, or did not dare. After a meritorious apostolate . . . to which we will offer once again the homage of our admiration, they died in order to give proof they had preached the truth, which is still very beautiful, but the Church of Japan died with them because before dying they neglected to place the torch of faith into the hands which were outstretched to receive it, and this will be deplored forever."

With the reopening of Japan by Commodore Perry in 1853, Roman Catholic missionaries re-entered the country six years later. In 1865 they were astonished to discover that, in the hills behind Nagasaki, Christian communities had survived during the intervening two centuries. Since they had had no ordained clergy, only the sacrament of baptism had been continued and celebrated by the laity. Missionaries of the Jesuits and the Paris Foreign Missions Society were among the first to return, followed by Dominicans and Franciscans from Spain and Germany, and Lazarists from France.

Unfortunately the discovery of the Nagasaki Christians led to a renewal of the Government's persecution of them during the five-year period, 1868–73. When the persecution commenced, ten students studying for the priesthood were sent to the major seminary at Penang in Malaya for their training. In 1870, 13 students were sent to Hongkong for the same purpose, and others were subsequently sent to Shanghai.

The first seminary to be re-established in Japan was in Nagasaki, founded in 1874 under the administration of the Sulpicians. In 1875 the Jesuits established the St. Francis Xavier Seminary in Tokyo. However, it was not until 19 years later that the latter seminary had one of its graduates ordained to the priesthood. Two other seminaries were opened in the period 1879–82 in Osaka and Hakodate, but these were subsequently closed.

Commencing in 1890 most of the major seminary students were being trained at Nagasaki, and it was not until 1932 that the major interdiocesan seminary in Tokyo was reopened. Meanwhile the Sulpicians transferred their seminary from Nagasaki to Fukuoka, where it is now serving as the regional seminary for Southern Japan.

In 1891 a Roman Catholic archdiocese and three dioceses were created in Japan, all administered by Europeans. The growth in the number of Japanese priests in recent decades has been slow inasmuch as the Roman Catholic Church has faced the same difficulties as have confronted Protestant missionaries in this country. Table 141 illustrates this point.

In 1913, Sophia University was founded in Tokyo by the Jesuits in accordance with a directive issued by Pope Pius X in 1908. Subsequently St. Francis Xavier Seminary was reconstituted and affiliated with it.

In 1927 Pius XI personally consecrated Msgr. Hayasaka at St. Peter's in Rome as the first local Bishop of Japan and placed him in charge of the Nagasaki Diocese where the majority of the Roman Catholics in Japan are residents. In 1936 and 1937 local priests were appointed to head the Archdiocese of Tokyo and the Kagoshima Apostolic Prefecture. Thus, with the outbreak of World War II the Roman Catholic Church in that country was in a better position to survive the pressure placed on all Christian organizations by the Japanese Government than it had been three centuries earlier. When the Religious Corporations Act became law in Japan in April 1940, all foreign heads of Roman Catholic dioceses resigned and were replaced by Japanese priests and bishops.

TABLE 141. GROWTH OF LOCAL JAP-
ANESE CLERGY (1892–1957)

| Year | Local Priests | Major Seminaries[a] | |
		Number	Students
1892	15	2	?
1907	33	2	21
1923	40	4	68
1933	73	1	115
1939	130	2	111
1948	176	2	165
1957	332	2	215

NOTE: [a] Exclusive of Scholasticates.

Following World War II some progress was made in increasing the number of Japanese priests. However, with the departure of large numbers of Roman Catholic priests from Communist China after 1950, many of them entered Japan. The result was that the Japanese Roman Catholic clergy continued to be outnumbered by foreign priests in a proportion of approximately 3:1, as shown in Table 142 relating to the period 1952–57.

In the period 1947–58 the number of members of the Roman Catholic Church in Japan rose from 120,000 to 254,000, an increase of over 100%; but this still is a small total in relation to the 90,000,000 population of the country. As a result of the large number (1,208) of foreign priests stationed in Japan, there is one priest for every 170 Catholics in the country. This is an unusually high ratio and it is indicative of the religious importance ascribed to Japan by the Propaganda Congregation since World War II.

Between 1947 and 1957 the total number of major and minor seminarians combined (secular and religious, Japanese and foreign) being trained in Japan increased almost ten-fold, i.e., from 58 to 519.

As in earlier centuries, the Society of Jesus was the leading religious community furthering the postwar missionary effort of the Roman Catholic Church in Japan. The growth in the number of Jesuits in this country in recent years is shown in Table 143.

The center of the Jesuit missionary effort is in Tokyo. In this capital city they administer three large institutions which are interrelated. The first is Sophia University which is located in central Tokyo. The second is the Interdiocesan Seminary for the secular clergy which they commenced to administer in 1946. Its Latin and philosophy courses are housed in buildings adjacent to Sophia University, and its theology department is located in the suburbs west of Tokyo, 40 minutes' drive away. The third institution is St. Mary's College, a Jesuit scholasticate which was founded in 1953 and which is located adjacent to the Interdiocesan Seminary's theology department in west Tokyo. An interesting summary of the recent activities of these

TABLE 142. COMPOSITION OF JAPANESE
ROMAN CATHOLIC CLERGY (1952–58)

	1952	1958
Japanese Priests	213	359
Foreign Priests	760	1,208
	973	1,567

TABLE 143. GROWTH OF SOCIETY OF JESUS IN JAPAN
(1946–57)

	1946	1957
Japanese Priests (S.J.)	6	12
Foreign Missionary Priests (S.J.)	83	187
Japanese Scholastics (S.J.)	4	58
Foreign Missionary Scholastics (S.J.)	5	92
	98	349

three institutions appeared in a bulletin published by the Jesuit Mission Bureau in Tokyo in 1958, from which the following has been abstracted:

At Saint Mary's College there are 48 young Jesuits studying theology and 13 studying philosophy. The latter commute daily by private bus to Sophia University. Next door, at the Tokyo Seminary, there are 63 seminarians in the theology course while 123 seminarians, in the philosophy and the preparatory Latin course, reside in their own house just ten minutes from Sophia University. The same fourteen professors of theology handle the teaching programs for Jesuit and secular seminarians. The rapid growth in the number of vocations to the priesthood in Japan has required constant expansion of living and study space. To meet this happy increase, the plans are on the drawing boards for additional wings at the Tokyo Seminary to bring all secular seminarians under one roof and thus to allow the Latin course seminarians the full use of the three-storied building near Sophia. Also in advanced stage are the plans for class rooms, library and auditorium for conjoint use by professors, seminarians of Tokyo Seminary and Jesuit scholastics of Saint Mary's College....

In 1956 ... the first group of Japanese Jesuit priests was ordained in Japan. And in 1957, after the hurried completion of two additions, the Jesuit House of Studies, St. Mary's College, was able to house all the young Jesuits.... The courses in the Sacred Sciences studied by the Jesuit scholastics of Saint Mary's College and by the seminarians of the Tokyo Seminary are integrated into the curriculum of Sophia University conducted by the Jesuits in Tokyo. At Sophia, the Holy See has erected a Pontifical Faculty of Theology and of Philosophy, and these two programs enjoy the approval and recognition of the Japanese Ministry of Education. Hence, the seminarians, both Jesuit and diocesan, have from now, in Japan, the unique advantage of receiving fully recognized civil degrees from the Bachelor's to the Doctorate inclusive, while at the same time they receive a training for the priesthood that meets the highest standards set by the Holy See....

The Jesuit priests serving in Japan represent 25 different nationalities, and the Society makes a practice of having a number of their European and North American scholastics receive a part of their scholasticate training at St. Mary's College in Tokyo. For example, of the 16 Jesuits who completed their training for the priesthood and were ordained in Japan in 1958, seven were Spaniards, four were Japanese, three were Americans, one came from Hungary and one was a Brazilian student of Japanese descent.

As in former centuries, the Franciscans have also resumed missionary work in Japan. In 1954, St. Anthony's Seminary was opened by them in Tokyo as a central scholasticate to serve as a training center in philosophy and theology for all the Japanese students who desire to enter this Order. The Franciscans also maintain a Bible institute which is attached to St. Joseph's Friary in Tokyo at which studies in Japanese history, law, etc., are being conducted, and whose faculty members have been translating the Old and New Testaments into modern Japanese.

Table 144 lists the major seminaries and scholasticates in Korea, Hongkong and Macao in 1956.

Roman Catholic missionaries in Korea have faced many of the same obstacles in fostering a local clergy as were encountered in Japan. Prior to the Japanese annexation of Korea in 1910, Roman Catholic priests were severely persecuted by the Korean Government. For example, in 1866 all the clergy were either killed or driven out of the country. Later, in 1908, there were a total of only ten local priests, and 61 men were being trained in the seminary.

TABLE 144.   MAJOR SEMINARIES AND SCHOLASTICATES IN KOREA, HONGKONG AND MACAO (1956)

Name	Location	Approx. Number of Major Seminary Students	Administration
Korea			
Holy Spirit	Seoul	243[a]	Secular
Hongkong			
Regional Seminary of Our Lady Queen of China	Aberdeen	80	Jesuits
Pontifical Seminary of St. Albert the Great	Hongkong	58[a]	Dominicans
Scholasticate[b]	Cheung Chau Island	10[a]	Salesians (St. John Bosco)
Scholasticate	Cheung Chau Island	12?[a]	Milan Missionaries[c]
St. Albert's Priory	Hongkong	37[a]	Dominicans
Missionary House of Studies[d]	Hongkong	12?[a]	Salesians (St. John Bosco)
Macao			
St. Joseph	Macao	28	Jesuits
Total: 8		480	

NOTES: [a] As of 1958.
[b] Philosophate, established in 1957.
[c] Fathers of the Pontifical Institute of Foreign Missions of Milan (P.I.M.E.)
[d] Established 1931.

The seminary at Seoul was founded in 1908 by the Missionary Benedictines of St. Ottilien, whose main monastery is in upper Bavaria. The activities of this Order in Northern Korea were altogether stopped with the entry of the Communists at the end of World War II. Following the outbreak of the Korean War in 1950, the Central Seminary in Seoul was destroyed. Reopened after the end of hostilities under the administration of the secular clergy, by 1958 it was training 243 students at the major seminary plus 232 students at the minor seminary level.

Early in 1959 it was announced that Cardinal Agagianian had approved the construction of a new major seminary to be located at Kwangju, in the southwestern corner of the Korean Peninsula.

Although the 1957 *Annuario pontificio* lists 29 major seminarians reported by the ecclesiastical circumscriptions comprising Formosa, it does not appear that there are any major seminaries or scholasticates on the island. Presumably these students are sent to either Hongkong, Macao or the Philippines for their training.

In 1841 the Imperial Chinese Government ceded the then small fishing village of Hongkong to Great Britain. The first Roman Catholic missionaries entered the Crown Colony in the same year. One year later the Native Seminary of the Immaculate Virgin was established. In 1867 the ecclesiastical direction of this Apostolic Prefecture was entrusted to the Milan Missionaries (Fathers of the Pontifical Institute of Foreign Missions of Milan, P.I.M.E.).

In 1926 the Jesuits commenced work in Hongkong and shortly thereafter established a regional seminary in the colony to supply the southern Chinese provinces of Kwantung and Kwangsi with local secular priests. This Seminary of Our Lady Queen of China was expanded after 1950 with the influx of Roman Catholic exiles from the Communist Chinese mainland. In the period 1950–56 the number of major seminarians enrolled in this institution increased from 25 to 80 students, and on several occasions it served as a refuge for entire seminary faculties and student bodies being evacuated from China. It offers a three-year course in philosophy (as well as the usual four years in theology), and its graduates are now serving throughout Southeast Asia.

Hongkong has also served as the place of refuge for the Pontifical Seminary of St. Albert the Great. This Dominican institution formerly was the Regional Seminary of Nam Dinh in Indochina and was transferred to Hongkong in 1954 to avoid being subject to the Communist regime in North Vietnam.

Since 1948, the Franciscans have maintained a "Studium biblicum Franciscanum" in Hongkong. It was originally established in Peking in 1945 for the purpose of translating the Bible into the Chinese language. In 1954, this organization published a three-volume text entitled, *Theses dogmaticæ* by P. Maurus Heinrichs, O.F.M. When reviewing this edition of Father Heinrich's work, Father Johann Hofinger, S.J., cited the need in Africa, Asia and Latin America for theological texts written in simple easy Latin for use in the seminaries and scholasticates in those areas. Father Hofinger believes there is a need to relate Christian concepts and terms (such as the Johannine *"logos"*) to the terms and concepts used in Taoism, etc., for a better understanding of the former by seminary students. Most of the texts now in use were written by Europeans, with very few having been prepared by the local clergy.

In Macao, St. Joseph's Seminary and its predecessors have had a long history going back to the early days of the Portuguese colonial advance in East Asia during the 16th century. With the progressive shrinkage of that empire to the three ports of Macao, Timor and Goa, and with the rise of Canton and Hongkong as the leading shipping centers of southern China, the importance of Macao has dwindled. The present St. Joseph's Seminary was founded in 1749, or shortly before, for the purpose of training priests destined for missionary work in China. Administered by the Jesuits, Portuguese and Chinese students have studied side by side in this institution. However, with the advent of the Communist regime in China, the future of this Seminary once more seems uncertain.

TABLE 145.   MAJOR SEMINARIES AND SCHOLASTICATES IN COMMUNIST CHINA (1950)

Name		Region	Mission	Approx. Number of Major Seminary Students	Administration
Major	Seminary	Anhwei	Wuhu	21	Jesuits
"	"	Chekiang	Ningpo	14	Lazarists
"	"	Fukien	Foochow	17	Dominicans
"	"	Honan	Kaifeng	31	Foreign Missions of Milan
"	"	Hopeh	Kinghsien	78	Jesuits
"	"	Hopeh	Pechino	96	Lazarists
"	"	Hupeh	Hankow	46	Franciscans
"	"	Kansu	Lanchow	12	Divine Word Fathers
"	"	Kiangsi	Yükiang	8	Lazarists
"	"	Kiangsu	Shanghai	38	Jesuits
"	"	Manchuria	Changchun	34	Assumptionists
"	"	Shansi	Hungtung	23	Secular Clergy
"	"	Shansi	Kweisui	73	Scheut Fathers
"	"	Shansi	Taiyüan	43	Franciscans
"	"	Shantung	Tsinan	35	Franciscans
"	"	Shantung	Yengchow	52	Divine Word Fathers
9 Major Seminaries		Various	Various	157	Secular Clergy
Subtotal: 25				778	
Scholasticates		Various	Various	33	Jesuits
"		"	"	12	Franciscans
"		"	"	10	Dominicans
"		"	"	2	Salesians (St. John Bosco)
"		"	"	6	Divine Word Fathers
Subtotal: 5				63	
Total: 30 (approx.)				841	

The seminaries in Communist China fall outside the scope of this Survey. However, the history of the efforts of the Roman Catholic Church to establish a local clergy in this country is of background interest. A list of the major seminaries and scholasticates in China as of 1950 (all of which were under the jurisdiction of the Propaganda) is contained in Table 145.

Christianity was introduced into China by the Nestorian clergy in both the 7th and 13th centuries, but both times these missionaries failed to establish an indigenous church. The result was that their efforts twice came to nought. As Msgr. Freri notes: "In the fourteenth century there were no less than eleven archbishops or bishops, with a corresponding number of priests in China, all Europeans, and the Christians numbered more than one hundred thousand; but we have no record that an effort was ever made to educate any native for the priesthood. In 1483 the last missionary to that unfortunate country was put to death, and when two centuries later the first Jesuit priests arrived in Peking they found no traces of Christianity."

Francis Xavier died in 1552 while on his way to China. His fellow Jesuit, Matteo Ricci (1552–1610), subsequently established the well-known Jesuit mission at the Court of Peking where he was placed by the Imperial Government in charge of the Bureau of Astronomy. For the first 50 years (1581–1631) the Jesuits were the sole missionaries in China. After that time they were followed by the Dominicans, Franciscans, Lazarists and other religious communities.

Basing his account on Father Huonder and French sources, Dr. C. Stanley Smith has written as follows:

. . . The Far East, until after the middle of the seventeenth century, had no established hierarchy. There were no native clergy and only one bishop at Macao, and he was not there all the time. The church authorities at Rome fully realized the weakness of the situation, especially after the persecution of the Christians in Japan and the expulsion of all foreign priests from that country. . . . Candidates for the priesthood who desired a more advanced education were usually sent outside the country, to Manila; to the general college at Penang or to Rome, or Naples; or, before the Revolution, to Paris. This method, however, was not satisfactory because few boys could afford to go abroad and many could not stand the change in climate which this involved. It is evident, also, that many of those who went abroad for their training did not become ordained to the priesthood. . . . A probable reason for the failure of the new native leadership to produce the fruits which were anticipated was the fact that the advice of Mgr. Pallu, that the Chinese bishops should be placed under the direction of Europeans, was not followed. . . .

The first system for obtaining a native clergy in China was inaugurated by the Jesuits of Peking. They proposed to ordain only mature men whom they would excuse from learning Latin. In 1615, their proposal won the approval of the Holy See who also approved the use of the liturgy in the vernacular. There were no theological books in Chinese, however, and the liturgy had to be translated. By the time this material was prepared there was no bishop in China to ordain. Finally, when there was both literature and bishop, the Papacy reversed its earlier ruling so that a century of agitation and preparation in the end proved a complete failure. Not entirely a failure, however, as much necessary and important translation work had meanwhile been accomplished by the Jesuit sinologue, Father Ludwig Buglio, which was to be the foundation for the education of an indigenous clergy. Among other things, the *Summa theologica* of Thomas Aquinas and a text-book on *Moral Theology* had been translated and published. . . .

Meanwhile, the Portuguese Jesuits in Macao had been attempting to carry on another system of training for a native clergy more in harmony with the decrees of the Council of Trent. . . . They proposed to select suitable native children, teach them Latin and train them in Macao, "according to European methods of training youths in Seminaries." This system was opposed by the Peking Jesuits. It was not very successful. In 1684, Father Couplet wrote of it that seventy years of experience had convinced them that they were losing time. Seminaries had been opened in Macao and Nanchang, but after much trouble and expense the only result was, "six or seven of those better gifted boys have been received in the Society of Jesus as Lay Brothers, to do manual work, which lay people might do just as well. . . ."

Since the Peking system did not have the sanction of the Papacy and the Macao system was not very much of a success, a third system was tried wherein the other two methods were combined. Men of mature age were to be ordained and to be taught enough Latin to read and explain the most essential parts of the Mass and the administration of the Sacraments, even though they themselves did not know enough Latin to understand much else. The first Chinese priest and bishop, Gregory Lopez (Lo Wen-tsao), was a product of this method. He had studied a little at the Dominican College of Saint Thomas in Manila before he was ordained, in 1656, to the priesthood . . . (he) was not consecrated, however, until 1685, largely because of the opposition of the Dominicans. . . .

In the period 1643–1742 the success of the Roman Catholic efforts in China was retarded by the Rites Controversy. The Jesuit missionaries under Ricci and his successors defended the practice of some Chinese priests of introducing into the liturgy some local practices which the Jesuits claimed were neither idolatrous or contrary to Roman Catholic dogma. The Dominicans and Lazarists opposed these practices on the grounds that they constituted aspects of ancestor worship and Confucianism. A part of the controversy reflected nationalist elements: the Jesuits were mostly Portuguese priests based in Macao, while the Dominicans were Spaniards looking to Manila for support. The congregations appealed to Rome. Finally in his bull *Ex quo singulari* dated July 11, 1742, Pope Benedict XIV ruled in favor of the Dominicans and Lazarists and forbade Roman Catholic priests in China to engage in such rites. It was not until December 8, 1939, that a decree of the Propaganda reversed this ruling. However, by that time (owing to the outbreak of World War II and the subsequent advent of Communism) this reversal had less effect than it otherwise might have. (In Japan the Vatican has permitted Roman Catholics to participate in certain Shinto rituals on the grounds that they are a patriotic exercise.)

In the 18th century there were only about 200,000 Roman Catholics in China. However, the Imperial Government commenced to practice religious toleration as a result of the treaties imposed on it by European powers beginning in 1844. This led to a rapid growth in the number of both Roman Catholics and Protestants. The Roman Catholics increased from approximately 300,000 in 1840 to 1,000,000 in 1907 and 2,000,000 in 1923. There was a corresponding increase in the number of local priests and major seminarians as shown in Table 146.

With the suppression of the Society of Jesus in 1773, the Lazarists took over their mission in Peking and established a seminary there. In 1842 the Jesuits returned to China and opened a seminary in Shanghai.

In the century 1850–1950 there was a considerable increase in the number of apostolic vicariates and prefectures in China. It was hoped that each vicariate would have its own seminary. Dr. Smith notes that in the summer of 1929, according to the Chancellor of the Catholic University in Peking, "it was planned to complete

TABLE 146.   GROWTH OF LOCAL CHINESE
CLERGY (1840–1949)

Year	Local Priests	Major Seminarians
1840	80	?
1907	502	?
1923	938	717
1939	2,022	853
1948	2,547	1,214
1949	3,350	957

the establishment of provincial seminaries from which the best students for the priesthood would be selected and sent to a national theological seminary to be established in connection with the Fu Jen University. He added that the professors for this highest of all theological seminaries would be chosen from the various Benedictine Orders throughout the world and that all professors must have their doctorate in philosophy and theology and have had at least ten years of teaching experience. . . ."

This plan was not immediately carried out. Instead, a few of the best students were sent to the Propaganda University in Rome for their advanced studies. In 1933 the administration of the University of Peking was transferred from the Benedictines to the Divine Word Fathers. Four years later the *Collegium sinicum ecclesiasticum* was established at the University to provide facilities for advanced studies in Chinese history, literature and languages for approximately 40 priests. In 1948–49 the total enrollment in all courses at the University of Peking amounted to 2,268 students. There also were Roman Catholic universities in Shanghai and Tientsin.

In the post-World War I period there was a trend toward consolidating major seminaries in China into regional institutions. By 1939, according to Father Beckmann, there were 12 of the latter type of institutions in operation.

The number of local priests in China quintupled during the period 1907–49 (from 502 to 3,350). According to Father Ledochowsky (who was then the Superior General of the Society of Jesus), in 1916, 35% of all the priests in China were indigenous. This proportion had increased to 41% by 1926 and over 50% shortly after World War II. In recognition of this trend, Pope Pius XI personally consecrated six Chinese bishops (one secular, one Jesuit, two Lazarists and two Franciscans) in Rome on October 28, 1926. However, at first none of the major vicariates were entrusted to their care.

According to Professor Freitag, in 1949, 33 of the 138 mission districts in China (or about one-quarter of the total) were then under the direction of local clergy, of whom 29 were secular priests and four were members of religious communities. Included among these 33 districts were four archdioceses, 23 dioceses and six apostolic prefectures. The elevation of Bishop Thomas Tien to the rank of Cardinal and Archbishop of Peking in 1946 was a further step. In China as a whole in 1946 there were a total of 20 archdioceses and 79 dioceses. In that year there were only three countries in the world (Italy, the United States and Brazil) which had a larger number of similar ecclesiastical circumscriptions.

With the advent of the Communist regime in China, the Roman Catholic Church was far better prepared for the ensuing period of persecution than it had been in previous centuries when it had been under attack. Subsequent to 1948, many major seminaries were either destroyed or closed, and some of their students went into exile in Hongkong, the Philippines and elsewhere.

In the last two months of 1956 a delegation of bishops and clerics from the Anglican Church in Australia visited Communist China in order to assess the status of the Chinese Christians. They were informed by the Roman Catholic Archbishop of Mukden, Pi Shu-Shih, that there were three Roman Catholic institutions in which major seminarians were then being trained. These were located in Peking, Nanking and Shanghai. Each of these institutions were said to be at about the same academic level and had about 60 students in attendance. The Peking seminary was training 34 "Latinists" and 27 students were reading theology and philosophy in preparation for the priesthood. The Archbishop stated these numbers were wholly inadequate for the needs of the Roman Catholic Church in China. However, the major difficulty, in his view, was not the small number of candidates applying for admission to the schools but rather the very grave shortage of teachers capable of serving on the seminary faculties.

Australia and New Zealand: The members and personnel of the Roman Catholic

TABLE 147.　MAJOR SEMINARIES AND SCHOLASTICATES IN AUSTRALIA AND NEW ZEALAND (1950)

Name	Location	Approx. Number of Major Seminary Students	Administration
Australia			
St. Francis Xavier	Adelaide	14	Secular
Pius XII	Brisbane	112	Secular
Corpus Christi	Melbourne	134	Jesuits
Archepiscopal Seminary, St. Patrick's College	Manly, Sydney	132[a]	Secular
Scholasticate	?	8	Pallotine Fathers
Scholasticate	?	22	St. Columban Fathers
Subtotal: 6		422	
New Zealand			
Holy Cross	Dunedin	70	Lazarists
Subtotal: 1			
Total: 7		492	

NOTE:　[a] Studying in Faculty of Theology.

Church in these two British Dominions technically still come under the authority of the Propaganda Congregation even though, generally speaking, they represent fully evolved Roman Catholic peoples. These two countries fall outside the scope of this Survey. Nevertheless, in order that the record of the Propaganda's activities in this field may be complete as set forth herein, there is presented in Table 147 a list of the major seminaries and scholasticates under the authority of the Propaganda which were located in these countries in 1950.

H. LATIN AMERICA

Since most of the countries in Latin America were colonies of Spain and Portugal from the 16th through the 18th centuries, the development of the Roman Catholic local clergy tended to follow a pattern similar to that which prevailed in the Philippines up to the 20th century. The annual contributions from the Spanish Crown for the construction of churches and chapels and for the missionary work of the Church in the early days in Latin America sometimes equalled the cost to it of maintaining the armies in the colonies.

In this connection Father Weyland has written:

An important factor in retarding the development of an indigenous clergy both in Portuguese and Spanish America was the enormous difference between the cultural level of the highly civilized Portuguese and Spaniards and that of the primitive Indians. They considered it necessary to Europeanize the Indians and to raise them to the level of Portuguese and Spanish 16th century culture before admitting them to the priesthood. They did not take into account that the native priests of the Iberian Peninsula in the early Christian centuries could not have measured up to this standard, and yet they proved to be valuable churchmen. . . . The majority of the early Spanish missionaries deemed it necessary to refuse Holy Communion to their Indian converts. . . . A royal decree of April 16, 1604, demands unequivocally that the Christian Indians without exception be given Holy Communion at least in the hour of death. . . . The Synod of Mexico (1555) and the two Synods of Lima (1552, 1567) expressly forbade the ordination of Indians and half-breeds. . . .

Father Anton Huonder, S.J., discusses how the restrictive practices of the religious communities in Latin America during the 17th and 18th centuries were overcome and an increasing proportion of secular priests of mixed blood (Mestizos) came to be ordained:

Since, at the beginning of the Spanish conquests in Mexico and South America, there was a dearth of secular priests, the monks of the various religious orders took over the regular parochial duties in numerous places. Once in possession of these parishes, the monks sought to perpetuate their possession and to preserve their influential position in the face of the secular clergy and even of the bishops. This led to a considerable tension between the secular and regular clergy and to constant collisions between the rights of bishops and the real or pretended privileges of the religious. This dispute, which was carried on with passionate vehemence on both sides, dragged on till the end of the 18th century, and fills one of the most disagreeable pages of Spanish colonial and mission history. For the purpose of strengthening their position against the powerful orders, the bishops now enlisted more and more native elements, especially Mestizos, and stationed them in as many parishes as possible. In doing so, they seem not to have been all too selective.

In 1751 Pope Benedict XIV decreed that the parishes in the Spanish colonies should from henceforth be placed in the hands of secular priests, and only in exceptional cases were they to be entrusted to the care of the religious clergy. Thus by 1793 in the case of the Archdiocese of Mexico, only six of the 253 Indian parishes were still in the hands of members of the religious communities. In this way the policies of the institutes were counteracted and the door was opened toward the establishment of a more numerous local clergy, which consisted chiefly of Creoles and Mestizos. According to Father Joseph Schmidlin, S.V.D., after the position of the secular clergy had been consolidated at the end of the 18th century, the number of local priests in Latin America showed a considerable increase. Later the obstacles against their being admitted as members of the religious communities were also removed. "The sole exception was the Jesuits' Reductions in Paraguay which still adhered to the old policy of rigid exclusion, yet were supposed to train 'model Christians.'"

Another factor which impeded the development of a strong local clergy in Latin America has been commented on by Edwin Ryan as follows: "All during the colonial period, the government at home (i.e., Spain) continued the pernicious practice of using the colonies as a dumping ground for priests who had given trouble in Spain. From time to time shiploads of such worthies were landed, accompanied by orders from the King that each be appointed to some ecclesiastical duties."

During the 16th century at least four seminaries were founded in Latin America. San Luis de Francia Seminary (named after the French King, Louis IX) was established in Santa Fé de Bogotá in 1582. Two years later, following the Council of Lima, seminaries were founded in Santiago, Chile (1584), Lima, Peru (1591), and San Luis de Quito (1594). The administration of these institutions was in the hands of the secular clergy. However, a number of the bishops found it necessary to staff their faculties with members of the religious institutes. Thus in the 17th century the seminary at Popayan, Colombia, was placed under the care of the Jesuits. The courses in these early seminaries were largely concerned with the scholasticism of the age, and lasted from three to five years, although occasionally men were ordained after only two years of training.

The Roman Catholic Church in Latin America never experienced a Counter Reformation as it did in Europe in the 16th century and in the Philippines at the beginning of the 20th century. Because of the weakness of the Latin American local clergy, the Vatican has sought to remedy the situation by sending missionaries and financial support from Europe and the United States. Approximately 40% of the total number of priests in South America at the present time are members of religious communities, and of this number more than half are foreigners. It is also stated that as many as one-half of the priests in Argentina today were born in Europe. But these efforts have not been outstandingly successful in creating a strong indigenous church leadership in most of these countries.

According to Father Albert J. Nevins, M.M., who is an expert on Roman Catholic affairs in Latin America,

more than 136 million people of Latin America claim to be Catholics, but even by the most generous estimates only about ten per cent can be called practicing Catholics. The sad fact is that Catholicism in Latin America is nothing more than a tradition for the vast majority of people there. . . . Latin America, which has more than four times the Catholic population of the United States, has fewer parishes than we do and almost half the number of priests. . . . At the best the Church is just about holding on. Facts do not warrant calling Latin America a Catholic continent. By tradition it is Catholic, but in actual practice the Latin American people as a whole live in neglect of their faith.

One indication of the vitality of the Roman Catholic Church in any country is the number of Roman Catholics in its population per priest. A relationship of 1,000 baptized members to one priest is generally considered to be the maximum desirable ratio. Table 148 indicates the extent to which the number of Catholics in most Latin American countries exceeds this norm.

TABLE 148.   NUMBER OF REPORTED ROMAN CATHOLICS PER PRIEST IN LATIN AMERICA (1958)

Area	10,000–12,000	7,000–10,000	5,000–7,000	4,000–5,000	3,000–4,000
Central America	Guatemala	El Salvador Honduras	Panama	Mexico Nicaragua Costa Rica	
Caribbean Area[b]		Cuba Dominican Republic	Haiti Puerto Rico		
South America			Venezuela Brazil Peru Paraguay	Bolivia	Colombia Ecuador Uruguay Argentina Chile[a]

NOTES: [a] 2,660 per priest.
[b] In the smaller units in the Caribbean area (not listed herein) the number of Roman Catholics per priest ranges from 500 to 2,650. On these same islands the missionary religious clergy outnumber the local secular clergy by a ratio of four to one.

By contrast, in Africa in 1957 all except two countries had less than 2,000 Roman Catholics per priest. The exceptions were Ruanda-Urundi (3,150) and Uganda (2,600) where the annual number of conversions to the Roman Catholic Church in recent years has been high. In Asia the number of Roman Catholics per priest in 1957 were: India, 935; Siam, 475; and Japan, 170.

There are a number of other factors peculiar to Latin America which account in part, at least, for the weakness of its local clergy. These factors have persisted in many of these countries throughout the 19th and 20th centuries. Among them, as cited by Father Stephen McKenna, C.SS.R., are "(a) The hostility shown toward the Church in the various countries has left in the minds of many well-meaning Catholics a low estimate of the priesthood and the religious life. (b) In South America . . . there is no strong middle-class from which in Europe, the United States and Canada such vocations have usually come. . . . (c) Many children in South America are born out of lawful wedlock, or of an invalid marriage, and thus they contract the stigma of illegitimacy, which is a canonical impediment to entering the clerical or religious state. (d) The rate of illiteracy in many countries is higher than 50 per cent. . . ."

One of the features which distinguishes the history and development of the seminaries in some countries in Latin America from elsewhere in the world is the number of times they have been suppressed by the national governments during the periods of popular or liberal reaction against the Roman Catholic Church which have occurred from time to time. These reactions have been more numerous and perhaps more violent in Mexico than in any other Latin American country. Father José Bravo Ugarte, S.J., has compiled some interesting data showing not only the steady development of the Roman Catholic seminaries in Mexico during the past four centuries but also the number of times the Mexican Government has confiscated their properties. Each time the seminaries were suppressed, they were subsequently replaced whenever this became possible. Table 149 summarizes this development and includes some institutions which were minor seminaries or are no longer in existence.

What these suppressions of Mexican seminaries meant in terms of the life of their faculties and students was graphically described in 1936 by another Jesuit, Father Wilfrid J. Parsons, S.J., as follows:

The Seminarians were dispersed and mostly went back to their parents. In three places, Mexico City, Saltillo, and Puebla, they were arrested in a body. . . . In Zacatecas the Seminarians have been dispersed fifteen times; their property has been confiscated, even their own personal belongings have been taken away from them. And still they persisted in their determination to go on for the priesthood. They would gather in one place, and shortly would have to leave for another.

In Puebla there are 126 Seminarians. The Major and Minor Seminaries have both been confiscated. Recently, the authorities got wind of their secret classes, and every Mayor in the State received a circular warning him to be on the lookout for them. The last place they were known to be was Tlaxcala, but they were rooted out of there and the building, a rented one, was confiscated. But I hear that they simply moved off somewhere else.

Of conditions in another State it would be cruel to reveal too much. It might give them away. But I have before me the official report of the Bishop. . . . The original Seminary

Table 149. Confiscation of Seminaries in Mexico (1857–1937)

Seminary		Years in which Seminary was Confiscated			
Year Founded	Diocese	Period of Reform (1855–62)	Reaction after the Deposition of Emperor Maximilian (1867–68)	Period of Revolution (1911–17)	Period of Religious Conflict (1924–40)
1538	Michoacán (I)				
1648	Puebla		1867	1914	1928
1678	Chiapas	1857		1914	1925
1681	Oaxaca	1860		1917	
1696	Guadalajara	1861	1867	1914	1924
1697	México	1861			1928
1751	Yucatán	1861	1868	1915	
1767	Durango	1860		1914	
1770	Michoacán (II)	1859	1867	1914	1926
1793	Monterrey	1862		1914	
1838	Sonora			1916	1932, 1935
1844	Californias				
1855	San Luis Potosí	1859		1914	
1854	León	1861		1915	1926
1864	Vera Cruz				1921
1865	Zamora			1914	
1865	Querétaro			1914	1927, 1932
1865	Tulancingo			1914	
1867	Chilapa				1934
1869	Zacatecas			1914	1926, 1931
1873	Tamaulipas			1913	1927
1882	Colima			1914	1925
1883	Sinaloa			1914	1926, 1937
1892	Tepic			1914	
1894	Cuernavaca				1925
1899	Aguascalientes			1914	1934
1900	Tabasco				
1903	Huajuapán			1914	1926
1904	Chihuahua				1934
1905	Saltillo			1914	1932
1911	Tehuantepec			1914	1926
1920	Tocámbaro				1926
1922	Huejutla				1926

was closed. . . . The Bishop took his Seminarians to the mountains and went on with their formation as well as he was able. . . . Three of these are studying Humanities under a professor in a friendly farmhouse. Three others are studying philosophy in another place. Nine are theological students with the Bishop himself in an inaccessible hiding place. . . .

Virtually all of the major seminaries and scholasticates now being operated in Latin America are under the jurisdiction of the Seminaries Congregation. The few exceptions are those located in areas under the jurisdiction of the Propaganda Congregation (i.e., remote, mountainous or tribal areas in South America as noted in the tables below). The reason why Latin America is not under the authority of the Propaganda is that when the Spanish colonial authorities were overthrown in the years 1810–24, some of the newly founded Latin American governments sought to exercise in their own countries the *patronato* rights which had formerly been enjoyed by the Hispanic Kings. In the course of resolving this problem, the Vatican decided that the Roman Catholic ecclesiastical authorities in virtually all of Latin

America should be considered as fully evolved hierarchies rather than as missionary circumscriptions.

With the departure of the Spanish viceroys, most of the then 35 Roman Catholic archbishops and bishops in Latin America (as well as the superiors of the religious orders and institutes) returned to Spain, leaving the Church behind them in confusion. The number of the secular clergy in the area dropped by 50%. Many of the seminaries were nationalized and affiliated with the secularized state universities. Furthermore some of the anticlerical governments required the seminaries to adopt unreasonably high entrance requirements in order that their enrollments might be held to a low number of students.

Although a high proportion of priests in Latin America today are of foreign birth and are members of religious communities, nevertheless a fair number of the major seminaries in this area are administered by the secular rather than the religious clergy. Where conditions permitted them to do so, local bishops sometimes entrusted the priests under their jurisdiction with the administration of the diocesan seminaries and avoided the tendency to turn this responsibility over to the various religious communities specializing in this type of work.

Because of the comparatively primitive and often chaotic conditions prevailing in Latin America throughout the 19th century, the development of strong seminaries was retarded. As a means of overcoming this situation, Pope Pius IX (at the suggestion of a Chilean bishop) established the Pontifical Latin American College in Rome on November 21, 1858. To this institution students in philosophy and theology are still being sent from all parts of Latin America for their training. The College is administered by the Jesuits.

Despite the hostility which a number of Latin American governments have occasionally displayed toward the Roman Catholic hierarchy in their own countries, including the wholesale suppression of the seminaries and the confiscation of the Church's properties, such hostile acts do not appear to have been as harmful to the Roman Catholic Church in the long run as has the general indifference of many of the people toward its teachings. In Mexico, for example, Church-State relations have often been bitter during the past century. Nevertheless the Roman Catholic Church in Mexico is currently experiencing a notable renaissance. One evidence of this is the large number of Mexican men who are now being trained for the secular clergy in the major seminaries as shown in Table 150.

From this table it will be noted that virtually all of the major seminaries in Mexico are under the administration of the secular clergy. During the previous periods of conflict between the Church and the Mexican Government, the attacks of the latter were often centered on the religious communities because of (1) a high proportion of their membership were foreign priests, and (2) the orders and institutes controlled considerable amounts of property which could be confiscated. A semi-

Table 150. Major Seminaries in Mexico (1956)

Name	Location	Approx. Number of Major Seminary Students	Administration
Interdiocesan			
Mexican National Seminary	Montezuma, New Mexico, USA	300	Jesuits
Archdiocesan			
Conciliar Seminary	Durango	67	Secular
St. Joseph	Guadalajara	282	Secular
Conciliar Seminary	México City, D.F.	119	Secular
Foreign Missions Seminary[a]	México City, D.F.	12	Holy Spirit Fathers of Mexico (?)
Major Seminary	Monterrey	55	Secular
Major Seminary	Morelia	129	Secular
Holy Cross	Oaxaca	37	Secular
Major Seminary	Puebla	140	Secular
Major Seminary	Jalapa	59	Secular
Major Seminary	Mérida, Yucatán	129	Secular
Diocesan			
St. Mary of Guadalupe	Aguascalientes	10?	Secular
Conciliar Seminary	San Cristóbal las Casas[c]	25	Secular
Assumption of Mary	Chihuahua	28	Secular
Major Seminary	Chilapa	69[b]	Secular
Major Seminary	Colima	46[b]	Secular
Major Seminary	Huajuapán	39	Secular
Major Seminary	Huejutla	64[b]	Secular
Most Holy Mother of Light and of the Immaculate Conception	León	104	Secular
Immaculate Conception	Papantla	6	Secular
Our Lady of Guadalupe	Querétaro	43[b]	Secular
Major Seminary	San Luis Potosí	54[b]	Secular
Major Seminary	Sinaloa	47	Secular
Major Seminary	Hermosillo, Sonora	20[b]	Secular
Conciliar Seminary	Tampico	31	Secular
Conciliar Seminary	Toluca	102	Secular
Immaculate Conception	Zacatecas	91	Secular
Conciliar Seminary	Zamora	105	Secular
Total: 28		2,213	

Notes: [a] Under jurisdiction of The Propaganda Congregation.   [b] As of 1952.   [c] Diocese of Chiapas.

nary administered by the local secular clergy is not as apt to become wealthy and is less likely to be suppressed.

Despite these setbacks, a number of religious congregations have established scholasticates in Mexico, as shown in Table 151, a list which is probably incomplete.

During the period of Church-State conflict which occurred in Mexico in the years 1926–40, approximately 22 seminaries had their properties confiscated, a few of them more than once during this period. During World War II, their recovery was gradual. Subsequently, however, the number of seminaries and students enrolled in them have increased very considerably, so that in 1956, of all the countries in Africa, Asia and Latin America, Mexico had the largest number (2,383) of men studying at the major seminary level for the priesthood.

The largest, and perhaps the most interesting of the institutions training the major seminarians is the Mexican National Seminary, located at Montezuma in New

Mexico, USA. At the height of the Church-State struggle in 1926–40 the Mexican hierarchy appealed on February 11, 1936, for support from the hierarchies in the United States and elsewhere. Their appeal stated that the Mexican Government had closed all the major seminaries in Mexico, was permitting only 197 priests to officiate in the entire country, and had confiscated the property of all the religious communities.

TABLE 151.   SCHOLASTICATES IN MEXICO (1957)

Type	Location	Approx. Number of Scholastics	Administration
Philosophate	Zapopan	20	Franciscans
Theologate	Monterrey	15	Franciscans
Scholasticate	México City	16	Marists
Collegium Maximum "Christ the King"[b]	México City	54	Jesuits
Philosophate	Zinacantepec	23	Claretians
St. Anthony's Seminary[a]	El Paso, Texas, USA	12	Franciscans
Philosophate	Las Cruces, New Mexico, USA	30	Franciscans
Total: 7		170	

NOTES: [a] Theologate, as of 1958.
 [b] Philosophate, as of 1956.

The response of the American hierarchy was to launch a campaign to establish a Mexican National Seminary which would be located in the United States and therefore not subject to political attack. Sunday, September 20, 1936, was designated by the American hierarchy as "Mexican Seminary Sunday," and a nation-wide collection for this purpose was held in the Roman Catholic churches in the United States. To this collection Pope Pius XI personally contributed $2,000, and a total of approximately $500,000 was raised.

With these funds a campus was purchased in New Mexico. Originally it had been a hotel constructed by the Atchison, Topeka & Santa Fe Railroad in 1900 or so. The building had cost approximately $2,000,000 and was intended to be a health resort utilizing the Montezuma Hot Springs which are located in the mountains some 35 miles east of Santa Fe. After the patronage of the hotel had declined, the site was first purchased by the Southern Baptist Convention which converted the property into a campus for Montezuma College. The latter was not a success and went out of existence some time before the property was purchased by representatives of the Roman Catholic Church.

Accordingly, in 1937, the Montezuma Seminary was opened under the administration of the Jesuits. Only Mexicans being trained for the secular clergy are enrolled and (aside from Latin) only Spanish is spoken by the faculty and students. The seminary is supervised directly by the Sacred Congregation of Seminaries and by a committee of seven American bishops, of which the Archbishop of Santa Fe, New Mexico, is Chairman. Approximately one-third of the institution's annual operating expenses are defrayed by the hierarchy in Mexico, and the remaining two-thirds (or approximately $125,000) is being contributed by the American Catholic hierarchy.

Once the Montezuma Seminary reached its capacity enrollment of 300, the policy was established of sending to it from Mexico only the most promising students. Its graduates are now serving in dioceses throughout Mexico. In the annual report of the Seminary for the academic year 1957–58 the Rector states: "With the present fourth year class the number of priests (graduated) from Montezuma Seminary will total 1,019, almost 25% of the secular Mexican clergy, and 20% of all priests in Mexico."

In 1958 the Seminary building was partially burned, and the Catholic Church Extension Society (whose offices are in Chicago) contributed toward the cost of the necessary repairs.

The location on American soil of this Mexican National Seminary serves as an "anchor to windward" and would afford some protection to the future of the Roman Catholic Church in Mexico if another period of conflict between Church and State were to occur in that country. In this respect the Montezuma Seminary serves in a capacity similar to that performed in the early period of the Reformation by the Jesuit-staffed English colleges at Valladolid, Seville and Madrid, the Scots colleges at Madrid and at Douai (in France), and the Irish colleges at Lisbon, Santiago, Salamanca, Seville and Poitiers to which seminarians from the British Isles were sent during the reign of King Henry VIII. Similarly, in recent years two of the Mexican Provinces of the Order of Friars Minor (Franciscans) have maintained scholasticates at Las Cruces in New Mexico and El Paso, Texas, to which Mexican scholastics are sent.

Table 152 lists the major seminaries in Central America. From this table it will be noted that within most of the countries in Central America, with the exception of Panama, there is located one central or national seminary.

TABLE 152. MAJOR SEMINARIES IN CENTRAL AMERICA (1957)

Name	Location	Approx. Number of Major Seminary Students	Administration
Guatemala Archdiocesan Seminary	Guatemala City	32	Secular
El Salvador St. Joseph of the Mountain	San Salvador	36	Jesuits
Honduras St. Joseph Interdiocesan	Tegucigalpa	21	Lazarists
Nicaragua National Seminary	Managua	16	Secular
Costa Rica Central Seminary	San José	46	Lazarists[a]
Total: 5		151	

NOTE: [a] German Province.

In Guatemala, the major seminary was reorganized in 1928 and now has a capacity of approximately 60 students which in recent years has sometimes been in full use, taking into consideration the minor seminarians who are also currently enrolled in a separate department in this institution.

In El Salvador, the St. Joseph of the Mountain Seminary located in its capital has served as a training center for students coming from Panama, Nicaragua, Honduras and Guatemala. During World War II a new building was commenced, and it was completed several years later.

In Panama the Lazarists operate a *seminario conciliar* which is at the minor seminary level. After having been closed, it was reopened in the 1930s, and several attempts have been made from time to time to establish a major seminary in the country. However, these have not been successful, and major seminary students from Panama are usually sent for their training to institutions in Colombia, Costa Rica or the United States.

Table 153 lists the major seminaries in the Caribbean area.

TABLE 153.   MAJOR SEMINARIES IN THE CARIBBEAN AREA (1957)

Name	Location	Approx. Number of Major Seminary Students	Administration
Cuba			
The Good Shepherd	Havana	30	Secular
Major Seminary	El Cobre	4	Secular
Jamaica			
St. Michael	Kingston	2	Jesuits
Haiti			
Our Lady of the Sacred Heart	Port-au-Prince	32	Jesuits
Dominican Republic			
Pontifical Seminary of St. Thomas Aquinas	Ciudad Trujillo	99	Jesuits
Martinique			
Holy Ghost	Fort-de-France	17	Secular
Trinidad			
Archdiocesan Seminary of St. John Vianney and The African Martyrs	Mt. St. Benedict, Tunapuna	15	Dominicans
Total: 7		199	

The University of Havana was established by the Dominicans in 1728. Forty years later, in 1768, this Order founded a seminary in Havana after the model of the one they had earlier established in Santiago de Cuba. Since this country was a Spanish colony until 1898, the number of indigenous priests trained in seminaries on the island was small, and the proportion of foreign priests (particularly from Spain) who were members of the religious orders and congregations was high. This disparity has continued into the 20th century, although many of the foreign missionary priests in Cuba are now being sent from North America. The Havana Seminary later came to be known as the Seminary of St. Charles and St. Ambrose and is now known as The Good Shepherd Seminary. It is administered by the secular clergy and is housed in a building constructed shortly after World War II.

The second seminary in Cuba was formerly located in Santiago and known as St. Albert the Great. At present it is situated in the old city of El Cobre (ten miles west of Santiago) and is part of the National Sanctuary of the Virgin of Charity, the Patroness of Cuba. Most of the students enrolled in this institution are at the minor seminary level, and its graduates serve in parishes in the eastern portion of the island. The Seminary is said to have a comparatively strong library.

There is no major seminary in Puerto Rico. The Jesuits maintain a minor seminary in Aibonito, whose graduates are sent for their instruction in philosophy and theology to the major seminaries in the Dominican Republic, Cuba and elsewhere. There have been a number of attempts to establish a major seminary in the Commonwealth, but so far without success.

In Jamaica, St. Michael's was a minor seminary until 1958 when courses in philosophy were added: this accounts for the small number (2) of its students at the major seminary level.

Formerly most Haitian candidates for the priesthood were sent for their training to major seminaries in France. Although the 1860 concordat between the Haitian Government and the Vatican permitted the establishment of major seminaries in Haiti, this did not take place at the time because there were so few Haitians choosing careers in the Church. Accordingly the Haitian Government entered into an arrangement whereby it would pay the cost of 20 scholarships for Haitian students in seminaries in France. In 1863–68, 14 Haitians were sent to the Grand séminaire d'Haiti which the Holy Ghost Fathers established in Paris. When the Haitian Government subsidy was stopped, the cost of these scholarships was defrayed by the Propaganda Congregation. In 1872 this seminary was transferred from Paris to the scholasticate of the Montfortain Fathers (The Company of Mary, S.M.M.), at Calvaire de Pont Chateau. During the next two decades, approximately ten Haitian priests were graduated each year from there. However, in the period 1893–96, this institution was closed as a result of anticlerical laws passed by the French Government. At this point a wealthy lady, Mme. de Keonartz, donated her chateau and large estate at Lampaul-Guimiliau in Brittany to the Church for use as a seminary. Up to World War I, approximately ten Haitian priests a year were graduated from this institution. During World War I only one Haitian student a year completed the course. In the postwar period, the hierarchy in France (striving to overcome the shortage of French clergy in that country) restricted the number of graduates of its seminaries in France who would be permitted to serve overseas. This impeded the study of Haitian seminarians at Lampaul. The institution still trains a few Haitians, but most of its graduates who now serve in Haiti are French priests.

In recent years, Jesuits from the Society's Province in Quebec established a major seminary in Haiti, Our Lady of the Sacred Heart, located in the capital, Port-au-Prince. It is now graduating approximately five students a year, and it is reported that the Haitian Government contributes $11,700 a year to this seminary for the support of its students. The Archdiocese of Port-au-Prince has a Negro auxiliary bishop, the sole Negro Roman Catholic bishop in Latin America.

The largest major seminary in the Caribbean area is the Pontifical Seminary of St. Thomas Aquinas located in Ciudad Trujillo, the capital of the Dominican Republic. This country takes its name from the Order of Preachers whose missions were for a long time the most important ones on the island. The capital of the country was formerly called Santo Domingo, and in 1518 the Dominicans founded a scholasticate there. In 1538 this institution was elevated by Pope Paul III to the rank of a Pontifical University. Favored by the Kings of Spain, the University (which continued to train priests) had alternating periods of prosperity and adversity. During times of troubles, it was occasionally closed.

By 1848 a separate major seminary was founded in Santo Domingo but it, too, had a checkered career. In 1908 the Eudist Fathers from France took over the task of administering it, but without a great deal of success. Subsequently the Jesuits assumed the task, and since then the seminary has prospered. When a new building for this institution was needed at a cost of $150,000 some years ago, the President of the Republic contributed toward its construction. The reconstituted Pontifical Seminary is now located in the neighborhood of the University City in Ciudad Trujillo. The Government contributes to its operating cost. Students from various countries in the Caribbean are sent to this Seminary for their training in philosophy and theology.

Approximately 40 years ago some Benedictine monks from Brazil founded a well-known abbey at Mt. St. Benedict on a mountainside near Port of Spain, the capital of Trinidad. In addition to European monks from Holland and elsewhere, the abbey includes among its members, Indians, Negroes, Chinese and men of mixed race. Also located at the Mount is the Archdiocesan Seminary of St. John Vianney and the African Martyrs which was established by the Dominicans in 1942. By 1958, six of its graduates had been ordained, and approximately 15 students were enrolled in the institution at the major seminary level.

Table 154 lists the major seminaries now training men for the priesthood in Colombia.

In addition to the 1,001 students enrolled in the major seminaries in Colombia in

Table 154. Major Seminaries in Colombia (1957)

Name	Location	Approx. Number of Major Seminary Students	Administration
St. Joseph	Bogotá	119	Secular
Colegio Ecclesiástica Aloisiana	Bogotá	49	Jesuits
St. Charles Borromeo	Cartagena	39	Eudists
Our Lady of the Rosary	Manizales	98	Sulpicians
Sacred Heart of Jesus	Medellín	142	Secular
St. Thomas Aquinas	Nueva Pamplona	39	Secular
St. Vincent de Paul	Popayan	25	Lazarists
San Luis Beltran	Barranquilla	15	Salesians (St. John Bosco)
St. Peter the Apostle	Cali	30	Eudists
Immaculate Conception	Garzón	28	Lazarists
San Joaquín	Ibagué	35	Lazarists
Christ the Priest	Palmira	19	Secular
Sacred Heart	Pasto	21	Eudists
St. Joseph	Santa Marta	40	Lazarists
St. Thomas Aquinas	Santa Rosa de Osos	56	Eudists
St. Charles Borromeo	San Gil	54	Lazarists
St. Pius X	Tunja	87	Secular
Our Lady of Miracles[a]	Bolívar	19	Burgos Fathers[b]
Pontifical Foreign Missions Institute[a]	Yarumal	86	Xaverians (M.X.Y.)
Total: 19		1,001	

Notes: [a] Under the jurisdiction of the Propaganda Fide Congregation.
[b] Seminary for Foreign Missions, Burgos, Spain.

Table 155. Scholasticates in Colombia (1955–57)

Type	Location	Approx. Number of Scholastics	Administration
Universidad Pontif. Xaveriana[a]	Bogotá	130	Jesuits
Theologate	Bogotá	60	Franciscans
Philosophate	Ubate	90	Franciscans
Holy Rosary Priory	Chiquinquirá	10[b]	Dominicans
Philosophate	Pasto	10?	Capuchins
Scholasticate	Usaquén	27	Eudists
Philosophate	Zipaquirá	46	Claretians
Theologate	Manizales	31	Claretians
Total: 8		404	

Notes: [a] Scholasticate section.
[b] As of 1949.

1957, there were also approximately 404 scholastics studying in eight scholasticates, as shown in Table 155.

As far back as 1563 the Dominicans founded a grammar school in Santa Fé de Bogotá which subsequently developed into an institution giving courses in philosophy. The Jesuits arrived in 1590 and were active in educational activities in the country until their expulsion in 1767. At present the Jesuits administer the Xaverian University in Bogota whose faculty of theology, according to Father Gustave Weigel, S.J., serves in some respects as a "house of studies" for the Colombian Province of the Society of Jesus.

As the tables indicate, there are approximately 1,405 men currently studying to be priests in Colombia. For a nation with a population of only 13,000,000 persons, this is a clear indication of the vitality of the Roman Catholic Church in this country today. The Lazarists and the Eudists are the most active religious community engaged in training the Colombian clergy.

One of the more interesting seminaries in Colombia is the Pontifical Foreign Missions Institute at Yarumal which is administered by the Xaverians (M.X.Y.). This institution was founded in 1927 by an energetic prelate, Bishop Miguel Angel Builes of Santa Rosa de Osos. At present, in addition to its 86 major seminarians, it has a total of 294 minor seminarians enrolled in its courses. The Yarumal Institute is devoted solely to training men for missionary activities. As such, it is one of the few institutions of its kind in South America and comes under the authority of the Propaganda Congregation. So far most of its graduates have been assigned to home missions work among the Indians in the northern lowlands of Colombia. The Yarumal Institute is located in the Province of Antioquia, of which Medellín is the capital. Many of the inhabitants of this Province are of Basque extraction and Antioquia alone supplies approximately two-thirds of the Roman Catholic clergy for all of Colombia. In terms of its religious and corporate life, the situation in Antioquia is said to resemble in some respects that of the Province of Quebec in Canada: many families have more than a dozen children from whom numerous "vocations" for the clergy are obtained.

Table 156 lists the major seminaries located in Venezuela.

TABLE 156.   MAJOR SEMINARIES IN VENEZUELA (1956)

Name	Location	Approx. Number of Major Seminary Students	Administration
Interdiocesan Seminary	Caracas	40	Eudists
St. Rose of Lima	Caracas	58	Jesuits
Archdiocesan Seminary	Mérida	17	Eudists
Divine Pastor	Barquisimeto	22	Lazarists
St. Thomas Aquinas	San Cristóbal	25	Eudists
Conciliar Seminary	Valencia	12?	Lazarists
Major Seminary	Upata	3	Capuchins
Total: 7		177	

Although Venezuela's population of approximately 6,000,000 persons is almost half that of Colombia, nevertheless Venezuela has only one-eighth as many major seminary students as its neighbor. In part, this situation arises as a result of the contrasting religious outlook of the two populations. It is also due to the fact that there has been much more conflict between Church and State in Venezuela than has been the case in Colombia.

In 1692 a seminary was opened under the direction of the secular clergy, and it was a part of the Royal and Pontifical University of Caracas until 1775. In 1837, according to M. R. Madden, "the Secretary of the Interior favored the separation of the seminary from the university since it gave too much of an ecclesiastical flavor to the university which should be 'national and scientific.' The clergy also wished this separation, which was accomplished in 1856, not for the same reason advanced by the Secretary but because the teaching of Bentham was ruinous to the spirit of the seminary."

At the time it was separated from the University, the Seminary of Santa Rosa was receiving income from certain chaplaincies. In order to replace these, the archbishop tried to impose a 3% tax on the income of all Church benefices within his jurisdiction, but even this proved to be an insufficient source of revenue.

The Seminary continued to function under the direction of the Archbishop of Caracas until it was suppressed by President Guzman Blanco in 1872. President Guzman was the dictator of Venezuela from 1870 to 1888. He closed this Seminary on the grounds that the isolation of its students and the nature of the doctrines being taught in it caused the students to be hostile to his Government. The President's conflict with the Archbishop of Caracas was heightened when Guzman sought to create a National Venezuelan Church. At this point all the Roman Catholic major seminaries and houses of study of the religious communities in Venezuela were closed. In 1891, three years after Guzman's downfall, the Government permitted the major seminaries to be reopened.

This permission was renewed in 1900 with a stipulation that such institutions would come under the supervision of the Ministry of Education. Seminaries in Venezuela are permitted to grant the degree of Bachelor of Philosophy, while the University of Caracas alone may award a doctorate.

Formerly the Interdiocesan Seminary in Caracas was administered by the Jesuits. However, they turned this institution over to the Eudists in 1954 at the time when the Society of Jesus commenced to administer the University.

Table 157 lists the major seminaries in Brazil.

From this table it will be noted that a total of 1,119 major seminarians were enrolled in 16 major seminaries in 1957. Of the major seminarians, 845 (or 77%) were enrolled in seminaries staffed by the secular clergy. Of the remaining 274 students, 268 were enrolled in four seminaries conducted by the Lazarists. A number of the 16 major seminaries have minor seminarians enrolled in separate departments.

In addition, as shown in Table 158, there were a total of 59 scholasticates maintained in Brazil by 31 religious orders and institutes in the same year, 1957. Many of these scholasticates were offering courses either in philosophy or theology, but not both. Recent enrollment statistics are available for only 13 of these institutions. Assuming, as seems reasonable, that an average of at least 15 students were enrolled at each of the remaining 46 scholasticates, this would suggest a total enrollment of 1,167 scholastics in these 59 institutions. Adding them to the 1,119 major semi-

narians previously listed, results in a total of 2,268 students at the major seminary
level in Brazil. This is the largest total of such students in any single country in
South America, but is slightly less than the number enrolled in Mexico.

TABLE 157.   MAJOR SEMINARIES IN BRAZIL (1957)

Name	Location	Approx. Number of Major Seminary Students	Administration
Our Lady of the Immaculate Conception	Belém do Pará	7	Secular
Archepiscopal Seminary of the Eucharistic Heart of Jesus	Belo Horizonte	77	Secular
Queen of Apostles	Curitíba	18	Lazarists
Sacred Heart of Jesus	Diamantina	33	Lazarists
St. Vincent	Fortaleza	103	Lazarists
St. Joseph	Manaus	8	Secular
St. Joseph	Mariana	114	Lazarists
Major Seminary	Olinda (Recife)	36	Secular
Major Seminary	Ponta Grossa	6	Redemptorists
Archepiscopal Seminary of Our Lady of the Conception	João Pessoa	9	Secular
Major Seminary	Viamão, Pôrto Alegre	307	Secular
Mary Immaculate	Ribeirão Prêto	24	Secular
Central Seminary of the Immaculate Conception	São Paulo	224	Secular
Central Seminary	Salvador	54	Secular
Rio Comprido	Rio de Janeiro	89	Secular
St. Joseph	Uberaba	10	Secular
Total: 16		1,119	

Of the approximately 61,000,000 people in Brazil, 93% are reported to be Roman
Catholics. Hence Brazil is the largest predominantly Roman Catholic country in the
world, exceeding (in terms of numbers of Roman Catholics) France, Italy and the
United States, etc. Paradoxically, it does not appear that the influence of the Roman
Catholic Church is nearly as strong in Brazil as it is in Colombia.

A part of the weakness of the Church in Brazil is due to the fact that during the
first three centuries (1500–1822) that Brazil was a Portuguese colony, the Portuguese
made few attempts to create a local clergy. Nor did they support the Church's missionary activities as vigorously as did the Spaniards elsewhere in South America.
The Jesuits were the first of the religious institutes to commence work in Brazil.
They were expelled in 1759 but later were permitted to return. Today the Franciscans and Capuchins are among the most prominent of the religious communities
conducting activities in this country.

During the 19th century a number of Brazilian seminarians were sent for their
training to Rome where they studied at the Pontifical Latin American College. By
1929 their number had increased to the point where it was found advisable to establish the Brazilian College in Rome, most of whose students take courses at the Gregorian University.

Within Brazil, there has been little in the way of vigorous theological research.
Many of the major seminaries have large minor seminaries attached to them, and
efforts are being made to expand these institutions. For example, the Redemptorists'

TABLE 158.   Scholasticates in Brazil (1957)

Institute	Locations of Scholasticates, etc.
Augustinians (Recollects)	Ribeirão Prêto
Barnabites	Belo Horizonte
Basilians	Ivaí
Benedictines (Brazilian Congregation)	Olinda, Santos, São Paulo, Rio de Janeiro
Benedictines (Congregation of St. Mary of Mt. of Olives)	Ribeirão Prêto
Camilians	São Paulo
Capuchins	Itambacuri, Garibaldi, Curitíba, Fortaleza, Maceió, Parnaíba, Marau, Engenheiro Gutierrez, Pôrto Alegre, Ijui, São Paulo, Alagoinhas
Carlists	Guapore, Casca
Carmelites	São Paulo
Claretians	Curitíba, Guarulhos[b]
Congregation of Our Lady of the Most Holy Sacrament (S.D.N.)	Manhumirim
Consolata Fathers	S. Manoel
Divine Word Fathers	Santo Amaro (São Paulo)[c]
Dominicans	São Paulo
Fathers of Sacred Heart of Jesus (P.S.C.J.)	Passa Quatro
Franciscans[e]	Divinopolis, Garibaldi, Curitíba, Olinda, Petrópolis, Salvador
Jesuits	S. Leopoldo (Pôrto Alegre)[f], Nova Friburgo[g]
Lazarists	Petrópolis[d]
Pallotines	S. João do Polesine
Passionists	Curitíba
Paulines	São Paulo
Picpus Fathers	Pindamonhangaba
Premonstratensians	Pirapora do Bom Jesus
Priests of the Sacred Heart of Jesus (S.C.J.)	Brusque, Recife, Taubaté
Redemptorists	Juiz de Fora, Tiete[a]
Sacramentines	Rio de Janeiro
Salesians	Campo Grande, (São João del Rei), Natal, São Paulo
Salvatorians	São Paulo
Servites	São Paulo
Sionites	São Paulo
Stigmatines	Ribeirão Prêto
Total: 31 Institutes	59 Scholasticates, etc.

Notes: [a] With 37 and 47 scholastics respectively (1955).
[b] With 35 theologians and 11 philosophers (scholastics), respectively, in 1955.
[c] 39 scholastics enrolled in 1958.
[d] 11 scholastics enrolled in 1958.
[e] A total of approximately 175 scholastics were enrolled in these six scholasticates in 1956.
[f] Colégio máximo "Christ the King," with 77 theological and 45 philosophy students in 1954 (a total of 122 students).
[g] Faculty of Philosophy "Our Lady Mediatrix," Colégio máximo Anchieta, Rio de Janeiro.

seminary at Ponta Grossa had only six major seminarians in 1957 (according to the Brazilian *Anuario* for that year), but it had approximately 81 minor seminarians who were enrolled there also. About $400,000 has already been spent by the Redemptorists in the construction of the buildings at Ponta Grossa. They will not be completed until 1960 and may cost an additional $50,000. It is planned that ultimately some 200 students will be enrolled in this one institution.

The Divine Word Fathers' scholasticate at Santo Amaro near São Paulo commenced courses for scholastics in 1942. It specializes in training priests for missionary work among non-Christians. In addition it provides classes in the Portuguese language for Divine Word priests coming from Europe to engage in missionary work in Brazil. Santo Amaro also is a center from which this congregation distributes missions literature to all parts of Brazil, including college and university campuses.

Because of the number of immigrants who have come to Brazil from Eastern Europe and the Middle East, there are a number of parishes in this country conducting services in the Byzantine, Antiochean and Armenian Rites. However, there are no seminaries in Brazil devoted exclusively to the training of priests for the Eastern Rites, and such students are occasionally sent to the Eastern Rite colleges in Rome. The Ukrainian-Rite Basilians maintain a scholasticate at Ivai in Brazil which is attended by students of the Ukrainian-Ruthenian Rite and also by students of some other Eastern Rites.

Table 159 lists the major seminaries and scholasticates in Ecuador.

There is now only one major seminary for the secular clergy in Ecuador. This is St. Joseph Interdiocesan Seminary of Quito which (including its predecessors) has

TABLE 159. MAJOR SEMINARIES AND SCHOLASTICATES IN ECUADOR (1957)

Name	Location	Approx. Number of Major Seminary Students	Administration
Seminaries			
St. Joseph Interdiocesan	Quito	115	Lazarists
Scholasticates			
St. Francis Convent	Quito	26	Franciscans
St. Dominic Priory	Quito	19	Dominicans
St. Augustine	Quito	5	Augustinians
Scholasticate	Quito	25	Salesians
Mercedarian Convent	Quito	21	Mercedarians
Scholasticate	Quito	18	Jesuits
Scholasticate	Quito	5	Oblates (C.O. CC.S.S.)
Saint Theresa	Quito	21	Lazarists
Scholasticate	Cuenca	27	Redemptorists
Pius XII Intermissional[a]	Ambato	17	Josephites[b]
Total: 11		299	

NOTES: [a] Under the jurisdiction of the Propaganda Congregation. [b] Josephites of Murialdo (Pious Turin Society of St. Joseph, C.S.J.).

been under the direction of the Lazarists since 1871. Its building was constructed in 1884 and was renovated in 1955. The 10 scholasticates are training 184 men for the religious clergy, or considerably more than are enrolled in St. Joseph's. Furthermore, in 1957 these 10 religious congregations had an additional 74 seminarians (not included in Table 159) who were enrolled in that year in institutions outside of Ecuador. Of this number, ten were Josephites studying in Viterbo, Italy, 23 were Salesians taking courses in theology in Bogotá, Colombia, and 33 were Jesuit scholastics studying in various countries. Ecuador as a whole has a better ratio of priests to Roman Catholics than do most other Latin American nations, but there is said to be little in the way of significant theological research being conducted in the country.

Table 160 lists the major seminaries and scholasticates in Peru.

The most important seminary is Saint Toribio in Lima which is administered by the Holy Spirit Fathers of Mexico. It was originally founded in 1591 by St. Toribio of Mogrovejo, the second Archbishop of Lima. The seminary benefits from its present relationship with the Faculty of Theology at the University of San Marcos, the latter having been founded in Lima by the Roman Catholic Church in 1551. While it is now a state institution, nevertheless its Faculty of Theology is empowered by the Sacred Congregation of Seminaries and Universities to grant pontifical degrees. In 1954 the Faculty had nine professors instructing 60 students.

TABLE 160.   MAJOR SEMINARIES AND SCHOLASTICATES IN PERU (1954)

Name	Location	Approx. Number of Major Seminary Students	Administration
St. Toribio	Lima	169	Holy Spirit Fathers of Mexico
St. Anthony	Cuzco	6	Secular
St. Christopher	Ayacucho	14	Salesians
St. Jerome	Arequipa	13	Secular
St. Charles and St. Marcelus	Trujillo	16	Claretians
Seminary of Jesus & Mary	Chachapoyas	11	Salesians
St. Dominic Priory	Cuzco	28[a]	Dominicans
Total: 7		257	

NOTE: [a] As of 1949.

The St. Anthony Seminary in Cuzco, Peru, was also originally established centuries ago (in 1596), and it was followed by the founding of the Saint Charles Seminary in Trujillo in 1624. Owing to the unsettled political conditions in the country, these seminaries have been faced with many problems, despite the predominant position of the Roman Catholic Church in Peru. Occasionally some of them have been closed, and the major seminary in Cuzco was only recently reopened.

Table 161 lists the major seminaries and scholasticates in Bolivia.

Over the years there have been many clashes between the Bolivian Government and the Roman Catholic Church. An interesting summary of the history of this conflict as it pertains to the major seminaries was written by Elizabeth Loughran. The author points out (1) how the Government sought to attack the Church by either

TABLE 161.   MAJOR SEMINARIES AND SCHOLASTICATES IN BOLIVIA (1957)

Name	Location	Approx. Number of Major Seminary Students	Administration
St. Jerome	La Paz	21	Salesians
St. Christopher	Sucre	11	Dominicans
House of Studies[a]	Cochabamba	4[a]	Augustinians
Scholasticate	Copacabana	10	Franciscans
Total: 4		46	

NOTE: [a] As of 1953.

closing or strictly regulating the seminaries; and (2) how the progress of these institutions was sometimes impeded by their admitting secular students (with the Church's approval):

. . . St. Christopher's in Sucre dates back to 1595, and was renowned for its excellence. In the middle of the eighteenth century, it had an enrollment of one hundred and fifty students; but, in 1767, when the Jesuits were expelled, both professors and students were taken from their work and pressed into service on the faculties of the university and its preparatory school. From that point, the principal seminary of the country fell into a decline. Forty years later, Archbishop Moxó found the seminary in a state of decadence and refused to assign any more students until both the course and the faculty were improved. . . . In 1826, Bolivar reopened St. Christopher's and made it the one general seminary of Bolivia; but since he allowed only twenty-four seminarians . . . it is clear that his intention was to control the number of priests. In 1830, President Santa Cruz reopened St. Jerome's but he destroyed the usefulness of both seminaries as preparatory institutions for the priesthood by secularizing them and making them part of the university system. . . . By 1857, the number of theological students in the whole country was reduced to seventeen. . . . In 1859, President Linares restored the direction of the seminaries to the dioceses. . . . Not many years later the bishops yielded to the entreaties of fathers of families to open the seminaries as colleges of liberal arts. . . . In 1900 the government in a campaign against Catholic education, passed new laws limiting the teaching to strictly theological courses with the view to abolishing Catholic training for the professions. Hostile as the government's action was meant to be, in the long run, it restored the seminaries to their rightful function in the plan of the Church. . . .

There has been a persistent shortage of priests in Bolivia for many years. Rev. Steven McKenna, C.SS.R., notes that "during the period from 1900 to 1930 only 45 priests were ordained for the See of La Paz (an average of 1.5 per year). At the present time (1947) there are only 227 native-born members of the diocesan clergy in

Bolivia, though Roman Catholicism is the predominant religion of the 3,500,000 inhabitants. The best way to realize what this means is to contrast the Archdioceses of La Paz and Philadelphia, which have about the same number of Catholics. In 1946 La Paz had 107 priests (sixty-three of whom were foreigners), while Philadelphia had 1,703. Even with the 216 priests from other countries the proportion of priests to the people in Bolivia is about one for 8,000."

The impoverished economic conditions in Bolivia are reflected in its seminaries. Formerly there was a major seminary at Cochabamba, but it was necessary to close this institution many years ago. Up to 1903 the Government contributed small annual subsidies to the seminaries in the form of scholarships for their students. However, since that year each diocese has been obliged to support its own institution. The buildings of the major and minor seminaries in Bolivia were reported in 1954 by Rev. Charles A. Brown, M.M., as being "physically most unattractive. No young fellow would want to spend even a night in one of them, let alone six or seven years of his life. There is also much to be desired as far as training the intellect and character (are concerned)."

A number of attempts have been made to correct this situation. For example, the administration of the St. Jerome Seminary in La Paz was placed in the hands of the Lazarists in 1905 and then transferred to the secular clergy in 1926. Ten years later its administration was returned to the Lazarists who staffed it until 1943. In that year all of the seminaries in Bolivia were reorganized as a result of studies conducted at the time by the Sacred Congregation of Seminaries and Universities. The administration of the St. Jerome Seminary was then transferred to the Salesians who are in charge of it at the present time.

The two major seminaries in La Paz and Sucre have been receiving 3% of the income from all the ecclesiastical benefices in their dioceses, together with the income from a number of *haciendas* (farm estates) which have been specifically bequeathed to them. However, it would seem evident that this income is insufficient to meet the fiscal needs of these institutions.

A further setback occurred when the building of St. Christopher's Seminary in Sucre was destroyed by an earthquake in 1947. For the next five years this institution functioned as a minor seminary, and its major seminary students were sent to St. Jerome in La Paz. By 1952 the building at Sucre was reconstructed, and the administration of the newly re-established major seminary was entrusted to the Dominicans.

Table 162 lists the major seminaries and scholasticates in Paraguay and Uruguay.

Originally Paraguay was included as a part of the Archdiocese of Buenos Aires. During the early missionary days, the Jesuits organized "reductions" which were villages in which the total life of the Indian residents was closely supervised by the members of the Society of Jesus. While this redounded to the benefit of the economic life of the population, the Jesuits virtually superseded the Government in large areas. At one point they were obliged to defend by force these "little republics" against the attacks of the Portuguese coming from Brazil.

At the end of the disastrous war which Paraguay waged from 1865 to 1870 against Brazil, Argentina and Uruguay combined, the Roman Catholic Church in Paraguay was so disorganized, according to Father McKenna, "that there were said to be only

TABLE 162.   MAJOR SEMINARIES AND SCHOLASTICATES IN PARAGUAY AND
URUGUAY (1957)

Name	Location	Approx. Number of Major Seminary Students	Administration
Paraguay			
Metropolitan Seminary	Asunción	48	Secular
St. Joseph	Concepción	18	Secular
Subtotal: 2		66	
Uruguay			
Interdiocesan Seminary of Christ the King	Montevideo	50	Jesuits
Scholasticate	Montevideo	10?	Capuchins
Subtotal: 2		60	
Total: 4		126	

seven priests in the whole country when peace was finally declared. Since that time Paraguay has been troubled by revolutions. . . . It is hardly a matter of surprise if Paraguay has had a shortage of clergy. For example, from 1881 to 1911 there were only 60 priests ordained" (i.e., an average of two a year).

In 1929 Paraguay was elevated into an independent ecclesiastical province with an archbishop at its head. The Metropolitan Seminary in Asunción, the capital, is the larger and more important of the two major seminaries in this country.

In Uruguay the Interdiocesan Seminary of Christ the King in Montevideo is the one major seminary training the secular clergy. Administered by the Jesuits, it was established largely as a result of the zeal of the first Bishop of Montevideo, Jacinto Vera, who was appointed to this post in 1878. In 1957, a large building of modern design was being planned for the seminary. A faculty of 14 staff the major and the minor seminaries which have had a total capacity of 150 students.

In Argentina there have been many changes in the hierarchy and circumscriptions of the Roman Catholic Church in recent years. At the same time there would appear to be much to be done in terms of revitalizing the Catholic faith of the people. An indication of this is contained in the study prepared by Rev. William J. Coleman, M.M., of the *Chimbote Report* (so named after a seaport town in Peru where some 300 delegates assembled in 1953 for an Interamerican Catholic Action Week, the purpose of which was to discuss ways and means of making the participation of the laity more effective in the work of the Church). According to the Report, 93% of the total population in Argentina have been baptized in the Roman Catholic faith: yet, "Sunday Mass attendance does not include 20% of the Catholic population, and in many dioceses may be as low as 10%. An average of Catholics who made their Easter duty would not be above 5% for the entire country. . . ." Among the reasons accounting for this situation, as cited in the Report, were the scarcity of clergy and lay Catholic leaders. Offsetting factors include the creation of new parishes in the more populated centers and an improvement in the quality of religious instruction in the schools. The political influence and vitality of the Roman Catholic Church in this country is noted by Father Coleman who comments that "it is admitted on all sides that the Catholic element of Argentina defeated the dictator, Perón. . . ."

Table 163 lists the major seminaries in Argentina.

TABLE 163.   MAJOR SEMINARIES IN ARGENTINA (1957)

Name	Location	Approx. Number of Major Seminary Students	Administration
Metropolitan Seminary	Buenos Aires	137	Jesuits
Our Lady of Loreto	Córdoba	108	Secular
Metropolitan Seminary	Paraná	41	Secular
St. Joseph	La Plata	130	Secular
Metropolitan Seminary	Santa Fé	40[a] [b]	Secular
St. Joseph	Tucumán	85[b]	Secular
Virgin of the Valley	Catamarca	46	Divine Word Fathers
Major Seminary	Azul	8	Secular
Pius XII	Mercedes	40[b]	Secular
Diocesan Seminary	Río Cuarto	16	Mallorca Missioners[c]
St. Charles Borromeo	Rosario	59	Secular
Total: 11		710	

NOTES: [a] Estimated.   [c] Missioners of the Sacred Heart, of
        [b] As of 1953.   Mallorca.

In addition to the 11 major seminaries listed in this table, there are 13 scholasticates in Argentina maintained by 11 religious communities, in which a total of approximately 402 scholasticates are enrolled. These are listed in Table 164.

The University of Córdoba was the third university to be founded in Latin America, having been established in 1613. Initially most of its courses were in theology preceded by a few arts courses. As such, it functioned as the first major seminary in Argentina. It was staffed by the Jesuits until their expulsion from Argentina in 1767 at which time its administration was taken over by the Franciscans. At present the separate seminary of Our Lady of Loreto in Córdoba is administered by the secular clergy.

The most important training center for the clergy in Argentina is the Metropolitan Seminary in Buenos Aires. Its origin goes back as far as 1622 when the administration of the original institution was placed in the care of the Jesuits. During the course of the next three centuries it experienced various financial vicissitudes. At one time (1780), the bishop of the diocese rented his own episcopal palace to a government dignitary for the latter's use in order that the Church might have sufficient funds to continue the operation of this seminary.

TABLE 164.　SCHOLASTICATES IN ARGENTINA (1952–58)

Religious Community	Location	Enrollment	
		Scholastics	Year
Capuchins	O'Higgins (Mercedes)	15[a]	1952
Capuchins	Villa Elisa (Mercedes)	15[a]	1952
Claretians	Villa Claret (Córdoba)	42	1955
Divine Word Fathers	Villa Calzada	37	1958
Franciscans	San Antonio de Padua	8	1956
Franciscans	San Lorenzo	20	1956
Jesuits[c]	San Miguel	144	1954
Marianists	Coronel Brandsen	15[a]	1954
Paulines	Florida	15[a]	1954
Betharram Fathers[b]	Adrogué	15[a]	1954
Redemptorists	Villa Allende (Córdoba)	46	1955
Salesians	Córdoba	15[a]	1954
Salesians (St. John Bosco)	Bernal	15[a]	1954
Total: 13		402	

NOTES:　[a] Estimated.　　　　　　　　　[c] St. Joseph's College.
[b] Priests of the Sacred Heart of Jesus of Betharram.

With the development of Argentina into a prosperous nation, the fortunes of the Roman Catholic Church in this country have also improved. The imposing building now occupied by the Metropolitan Seminary was constructed in the period 1897–1905, and the Government contributed a portion of its cost. The faculty of 28 is staffed by the Jesuits, and it is now the largest seminary in the country. Attached to it is a minor seminary with 171 students, and the Theological Faculty of the Immaculate Conception. The latter is a faculty of ecclesiastical studies at the graduate level which was canonically erected in 1944. Buenos Aires is now said to be the leading center of Roman Catholic theological inquiry and discussion in Latin America.

The Government is reported to be contributing annual subsidies toward the operating costs of a number of the seminaries in Argentina. In the case of Spain and other countries where the religious communities have had their properties expropriated from time to time, provisions for these subsidies are occasionally included in concordats between the Church and the government as recompense for such expropriations.

Table 165 lists the seminaries and scholasticates in Chile.

In Chile there would appear to be an interesting paradox with respect to the number of priests and the influence of the Roman Catholic Church within the country. Along with Colombia and Ecuador, Chile has the highest proportion of priests in South America, namely, one for every 2,660 persons. However, despite this comparatively favorable ratio, the vast majority of the Chilean Catholics, according to Father Coleman (writing in 1954), "have no real notion of what a Catholic is or should be. If we take the statistics of Chile as a test and measure of the practical Catholicism of the other 19 republics of Latin America, and it would seem that this

TABLE 165. Major Seminaries and Scholasticates in Chile (1957)

Name	Location	Approx. Number of Major Seminary Students	Administration
Seminaries			
Pontifical Seminary	Santiago	127	Secular
Immaculate Conception	Concepción	43	Secular
Immaculate Conception	Ancud	6	Secular
Scholasticates			
Archbishop Valenzuela	Santiago	27	Mercedarians
St. Pius X	Santiago	15[a]	Oblates of Mary Immaculate
Scholasticate	Chillán	50	Franciscans
Scholasticate	La Granja	45	Franciscans
Philosophate	Talagante	20[b]	Claretians
St. Joseph of Mariquina[c]	Villarrica	14	Capuchins
Scholasticate[c]	Los Angeles	20	Capuchins
Total: 10		367	

Notes: [a] Estimated. [c] Under jurisdiction of the Propaganda Congregation.
[b] As of 1955.

would do no great injustice to any one country, then we find that according to the careful and courageous survey of Father Hurtado there are $3\frac{1}{2}$% of the men and $9\frac{1}{2}$% of the women who go to Mass on Sunday while 14% fulfill the Easter duty which would make them, canonically speaking, Catholics. Half the people die without the Last Sacraments and at least half are married outside the Church."

One of the reasons accounting for this situation is the fact that approximately one-half the number of priests in the country are stationed in the two dioceses of Santiago and Valparaíso which have only one-fourth of the total number of Roman Catholics in Chile. Another reason is that the clergy has a high proportion of foreign priests. In 1956 as many as 1,093 of the 1,878 priests in the country were members of religious communities, the majority of whom had come from the United States and Europe. In 1945 not a single Chilean priest was ordained in five dioceses in Chile which together had a combined population of over 1,000,000 Roman Catholics.

The leading institution training priests for the secular clergy in Chile is the Pontifical Seminary. In 1935 a Faculty of Theology was established at the Catholic University of Chile, also located in Santiago, with the result that there is said to be considerable interest in theological matters in this city.

The second leading Chilean seminary is the Conciliar Seminary of the Immaculate Conception located in Concepción, which was also established many years ago. At one point it was united with the Seminary in Santiago owing to a scarcity of students and funds. In the latter half of the 18th century, one Chilean bishop (Alday y Aspee, who was a brilliant scholar) is said to have accomplished more for the benefit of the training of a local clergy in this country than has anyone else, before or since.

The Franciscans and Capuchins have been among the most active religious communities in Chile. The Bavarian Province of the latter Order maintains scholasticates in Villarrica and Los Angeles which come under the authority of the Propaganda Congregation inasmuch as their students are being trained to serve in the missionary area of Araucanía in Chile.

Latin America Over-all: In 1948 a leading American Jesuit with wide experience in Latin America, Father Gustave Weigel, S.J., commented as follows on the state of theological inquiry and research as it has been conducted in recent years in the Roman Catholic Universities and Faculties of Theology in South America:

First of all, it must be admitted that South American theology, whether of yesterday or today, has made no transcendental contribution; on the other hand, it has not been reduced to sterile stagnation. No great movement can be discerned, although genuine life is evident in many places. . . . A consciousness is being awakened everywhere in favor of a vital, progressive, and scientific theology. The old ideal of knowing by memory what the text-book says and confounding such knowledge with theological insight is rapidly giving way to the recognition that theology is a living thing that can be grasped only by a faithful and laborious meditation of the various sources of faith, according to a rigorous scientific method. . . .

The evolution of South American culture makes the present-day Sudamericano disinclined to metaphysical penetration. . . . He is highly intelligent but he has greater faith in spontaneous intuitions than in detailed analytical thought. The result is that even when a spirit of investigation is inculcated into young men, their environment is rather disdainful of their labors. One practical consequence of this attitude is that no money will be devoted to scholarship, and the theologians, who rarely have adequate incomes or supporting foundations, are thus deprived of the financial means required for their research. . . . Even if the books are found and the study finally terminated, the theologians will have great difficulties with publishers and the press. The ordinary publishing houses, even when under Catholic auspices, are not interested in scholarly work, which appeals to so small a public.

While it may be difficult for South American theologians to find publishers for their books, there are said to be a number of theological reviews and periodicals of good quality (particularly in Brazil and Argentina) in which they may make their views known.

In August 1954 the Maryknoll Fathers (who have been active in Latin America) held a conference in Lima, Peru, which was attended by a number of the leading members of this society and at which the relative merits of various types of missionary activity were discussed. Among the papers presented and the remarks of the participants relating to the problems confronting the major seminaries in Latin America were the following comments:

Father Brown:

The most basic difficulty, to my mind, is the lack of a true concept of just what the priesthood is. To the average South American the priest is nothing more than a paid servant who for so many "pesos" will perform certain external rites demanded by tradition. With such a concept it's no surprise to find phrases in fairly common use like "los inutiles al colegio militar y los frascados al seminario." (The useless ones to the military college and the failures to the seminary.) . . . The poorer families . . . are usually so "strapped" economically that, not only can't they undertake the financial underwriting of a seminary education for their son, but also suffer economically by the loss of another possible source of family income.

Father Comber:

The tenure of the foreign missioner is uncertain. It is especially so in the age of communism. In two of the five countries in Latin America in which we are working, the pressure from Communists is already very great. I do not speak of this as a reason to hold up mission projects because of this uncertainty but as an argument for the immediate development of a National Clergy even when conditions do not seem to be ideal. . . .

Regarding the staff of a major seminary, I do not think that we have to have a large major seminary staff until we have a large number of seminarians. . . . Just as there are many parishes that are understaffed and many without priests, so, too, the major seminary would make sacrifices and adjustments until the time when there would be a full enrollment. I think that two or three priests should be sufficient for a major seminary of twenty or twenty-five students. It would mean that these priests would have to teach more than one subject and that there would have to be cycle classes and other inconveniences but when we have thirty-five priests ministering to almost a million people (as in Puno) we cannot afford to put a dozen men in seminary work until the number of seminarians warrants it. . . .

Father Considine: "I think the thought of us all is that the Church in Latin America is going to be manned locally or it's not going to be manned at all. . . . You can talk all you want about the shortage of vocations, about the Holy Ghost who must give the inspiration. But the Holy Ghost works in the matter of vocations much the same as in everything else. He won't work miracles; nothing will happen if we don't do something about it. . . . We get vocations if we work hard for them; they require persistent effort. . . ."

The 216 major seminaries and scholasticates in Latin America, as previously listed in this chapter, have a combined enrollment of 8,808 students taking courses in philosophy and theology. This is an impressive total until it is related to the fact that in 1957 there were approximately 170,572,000 Roman Catholics in Latin America whose spiritual needs were being served by 35,613 priests. The grave shortage in Latin American priests has already been noted. In addition, assuming the career of each priest lasts an average of 33 years, this would suggest an attrition rate of approximately 3% a year among the clergy owing to death, old age, and other factors. On this basis the major seminaries in Latin America would need to graduate 1,068 students each year merely in order to replace the ranks of the clergy. Assuming that each of these institutions has a six-year course and that two-thirds of the students enrolled in them are ultimately ordained, on this basis the 216 Latin American seminaries and scholasticates would be graduating 979 priests a year, or 9% less than the number needed to replace the assumed attrition from the clergy's ranks each year. These assumptions may not apply in some of these countries, and the conclusion derived therefrom is intended to be indicative only. Furthermore, no allowance is made for the influx of missionary priests coming from abroad each year.

However, a further factor needs to be taken into account. Of the 8,808 major seminary students in Latin America, 7,186, or 82%, are enrolled in institutions located in four countries: Mexico, Colombia, Brazil and Argentina. The seminaries and scholasticates in Mexico and Colombia are training all or a very high proportion of the number of priests needed as replacements each year in the ranks of the clergy in those countries, but this is not the case in Brazil or Argentina. On the other hand, of the remaining 1,622 seminary students in other countries elsewhere in Latin America it may be assumed (on the same basis as above) that 180 of these students will annually join the ranks of the clergy in those countries. In 1957 these countries had a total of 11,492 priests, of whom (at an assumed attrition rate of 3%) 345 will need to be replaced each year. This is almost double the number that are being graduated annually from their seminaries.

Put in another way, it appears that approximately 48% of the major seminary students in Latin America as reported in 1957 by diocesan authorities were in two countries, Mexico and Colombia. On the other hand, two-thirds of the circumscriptions in Latin America in that year reported none or only one ordinand (i.e., a fourth-year student in theology) being trained for service in the secular clergy. Approximately 50% of the circumscriptions had no secular priests ordained in 1957. Furthermore, no allowance has been made in these calculations for the prospective increase in the populations of these countries which on the average is presently at the rate of 2% a year throughout Latin America.

In this perspective, it would appear that the problems confronting the Latin American seminaries are serious, and that the role of the foreign missionary priest in this area is likely to be a continuing one. This was recognized by Pope Pius XII in a speech which he made on September 23, 1958 (15 days before his death) in which he described the shortage of priests in Latin America as "a most urgent problem." The speech was made to a congress of rectors of major seminaries in 18 Latin

American countries and of the Spanish-American Colleges of Madrid and Louvain. The purpose of the congress was to study ways and means of coordinating the seminaries' activities.

I. Over-all Aspects

Of the total of 97,748 priests, brothers and sisters serving in Roman Catholic foreign missionary areas under the Propaganda in Africa, Asia, Latin America and elsewhere in 1950, a total of 53,521, or 54%, were indigenous to those areas. Table 166 indicates the trend in recent years toward the formation of an indigenous clergy in Roman Catholic missionary areas.

TABLE 166. PERCENTAGE OF TOTAL NUMBER OF FOREIGN AND LOCAL PRIESTS, BROTHERS AND SISTERS IN MISSION LANDS (1925–50)

Year	Foreign	Local
1925	60	40
1936	54	46
1950	46	54

Thus during the quarter century 1925–50 there has been only a moderate increase in the proportion of local to foreign priests serving under the jurisdiction of the Propaganda. Yet in the same 25 years the total number of local priests, brothers and sisters serving in Roman Catholic missionary areas rose from 16,406 to 53,521, an increase of 240%. The reason why this increase still resulted in only a bare majority (54%) of the priests, brothers and sisters in mission lands being indigenous to those areas in 1950 is the fact that in the years 1925–50 the number of foreign (largely European) priests, brothers and sisters serving under the authority of the Propaganda rose from 22,477 to 44,227 (an increase of almost 100%).

One way of indicating the extent to which the Roman Catholic Church has developed an indigenous ecclesiastical leadership in Africa, Asia and Latin America is to trace the growth in the local hierarchies, i.e., the number of indigenous bishops and cardinals appointed in recent years from the ranks of the local clergy.

With respect to the bishops, in 1922 there were only 25 local bishops serving in mission lands under the authority of the Propaganda. By 1939 this had increased to 70. During the year 1955, 13 local bishops were appointed (one in the Sudan, one in the Cameroons, five in India, two each in Burma and Malaya, and one each in Japan and Korea). In 1956 there were 113 local bishops, an increase of 88 over the number in 1922. These 113 bishops were in charge of dioceses or missionary districts in the countries listed in Table 167.

The significance of this total of 113 bishops can be measured against the number of foreign clergy of episcopal rank serving in the missionary areas. As of July 1956

TABLE 167. DISTRIBUTION OF INDIGENOUS
BISHOPS (1956)[a]

Africa	17
India	33
Ceylon	3
Indonesia	3
China	33[b]
Viet Nam	9
Japan	9
Elsewhere	6
	113

NOTES: [a] Under the Formosa, and some
authority of the Prop- of the others were
aganda Congregation. elsewhere outside of
[b] Of whom six were in China.

there were 557 archdioceses, dioceses and apostolic vicariates under the jurisdiction
of the Propaganda, almost all of which were being administered by prelates having
the rank of bishop or higher. Thus only one out of every five Roman Catholic clergy
of episcopal rank serving in mission lands was indigenous.

With respect to the indigenous Cardinals in Africa, Asia and Latin America, in
October 1958 Pope John XXIII named 23 new Cardinals from all parts of the world,
thereby indicating his intention to raise the membership in the College of Cardinals to 75. Of the 23 nominated, only two were from Africa, Asia and Latin America. Of the 75 Cardinals and Cardinals-Designate, 15 were nationals from underdeveloped countries, or a ratio of one out of every five Cardinals. This is the same pro-

TABLE 168. INDIGENOUS ROMAN CATHOLIC CARDINALS IN AFRICA, ASIA AND LATIN AMERICA (NOVEMBER 1958)

Name	Office	Nationality	Created Cardinal
Africa			
None		[a]	
Middle East			
Ignatius Gabriel Tappouni	Patriarch of Antioch	Syrian	1935
Gregory Peter XV Agagianian	Patriarch of Cilicia of the Armenians	Armenian	1946
Southern Asia			
Valerian Gracias	Archbishop of Bombay	Indian	1953
Southeast Asia			
None			
East Asia			
Thomas Tien	Archbishop of Peking	Chinese	1946
Latin America			
Emanuel Arteaga y Betancourt	Archbishop of Havana	Cuban	1946
Crisanto Luque	Archbishop of Bogotá	Colombian	1953
Carlos Maria de la Torre	Archbishop of Quito	Ecuadorean	1953
Augusto Alvaro da Silva	Archbishop of São Salvador da Bahia	Brazilian	1953
Jaime de Barros Camara	Archbishop of Rio de Janeiro	Brazilian	1946
Carlos Camelo de Vasconcellos Motta	Archbishop of São Paulo	Brazilian	1946
Jacobo Luigi Copello	Archbishop of Buenos Aires	Argentinian	1935
Antonio Caggiano	Archbishop of Rosario	Argentinian	1946
José M. Caro Rodriquez[b]	Archbishop of Santiago	Chilean	1946
José Garibi y Rivera[c]	Archbishop of Guadalajara	Mexican	1958
Antonio Maria Barbieri[c]	Archbishop of Montevideo	Uruguayan	1958

NOTES: [a] Teodosio C. de Gouveia, a Portuguese, is   [b] Deceased December 4, 1958.
Archbishop of Lourenço Marques (the capital of Mozam-   [c] Cardinal-Designate.
bique) and Cardinal of Portuguese East Africa.

portion as in the case of the bishops serving under the Propaganda. On the other hand, more than two out of every five Catholics in the world are residents of Africa, Asia and Latin America.

Of the 15 Cardinals in Africa, Asia and Latin America, 13 were created after World War II, and 11 of the 13 were Latin Americans. The list of indigenous Cardinals is shown in Table 168.

The quality of the ecclesiastical leadership of the Roman Catholic Church in Africa and Asia was assessed at the 1954 Fordham Conference (previously cited). This analysis was based not on the aggregate number of the clergy or members of the Roman Catholic Church in these countries, but rather on the qualitative aspects of their indigenous leadership. Subsequently a Jesuit editor in Bogotá, Colombia, with considerable experience in this field, prepared a similar list relating to the countries in Latin America. The estimates from these two sources are set forth in Table 169.

Table 169 provides a summary indication of the quality of the leadership of the Roman Catholic Church in the underdeveloped countries as unofficially evaluated by Roman Catholic experts. These estimates are considered by a number of Protestant mission authorities to be both realistic and conservative. Over-all, it would appear that the indigenous leadership of the Roman Catholic Church in the underdeveloped countries tends to be strongest in a few of the Latin American countries, and weakest as a whole in Africa, Southern and Southeastern Asia and in parts of Latin America.

With respect to the clergy of the future, it is of interest to note that there has been a steady growth in the number of major seminaries and seminarians in Africa, Asia, and Latin America during the past three decades. Statistics illustrating this growth are available only in connection with seminaries under the jursdiction of the Propaganda; and it seems likely that there has not been a comparable growth in the major seminaries and seminarians under the jurisdiction of the Oriental and Seminaries Congregations in Africa and Asia. With respect to the students studying in major seminaries under the jurisdiction of the Propaganda, the total in 1926 is reported to have been 1,770. In the ensuing 13 years, this number increased by 87% to a total of 3,319 in 1939. In the subsequent period 1939–58, the growth continued, as set forth in Table 170.

Table 170 discloses that since the eve of World War II there has been an increase of about one-fourth in the number of major seminaries in the missionary territories but only a small increase in the number of minor seminaries. Also, there has been a sharper percentage increase in the number of both major and minor seminary students than there has been in the number of their respective training institutions. This would indicate that most of the individual major and minor seminaries in 1958 had a larger enrollment than they had in the prewar years. Furthermore, in view of

TABLE 169. ESTIMATED QUALITY OF INDIGENOUS
LEADERSHIP OF ROMAN CATHOLIC CHURCH IN AFRICA,
ASIA AND LATIN AMERICA

	Strong	Moderately Strong	Weak
Africa			
East Africa		x	
West Africa			x
Belgian Congo		x	
Southern Africa			x
Southern Asia			
India		x	
Pakistan			x
Ceylon		x	
Southeast Asia			
Burma			x
Thailand			x
Malaya			x
Indonesia			x
Viet Nam		x	
Philippines			x
East Asia			
Japan	x		
Korea		x	
Formosa		x	
Hongkong	x		
Central America			
Mexico	x		
Guatemala			x
El Salvador			x
Nicaragua			x
Costa Rica	x		
Panama			x
Caribbean Area			
Cuba			x
Puerto Rico			x
Haiti			x
Dominican Republic			x
South America			
Colombia	x		
Venezuela			x
Brazil		x	
Ecuador		x	
Peru		x	
Bolivia			x
Paraguay			x
Uruguay	x		
Argentina	x		
Chile	x		

the effort during the past few decades to consolidate local major seminaries into interdiocesan and regional institutions, the fact that the number of major seminaries still increased substantially in the period 1939–58 (whereas the percentage increase in the number of minor seminaries was considerably less) suggests that a comparatively greater emphasis has been placed in recent years by the Propaganda on the development of the major rather than the minor seminaries.

TABLE 170.   GROWTH IN SEMINARIES UNDER THE PROPAGANDA CONGREGATION (1939–58)

	1939	1958	Increase
Seminaries			
Major	84	105	24%
Minor	268	296	10%
Seminarians			
Major	3,319	4,500[a]	36%
Minor	11,877	18,300[a]	54%

NOTE: [a] As of 1957.

TABLE 171.   LEADING RELIGIOUS COMMUNITIES, ETC., ADMINISTERING SEMINARIES AND SCHOLASTICATES IN AFRICA, ASIA AND LATIN AMERICA (1956–58)

Community	Number of Seminaries and Scholasticates	Enrollment Major Seminary Students	Average
Secular Clergy	77	4,809	62
Jesuits	40	3,179	80
Lazarists	24	1,040	43
Franciscans	26	706	27
White Fathers	9	482	54
Dominicans	13	390	30
Discalced Carmelites	2	365	182
Capuchins	22	302	14
Holy Ghost Fathers	8	299	37
Divine Word Fathers	9	296	33
Sulpicians	4	274	68
Paris Foreign Missions Society	4	257	64
Eudists	8	255	32
Claretians	10	242	27
Redemptorists	6	234	39
Salesians (St. John Bosco)	8	230	29
Scheut Fathers	3	187	62
Benedictines	8	181	23

With respect to the number of students enrolled in all the major seminaries and scholasticates in Africa, Asia and Latin America which come under the authority of the Propaganda, Oriental and Seminaries Congregations (and which have been previously listed in this chapter), Table 171 indicates the relative importance of the effort of the secular clergy and the 17 leading religious communities which are in charge of these institutions. Among the institutes the Jesuits are in first place, training more than three times as many major seminarians as are the Lazarists who are in second place. Furthermore the average enrollment of 80 students per Jesuit institution is about double the average enrollment at the institutions staffed by most of the other religious communities listed in the table.

Table 172 indicates the number of theological schools and major seminaries currently being maintained by the Roman Catholic, Protestant and Eastern Churches in Africa, Asia and Latin America, together with the total number of students enrolled at the theological and major seminary level in these institutions.

TABLE 172.   COMPARISON OF NUMBER OF ROMAN CATHOLIC, PROTESTANT AND EASTERN CHURCH SEMINARIES AND STUDENTS
(1956–58)

	Theological Schools, Major Seminaries, etc.				Theological Students, Major Seminarians, etc.			
	Roman Catholic	Protestant	Eastern Church	Total	Roman Catholic	Protestant	Eastern Church	Total
Africa	53	71	2	126	1,907	1,674	160	3,741
Middle East	14	1	9	24	225	12	175	412
Southern Asia	33	35	2	70	2,080	702	28	2,810
Southeast Asia[a]	35	32		67	1,458	840		2,298
East Asia[a]	15	28		43	846	2,218		3,064
Latin America	216	35		251	8,808	748		9,556
	366	202	13	581	15,324	6,194	363	21,881

NOTE: [a] Exclusive of Australia, New Zealand and Communist China.

Table 172 discloses that in terms of the total number of institutions and ordinand students being trained in them, the Roman Catholic Church has considerably surpassed the efforts of the Protestant missions in Africa, Asia and Latin America as a whole. The number of Roman Catholic and Protestant students in Africa are almost equal, and the number of Protestant students in East Asia (notably in Korea) exceeds the number of Roman Catholic students by a margin of more than two to one. In southern Asia (i.e., India), on the other hand, Roman Catholic major seminarians and scholastics outnumber Protestant theological students by three to one, and in Latin America by a margin of ten to one. For Africa, Asia and Latin America as a whole, the ratio of Roman Catholic to Protestant students is 2.5:1. Among the reasons for this preponderance, the following factors might be cited:

1. The modern phase of the Roman Catholic foreign missionary enterprise has been conducted for approximately 450 years, whereas few Protestant missions are more than 150 years old. With respect to the efforts to develop a local clergy, the previously quoted directives of the Propaganda were issued during a period of 300 years, whereas Protestant foreign mission boards placed little or no emphasis on the establishment of theological schools in the younger church areas until about 40 years ago.

2. The central organization of the Roman Catholic Church has enabled the Vatican to emphasize the importance of providing adequate training for a local clergy during the decades when individual and competing Protestant foreign mission boards were chiefly concerned with establishing mission stations abroad and sending their European and American missionaries overseas to staff them.

3. Among a number of the Roman Catholic religious communities, particularly the

Jesuits, there has been a greater and more sustained interest in obtaining a high level of scholarship in the major seminaries and scholasticates they administer than has generally been true in the case of Protestant foreign mission boards supporting theological schools overseas.

On the other hand, as noted in Chapter 1, there are six times as many Roman Catholics in Africa, Asia and Latin America combined as there are Protestants. Viewed in this light, the data in Table 172 suggests that in relation to the number of members of their churches and religious communities, the Protestants until recently have devoted a proportionately greater effort in establishing theological schools and enrolling ordinand students in the younger church areas than has the Roman Catholic Church. Writing in 1930, Father Schmidlin noted: "The fact that the Protestant missions have a still stronger tendency toward ecclesiastical emancipation, and usually realize this aim more rapidly and generally than the Catholic, is not the least factor in their great success in the domain of wide-spread Christianization, and partly offsets the internal difficulties which hamper the Protestant mission organization as such. . . . That the Protestant and schismatic missions pursue this object more consistently, and, having less difficulties to overcome, obtain a numerically (but not qualitatively) greater success, is well known."

Father Schmidlin's comment may have been accurate during the first two decades of the 20th century. However, the strengthening of the Roman Catholic missionary efforts and seminaries during the pontificates of Popes Pius XI and XII (i.e., from 1922 to 1958) as recounted in this chapter suggests that the activities of the Roman Catholic Church in this respect in recent years may have been proceeding at a greater rate than those of the Protestant churches along the same lines.

It is not possible to compare in detail the quality of the training provided at the Roman Catholic major seminaries with that provided in Protestant theological schools. In the first place the caliber of the teaching and the quality of students vary considerably from one major Roman Catholic seminary to another, as is true in the case of Protestant theological schools, making an over-all qualitative appraisal difficult. Secondly, the courses offered and the educational philosophy adhered to in Roman Catholic seminaries differ so greatly from those in Protestant theological schools that it is not easy to envisage how a common academic yardstick could be devised with which one could accurately appraise their relative merits. Yet, it is probably fair to say that the coordination of the studies in the minor and major seminaries, resulting in a longer period of training under the Church's auspices for candidates for the priesthood, probably results on the average in more highly trained students graduating from the major Roman Catholic seminaries in Africa, Asia and Latin America than from a majority of the Protestant theological schools.

Very few foreign missionaries in the field, either Protestant or Roman Catholic, have taken the trouble to study objectively and in detail the missionary activities of *both* of these churches within the particular area in which they are stationed, and then report their comparisons and findings to the public. An exception is Dean Horner of the Presbyterian Theological Seminary in Louisville, Kentucky, who served in the Cameroons from 1939 to 1949. During those ten years he observed at close range (among other missionary activities) the two Presbyterian theological schools (French and American) training pastors in the Cameroons and compared them with the St. Lawrence Seminary at Otélé which is staffed by Benedictine monks from Engelberg, Switzerland. Dean Horner summed up his views on Protestant and Roman Catholic seminary training in the Cameroons as follows:

In summary, Catholic missions emphasize theological training to a greater degree than general education, and from the academic standpoint, their effort in Cameroun is clearly superior to that of the Protestants. The Catholic major seminary is staffed with a corps of thoroughly trained professors, specialists in their respective fields. The quality of instruction is equal to that in most Catholic seminaries of Europe or America. A strong faculty and adequate equipment permit the enrollment of new classes regularly so that junior and senior students are taught simultaneously. By comparison the Protestant seminaries are "step children" of their respective missions, understaffed and neglected because of other emphases, taught by men who have little or no specialized training for such work and who are harassed by other pressing duties.

On the other hand the Catholic seminary curriculum is quite as lacking as the Protestant in any specific approach to the disturbed African social scene. It seems to be in even more danger of sterility at the point of training men to bear effective Christian witness in modern society. Moreover, the comparative isolation of Catholic theological students from normal African life for the greater part of twelve formative years is likely to have devastating effects on relationships with their own people. It is inconceivable that any but the most alert and inquisitive among them can comprehend the problems of present-day Africa in any adequate perspective.

The centralized control of the Vatican over the seminaries' curricula tends to make it possible for this Church to maintain the scholastic standards of its educational institutions more consistently than is presently possible among the Protestant theological schools in Africa, Asia and Latin America. Protestants might do well to note the fact that the average enrollment (42) of major seminary students in the typical Roman Catholic seminary in these three continents is 40% larger than that of its Protestant counterpart, thereby permitting a more effective use of faculty personnel and plant facilities.

Perhaps the greatest difference between Roman Catholic and Protestant seminaries is the stress placed by the former on the spiritual formation of their students. With the possible exception of some Anglican theological schools, the great majority of the Protestant seminaries appear to be seriously neglecting this most important phase in the training of a minister. The deficiencies of the Protestant schools may even be greater on this account than in their failure to insist on high academic standards in their curricula.

This point was emphasized by Rev. William L. Sullivan who was in an excellent position to judge such matters. During the years he was a Paulist Father, he taught dogmatic theology at St. Thomas' College, a scholasticate which this society then maintained in Washington, D.C. He became involved in the controversy over "modernism" which took place at the Catholic University of America at that time, and in 1909 he reluctantly resigned his membership in the Roman Catholic Church. In 1912 he became a minister in the Unitarian Church, in which capacity he served with distinction until his death in 1935. In his autobiography Dr. Sullivan compares Roman Catholic and Protestant seminaries as follows: "It will be seen from this that the Catholic Church takes seriously the preparation of the soul of its aspirant to her clergy. Would that Protestant seminaries followed her example! It has never failed to give me a sense of dismay to see how many of them are content with administering the pedantry of the minister's office to their students, leaving almost unnoticed the systematic freshening and fortifying of their souls."

On the other hand, to the extent that the Roman Catholic seminaries are concerned with the intellectual development of their students, the faculties of these institutions are more seriously confronted with one philosophical problem than are the faculties of most of the Protestant theological schools in these areas. This is how best to inculcate among their students a living belief in, rather than an unreasoning acceptance of, both the directives of the Church and the theological system (e.g., Thomism) upon which its intellectual unity is based, yet whose basic tenets the students and faculties are not permitted to question.

Finally it is worth noting that the statistics cited above relating to the number of major Roman Catholic seminaries and scholasticates actually in operation convey little or nothing of the human aspects of this missionary effort. If it took a long while for the major seminaries to be established in Europe following the Council of Trent, it is all the more understandable why a greater length of time was needed to accomplish the same objectives in Africa, Asia and Latin America. Furthermore the record shows that in many of the underdeveloped countries foreign missionaries have been persecuted and their missions suppressed by local governments throughout the past four hundred years in the belief that they were the forerunners or vestiges of unwanted colonial powers. The lag on the part of some of the missionary members of the religious communities in responding to the directives of the Vatican probably arose, in part at least, from a factor that has also hindered Protestant mission boards in establishing theological schools in the younger church areas. This is a lack of an adequate and sufficiently continuous line of communication between headquarters and the field.

Despite the friction which occasionally arose between the religious communities, and between them and Rome, the efforts of the Vatican and the communities to create a local clergy have achieved the very considerable results outlined in this chapter; and for this all Christians should be thankful.

Less than a month before he died, Pope Pius XI stated that he considered his encyclical *Ad catholici sacerdotii* dated December 20, 1935, was the most important pronouncement he had made during his pontificate. In it he said: "No matter how we seek, we shall always discover ourselves unable to contribute to anything greater than to the forming of good priests. In truth nothing is more acceptable to God, of more honor to the Church, or more profitable to souls. . . ."

Part Three:

THE SEMINARIES OF THE EASTERN CHURCHES

CHAPTER 15

THE SEMINARIES OF THE EASTERN CHURCHES IN AFRICA, ASIA AND LATIN AMERICA

A. GENERAL

As mentioned in the previous chapters relating to the seminaries of the Roman Catholic Church, the conclusions and recommendations of this Survey are limited to the Protestant theological schools in Africa, Asia and Latin America. There are no Eastern Church seminaries in Latin America. However, in order to complete this Survey of the Christian seminaries in Africa and Asia, the following chapter is devoted to a listing and discussion of the seminaries maintained by the various Eastern Churches in those two continents. The seminaries of the Eastern Churches in Europe and North America do not come within the scope of this Survey.

In order to present a balanced picture of the seminaries of the various Eastern Churches, it is necessary to relate them to the history and background of the ecclesiastical groups which support them. But here a difficulty arises. The origin of many of the Eastern Churches is shrouded in the distant past; and political, social and other nonreligious factors were of great importance in causing them to become independent. Thus any attempt to summarize 1500 years of the history of a church in a few sentences or paragraphs must necessarily result in oversimplifications of statements and interpretations. Those interested in obtaining fuller accounts of the activities of these churches may find the titles of a number of scholarly works in this field listed in the bibliography at the end of this Survey.

Almost all of the Eastern Churches have the word "orthodox" as part of their names. As a means of classifying them, these Churches are divided by some authors into three main groups—Orthodox, Monophysite and Nestorian. Such a division is not entirely satisfactory. Several of the Eastern Churches which are usually called "Monophysite" or "Nestorian" deny the accuracy of those designations or the assertion that they are "heretical." They claim, on the other hand, that they are following the creed of Nicaea as confirmed by the Synod of Ephesus (449) rather than the formula evolved at the Council of Chalcedon two years later. There is also said to be considerable doubt whether the so-called "Eutychian" Monophysitism is still adhered to by some Monophysites today. Finally it should be noted that the schisms which resulted in the creation of some of these Churches took place over a lengthy period of time, so that it is not always accurate to cite a single date as the one point in time at which the schism became definite or complete. Table 173 lists the membership statistics of the various Eastern Churches. This table and the remarks which follow should be interpreted in the light of these comments.

The various Eastern Churches are listed in this table which has been adapted and revised from the data presented by the Roman Catholic experts Donald Attwater (in his interesting two-volume work *The Christian Churches of the East,* which was published in 1948) and Pierre Rondot. The membership statistics are for the most part those presented in the 1957 edition of the *World Christian Handbook.*

As noted in Table 173, there are four Greek Orthodox Patriarchates in the Middle East and Africa. These are the Patriarchates of Constantinople, Antioch (with its Patriarch currently residing at Damascus), Jerusalem and Alexandria. Among these the Ecumenical Patriarch of Constantinople has a degree of precedence which is based in history on the importance of the City of Constantinople when it served as the capital of the Roman and Byzantine Empires. The rupture between the Roman Catholic Church and the Greek Orthodox Church was not final until after 1350, although July 16, 1054, is often used to indicate the most important date in the development of the schism between the two Churches. On that day the Cardinal Legates from Rome publicly placed on the high altar of St. Sophia Cathedral in Constantinople a letter from Pope Leo IX excommunicating the Patriarch Michael Cerularius on the grounds of his failure to conform to the Vatican's interpretation of various theological and jurisdictional matters.

The so-called Monophysite churches were the second large church group still existing today to split off from the original Christian Church. At the Council held in the year 451 at Chalcedon (a town located across the Bosporus from Constantinople), the Monophysite doctrine was discussed at length and condemned as heresy. The doctrine asserts that Christ possessed a two-fold nature before his incarnation but a single nature after his incarnation, that nature being divine. However, the Council of Chalcedon declared—largely as a result of the influence of Pope Leo the Great— that Christ had two natures, unmixed and unchangeable, but indistinguishable and inseparable. For political as well as religious reasons the Patriarch of Alexandria declined to accept the Council's decision. Thus the Coptic Orthodox Church of Egypt came into being, followed by the formation of the Armenian Orthodox and Ethiopian Orthodox and the Syrian Orthodox Churches during the next few decades. Eleven hundred years later the Syrian Orthodox Church of Malabar was established

TABLE 173. THE MEMBERSHIP AND LANGUAGES OF THE EASTERN CHURCHES (1957)

Church	Approx. Number of Members	Location	Approx. Date of Separation from Rome	Language	
				Liturgical	Vernacular
Orthodox					
Europe					
Patriarchate of Moscow	90,000,000?	USSR	1472	Slavonic	Russian
Patriarchate of Rumania	13,670,000	Rumania	"	Rumanian	Rumanian
Church of Greece	7,473,000	Greece	"	Greek	Greek
Serbian Patriarchate	8,019,000	Yugoslavia	"	Slavonic	Serbian
Exarchate of Bulgaria	6,000,000	Bulgaria	"	Slavonic	Bulgarian
Others*a*	4,140,000	*a*	various	various	various
Middle East and Africa					
Patriarchate of Constantinople	103,000	Turkey	1472	Greek	Greek
Patriarchate of Antioch	296,000	Syria, Lebanon	1517	Arabic	Arabic
Patriarchate of Alexandria	89,000	Egypt	1534	Greek	Arabic
Patriarchate of Jerusalem	30,000	Jordan, Israel	1534	Greek	Arabic
*Others*b*					
Ethiopian Orthodox Church	7,000,000	Ethiopia	550	Ge'ez	Amharic
Coptic Orthodox Church	2,000,000	Egypt	451	Coptic	Arabic
Armenian Orthodox Church	2,500,000?	USSR, Mid East	491	Armenian	Armenian
Syrian Orthodox Church	90,000	Syria, Iraq	543	Syriac	Arabic
Syrian Orthodox Church of Malabar	800,000	India	1653	Syriac	Malayalam
The Church of the East (Assyrian)	50,000	Iraq, Syria	431	Syriac	Syriac
Church of Trichur (Mellusian)	10,000?	India	1874	Syriac	Malayalam

NOTES: *a* Includes the Orthodox Churches of Cyprus, Albania, Finland, Poland, Germany, Hungary, Czechoslovakia and Japan, totaling about 1,640,000 members. The various Orthodox Churches in the USA have a total of approximately 2,500,000 members. *b* Monophysite, Nestorian, etc., as defined (see text).

in southern India among the descendants of the early "St. Thomas" Christians as a result of their reaction against the attempts of the Portuguese Archbishop of Goa to convert them by force to membership in the Roman Catholic Church. Some elements within some of these Orthodox churches no longer stress or even subscribe to the Monophysite doctrine.

The Nestorian Churches were the first religious group still existing today to break off from the original Christian Church. The story of their origin is complicated and can only be told very briefly here. At the third Ecumenical Council held in the year 431 at Ephesus (a port on the Aegean coast of Turkey, south of Smyrna), Bishop Nestorius of Constantinople was condemned and deposed in large part for his reluctance to refer in his sermons to the Virgin Mary as *theotokos* (i.e., Mother of God), rather than the phrase he preferred to use *christotokos* (i.e., Mother of Christ). "The Holy Apostolic and Catholic Church of the East," or Assyrian Church, as it is now called, became the national church in the Persian Empire. The Persian Emperors were constantly at war with the Roman Emperors in that era, and the Nestorian Church in Persia was able to disown any ties with the Church at Rome. Early in the 14th century the Nestorian Patriarch is reputed to have had 25 metropolitans and about 250 bishops under his jurisdiction, with the members of this Church extending throughout Asia from Mesopotamia to the

China Sea. However, the onslaught of the Mongols under Genghis Khan and his Muslim successors, notably Tamerlane, all but exterminated the membership of this Church. A few small remnants gathered in the mountains of Kurdistan and Anatolia under their spiritual leader who was known as the "Patriarch of the East and of the Assyrian CXIX."

The early development of the training schools and seminaries for the clergy in the West has been noted in Chapter 13. During the first few centuries of the Christian era a parallel development occurred in the Eastern Mediterranean area. Indeed, it is probably fair to say that until the middle of the fifth century the schools training priests in the Eastern provinces of the Roman Empire and in Persia were fully as important as those educating the clergy in the West.

Probably the earliest and the most famous of all these institutions was the Catechetical School which was established in Alexandria, Egypt, in the year 180. Its first three superintendents were Pantaenus, Clement and Origen. Origen was perhaps the greatest scholar of the ancient Church and served as head of this School from 204 to 232. In the latter year he was removed from this position by his bishop on the grounds that he had been ordained outside of the latter's diocesan jurisdiction, and for other reasons.

Attendance at the Catechetical School was voluntary, and the superintendents were unsalaried. The professors on the faculty sometimes became priests and bishops. However, in its earlier years the instruction was rather general, dealing mostly in apologetics and was initially aimed at training only catechumens (i.e., those receiving rudimentary instruction in Christianity). According to Charles Bigg,

there were no buildings appropriated to the purpose. The master received his pupils in his own house, and Origen was often engaged till late at night in teaching his classes or giving private advice or instruction to those who needed it. The students were of both sexes, of very different ages. Some were converts preparing for baptism, some idolaters seeking for light, some Christians reading as we should say for orders or for the cultivation of their understandings. There was as yet no rigid system, no definite classification of Catechumens, such as that which grew up a century later. The teacher was left free to deal with his task, as the circumstances of his pupils or his own genius led him. But the general course of instruction pursued in the Alexandrine school we are fortunately able to discover with great accuracy and fullness of detail. Those who were not capable of anything more were taught the facts of the Creed, with such comment and explanation as seemed desirable. Others, Origen tells us, were taught dialectically.

Later on the Catechetical School trained an increasing number of men destined for the priesthood and added to its "curriculum" courses in science, philosophy, rhetoric, etc. Although the number of students was not large, it nevertheless became a center of learning. The School continued in operation until the year 391.

Unfortunately, Origen's successors as superintendent (Heraclas, Dionysius, Theognostus, Pierius, Seraphon, Peter, the blind Didymus, and lastly Rhodon) were not of the same high intellectual caliber. The Catechetical School was closed in part as a result of the destruction of the famous library of the Serapeum (a former temple in Alexandria) by some ignorant and fanatical Egyptian monks.

As noted by Charles Augustus Briggs, "with Rhodon the school of Alexandria came to an end. Political interference, ecclesiastical domination, and popular outbreaks, which were common occurrences, combined to reduce the school to severe straits and eventually to destroy it. The monks, rigid ascetics, and inclined to be hostile toward philosophy and Greek learning, were not favourable to the historic principles of the school, which had enabled its teachers to work in harmony with the teachers of the university."

Owing to the hostile actions taken against him by the bishops of Alexandria, Origen withdrew to Caesarea (near the present-day port of Haifa) where he served as principal of another catechetical school. This institution had been founded as early as 215. During most of the years from 232 to 254 Origen taught here, and its fame soon rivaled that of the School at Alexandria. After his martyrdom, Origen was succeeded as principal by Pamphilus (ca. 240–309) who (according to Briggs) "enlarged Origen's collection of books and made of it a great library, gathering manuscripts from all parts of the world, employing copyists and transcribing many works with his own hand." After Pamphilus died, the school at Caesarea declined into oblivion.

During this same period, small clergy training schools were established in Gaza and Jerusalem. The former was an outgrowth of the Alexandrian School. The latter flourished under the leadership of Cyril, whose catechetical lectures have been preserved and illustrate the style of instruction used in the bishops' schools in those days.

A better known training center for the clergy was founded by the Presbyter Lucian in 290 at Antioch (in present-day Turkey). It tended to emphasize a historical and grammatical (exegetical) study of the Scriptures rather than the allegorical, speculative interpretation favored at Alexandria. In philosophy the school at Antioch taught the Aristotelian method, in contrast to the Platonic approach stressed in Alexandria. Dr. Lewis J. Sherrill points out: "When Nestorianism was condemned by the church in 451, the school fell into disfavor, for it was claimed that the Nestorians had built with materials from the theology of Antioch. But the (Nestorian) tendency passed into the Persian schools of Edessa and Nisibis."

In the year 363 (or thereabouts) another school was founded at Edessa which is today the city of Urfa, northeast of Antioch. This institution trained Nestorian clergy for service in Syria, Mesopotamia and Persia. In 378 the school was reorganized by Ephraem the Syrian under whose leadership it gained a high reputation for learning in the theological and other fields of study. One of its strengths is said to have been the fact that free inquiry was permitted on the part of its faculty and students. As Roscoe notes, "it must not be thought that all these theological schools were orthodox, as we would judge it to-day, for a great deal of philosophical inquiry, as well as theological education, was carried on, both theoretically and practically. This keen opposition to each other gave a great impetus to the discovery of doctrinal truth."

The Edessa school suffered as a result of the theological controversies which finally culminated in the Council of Chalcedon in 451. In the year 411–435 the principal of the school was Rabbula, an able bishop who opposed Nestorianism and used his influence against the native Syrian tendencies in favor of the Greek. According to Briggs, "one of his measures is said to have been the removal of the teachers of the theological school, for their Nestorian tendencies. By such measures he alienated the Syriac Christians; and the division that ensued, especially after his death, carried the greater part of the Syrians into heterodoxy. The Eastern Syrians became Nestorians, the Western Monophysites." The school at Edessa continued its identification with Nestorianism and lasted until 489 when it was disbanded under the orders of the Emperor Zeno. Its scholars were banished and scattered over Persia.

One of the direct results of this diaspora was the refounding of the clergy training school at Nisibis in Mesopotamia. It had originally been established some time earlier but had subsequently been closed, possibly when the Persians captured the city in 363. Nisibis became a center of Nestorianism when those Christians who held these views were persecuted as heretics in the Roman Empire and consequently emigrated to the Persian Empire to begin life anew. Some of the scholars who left Edessa in 489 came to Nisibis where the training school was reopened. It reached its highest point at the end of the 6th century when some 800 students were enrolled. Virtually all of these men were being trained for service in the Nestorian clergy in Persia and elsewhere throughout Asia. According to the statutes of the school which were adopted in 496 and promulgated once again in 602, the students and teachers shared a communal life which was strictly regulated. Instruction was free of charge, but the students (both lay and clerical) were obliged to take care of their own living expenses during the three-year course. The instruction tended to follow the Antiochian emphasis on exegesis of the Scriptures, and the courses are said to have been more systematically presented than was the case at most of the training institutions of that era. However, by the 9th century the school fell into disrepute, and with the rise of Islam and the later Mongol invasions, both this institution and, for the most part, the Nestorian Church itself passed out of existence.

As the Byzantine Empire became the most important center of Christianity in the Eastern Mediterranean area, church scholars emigrated to Constantinople. Under the Ecumenical Patriarch, this city became a leading center for the training of the clergy of the Greek Orthodox Church. However, no outstanding theologians were produced; and with the capture of Constantinople by the Ottoman Turks in 1453, the Eastern Churches in the Middle East entered into a period of comparative eclipse.

Meanwhile the Russian Orthodox Church continued to grow until the overthrow of the Tsarist Government in 1917 and the subsequent persecution of that Church by the Communist regime. Although there are reported to be 22,000 congregations and 32,000 priests in the Russian, Ukrainian and Armenian Orthodox Churches in the USSR today, the accuracy of these figures is problematic, as is the estimate of 90,000,000 members in the Russian Orthodox Church at the present time. It is of interest to note briefly the missionary efforts of the Russian Orthodox Church in the Middle East and East Asia during the past five centuries.

From the 14th century onward (i.e., after the overthrow of the Mongol domination of Russia), the main thrusts of the missionary efforts of the Russian Orthodox Church were in three directions. First and foremost, its missionaries moved eastward through Siberia, Kamchatka, China, Japan and on to Alaska. Second, they spread southeast through Central Asia and the Muslim Khanates among the Kazakh and Kirghiz peoples in that area. Third, Russian pilgrims annually traveled south to visit the Holy Land in considerable numbers, and the Tsarist Government recognized the political uses which could be made of this fact.

Because Siberia in the 19th century was sparsely populated, the missionary efforts of the Russian Orthodox Church among the Yakut and Samoyed peoples, etc., were on a comparatively small scale. In Japan, on the other hand, Ivan Kasatkin, known as Bishop Nicolai, achieved a considerable success following the establishment of a Russian Orthodox mission there in 1871. The indigenous membership of the Russian Orthodox Church in Japan was larger in proportion to the number of foreign missionaries associated with it than was the case with any other Christian church in the country at that time. A Roman Catholic missionary expert, Father Schmidlin, ascribes this success "to the fact that its founder and leader, Nicolai, kept himself as far as possible in the background and put forward the native mission personnel to whose development he devoted his chief efforts." In this connection Nicolai founded a seminary in Japan in 1873, two years after his arrival. According to Father Glazik, by 1900 there were 28 Russian Orthodox Japanese priests, but the total subsequently remained at about this number. The seminary (which once had as many as 70 students) was closed in 1918 and never reopened, owing in part to a lack of financial support from abroad. When Archbishop Nicolai died in 1912, it was estimated there were 30,000 Russian Orthodox converts in Japan. Yet in 1939 there were only 41,000 members, despite the large increase in the population of the country during the previous three decades. It would appear that a part of the reason for the failure of this Church to continue its early growth may have been due to a departure from the principles of organization on which it was founded.

The efforts of the Russian Orthodox Church to convert the Muslims in the Central Asian Khanates have been commented on by Donald Attwater as follows: "There is no doubt that the Russian missionary 'technique' is of great interest, and it has received very little attention in the West. Among its methods was the ordination of 'native' priests at the earliest possible moment and the use of the local vernacular language in public worship; it was found by experience, e.g., among the Tartars, that until this last was introduced no solid progress was made at all. In this matter a great modern worker was Nicholas Ilminsky (d. 1891), a layman who was a most remarkable linguist and a collaborator with the Metropolitan Innocent. In fifty years his translation committee published over $1\frac{1}{2}$ million copies of religious books in twenty-two non-Russian languages."

Toward the south, the Tsarist Government and the Russian Orthodox Church exerted some influence in Syria and the Holy Land in the era preceding World War I. By the year 1913 the Imperial Orthodox Society of Palestine had established a number of churches and hostels for pilgrims within the jurisdiction of the Greek Orthodox Patriarchates of Antioch and Jerusalem. In addition, the Society is reported to have supported 120 small community schools throughout the Levant in which approximately 20,000 school children were enrolled; but, unlike the Russian Orthodox mission to Japan, no seminary was established as a part of their effort to penetrate the Middle East.

With the collapse of Russian Orthodox foreign missionary efforts in 1918, it was not until after World War II that this Church (presumably with the approval of the Soviet Government) resumed its attempts to influence the activities of the Greek Orthodox, Armenian Orthodox and the other Eastern Churches in the Middle East, Eastern Europe and elsewhere.

Today the typical seminary maintained by the Eastern Churches differs somewhat from those supported in the Middle East by the Roman Catholic and Protestant Churches. Whereas there is usually a clear distinction between major and minor Roman Catholic seminaries, the seminaries of the Eastern Churches tend to train students continuously from an early age on up to the time of their ordination. Thus the latter institutions often operate at both the upper primary and secondary levels, with some having small faculties composed of men serving only part time. Furthermore, with one or two exceptions the curricula of the seminaries of the Eastern Churches are less formalized, and their educational level tends to be somewhat lower than their Roman Catholic and Protestant counterparts in the Middle East. A number of the seminaries have between 60 and 100 students enrolled for study, but it is not easy to ascertain with accuracy what proportion of these may properly be called theological students in the same sense that this term has been used in connection with Protestant and Roman Catholic students preparing for the ministry. Accordingly in the tables below, the number of faculty members and theological students listed as teaching and studying at each of the seminaries of the Eastern Churches represents in some cases an estimate of the number of only those teachers and ordinands at that institution who are engaged in studies at a theological level, and excludes those who are at the pretheological level.

B. AFRICA

Table 174 lists the seminaries of the Eastern Churches in Africa.

Coptic Theological College: Approximately 2,000,000 persons out of a total population of 23,000,000 in Egypt are members of the Coptic Orthodox Church. Thus there are about 30 Copts for every one member of the Greek Orthodox Patriarchate

TABLE 174.   SEMINARIES OF THE EASTERN CHURCHES IN AFRICA (1957)

| | | Approx. Number of | | |
| | | | Theol. | |
Name	Location	Faculty	Students	Supporting Church
Egypt				
Coptic Theological College	Cairo	14	110	Coptic Orthodox Church
St. Photius Seminary[c]	Alexandria	Proposed[c]		Greek Orthodox Patriarchate of Alexandria
Ethiopia				
Theological School of the Holy Trinity	Addis Ababa	6[a]	50[b]	Ethiopian Orthodox Church
Total: 2 (in operation)		20	160	

NOTES: [a] Plus part-time and additional faculty members teaching at other levels of study.   [b] Plus other students at lower or higher level of training.   [c] See text.

of Alexandria. The Copts are most numerous in the towns of Middle Egypt, particularly at Assiout and Achmim. The name "Copt" is said to be a corruption of the Greek word meaning "Egyptian." The leader of this Church, the Coptic Patriarch of Alexandria, now resides at Cairo.

The members of the Coptic Church have always been drawn from the native Egyptian population, whereas the Greek Orthodox Church in Egypt has drawn its membership largely from Greeks settled in the larger cities. The Copts in past centuries have in general adhered to the Monophysite doctrine though not all of them have supported it at all times. They have also pointed to the dependence from time to time of the Greek Orthodox Church in Egypt upon the Ecumenical Patriarch in Constantinople. With the Arab invasion of Egypt and the adoption of Islam as the national religion of Egypt in the 7th century, the Copts at first supported the Arabs against the Greeks. Later the Copts were mercilessly persecuted by the Muslims, and in subsequent centuries the latter have customarily exerted considerable pressure on all the Christian churches in Egypt. For example, in the summer of 1957, to cite a recent instance, the Egyptian Government confiscated the landed estates belonging to the Coptic Church, and offered Government bonds in exchange therefor.

Like some religious minorities in other countries, the Copts in Egypt have over the centuries devoted more attention to the education of their children than has the rest of the population. One result has been that they obtained a disproportionate influence in trade and government service. In recent decades, however, the general raising of the educational level of the Muslim population in Egypt has tended to narrow the Copts' advantage in this respect.

On the other hand, the emphasis of the Copts on the secular education of their children was not accompanied by a similar emphasis on the theological training of the Coptic clergy. Thus Coptic laymen have traditionally been better educated than their clergy. Shortly after World War II, the Roman Catholic expert, Donald Attwater, wrote: "The great reproach against the Coptic clergy is their lack of education—which is not their fault, for the only seminary has never yet functioned properly. Many of the priests cannot read their liturgical language . . . some even cannot read Arabic. Clerical education has been one of the concerns of the reforming party, but they want to send ecclesiastical students to England—where they run the risk of being protestantized; the late patriarch favoured Orthodox colleges. Priests are mostly drawn from the artisan class (for which reason alone the bourgeois laity despise them), and are always married before ordination . . . ."

The difficulties of the Coptic Church today result not only from the pressures of the Egyptian Government and Islam but also are accounted for in part by the loss of some of their members each year to Protestantism. According to one authority, William Worrell, "conversions to Protestantism are probably not due to the appeal of another doctrine or theology, or another form of worship, but to the effect of attendance at (Protestant) mission schools, where a good modern education can be obtained in preparation for the economic struggle of life in the teeming Egyptian world. . . . Reform movements are in the hands of the (Coptic) laity and in the very nature of the case opposed by the clergy, who cannot put themselves in line with modern life." Another factor worth noting is the tradition in the Coptic and other Eastern Churches of having some lay theological teachers on the faculties of their seminaries.

Over a century ago J. R. T. Lieder of the Church Missionary Society of England established a boarding school for Coptic boys in Egypt which by 1842 had grown into a theological seminary for the Coptic clergy. One of its graduates subsequently became the Abuna, or head, of the Ethiopian Church. However, the quality of candidates for this theological school proved to be poor, and some Coptic bishops refused to ordain its graduates on the grounds that they had been trained in a Protestant institution. Accordingly the school was closed in 1848. A successor seminary lasted from 1854 to 1861.

In 1875 Cyril V was elected Patriarch of the Coptic Orthodox Church. Shortly thereafter a new seminary was founded in Cairo and placed under the direction of a learned and unusually able scholar by the name of Philotheus. The latter was assisted by four other teachers, and in the first year 12 students were enrolled. However, the Patriarch became dissatisfied with the head of the seminary and the teaching therein, so he abolished the institution. Once again the priests were left without any school to prepare them for their life's work.

In 1890 a number of Coptic laymen established a society in the hopes of bringing about needed reforms within their Church, including the enforcement of higher educational standards for the clergy. The Coptic priests were antagonistic and suspicious, but in 1895 the seminary was reopened. Unfortunately, according to Butcher, the initial faculty members were entirely unfit for their duties and ultimately had to be replaced by more capable teachers. It is not clear how long the institution remained open.

According to Attwater, the same Patriarch, Cyril V, "died at a great age in 1927, having governed his church for fifty-two years and having on the whole successfully opposed all reforms, good and bad, which the notables had tried to impose on him . . . a new patriarch, John XIX, formerly metropolitan of Bohaireh and a monk of al-Baramus, was appointed in December, 1928. He was the leader of the conservative party, but promised to reorganize the Cairo ecclesiastical school, to send promising clerical students abroad for studies, and other reforms, including a 'constitution' for his church."

The present Coptic Theological College was formerly located in antiquated buildings at Mahmasha, one of the native quarters of Cairo. In October, 1953, it was transferred to the new Anba Rueiss Building on Ramsis Street in Abbassia, a more modern section of the city. The new three-story building was paid for by the Coptic Community Council (Megliss Milli) at a reported cost of over $400,000. It contains seminar and lecture rooms, an amphitheater, "a fair library," a chapel, refectory, laboratory and dormitories. The funds obtained to construct this building were largely in the form of contributions received from individual members of the Coptic laity who are interested in furthering the renaissance of this Church.

The institution consists of four departments and currently has a faculty of 22 full-time professors and teachers, plus 15 part-time instructors. A number of the faculty have been trained abroad and are well regarded in their fields. The current student body totals approximately 200 men. In recent years about a dozen students from Ethiopia have usually been enrolled. The ordinands amount to approximately 110 of the total, and the equivalent of about 14 full-time members of the faculty devote their time to the training of students at the theological level.

The first department, the Theological College itself, offers a four-year course for students who enter with the baccalaureate degree (which is equivalent to the entrance requirements for the Government universities). This course leads to a diploma qualifying these graduates for appointment as priests in the service of the Coptic Church. The Rector of the College is the Abuna Ibrahim Atiya who succeeded a layman, Habib Guirguis, to this position after the death of the latter. The sub-rector, Dr. Wahib Atallah, recently acquired his doctoral degree from Manchester University under the guidance of the famous Coptic scholar Wilhelm Till. Another faculty member is Father El Souriani Makary, a monk who served as a delegate of the Coptic Orthodox Church to the Second Assembly of the World Council of Churches which was held in Evanston, Illinois, in 1954.

The second department provides an intermediate course for students who have only a preparatory school (i.e., presecondary) certificate. Many of these students are destined for service as pastors in rural areas. They take a five-year course at a somewhat lower academic level than that offered in the College.

The third department trains choir leaders and offers a six-year course. It is to be renamed the St. Didymus School, in honor of the famous blind Director of the Alexandria Institute of Catechetical Studies during the 4th century.

The fourth department is the Higher Institute of Coptic Studies which was founded in 1955. The Institute is not a seminary but rather an educational and research center at the graduate level for the study of the cultural content of Coptic life. It admits students from a number of Eastern Churches beside the Coptic Church, and has some Roman Catholic, Jewish and Muslim students. The Director of the Institute is Dr. Aziz S. Atiya, Chairman of the Department of Medieval History at the Alexandria University. The Institute has four or five faculty members on its staff. It lists courses in the Egyptian language, historical studies, archaeology, arts, ecclesiastical law, sociology, church music, Ethiopian studies, Semitic languages and.literature, African studies, theology, etc. However, because of the shortage of competent theologians, the Institute has had difficulty in finding a suitable professor to teach the last-named subject. Ultimately it is hoped that the Institute will serve to raise the general intellectual level of the Church and the Coptic population in Egypt.

The joint library of the institution contains about 4,500 volumes. Also housed in this building are the administrative offices of the Coptic Sunday Schools system.

The principal language of instruction at this institution is Arabic. The ordinand students are also taught either Coptic or Ge'ez, the ancient languages of Egypt and Ethiopia, respectively, which are now used as the liturgical languages in the Coptic and Ethiopian Churches in those countries. Ge'ez has not been generally spoken by the Ethiopian people for over 1,000 years. Other languages taught include Greek, Hebrew and English.

In addition to the institution described above, there is said to be a center at or near Hélonan, another suburb of Cairo, where the monks for six monasteries of the

Coptic Church are trained. A seventh monastery reportedly has a school of its own, but there is little information readily available concerning these centers. Possibly they might be compared to the scholasticates which are maintained by the religious communities of the Roman Catholic Church, but in the absence of factual data it is not possible to be precise concerning them. The influence of the monks in the Coptic Church is considerable inasmuch as the Patriarchs and Bishops are always chosen from among their ranks.

It would appear that subsequent to the time Attwater wrote his comment on the Coptic clergy, quoted above, there has been a revival in the intellectual life of this Church, centered largely in its training institutions in Cairo.

St. Photius Seminary: The Greek Orthodox Patriarchate of Alexandria has been weakened by the fact that its members have been subjected from time to time to pressure from Islam and the Egyptian Government. The majority of the priests in this Patriarchate are of Greek nationality. Because Greek Orthodoxy has appeared to many Egyptians as an instrument of foreign influence, its task has been particularly difficult. Over the years there has been a continuing emigration of the Greek-speaking population in Egypt to other countries.

Until 1926 there was no seminary maintained by the Patriarchate of Alexandria. In that year Patriarch Meletios II founded the St. Athanasius Seminary in Alexandria. This institution offered a six-year course training men to become pastors, choir masters and secular school teachers. In 1929 it had 46 students (36 Greeks and 10 Syrians). However, its educational level was fairly low and only about one-quarter of the curriculum was devoted to ecclesiastical subjects. The most promising candidates for the priesthood were sent to be trained at the Greek Orthodox Seminary at Halki (near Istanbul) or at the Theological Faculty of the University of Athens in Greece. The St. Athanasius Seminary was closed in 1936 by Patriarch Nicholas II. During the decade of its existence only 63 of the 100 students who entered it were graduated. Of these 63 graduates, only 20 became priests. The total expense to the Patriarchate amounted to 23,500 Egyptian pounds (or more than 1,000 pounds spent for each of these 20 priests).

For a number of years there have been plans announced from time to time by the Patriarch Christoforos looking toward the establishment of St. Photius Seminary in Alexandria. There have also been discussions for the purpose of founding a joint seminary in Alexandria to serve students from the Greek Orthodox Patriarchates of Antioch and Jerusalem as well as Alexandria. However, none of these plans have materialized. The result, according to one informant, is that the larger number of the priests currently serving in the Alexandria Patriarchate receive only primary religious training and consequently "have only 'notions' of religious knowledge."

Theological School of the Holy Trinity: The Ethiopian Orthodox Church has the largest membership of any of the Eastern Churches in Africa or Asia.

When the Monophysite Churches were established during the half century following the Council of Chalcedon (451) these Churches were cut off from the main stream of church life in the Eastern Mediterranean area. Various other factors served to accelerate the isolation of the Ethiopian Orthodox Church during the next 1,000 years. Among them was the fact that much of Ethiopia is a highland or plateau area. It has few natural transportation routes and lies to the east of the main north and south trade routes along the White Nile southward to Lakes Albert and Tanganyika. The rise of Islam in the 7th and 8th centuries in Arabia and Egypt served further to cut off the Ethiopian Church from the other Christian churches. Throughout this long period of isolation, the Ethiopian Church served as one of the principal cultural and unifying agencies in the country.

At present the population of Ethiopia numbers approximately 19,500,000, of whom between 5,000,000 and 8,000,000 are estimated to be members of the Ethiopian Orthodox Church. There are about 5,000,000 Muslims in the country, largely in the northern and eastern areas. Most of the remainder of the population are pagans residing in the Galla area and elsewhere in the southwestern section of Ethiopia. Protestant churches have about 96,000 members, and there are approximately 60,000 Roman Catholics in the country.

The skeptical attitude of the Ethiopian Church toward the Roman Catholic Church is said to have increased during the Italian occupation of the country during the years 1935–41. In addition, the Ethiopian Church claims with some foundation in fact that during the past century Protestant missionaries in their country have tended to proselyte members of the Ethiopian Church rather than Muslims or pagans.

Since its establishment, the Ethiopian Orthodox Church has constantly maintained a relationship with the Coptic Orthodox Church of Egypt inasmuch as both subscribe to Monophysite doctrines. Customarily when the Abuna (i.e., the leading church official) died in Ethiopia, the Emperor would inform the Coptic Patriarch of Alexandria and request the latter to send a replacement. This replacement would usually be an Egyptian Copt. For example, in 1881 the Coptic Patriarch of Alexandria, Cyril V, consecrated four Egyptian Copts as bishops and sent them to administer dioceses in Ethiopia.

In 1922 discussions were commenced looking toward a revision in this relationship. The present Emperor, Haile Selassie, serves as the official head of the Ethiopian Orthodox Church and takes a considerable interest in its affairs. However, it was not until 1948 that he was able to conclude an agreement with the Coptic Patriarch of Alexandria whereby the successors to the position of Abuna (or Metropolitan) in Ethiopia would be elected by the Synod and confirmed by the Emperor from among the Ethiopian bishops or monks. The new Abuna was to be sent to Cairo for his consecration. In 1948 the Patriarch consecrated six Ethiopian bishops who had been chosen from among the monks of that Church. In this way the Ethiopian Church recognized the power of Coptic episcopal succession but freed itself from the administrative supervision of the Coptic Church. Finally, in 1959 a new agreement was concluded whereby the Archbishop of the Ethiopian Orthodox Church (Abuna Basilios) was elected to the position of Patriarch of Ethiopia, with the power to consecrate his own archbishops and bishops. Thus this Church has now completed the process of establishing its ecclesiastical independence within the Monophysite world.

It has been estimated that as many as one-fifth of the Coptic male population in Ethiopia are serving as priests and *debteras* (full-time lay offcers and choir members). Thus Ethiopia is one of the few countries in the world with a surfeit rather than a shortage of Christian clergy. Commenting in 1950 on the quality of the lower clergy of the Ethiopian Church, a Protestant specialist, Dr. J. Spencer Trimingham, wrote: "The root cause of the weakness of the Church in raising the spiritual life of the people is the backward condition of the clergy. They are chosen from traditional priestly families and so form almost a Levitical caste. They are ordained without any training and consequently are ignorant, superstitious and lazy."

The situation among its clergy was also described by Rev. Gregory Wilkins, S.S.M. (Society of the Sacred Mission). Father Wilkins is an Anglican priest who taught at the Theological School of the Holy Trinity in Addis Ababa during 1955 and subsequently wrote as follows:

There seem to be few qualifications required for ordination; not even a lower age limit as in the Church in the West. Quite young boys are ordained, and even a number of the scholars in the school where I was were in orders; some of them were only twelve years old. Nor has there been much in the way of intellectual requirements from ordinands, apart from some knowledge of Ge'ez, the dead language in which the liturgical and other church books are written. Even on this point it is enough to be able to read it, that is, to make the correct sounds! A knowledge of the meaning may be a good thing, but is not essential. . . .

In Ethiopia the layman . . . has far more to do in matters which in England are kept much more strictly in the hands of the clergy . . . At the college where I stayed, much of the religious instruction was given by laymen. . . . The danger is that if the present trend continues there will very soon develop a serious division between an educated laity and an uneducated priesthood. At present there is among the priests an almost complete absence of education in the modern Western sense. . . . So the . . . most serious aspect of it all is the tendency, only too clearly seen, for the priests to be 'uneducated' in our sense of that word, while the 'educated' are to be found outside the priestly ranks. The good student is quite readily sent abroad to a European or an American university . . . (but) not one comes abroad to study in order to go back and become a priest.

I believe that a very few have been sent to Greece with future ordination in mind; but several times as many have been sent abroad to learn, to take only one example, engineering. Here then is the great and pressing danger, the danger of a secularised and educated laity coming to feel superior to and contemptuous of an uneducated priesthood.

Some of those in authority in Ethiopia are aware of this danger, and among the most aware is the Emperor himself. His interest in and enthusiasm for education may be judged from the fact that he is himself Minister of Education in his own government. One of his own acts has been to found the Theological College of the Holy Trinity where I lived for the nine weeks that I was in the country.

When the Emperor Haile Selassie returned to head the Government in Addis Ababa in 1942, he recognized that a number of reforms in the Ethiopian Church were needed. In 1943 the Emperor obtained the services of Dr. Mourad Kamel to organize a seminary in Addis Ababa to train deacons and priests for the Ethiopian Church. Dr. Kamel, an Egyptian Copt, brought three other graduates of the Coptic Theological College in Cairo with him from Egypt to serve on the faculty of the new institution. The seminary was opened in December 1944 and was administered by the Ministry of Education with the guidance of His Beatitude Abuna Theophelos. Six months later a total of 220 students from all the provinces of Ethiopia were enrolled. However, there is said to have been some difficulty in placing the graduates of the first few classes in positions within the Church, and it was concluded that a change in the administration of the seminary was needed.

Accordingly in 1951 Rev. Kunnumporath Mathew Simon, a priest of the Syrian Orthodox Church of Malabar was selected to reorganize the institution. As a member of another Monophysite Church, Father Simon had studied theology at Kelham, England, and in the United States.

The Theological School of the Holy Trinity is now the official seminary of the Ethiopian Orthodox Church. It is managed by a board of seven members appointed by the Emperor, with His Grace Abdul Theophilos (the Deputy Archbishop) as its Chairman. Four of the seven members of the board are ministers of the Crown, and the operating costs of the institution are defrayed by the Government.

Until recently the seminary was housed in prefabricated huts which had been set up by the Italian Army in the 1930s to serve as military barracks in Addis Ababa. Some of the classrooms and offices of the seminary are still maintained in these somewhat dilapidated structures; others are now located in a small two-story building which once served as the Government's office for the liberation of slaves. The seminary now has new dormitory buildings located close to the Church of the Holy Trinity, the principal church in Addis Ababa. These dormitories can house a total of 289 students.

According to Father K. M. Simon, "our library is really a nominal one only. . . . The total number of theological books may come to a little over three thousand. But a large number of these are not really worthwhile books. We have also at the moment not a good place to be used as a library. This is included in our plan of the second stage, but the money for the second stage (which includes the lecture blocks, auditorium, administration block, library) has still to be found."

The reorganization of the seminary in 1951 necessitated the establishment of classes at the primary level. In these classes, boys commence their studies at an early age and continue them until their ordination. As students progressed, classes at a higher level were added to the curriculum from year to year. Thus in the first few years of Father Simon's administration, the seminary was not equipped to train students at the upper secondary level. Accordingly the most promising ordinands (usually more than a dozen each year) were sent to the seminaries at Cairo, Halki and at Athens to complete their studies.

Commenting on the situation, Father Wilkins noted that there were about 250 students enrolled in this institution in 1955:

Of these some hundred and fifty are boarders, selected and sent there and paid for by the government. All expenses are paid; food, lodging, clothes, and even fares home for the holidays, are found. The rest of the students live in Addis Ababa and attend the classes. The zeal of students and the difficulties that arise from poverty may be gauged by the fact that some of the non-boarders have no homes in Addis Ababa; they sleep in churchyards, or anywhere else that they can find. As for food, it is no disgrace in Ethiopia to be a beggar, and the boarders are generous.

The range of ages among the students is very great. There are boys of ten in the lowest classes; but you may find in the same class men who are in the twenties. The Bishop of Harar is a great patron and friend of the College. Partly as a result of his influence, there are a number of young deacons and priests coming to it to be educated. There are also a number of young monks sent there by their abbots.

According to Father Simon (writing in 1957),

the vast majority of new students are residents and they need not necessarily be deacons or priests. . . . Up to now no less than 300 have been graduated and they are now serving the church in various capacities, some as priests, but a good many as religious teachers in the many schools in Addis Ababa and the other parts of the Empire.

Four years ago we changed our policy and converted the school gradually to a full-fledged secondary school with a religious setting. We started with the 8th grade and only this year we completed the 12th grade, thus making it a full theological secondary school. Here we teach the full curriculum as set by the Ministry of Education, plus as much of the religious subjects as we can. A real religious atmosphere is maintained in order to help the student to develop a true sense of vocation for the sacred ministry. . . . The students of the secondary will at the end of the year appear for the general S. L. certificate examination of the Ministry of Education and London Matriculation.

Father Wilkins notes that "the subjects studied are much as in similar schools in England, but with two additions. The first is that as a theological foundation the boys have to learn Church music, and Ge'ez, the Church language. . . . The second addition to the curriculum is English. In primary schools under the direction of the Ministry of Education, and this means all except the little village schools, English is a compulsory subject. In all other schools and colleges the teaching of English is continued if necessary, and—this is the interesting point—all instruction must be given in English."

In addition to the regular secondary classes, this institution is also currently conducting a two-year course for religious teachers. These men serve as chaplains in the secular schools and colleges.

The faculty of the Holy Trinity School now consists of about 15 professors and lecturers, the majority of whom are teaching academic subjects at the primary and lower secondary levels. In addition to Father Simon, there are three other Indians serving on the faculty, plus four Egyptians (Copts) and seven young Ethiopians who have been educated abroad. It is of interest to note that few of the latter are priests.

It was planned to open a theological college in September 1958 as part of this institution, with Father Simon serving as its director and a 4½-year theological course being offered. However, the opening was postponed until October 1959 when 12 students commenced the course. Trinity Theological College is being associated with the new University of Addis Ababa immediately adjacent to it, and will serve as its theological faculty. The graduates of the theological course will receive a B.D. degree.

In 1957 Father Simon pointed out:

This will be the only theological institution of university level in the whole of the Monophysite world. . . . We are hoping to become the main center to turn out missionaries for this continent . . . a hope to recruit some really fine theologians from different parts of the world to be professors in the college. . . .

The next year along with the college (we) also plan to start a youth training center and later a training center for workers among women. Further, in order to get the thousands of clergy set in line with the thinking of the time, we also plan to start regular "refresher" courses for the existing clergy during the long vacation. . . .

We have a nice plan for our lecture blocks, auditorium, library, administration block as well as staff quarters, but lack of funds is holding everything up. Our church is reported to be immensely rich. It certainly has much land. But since from old times these are distributed among the thousands of clergy who get their subsistence by working on the land, there is not much money which could be actually gathered and used for a common cause like this. Actually most of the churches have many priests attached to it and some big churches even up to 200. Further the clergy has still to be educated even in administration of property and the use of money. His Majesty is trying to reorganize all. But it is bound to take time. In the Orient, all things happen slowly. Only the time is not on our side. The Muslims are organizing themselves. There are over 100 million pagans in this continent and if we do not rise to the occasion, not only that these millions will be lost to the church, but we might lose some of our own too. . . .

C. MIDDLE EAST

Table 175 lists the seminaries of the Eastern Churches which are located in the Middle East.

Greek Orthodox Seminary, Halki: The fortunes of the Greek Orthodox Ecumenical Patriarchate of Constantinople declined precipitously with the collapse of the Byzantine Empire when Constantinople was captured by the Turks in 1453. Since that time the Orthodox Christians in Turkey (largely of Greek extraction and living in the neighborhood of Istanbul, the Turkish name for Constantinople) have been

TABLE 175. SEMINARIES OF THE EASTERN CHURCHES IN THE MIDDLE EAST (1957)

Name	Location	Approx. Number of		Supporting Church
		Faculty	Theol. Students	
Turkey				
Greek Orthodox Seminary	Halki, Istanbul	11[a]	50[a]	Greek Orthodox Patriarchate of Constantinople
Armenian Theological Seminary	Uskudar, Istanbul	6[a]	20[a]	Armenian Orthodox Church
Syrian Orthodox Seminary	Mardin	3	10	Syrian Orthodox Church
Lebanon				
Armenian Theological Seminary	Antelias (Bikfaya)	5[a]	15[a]	Armenian Orthodox Church
(Independent Armenian) Seminary	Beit Meri	3	12	Independent Armenians of Lebanon
Holy Trinity	Belmonte, Tripoli	5	20[a]	Greek Orthodox Patriarchate of Antioch
Jordan				
St. Demetrius	Jerusalem	5[a]	25[a]	Greek Orthodox Patriarchate of Jerusalem
St. James	Jerusalem	4[a]	8[a]	Armenian Orthodox Church
Iraq				
Mar Ephraem	Mosul	4[a]	15[a]	Syrian Orthodox Church
Assyrian Seminary[b]	Kirkuk	Proposed[b]		Church of the East (Assyrian)
Total: 9 (in operation)		46	175	

NOTES: [a] Plus others at a lower level of training or teaching.
[b] See text.

treated as a religious minority, sometimes harshly. In the war of 1921–23 in which Greece was defeated by Turkey, nearly 1,500,000 Greeks, most of them members of the Greek Orthodox Church, were deported from Anatolia and Asia Minor to Greece. Thus, as Dr. K. S. Latourette notes, "the constituency over which the Ecumenical Patriarch exercised direct jurisdiction shrank to very small proportions, and that office, once vying with the Papacy in power, now had little but the tantalizing memories of a great past."

For almost four centuries following the fall of Constantinople there was no organized training provided for the priests serving in this Patriarchate. In 1839 a seminary was established in Constantinople, but it was closed a year later owing to a lack of funds. The present Seminary was founded in 1845 on the island of Halki near Istanbul by the Patriarch Germanos IV. Thus it is the oldest of the Greek Orthodox seminaries in the Middle East. It has had a comparatively good academic standing. Prior to World War I it attracted students from all parts of the Middle East and many of the higher clergy also came from Greece to study there. However, over the years, it has trained only a small proportion of the parochial clergy under the jurisdiction of this Patriarchate.

The Seminary was closed during World War I. In 1923 it was reopened with the first class graduating in 1930 after completing a seven-year course. In this period Halki operated at the level of a provincial seminary. The late Patriarch, Photius II, is reported to have worked diligently during the 1930s to raise the intellectual standards of his clergy and to enable Halki to regain something of its former status. He also sent some students to the Theological Faculty of the University of Athens and to Orthodox seminaries elsewhere in Europe for their training.

The activities of the Halki Seminary have been somewhat restricted in recent years by the actions of the Turkish Government and people. In 1951 it had only 20 students enrolled because of Government regulations reducing the number of foreign students permitted to enter the country. At one point the school was threatened with closing. However, the Government reconsidered and once again permitted students and professors to come into the country from abroad. It also accorded Halki the academic rating of a university.

The Seminary was slightly damaged in the anti-Greek riots which occurred in September, 1955, over the issue of the political disposition of Cyprus. A fire destroyed some of the furnishings at Halki, but no lives were lost. The library and other buildings were largely undamaged, except for broken windows. Since then the Seminary has been subjected to some threats and restrictions, but it continues its work generally undisturbed.

The island of Halki is located at the mouth of the Bosporus, about 25 miles' distance (approximately one hour by boat) from Istanbul. It has a winter population of 5,000 and a summer population of about 15,000 inasmuch as it is a summer resort. The Seminary campus consists of about five acres located on a hill about 20 minutes' walk above the harbor. Its facilities consist primarily of one large three-story stone building surrounded by gardens and an orchard. In this building are the classrooms, library, refectory, chapel, etc. It has dormitory accommodations for approximately 90 students. A part of the building has also been used as the summer residence of the Ecumenical Patriarch.

Like most of the theological schools of the Eastern Churches, Halki offers courses at both the seminary and preseminary level. The "gymnasium" or "lycée" section consists of three years of basic training. Six years of elementary schooling are required for admission into it. There are about nine professors teaching these courses.

The advanced school at Halki consists of four years of theological study at a university level. A Master of Theology degree is awarded, and this degree is accepted on a par with similar degrees from the universities at Athens and Saloniki. Approximately 11 professors are teaching in this school, the entrants to which must have had three years at the lycée level. Thus a total of seven years' study is offered. As a rule most of the students continue from the lycée through the upper classes.

The language of instruction in the lower classes is modern Greek. In the upper classes ancient Greek is taught. Classes also are conducted in Turkish.

The Seminary is administered by a dean who is directly responsible to the Ecumenical Patriarch and the Holy Synod of this Patriarchate. The institution's financial needs are met with funds provided by the Patriarchate.

The strength of Halki is said to be in the caliber of its faculty. All, or nearly all, of the professors are graduates of universities in Europe and the United States. By contrast, the professors of the two other Greek Orthodox seminaries in the Middle East are said to be not as highly educated. A number of guest lecturers from Europe have also served at Halki.

There are approximately 50 men enrolled at the advanced level for a Master of Theology degree. In addition, there are about 60 students at the lycée level, making a total of approximately 110 students currently enrolled in the institution. It is estimated that 95 out of every 100 students awarded a Master of Theology degree become ordained priests, with the balance entering teaching careers. A fairly strict life is imposed on the students, and some applicants for admission are rejected.

One of the unusual features of this Seminary is the international composition of its student body. Approximately two-thirds of the students are of non-Greek descent. In each of the last few years students have been enrolled from Ethiopia, Uganda, South India, Finland and Cyprus. Occasionally students from Germany, France, England and the United States are trained here also. Thus the number of students coming from the jurisdiction of the Ecumenical Patriarch is only about one-third of the total. Students from abroad receive board, lodging and tuition free of charge. Their own churches normally provide them with their travel, clothing and personal expenses.

The Seminary has a comparatively large library of about 50,000 volumes. Students also have access to the library of the Ecumenical Patriarchate located in Istanbul. Most of the books at Halki are in Greek, but there are said to have been comparatively few accessions to the Seminary's collection since World War I. Thus it would appear to be in need of recently published theological literature in the Arabic and Greek languages.

Halki has trained men who later became Greek Orthodox patriarchs, metropolitans and bishops serving not only in the Middle East but also in Europe (Greece and Yugoslavia) and in the United States. It is generally recognized that this institution is the leading seminary among those in Africa, the Middle East and Southern Asia which are maintained by the various Eastern Churches.

Armenian Theological Seminary, Uskudar: This is one of three seminaries maintained in the Middle East by the Armenian Orthodox Church.

This Church was founded by St. Gregory the Illuminator who was born in Armenia in the third century. In the year 301, Armenia proclaimed Christianity as its official religion, some 12 years before the conversion of the Roman Emperor Constantine I. Subsequently the leaders of this Church adhered to the Monophysite doctrine. Accordingly it was split off from the main body of the Church following the Council of Chalcedon in 451. At one point it was reunited with the Greek Orthodox Church, but subsequently it split off again. At the Council of Florence in 1439, a number of the groups within the Armenian Church abandoned the Monophysite doctrine and joined the Roman Catholic Church: these groups now constitute the members of the Armenian Rite of the Roman Catholic Church.

Like most of the other Eastern Churches, the continuation of the Armenian Orthodox Church has been based largely on national and racial factors. It has suffered throughout the years owing to the fact that Armenia has been a battleground for centuries between the Turks, Persians and Russians.

At present, this Church is also rent by political differences occasioned by the fact that its leading prelate, who is known as the Supreme Catholicos, resides at Etchmiadzin, close to Mt. Ararat, in the Armenian Republic of the USSR. The Armenian Orthodox Church also has two patriarchates, one located in Constantinople and the other in Jerusalem; and it has a Catholicate (of Sis) located in Lebanon. In theory, a patriarch or catholicos who has been elected to office by his brotherhood should be consecrated by the Supreme Catholicos at Etchmiadzin. However, in recent years the political opposition of some Armenians residing in the Middle East to any ecclesiastical link with Etchmiadzin has caused difficulties in this practice.

Among the patriarchates of the Armenian Orthodox Church, the one at Constantinople was the most severely hurt by the massacres of scores of thousands of Armenians by the Turkish Government before, during and after World War I. Today this Patriarch has under his jurisdiction a comparatively small number of Armenians residing in the Turkish Republic and in the Balkans.

In the years prior to the Armenian massacres, this Patriarch maintained a flourishing seminary at the Armash Monastery. It was founded in 1889 and the first class was graduated in 1895. A celebrated scholar, Bishop Elisha Tourian, served as Principal. However, with the outbreak of World War I in 1914, the institution was closed. Bishop Tourian subsequently served as the Armenian Patriarch of Constantinople and still later as Principal of the St. James Seminary in Jerusalem.

The present Seminary of this Patriarchate was established in 1953 by the Patriarch, Archbishop Karekin Chachadourian. It is located in Uskudar, directly across the Bosporus from Istanbul. The majority of its buildings are comparatively modern and include a library, refectory, dormitories and a fairly large auditorium for meetings and plays. About 80 students are trained at various levels of instruction, of whom it is estimated about one-fourth might be considered as students at a theological level. Four years of preparatory work are followed by three years of advanced studies. Candidates for both the celibate (monastic) and the married (parish) clergy are trained in this institution.

Syrian Orthodox Seminary, Mardin: The Syrian Orthodox Church is another of the churches which was severed from the other Christian churches after the Council of Chalcedon. Although it is sometimes classified as a Monophysite church, it does not adhere to *Eutychian* doctrine; and the theological controversy at the Council of Chalcedon did not affect the Syrian population as deeply as it did in the case of the Copts in Egypt. However, this Church was founded on the same basis, namely, a political opposition to Constantinople. The Emperor Justinian I came close to eliminating all of the Monophysite bishops in the Middle East, but his wife, the Empress Theodora, favored the "heresy." Accordingly she arranged for the secret consecration of Jacob Baradaeus as Bishop of Nisibis in the year 543 by the Monophysite Patriarch of Alexandria. During the next 35 years Baradaeus traveled throughout the Middle East organizing Monophysite communities. The Syrian Orthodox Church is sometimes called the Syrian "Jacobite" Church in recognition of the contributions which Baradaeus made to its development. It flourished for a considerable period of time, and at its height in the 13th century is said to have comprised 120 dioceses. This Church suffered greatly from the persecutions occasioned by the conquests of Tamerlane in the 14th century, which were followed by internal dissension and the conversion of many of its members to Islam.

At first, the Patriarch of the Syrian Orthodox Church resided at Antioch. Later his residence was transferred to Mesopotamia and then to Mardin, a city in the southeastern corner of Turkey, some 150 miles northwest of Mosul (Iraq). In 1875, and thereafter, the Angelican Church is reported to have sent a number of missions to assist the Syrian Orthodox Church in response to requests from its Patriarch who was concerned with the increasing number of Jesuit missions coming into the area under his jurisdiction. In the years following World War II his residence was in Syria, at Homs, a city 100 miles northeast of Beirut. At Homs the former Patriarch Ignatios Ephraem I Barsom (who died in 1957) maintained the Patriarchal Library of approximately 1,500 books and manuscripts written in the Arabic, Turkish, Armenian, Latin, French, English, Italian and Syriac languages. In 1959 it was decided to move the seat of the Patriarchate from Homs to Damascus.

In modern times the intellectual standards of the Syrian Orthodox clergy have been low owing to the lack of training facilities for them. In addition the poverty of the Church as a whole has required many of its parish priests to supplement their income through part-time work as farmers or in trade. The monks on the other hand devote all their time to church work and, unlike the parish priests, are subject to being transferred from one post to another whenever and as often as the Church officials decide.

The Syrian Orthodox Seminary outside of Mardin has the Arabic name of Deir-ez-Sa'faran. It is the oldest seminary of this Church, dating perhaps from the fourth or fifth century. However, it has not been continuously operated since that time. The school was reopened in 1896 as a result of the efforts of Archbishop Dionysios Behnam of Mosul, but had to be closed again in 1914 upon the outbreak of World War I. At present there are ten students enrolled in it, all of whom are boarders studying to be monks. The faculty consists of three persons, with Bishop Dolabani in charge. A five-year course of religious studies is offered. The languages of instruction are Turkish and Syriac. Academic requirements are low inasmuch as the handful of students are at the elementary and lower secondary level. At present there are only two classes proceeding through the five-year course. The library of this institution is said to possess a number of old books.

Armenian Theological Seminary, Antelias (Bikfaya): The members of the Armenian Orthodox Church in Syria and Lebanon are organized in the Catholicate of Sis (i.e., Cilicia, the ancient name of a district in Turkey).

The 1951 Bulletin of the Armenian Theological Seminary of the Catholicate of Cilicia contains an interesting summary of the origin and development of this institution, from which the following excerpts have been abstracted:

After World War I and during readjustments under refugee conditions of living, the Armenian Orthodox Church was unable to train an adequate number of leaders for its people. In the chaotic years of persecution from 1914 to 1922, clergymen, teachers, and other national leaders were executed. Schools, seminaries, and churches were abandoned by people fleeing in panic and despair. Famous religious centers of learning, the Academy of Etchmiadzin, the Seminary of Armash, the Clerical College of Sis, and other religious institutions were closed. . . .

The American Near East Relief, which later took the name of the Near East Foundation, was helping the Armenian refugees to settle in Syria and Lebanon. The Foundation had bought a property of 14,000 square meters in Antelias (a village about four miles from the city of Beirut . . . overlooking the Mediterranean Sea), where since 1922 it had been caring for numerous Armenian orphans. Catholicos Sahag II who had visited the orphanage on several occasions, thought that these buildings and grounds, which were no longer needed for an orphanage after 1928, would be a suitable place for the Holy See. With this purpose in mind, he petitioned the executive committee of the Near East Foundation in the United States asking them to put the Antelias Orphanage under his disposition, to be used as the seat of the catholicate, and thus to re-establish the See of Cilicia. A seminary was also needed to train priests and teachers to meet the religious and educational needs of the Armenians in Syria and Lebanon. . . .

Conferences with some notable Armenians in the United States were held by the representatives of the Near East Foundation concerning the Antelias project and every one favored the plan for a "religious training school." As the result the executive committee of the Near East Foundation decided to transfer the Antelias Orphanage to His Holiness for a period of five years to be used as a school for training priests and teachers. Upon this decision an Antelias Committee was formed to provide means for the maintenance of the proposed seminary. Dr. Robert E. Speer, who became chairman, was elected by the Committee on Cooperation in the Near East to represent that body. . . . The executive committee of the Near East Foundation agreed to contribute between $6,000 and $7,000 annually and the Armenian benefactors, $5,000.

The Antelias Committee elected the Very Reverend Shahe Vartabed Kasparian (later archbishop), the rector of the Armenian Holy Trinity Church in Boston, Massachusetts, dean of the seminary. As a graduate of Armash Seminary in Constantinople, and of the Episcopal Theological School, Cambridge, Massachusetts, he was well prepared for this office. . . .

Archbishop Papken Gulesserian (later Papken I, coadjutor catholicos of Cilicia), a graduate of Armash Seminary and a famous scholar who was teaching in the Armenian Seminary of St. James, Jerusalem, was appointed as locum tenens by Sahag II. . . . By September, 1930, the teachers were engaged; a service staff of eight was chosen and its duties assigned. . . . The Reverend Theodore A. Elmer, a graduate of Princeton University and Princeton Theological Seminary, was appointed by the Near East Foundation "as an assistant to Dean Kasparian in the educational work of the school."

The French High Commission (Lebanon was then under the French mandate) showed great interest in the seminary by granting a subvention of 10,000 francs a year, beginning with April 1931, and by assigning a teacher of French free of charge. . . .

On June 16, 1935, the first class completed the five-year course plan. Sixteen students were graduated, two of whom, Father Zarah Payaslian and Father Terenig Poladian (now bishops) were ordained to the sacred priesthood. The other fourteen began to teach in the Armenian community schools.

Upon the completion of the five-year course plan the seminary underwent basic changes. As a consequence of the liquidation of its mission in the Near East, the Near East Foundation discontinued its annual appropriation and the seminary was left dependent on the meager resources of the catholicate. Despite this, the property of the seminary remained at the disposition of the catholicate until 1937. A change was made in the curriculum; the course of study was extended to seven years. The first four years were assigned to secondary education, and the last three to theological studies. The number of students, previously 43 to 45, was restricted to 20 to 22. The budgets of the seminary and of the catholicate were combined for the sake of economy.

Unfortunately, in November, 1935, the Dean of the seminary, Archbishop Shahe Kasparian had died. . . . The eighty-eight-year-old catholicos Sahag II . . . appointed Archbishop Bedros Sarajian as his locum tenens. The latter opened a campaign to secure financial means for the purchase of the Antelias property and for the support of the seminary and the catholicate. Many Armenians responded to the call. Mr. & Mrs. Simon and Mathilde Kayekjian of Cairo, Egypt, made possible the purchase of the property from the

Near East Foundation by a generous donation of $19,000. From the contributions of the people, a sum of $30,000 was raised, with which a seminary building and a residence for the catholicos were erected. Some other buildings were also restored.

In 1939 His Holiness Sahag II died. He was succeeded by Archbishop Bedros Sarajian, who died shortly afterwards. On May 10, 1943, Archbishop Karekin Hovsepian, the primate of the Armenian Church in North America, a great and renowned scholar, was unanimously elected catholicos of the House of Cilicia. Before his coming to Antelias, which took about two years, his golden jubilee was celebrated in the United States and Egypt, and all the proceeds amounting to about $100,000 were allotted to the seminary. The number of the students and the members of the faculty were increased.

Terenig Vartabed Poladian, who was a student in New York, N. Y. . . . was appointed dean of the seminary in 1946. In the summer of 1948 the dean visited England and the United States where he found several benefactors for the seminary and raised a sum of $50,000 for its maintenance. The following year he went to Egypt and raised 8,000 Egyptian pounds for the same purpose. In 1950, the number of the students was raised to seventy-two.

Concerning the location of the Seminary, the Bulletin points out that it is situated within the premises of the headquarters of the Catholicate of Sis, next to the Cathedral of St. Gregory the Illuminator:

The cathedral was constructed during 1938–40 through the generous donation of an Armenian who kept his name secret even after the building was completed. The name of the "anonymous donor," Sarkis Kenadjian of Istanbul, was made public by his son only after his father's death. The cathedral . . . can accommodate approximately one thousand people. . . .

The seminary building was constructed in 1939. . . . It can accommodate thirty students. On the first floor is the assembly hall and two rooms where the students play indoor games. On the second floor are four classrooms and the dean's office. The dormitory is on the third floor.

The library was founded in 1931. . . . It contains approximately eight thousand bound volumes and three thousand pamphlets. Nearly twenty-five periodicals and thirty dailies are currently received. There is also a collection of manuscript material. Literary and philological reviews and periodicals in Armenian constitute an important collection of the library. . . . The volumes are shelved in wooden closets covered with glass. Steel stacks are needed to keep the books from insect damage and decay. The library is open daily except Sunday during the seminary year from 1 P.M. to 4 P.M. There is a great need for books in English, French, and Armenian on biblical, philosophical, theological, educational, historical, sociological, and psychological subjects, as well as for dictionaries and encyclopedias. There is no annual appropriation for the support of the library.

The printing press was established in 1932 by Catholicos Papken I for printing various religious, educational, philological, and literary publications. So far, more than twenty-five volumes have been printed by the press. HASK, "the official, religious, educational, literary, and philological monthly review" of the catholicate is regularly published here. The printing press also provides facilities for printing all the necessary books and pamphlets for the seminary.

The Bulletin then points out that the Seminary has three sections: a Primary School, the School of Theology, and a Special Class for Married Priests:

The Armenians have few secondary schools. In view of this situation, the seminary has a four-year Preparatory Institute for secondary education dealing mainly with languages, sciences, mathematics and history. . . . Local conditions and public opinion demand the teaching of four languages, Armenian, Arabic, French, and English. . . .

After graduating from the Preparatory Institute of the seminary, those students preparing for the priesthood or for teaching, continue their education in religious and philosophical studies, in the School of Theology which has a course of three years. . . .

The candidate, after graduating from the School of Theology and being ordained a celibate priest, must prepare a dissertation on a subject related to the field of his special interest. To this he shall devote at least the equivalent of one year of study, usually in seminars. . . . Those who volunteer for the celibacy are ordained to the sacred priesthood upon the completion of the seven-year program of the seminary. After their ordination they may continue for one or more years, working toward the degree of Bachelor of Sacred Theology.

On the other hand, those who prefer the married priesthood spend a few years in teaching after completing the seminary, and participate in the performance of church services. Within this period they marry, and after gaining some experience in teaching and community life, and becoming the father of one child, they are ordained to the priesthood. This is according to the canons of the Armenian Church. . . .

In October 1949, His Holiness, Catholicos Karekin Hovsepian, established a new class devoted solely to the preparation of married men who desire to become priests. So far twelve members have been accepted. The program of study of this special class is from two to three years depending upon the previous education and experience of each candidate. . . .

So far (i.e., up to 1951) the seminary has had eighty-seven graduates from the Preparatory Institute and the School of Theology. Of these, twenty-five have become clergymen, serving as prelates and rectors. . . . (Other) students . . . are now teaching in various Armenian institutions and schools, in Syria, Lebanon, Palestine, Cyprus, and Armenia. . . . The seminary sends each year one or two of its graduates to seminaries and universities in Lebanon, Europe, and the United States. . . . Graduates have received master's and doctor's degrees from Université Libre of Brussels, and the Université Catholique of Louvain in Belgium; from the General Theological Seminary, the Union Theological Seminary, Columbia University, and New York University in the United States.

One of the features of this Seminary, according to its Bulletin, is the financial support it has received from Armenians living in various parts of the world:

In 1944, when His Holiness, Karekin Hovsepian, the catholicos-elect of the House of Cilicia, was in the United States, he founded the Armenian Seminary Association, to render financial help to the seminary. In 1948, the dean, Bishop Terenig Poladian, reorganized the association. He founded more chapters in the United States and in Europe. At present the association has branches in Egypt, England, France, and the United States. The central committee of the United States is in New York City. . . . France has branches in Paris, Nice, and Marseilles. There are two English branches, in London and Manchester. Egypt has chapters in Cairo and Alexandria. Each chapter raises a sum annually for the maintenance of the seminary. Some chapters have adopted a student or two and pay their yearly expenses. . . .

. . . The Board of Trustees of the Gullabi Gulbenkian Foundation in New York, N.Y., U.S.A., donates $4,500 annually to the seminary (and it) donated $40,000 to construct another seminary building which will be completed during the summer of 1951.

The Bulletin also listed the major capital needs of the Seminary in 1951, among which were a new library building (cost: $25,000), a museum ($25,000), and "books and periodicals for the library, annually $600."

When the former Catholicos of Sis died in 1955, Bishop Zarah of Aleppo was elected as his successor. This election was recognized by the Syrian and Lebanese Governments despite the opposition of the Supreme Catholicos at Etchmiadzin. Bishop Zarah's consecration as Catholicos took place in September, 1956. The churches under his jurisdiction are sometimes referred to as the Independent Armenian Catholicate, with headquarters at Beirut, Lebanon. In the latter part of 1957 the Armenian National Apostolic Church of America transferred its allegiance from the Supreme Catholicos at Etchmiadzin to the Independent Armenian Catholicate at Beirut.

In the last few years the total enrollment at the Seminary of the Catholicate of Sis has reached approximately 75 students, and about eight full-time members have served on its faculty. Until recently this institution was considered to be the leading seminary supported by any of the Eastern Churches in Lebanon. However, the Seminary has steadily grown weaker during the past two years as a result of the external and internal problems of the Catholicate.

The external problem, according to some (but not all) sources, is that of keeping the Catholicate free of Communist infiltration. An internal problem was created during the summer of 1956 by the dissident activities of Bishop Khat (a former locum tenens of the Catholicate for a long period). He attempted to take over the direction of the Armenian Theological Seminary at Antelias and declined to be removed from its premises. The Catholicos appealed to the Lebanese Government for assistance, and at dawn on October 15, 1956, the Seminary was occupied by the police. Bishop Khat and his followers later moved to Beit Meri (see below).

Shortly thereafter the Armenian Theological Seminary was transferred by Bishop Zarah from Antelias to Bikfaya where its educational activities have been resumed. Bikfaya is located in the mountains approximately ten miles in the interior from

Antelias. Formerly the Armenian Theological Seminary operated nine months of each year at Antelias and two months in the summer at Bikfaya, with the students having a one-month vacation at the end of the academic year. While the accommodations at Bikfaya were not originally intended to serve as a year-round location for the Seminary, the institution is now using them for this purpose in order to remove its students from the atmosphere of dissension which has prevailed at Antelias. Approximately 45 seminarians are now enrolled at Bikfaya, of whom an estimated one-third, or 15, are engaged in theological studies.

(Independent Armenian) Seminary, Beit Meri: Following their ejection from the seminary campus at Antelias in October, 1956, Bishop Khat and about 20 seminarians are reported to have set up a small training institution at Beit Meri. It had a faculty of two or three persons. With the refusal of the Lebanese Government to recognize Bishop Khat's group as the "Independent Orthodox Armenians of Lebanon," the future of this institution is uncertain, and the number of its students is said to have dwindled to approximately a dozen. As of mid-1957, the Seminary was still in existence, though it was expected by some that it might be transferred to Syria where there is said to be a movement looking toward the creation of an Armenian Orthodox Church in Syria which would be independent of the Armenian Orthodox Church in Lebanon. Bishop Khat and his followers have been recognized by the Supreme Catholicos in Etchmiadzin, USSR, as a lawful group within this Church.

Holy Trinity Seminary, Tripoli: When the city of Antioch and the surrounding territory were ceded by the French authorities in Syria to the Republic of Turkey in 1939, the Greek Orthodox Patriarch of Antioch transferred his residence from Antioch to Damascus in Syria. Both Lebanon and Syria are within the jurisdiction of this Patriarchate, and the number of Greek Orthodox Christians in these two countries amounts to about 296,000 persons.

It is stated that the Greek Orthodox Patriarch of Antioch visited the USSR in 1945 to participate in the election of the Russian Orthodox Patriarch Alexis of Moscow. This same Patriarch (who was an Arab) also sent some delegates to a conference which was held in Moscow in 1948; and in 1951 he is stated to have made a second trip to the USSR. On the latter occasion, according to M. Gaston Zananiri, he issued a declaration, which was printed in the international press, containing the following statements: ". . . Recently the efforts in the camps of the forces hostile to peace have been redoubled in order to weaken the Patriarchate of Antioch. After their voyage to Rome in 1950 for the celebration of the so-called Holy Year, the Catholics of Syria and Lebanon returned bringing considerable sums of money from the Vatican in order to carry on the struggle against Orthodoxy. . . . It is regrettable that the union of all the Orthodox Churches in the struggle for peace is impeded by influences which are hostile to the establishment of peace in the entire world. . . .

On my recent trip in Greece I became convinced that in this country, which annually receives subsidies from America, the Orthodox Church does not intervene in the cause for peace. . . ."

The one seminary maintained by the Greek Orthodox Patriarchate of Antioch is located at Belmonte (Balamant), near Tripoli, Lebanon, approximately two hours' traveling time north of Beirut. It is maintained in an old monastery building where instruction for ordinands was commenced in 1904. The Seminary was closed in 1912 and not reopened until 1929. Subsequently it was closed again and reopened after World War II.

Approximately 40 students are enrolled, of whom perhaps one-half might be considered to be students studying at a theological level. The course of study is taught by a deacon and four assistants. It comprises a four-year course which is generally below the level of instruction at Halki. About 8–12 men are graduated each year, most of whom subsequently serve as parish priests. The students lead a rather relaxed, monastic type of life, and many facilities and equipment are said to be lacking. The languages of instruction are Arabic and liturgical Greek.

The Greek Orthodox Patriarchate of Antioch also maintains the Seminary of St. Elias Bettina and the College of Annunciation in Beirut. However, it does not appear that either of these are theological schools providing a full training course for ordinands. In addition there are said to have been proposals occasionally made to establish a regular seminary of this Patriarchate in Beirut, but these plans are still believed to be in only the discussion stage.

St. Demetrius Seminary, Jerusalem: It is estimated that there are only about 30,000 members of the Greek Orthodox Patriarchate of Jerusalem, whose jurisdiction comprises Israel, Jordan and Saudi Arabia. There has long been tension between the Arabic-speaking members of this Patriarchate and its Greek hierarchy, particularly since few, if any, Arabic-speaking bishops have been consecrated by the latter in recent years.

The history of the Theological College in the Convent of the Cross (which was the predecessor of the present St. Demetrius Seminary) was summarized shortly before World War I by Archdeacon Dowling as follows:

The education of the Clergy is supplied mainly by the Theological College in the Convent (note: monastery) of the Cross (Deir el-Musallebeh) (according to the Greeks, the traditional site of the tree of which our Lord's Cross was formed). It is situated in a shallow stone wady, about 1½ miles west of the city walls. During the period of the Crusading Kingdom of Jerusalem, this ancient pile of buildings was one of eleven religious houses, once the property of the Georgians. It is said to have been founded in the fifth century. . . .

The Patriarch Kyrillus II opened the College in 1855, and after being three times closed, it was re-opened by the Patriarch Gerasimus in September, 1893. (There were in

1898 60 students). The Course of Instruction has, up to this date, extended over seven years. . . . The eight Professors are preferably, but not necessarily, Ecclesiastics. . . . The Students are frequently nephews, or near relatives, of Greek monks in the Convent of St. Constantine. They are admitted between the ages of 15 and 22 years. After admission the Course of Education is absolutely free. . . .

The well-catalogued Library contains several English Theological and other works. . . . Anglican theology is better represented in this College than in that of the more celebrated Orthodox Greek College at Halki. . . .

In the year preceding World War I the Greek Orthodox Patriarchate of Jerusalem was dependent for as much as 64% of its annual income from Russian sources. This took two forms: first the offerings of Russian pilgrims visiting Jerusalem; and second, the income received by the Patriarchate from large estates it owned in Bessarabia. The Russian Orthodox Church utilized its influence in the Patriarchate to support the Arabic-speaking clergy who were opposed to the Greek members of its hierarchy. However, with the cessation of these pilgrimages in 1914 and the awarding of Bessarabia to Roumania in 1918, the Patriarchate was entirely cut off from these sources of income. Consequently it was threatened with bankruptcy, inasmuch as it had also contracted debts totalling £500,000 which it could not repay. One result was that the Theological College in the Convent of the Cross was closed in 1920.

The new British Government in Palestine appointed a Commission under the direction of Sir Anton Bertram (who was then Chief Justice of Ceylon) to manage the fiscal affairs of the Patriarchate. The Commission surveyed the entire operation of the Patriarchate, and in its report published in 1921, the following recommendation was expressed: "In conclusion, we may be permitted to express the hope . . . in particular that means will be found to reopen the theological school of the Monastery of the Holy Cross, which in recent years was one of the most valuable institutions of the Patriarchate of Jerusalem."

The Bertram Commission (with some changes in its personnel) issued a second report in 1926 concerning the Patriarchate's finances. Again, the conclusions expressed in the report stressed the importance of reopening the Holy Cross seminary:

Every one is anxious that this school should be reopened. The reason why it remains closed is simply lack of funds. As we have said, it was once the pride of the Patriarchate. . . . The generation now growing up to succeed its pupils must be greatly handicapped by the absence of such a training, and it is difficult to see how the Brotherhood (of the Holy Cross) will ever recover a proper standard of culture and theology until this school is reopened. Nothing would do more to restore harmony and satisfaction in the Church than the provision of the necessary funds for the reopening of this Theological School, including a department for the training of the local clergy. Such a school is urgently needed on all grounds. The Theological School of the Ecumenical Patriarchate at Halki is now closed, and in recent years the centres at which it was possible to obtain a sound theological training among the Orthodox Countries in the Near East have been largely reduced. . . . Unfortunately it seems impossible to hope that in the present circumstances of the Church it could be re-established from local resources. If other sections of Christendom were moved to do something to assist the ancient Patriarchate of Jerusalem in its present distress, that assistance could take no more practical shape than the re-establishment of this institution.

There were no training facilities available in Jerusalem for the clergy of the Greek Orthodox Patriarchate for 32 years (1920–52). The advent of World War II delayed the re-establishment of a seminary, as did the Arab-Israel War of 1948 and the necessity for this Patriarchate to care for many Arab-speaking refugees of the Greek Orthodox faith. By the early 1950s the number of Greek Orthodox priests who had been educated at the former Theological College in the Monastery of the Cross was reduced to a very small proportion of the total of its clergy. After World War II the Russian Orthodox Patriarch of Moscow was reported to have been interested in the affairs of this Patriarchate but is said to have made little progress in the face of the opposition of the Brotherhood of the Holy Sepulcher.

The present St. Demetrius Seminary was opened in 1952. The partition of the City of Jerusalem following the Arab-Israel War resulted in the Monastery of the Holy Cross being situated in Israel. Since most of the seminary students are Arabs, St. Demetrius was opened in the Monastery of St. Constantine and St. Helena which is located in the Orthodox quarter of the Old City, in the Jordanian sector of Jerusalem. An old stone, two-story building serves as the principal structure of the institution. The neighborhood is fairly crowded, and the seminary lacks sufficient out-of-doors space in which its students may exercise.

In the academic year 1957–58 a total of 68 students were enrolled, of whom 58 were boarders and ten were day pupils. Of the student body an estimated 25 are studying at a theological level. During the period 1952–57 a total of 42 students were graduated, or an average of eight per year. As students progress from the lower to the upper classes, the number enrolled in the individual classes decreases.

The primary purpose of St. Demetrius is to provide an educated Arab-speaking clergy for rural Greek Orthodox parishes. The course lasts five years, following which those who wish to become ministers may be ordained immediately after graduation. Often, however, two or three years' practical work, as teachers and otherwise, is required of students before the final decision is made concerning their ordination. When a student signifies his intention to become a priest, he thereafter wears a cassock and allows his hair and beard to grow.

The director of the Seminary, Professor Nicholas George Pizanias, is directly responsible to the Patriarch Benedictos and to the Holy Synod of the Jerusalem Patriarchate. A total of ten professors and teachers, principally Greek, serve on the faculty. The full-time professors are paid salaries amounting to approximately $20 a month. The Seminary follows the educational program of colleges (secondary schools) in Greece. Its graduates are qualified for university entrance, and some of them pursue further theological studies at Halki or in Athens. In addition to the Greek language, Arabic and English are taught.

According to the Patriarch Benedictos, the library of this Seminary consists of 134 books, of which 100 are for the use of the students. Copies of the lectures and texts used in the courses at St. Demetrius have been mimeographed and distributed whenever this was considered essential. One of the greatest needs of its library is said to be for several hundred carefully selected modern books in the Greek, Arabic and English languages.

Students at this Seminary are not required to pay any tuition, board or lodging fees. The operating costs of the institution are provided by the Patriarchate. A small number of donations are received from friends in Greece and elsewhere, and also from the World Council of Churches. The American Friends of the Orthodox Patriarchate of Jerusalem, Inc. (see below) contributed about $2,000 to help open St. Demetrius in 1952. The parishes within this Patriarchate are so poor that many of them are supported from the central treasury of the Patriarchate and consequently have no funds to donate to the maintenance of the Seminary.

St. James Seminary, Jerusalem: The history of the Jerusalem Patriarchate of the Armenian Orthodox Church goes back to the 4th century when some Armenian soldiers in the Roman legions stationed in Jerusalem established a small monastery there. In the 10th century it was made a part of the present Monastery of St. James which is located on Mt. Zion. This Monastery sheltered many crusaders from Western Europe who found themselves unable to return home. Following the crusades, when the Muslim Arabs returned to power in the Holy Land, the Armenian bishopric in Jerusalem was elevated to a patriarchate and the Monastery of St. James served as a hostel for many pilgrims during the ensuing centuries. Then, after World War I, when tens of thousands of Armenian refugees who had survived the massacres in Turkey were seeking new homes, several thousand of them went to Jerusalem where they were quartered temporarily in the large buildings of Saint James. These persons gradually established themselves in their own businesses and homes, so that in 1947 there were about 5,000 Armenians in Palestine and a few others in what was then Transjordan. Most of the Armenians now residing in Jerusalem live in a large compound in the southwestern section of the City within the old walls. In the monastery compound itself are the Church of Saint James and the Seminary of the same name.

The saintly and scholarly Patriarch of Jerusalem in the post-World War I era, Yeghishe (Elisha) Tourian, who had previously been Patriarch of Constantinople, did much to raise the prestige of the Patriarchate. He revived the Armenian press in the Monastery, and also reopened the theological school, receiving aid for these purposes from wealthy Armenians in America. Patriarch Tourian sought to revive at Jerusalem the work of the former Armenian seminary at Armash in Turkey. Rt. Rev. Papken Gulessarian, formerly Bishop of Ancora, was brought over from America to be the head of the St. James Seminary. Stress was laid on providing the students with a working knowledge of both English and French in order to give them access to modern theological literature. An American priest of the Protestant Episcopal Church, Rev. Charles T. Bridgeman, was added to the staff to help with English studies, and English clergy have since continued to assist in the same way.

The Jerusalem Patriarchate became the outstanding Armenian cultural center in the free world, and its publications were sent to parishes of this Church in various countries. In the same period the Seminary enjoyed a period of considerable prosperity. However, the Arab-Israel War of 1948 weakened the Patriarchate considerably, as much of its income came from land located in that part of the modern suburbs of Jerusalem which was occupied by the Israelis. At the same time the Monastery of St. James was once again obliged to take in large numbers of refugees. The Patriarchate is said to be recovering from this setback but still is encountering fiscal difficulties.

The jurisdiction of the Armenian Patriarchate of Jerusalem covers Israel and the Hashemite Kingdom of Jordan. Patriarch Yeghishe Tourian, who died in 1932, was followed by Mesrob Nishanian until 1944, and by Guregh Israelian until 1949. The present Patriarch-elect is Archbishop Tiran Nersoyan whose confirmation by the King of Jordan has been held up because of objections raised by the former locum tenens, Archbishop Yeghishe Derderian. The Patriarch-elect was trained in the Jerusalem Seminary and at the College of the Resurrection, Mirfield, England. After being a Bishop in Paris he was subsequently the Bishop of the major part of the Armenian Church in the United States, during which time he became an American citizen.

The St. James Seminary has two buildings, one consisting of classrooms and a study hall, and the other containing the deanery, refectory, a dormitory for the pretheological students, and individual rooms for deacons. The building used for the theological classes is somewhat antiquated inasmuch as it was originally intended to serve as a hostel for pilgrims, and it was also damaged in the Arab-Israel war.

Approximately 26 students were enrolled in the Seminary in the academic year 1957–58. Of this number, 18 young men were studying at the pretheological level and 8 students comprised the theological training class. These totals are somewhat lower than the enrollments of previous years. Of the 84 students who entered in the period 1951–56, about half subsequently adopted secular careers. The students come from various countries in the Middle East. Men are trained to serve both as married, secular clergymen doing parish work, and as celibate monks residing in the monasteries of the Patriarchate. The prelates and bishops are selected from the celibate priests or monks. A majority of the members of the present hierarchy in the various patriarchates and dioceses of the Armenian Orthodox Church are graduates of this institution since it was revived in 1923.

The curriculum covers a nine-year period. Boys enter at the age of 14 and spend the first five years taking courses at the pretheological level. Later those who intend to become celibate priests take their vows, join the Brotherhood and are ordained deacons. The men who intend to enter the married priesthood, a decision they must make before being ordained deacons, either take up work as teachers until married, or go to the Seminary at Antelias (Bikfaya) which makes provision for the training of married men.

The final four years at St. James are spent in theological studies at a postsecondary level. The languages of instruction are Armenian and Arabic, but the men are also equipped to use books in English and French, and normally acquire some proficiency in Greek.

The faculty of this Seminary consists of approximately seven full-time men, plus four part-time teachers, and includes bishops, monks and laymen. The Dean, Very Rev. Father Torkom Manougian, is directly responsible to the Patriarch.

One of the important features of the St. James Seminary is the fact that it has access to the Gulbenkian Library donated by the late Armenian oil magnate, Calouste S. Gulbenkian. The handsome library building was dedicated in 1932 and it contains about 50,000 volumes written in the Armenian, French, German, Greek and Latin languages. It is said to be the best library in the Kingdom of Jordan. Nevertheless, during the past 25 years much of its foreign material has become out of date. There are also some 4,000 manuscripts of considerable value in the library, including priceless illuminated medieval manuscripts.

Connected with the library is a modern printing plant in which many religious and liturgical books in the Armenian language are produced. The official monthly magazine of the Patriarchate is entitled *Zion,* and in the past it has taken a liberal line, pointing the way toward reforms within this Church.

The St. James Seminary is financed with income obtained from the remaining property owned by the Monastery of St. James and also through donations made to it by Armenians throughout the world. Its most important capital need is said to be a new and adequate building. Under more stable conditions it might be expected that this institution would be able to recover the high status it formerly enjoyed.

Seminary of Mar Ephraem, Mosul, Iraq: The Syrian Orthodox Seminary of Mar Ephraem was founded by Patriarch Ephraem I in Zahleh, Lebanon, in 1938. It was transferred to Mosul in 1945 because the Syrian Orthodox Church is stronger in Iraq than it is in Lebanon. Today this is the leading seminary of this Church, with one-half of its expenses being defrayed by the Diocese of Mosul and the remaining one-half by the other Syrian Orthodox dioceses. At present there are about 30 students enrolled in it, all boarders taking a seven-year course (after elementary school) leading to a diploma. Studies are pursued throughout the 12 months of the year, and lodging and tuition are provided free of cost to the students. The Director of the Seminary is Archbishop Grigorios who is assisted by two monks and two deacons. The courses are conducted in Arabic, Syriac and English. The library of this institution is said to be good and contains a number of valuable parchments, documents in Aramaic, etc. The graduates of the Seminary become parish priests, monks and teachers in church schools, most of whom serve in Iraq.

Assyrian Seminary, Kirkuk: After the outbreak of World War II, the present Patriarch of the Church of the East (Assyrian), Mar Shimun XXIII, came from Iraq to the United States in 1940. He subsequently resided in Chicago and at Turlock, California, where the Mar Addai Cathedral Church of the East is located. It is estimated that perhaps 22,000 members of this Church reside in Iraq, 10,000 in the Khabour area of northeastern Syria, and a few thousand each in Iran, Egypt and the United States.

This Church has had no seminary in the Middle East in recent times, with the result that its clergy are stated to be often quite illiterate and are not expected to be able to do much more than to celebrate the liturgy. The parish priests usually are married, and the office often descends from father to son. The office of Patriarch is transmitted from uncle to nephew, thus making it as nearly hereditary as possible under the rule whereby this position must be filled by a celibate.

At the end of 1957 there were plans to establish a seminary of the Assyrian Church at Kirkuk in Iraq. A number of students plan to enroll in the seminary, when and if it opens. It is reported that two or three boys were assembled, but that instruction had not as yet begun. According to Metropolitan Yosip of Iraq, it was contemplated that a small building might be used for the seminary with "nothing to speak of in the way of a library."

D. SOUTHERN ASIA

The seminaries of the Eastern Churches which are located in Southern Asia are listed in Table 176.

The two seminaries of the Syrian Orthodox Church of Malabar are both small and have reflected the hostility which once existed between the Catholicate and Patriarchate branches of this Church. Prior to 1653, when a number of the so-called "St. Thomas Christians" in southern India revolted against the attempts of the Portuguese Roman Catholic Archbishop of Goa to dominate their hierarchy, there had been no hierarchical connection between these Indian Christians and the Syrian Orthodox patriarch of Antioch. However, after that event, the Malabar Christians who refused to join the Roman Catholic Church appealed to the Syrian patriarch for support. In response he sent a Syrian Orthodox bishop who was followed during the next century by other prelates coming from Antioch. Their policy was to strengthen the links between the Syrian Orthodox Church in India with the Syrian Patriarchate at Antioch. As nationalist tendencies in India increased, this policy ultimately led to a clash in the Church which came to a head in 1909–12.

TABLE 176.   SEMINARIES OF THE EASTERN CHURCHES IN SOUTHERN ASIA (1957)

Name	Location	Approx. Number of		Supporting Church
		Faculty	Theol. Students	
India				
Orthodox Theological Seminary	Kottayam	5	20[a]	Syrian Orthodox Church of Malabar
Patriarchate Seminary	Omalloor	2	8[a]	Syrian Orthodox Church of Malabar
Theological Seminary[b]	Trichur	Proposed[b]		Church of Trichur (Mellusian)
Total: 2 (in operation)		7	28	

NOTES: [a] Plus other students at lower level of training.
[b] See text.

In 1955 a Belgian Jesuit specialist on religious affairs in India, Father E. R. Hambye, S. J., wrote an interesting account of the strife within the Syrian Orthodox Church of Malabar since 1912, as follows:

. . . . One section secured from a forcibly deposed patriarch, Mar Abdelmassih II, the recognition of the head of the Malabar Jacobites, as a catholicos, as a sort of quasi-patriarch of their own. . . . The other section did not want such a large measure of independance and remained faithful to the direct jurisdiction of the patriarch. Hence the existence of two opposite parties . . . the first being called the catholicos' party, the other the patriarch's.

Some indication of the comparative size of the two groups in 1957 is shown in the following estimates:

Branch	Members	Bishops	Priests	Seminarians	Churches, Chapels
Catholicate	450,000	10	215	60	380
Patriarchate	350,000	6	180	45	325

Father Hambye continues:

The catholicos, Mar Basilios III (since 1929), resides at Kottayam. . . . The Jacobites, who remained faithful to the patriarch of Antioch, depend at present on an Indian metropolitan, but there has also been a delegate of the patriarch since 1908. . . . He lives in India since 1927, and he resides at Omalloor. . . . The patriarch's followers are particularly strong in Northern Travancore and in the former State of Cochin. The catholicos' people thickly populate Central and Southern Travancore.

Thanks to their early progress in education, the Jacobites still count among the most active communities of the land. . . . The elite of the Jacobite laity is by far better educated and more influential than its clergy. This unfortunate situation, leading doubtless to a danger of dechristianization, is mainly due to the decadence into which the training institutions for the clerics have fallen. This decadence is also the outcome of the discord between the two parties. Many seminaries have been obliged to close down, others do not keep a decent level of clerical education. Thus the average priest is poorly trained and knows little, if anything, about a solid theology, even the objective history of his community, his liturgy, his pastoral duties. No wonder that for the past twenty years there has been a marked deterioration in the internal life of the Church. . . .

Fortunately the litigation between the Catholicate and Patriarchate branches of the Jacobite Church was terminated by the Indian Supreme Court which, on September 12, 1958, handed down a unanimous decision in favor of the Catholicate; and this decision subsequently led to the uniting of these two branches in December 1958 into one church known as the Syrian Orthodox Church of Malabar.

Early in the 1800s, i.e., about a century before the split occurred between the Catholicate and Patriarchate branches, the Church Missionary Society (Anglican) commenced providing support to the Syrian Orthodox Church in India. Some of this assistance took the form of furnishing educational opportunities for Jacobite students at Protestant institutions in India. After several decades a small group in the Syrian Orthodox Church transferred their allegiance to the Angelican Church. A larger group, which came to be known as the Mar Thoma Syrian Church of Malabar, split off from the Syrian Orthodox Church between 1850 and 1880. The members of the Mar Thoma Church adopted a theology which falls between the Protestant and the Syrian Orthodox position in such matters. The Mar Thomites also revised their liturgy somewhat but retained the type of vestments traditionally used by the priests of the Syrian Orthodox Church of Malabar. The center of the Mar Thoma Church is in Kottayam in Travancore-Cochin (Kerala) where the Catholicos of the Syrian Orthodox Church of Malabar also resides. The Mar Thoma seminary is located less than one mile away from the Catholicate Seminary in Kottayam, but there is little or no contact between them. The Mar Thoma seminary is affiliated with the Serampore Senate (and so listed in this Survey), whereas the Catholicate Seminary is not. The Syrian Orthodox tend to regard the Mar Thomites as being closer to a Protestant-type church than an Eastern Church. Metropolitan Juhanon of the Mar Thoma Church is one of the six presidents of the World Council of Churches (which has had a number of presidents coming from Eastern Churches).

Orthodox Theological Seminary, Kottayam: This Seminary maintained by the Catholicos of the Syrian Orthodox Church of Malabar was founded in Kottayam in

1813. By 1816 its building was half finished, and 25 students had been enrolled. During its first few decades the Seminary received support from the Church Missionary Society (Angelican) until such assistance was terminated in about 1850. It continued to train students thereafter, although during occasional periods its doors were closed. In 1942 the Seminary was reopened with a first class of six students. During the academic year 1956–57 there were 35 students enrolled, of whom an estimated 20 might be considered as students being trained at a theological level. There were five full-time faculty members, two of whom had studied outside of India.

According to Father Korah Philipos, who served on the faculty of this Seminary in the period 1942–56, its entire curriculum was recently revised and modernized. Most of the instruction is carried on in English, with the balance in Malayalam and classical Syriac, the liturgical language of this Church. The course lasts four years, at the end of which a graduating student receives a diploma. No degrees are offered inasmuch as this institution is not affiliated with either the Serampore Senate or a university. However, in 1956, one or two of its students took the B.D. examination offered by the Serampore Senate.

The library contains about 5,000 volumes. Very few books are said to have been purchased for it since World War II. Nor does it subscribe to any magazines.

Patriarchate Seminary, Omalloor: The Seminary maintained by the Patriarchate branch of the Syrian Orthodox Church of Malabar was founded in 1934 at St. Ignatius' Monastery at Omalloor, near Pathanamthitta, in Travancore. About 14 students are enrolled, of whom an estimated eight might be considered as students at a theological level. However, it is said not to have a regular curriculum, and the faculty consists of one or two resident priests. Students attend for one, two or three years, and the teaching stresses Syriac, the liturgy of the Church, *exegesis* and dogma.

Theological Seminary, Trichur: The Church of Trichur, or Mellusian Church, is a small off-shoot of the Nestorian Church. Trichur is located in Travancore-Cochin in the Malabar coastal area about 80 miles north of Kottayam. The Church of Trichur was without a head from 1874 to 1908 when the Nestorian (Assyrian) Catholicos is stated to have sent them a bishop who commenced a protestantizing policy which was resisted by some of the members of this Church. There are believed to be only about 10,000 Mellusians at the present time, most of whom live in the northern part of Kerala (Travancore-Cochin). They are a comparatively wealthy group who are active in trade but are gradually being absorbed by the surrounding population.

In 1956 the Mellusians constructed a fairly large building, and there were plans to establish a seminary there. It is not known at the present writing whether this intention was carried out.

E. OVER-ALL ASPECTS

In 1923 a book entitled *The Uniate Eastern Churches* was written by Adrian Fortescue, formerly Professor of Ecclesiastical History at St. Edmund's College in Ware, England. In it, Professor Fortescue, a Roman Catholic expert on the Eastern Churches, reached an adverse and perhaps unduly harsh verdict concerning the "schismatical" clergy of the Eastern Churches as follows:

> The lack of education among the schismatical Eastern clergy is the invariable reproach of Western travellers. . . . Today no one would cite a Jacobite parish-priest, a Coptic monk, as a shining example of learning, or as the exponent of a high moral ideal; though he is often sincerely pious. . . . There are no theological works produced by modern schismatical Copts or Jacobites; generally their clergy can hardly read, and do not understand their own liturgical language. Nor is much in this way produced by the Armenians or the Orthodox. What they do produce is generally a rather naive reproduction of western ideas at second hand.
>
> . . . . There is no question that the Uniate Clergy (Roman Catholic) have had an immeasurably better education than the others. In this matter they have every advantage from their union with the more highly developed West. . . . Most of them know at least some Latin, many can talk quite good French. This opens to them vast fields of knowledge, closed to the schismatics who know nothing but Arabic. . . .
>
> The schismatic (Eastern clergy) generally has had no education, and has learned no theology at all. As a simple test of this, ask (Roman Catholic) priests in the Levant about the great questions which lie beneath their differences, about Nestorianism, Monophysism, the idea of the Church and the Papacy. You will not find one Uniate who is not able to give you a general, fairly accurate, if perhaps rather old fashioned statement on these points, and a defense of what he believes. You will find few schismatics who know anything about them at all, who even know what these questions mean.

While the educational status of the clergy of the Eastern Churches in the post-World War I period may have been as Professor Fortescue describes it, nevertheless it would appear that in the subsequent 40 years the situation has improved considerably. In support of this one can point to the comparatively high standards maintained by the Greek Orthodox Seminary at Halki, to the renaissance in recent years in the training of Coptic priests in Egypt, and to the development of the theological school, Holy Trinity College, in Addis Ababa. Furthermore, the two Protestant seminaries at Beirut and Cairo are among the weakest of all the Protestant theological schools in Africa, Asia and Latin America, due, in part at least, to the difficulties encountered by all Christian churches in Islamic countries. On the other hand it also seems clear that the seminaries of the Eastern Churches as a whole are qualitatively inferior to the Roman Catholic and Protestant seminaries as a whole in Africa, Asia and Latin America.

The growth of the Protestant and Roman Catholic seminaries in Africa and Asia has taken place almost entirely within the past 100 years. The various Eastern

Churches in northeastern Africa and the Middle East have suffered from the turmoil which has beset this area throughout most of this period. Accordingly in the
20th century they have not experienced increases in their income comparable to
that which the churches in the other two major branches of Christianity have enjoyed. A large proportion of the free funds of the Eastern Churches have had to be
devoted for relief rather than educational purposes. Consequently the task of
strengthening their seminaries has been relatively more difficult for them to undertake.

On the other hand, not all such measures require the expenditures of large
sums of money. A recent editorial in the *Greek Orthodox Theological Review* by Rt.
Rev. Athenagoras, Dean of the Holy Cross Orthodox Theological School in Brookline, Massachusetts, points to some steps which might be taken by Orthodox
Churches throughout the world:

Among the many needs and challenges that face Christian Orthodoxy there is one that
deserves serious and even vigorous attention and consideration. This is the somewhat
belated necessity of organizing from among the Orthodox Churches an international educational organization for the purpose of guiding the accreditational and academic status
of Orthodox Theological Schools throughout the world. . . . It is rather unfortunate that
through the years the Eastern Orthodox Theological Schools—Holy Cross in Brookline,
Massachusetts, St. Vladimir's in New York City, St. Sergius in Paris, the Theological
School of Halki, Constantinople, to mention only several—have been pursuing their
particular ways without any real understanding of, if not concern for, the existence and
program of the others. The result has been a kind of *decentralized ignorance* (note: Bishop
Athenagoras' italics) on the part of each. . . . That an accrediting agency comprising the
representatives of all Orthodox Theological Schools is needed is a mere understatement.
With the growth of Orthodoxy and with the consequent increased demand for Orthodox
clergymen and lay workers, the Orthodox Theological Schools begin to assume an ever increasing role of importance in education. . . . We do not propose . . . to create an agency
for the purpose of either the standardization or regimentation of the different phases of
Orthodox Theological preparation pursued in the different schools. . . . What we do
propose at this time is the calling of a conference for the purpose of considering the creation of the "International Association of Orthodox Theological Schools."

The Bishop points out: "Such common Eastern Orthodox problems and policies,
for example, as academic degrees and honors, transfer credit of students changing
from one Orthodox Theological School to another, exchange students and lecturers, scholarship programs, and even the inauguration of specific degrees in Orthodox Theology, would perhaps be discussed during such a conference."

In 1950 the American Friends of the Greek Orthodox Patriarchate of Jerusalem,
Inc. was formed in Cambridge, Massachusetts, in order to raise funds in the United
States for the financial needs of this Patriarchate. In the ensuing seven years a total

of approximately $17,000 was obtained, which was used principally to support the system of elementary schools operated by the Patriarchate. In this connection an Episcopalian, Rev. Charles T. Bridgeman, wrote a paper summarizing his views relating to the ways and means by which he felt American Protestants might properly assist in the strengthening of the clergy of the Eastern Churches:

There are outstanding leaders in the Eastern Churches who are aware of the need for more effective spiritual leadership. They are hampered in their thinking both by a strong conservatism which pervades many of the clergy and by lack of funds. . . . At the present time, too many (Orthodox) theological students receive informal private training on the basis of little more than primary education. In their theological training, therefore, they do well if they acquire a fair knowledge of the vernacular and classical language of their people and liturgy, singing and music, rudimentary Biblical knowledge, the doctrine of the Christian Church as represented by their own denominational viewpoint, some knowledge of their own Church fathers, the canon law of their Church in its simpler aspects, and Church history as seen from their viewpoint. A certain number of the candidates may have a little knowledge of French or English but hardly enough to read these languages readily. Many parish priests do not even have as much training as indicated above, being merely loyal sons of the Church who, after having been choir singers or primary school teachers, have been ordained to the priesthood to supply vacant parishes. . . . The training (elsewhere), such as it is, is given privately by some older priest, whose own scholarship may be very meagre.

Obviously, the *first step* towards a *high level* of education must begin by making sure that candidates have a sound basic training. . . .

Very few young men directly influenced by (Protestant) missionary schools have ever found their way into the priesthood of the ancient Churches. This is partly because, though many have remained technically members of their ancestral Churches, they have been educated outside its orbit and have little knowledge of or sympathy with the old ways. And it is partly because the families which have sent young men to secure a good modern education have thought it a waste of good money and of time spent on education to allow their educated sons to give themselves to so "unrewarding" a vocation as that of a priest.

The majority of the theological students, and all those aspiring to be more than simple parish married priests, are destined to become monks and find their life in monastic communities. Eastern monasticism in each religious community has its own special spiritual ideals and discipline which a theological student must share in and learn to appreciate from the very beginning of his training.

It would be naïve to assume that it would be enough to create a Western-type "union" theological school and invite the various Eastern Churches to send their young men for training. And to suggest a school run on traditional Protestant lines would court immediate rejection by the ecclesiastical authorities. . . . A sound system of theological education for the ancient Churches cannot rely on Western teachers or people trained only in Western ideas. . . . Western teachers sent out to assist in Eastern theological education, though they may be very competent in their own sphere, must learn to approach the theological world of the East with respect and deference. . . . Teachers of Holy Scripture trained in the West assume without question the validity of Higher Criticism. The East knows little of this approach. For a foreign teacher to jump without due preparation into the problems of modern scholarship would lead to misunderstanding and rejection.

All too frequently the students (who) are educated (overseas) away from their people . . . either give up their vocation or have a strong compulsion to remain abroad serving their people resident in America, England or France. In either case, they are of no use in the upbuilding of their people in the Middle East. Foreign studies, if envisaged at all, should be for the most promising youths and then only after they have finished their normal theological course, been ordained and agree to return to serve their people back home.

Eastern leaders drafted into cooperation with Western teachers will not wish to abate one jot or one tittle of their traditional worship and doctrine. Nor should they be asked to do so. . . . It must be remembered that for generations the Eastern Churches have been trying to defend themselves from two alien mentalities: that fostered by the Roman Catholics and that fostered by the Protestant missions. Both these foreign missionary endeavours have been at work in the East, and despite good intentions and sincere conviction, they have tended to foster foreign ideals and neglect the Eastern Christian tradition with its organized Church life and distinctive spiritual emphasis.

Any attempt to help the Eastern Churches secure a better educated priesthood must be strictly guided by *the ideal of keeping alive the ancient faith, worship and customs* of the various Eastern bodies. It must also be done in closest cooperation with the existing authorities on the Eastern Churches, *and under their guidance.* . . .

There are two possible approaches—to assist each ancient Church to conduct its own school in its own way, or to plan a kind of "Theological university" with common lectures in subjects capable of being treated that way, and separate residence "colleges" where each Church could house its own students, provide them with their proper religious services and superintend their special theological studies.

This latter suggestion might for example be worked out in a place like Jerusalem, where all the major communities have strong convents. If this type of schedule could not be arranged, then it would seem best to concentrate on giving support to small denominational schools in each religious community and leave to the future the provision of advanced education in a common school. *But, too much stress cannot be laid on the fact that a simple "union" school devoted to the subjects of common interest would be quite inadequate and inacceptable.*

The Eastern Churches need new leaders. *It is worth more to provide the Churches with one trained priest than to give it twenty trained laymen*—for the priests are natural leaders of the people.* . . .

Many times in the last quarter of a century Westerners have broached to the East the question of giving them assistance in theological education. Vast schemes have been discussed with Eastern Church leaders. But, nothing has ever been heard of them again. The East has rightly grown suspicious of the Western sincerity in making such advances. It would be unfortunate if representatives of American Churches were to go abroad filled with visionary plans which they were unwilling or unable to implement when time for action actually came. The critical factor is that of *adequate funds* and *generosity* in allowing Eastern Church leaders to guide their expenditure. The above remarks are designed to forewarn any interested in the question that they must think through beforehand the problems involved and not approach Eastern leaders until they are clear in their own minds how far they are prepared to go. And further it is hoped that the possibility of securing funds be advanced to a real probability or even certainty before raising hopes in the minds of the authorities of Churches which sorely need help.

As mentioned in the beginning of this chapter, the conclusions and recommendations of this Survey are limited to Protestant theological schools. As will be noted later, one of the recommendations of this Survey calls for the inauguration of a large-scale program for translating theological texts into the languages of major importance to the Protestant missionary enterprise.

Aside from liturgical Greek, Ge'ez and Syriac, the principal language used in the seminaries of the Eastern Churches is Arabic. In addition a small number of these institutions employ English (in a few courses), modern Greek, Armenian, Malayalam and Amharic.

For the reasons listed earlier in this Survey, Arabic was not suggested as being one of the languages of major importance to the Protestant missionary enterprise. On the other hand, it would appear that one of the ways in which assistance might be furnished to the seminaries of the Eastern Churches in an acceptable form would be the strengthening of their libraries, and particularly through the translation of suitable theological texts into Arabic. If the Translation Program recommended in this Survey is successfully launched, and if the seminaries of the Eastern Churches initiated requests for the translation of suitable texts into Arabic, it is believed that the furnishing of such texts at cost prices to those seminaries would be entirely consistent with the purposes of the Translation Program as a whole.

Part Four:
CONCLUSION

CHAPTER 16

THE SUPPORT GIVEN TO PROTESTANT THEOLOGICAL SCHOOLS BY FOREIGN MISSION BOARDS

A. IN THEORY

If the high-level pronouncements of the mission boards and agencies actually served as reliable guides to their practices in the field, one would gain the impression that they place heavy stress on the importance of theological education in Africa, Asia and Latin America. All of the following statements have been made by these agencies in published reports in recent years.

International Missionary Council: The findings of the International Missionary Council (IMC) Conference held at Tambaram, Madras, India, in 1938 include the following statement:

Almost all the younger churches are dissatisfied with the present system of training for the ministry and with its results. In many reports received from different parts of the world, it is stated that there are ministers of a poor standard of education, who are unable to win the respect of the laity and to lead the churches, that some are out of touch with the realities of life and the needs of their people and are not distinguished by zeal for Christian service in the community. From every field has come the conviction that a highly trained ministry is necessary for the well-being of the Church. . . . One of the difficulties by which we are faced is the large number of small, isolated and ill-staffed institutions, in which the standard of work is inevitably low. It is our firm conviction that in almost every case theological training should not be attempted except on a cooperative basis, with a number of churches participating. . . . Although the main financial burden of this work may for many years fall on the sending churches, it is of vital importance that in all theological institutions control should progressively pass to the churches in the field. . . . It is our conviction that the present condition of theological education is one of the greatest weaknesses in the whole Christian enterprise, and that no great improvement can be expected until churches and mission boards pay far greater attention to this work,

547

particularly to the need for cooperative and united effort, and contribute more largely in funds and in personnel in order that it may be effectively carried out.

The IMC Conference held at Whitby, Canada, in 1947 made the following finding: "Among all the tasks to which, in partnership, the younger and older churches are called to put their hand, absolute primacy must be accorded to the training in the younger churches of leaders fully equipped to bear the heaviest burdens."

At the IMC Conference held in Willingen, Germany, in 1952, the Conference declared: "The present situation calls, however, for re-examination of the number and character of institutions in relation to the Church's total task and resources. Colleges, schools, and hospitals were founded, mostly from the West, and in accordance with western patterns. In the changed circumstances of our time there is urgent need to ask whether resources claimed by some of these institutions should not be released for use in new enterprises, closer to the local church, and more central to its missionary task."

Part II of the IMC African Survey published in 1954 made as its first recommendation the following: "We believe that not less than one-fourth of missionary personnel and effort should be wholeheartedly directed to the training of ministers and of lay workers in the churches. . . ."

The following statements have been made in recent years by individual mission boards in their published reports:

Methodists: "Perhaps the greatest contribution missionaries have made is the training and encouraging of Asian leaders to carry the responsibility of the church. . . . It is an accepted mission philosophy that western missionaries are on the field to help in building a Christian church 'of the people, by the people and for the people'."

Presbyterians USA: "The provision of an adequate leadership in the indigenous churches . . . has become the crucial problem which the churches and the Board face together. . . ."

United Lutherans: "More intensive training in leadership by the Indian people themselves will serve both to give proper status to foreign missionaries as serving under the India Church, and to provide even more than we now have of highly . qualified Indian leaders against the time when missionaries are no longer needed or accepted by the government."

Protestant Episcopal: "The enlistment and training of a native leadership in the overseas fields is a matter which has been given first consideration. In this program, theological education has been given a place of highest priority. The goal in every field is a national Church, with its own leadership, able to take its place within the Anglican Communion."

Congregational: "We are called upon to live and work in a revolutionary world. So far as India is concerned, there will be advantages in working through Indians more and, if necessary, through missionaries less. If this be so, let us *use* the revolution. We have been talking for nearly a century about a self-governing, self-propagating, self-supporting church. Now, let us provide *skills* in the form of trained and inspired Indians, and *tools* in the form of buildings, medical equipment, books, etc. Let us tell our churches in America that these are the things which can help India to know Christ."

B. In Practice

The question arises: what proportion of the American foreign mission boards' expenditures and personnel are devoted to the support of theological education overseas? As mentioned earlier, no figures relating to such expenditures by mission boards generally are available because none of these agencies have customarily analyzed their operations from a functional standpoint. Since an undue amount of time and effort would be necessary in order to obtain such data on a broad basis, it seemed best to limit this inquiry to the practices of a few leading American mission boards which are ecumenically motivated. Consequently eight boards were selected by the IMC which asked them to analyze their expenditures in support of theological education overseas during their most recently completed fiscal years. In most instances this was the calendar year 1955. The results received are set forth in Table 177.

TABLE 177. EXPENDITURES OF SELECTED MISSION BOARDS FOR THEOLOGICAL EDUCATION OVERSEAS (1955)

| | (Column A) | (Column B) | |
Denomination	Total Foreign Mission Expenditures	Total Spent for Theological Education Overseas	Percentage of Column B to Column A
Methodists	$12,133,975[a]	$709,976	6
Presbyterians USA	8,076,809	300,413	4
American Baptists	2,762,949[b]	116,339[b]	5
United Lutherans	2,571,658	250,423	10
Congregational	2,331,690	134,468	6
Protestant Episcopal	2,294,973	253,274	11
Disciples[c]	2,229,237	137,700	6
Evangelical and Reformed	1,081,937	24,089	2
	$33,483,228	$1,926,682	5.8

NOTES: [a] Includes disbursements of the "Opportunity Fund" and of the "Department of Work in Foreign Fields of the Women's Division of Christian Service," but excludes certain other funds of the Division of World Missions designated for specific purposes of a nonbudgetary nature.
[b] Includes disbursements of the Women's American Baptist Foreign Mission Society. Column A fiscal year ending 4/30/55, column B ending 4/30/56.
[c] Consists of "Foreign Missions" expenditures, plus an estimated $250,000 of related overhead expenses, of the United Christian Missionary Society for fiscal year ending June 30, 1955.

The figures in Table 177 disclose that, on the average, less than 6% of the foreign missions expenditures each year of the eight leading ecumenically minded boards in the USA are devoted to theological education overseas. These eight boards account for about one-quarter of the total disbursements made by all the North American Protestant foreign mission boards each year. The $1,926,682 spent by the eight boards in a typical year in support of seminaries in Africa, Asia and Latin America probably represents at least 80% or more of the sums remitted each year from the United States for this one purpose: the sects are primarily evangelical in their work overseas, and such funds as they disburse for educational purposes are generally directed toward Bible schools rather than seminaries.

It appears that the British missionary societies devote an even smaller proportion of their annual budgets to theological education overseas than do the American boards. Six of the leading British societies were requested by the IMC to report the total of their expenditures in support of foreign seminaries in the most recent year for which such figures were available. The data contained in their replies are listed in Table 178, together with the totals of their annual expenditures as previously set forth in Table 9.

Table 178.   Annual Expenditures of Six British Missionary Societies for Theological Education Overseas

	Total	For Theological Education	%
Methodist Missionary Society	$2,253,000	$12,891	0.57
Church Missionary Society (Low Anglican)	1,529,000	6,882	0.45
Society for the Propagation of the Gospel (High Anglican)	877,000	17,226[a]	1.96
London Missionary Society (Congregational)	780,000	8,524	1.09
Baptist Missionary Society	642,000	8,123	1.27
Church of Scotland Foreign Missions Committee (Presbyterian)	540,000	5,488[b]	1.02

Notes: [a] Plus $58,520 nonrecurring expenditures in that year amounting to an additional 6.67% of its total income.   [b] Plus $7,072 nonrecurring expenditures amounting to an additional 1.31% of its total income.

It is possible that the comparatively low percentages listed in Table 178 do not fully reflect (1) the allowances paid by some of the societies to individual seminary faculty personnel directly supported by them, or (2) the grants made by some of the societies to diocesan authorities who in turn utilize these funds to support theological schools in Africa and Asia. However, even after allowing for these factors, the percentages of the societies' budgets devoted to this type of endeavor seem to be unjustifiably low.

Another example of the persistent tendency on the part of American mission boards and agencies to minimize their support of theological education overseas is seen in the financial reports of the Interboard Committee for Christian Work in Japan whose function has previously been described in this Survey. It is of interest to note that of the total of approximately $2,000,000 which the Committee planned to transmit to the Kyodan in 1957, only $37,000, or less than 2%, was to be devoted to theological education.

The question arises: for what purposes do the American mission boards spend the other 94% of their yearly disbursements? These can be stated only in general terms because in missionary areas it is impossible to draw tidy boundaries between the various elements in the life of the church.

The annual reports of the mission boards and agencies list numerous expenses and activities in which they are directly or indirectly engaged. These include hospitals, the shipping of supplies to the field, boys' and girls' clubs, supervision of work overseas, support to colleges, retired missionaries' allowances, orphanages, religious journalism, cost of promotion and services to churches in the USA, scholarships for volunteers, training institutes for missionaries, training centers in animal husbandry, audio-visual aid, medical care of missionaries, summer training programs, support to primary and secondary schools, general administrative expenses, repairs to and maintenance of mission property, student hostels, evangelism, old peoples' homes, screening of missionary applicants, contributions to younger churches, specialized schools for the deaf, conferences overseas, recreation centers, classes in cooking, dressmaking, child care, medical and dental assistance, night school courses, procurement expense, community betterment organizations, homes for "fallen women," etc.

To cite one board, the Presbyterians USA report that

as of the end of 1955, missionaries and fraternal workers totaled 1,061. . . . Either singly or cooperatively, the Board maintained 640 schools of primary and secondary grade and 44 colleges and universities, in which there were 7,306 teachers and a total enrollment of 182,394. On a similar basis, it maintained 46 hospitals with a staff of 1,123 doctors and nurses. . . . The Central Brazil Mission owns three very large tracts of land, suitable for agriculture. . . . Pig-and-cattle raising, butter-making, and early-corn producing may seem a far cry from the conversion of sinful men and women to Christ, but actually these are only the hyphen between the agricultural missionary and Christ. . . . Many people who could not possibly be approached directly have been attracted to the Gospel by this means.

To cite one area: it is reported that in Latin America alone, the 1,619 technical (i.e., Point IV) aid services of the 66 religious agencies of all Protestant denominations which are operating in this area involve the maintenance of field staffs aggregating approximately 2,100 full-time missionary and local personnel.

Writing over 20 years ago (in 1935), Professor Kenneth Scott Latourette observed: "In general . . . Protestant missions have had much more marked success in fostering education, in introducing modern medicine and in pioneering in fighting social ills than in the tasks which most missionaries and mission boards have declared to be central."

Since the boards do not make financial analyses of their operations, function by function, the only way one can gauge the present relative importance they place on each of their various activities is to review the occupational distribution of their personnel. Such figures are not readily available. Table 179 presents the most comprehensive estimates which are available along these lines. They were published by two agencies and from slightly different angles of approach. The first is adapted from a bulletin prepared by the Missionary Research Library (MRL) and relates to the functional distribution of North American foreign mission personnel in 1956 based on data for 1952. The second is adapted from the report for 1957 of the Division of Foreign Missions (DFM) which lists the vocational classifications of 850 new missionaries sent out from the United States by 45 leading boards and agencies in 1956, a representative year.

TABLE 179. OCCUPATIONAL DISTRIBUTION OF MISSIONARIES IN THE FIELD
(1956–57)

	MRL		DFM	
	Number	%	Number	%
Evangelists and Church Workers	8,894	46	275	33
Educators (Secular and Religious)	3,286	17	265	31
Doctors, Dentists, Nurses, etc.	2,320	12	139	16
Technical, Social and Miscellaneous	4,833	25	171	20
	19,333	100	850	100

Of the estimated 1956 total of 19,333 missionaries in the field, 60% were women. Of the women, over one-half (i.e., more than 30% of the total number of missionaries) were single women. Only 28% (or about 5,400 missionaries) were ordained ministers, a decrease from the 34% estimated for 1952. Furthermore, of the 850 missionaries sent out in 1956, only 21% were ordained ministers, whereas 56% were women.

It has been previously estimated in this Survey that at the 202 theological schools in Africa, Asia and Latin America there are about 433 western missionaries serving as full-time members of their faculties. Assuming this estimate is reasonably accurate, such a number amounts to less than 2% of the 25,058 North American missionaries presently serving in the field. Even if (from the purely quantitative viewpoint) the number of western faculty personnel were increased by 100%, this would still result in only 4% of the total number of North American missionaries being so occupied. Such percentages are a far cry from the "absolute primacy" for theological education to which the mission boards allegedly subscribe.

C. SOME REASONS FOR THE NEGLECT OF THEOLOGICAL EDUCATION

At the missionary conference held by the Presbyterians USA at Lake Mohonk in April 1956 which was attended by 137 delegates and staff members, etc., Dr. Henry P. Van Dusen stated: ". . . I cannot think of one single instance in a country where our Christian education is not notably stronger than our Christian theological education. . . . Theological education on the whole has been the stepchild or orphan of the Christian world mission. Why that has been I am not quite sure."

The following are some reasons which might be cited as having contributed to this situation.

1. *The mission boards themselves have not been entirely convinced of the importance of increasing their support for seminaries overseas.*

As previously noted, despite the lip service which is paid by the mission boards to the importance of theological education, an average of 94% of their expenditures are devoted to other purposes.

A clear-cut example of the dichotomy in the thinking of the boards in the past is to be found in the proceedings of the Lake Mohonk Conference itself. In the special issue of the *New Day Outlook,* published shortly after the Conference by the Presbyterians USA, the headline and text of the principal article reads:

FRESH STRATEGY FOR OVERSEAS WORK VOTED AT LAKE MOHONK. The Consultation approved "evangelism beyond the Church" and "the recruiting, training and use of leaders" as being "two fundamental emphases that must have top priority." ... In addition to the priorities of first importance, the Consultation highlighted two other emphases in future planning; (1) undergirding the life of the Church through stewardship education and church extension; and (2) taking the gospel to the community through rural reconstruction, community services, mobile medical services and cooperatives. ... A total of 450 new personnel, for specific tasks not now properly manned was requested. ... Although the Board will require months to work out the financial details of a five-year plan (1957–61), it made record at a meeting immediately following the Consultation that an increase of $1,200,000 (120%) in its annual field work appropriations is called for, not including the cost of additional personnel, and that capital needs requested total $7,300,000.

Thus the conference outlined an omnibus program in which theological education was one of the two activities accorded a "top priority." However, a reading of the conference transcript discloses that the vocational classifications of the 452 new personnel requested to carry out this program in 1957–61 was that shown in Table 180.

Thus a total of three out of the 267 workers (exclusive of wives), or roughly 1% of the total requested personnel, were designated for theological education. No other category was accorded a lower priority, with the exception of the one medical committee secretary and the two laboratory and X-ray technicians. A reading of the transcript also discloses that, except for statements made by Drs. Van Dusen and John A. Mackay, very little of the recorded discussion was devoted to theological education. One wonders how such a conference could accord a "top priority" to theological education with most of the recorded proceedings devoted to a discussion of other matters.

In fairness to the Presbyterians it may be noted that (1) the requests for personnel for 1957–61 as shown in Table 180 were the requests sent in from the field;

(2) their mission board was not necessarily committed to adding to their overseas staff precisely along these lines; (3) only a comparatively small proportion of missionary personnel would still be serving on seminary faculties even if the board's support of theological education overseas was greatly strengthened; and (4) it would be possible for the board to make financial contributions in 1957–61 in support of theological education overseas which would balance or outweigh in significance the fact that only 1% of the projected 452 new personnel were to be engaged in train-

TABLE 180.   Presbyterian USA Personnel Requests for 1957–61

Ordained Men:	
Rural and Urban Evangelism	84
Industrial Evangelism	11
Youth and Student Work	7
Theological Education	3
Single Women for Religious Education, Evangelism and Church Work	21
Men and Women for Secular Education	70
Doctors	15
Nurses	20
Business Administrators	4
Hospital Administrators	3
Agriculturists, Country Agents, Extension Workers	7
Social Service, Cooperatives and Community Workers	5
Broadcasting and Films	6
Literacy and Literature Specialists	5
Laboratory and X-Ray Technicians	2
For Reading Rooms	3
Secretary of Medical Committee	1
	267
Plus wives	185
	452

ing a local ministry. Nonetheless, it is believed that the over-all pattern of these personnel requests is indicative of much of the thinking which presently pervades missionary circles.

Finally one might cite the following statements made in Parts II and III of the IMC African Survey :"Missions often have not considered ministerial training a 'must.' While continuing other kinds of work, sometimes in reduced form, they simply halted ministerial training. To them it was not really important, when put in the scales with general church work, general education, medical service, or mission administration. . . . The present reigns. There is not enough consideration of the future. . . . The discovery of one good minister and his development, providing for thirty years of significant service, would seem to be worth more to Christ and His church than one year of present service by the potential discoverer and sponsor. . . ."

The same type of adverse comment, according to Part III, is being made by the Bantus in South Africa: "A . . . criticism was voiced at the meeting of African elders when a layman said: 'How can you expect us to take the Church really seriously? Have you done that yourselves? Do you not in fact spend much more money on (secular) education than upon the building of the African Church? Is it not true that you find it difficult to set sufficient men free for teaching in theological colleges because you put other educational activities first?'."

2. *Some mission boards tend to plan their operations primarily with a view toward sending out western missionaries to make converts in "new" geographic areas rather than helping ministers in the younger churches to make such converts.*

Rev. R. Kenneth Strachan, Chairman of the Latin American Committee of the Interdenominational Foreign Missions Association of North America (IFMA), has stated: "The dilemma in which we find ourselves is that on the one hand our entire missionary movement is geared psychologically to the sending out of increasing numbers of foreign missionaries; on the other hand, the present world situation calls for a disassociation of the Christian witness from Western imperialism, for the establishment of a strong indigenous church and for the transfer of leadership from the foreigner to the national."

Dr. Winburn T. Thomas and Bishop Rajah B. Manikam have written:

Missionary promotion and education in the sending lands have been centered upon missionary personnel and their individual accomplishments. . . . Unfortunately, the present Protestant approach to the non-Christian world overseas is essentially the same as it was in the early days of missions. Each denominational or confessional agency goes where it wills. In pioneering days, such a method was not a serious handicap; there were so many unworked fields that any group might choose for itself the place of primary interest. No longer is this true. There is (a) surfeit of workers in some regions, scarcity in others. In contrast, the Roman Catholic Church has a global program. For example, the Vatican admittedly has set out to win the Batak people in Sumatra.

World Protestantism is slow to accept the leadership and planning that the International Missionary Council could provide by way of a united, comprehensive approach to missions. Until such an over-all program is followed, the Protestant groups will continue to misdirect and dissipate their resources. Unless global, interdenominational planning is adopted, the Protestant churches probably will continue to send people and money to areas that have sentimental appeal or that are important economically or politically for their homelands. And, because the younger churches, like the older ones, are partly conditioned by nationalism, they will accept a similar pattern for themselves.

Dr. Winburn T. Thomas writes from Djakarta concerning the experience of the Board of Missions of the Netherlands Reformed Church in its work in Indonesia, as follows:

In 1939, Oegstgeest was allocating but 3% of its total Indonesian budget to theological training (not including salaries of missionary staff). In 1951, this item received 8% of the total Indonesian budget. . . . While the Directors point out that this is progress, they admit that "this distribution of funds is inadequate to render missions superfluous by training Indonesians." They recognize that as early as 1926, Dr. John R. Mott had noted the small number of Indonesian-trained Christian leaders. The report explains the lack thus:

"The Dutch mission boards and the supporting communities concentrate undue attention upon the Dutch missionary. . . . We often have argued that the younger churches should be independent, yet we have withheld the funds needed to train leaders, in order to send out more Europeans."

Among the various American mission boards, the Presbyterians USA are considered by some to be among the most alert to the need for planning their operations on functional as well as geographic lines. This Board has already set up some "functional portfolios" in addition to the various "area portfolios" it maintains. However, a reading of the reports of this and other boards leads one to the belief that the boards still conceive of their main mission as the making of converts through the efforts of western missionaries working in the younger church areas.

The 1955 report of the Foreign Missions Board of the Evangelical and Reformed Church states: "The Evangelical and Reformed Church has never accepted any geographical mission responsibility in Indonesia, but we have ecumenical concerns that make us sensitive to that great area of need so largely neglected today by mission boards. . . . During the past two centuries the Dutch missionaries did very effective work, but few of them have found it possible to continue since 1950. In no land, perhaps, is the need for Christian ministers so evident."

The 1956 report of the American Baptists points out that the "area of emphasis" in 1955 of this denomination's "World Fellowship Offering" was Europe. "The area of special emphasis in 1956 is the Burma Mission. . . ."

Perhaps the most clear-cut example of the geographic orientation in the boards' thinking is seen in the case of the Methodists. At the 16th annual meeting of this Board held at Buck Hill Falls, Pennsylvania, in January 1956, a plan for the 1957–60 quadrennium was adopted. According to the *Journal* of this meeting,

the central element in the plans for the new quadrennium, of course, is the need for missionary personnel. The askings from the fields to the Division of World Missions call for 1,300 missionaries. That number is about 300 more than were provided for in the appropriation for the fiscal year 1955–56. . . . In every field the church confronts vital opportunities. The basic assumption of the plan for the quadrennium is the ability to supply all fields the increasing support which is essential to healthful growth, and then beyond that to move with special power at the places of special opportunity. . . . We hope to find an increased effectiveness in our witness to Christ: broad enough to include every function of our mission—education, medicine, social work, agriculture, administration, as well as worship; narrow enough always to keep central the need of every person to know Jesus Christ as Savior and Lord. . . . We face four special opportunities in terms of four specific geographical areas. There are places where the hour of decision is upon the church. . . . This is the time to strike. Moreover, missionaries are eagerly wanted in each of these fields. . . .

1. *Sarawak*. . . . Sarawak is the British controlled northwest corner of the island of Borneo. . . . The Iban across the years . . . were the "wild men of Borneo"; until very recently

almost inaccessible to missionary influence. Today . . . they are clamoring for entrance into The Methodist Church. . . . The thrilling opportunity which they offer us for serving them is matched, however, by the opportunity for failure. Islam is in the country. The Roman Catholics are seeking to enter. . . . When a people thus move out of an animist culture into a new world, their first choices tend amazingly to be their final choices. . . . Christ's call to Methodism to move with power among these people is unmistakably clear.

2. *Korea.* Korea may possibly become, in our lifetime, the first predominantly Protestant nation of Asia. . . .

3. *Belgian Congo.* The Christian Church may face in Africa the most massive single opportunity of its history. . . . It is also quite possible that this vast region might become solidly Muslim or fanatically Communist. . . .

4. *Bolivia.* Bolivia is one of the most beautiful countries in the world and one of the most difficult to live in. . . . After decades of desperate labor, suddenly now the opportunity opens before us. . . .

3. *Mission boards permit their personnel to remain frozen in "old" areas where the missionary enterprise has consistently failed to make a significant number of converts, even after centuries of effort.*

In addition to the tendency of the major boards to conduct at one time as many activities in as many of the major missionary areas as possible, there also seems to be a tendency for most boards to be reluctant to withdraw from a country, no matter how discouraging their efforts in that area over the years may have been. Thus, numbers of their personnel are in some instances stationed indefinitely in areas where they themselves can point to comparatively little concrete evidence of success, and occasionally admit their failure. Sometimes these missionaries continue their work in unfruitful areas primarily because after long years they have attained a personal identification with the people and a competence in the local language. This is understandable enough, but does not necessarily constitute an effective use of missionary resources.

The Methodists report concerning their work in North Africa in 1955 that "at our annual conference held in November at the mission station in Il Maten, Algeria, we were confronted with the painful realization that in terms of converts the churches and the mission work in general has none to report. Our new presiding bishop . . . called the conference to prayer. From this point our doors seemed to open for a more encouraging future for the church work in North Africa. Dr. Elmer Douglas proposed an 'Evangelism Retreat'."

The number of converts won over to Protestantism is doubtless not the only yardstick with which to measure the success of a mission in the field over the years. Yet it is interesting to note that after 46 years of effort among the Muslims in North Africa, the Methodists have succeeded in winning a total of only 371 church members, or an average of eight such converts a year. At present nine Methodist preachers are maintaining approximately 15 mission stations and other conference-wide projects in Algeria and Tunis. Thus the number of preachers is about equal to the average number of converts made annually over the years. During the last 20 years, according to Dr. Eugene Smith, the Board has given serious consideration to closing down these activities, which he once thought should be done. However, about 15 years ago the Board sent a commission of laymen to study their North African work. The commission concluded it should be continued for the following reasons:

1. The Church's Christian obligation to the Muslims concerning which the Church is said to have been delinquent since the Crusades.

2. No other Protestant church has been working among the native Algerians and Tunisians (the French Reformed Church confines its activities to the French in North Africa).

3. If the Methodists were to withdraw, the Methodist pastors and congregations there would need outside financial support if they were to continue their activities.

The Presbyterians are also active in the Muslim Middle East and are faced with the same problem as the Methodists. When, however (at the Lake Mohonk conference), "the question was asked as to whether the slow growth of the Church in the Near East justified abandonment or curtailment of the Christian mission there, many voices were raised to ask for an advance instead."

For the year ending December 31, 1956, 22 out of 51 mission boards and agencies associated with the Division of Foreign Missions (DFM) reported that an aggregate of $2,499,688 had been devoted by them in the form of "recurring overseas expenditures" to their activities in the Near East and North Africa. It seems likely that a considerably larger total than this is being spent annually by all the North American agencies active in this area. Assuming the 951 missionaries maintained by the North American boards in North Africa and the Middle East in that year cost these boards an average of $4,000 per capita, this would indicate that the expenditures for mission personnel in this area amount to $3,804,000 a year, without allowing for grants for equipment or capital purposes. Thus, whatever the actual total may be, it is clear that a very considerable sum of money is being spent each year by Protestant agencies in furtherance of their missionary efforts to convert the Muslims in this area.

The Christian enterprise has made little or no progress during the past millenium in obtaining a significant number of converts from Islam, and it is difficult to elicit objective, factual reasons why Protestantism might be reasonably expected to achieve a greater success in this direction during the next century. It is astonishing to read in *The Call of the Minaret* the argument of one of the leading Protestant experts on Islam:

The question of converts, their number and their trials, is often raised in the home Church whenever the missionary effort among Muslims is discussed. . . . There are some who, in days of urgency everywhere and limitations of resources and manpower, tend to approve the diversion of personnel and funds away from Muslim areas to more receptive territories. . . . The first point to be made is that no Christian mission is constituted in its success, and none, therefore, is invalidated by numerical failure. The whole point of the argument has been missed if it is not clear that there is a Christian obligation to Islam which neither begins nor ends in how Muslims respond. . . . This is a categorical imperative. It should be plain to Mission Boards and subscribing Churches that the mission is not a calculus of success, but an obligation in love. Statistics do not make it, nor can they unmake it. Nor is it always a Christian thing to ask to know where we are going. It is not ours to see the full consequences or conditions of our duty. . . . As long as Christ is Christ, and the Church knows both itself and Him, there will be a mission to Islam.

According to St. Mark (16:15) Christ bade his apostles: "Go ye into all the world and preach the gospel to every creature." Such a mandate does not imply that the preaching of the gospel must necessarily take place in all areas at the same time. A case can be made for sending two or three experts to Muslim countries to study Islam and maintain Protestant contacts there. But the theory that the "obligation of the Christian witness" should be demonstrated by a large number of boards simultaneously sending out the maximum number of missionary personnel from the West on a pangeographical basis to all parts of the globe has resulted in a costly dispersion of the Protestant missionary effort. With the far greater missionary opportunities presently opening up in Korea and in Africa south of the Sahara, might it not be wiser for Protestantism to defer its support of a multimillion dollar missionary enterprise to Islam until a later time and utilize its resources more fruitfully elsewhere? Or, if because of its pluralist structure Protestantism is incapable of achieving flexibility in the choice of the geographical emphases of its missionary effort, might not the mission boards devote their budgets for the Middle East to better purpose and in all likelihood with more effective results by strengthening the indigenous Eastern Churches, particularly with regard to their seminaries?

4. *Once a mission board commences to support a project of any type, it is for internal organizational reasons exceedingly difficult for that board to cut off such assistance in order to shift its support to some relatively "newer" activity, such as theological education.*

The position of the boards in this respect has been expressed by Dr. Eugene Smith as follows:

The monies within our Board of Missions have, actually, far less fluidity than may seem at first glance. One-half of the income of our Division of World Missions comes in designated gifts. For these gifts we act only as the banker, sending them immediately to the mission fields and to the specific projects for which they were designated by the donor. . . . We would not serve the interests of the Kingdom by closing hospitals, by shutting down evangelistic work, cutting out the salaries of national leaders, or in closing primary schools that a higher priority might be put upon theological education. The amount of our undesignated income which is free for use in special priorities is, actually, quite small. Our situation is radically different from so many foundations in the United States which make capital grants but avoid becoming involved in recurring institutional budgets.

According to one missionary of considerable experience, when the typical foreign mission board makes up its yearly budget allocating funds for overseas work, this can become a rather "painful process." The needs of each of the missionary areas of the world are usually summarized by the boards' area specialists; and then at group meetings these needs are adjusted with each other to fit within an over-all budget. If a specialist is stubborn, the sessions may become tense and a "pulling and hawing" ensue. After the over-all budget is completed by the staff, it is then presented for review and approval at the annual meeting of the society, board or convention. At these meetings, sometimes 50 or 100 people attend and vote. Occasionally a bishop or a well-known cleric or lay leader interested, for example, in Asia will arise and make a strong, extemporaneous plea for the inclusion within the budget of a new $50,000 or $100,000 project in this area. Moved by his eloquence the meeting is apt to approve the budget subject to the inclusion of this special project within the over-all limits, thus requiring the other appropriations to be reduced. Or, if a popular project is deliberately omitted from the budget as presented to the meeting, one can fairly certainly count on pleas being made from the floor to reincorporate it. This accounts in part for the inability of the headquarters staff to effect significant shifts in the budget allocations from year to year.

Furthermore, the secretary of a typical mission board may have enough power to cut out or reduce one or two budget allocations; but if he were to attempt to accomplish more along these lines, this would be apt to create such a disturbance within the denomination that it would almost certainly result in the failure of such an over-all effort on his part. Within most mission organizations there appears to be a strong pressure from national groups overseas to maintain established institutional programs abroad even after the need which led to their creation has diminished or disappeared. The fundamental reason for this seems to be that owing to the voluntary basis of the general membership in the Protestant churches, one cannot run a denominational organization autocratically as one might administer a business corporation.

Sometimes if a board receives a substantial bequest for a specific project or activity, the tendency may be to shift undesignated income away from such activity for some other project. In the case of the Methodists, for example, the receipt of the Swope-Wendell Fund (for the Board of Founders of Nanking Theological Seminary) is said to have been cited in the past by some leaders in that denomination as a reason for not increasing the Division's appropriations for theological education overseas.

Among the smaller denominations, the Evangelical and Reformed Church is said to use a somewhat different system in preparing its annual foreign missions budget. Having only one secretary generally responsible for this task, there is less "pulling and hawing" involved. However, he is still subject to the conflicting pressures of the different Evangelical and Reformed missionaries in the field. The Congregational Christian Church is stated to have a small "prudential committee" of a semi-independent corporation reviewing competing requests from the field, and it may be that this is the most expeditious way of solving the problem of achieving a flexible approach in the allocation of mission expenditures. However, in the case of the Congregational Church, the flexibility of its operations in the field has been hampered by the fact that this denomination has in recent years apparently not fared as well financially as have some other denominations.

In the case of the American Baptists, this comparatively decentralized denomination is experiencing severe competition for new members within the United States from the fast-growing Southern Baptist Convention; and the two American Baptist Foreign Mission Societies were only recently reorganized and partially integrated after many years of preparatory planning.

Another factor accounting for a reduction in the flexibility of the planning of foreign mission boards is the long-range basis on which their operations are projected. For example the United Lutherans plan two years ahead, and the Methodists quadrennially. Still another factor is that within a denomination as a whole there may be a preference to emphasize some other activity at the expense of foreign missions, or to increase home missions as compared to activities overseas.

Of all the major, ecumenically minded boards, the Methodists appear to have been the most successful in recent years in increasing their denominational appropriations for their foreign mission activities as a whole. Among the reasons cited by others for this are the following:

1. A more intelligent promotional campaign within the denomination, avoiding the old-fashioned emphasis on the romantic aspect of missions and stressing the concrete facts constituting the over-all missionary situation today. This type of approach is said to appeal more to the business-minded leaders among the laity who are often in a better position to make substantial contributions.

2. The Methodists have a promotional device which they call "Advance Specials," whereby each church or contributor after making their regular donation to the Board's needs may make additional gifts especially designated for a project of their own choosing. Such projects are often specifically suggested to them by the Division's staff.

3. Because of the increasing amounts available to the Methodist Division of Foreign

Missions in recent years, it has been able to establish what it calls an "Opportunity Fund" to which are assigned all surplus funds available after regular annual appropriations have been met. With a grant from this fund a smaller "Pioneer Fund" was established in order to finance the cost of engaging in experimental projects. It was from the Opportunity Fund that the Methodists' $50,000 contribution to the Commission on Ministerial Training in Africa of the IMC-DFM Africa Committee was made.

5. *Missionaries in the field are often even less persuaded than are the mission boards of the importance of training a local ministry.*

A number of authorities may be cited in support of this statement. According to the *Laymen's Inquiry,* "the other cause of difficulty is the natural reluctance of missionaries to withdraw from fields of labor to which they have devoted the best years of their lives. This reluctance is all too likely to result in the rationalization that the Christian nationals are not yet ready for responsibility, although to a disinterested observer competent native leadership appears to be available."

Part II of the IMC Survey states: "It is far too easy for a missionary to assume a burden of useful work, which no one else can presently carry so well as he, and to devote himself so fully to doing that work that he holds himself increasingly indispensable and is more convinced that an African cannot do it. . . . 'We just haven't been able to spare the staff for training at higher levels' is the common formula, spoken either in anxious and penitent confession, or in self-justification which reveals more than it covers. In hard practice, missions have considered other things more important than (ministerial) training."

Professor M. Searle Bates has written: "Some missionaries are half-drugged by that sense of their own indispensability and of African inadequacy." Many missionaries in the field are said to believe that too much money is being allocated by their own boards to education, both secular and theological, inasmuch as they are more concerned with evangelism, medical and agricultural programs, etc.

In fairness to the missionaries in the field, one must recognize that they are constantly faced with an almost infinite variety and extent of human misery and distress. It is doubtless much more dramatic and immediately satisfying to set a native's broken arm, for example, than it is to attempt to train a catechist to appreciate the importance of the distinction between "Homoousian" and "Homoiousian." Many missionaries in the field are so isolated in the hills or on the desert's edge or in the jungle, that they are cut off from a flow of news of the outside world. Working in many instances sacrificially hard to maintain a hospital or a school, it is understandable that they should object when an order arrives from a mission board overseas directing them to shift their activities to some other project. The basic difficulty would seem to be in part owing to a lack of constant and adequate communication between headquarters and the field.

That this condition is a chronic one of long standing may be seen in the statement made a quarter of a century ago by the *Laymen's Inquiry:*

We are convinced that one of the most urgent needs of the missionary enterprise is the adoption and rigid enforcement, in all fields, of a definite policy of concentration of personnel and resources. Experience shows that this cannot be accomplished by the missionaries in the field. The forces which make for the maintenance of the status quo are too strong for them. Plans for concentration are usually unwelcome to nationals employed in religious work. In situations where they have voice or influence and especially where the boards give discretion to the field in the allocation of funds, the mission-employed workers strongly resist the contraction of established work, no matter how unpromising it may be. Vigorous and determined action on the part of the mission boards in America is imperative.

6. *The younger churches are also not fully aware of the importance of increasing their efforts to train their own clergy.*

The 1932 *Laymen's Inquiry* pointed out: "The greatest trouble with the indigenous church is the weakness of its pastorial leadership. The Commission believes that one of the reasons why the ministry is so commonplace is because it has appeared to be a career where a man could secure an easy—though meager—means of support, free from dependence upon those he was supposed to serve."

Thirteen years later the Ranson report stated:

At the present time the main burden of maintaining theological schools and colleges rests upon the missionary societies of the older churches. The resources of the Church in India . . . have, very properly, been directed primarily to the support of directly pastoral and evangelistic work and only in a very limited measure to the maintenance of training institutions. The result has been a tendency in the indigenous churches (a) to regard theological education as a somewhat remote responsibility, and (b) to feel that the continuing support of the missionary societies relieves them of the duty of contributing generously to theological institutions. On the side of the missionary societies it has resulted, in many cases, in the administration of theological education primarily as a "mission" concern and an inadequate representation of the indigenous Church in the shaping of policy and the general administration of theological institutions.

Six years later (1951) Bishop Neill concluded in Part I of the IMC Survey: "So far the African churches have not really taken very much interest in theological education."

Five years later Dr. William Stewart, a member of the Serampore faculty, wrote: "The Church in Asia must awaken to the dangerous extent to which it has been unconsciously depending on the theological contribution of missionaries from overseas and understand it as a matter of its very life that provision to train men . . . in theology from within its own ranks should be more adequately made."

The top leaders of the younger churches in Asian countries are said to recognize the importance of theological education, but it appears that many of their subordinates do not. According to the Ranson report, "churches and missions are so pressed for men of capacity, who can assume positions of responsible leadership, that when a young minister of marked ability appears he is almost invariably snapped up for some immediate practical task which is regarded as more urgent and important than any kind of advanced study. In many cases these tasks are primarily administrative, rather than pastoral or scholarly. The historical development of devolution has resulted in a tendency in the Church to regard the work of the administrator as more important than the pastoral and preaching offices."

As Dr. Keith Bridston has pointed out, "having gotten along without adequate theological training for so long, the national leadership of these places has the impression that theological education on a higher level is an unnecessary luxury."

Another problem of the younger churches is the low salaries which they pay to their pastors and the effect this has on recruiting an adequate number of seminary students. In the long run, it would seem that the only fundamental way of solving the problem of low salaries in those countries in Africa, Asia and Latin America where literacy and educational standards are comparatively low, will be through raising the *quality* of ministerial personnel to the point where their congregations, either spontaneously or with a minimum of outside suggestion or pressure, will increase the salaries they pay their pastors. As the general educational level of the pastors is raised, so should they be enabled to help their congregations more, and ultimately at an improved financial recompense to themselves. Improving the quality of pastors will involve making the seminaries recruitment-conscious and improving the caliber of their faculties.

A further way in which the younger churches tend to repeat some of the errors of the older churches is in needless competition. The Methodists' report, for example, dealing with their Sumatra Provisional Annual Conference has this to say:

The . . . relationships between the Hurai Kristen Batak Protestant Church (Lutherans, largely located on the central plateau of Sumatra) and the Methodist Church (largely along the coastal lowlands) is another problem . . . (which stems) from the fact that the larger Batak Church has moved into areas where the Methodists have been working, and have tended to build churches near our own. They claim they have a right to do so, in light of the fact that almost all of the people who have moved into that area have come from the Batak land and are really members of the Batak Church. The Methodists have, on the other hand, established two or three small mission chapels within the borders of the Batak Church itself. This has been viewed with great apprehension on the part of the Batak leaders.

Would it not in the long run be wiser for the Batak Church and the Methodist

Conferences (and other younger churches) to devote their available resources to the support of the Nommensen (and other) seminaries, rather than the engendering of long-term antagonisms through the building of chapels within each other's territories?

It is doubtless true that a Korean may be more readily listened to by the people in Ceylon than would an Englishman, or a Filipino may gain an audience more easily in Indonesia than would an American, etc. Yet, in connection with the launching of the East Asia Christian Conference might it not be wise for the younger churches to devote such surplus funds as they possess to the training of their own future leaders (or the leaders of other younger churches)—instead of sending medical and agricultural specialists from one underdeveloped country to another?

7. *The seminaries in Africa, Asia and Latin America have themselves been remiss in presenting their claims for increased support.*

The theological scholars in any religion are not apt to be aggressive, dynamic salesmen skilled in the art of applying pressure effectively upon ecclesiastical executives. One mission board executive comments as follows on the types of contact which are apt to arise between them and seminary administrators :"Outnumbered in the first case, they (the seminary administrators) seem to accept an in-law status, to hold back from the techniques of publicity and group pressure, and to act in a noncompetitive way when plans and budgets are being drawn up."

Some seminaries, particularly a few of those of the more conservative Anglican ones, tend to resemble a monastery rather than an educational center where students can learn wherein Christianity is relevant to the solution of the problems of the 20th century. As such they are not likely to present their needs to mission boards or to the public in an effective manner. Furthermore the lack of cooperation among seminaries has precluded the joint presentation by the schools of financial appeals to the younger churches and to donors in their own countries.

One seminary which seems to be a leader in this respect is the United Theological College at Bangalore. According to its 1954 Yearbook,

in reviewing the work of the past year . . . in one respect there is reason for grave disquiet. . . . The financial support of the College has been left so largely to bodies lying outside of India. In the matter of contributions from Indian churches and individuals we must unhappily report not an advance but an actual decline. . . . Our contributions from Indian and Ceylonese sources are actually growing less. In 1946 we received from churches and missions in India and Ceylon about Rs 600, and from individual contributions nearly Rs 1,000. In 1953 from both these sources taken together the total was only slightly above Rs 700. . . . It is disturbing that no real progress is apparent in securing material aid from the churches whose ministry is being trained. It cannot lightly be assumed that the present opportunities for securing finance and personnel from abroad will always continue uninterrupted. For the future health of the Christian church in India and Ceylon it is surely of great importance that the continuance of the present work should not depend solely upon the accidents of international relations.

The 1956–57 Yearbook of the same college states:

It is most important that the Churches in India and Ceylon should take greater responsibility for theological education. One of the most vital needs of the Church's life should not be dependent for long on funds from overseas. . . . Our appeal is being considered by some of the CSI (Church of South India) dioceses and other churches also. But in some quarters there seems to be hesitation as to the importance of such higher grade theological institutions. The Churches have to make up their mind as to what kind of theological institutions they need for the training of different types of ministers. Are the graduate level institutions a luxury an indigenous church can dispense with? Or are they also as vital as the other institutions?

The minutes of the meeting held at Nagpur in December 1955 by the Board of Theological Education of the National Christian Council of India state: "During 1956 an attempt will be made to survey carefully the needs of all our theological institutions with a view to presenting a consolidated appeal to all friends of the Church of Christ in India." This effort culminated in 1957 in the joint appeal for a total of $1,496,960 to be divided among a considerable number of the theological schools and colleges in India, as previously outlined in chapter 4. It would appear that this joint appeal has in all likelihood attracted a greater degree of attention to these seminaries' needs than would otherwise have been the case.

The instances cited above constitute steps forward. It is also of interest to recall the comment made earlier in this Survey, i.e., that the majority of the strongest seminaries in Africa, Asia and Latin America are those which have citizens of their own countries serving as their principals: it is these men who have had the greatest success in alerting their own local churches to their seminaries' needs.

These seven reasons which have been cited as some of the factors contributing to the neglect of theological education are not listed simply for the purpose of criticizing one agency or institution as against another. Rather, the reasons are set forth in an attempt to explain, in part at least, how "the stepchild or orphan of the Christian world mission" came to be that way.

CHAPTER 17

RECOMMENDATIONS

A. General Conclusions

In 1955 Bishop Rajah B. Manikam wrote that "while a number of surveys of theological education have been completed, few of them have been pressed to practical conclusions."

It would be superfluous for one more Protestant to add further remarks to those which have already been noted in the present Survey concerning the need for improving the theological schools now being operated in Africa, Asia and Latin America. Consequently the following comments are directed toward the steps which might be taken at this time to meet such needs and to bring about some improvement in their status.

Ideas, whether related to nationalism or religion, which have been endorsed by the leaders in countries having relatively low literacy and education standards tend to have a wider currency and acceptability than they do in the case of societies where more of the people are themselves able to deal with intellectual concepts. In this connection Dr. R. Pierce Beaver recently wrote as follows (after spending a year in Asia studying various religions at first hand):

The most obvious new emphasis required under present conditions is witness to intellectuals, including both the secularized intelligentsia and the devotees of the religions, especially those adhering to the reform movements. This has always been an obligation of missionaries, but it has been sadly neglected. It has been so much easier on the missionary's mind and his pride to work with peasants, and the statistical returns have appeared to be so much greater. . . . The lay role in the revival of religions, the intellectual and spiritual ferment of national reconstruction, and the charge that missionaries avoid an engagement with the intellectuals while they stress mass movements, all urgently challenge the representatives of the churches to undertake a new type of witness. . . .

The leaders in Africa, Asia and Latin America are not necessarily those persons in the upper social classes but include, in particular, the labor union leaders, government administrators at the lower bureaucratic echelons, school teachers, etc. As the level of education rises and foreign missionaries continue to be squeezed out of these countries, the intellectual challenge presented to the ministers in the younger churches will be increased. Such a challenge in the long run can be met only through bringing about an improvement now in the training of the future intellectual Christian leaders who, hopefully, may be able to cope with these problems as they arise.

Up to now the mission boards have often tended to be more interested in bandages rather than books, in hospitals rather than libraries, and in secular education as compared to the training of men for the ministry. This order of priority is of interest because, while Christ both healed and taught, His principal emphasis was on teaching. Christianity has always existed, and in all likelihood will continue to move forward, primarily on the basis of what Christ taught and not because of His successes in the field of public health. The essence of the missionary enterprise would seem to be in the propagation of the faith, and not in Point IV activities. With the level of education rising in most countries, it seems reasonable to believe that the growth of faith, as well as the development of reason, will in the future be accomplished less through simple evangelism, however zealous, and more through the theological training of the most capable youths in each country and through an increase in the dissemination and reading of scholarly texts.

With respect to the recruitment of students for Protestant theological schools overseas, it is of interest to note that the poorer quality seminaries throughout the world report difficulties in obtaining an adequate number of recruits. By contrast, the strongest seminaries are not confronted with a shortage of applicants. The recruitment problem is not an easy one to solve, yet this difficulty would appear to be based more than anything else on the low level of instruction offered at the seminaries and the poor caliber of their professors. It is believed that the basic problem in this respect is qualitative rather than quantitative, and that candidates for admission to seminaries should be rigorously screened even when there is a shortage of student applicants. An attempt should also be made to recruit capable ministers and laymen to serve as professors on the schools' faculties. Such a course would appear to offer more prospects of success than would a broad effort to obtain additional numbers of candidates merely to alleviate the alleged quantitative shortage of ministers.

It would seem to be almost axiomatic that the more thorough the training given to carefully selected seminary students, the greater will be the success in the long run of any church, whether young or old. The record achieved by the Society of Jesus in this respect, and the failure of the various Eastern Churches to recover their former eminence, may in part be attributed to the degree to which each of these organizations have provided for the theological education of their future leaders.

It would appear that the key to the success of theological education overseas is not in the construction of expensive buildings but rather in the strengthening of the seminary faculties. A strong African, Asian or Latin American seminary principal has the best opportunity for obtaining the support of the local churches in his area and attracting the most capable indigenous faculty personnel. If the schools' faculties can be strengthened and selective recruitment programs inaugurated, the problem of the "shortage" of ordinand students might be at least partially solved. Throughout history the impact and influence of educational institutions in all fields and countries have depended primarily on the caliber of their individual teachers and students rather than on the excellence of their structural facilities or the size of their enrollments.

The cause of Protestant Christianity in Africa, Asia and Latin America has been hindered both by the large number of denominations competing with each other and by the dispersion of their efforts in numerous and costly activities of doubtful essentiality. It is believed that the key workers in the Protestant church structure are the ordained ministers, and that the stress of the church's emphasis in the entire field of education should be placed upon their training.

The promotion of mergers among seminaries is always a difficult task. Only the intervention of a national government during a total war (as in the case of the Kyodan Church in Japan) or a total political revolution (as in the case of Communist China) has up to now been sufficient to oblige Protestant denominations to rationalize the operation of their seminaries in the younger church areas to any significant extent. As the recent example of the Burma Divinity School indicates, about as "ecumenical" as most denominational theological schools now seem willing to be is for them to permit professors and students of another denomination to teach and study at their presently established schools. The structure of Protestantism is filled with so many interlocking and slow-turning wheels that even though such mergers undoubtedly are desirable, nevertheless it simply is not realistic to expect a large number of mission boards, seminaries and younger church administrators to accept suggestions concerning the consolidation of many theological schools within a short space of time.

Furthermore, the prospective sharp increases in the populations of most of the countries in Africa, Asia and Latin America during the next four decades suggests that, if the proportion of their Christian populations merely remains the same, even though the number of their Protestant seminaries is not decreased, the enrollment in most of these seminaries will be considerably increased. (With respect, for example, to the 32 seminaries in India—virtually all of which are now too small in size—at its present annual rate of growth of 1.5%, the population of that country—which now amounts to roughly 375,000,000 persons—is expected in the next 40–45 years to increase to 750,000,000, i.e., doubling in size.) On the other hand, it is believed that the boards should do what they can to foster such mergers wherever the possibilities seem favorable and whenever they can be effectively promoted. There are already an abundant number of seminaries in most areas, and the tendency of the more evangelical mission boards is to open new schools. What is needed most is a smaller number of better seminaries. If a determined effort is made to select only those candidates for the ministry who are the most capable and best qualified men, such students can ordinarily be sent to the nearest seminary, even in a neighboring country, at less expense than is involved in founding a new institution. With the means of transportation constantly improving everywhere, the boards might do well to assist seminaries that are already in being rather than engage in the time-consuming effort of assembling new faculties to be located in remote areas. The cost of launching new seminaries of the requisite caliber is in general disproportionately high.

It would also be less costly to build on strength rather than on weakness. With any type of organization, more can be done where a strong nucleus already exists than in instances where administrative personnel are weak. A significant improvement in theological education overseas cannot be made merely by assisting the weaker institutions to rise to the level of the stronger ones in those same countries. The stronger schools should be enabled to make advances to the point where they would attract students of higher quality to enroll in them. A by-product of such a policy is that it tends to require the weaker seminaries to take similar steps or else fall behind in the competitive process.

In 1949 Dr. Henry P. Van Dusen wrote the following in an article entitled *United Strategy in Christian Missions—The Next Step:*

The impatient, those who discern the trend of advance but not its step by step logic, those who envision the ultimate goal but not the tedious stairway toward its achievement, cry for instant and complete organic union of our Churches—or, in any event, of their mission boards. In the World Mission we should be guided less by obedience to *a priori* conceptions describing what someday should be, than by discernment of their inner logic of growth prescribing what today must be. . . .

What is next required is . . . the extension to the Christian World Mission as a whole of the structure and practice now tried and proved in union Christian higher education, medicine, theological training on the field, and in united boards at home. . . .

What concretely would this imply? . . . A *united strategy*—the planning of the entire world evangelistic enterprise of the Churches as one organic movement, determined in the light of the total task and the total resources available . . . (and) . . . A *united program,* made possible by the pooling of all resources—men and money—and their deployment according to a united plan for largest effectiveness. . . . It implies a shift of the center of gravity from individual mission boards to one, or several, united boards.

It is clear from this Survey that an ecumenical program for the strengthening of the theological schools in Africa, Asia and Latin America is overdue. It should be lodged at the apex of the missionary structure, the IMC. The Protestant mission world is replete with organizations and committees, the gearing together of which is a ponderous affair. The need to refer back to New York, London, Paris, etc., for ultimate decisions results in costly delays. It is virtually impossible to obtain united mission action on a world-wide project, except at the apex, and only if the necessary funds for the project are pledged or made available prior to its launching.

It is therefore believed that the IMC should organize a Theological Education Committee (TEC) which would have the sole power of administering funds donated to the IMC for the support of theological schools in Africa, Asia and Latin America. The membership of the TEC should be approximately 20 in number and composed of outstanding leaders in this field. Among them should be leaders from overseas, for, as Prime Minister Nehru has pointed out, "one still finds a lack of realization in European countries or in America that Asian problems cannot be decided without Asia; without Asian opinion or without Asian co-operation. They still continue the attempt to decide the problems of Asia somewhere in London, in New York or in Paris, or wherever it may be. This is resented here as a matter of principle. What is more, that decision does not really carry any effect."

It is suggested that the persons who might be considered for membership on the TEC should include leaders from the younger and older churches, and from the leading denominational mission boards, who have demonstrated their interest in theological education. It is believed that it would be preferable to exclude from membership on the committee the administrative heads of seminaries which might receive assistance from the TEC in one form or another.

It is believed that a minimum of $4,000,000 should be placed at the disposal of the TEC to be spent over a five-year period if a significant improvement is to be made in the quality of the instruction offered at seminaries in the younger church areas. Such a program might be accomplished in various ways and the following suggestions are offered for consideration.

TABLE 181. SUGGESTED ALLOCATION OF TEC FUNDS

	Annually	5-Year Total	Allocation
Seminary Program	$540,000	$2,700,000	68%
Texts Program	200,000	1,000,000	25%
Administration	60,000	300,000	7%
	$800,000	$4,000,000	100%

A comprehensive program might fall into two main categories, seminaries and texts, as shown in Table 181. There would be no need for precisely these amounts to be allocated in this way or for precisely one-fifth of the total funds allotted to the seminary and texts activities to be spent in each of the five years of the program. In all likelihood there would be very few grants, perhaps none, made by the TEC in its first year of operations.

B. SEMINARY PROGRAM

The Choice of Seminaries for Support: It seems likely that virtually all of the suggested $2,700,000 budget for the Seminary Program would be devoted to grants to individual theological schools. In order to make a significant impact upon the operations of an individual seminary overseas, a sizeable grant would be necessary. Thus, with the funds available to the TEC for its Seminary Program over a five-year period there would be approximately 20 seminaries to which it might make institutional grants on this basis. It might be preferable to select some seminaries to receive major grants, thereby enabling minor grants to be made to a somewhat larger number of schools. In any event it is believed that the total number of schools receiving major or minor institutional grants should be no more than approximately 20. Only in this way can the TEC raise the level of selected seminaries to an area-wide rather than a local significance.

It is recognized that the generally lower level of theological education in Africa, plus the fact that some of the seminaries located near the new university colleges might need to be built up almost *de novo,* could result in a larger share of the Seminary Program funds being devoted to Africa. Conversely a somewhat smaller proportion might be devoted to seminaries in Southeast Asia which are in the area of especial interest to the Board of Founders of Nanking Theological Seminary.

It is of interest to note what seminaries have stated in their printed literature they would be able to accomplish in the way of plant expansion at a cost of $100,-000 or less. For example, for $75,000 Serampore College proposes to erect "a chapel ($18,000), classrooms and offices ($25,000), faculty residences ($25,000), and married students quarters ($7,000)." The Union Theological School at Makassar in the Celebes proposes to build for $62,500 "three classrooms ($8,000), two houses for teachers and married students ($16,500), one main office and library ($11,000), one chapel ($12,500) and furnishings for these buildings ($14,500)." On the other hand, it has been estimated by mission board sources that the cost of moving Trinity College from Kumasi to a site near the University College of Ghana at Accra would amount to as much as $250,000, with not much money to be expected from the sale of the old site. The proposed transfer of the Union Theological Seminary from Manila to Quezon City could ultimately involve an even larger expenditure. Building costs vary from area to area, but it is clear that the TEC should seek to avoid as far as possible the underwriting of the cost of relocating and constructing completely new plant facilities. An exception might be considered in the case of a seminary wishing to merge with one of the key seminaries.

In connection with the attempt to raise the scholarship level of these schools, a question which arises is the advisability of making grants for endowment purposes. It is estimated that from 30% to 60% of the present income of the majority of the seminaries is derived directly or indirectly from contributions of foreign mission boards. The Ranson Report stated that the theological schools in India receive approximately 75% of their cash income from missionary societies in addition to the services of the missionary members of the staff. "Comparatively few institutions possess any endowments, though in some cases these are fairly large. About 16% of the aggregate income of the theological schools is derived from this source." At a meeting of the Theological Education Committee of the National Council of Churches in India held in December 1955 the Committee "expressed its conviction that it is urgent to secure for theological institutions more stable support than annual grants from foreign mission boards and individual contributions . . . partial endowment of theological education is necessary in India as in the West." Since only a handful of the seminaries overseas possess income-producing endowments, the problem is a real one.

Despite the plea cited above, it is believed that the TEC would be well advised not to make grants for endowment purposes, for two reasons. The first is the unstable monetary conditions prevailing in many of the countries in Africa, Asia and Latin America. This can be measured most simply in terms of the percentage increases in the cost of living in those countries during the past decade in relation to the comparable increase in the United States during the same period, as shown in Table 182.

TABLE 182. PERCENTAGE INCREASES IN COST OF LIVING IN SELECTED COUNTRIES (1946–56)

North America	%	Africa	%
USA	40	French Equatorial Africa	371
		Kenya	66
		Southern Rhodesia	57
		Belgian Congo	49
Southern Asia	%	Southeast Asia	%
India	39	Thailand	73
Pakistan	8	Burma	11
East Asia	%	Latin America	%
Korea	3070	Argentina	463
Formosa	1080	Brazil	289
Japan	556	Mexico	114

The second reason for not making grants for seminary endowments is simpler. At a 4% return, and despite the fact that the typical seminary has an operating income of slightly less than $20,000 a year, the $80,000 annual income which might be derived if as much as $2,000,000 were granted for endowment purposes would merely serve to double the budgets of only four seminaries, or provide a 20% increase for 20 seminaries.

The question then arises as to how the level of scholarship at these 20 schools can be raised if capital grants are not used primarily for a merely quantitative expansion of their facilities or for endowment. Some of the TEC's grants undoubtedly will be needed for the seminaries' building needs; but it is hoped that as large a percentage of its funds as possible will be disbursed directly for the purpose of stimulating and deepening the intellectual and spiritual life of these schools.

The key to the success of any educational institution is in the excellence of (1) its faculty and administrative leaders and (2) its student body. In the long run the salvation of the theological schools in each of the countries in Africa, Asia and Latin America will depend primarily upon their ability to engage truly able principals and faculty members who are citizens of their own countries rather than foreigners. However, there are at the present time few sufficiently qualified citizens of the countries in Africa, Asia and Latin America to whom the TEC might turn in order to augment the seminary faculties. Some foreign scholars now teaching in secular institutions overseas or some outstandingly successful indigenous pastors might be attracted to posts on seminary faculties. If the TEC were to make grants for the construction of attractive faculty housing to be assigned to the seminary professors on a rent-free basis, this might be of assistance. The success of the Union Theological Seminary in New York City along these lines might well be noted by seminaries overseas in their endeavor to attract scholars of proven reputation.

A more fundamental step would be for the TEC to take steps now to provide postgraduate training for some of the most capable of the indigenous graduates of these schools overseas who intend to adopt a career in seminary teaching. Such graduate students would need to study for a period of one to three years at centers in Europe and America, and it would be important to have the students agree that upon the completion of such studies they would return to their own countries to enter full-time teaching careers. Too often foreign students have found living conditions abroad more satisfactory than at home, with the result that they become expatriates and deny their homelands the benefits of their abilities and services.

It is believed that if grants are awarded to enable the seminaries to engage new faculty members, contributions should be made only when there is a reasonable prospect that the seminaries will be successful in obtaining scholars of good caliber to serve in this capacity. Outstanding professors in American and European seminaries might be enabled to teach during their sabbatical years at theological schools overseas. For example, the visit to Indonesia in 1956 of Dean Elmer Homrighausen of the Princeton Theological Seminary was welcomed by the Indonesians and is stated to have achieved valuable results. As Dr. Winburn T. Thomas has pointed out, "in the long run, the distinctive contribution of American theological method can be made relevant to Indonesia only by the appointment of theological teachers to the Indonesian training institutions. The appointees must be specialists in these new fields, but at the same time academically grounded in the classic theological discipline if they are to hold their own with the continental scholars who now teach in these same institutions."

Continental European professors are generally paid lower salaries than their counterparts in the United States so that it might be helpful to follow the pattern set by the Lutheran churches which staff the faculties of their seminaries in the younger church areas with Europeans rather than with Americans in many instances. The selection of American professors might well be made in consultation with the American Association of Theological Schools in connection with its current Faculty Fellowship Program.

Such sabbatical visiting professorships should be attractive assignments for the professors involved and would serve to enlarge their horizons. Upon their return to Europe and the United States the professors might help to "sell" in their own countries the cause of theological education overseas. In this connection it is interesting to note that in 1956 the Department of World Missions of the Evangelical United Brethren Church inaugurated a plan to send professors on sabbatical leave from this denomination's seminaries in the United States on guest lectureships at foreign theological schools.

These visiting professorships would tend to repay in part the benefits which American seminaries have derived from having recently had distinguished scholars from abroad serving on their faculties for a period of a year or more. Since World War II there has been some competition between some of the leading theological schools in the United States with respect to the number of eminent foreign scholars they might attract as visiting professors to their staffs. The engagement of these foreign professors is often stressed in the seminaries' promotional literature. While the American seminaries have no doubt benefited from this process, the concomitant cost has been that the younger churches have been deprived for a varying length of time of the services of some of their outstanding leaders, a loss which they can ill afford. Hence it is believed that in the interests of the Christian enterprise as a whole the time has come to reverse this process.

Despite the desirability of having only outstanding European and American professors chosen for these posts overseas, it seems likely that because of their age and other factors it might be difficult to recruit a sufficient number of them. If so, it is suggested that the TEC might well seek to recruit equally able but younger members of European and American seminary faculties. In some instances it might be profitable to canvass European or American graduate students seeking their doctoral degrees in this field: the TEC might engage their services on the faculties of seminaries overseas for a period of several years prior to their assuming teaching posts at home.

These suggestions imply the necessity of having the TEC Executive and Associate Directors engage in a considerable amount of faculty recruiting work. Because the supply of outstanding theological scholars in the United States is low in relation to the demand therefor, the competition among the seminaries in this country for their services is keen. If a minimum of only one able professor were engaged by the TEC for each of the 20 key seminaries overseas, this would represent a substantial depletion in the supply of such scholars in Europe and America.

Once the 20 key seminaries have been selected, one way of creating an interest in them on the part of European and American seminaries would be for the TEC to request 20 of the schools in the West to "adopt" any one of the 20 seminaries overseas: this might follow the pattern in accordance with which American cities "adopted' European cities of the same name (e.g., Reading, Pennsylvania, and Reading, England) in the years of relief and reconstruction immediately following World War II. If the TEC could induce 20 outstanding European and American seminaries to express such an interest, the TEC might assign each of them to its most logical counterpart among the 20 seminaries overseas. It might then be possible to persuade each of the 20 European and American seminaries to assume the responsibility of having at least one or another of its outstanding faculty members serving at all times during a five-year period on the faculty of its counterpart seminary overseas, with the TEC underwriting the cost of his replacement while abroad. The counterpart seminary overseas would also have the benefit of being able, if it wished, to look to a specific European or American seminary (as well as the TEC) for guidance in solving its scholastic and administrative problems.

The question arises whether European and American faculty personnel would be able to speak the languages used in seminaries overseas. While the selection of these schools is still to be made, it would appear that among some, at least, of the institutions likely to be chosen, English is used as a primary or secondary language of instruction.

Another method of raising the stature of the key seminaries would be through the making of small expendable grants enabling them to become the accrediting institution for the seminaries in their own countries and areas in much the same way that the Serampore Senate operates in India. Once an accreditation system was established, the operating costs should be underwritten by the member institutions.

Most seminaries overseas are in need of audio-visual equipment which would be of use in classroom instruction. It might be feasible for the TEC to pool a number of orders for such equipment and obtain these items from one supplier at one time (and possibly at a substantial discount).

In the long run it would seem to be highly desirable, and indeed inevitable, that a postgraduate theological department should be established at an existing key seminary in Asia for the purpose of training Asians in Asia to serve on theological school faculties. In the over-all budget for the Seminary Program a small provision might be earmarked for the proposed Higher Theological Faculty in Asia which was suggested at the Bangkok Theological Conference in February-March 1956. Dr. Guansing's committee, as previously noted, anticipated that the setting up of such a faculty of five members would entail nonrecurring capital expenses of $125,-

500. It is not at all clear why such a faculty should need to erect a new plant when it might be better situated if attached to an existing seminary of high standing.

Another problem is how such a higher faculty could be staffed with outstanding Asian professors without seriously weakening existing Asian seminaries in the process. A possible solution might be achieved through rotating faculty appointments. While the case for launching a new institution such as this at the present time may not as yet be complete, nevertheless the TEC might explore the possibilities and assist in the development of the project. It is also believed that before it is launched, some financial (as well as institutional) support should be received from the younger Asian churches and their seminaries as evidence of their determination to support such a venture adequately and fully.

In addition to strengthening the faculties and the instruction at key seminaries, the TEC might explore the problem of recruiting more able students to enter these institutions. Some schools are not as aggressive along these lines as they might be, and others stress the number of their entrants rather than their quality. It is believed that the emphasis should always be placed on the high caliber of the students, and in order to make it possible for the needy among them to study at seminary, scholarship funds might be made available by the TEC to selected seminaries.

On the other hand, it would probably be unwise for the TEC to arrange to send a considerable number of foreign seminarians to study for their B.D. degrees in divinity schools in Europe or the United States. The differences in the standards of living and the cultural backgrounds between the countries are too great, and the outstanding among such students would be tempted to remain away from home. Nor does such training serve well to fit a man for pastoral duties in Africa, Asia or Latin America. Such students are best trained in their own or nearby countries, and it would appear that the Program of Advanced Religious Studies at Union Theological Seminary in New York City for the rising leaders and graduate students of the younger churches is about as far as it is desirable to proceed along these lines in an organized way.

The staff of the TEC might wish to study the curricula of the theological schools with a view toward making suggestions as to how they can be improved. In particular, there is a need to develop ways and means whereby their courses can be made more relevant to the moral and social problems which are evolving in the rural and especially the urban life of the people in Africa, Asia and Latin America today.

Finally, the TEC might do well to study in some detail the activities of Roman Catholic major seminaries with respect to the spiritual formation of their student candidates for the priesthood: in this field, Protestant theological schools would appear to be deficient, and it seems likely they could increase their emphases along these lines without in any way impinging upon their present liturgical observances or theological doctrines.

The Texts Program discussed below could be of benefit to virtually all the seminaries in Africa, Asia and Latin America. Consequently this would enable the TEC to concentrate the major portion of its funds in the Seminary Program for capital grants to the 20 key institutions. There would undoubtedly be a tendency for some to suggest that the Seminary Program should support summer institutes for the training of pastors already engaged in parish work. While these activities may sometimes have their uses, it is believed that one of the most difficult tasks of the TEC would be to minimize its support for such undertakings and to focus its interest primarily and essentially on the intensive training of men preparing for careers in the ordained ministry. The cardinal feature of the suggested Seminary Program is the concentration of substantial support for a few key seminaries and the avoidance of the error of trying to do too much with too little.

C. TEXTS PROGRAM

A Texts Program should be designed to strengthen the libraries of virtually all the seminaries in the younger church areas and to improve the teaching in the classrooms of many of them. The Program would call for a very considerable increase in the efforts which have been made to date by the foreign mission boards and agencies in this particular field.

Budget and Administration: The budget of the Texts Program might be allocated as shown in Table 183.

TABLE 183.   SUGGESTED FIVE-YEAR TEXTS PROGRAM

Distribution of scholarly books and periodicals in English	$350,000
Writing, translation and distribution of books in foreign languages	650,000
	$1,000,000

One of the initial steps might be to make a first-hand inspection of the theological texts activities now being conducted by the various interboard agencies. In this and the other aspects of the TEC Texts Program, it would be important to keep the focus confined strictly to texts used in the training of ministers and not allow the TEC funds to be diverted to the other literature activities (e.g., the production of literacy or Sunday school texts) now being conducted by many of these agencies.

During visits to seminaries overseas, the schools might be advised concerning cataloguing and classification problems in their libraries. Short periods of training in library procedures for some of the permanent members of their faculties might be provided. Indeed at a later date the TEC might wish to explore the advisability of establishing a small library training school at one of the key seminaries having a large library.

It may be desirable for the TEC to arrange for the preparation of two basic seminary library lists of 1,000 and 2,500 volumes respectively. These model lists would consist of the books which "every good seminary library should have," comparable to the Shaw list (*List of Books for College Libraries*). The Missionary Research Library at the request in June 1956 of the Board of Founders of Nanking Theological Seminary has been preparing one such model list of 500–1,000 titles. Various topical bibliographical lists in individual fields have also been prepared in recent years by the seminary libraries at Princeton and Andover-Newton.

It might be helpful if the TEC were to send out a questionnaire to the various seminaries overseas. Such a questionnaire could include the model list of 1,000 library books, and the seminaries would be requested to return the list having checked off those titles which they already possess (indicating the language in which they are printed, if not in English). Another such list to be returned might comprise the names of the periodicals to which they are at present subscribing. The seminaries might be forewarned that those institutions which failed to return the questionnaires within two months' time might be excluded from participation in the Texts Program. The tabulated results of such a questionnaire could be of considerable value in planning the distribution and translation programs of the TEC.

Distribution of Scholarly Books and Periodicals in English: There are well over 100 seminaries in Africa, Asia and Latin America where English is spoken or read either as a primary or secondary language which would benefit from a strengthening of their library resources in English. It is assumed that 150 seminaries might wish to participate in this Program. If, on the other hand, only 100 schools participated in the distribution of English books already in print, the estimated cost of this portion of the Program would be reduced by one-third.

The procedure of presenting books to libraries has some disadvantages. But it is useful because of its flexibility (no fixed number of volumes being necessary in all instances), its avoidance of a continuing commitment for staff, rent, etc., its almost universal approval by local governments and people, and the fact that the recipient institutions can be of all types. Thus a small number of basic sets of books might be sent to the smaller institutions and a larger number to the more important theological schools.

While many important books on theological topics are technically still "in print," it is recognized that it might be difficult for the TEC to obtain as many as 150 copies of them. Furthermore, it would seem advisable for the TEC to purchase collections and sets of the important authors, rather than to attempt to obtain in all cases the so-called "best" individual compendium of the writings of each author.

With respect to books which are almost or entirely out of print, $150,000 (or some such amount) might be earmarked in the Texts Program to pay for the cost of reprinting them. In this connection, certain assumptions have been made. The first is that books to be reprinted would contain an average of 100,000 words each. The second is that the royalties to be paid would be inconsequential in amount.

It costs comparatively little more to produce some 2,000 copies of a book in a simple cloth binding than it costs to produce 500 copies. A book which retails at $5 may cost as little as $1 to manufacture, the other $4 representing the publisher's cost of discount to booksellers (that item alone being $2), royalty, editing, selling, advertising, shipping, storing, billing, bad debts, general overhead, allowance for losses on books which do not sell out the full number printed, and publisher's profit. In a guaranteed program which is a nonprofit plan of reprints not for commercial sale, one saves not only the profit factor and the factor of loss resulting from unsold copies, but also many other of the normal elements of the publisher's cost.

It is estimated that the payment of $2,500 would normally cover in full the printing and shipping costs of 2,000 copies of most theological books. Assuming that a sum in the order of $150,000 were devoted for this purpose, such an amount would enable the reprinting of 60 titles, at a cost of $1.25 per copy. Printing costs in the underdeveloped countries would amount to only a fraction of this cost. On the other hand, to the extent that such books were sold to the general public in those countries the currency and export regulations of those governments make it highly desirable that the reprinting of theological books in English be handled through one or two of the leading American publishing firms (e.g., Dover Publications, Inc., etc.) which specialize in this field.

The production of, say, 2,000 copies of each title would on the average make it possible to send a dozen copies of each title to 150 seminaries. While there is no clear dividing line in the theological field between library books and classroom texts, it might be desirable for the recipient seminaries to retain ownership of the dozen copies of the titles they would receive and use them for classroom instruction. Those titles which met with the greatest favor and which the seminary students wished to include in their personal libraries after graduation could be printed by the TEC in greater quantities at only a minor additional cost. Those titles not suitable for use as classroom texts might be printed in quantities of less than 2,000 each. Surplus copies might be sold through the TEC at cost to seminaries in the United States and Europe.

The TEC might also wish to investigate the possibility of making available to the 20 key seminaries microfilms, microtexts, etc., already in print, together with the new microfilms of back issues of periodicals which the American Theological Library Association has been enabled to produce in 1957–59.

It might be advisable to have a proviso that, whenever possible, the seminaries receiving these books should as a quid pro quo undertake to fulfill certain conditions. One of these would be that they would agree to spend not less than 8% of their instructional budgets for the expenses of their libraries (acquisitions, salaries, binding, etc.). This would compare with an average (in 1950–51) of 12–14% spent for this purpose by the accredited seminaries in the United States. The fully accredited American seminaries are expected to spend not less than $10,000 per year for their library budgets, or $35 per student, whichever is larger. It is also expected that $2,500 of this amount in the budget will be spent annually for books and periodicals. However, some of the smaller American accredited seminaries (with 4–7 faculty members) in 1951 were spending only about $4,500 a year on their libraries. If 8% of the instructional budget of the typical seminary overseas was devoted to this purpose, this would amount to total library expenditures on their part of approximately $1,500 a year.

The recipient seminaries should also be required to certify that their library facilities are such that the books presented to them by the TEC would be carefully protected from mildew, leaking roofs, shelves infested with termites, etc. Conceivably the TEC might in some instances consider the possibility of sending to a few of the schools located in the most remote tropical areas metal book cases in which to retain the books that are distributed to them.

Inasmuch as many of the theological schools overseas are not only somewhat isolated from the main streams of activity in their own countries, but, more particularly, are separated from the activities of Protestantism in the rest of the world, the periodicals program outlined below anticipates the expenditure of $50,000 over a five-year period. An expenditure of $10,000 a year for this purpose for 150 schools would make it possible to enter magazine subscriptions annually costing a total of approximately $65 per school. At the same cost, an even larger number of periodicals might be obtained if the TEC were able to place block subscriptions with publishers at reduced rates. At current subscription rates and allowing $65 per school, each seminary would be enabled to receive one-half or more of the outstanding theological periodicals listed in alphabetical order in Table 184.

TABLE 184.   Some Outstanding Theological Periodicals

In English	In European Languages
Christian Century	L'Actualité missionnaire
Christianity and Crisis	Allgemeine Missionsnachrichten
Ecumenical Review	Christ und Welt
Hibbert Journal	Kerygma und Dogma
International Review of Missions	Novum testamentum
Interpretation	La Nueva democracia
Religion in Life	Revue biblique
Theology Today	Theologische Zeitschrift
	Zeitschrift für Theologie und Kirche

The list of periodicals set forth in this table is entirely tentative and is intended to be indicative only. It has been prepared in consultation with the librarians of the Union Theological Seminary and the Missionary Research Library in New York City. Other titles might be added to the list, and it could easily be varied to meet the needs of seminaries already subscribing to some or all of these publications.

That it is a modest list in length is indicated by the fact that the Union Seminary Library subscribes to over 500 magazines and its affiliated Missionary Research Library subscribes to a different list of 500 periodicals. An outstanding secular review might well be included in the list even if it involved eliminating a theological journal from it.

It may be advisable that these periodicals should be sent to the seminaries as a conditional gift. It would be preferable if three-year subscriptions were presented gratis to the schools on the understanding that the seminaries would agree at the end of this period either to renew these subscriptions for a two-year period at their own cost or to make an equivalent expenditure for other periodicals of their own choice for the same length of time. During the last two years of the five-year program, the TEC might then contribute additional subscriptions of different periodicals to the schools as the experience of the program at that time might indicate; or such funds as are then available might be utilized to inaugurate the publication by an Asian seminary of the *Journal of Theology* as recommended at the 1956 Bangkok Theological Conference.

Translation and Distribution of Books in Foreign Languages: It is recommended that the sum of $650,000 or thereabouts be spent for the translation and distribution of theological texts in foreign languages and the stimulation of original writing in the areas concerned.

The choice of titles might focus on the types recommended by Bishop Neill in Part I of the IMC African Survey, in which he advocated the production of:

> Simple commentaries on the Bible.
> Short books on single doctrines of the Christian faith.
> Short books on periods of Church history.
> Biographies of Christian leaders of all ages.

Two problems emerge: (1) the writing and/or editing of the basic text (presumably most often in English); and (2) accomplishing their translation into the foreign languages within a reasonably short period of time.

There are two approaches to the editing problem. The first emphasizes the need for a high degree of perfection and the second, a need for speed in completing the project. As Professor James Welch of Ibadan University College and others have pointed out, the African mind is concrete rather than speculative, and is more at home in Hebrew than in Greek modes of thought. Lacking the heritage of European culture, Africans sometimes find it difficult to appreciate the allusions and historical references made in theological texts originally written in European languages. Accordingly the suggestion is sometimes advanced that especially written texts interpreting Christian theology in the light of African beliefs about God, etc., should be prepared. Similar comments have been made concerning texts to be used in India and elsewhere abroad.

The difficulty here is that it apparently requires a number of years to persuade a theologian to write and complete such a text, as the experience to date of the Christian Students' Library in India indicates. It is believed that adapted texts would be desirable; but the pace of events in Africa, Asia and Latin America today is so rapid that considerably greater emphasis on speed of preparation is needed.

Once the English texts have been agreed upon, there arises the problem of translating them promptly. Here again the tendency of translators is to attempt to achieve a high degree of perfection, which is a commendable policy when time is not of the essence. The record to date of the Nanking Theological Seminary translation project indicates how difficult it is to achieve rapid progress along these lines. On the other hand, the truly remarkable success of Franklin Publications, Inc., in promoting the publication in Islamic countries of translations of a considerable number of nontheological books shows what can be done when the translation and production of texts is placed in the hands of experts in the publishing field rather than missionaries. The "crash program" which Dr. Harold Bosley and others have been calling for is believed to be warranted.

With respect to the cost of translating texts into foreign languages the rates for translation, checking and revision, combined, paid by existing organizations with translation programs, such as Franklin Publications and the ministries of education in the various countries, are of the following general order for a book of 100,000 words: Persian, $700; Bengali, $600; Urdu, $500; Indonesian, $800; and Arabic, $1,300. The experience of the regional committees sponsoring the translation of the books in the Christian Students' Library series into the Indian vernaculars has been that such translations cost on the average $200–300 per title. On the other hand, the cost of translating theological texts into the three Latin languages of importance to the seminaries (French, Spanish and Portuguese) might amount to $2,000–3,000 per text. Thus it would appear as a rough guide that $1,000 might be allowed as an average cost of translating each text into a foreign language.

It is believed that the task of translation should be entrusted to the best qualified translators available, and not necessarily to seminary professors alone. The administrative problem of arranging for these translations might be simplified, however, if one organization or institution in each language area were entrusted with the responsibility of coordinating the efforts of others to complete such translations within a specified period of time. In India, for example, it would seem logical that either the National Christian Council or the United Theological College at Bangalore, where the Christian Students' Library project is being conducted, would be a logical headquarters to supervise an over-all translation program in that country.

To the editing and translation costs there must be added the printing expenses for each title. Contrary to the suggestions made above with respect to the advisability of printing English texts in the United States and/or Great Britain, it is believed that it would be advantageous for the TEC to have its translated texts printed and distributed by publishers in Africa, Asia and Latin America producing and distributing books written in those foreign languages. It is said to be quite as simple to print a book in Tamil, for example, as it is in English; and the cost of printing such a book in Tamil would be much lower in southern India than it would be in the United States. A text in English which costs $1.25 to print in New York City costs approximately as follows to print in the local language used in the following leading cities overseas: Teheran, 30¢; Cairo, 35¢; Lahore, 40¢; Djakarta, 65¢. The cost of printing texts in ideographic scripts such as Chinese, Japanese and Korean might run a good bit higher than in the case of the alphabetically written languages. Thus an average of 75¢ as the printing cost per book would appear to be a conservative estimate to use in Africa, Asia and Latin America, including the major publishing centers of Manila, Hongkong and Toyko. The printing of 2,000 copies of a book at 75¢ a copy would cost approximately $1,500. Thus the total cost of translating and printing such a text would on the average amount to $2,500 per title. If $65,000 were allotted for each of the eight foreign languages of major importance to seminaries as listed in chapter 10, and if $2,500 were spent in the translating, editing and printing of each title, this would enable 26 titles to be produced in each of these languages. This would seem to be an adequate number to aim at achieving during a five-year program.

The texts which might be translated into the foreign languages would not only be of assistance to the regional theological schools but also to many of the estimated 325 Bible schools overseas. In addition, surplus copies could have an important value in enabling the Christian message to be brought to the intellectual leaders in the underdeveloped countries, particularly those persons who are not already Christians. The costs of such a program are high, and because of this fact it has hitherto not been possible for individual mission boards and interboard agencies to make much progress along these lines. Progress could be made on a united basis as outlined above.

D. UNDERWRITING THE COST

It has already been noted in this Survey that the total of the contributions made by the eight leading foreign mission boards in the United States in support of theological education in the younger church areas currently amounts to approximately $1,926,000 in a typical year.

It has been suggested that if significant progress is to be made in the upgrading of theological education overseas, a program would require a minimum expenditure during a five-year period of an additional $4,000,000 over and above that which is now being spent by the boards each year for this purpose. One way in which this $4,000,000 might be raised would be if a donor were to contribute $2,000,000 toward this project on the understanding that the eight leading boards would match this sum dollar for dollar with grants and/or pledges to the IMC totaling $2,000,000 over a five-year period.

TABLE 185. SUGGESTED CONTRIBUTIONS OF EIGHT LEADING MISSION BOARDS

| Denomination | Suggested Annual Contributions | | Present % of Expenditure[a] Devoted to Theological Education | Total of Five Years' Contributions |
	Amount	% of Expenditure[a]		
Methodists	$150,000	1.24	6	$750,000
Presbyterians USA	100,000	1.24	4	500,000
American Baptists	35,000	1.27	5	175,000
United Lutherans	20,000	.78	10	100,000
Congregational	30,000	1.29	6	150,000
Protestant Episcopal	20,000	.87	11	100,000
Disciples	30,000	1.35	6	150,000
Evangelical and Reformed	15,000	1.39	2	75,000
	$400,000	1.14	5.8	$2,000,000

NOTE: [a] As a percentage of this denomination's foreign missions budget as presented in chapter 16 of this Survey.

The question arises, could the boards afford to contribute $2,000,000 within this period of time? It is believed that they could do so without difficulty, and that the raising of these funds would not necessarily oblige them to curtail their other activities or even to reduce the number of their personnel in the field. The data in Table 185 indicates the basis for this belief.

In this table it will be noted that six of the eight boards would be requested to contribute approximately 1.25% of their current annual income for five years. The other two boards (United Lutheran and Protestant Episcopal) would be asked to contribute roughly .82% each year, or only two-thirds as much as the other six. The reason is that these two boards already are contributing 10% and 11% of their budgets for theological education overseas. Even if all eight boards were to agree to make the contributions suggested, the percentage of their combined budgets devoted to theological education would still be less than 7% (i.e., 6.94%).

It is believed that, like most philanthropic foundations, the mission boards are often immune to appeals for action when such requests are amorphous in structure and only hortatory in essence.

It is recommended that the boards should be requested by the IMC to contribute the specific dollar sums mentioned in the table above. When making their contributions and pledges to the IMC the boards should be asked to certify that the total of their regular annual contributions (other than those to the IMC) in support of theological education overseas during the five-year period 1958–62 would be no lower than they were in 1956 or 1957.

Other foreign mission boards in the USA and elsewhere (in addition to the eight leading boards) should be invited to contribute to the work of the TEC. If a board did not wish to contribute to the support of seminaries receiving support from other boards, it might designate its contributions solely for the Texts Program—which should be of benefit to all seminaries impartially.

During the past decade the great majority of the mission boards have seldom if ever been more prosperous than they are now. In every case (except that of the American Baptists) the suggested annual contributions of the individual eight boards to the IMC would amount to only a fraction of the average annual increases in their income during the years 1949–56 as shown in Table 186.

TABLE 186. TOTAL INCOME OF EIGHT FOREIGN MISSION BOARDS (1949–56)[a]
(In Millions of Dollars)

Denomination[b]	1949	1950	1951	1952	1953	1954	1955	1956	Increase 1956 vs. 1949 $	%	Average Per Year
Methodist	6.9	8.4	9.9	9.5	9.7	11.2	12.9	12.0	5.1	74	0.7
Presbyterian USA	5.6	5.8	6.6	5.9	6.1	6.6	8.0	8.6	3.0	54	0.4
American Baptist	2.4	2.0	1.9	2.2	2.4	2.4	2.4	2.7	0.3	13	0.04
United Lutheran	1.4	1.7	1.9	2.0	2.2	2.3	2.1	2.8	1.4	100	0.2
Congregational	1.5	1.5	1.7	1.7	1.7	1.8	2.0	2.0	0.5	33	0.1
Protestant Episcopal[c]	1.2	1.9	2.2	1.9	2.1	2.2	2.4	2.5	1.3	108	0.2
Disciples	0.7	0.7	0.8	0.8[d]	0.8[d]	1.0	1.1	1.2	0.5	71	0.1
Evangelical & Reformed	0.6	0.8	0.7	0.7	0.9	1.0	1.0	1.0	0.4	67	0.1
	20.3	22.8	25.7	24.7	25.9	28.5	31.9	32.8	12.5	62	1.8

NOTES: [a] Source: Annual Reports of DFM.
[b] Figures include the income of women's divisions, societies, etc., of each denomination's board.
[c] Expenditures; income figures not reported by DFM.
[d] Figures from previous year's report.

It is believed that the income of the individual boards in 1957 was increased over 1956 in some cases by at least the same amount as the average annual increase experienced by them in the years 1949–56. The Presbyterians USA, for example, adopted in November 1956 a budget of $9,112,398 for overseas missionary work in 1957, the largest budget in the Board's 120-year history. The annual budget adopted in March 1957 by the American Board of Commissioners for Foreign Missions (Congregational Church) amounted to $2,348,771 (or $231,904 over that of 1956): this was the largest in the organization's 150-year history. The United Lutherans are asking their members to "double their contributions in 1958 for its world-wide work," an increase from $7,633,600 in 1957 to $15,000,000 in 1958, with an increase of $1,205,-000 for foreign missions in 1958. The success of the Methodists' "Bishops Appeal for Korea" in 1954 in raising $1,653,000 for this special additional project gives some indication of what the denominations and boards can accomplish when they are so minded.

It would appear that a major criticism which might be made of the tentative proposals as outlined in this Survey is that they are too small in scope, particularly with reference to the approximately $2,700,000 which might be allocated for institutional grants to individual seminaries. If as many as 20 seminaries overseas were designated as key institutions, this would result in an average of only $135,000 being available for institutional grants to each. By contrast, if the Southern Baptists can contribute $450,000 for the construction of one building for their seminary in Buenos Aires, this indicates the comparatively modest dimensions of the program suggested above.

No opportunity should be missed to induce the boards to maintain and increase the level of their total support for theological education at the same or higher levels after the initial five-year program (1958–62) of the TEC has been completed. An additional objective would be to obtain a continuation of the boards' grants for the work of the TEC after 1962 if this should seem desirable at that time. Such grants to the TEC might well be needed to finance a continuation of the proposed sending of European and American professors to serve on the faculties of the 20 key seminaries overseas.

A part of the effort to secure additional grants from mission boards might involve the obtaining of reports from the seminaries concerning the accomplishments made possible as a result of the support they had received from the TEC. The use of movies or photographs depicting the activities of the theological schools overseas might also be helpful in promoting an awareness of their needs.

The Protestant, Roman Catholic and Eastern Churches each have much to learn from the experience and successes of the others. The emphasis placed by the Vatican in recent decades on creating regional major seminaries is worth noting, and it is hoped that the recommended support of 20 key theological schools by the TEC may achieve comparable results. In some respects the creation of the TEC might be considered as constituting a counterpart within Protestantism of the Sacred Congregation of Seminaries and Universities within the Roman Catholic Church (in so far as the activities of the latter pertain to the operation of the major seminaries of that Church which are located in Africa, Asia and Latin America). There would, however, be this significant difference between the two organizations. The activities of the Seminaries Congregation in training men for the priesthood are limited in one respect to the definitions of the Roman Catholic faith as formulated by the Supreme Sacred Congregation of the Holy Office. The IMC has no similar power to influence the beliefs of Protestant denominations; nor would it wish to obtain such power (assuming this were possible, which it is not). But the TEC would have the opportunity of going beyond what up to now has been the essentially passive role of the Seminaries Congregation. The TEC would be concerned primarily with the fostering of new developments in theological education rather than simply the maintenance of accepted norms.

In the event that the Roman Catholic or any of the Eastern Churches desired to purchase at cost prices theological texts which had been written or translated under the auspices of the TEC, the latter, if it wished, could accommodate such requests and thereby help to strengthen in a very small yet concrete way the friendly ties which already exist between the various branches of Christianity.

If the ecumenical movement is ever to become something more than a primarily intra-Protestant activity, a greater initial measure of progress toward unity among the three major branches of Christianity might be achieved if the Protestant Churches were to take the initiative in making definite offers to the Roman Catholic and Eastern Churches to cooperate with them in specific projects of a religious nature designed to achieve the common good. Such offers—even in the instance of modest ventures, such as joint translations or preparations of new theological texts, or an occasional temporary exchange of faculty personnel, etc.—might not meet with encouraging responses at the outset. But the offers should be made, and the idea of cooperation among the seminaries of the Protestant, Roman Catholic and Eastern Churches should be planted wherever possible: for, indeed, the hope of the harvest is in the seedbed.

Christian Students' Library
Progress as of May, 1957

Published
1. S. Estborn: The Christian Doctrine of Salvation
2. A. T. Hanson: The Revelation of St. John the Divine
3. W. Scopes: The Parables of Jesus
4. H. C. Lefever: The History of the Reformation
5–6. Marcus Ward: The Outlines of Christian Theology, Vols. 1 & 2
7. Peter May: The Doctrine of the Trinity
8. A. F. Carleton: How Shall I Study the Psalms
9. A. T. Hanson: Jonah and Daniel
10. T. C. Witney and B. F. Price: Amos
11. A. B. Elliott: Hebrews

In Press
12. H. K. Moulton: Acts
13. G. Paul: St. Mark
14. W. B. Harris: I Corinthians

Manuscripts under Consideration or to Be Received
1. W. Stewart: Nature and Function of the Church
2. P. B. Harvey: Theology of the New Testament
3. P. D. Devanandan: Major Religions in India
4. E. E. White: An Introduction to the Study of Indian Music
5. E. Sambayya: Introduction to Moral Theology
6. L. M. Schiff: Christian in Society

Other Manuscripts in Preparation
1. M. H. Harrison: History of the Hebrew
2. S. Thoburn: Introduction to Old Testament (Revision of a MS by C. Keller)
3. D. H. Mason: Old Testament Prophets (Revision of a book by W. Hazen)
4. A. E. Inbanathan: Isaiah 1–39
5. D. Christudas: The Inter-Testamental Period
6. J. Reid Graham: The Life and Teaching of Jesus
7. R. Tauscher: Romans
8. J. E. L. Newbigin: Eschatology
9. W. W. Winfield: Atonement
10. J. R. Chandran: Outlines of Church History
11. C. B. Firth: History of Christianity in India
12. P. D. Devanandan: Hinduism
13. M. L. Dolbeer: Pastoral Psychology
14. C. Hargreaves: Miracles of Jesus

Additional Titles Accepted by Authors
1. M. H. Harrison: Theology of the Old Testament
2. A. B. Masillamony: Eighth Century Prophets
3. D. T. Niles: Psalms
4. H. K. Moulton: Introduction to the New Testament
5. R. D. Immanuel: St. Luke
6. F. Muliyil: Teaching of Greek in Asia
7. V. P. Thomas: The Person of Christ
8. Peter de D. May: The Doctrine of the Holy Spirit
9. S. W. Sawarimuthu: Gospel and Bhakti
10. L. M. Schiff: The Christian in Society
11. C. Arangaden: Christian Social Ethics
12. J. R. Chandran: Christian Ethics
13. P. D. Devanandan: Primitive Religion
14. W. G. Mulligan: Theism
15. T. S. Garrett: A Handbook of Worship
16. T. Sitther: Homiletics
17. W. Scopes: Homiletics
18. V. T. Kurien: Pastoralia, Part I—The Minister of the Word and Sacraments
19. M. H. Harper: Pastoralia, Part II—Shepherds and Stewards
20. W. Perston: Fourth Gospel (work suspended)

Christian Students' Library
Progress as of May, 1957

Additional Titles Accepted by Authors (Cont'd.)
21. A. T. Hanson: Genesis
22. B. F. Price: Exodus
23. Miss E. L. Wood: Jeremiah
24. W. B. Harris: Romans
25. W. Q. Lash: The Christian Doctrine of Prayer
26. A. M. Hollis: Holy Spirit
27. C. E. Abraham: History of Christianity in India
28. D. Chellappa and Sister Gertrude: Selections from Basic Christian Documents
29. M. M. Thomas and J. R. Chandran: History of the Ecumenical Movement
30. R. D. Paul and Victor Koilpillai: Christian Biographies
31. P. David: Hinduism
32. C. Muelder: Islam
33. K. W. Anand: Islam in India
34. J. D. Brown: Islam in Pakistan
35. A. E. Frederick: Modern Religious Movements in India

Titles not yet Accepted
1. I Samuel
2. Pastoral Epistles
3. I Peter
4. Life and Letters of St. Paul
5. The Christian Doctrine of God
6. History of the Church in the First Five Centuries
7. Modern Church History
8. Mahayana Buddhism
9. Hinayana Buddhism
10. The Background of Indian Thought
11. Religious Syncretism in Asia
12. Evangelism
13. Psychology
14. Law as Applicable to Indian Christians
15. Christian Marriage
16. A Book of Sermons Preached in India
17. A Book of Christian Biographies
18. An Introduction to Psychology
19. Law as Applicable to Indian Christians
20. Christian Ministry to the Sick

APPENDIX A2

NANKING THEOLOGICAL SEMINARY—LITERATURE PROGRAM: "THE CHRISTIAN CLASSICS LIBRARY"
FIRST SERIES—CLASSICS OF EARLY CHRISTIANITY—AS OF MAY 1957

Title	Author	Contents	Status
1. The Sub-Apostolic Age	Prof. Cyril Richardson	Apostolic Fathers, Austin Martyr, etc.	MS in Nanking
2. The Later Ante-Nicene Period	Prof. Massey Shepherd	Irenaeus, Hippolytus, Cyprian, Lachtantius	Translation just begun
3. Tertullian	Prof. Marvin M. Deems		MS in Nanking
4. The Christian School of Alexandria	Prof. Albert C. Outler	Clement and Origen	Not begun yet
5. Eusebius	Prof. Paul Schubert	Ecclesiastical History	MS in Nanking
6. Other Historical and Biographical Material	Roman Catholic Scholars	Lives of Anthony, Pachomius, St. Martin, Lausiac History, etc.	Not begun
7. The Arian Controversy	Prof. Robert P. Casey	Athanasius, His Opponents and Successors	Some MS in Nanking
8. The Eastern Church	Prof. G. P. Fedotov	Gregory of Nyassa, Dionysius, Maxim the Confessor, John of Damascus	Most MS in hand
9. Augustine, Jerome	Prof. E. R. Hardy, Jr.	Confessions, Letters of Jerome, Life of St. Hilarion, etc.	MS in Nanking
10. Augustine	Roman Catholic Scholars	Further Works	Not begun
11–12. Augustine: City of God	Prof. F. K. Loetscher		MS in Nanking
13. The Latin Church	Prof. E. R. Hardy, Jr.	Ambrose, Leo, Gregory, etc.	MS in hand
14. Mediaeval Thought	Rev. W. Norman Pittenger	Boethius, Anselm, Abailard, etc.	Most MS in hand
15–17. Thomas Aquinas	Roman Catholic Scholars		Not begun
18. Mediaeval Devotion	Prof. Douglas V. Steere	(1) Thomas À Kempis	Translated
		(2) Little Flowers	MS in Nanking
		(3) St. Bernard's De Consideratione	Not yet transl.
19. Devotional Anthology	Prof. Douglas V. Steere	Eckhart, Tauler, etc.	Not begun
20. Patristic and Mediaeval Sermons	Prof. Ray C. Petry	(See Petry's *No Uncertain Sound*)	MS in hand

APPENDIX A2 (Cont'd.)

NANKING THEOLOGICAL SEMINARY—LITERATURE PROGRAM: "THE CHRISTIAN CLASSICS LIBRARY"
SECOND SERIES—CLASSICS OF PROTESTANT CHRISTIANITY—AS OF MAY 1957

Title	Author	Contents	Status
1. The Late Middle Ages	Prof. M. Spinka	Huss, Wyclif, etc.	Not begun
2. Luther and Melancthon	Pres. Abdel Ross Wentz		Larger part of
3. " " "	" " " "		MS in hand
4. Calvin	Prof. J. T. McNeill		Published
5. "	" " " "		Nearly ready
6. "	" " " "		MS in hand
7. The Christian Humanist	Prof. C. R. Thompson	Erasmus, etc.	Not begun
8. The Radical Reformation	Prof. R. H. Bainton	Anabaptist, Mennonite, etc., thought of the Reformation Period	Not begun
9. The Quakers	Prof. Henry Cadbury	Fox's Journal, etc.	Not begun
10. Anglican Thought	Rev. C. W. Lowry	Hooker, etc.	Not begun
11. British Presbyterianism and Puritanism	Prof. W. S. Hudson	Knox, Baxter, Milton, etc.	Parts of MS in hand
12. 17th and 18th Century Rationalism	Prof. George Thomas	Descartes, Locke, Tindal, Butler, Hume, Kant	MS mostly in hand
13. 18th and 19th Century Idealism	Prof. E. S. Brightman	Berkeley, Kant, Hegel	MS partly finished
14. "	" " " "	Lotze, Emerson, Bowne, Royce, etc.	"
15. Pietism and Devotional Literature	Prof. Douglas V. Steere	Boehme, Spener, Zinzendorf, Arndt, Law, etc.	Not begun
16. John Wesley	Pres. Umphrey Lee	Journal, etc.	Published
17. Jonathan Edwards	Prof. J. Haroutunian		MS in hand
18. Schleiermacher	Prof. William Pauck	The Christian Faith	Not begun
19. Ritschl and Harnack	Prof. Paul Lehmann		R not begun H tr. in Nanking
20. John Henry Newman	Prof. E. R. Hardy, Jr.		MS in hand
21. The Romantic Movement	Prof. Walter M. Horton	Coleridge, Martineau, Bushnell	Just a beginning
22. 19th Century Social Christianity	Dean W. G. Muelder	Rauschenbusch	Published
23. "	" " " "	Troeltsch: Social Teachings	MS in hand
24. Kirkegaard	Prof. Karl Loewith		Tr. proceeding
25. Protestant Sermons	Prof. G. W. Stafford, ed.		Not begun
26. Confessions, Catechisms, and Church Councils	Prof. J. H. Nichols, ed.		Published

NANKING THEOLOGICAL SEMINARY—LITERATURE PROGRAM: "THE CHRISTIAN CLASSICS LIBRARY"
THIRD SERIES—MODERN WORKS—AS OF MAY 1957

Title	Author	Contents	Status
1. Barth and Brunner	Prof. David E. Roberts, ed.		Not begun
2. The Theology of Friedrich von Hugel	Pres. H. P. Van Dusen, ed.		Not begun
3. Recent Eastern Thought: Berdyaev	Prof. Matthew Spinka, ed.		Not begun
4. F. R. Tennant	Prof. E. Jerome Johanson, ed.		Not begun
5. William Temple	Rev. Charles W. Lowry, ed.		Published
6. Contemporary Social Theory	No editor assigned	Oxford Conference Reports, etc.	Not begun
7. Documents of Protestant Missions	Prof. K. S. Latourette, ed.		Not begun
8. Nature and Destiny of Man	Reinhold Niebuhr		MS in hand

World Christian Books
Progress as of September 30, 1958 of First Series of 24 Titles in English Published in Great Britain

No.	Title	Author	Publ. Date	Copies Sold
1.	The Christians' God	Stephen Neill	10/54	27,201
2.	Christian Giving	V. S. Azariah	10/54	22,906
3.	Mark's Witness to Jesus Christ	E. Lohse	2/55	16,878
4.	Christianity and Science	Charles E. Raven	2/55	20,352
5.	The Christian as Citizen	John C. Bennett	6/55	15,730
6.	The Christian Character	Stephen Neill	6/55	17,577
7.	Reading the Bible Today	D. T. Niles	10/55	15,892
8.	John's Witness to Jesus	George Appleton	10/55	12,270
9.	From Brahma to Christ	L. Tilak	2/56	10,281
10.	Beginning from Jerusalem	John Foster	2/56	11,507
11.	Jesus and His People	Paul Minear	5/56	8,242
12.	Did Jesus Rise from the Dead?	James Martin	5/56	10,275
13.	The Cross is Heaven	A. J. Appasamy	11/56	8,011
14.	Who is Jesus Christ?	Stephen Neill	11/56	8,634
15.	A Letter of Wise Counsel	E. A. Maycock	1/57	5,774
16.	Religious Liberty	Giovanni Miegge	1/57	6,048
17.	Living with the Gospel	D. T. Niles	5/57	5,739
18.	Livingstone in Africa	Cecil Northcott	5/57	5,901
19.	Christ's Messengers	C. F. D. Moule	9/57	5,346
20.	Japanese Witnesses for Christ	Norimichi Ebizawa	9/57	4,239
21.	One Lord, One Church	J. Robert Nelson	1/58	3,971
22.	The People of God in the Old Testament	H. J. Kraus	1/58	3,790
23.	Matthew's Witness to Jesus Christ	H. N. Ridderbos	4/58	3,725
24.	The Psalms as Christian Praise	R. B. Y. Scott	4/58	4,045
				254,334

APPENDIX B

THEOLOGICAL SCHOOLS IN AFRICA, ASIA AND LATIN AMERICA MAINTAINED BY THE SOUTHERN BAPTIST CONVENTION (1958)

Area	Name	Location	Full-Time Faculty	Theol. Students
Africa				
Nigeria	Nigerian Baptist Theological Seminary	Ogbomosho	10[a]	100[b]
Southern Rhodesia	African Baptist Theological Seminary	Gwelo	2	30
Southeast Asia				
Thailand	Thailand Baptist Theological Center	Bangkok	2[a]	9[b]
Malaya	Malaya Baptist Theological Seminary	Penang	4[a]	12[b]
Indonesia	Baptist Theological Seminary of Indonesia	Semarang	3	15[b]
Philippines	Philippines Baptist Theological Seminary	Baguio	5[a]	18[b]
East Asia				
Japan	Seinan Gakuin University Theological Department	Fukuoka	5[a]	45[b]
Korea	Korea Baptist Seminary	Taejon	4[a]	90[b]
Formosa	Taiwan Baptist Theological Seminary	Taipeh	6	35[b]
Hongkong	Hongkong Baptist Theological Seminary	Hongkong	4[a]	30[b]
Latin America				
Mexico	Mexican Baptist Seminary	Torreón	5[a]	20[b]
Colombia	International Baptist Theological Seminary	Cali	3	11[b]
Brazil, North	North Brazil Baptist Theological Seminary	Recife	4	31[b]
Brazil, South	South Brazil Baptist Theological Seminary	Rio de Janeiro	4[a]	60[b]
Argentina	International Baptist Theological Seminary	Buenos Aires	6[a]	40[b]
Chile	Baptist Theological Seminary	Santiago	3	12[b]
Total: 16			70	558

NOTES: [a] Plus others teaching at lower level.
[b] Plus other students at a lower level of training.

The 1956 Annual of the Southern Baptist Convention states that there are 2,250 Southern Baptist churches overseas, of which 1,424 are self-supporting, employing a total of 130 missionary pastors and 1,541 local pastors.

In addition to the 16 theological schools listed above, the Southern Baptists are operating eight "institutes" at the preseminary or Bible school level (which are listed in chapter 9) plus two institutes in Africa (one at Kumasi, Ghana, and the other at Kaduna in Nigeria) and an institute at Davao City in the Philippines.

THE ESTABLISHMENT OF THE THEOLOGICAL EDUCATION FUND COMMITTEE

As mentioned in the foreword, the Assembly of the International Missionary Council which met at the University College of Ghana from December 28, 1957, to January 8, 1958, authorized the establishment of a Theological Education Fund and the appointment of a committee to administer its affairs. The following are excerpts from the minutes of the actions taken by the Assembly in this connection:

IV. The Assembly notes the following statement made ... regarding the administration of the Fund ... :

"It is recommended that the Council set up a 'Theological Education Fund Committee' of approximately 20 members charged with the responsibility of supervising the project. The membership of the Committee would include Protestant leaders of various denominations from both the younger and older church areas, as well as representatives of the mission boards contributing to the project. Two executives would be employed full-time by the Committee to administer the two main phases of the project, namely making grants to a few key seminaries and carrying out a Text Program.

"The Committee would:

"1. Select for individual institutional support those seminaries which on the basis of their strategic location, the excellence of their present work, and their plans for development, offer the greatest possibilities for qualitative growth in the future. It would pursue a policy of concentration by limiting its institutional grants to approximately twenty seminaries throughout the younger church areas, thereby endeavoring to build on strength rather than weakness. The main thrust of the program would, as far as practicable, be toward improving the level of scholarship at the institutions, rather than in defraying the cost of constructing new buildings at the seminaries, although grants for the latter purpose would not be precluded. The Committee would normally give preference to institutions receiving support from several denominations, having due regard to the facts of the situation in the country concerned. The Committee would not attempt to create new seminaries, and ordinarily would not place its major emphasis on attempts to unite existing institutions, desirable as such mergers may be. On the other hand, it would not be precluded from assisting certain new undertakings, such as the proposed Higher Theological Faculty in Asia, etc. It would also make grants only in response to carefully formulated requests carrying the full support of the governing body of the institution concerned.

"2. Spend approximately $1,000,000 in furtherance of the Text Program outlined in detail in the Survey. This Program would be designed to improve the condition of the libraries of theological schools generally which desire to participate in the project. It would also enable the translation of suitable theological texts into those foreign languages which are of major importance to the Protestant missionary enterprise."

V. For the further guidance of the Theological Education Fund Committee (hereafter referred to as the TEFC) the Assembly adopts the following supplementary statement of policy:

1. Grants should be designed to develop and strengthen indigenous theological education. They should stimulate local responsibility, encourage creative theological thinking and provide a higher standard of scholarship and training which is suited to the needs of the churches to be served.

2. The present resources of the Fund shall be designed to be used over a period of five years.

3. Grants from the Fund shall normally be made in the first instance on the basis of a five-year plan.

4. The phrase "in Asia, Africa and Latin America" shall not be interpreted as excluding church institutions otherwise qualified in such areas as the South or Southwest Pacific Islands, the British West Indies, Madagascar, etc.

5. Care should be taken to avoid making any institution dependent upon the Fund.

6. Every effort should be made to maintain liaison with the Board of Founders of Nanking Theological Seminary (New York), or other bodies with a similar program with a view to achieving reasonable coordination of program.

VI. The Assembly agrees to appoint a Theological Education Fund Committee of approximately twenty members, and to designate the Chairman thereof. The Assembly instructs the TEFC to administer the Fund in accordance with the principles stated. . . .

The list of the members of the Theological Education Fund Committee as it was constituted in the fall of 1958 was as follows:

Baëta, Christian G.	Senior Lecturer, University College of Ghana, Achimota
Bentley, Jonathan B.	Director, Overseas Department, National Council of the Protestant Episcopal Church, New York City
Carleton, Alford	Executive Vice President, American Board of Commissioners for Foreign Missions, Boston
Dougall, J.W.C.	General Secretary, Foreign Missions Committee, Church of Scotland, Edinburgh
French, Clara	Executive Secretary for Southeast Asia and China, Woman's Division of Christian Service, Board of Missions, The Methodist Church, New York City
Freytag, Walter	General Secretary, German Evangelical Missionary Council, Hamburg

Fry, Franklin C.	President, United Lutheran Church in America, New York City
Horton, Mrs. Douglas	Former Vice President, National Council of Churches (USA); Cambridge, Mass.
Kim, Helen	President, Ewha Woman's College, Seoul
Mackay, John A.	President, Princeton Theological Seminary, Princeton, New Jersey
Milford, T. R.	Master of the Temple (Church of England), London
Moraes, Benjamin	Former Moderator, Presbyterian Church of Brazil, Rio de Janeiro
Moses, David G.	Principal, Hislop College, Nagpur
Pope, Liston	Dean, Yale Divinity School, New Haven, Conn.
Rodrigues, Proculo	Bishop, United Church of Christ in the Philippines, Manila
Sitompul, Karimuda	Associate General Secretary, National Council of Churches of Indonesia; Pearadja Tarutung, Sumatra
Sly, Virgil A.	Executive Chairman, Division of World Missions, The United Christian Missionary Society (Disciples), Indianapolis, Indiana
Smith, Eugene L.	General Secretary, Division of World Missions, Board of Missions, The Methodist Church, New York City
Smith, John C.	Associate General Secretary, Commission on Ecumenical Mission and Relations, The United Presbyterian Church in the USA, New York City
Sundkler, Bengt G.M.	Professor of Missions and Church History, University of Upsala, Sweden
Thomson, James S.	Professor of Theology, McGill University, Montreal
Van Dusen, Henry P.	President, Union Theological Seminary, New York City
Willingham, Edward B.	General Secretary, American Baptist Foreign Missionary Society, New York City
Yuasa, Hachiro	President, Japan International Christian University, Tokyo

In addition to the 24 members of the Theological Education Fund Committee listed above, a place is being held open on the Committee for an additional member, to be selected, representing a church in Africa. On this basis a majority of the Committee of 25 are representatives of churches outside of the United States, with one-third of the members being citizens of countries located in Africa, Asia and Latin America. Approximately 12 different European and American denominations are represented on the Committee, with no one of them contributing more than three members. Among the ex officio members is the Chairman (and General Secretary-Elect) of the IMC, the Right Reverend J. E. Lesslie Newbigin, a Bishop of the Church of South India.

Serving under the Committee in the fall of 1958 were its Director, Dr. Charles W. Ranson (formerly General Secretary of the International Missionary Council) and its Associate Director, Dr. Charles W. Forman (Associate Professor of Missions at the Yale Divinity School).

ACKNOWLEDGMENTS AND
BIBLIOGRAPHY

The following bibliography is incomplete. It does not list most of the annual reports, bulletins, catalogues and leaflets issued by mission boards, seminaries, Christian literature societies, etc., which were consulted. The reason for this omission is that when the chapters of this Survey relating to the Protestant theological schools were written it was not intended that they should be published. Later when the manuscript was being revised for publication it was not practical to attempt to list more than the most important sources used. On the other hand, the bibliographies for chapters 12 through 15 (those relating to the Roman Catholic and Eastern Churches) are complete, in the sense that most of the sources relied upon in the text are listed.

The majority of the documents consulted are to be found in one or another of the libraries of the following institutions: New York Public Library, Missionary Research Library, Union Theological Seminary, Catholic University of America, Yale Divinity School and Fordham University. The remainder, principally Roman Catholic directories, were kindly loaned to the author for short periods of time by members of that Church.

The absence of footnotes in the text is regretted. There are several reasons for this. The first has already been noted—namely, that the original draft of the Protestant chapters was written for only a limited number of readers. Second, a considerable proportion of the information in the text was obtained in the course of interviews with a number of informants. Not all of the informants were in agreement on a given subject, and it has sometimes been necessary to select a middle ground between their statements: in these instances the footnotes, if used, would have necessarily had to include explanations as well. Third, a good deal of additional information was obtained in written correspondence. Some of this was directly with the author, but some information was supplied by informants in response to inquiries sent out by others at the author's request. Here again accurate footnotes would be cumbersome and would refer to material which is not available in library collections. Fourth, a number of informants supplied opinions and information of a nonconfidential nature, but with which they did not wish to be personally identified in the text.

Within the limits cited above, all sources which have been quoted have also been identified by name in the text, and the documents from which such quotations were taken are listed in the bibliography below. While the omission of footnotes may result in the text appearing to be less learned, it is hoped that by the same token it may thereby have been made more readable.

This Survey could not have been written without extensive assistance from many persons. A total of 107 informants kindly furnished information used in the chapters relating to the seminaries of the Protestant and Eastern Churches. Their names are listed below. Of this number, 97 were interviewed orally, and their names are starred. In addition, over a score of the individual members of the clergy of the Roman Catholic Church were helpful in providing information concerning the seminaries of their Church. To all of these informants the author would like to express his appreciation once again. Any comments included in the text which are not quotations directly or indirectly attributed to individual sources reflect the views of the author, and these opinions are not necessarily identical with those expressed by the informants.

Those names preceded by two stars in the list of informants denote experts who consented to read individual sections of the manuscript falling within their particular sphere of competence. As a result of their diligence and patience, a number of errors of fact and interpretation in the original manuscript were eliminated. The responsibility for any errors which may remain in the text should be attributed to the author alone. The author will welcome any criticism or corrections which readers may wish to send to him in care of the publisher.

Particular thanks are due to those informants who either wrote a number of letters soliciting information on the author's behalf, or who made available to him unpublished material they had personally assembled, including the returns from questionnaires they had previously sent out to others. Among these are Messrs. Dorman, Forman, Larson, Tobias and C. S. Smith. The last-named, the late Dr. C. Stanley Smith, was especially helpful, not only in connection with the seminaries in Southeast and East Asia (concerning which institutions he was the leading expert) but also those in Latin America, to which he had recently been devoting his time and study. Many other persons should be mentioned here and thanked by name, but space will not permit. The Director of the Theological Education Fund, Dr. Charles W. Ranson, was a constant source of help on many occasions: the degree to which he devoted his patience, wisdom and good humor to the author's problems along the way are much appreciated.

Especial thanks are also due to Miss Jytte B. Freuchen, the author's secretary, who typed the entire manuscript the equivalent of three times, totaling well over a million words of typescript. In addition she was of invaluable assistance in editing and conforming the text, and in preparing the bibliography, etc. Her patience with the seemingly endless number of revisions which were handed to her was matched only by the speed and accuracy with which she incorporated them into the text.

Finally the author would like to express his appreciation to Mrs. Evelyn Nethercott for the precision and artistry with which she prepared the maps to be found in this book; and to Miss Patricia G. Healy for her remarkably accurate work in proofreading the galleys and preparing the Index.

There follows a list of the individuals who kindly provided helpful information, together with the title of the principal position held by them at the time they furnished this assistance.

INFORMANTS

*ABRAHAM, C. E. Principal, Serampore College, Calcutta

*ALBAUGH, DANA Director, Overseas Department, American Baptist Foreign Mission Society, New York City

*ANDERSON, PAUL B. Associate Executive Secretary, International Committee, YMCA, New York City

*ANSPACH, P. P. Secretary, Board of Foreign Missions, United Lutheran Church, New York City

*ASKE, SIGURD Associate Secretary, Lutheran World Federation, Geneva

**ATIYA, AZIZ S. Director, Higher Institute of Coptic Studies, Cairo

*BADEAU, JOHN S. President, Near East Foundation, New York City

*BAËTA, CHRISTIAN G. Senior Lecturer, University College of Ghana, Achimota

*BAEZ-CAMARGO, GONZALO Professor of Christian Literature and Journalism, Union Theological Seminary, Mexico City

*BATES, M. SEARLE Professor of Missions, Union Theological Seminary, New York City

*BEACH, ROBERT F. Librarian, Union Theological Seminary, New York City

BENEDICTOS Greek Orthodox Patriarch of Jerusalem

*BENTLEY, JONATHAN B. Bishop, Director of Overseas Department, National Council, Protestant Episcopal Church, New York City

BILL, RENÉ H. Swiss Mission in South Africa, Pretoria, Transvaal.

*BIRKELI, FRIDTJOV Director, Department of World Missions, Lutheran World Federation, Geneva

*BRANSCOMB, HARVIE B. Chancellor, Vanderbilt University, Nashville

**BRIDGEMAN, CHARLES T. Vicar, Trinity Church, New York City

*BRIDSTON, KEITH R. Secretary of Department on Faith and Order, World Council of Churches, Geneva

*BRUMBAUGH, THOBURN T. Administrative Secretary for East Asia, Methodist Division of World Missions, New York City

*BURGER, FRANCIS Traveling Secretary, Student Christian Association of South Africa, Stellenbosch

**CARLETON, ALFORD Executive Vice President, American Board of Commissioners for Foreign Missions, Boston

**CARPENTER, GEORGE Secretary, International Missionary Council, New York City

**CARTWRIGHT, FRANK T. Executive Secretary, Board of Founders of Nanking Theological Seminary, New York City

*CHANDRAN, J. RUSSELL Principal, United Theological College, Bangalore

*DAGADU, PETER K. Secretary, Christian Council of Ghana, Accra

**DECKER, JOHN W. Secretary, International Missionary Council, New York City

*DODDS, J. LEROY Secretary for India, Board of Foreign Missions, Presbyterian Church USA, New York City

DORMAN, HARRY G., JR. Executive Secretary, Near East Christian Council, Beirut, Lebanon

*ECKLUND, HELEN M. Associate Staff Secretary, Committee on Cooperation in Latin America, Division of Foreign Missions, National Council of Churches (USA), New York City

EDDY, G. THACKRAY Chairman, The Methodist Church, Accra, Ghana

*ELLIS, JAMES E. Administrative Secretary, Latin American Fields, Methodist Division of World Missions, New York City

*ERB, EARL S. Executive Secretary, Board of Foreign Missions, United Lutheran Church, New York City

*FENN, WILLIAM P. Executive Secretary, United Board for Christian Higher Education in Asia, New York City

**FORMAN, CHARLES W. Associate Director, Theological Education Fund, International Missionary Council, New York City

*FREYTAG, WALTER General Secretary, German Evangelical Missionary Council, Hamburg

FROST, STANLEY B. Dean, Faculty of Divinity, McGill University, Montreal

*GERICKE, J. S. Vice Chancellor, University of Stellenbosch, Union of South Africa

*GOTWALD, LUTHER Executive Secretary, Division of Foreign Missions, National Council of Churches (USA), New York City

**GRIGORIOS, PAULOS BEHNAM Archbishop of Mosul and Baghdad, Syrian Orthodox Church, Mosul, Iraq

**HAHN, YOUNG K. Dean, Yonsei University, Seoul

*HASTINGS, SELVIN URIAH Moravian Church in Jamaica, The West Indies

*HOWELLS, ADELAKUN W. Bishop, Church of the Province of West Africa (Anglican), Lagos, Nigeria

*JAMES Metropolitan of Melita; Representative of the Ecumenical Patriarch of Constantinople to the World Council of Churches, Geneva

*JOHNSON, KATHERINE Secretary, Interboard Committee for Christian Work in Japan, New York City

*JOHNSON, WARREN C. Secretary, Board of Foreign Missions, United Lutheran Church, New York City

*JONES, FRANCIS P. Secretary, Literature Program, Board of Founders of Nanking Theological Seminary, New York City

*JONES, TRACEY K. Executive Secretary for Southeast Asia and China, Methodist Division of World Missions, New York City

*KIM, HELEN President, Ewha Woman's University, Seoul

*KRAELING, CARL H. Director, The Oriental Institute, University of Chicago

*LARSON, WILBUR Secretary for Latin America, American Baptist Home Mission Society, New York City

**LATOURETTE, KENNETH S. Professor of Missions, emeritus, Yale Divinity School, New Haven

*LATUIHAMALLO, PETER D. former Rector, Djakarta Theological College, Djakarta

*Leber, Charles T. General Secretary, Commission on Ecumenical Mission and Relations, United Presbyterian Church USA, New York City

*Liggett, Thomas President, Evangelical Seminary of Puerto Rico, Rio Piedras

*Long, Charles H., Jr. Director, Yale-in-China Association, Kowloon, Hongkong

*Lorimer, John United Presbyterian Mission, Mansura, Egypt

Loutfi, Germanos Conseil supérieur de la Communauté grecque-orthodoxe égyptienne, Cairo

*McGill, Willis A. United Presbyterian Mission, Cairo

*Mackay, John A. President, Princeton Theological Seminary, Princeton, N.J.

*Manikam, Rajah B. Bishop of Tranquebar, Federation of Evangelical Lutheran Churches, India

Marantika, Simon General Secretary, National Council of Churches in Indonesia, Djakarta

**Mathews, James K. Associate General Secretary, Division of World Missions, Board of Missions, The Methodist Church, New York City

*Maxwell, Raymond E. Secretary for Orthodox Churches and Countries, World Council of Churches, Geneva

*Merwin, Wallace C. Executive Secretary, Far Eastern Joint Office, Division of Foreign Missions, National Council of Churches (USA), New York City

*Morgan, Barney Board of National Missions, Presbyterian Church USA, New York City

*Moses, David G. Principal, Hislop College, Nagpur, India

**Neill, Stephen C. Bishop, Church of England, London

*Nelson, J. Robert Dean, Vanderbilt Divinity School, Nashville

*Neudoerffer, J. Frederick Secretary, Board of Foreign Missions, United Lutheran Church, New York City

*Newbigin, J. Lesslie Bishop, Diocese of Madura and Ramnad, Church of South India, Tallakulam, Madurai

**Nida, Eugene A. Secretary, Translations Department, American Bible Society, New York City

*Nielsen, Eric W. Secretary, International Missionary Council, London

Nsubuga, D. K. Warden, Bishop Tucker Theological Seminary, Mukono, Kampala, Uganda

*Overton, Douglas Executive Director, Japan Society, New York City

*Philipos, Korah General Secretary, Syrian Orthodox Church of Malabar (Catholicate), Kottayam

*Pickens, Claude L. Assistant Secretary, Overseas Department, National Council, Protestant Episcopal Church, New York City

**Pope, Liston Dean, Yale Divinity School, New Haven

**Price, Frank W. Director, Missionary Research Library, New York City

**Ranson, Charles W. Director, Theological Education Fund, International Missionary Council, New York City

*Rolander, Oscar Secretary, National Lutheran Council, New York City

*Ross, Emory Chairman, African-American Institute, New York City

*RYCROFT, W. STANLEY Secretary for Latin America, Board of Foreign Missions, Presbyterian Church USA, New York City

*SAHAI, GEORGE S. Principal, Leonard Theological College, Jabalpur, India

SARAFIAN, RICHARD Episcopal Theological Seminary, Cambridge, Massachusetts

*SCOTT, ROLAND W. Executive Secretary, Joint Office for Southern Asia and the Near East, Division of Foreign Missions, National Council of Churches (USA), New York City

*SHACKLOCK, FLOYD Executive Secretary, Committee on World Literacy and Christian Literature, Division of Foreign Missions, National Council of Churches (USA), New York City

*SHAULL, RICHARD Dean, Presbyterian Theological Seminary of Campinas, São Paulo, Brazil

SHORT, FRANK Secretary, Conference of Missionary Societies in Great Britain and Ireland, London

**SIMON, K. MATHEW Director, The Theological School of the Holy Trinity, Addis Ababa

**SLY, VIRGIL A. Executive Chairman, Division of World Missions, United Christian Missionary Society (Disciples of Christ), Indianapolis, Indiana

**SMITH, C. STANLEY Field Representative in Southeast Asia, Board of Founders of Nanking Theological Seminary, New York City

**SMITH, DATUS C., JR. President, Franklin Publications, Inc., New York City

**SMITH, EUGENE L. General Secretary, Division of World Missions, Board of Missions, The Methodist Church, New York City

**SMITH, JOHN COVENTRY Associate General Secretary, Commission on Ecumenical Mission and Relations, United Presbyterian Church USA, New York City

*SMITH, MORTON Professor of Ancient History, Columbia University, New York City

SMITH, P. E. S. Home Mission Secretary, The Dutch Reformed Church Mission in South Africa, Cape Town

STANWAY, ALFRED Bishop, Diocese of Central Tanganyika (Anglican), Dodoura, Tanganyika

**TOBIAS, ROBERT Associate Executive Secretary, Council on Christian Unity, Disciples of Christ, Indianapolis

*TUCKER, THEODORE L. Executive Secretary, Africa Committee, Division of Foreign Missions, National Council of Churches (USA), New York City

**VAN DUSEN, HENRY P. President, Union Theological Seminary, New York City

*VISSER 'T HOOFT, W. A. General Secretary, World Council of Churches, Geneva

**WADDAMS, HERBERT M. General Secretary, Church of England Council on Foreign Relations, London

*WADE, EUSTACE H. Archdeacon of Durban City, Natal, South Africa

*WILLAND, PITT S. Episcopal Theological Seminary, Cambridge, Massachusetts

**WILLINGHAM, EDWARD B. General Secretary, American Baptist Foreign Mission Society, New York City

*WYSNER, GLORA M. Secretary, International Missionary Council, New York City

*YODER, HOWARD W. Staff Secretary, Committee on Cooperation in Latin America, Division of Foreign Missions, National Council of Churches (USA), New York City

In addition the author would like to express his appreciation for the information and helpful assistance which he received from over a score of individual members of the Roman Catholic hierarchy, secular clergy and of the following religious communities: the Capuchins, Carmelites, Claretians, Divine Word Fathers, Dominicans, Eudists, Franciscans, Holy Cross Fathers, Holy Ghost Fathers, Jesuits, Lazarists (Vincentians), Marists, Maryknoll Fathers, Oblates of Mary Immaculate, Redemptorists and Sulpicians.

The following is a list of the informants and principal documents cited in the various chapters.

PREFACE

Hailey, Lord, *An African Survey—A Study of Problems Arising in Africa South of the Sahara,* rev., Oxford University Press, London, 1957.

Index generalis 1954-55 (General Yearbook of Universities), Dunod, Paris, 1955.

Minerva—Jahrbuch der gelehrten Welt, Abteilung Universitäten und Fachhochschulen, 3 vols., Walter de Gruyter & Co., Berlin, 1952-56.

The World of Learning, 8th ed., Europa Publication Ltd., London, 1957.

World Survey of Education—Handbook of Educational Organization and Statistics, UNESCO, Paris, 1955.

Chapter 1. *Introduction*

Informants: Messrs. Decker, Gotwald and Price.

Beaver, R. Pierce, *The Evangelical Foreign Missions Association,* Missionary Research Library, New York City, April 1952.

Beaver, R. Pierce, *Theological Education in the Younger Churches—A Review of the Literature,* Commission on Cooperation in Latin America, New York City, 1953 (unpublished).

C.S.M.C. World Mission Map, Catholic Students' Mission Crusade, USA National Center, Cincinnati, Ohio.

The Commission (Southern Baptist World Journal), July 1958.

Directory of Foreign Mission Agencies, rev., Missionary Research Library, New York City, 1958.

Division of Foreign Missions Annual Reports 1955-57, National Council of Churches, New York City.

Latourette, Kenneth S., *A History of Christianity,* Harper & Brothers, New York City, 1953.

Mead, Frank S., *Handbook of Denominations in the United States,* rev., Abingdon Press, Nashville, Tenn., 1956.

Missionary Research Library Bulletins, vol. IV, No. 7; vol. V, Nos. 7 and 14; vol. VII, No. 9; vol. VIII, Nos. 7 and 10; vol. IX, No. 4; vol. IX, No. 10.
Southern Baptist Convention Annuals, 1955 and 1956.
World Christian Handbook, World Dominion Press, London, 1957.

Chapter 2. *Africa*

Informants: North Africa—Messrs. Badeau, Lorimer and McGill.
    East Africa—Messrs. Carpenter, Erb, Forman, Nsubuga and Stanway.
    West Africa—Messrs. Aske, Baëta, Bentley, Dagadu, Eddy, Forman, Frost, Howells, Neill and Rolander.
    Latin Africa—Messrs. Albaugh, Aske, Bates, Birkeli, Forman, Leber, Ranson, Rolander, Ross, Sly and Tucker.
    Southern Africa—Messrs. Bill, Branscomb, Burger, Carleton, Gericke, Nielsen, Short, E. L. Smith, P. E. S. Smith and Wade.

Bouffard, Adrien, *Perspectives sur le monde,* L'Union missionnaire du clergé, Quebec, 1957.
Brown, David, "Theological Training in the Southern Sudan," *Truly Called,* Douglas Webster, ed., The Highway Press, London, 1954.
The Church in Changing Africa—Report of the All-Africa Church Conference, Ibadan, Nigeria, January 10–19, 1958, International Missionary Council, New York City, 1958.
Commonwealth Universities Yearbook 1958, The Association of Universities of the British Commonwealth, London.
Cunningham, Robert J., *A Thumbnail Sketch of North and Northeast Africa—A Contemporary Survey of the Peoples and the Church,* World Horizon Reports, No. 16, 1956.
Ewing, J. Franklin, ed., *Local Leadership in Mission Lands*—Proceedings of the Fordham University Conference of Mission Specialists, Second Annual Meeting, January 23–24, 1954, Fordham University Press, New York City, 1954.
Fueter, Paul D., "The All-African Lutheran Conference, Marangu," *International Review of Missions,* July 1956.
Gerdener, G. B. A., *Recent Developments in the South African Mission Field,* Marshall, Morgan & Scott, London, 1958.
God's Kingdom in Multi-Racial South Africa—A Report on the Inter-Racial Conference of Church Leaders, Johannesburg, 7 to 10 December, 1954, South African Institute of Race Relations, Johannesburg, 1955.
Gunther, John, *Inside Africa,* Harper & Brothers, New York City, 1953.
Hailey, Lord, *An African Survey—A Study of Problems Arising in Africa South of the Sahara,* rev., Oxford University Press, London, 1957.
Harney, Martin P., S.J., *The Jesuits in History,* The America Press, New York City, 1941.
Horner, Norman A., *Protestant and Roman Catholic Missions among the Bantu of Cameroun—A Comparative Study,* a doctoral dissertation presented in 1956 to the Hartford Seminary Foundation, Hartford, Conn. (unpublished, used with permission).
Marangu Conference Proceedings, Lutheran World Federation, Geneva, 1956.
Paton, David M., *Church and Race in South Africa,* SCM Press Ltd., London, 1958.

Report on the First Consultative Conference on the Training of the Ministry in Africa, Leopoldville, 1956 (mimeographed).

Report of the Second Consultative Conference on the Training of the Ministry in Africa, Douala,
1958 (mimeographed).

Report of Visitation to University College, Ibadan, 1957, Ibadan University Press, 1957.

Resources and Needs for Training Facilities for Africans in British Africa, Ethiopia and Liberia,
Ruth Sloan Associates, Inc., Washington, D.C., September 30, 1955.

Richter, Julius, *A History of the Protestant Missions in the Near East,* Fleming H. Revell
Co., New York City, 1910.

Survey of the Training of the Ministry in Africa, Part I (East and West Africa) 1950, Part II
(Latin Africa) and Part III (Southern Africa) 1954, International Missionary Council,
London and New York.

Survey of the Training of the Ministry in Madagascar, International Missionary Council,
London and New York, 1957.

Taylor, John V., lecture given at the Ecumenical Institute, Bossey, Switzerland in 1955
concerning Bishop Tucker College (mimeographed).

Trimingham, J. Spencer, *The Christian Church in Post-War Sudan,* World Dominion Press,
London, 1949 (Post-War Survey Series No. 4).

Wysner, Glora, comment on Carpenter, George, "The Role of Christianity and Islam in
Contemporary Africa," *Africa Today* (C. Grove Haines, ed.), Johns Hopkins Press,
Baltimore, 1955.

Chapter 3. *The Middle East*

Informants: Messrs. Badeau, Carleton, Dodds, Scott, C. S. Smith and Willand.

Addison, James T., *The Christian Approach to the Moslem,* Columbia University Press, New
York City, 1942.

Clyde, Walter R., "The Near East School of Theology," *Western Watch,* vol. IX, No. 3,
September 15, 1958, Western Theological Seminary, Pittsburgh, Pa.

Richter, Julius, *A History of Protestant Missions in the Near East,* Fleming H. Revell Co.,
New York City, 1910.

Chapter 4. *Southern Asia*

Informants: Messrs. Abraham, Chandran, Dodds, Gotwald, Manikam, Mathews, Moses,
          Nelson, Neudoerffer, Newbigin, Pickens, Ranson, Sahai, Scott and E. L.
          Smith.

Beaver, R. Pierce, *Some Observations on a Visit to Religious Centers in India and Other Parts of
Asia from December 6, 1956 to March 24, 1957*—A Report to the Federated Theological
Faculty and the Committee on the Haskell and Barrows Lectures, Chicago, 1957.

Harrison, M. H., *After Ten Years—A Report on Theological Education in India,* The Board of Theological Education, National Christian Council of India, 1957.

Minutes of a Meeting of the L. Th. Commission in the Hindi Area, held at Bareilly, U.P., August 12–13, 1957, National Christian Council of India, 1957.

Ranson, Charles W., *The Christian Ministry in India,* United Society for Christian Literature, Lutterworth Press, London, 1945–46.

Stewart, William, "Training the Ministry in South and Southeast Asia," *International Review of Missions,* October 1956.

Chapter 5. *Southeast Asia*

Informants: Messrs. Bentley, Bridston, Cartwright, Decker, Freytag, T. K. Jones, Latuihamallo, Marantika, Merwin, Pope, Short and C. S. Smith.

Anderson, S. R., and C. Stanley Smith, *The Anderson-Smith Report on Theological Education in Southeast Asia—The Report of a Survey Commission, 1951–52,* Board of Founders of Nanking Theological Seminary, New York City, 1953.

Merwin, Wallace C., field reports to Division of Foreign Missions, National Council of Churches (USA), New York City.

Pacific Islands Yearbook 1956, Pacific Publications Pty., Ltd., Sydney, Australia, 1956.

Rasker, A. J., "Higher Theological Training in Indonesia," *International Review of Missions,* October 1949.

Report of Conference on Theological Education in Southeast Asia, Bangkok, 1956.

Rotz, Henry Welton, *A Study of the Recruitment, Training, Support and Performance of Church Leaders in Three Protestant Denominations in the Philippine Federation of Christian Churches,* a doctoral dissertation presented in 1955 to the Graduate School of Cornell University, Ithaca, New York (unpublished, used with permission).

Smith, C. Stanley, field reports to Board of Founders of Nanking Theological Seminary, New York City.

Smith, C. Stanley, *Theologcal Schools in Southeast Asia—*Handbook for the Conference on Theological Education in Southeast Asia, Bangkok, Thailand, February 21-March 7, 1956, Singapore, 1957.

Stewart, William, "Training the Ministry in South and Southeast Asia," *International Review of Missions,* October 1956.

Thomas, Winburn, and Bishop Rajah B. Manikam, *The Church in Southeast Asia,* Friendship Press, New York City, 1956.

Thomas, Winburn, field reports to Division of Foreign Missions, National Council of Churches (USA), New York City, and to the *Christian Century,* Chicago.

Van Dusen, Henry P., lecture to Division of Foreign Missions, National Council of Churches (USA), New York City, 1953.

Wentzel, Constance W., *A Half Century in the Philippines,* National Council, Protestant Episcopal Church, New York City, 1952.

Chapter 6. *East Asia*

Informants: Miss K. Johnson, Miss Kim and Messrs. Anspach, Brumbaugh, Fenn, Hahn, W. C. Johnson, Long, Overton, Pickens, C. S. Smith, E. L. Smith, J. C. Smith and Willingham.

Education for Service in the Christian Church in China—The Report of a Survey Commission, 1935, Board of Founders, Nanking Theological Seminary, New York City, undated.

James, Francis, "How the Church in China Trains its People," *Episcopal Church News,* April 28, 1957.

Japan Christian Yearbook 1956, Christian Literature Society, Tokyo.

Kuwada, Hidenobu, "Protestant Theological Education in Japan," *International Review of Missions,* October 1957.

Manikam, Rajah B., Bishop, report dated July 10, 1956, to International Missionary Council concerning visit to China (unpublished).

Year Book of Christianity 1957, Christian Literature Society, Seoul, Korea.

Chapter 7. *Latin America*

Informants: Miss Ecklund and Messrs. Baez-Camargo, Bentley, Ellis, Erb, Hastings, Larson, Liggett, Mackay, Morgan, Neill, Ranson, Rycroft, Shaull, Van Dusen and Yoder.

Baez-Camargo, Gonzalo, "Church, State and Religious Liberty in Latin America," *World Dominion,* vol. 34, January 1956.

Bingle, Ernest J., *Cuba to Surinam—Report of a Journey in the Caribbean,* September 10 to November 5, 1954 (unpublished).

Cardona, José A., *Factual Conditions of Theological Education in Haiti, the Dominican Republic and Puerto Rico* (unpublished).

Cook, Herbert J., *Ministerial Training in the Caribbean Area* (unpublished).

Considine, John J., M.M., *Call for Forty Thousand,* Longmans Green & Co., New York City, 1946.

Mackay, John A., "A Theological Meditation on Latin America," *Theology Today,* July 1947.

Ospena, Eduardo, *The Protestant Denomination in Colombia—A Historical Sketch with a Particular Study of the So-called "Religious Persecution,"* National Press, Bogotá, 1954.

Chapter 8. *Summary of the Theological Schools*

Hocking, William Ernest, *Re-Thinking Missions—A Laymen's Inquiry after One Hundred Years,* Harper & Brothers, New York City, 1932.

Latourette, Kenneth S., "Re-Thinking Missions after Twenty-Five Years," *International Review of Missions,* April 1957.

Laymen's Foreign Missions Inquiry, Fact Finders Supplement, Orville A. Petty, ed., 7 vols., Harper & Brothers, New York City, 1933.

Moses, David G., *The Outreach in Southern Asia,* Committee for Southern Asia, Division of Foreign Missions, National Council of Churches (USA), New York City, 1957.

National Council of Churches Yearbook 1956 (USA), New York City.

Thomas, Winburn, "Teaching Theology in Asia," *Theology Today,* July 1956.

Chapter 9. *The Number and Role of the Bible Schools*

Bridston, Keith, *An Ecumenical Survey of the Discussion on Theological Training — A Preparatory Paper for the Consultation on Theological Education, Arnoldshain, Frankfurt, July 1956.*

National Christian Council of India Conference Proceedings, Bangalore, 1956.

Chapter 10. *The Lack of Texts*

Informants: Messrs. Baez-Camargo, Bates, Bentley, Carpenter, Gotwald, Leber, Merwin, Morgan, Neudoerffer, Newbigin, Nida, Rycroft, Scott, Shacklock, Shaull and D. C. Smith.

American Association of Theological Schools Biennial Report 1952–53.

American Association of Theological Schools Statistical Report 1954–55.

Birkeli, Fridtjov, "The Church in Madagascar," *International Review of Missions,* April 1957.

Conference on American Books Abroad held in Princeton, N.J., September 1955, proceedings (held under the auspices of National Book Committee of the American Library Association).

Dezza, Paul, S.J., *Catalogus catholicorum institutorum de studiis superioribus,* Catholicarum universitatum foederatio, Roma, 1957.

Hailey, Lord, *An African Survey — A Study of Problems Arising in Africa South of the Sahara,* rev., Oxford University Press, London, 1957.

Jothipakiam, V., "The Training of Christian Church Leaders in India," *International Review of Missions,* October 1950.

Minutes of a Meeting of the L. Th. Commission in the Hindi Area, held at Bareilly, U.P., August 12–13, 1957, National Christian Council of India, 1957.

Morgan, F. Bruce, "Theological Education, East and West," *Theology Today,* April 1952.

Pei, Mario, *Languages for War and Peace,* S. F. Vanni, New York City, 1945.

Pei, Mario, *The Story of Language,* J. B. Lippincott, Philadelphia, 1949.

Tucker, Henry St. George, *The History of the Episcopal Church in Japan,* Charles Scribner's Sons, New York City, 1938.

Van Dusen, Henry P., lecture to Division of Foreign Missions, National Council of Churches (USA), New York City, 1953.

von Sicard, Harald, "Language and Theological Training in Africa," *International Review of Missions,* April 1955.

Wemyss, Stanley, *The Languages of the World,* Philadelphia, 1950.

World Almanac 1958 (The Principal Languages of the World by Professor Sidney S. Culbert), New York World-Telegram, New York City, 1958.

World Illiteracy at Mid-Century—A Statistical Study, UNESCO, 1957.

Chapter 11. *Interboard Agencies Assisting Theological Schools*

Informants: Messrs. Baez-Camargo, Carpenter, Cartwright, Chandran, F. P. Jones, Merwin, Neill, Scott, Shacklock and Yoder.

Jennison, Peter S., *American Books in the Near East, Central Africa and Asia*—Report of the Second Conference on American Books Abroad, sponsored by the National Book Committee, Arden House, Harriman, New York, October 31-November 1, 1957, R. W. Bowker Co., New York City.

Ward, Marcus, "The Christian Students' Library," *International Review of Missions,* October 1952.

Chapter 12. *The Administrative Structure of the Foreign Missions and Eastern Rites of the Roman Catholic Church*

Chapter 13. *The Development and Administration of the Roman Catholic Major Seminaries and Scholasticates*

Chapter 14. *The Efforts of the Roman Catholic Church to Create and Train a Local Clergy in Africa, Asia and Latin America*

Informants: Members of the Roman Catholic hierarchy, secular clergy and of the following religious communities: the Capuchins, Carmelites, Claretians, Divine Word Fathers, Dominicans, Eudists, Franciscans, Holy Cross Fathers, Holy Ghost Fathers, Jesuits, Lazarists (Vincentians), Marists, Maryknoll Fathers, Oblates of Mary Immaculate, Redemptorists and Sulpicians. Any comments in this Survey which are not directly attributed in the text to individual sources reflect the views of the author; and such comments are not necessarily identical with those expressed by the informants.

The data contained in the tables in chapter 14 listing the number of students enrolled in the seminaries and scholasticates was obtained and assembled from a variety of sources, as noted in the bibliography presented below. In those few cases where the data in a table differs from that reported in the directory for an individual country in a given year, this reflects modifications made by the author in the light of other evidence at hand. With respect to the seminaries in Latin America, some of the data was obtained in correspondence with the Consejo Episcopal Latinoamericano (CELAM) in Bogotá, Colombia.

Acta apostolicæ sedis—Commentarium officiale, Typis Polyglottis Vaticanis, Romæ, 1909 to date.

Acta sanctæ sedis, Typographía Polyglotta, Romæ, 1865–1908.

"L'Afrique en chiffres," *Agenzia Internazionale Fides Doc.,* vol. III, No. 34, p. 298, May 27, 1957.

Annuaire catholique d'Egypte 1946, Edité par la Délégation apostolique en Egypte, Association catholique de la Jeunesse Egyptienne, Cairo.

Annuaire catholique de France, Les Presses Continentales, Paris, 1957.

Annuaire des missions catholiques au Congo Belge et au Ruanda Urundi, L'Edition universelle, S. A., Brussels, 1949.

Annuaire des missions catholiques de la Délégation apostolique de Dakar, 1957, L'Office nationale de Propaganda catholique, Paris.

Annuário católico de Portugal 1953, Lopez da Cruz, ed., Graficas da Radio Renascença, Lisboa.

Annuário católico do Brasil 1957, Publicado pela Conferencia nacional dos Bispos do Brasil, Palácio São Joaquim, Rio de Janeiro.

Annuário do ultramar Português 1952, Edicão da Impresa nacional de Publicidade, Diario de Noticias, Lisboa.

Annuario pontificio, 1950 & 1957, Tipographía Vaticana, Vatican City.

Annuarium ordinis fratrum minorum, II, 1956–57, Typographía "Pax et Bonum," Romæ.

Anson, Peter F., *The Religious Orders and Congregations of Great Britain and Ireland,* Stanbrook Abbey Press, Worcester, England, 1949.

Anuario catolico del Uruguay 1958, Suplemento de Tribuna católica, Publicación oficial de la Acción católica del Uruguay, Montevideo.

Anuário de la Iglesia católica en Colombia 1957, Secretariado permanente del Episcopado, Bogotá.

Anuario de Macau 1951–52, Imprensa nacional, Macau, 1952.

Anuario eclesiástico de Bolivia 1953, Por Felipe Lopez Menendez, Talleres Gráficos Bolivianos, La Paz.

Anuario eclesiástico del Perú 1954, Editorial Lumen S.A., Lima.

Anuario eclesiástico Venezolano 1956, R.P.J. Cunillera, ed., Caracas, Venezuela.

Arens, Bernard, S.J., *Handbuch der katholischen Missionen,* 2nd ed., Herder & Co., Freiburg im Breisgau, 1925.

Argentina católica, Julian Alameda, ed., PP. Benedictinos, Buenos Aires, 1935.

Atlas Societatis verbi divini, P. Henrico Emmerich, ed., Typis ad S. Gabrielem, Mödling prope Vindobonam, Austria, 1952.

L'Attivita della Santa Sede (Pubblicazione non ufficiale), Tipografía Poliglotta Vaticana, 1943–1954.

Attwater, Donald, *The Christian Churches of the East,* vols. I–II, rev., Bruce Publishing Co., Milwaukee, 1948.

Attwater, Donald, ed., *Orbis catholicus,* Burns, Oates & Washbourne Ltd., London, 1938.

Australasian Catholic Directory for 1955, St. Mary's Cathedral, Sydney.

Barrett, E. Boyd, *The Jesuit Enigma,* Boni and Liveright, New York, 1927.

Beckmann, Johannes, S.M.B., *Der einheimische Klerus in den Missionsländern — Eine Übersicht,* Verlag der Paulusdruckerei, Freiburg, Switzerland, 1943.

Beckmann, Johannes, ed., S.M.B., *Der einheimische Klerus in Geschichte und Gegenwart,* Administration der neuen Zeitschrift für Missionswissenschaft, Schöneck-Bekenried, Switzerland, 1950.

Beckmann, Johannes, S.M.B., "Einheimischer Klerus und Rassenfrage," *Neue Zeitschrift für Missionswissenschaft,* Vol. XI, No. 1, 1955.

Beckmann, Johannes, S.M.B., *Die katholische Kirche im neuen Afrika,* Verlagsanstalt Benziger & Co. A. G., Einsiedeln/Köln, 1947.

Benedict XV, Pope, "Maximum illud," Nov. 30, 1919, *Selected Papal Encyclicals and Letters,* Vol. 1, Catholic Truth Society, London, 1939.

Binsfield, Edmund L., C.PP.S., "Church Legislation on the Reading of Periodicals and Papers in the Major Seminary Library," *The Jurist* (Catholic University of America), Vol. 13, pp 298–332, July, 1953.

Bolduc, P. Gatien, *Les études dans les religieux cléricales — Abrège historique et commentaire canonique,* Catholic University of America Press, Washington, D.C., 1942.

Boletim do Ordinariato dos católicos de Ritos Orientáis do Brasil, No. 2, 1955, Rio de Janeiro.

Bouffard, Adrien, *Perspectives sur le monde,* L'Union missionnaire du Clergé, Quebec, 1957.

Bougaud, Louis V. E., *History of St. Vincent de Paul,* Longmans Green & Co., New York City, 1908.

Bouniol, J., W.F., *The White Fathers and Their Missions,* Sands & Co., London, 1929.

Bourne, Francis, Cardinal, *Ecclesiastical Training — Being a Short Treatise on the Spiritual Formation of Aspirants to the Priesthood,* Burns, Oates & Washbourne Ltd., London, 1926.

Boxer, C. R., *The Christian Century in Japan,* University of California Press, Berkeley, 1951.

"Brasilien — Das grösste katholische Land," *Herder-Korrespondenz,* Vol. 10, March 1956, pp. 280–85.

Bravo Ugarte, José, S.J., *Memorias de la Academia mexicana de la historia,* Tomo XI, No. 2, April–June, 1952.

Briggs, Charles Augustus, *History of the Study of Theology,* 2 vols. Charles Scribner's Sons, New York City, 1916.

Brou, Alexandre, S.J., *Cent ans de missions 1815–1934 — Les Jésuites missionaires au XIXe et XXe siècles,* Editions Spes, Paris, 1935.

Brown, Charles A., M.M., *Vocations and the Training of Clergy,* Paper 10A, Maryknoll Conference, Lima, Peru, 1954.

Burke, Thomas J.M., ed., *Beyond all Horizons — Jesuits and the Missions,* Hanover House, Garden City, N.Y., 1957.

Calendario de la Altagracia, 1958, Publicación anual para la República Dominicana, con Licencia eclésiastica, Curia arquidiócesiana, Ciudad Trujillo, 1958.

Cardinal Mercier's Conferences Delivered to His Seminarists at Mechlin in 1907, Benziger Brothers, New York, 1910.

Catalogue des maisons et du personnel de la Congrégation de la Mission 1958.

Catalogus, C.SS.R., 1955, Cum statu personali diei 25 Febr. 1955, Lovanii Typ. ad S. Alfonsi (Redemptorists).

Catalogus Congregationis missionariorum filiorum Immaculati Cordis Beatae Mariae Virginis, (C.M.F.), Romae, MCMLV (Claretians).

Catalogus generalis ordinis praedicatorum (mense Aprili MCMXLIX), Reverendissimi Patris Fr. Emmanuelis Suarez, Magistri generalis ordinis, Jussu editus, Societa Tipogr. Castaldi, Romae.

Catalogus sodalium Societatis Verbi Divini ineunte Anno 1958, Ex Typographia Domus Missionum ad S. Michaelem Archangelum, Steylensis.

Catholic Encyclopedia, The Encyclopedia Press, New York City, 1907 & 1913.

Catholic Church and Southern Africa—A Series of Essays, The Catholic Archdiocese of Cape Town, 1951.

Catholic Directory for India, 1956, J. Fernandes, ed., Archbishop's House, New Delhi.

Catholic Directory of India, Pakistan, Burma and Ceylon, 1948, The Good Pastor Press, Madras, 1948.

Catholic Directory of Japan, 1958, Office of the Secretary General, The National Catholic Committee of Japan, Tokyo.

Catholic Directory of the British Caribbean, 1958, Catholic Opinion Press, Kingston, Jamaica, British West Indies.

Catholic Directory of the Philippines, 1956, Catholic Trade School, Manila, P.I.

Catholicisme, hier aujourd'hui demain, 7 vols., Paris, 1952.

"Catholics Assess Evangelical Work" (Chile), *Christian Century,* Jan. 1, 1958, p. 23.

Cavilli, F., "I problemi del cattolicismo nel America Latina," *La Civiltà cattolica,* Vol. 106, Sept. 3, 1955.

Centenaire de la Congrégation du Très Saint Sacrement (1856-13 mai-1956) Curie Généralice, Rome, 1956.

Champagne, Joseph E., *Manual of Missionary Action,* University of Ottawa Press, 1948.

Charon, Cyrille, "Le Séminaire Saint-Anne à Jérusalem," *Echos d'Orient,* Vol. XII, 1909, pp. 234–41, 298–308.

"Church (The)—From India across the Pacific," *International Fides Service* Supplement No. 17, September 28, 1957, Rome.

Clark, Francis X., *The Purpose of Missions—A Study of Mission Documents of the Holy See 1909-46,* Academia Studies, June, 1948.

Codex iuris canonici, Pii X Pontificis maximi, iussu digestus, Benedicti Papae XV, auctoritate promulgatus, Typis Polyglottis Vaticanis, Romae, 1917.

Coleman, William J., M.M., *Latin-American Catholicism, A Self-Evaluation, A Study of the Chimbote Report,* World Horizon Reports No. 23, 1958, Maryknoll Publications, Maryknoll, New York.

Coleman, William J., M.M., *The State of Catholicism in Latin America Today,* Paper 1A, Maryknoll Conference, Lima, Peru, 1954.

Collectanea S. Congregationios de Propaganda Fide seu decreta instructiones rescripta pro apostolicis missionibus, Vol. 1, Ann. 1622–1866, NN 1–1299, Typographía Polyglotta S.C. de Propaganda Fide, Rome, 1907.

Comber, John W., M.M., *The Major Seminary,* Paper 10C, Maryknoll Conference, Lima, Peru, 1954.

Compton, Piers, *The Great Religious Orders,* Elkin Mathews & Marrot, London, 1931.

Congregación de Jesus y Maria, Vice-Provincia de Venezuela Personal 1957-58, Editorial San Juan Eudes, Usaquén, Colombia.

Congrégation du T-S Rédempteur, par un Père Rédemptoriste, Librairie Letouzey et Ané, Paris, 1922.

Considine, John J., M.M., *Africa, World of New Men,* Dodd, Mead & Co., New York City, 1954.

Considine, John J., M.M., *An Outline of Missiography,* Academia Studies, Vol. 1, No. 8, 1943–44, America Press, New York City.

Conspectus missionum Ordinis fratrum minorum, iussu Revmi P. Augustini Sepinski, Ministri generalis totius Ordinis fratrum minorum compositus, Secretariatus missionum O.F.M., Romae, 1957.

Cox, Joseph Godfrey, *The Administration of Seminaries—Historical Synopsis and Commentary,* Catholic University of America, Washington, D.C., 1931.

Cunningham, Robert J., *A Brief Survey of Southern Africa—A Contemporary Review of the Peoples and the Church,* World Horizon Reports, No. 14, 1956, Maryknoll Publications.

Cunningham, Robert J., *A Thumbnail Sketch of North and Northeast Africa—A Contemporary Survey of the Peoples and the Church,* World Horizon Reports, No. 16, 1956.

Da Mondreganes, P. Pio Maria, *Manuale di Missionologia,* Stabilimento Grafico Marietti, Torino, 1950.

De La Costa, H., "Capacity for Leadership in Philippine Clergy and Laity," *Worldmission,* Vol. 4, No. 2, Summer 1953.

De Melo, Carlos M., S.J., *The Recruitment and Formation of the Native Clergy in India (16th-19th Century)—An Historico-Canonical Study,* Agencia Geral do Ultramar, Lisbon, 1955.

de Reefer, J., "The Historical Background of our Mission Hierarchy," *Worldmission,* Vol. 4, No. 3, Fall 1953.

de Reeper, John, M.H.F., "Missionary Societies without Vows and Title of Ordination," *The Jurist* (Catholic University of America), Vol. XVI, Jan.–Oct. 1956.

Devas, Raymund, O.P., *The Dominican Revival in the 19th Century,* Longmans Green & Co., New York City, 1913.

Dezza, Paul, S.J., *Catologus catholicorum institutorum de studiis superioribus,* Catholicarum universitatum foederatio, Roma, 1957.

Dietz, Frederick C., *How the Church Conducts its World Missions,* Academia Studies, Vol. VI, No. 3, 1948–49.

Directiones et aliae indicationes domorum ordinis fratrum minorum, Ex Typographia Collegii S. Bonaventurae, Quaracchi, Florentiae, 1956.

Directoire des grands séminaires confiés aux prêtres de la mission, 2nd ed., Imprimerie de D. Dumoulin & Cie., Paris, 1895 (reprinted at St. Vincent's Seminary, Germantown, Philadelphia, Pa., 1942).

Directorio de la Iglesia en México 1952, José A. Romero and Juan A. Mejia, eds. Bueña Prensa, Mexico, D.F.

Directorium seminariorum (in Sinis), Missionariis Congregationis Immaculati Cordis Mariae (Scheut), Peking, 1949.

Dirks, Walter, *The Monk and the World,* David McKay Co., New York City, 1954.

Domus religiosae Ordinis fratrum minorum Capuccinorum necnon monasteria monialium Capuccinarum cum directionibus tabellariis, Apud Curiam generalem, O.F.M. Cap., Romae, 1952.

Drane, Augusta T., *Christian Schools and Scholars, or Sketches of Education from the Christian Era to the Council of Trent,* 2 vols., Longmans Green & Co., London, 1867.

du Bois, A., C.R.S.P., *Les Barnabites, clercs réguliers de St. Paul 1533,* Librairie Letouzey et Ané, Paris, 1924.

Dubay, Thomas, S.M., *The Seminary Rule,* The Newman Press, Westminster, Md., 1954.

Dugon, Robert M., C.S.Sp., "Cent ans d'efforts pour former trente prêtres africains," *Spiritains,* No. 5, Sept.-Oct. 1957.

Dunne, Peter M., S.J., "The Church in Latin America," *The Catholic Church in World Affairs,* Waldemar Gurian, ed., University of Notre Dame Press, Indiana, 1954.

Elenchus seminariorum cum appendice et imaginibus phototypicis, Sacra Congregatio de seminariis et studiorum universitatibus (Typis Polyglottis Vaticanis), 1934.

Ellis, John Tracy, *American Catholics and the Intellectual Life,* The Heritage Foundation, Inc., Chicago, 1956.

Emmerich, F., O.F.M., "The Catholic Church in West Pakistan," *Worldmission,* Vol. 4, Spring 1953.

Enchiridion clericorum—Documenta ecclesiae sacrorum alumnis instituendis, S. Congregatio de Seminariis et Studiorum Universitatibus, ed., Typis Polyglottis Vaticanis, 1938.

Enchiridion de statibus perfectionis—Documenta ecclesiae sodalibus instituendis—Collectanea Sacrae Congregationis de Religiosis, Officium Libri catholici, Romae, 1949.

Enciclopedia cattólica, Vatican City, 1950-53.

Enciclopedia universal ilustrada, Espasa-Calpe, S.A., Madrid, 1927.

Espinosa, J. Manuel, "The Role of Catholic Culture in Uruguay," *The Catholic Historical Review,* Vol. 26, No. 1, April 1940.

Estado del Clero, 1958, Imprenta Lehmann, San José, Costa Rica.

Etat de la Compagnie de Saint Sulpice, 1956-57, Paris, 1957.

Etat des œuvres de la Congrégation du Saint Espirit, No. 13, Feb. 1956, La Chapelle, Montligeon (Orne) France.

Etteldorf, Raymond, *The Catholic Church in the Middle East,* Macmillan & Co., New York, 1959 (Msgr. Etteldorf is an official of the Sacred Congregation for the Oriental Church).

Ewing, J. Franklin, ed., *Local Leadership in Mission Lands,* Proceedings of the Fordham

University Conference of Mission Specialists, Second Annual Meeting January 23–24, 1954, Fordham University Press, New York City, 1954.

Fehrenbacher, D. Bruno, O.S.B., "The Benedictine Syrian Seminary," *The Eastern Churches Quarterly*, Vol. IX, No. 1, Spring 1951.

Fischer, Herman, S.V.D., *Life of Arnold Janssen, Founder of the Society of the Divine Word*, Mission Press S.V.D., Techny, Illinois, 1925.

Fortescue, Adrian, *The Uniate Eastern Churches*, Frederick Ungar Publishing Co., New York City, 1923.

Freitag, Anton, "Die Fortschritte des einheimischen Klerus und der einheimischen Hierarchie in den Missionsländern in den letzten dreisig Jahren (1920–50)," *Der einheimische Klerus in Geschichte und Gegenwart*, Johannes Beckmann, ed., op. cit.

Freitag, Anton, *Die neue Missionsära—Das Zeitalter der einheimischen Kirche*, 2nd ed., Steyler Verlagsbuchhandlung, Kaldenkirchen, 1953.

Freri, Joseph, *Native Clergy for Mission Countries*, Press of the Society for the Propagation of the Faith, New York City.

Freriks, Celestine A., *Religious Congregations in their External Relations—A Dissertation* submitted to the Faculty of Theology of the Catholic University of America, Washington, D.C., 1916.

Fülöp-Miller, René, *The Power and Secret of the Jesuits*, Viking Press, New York City, 1930.

75 Jahre im Dienste des göttlichen Wortes—Gedenkblätter zum 75 jährigen Jubiläum des Steyler Missionswerkes, herausgegeben von der Gesellschaft des göttlichen Wortes, Steyler Missionsdruckerei, 1950.

Gautier, Jean, *Ces messieurs de Saint-Sulpice*, Librairie Arthème Fayard, Paris, 1957.

Gay, Jean, C.S.Sp., *La Doctrine missionnaire du Vénérable Père Libermann*, Imprimerie catholique, Basse-Terre, Guadeloupe, 1943.

Gérin, Marcel, *Le Gouvernement des missions*, Faculté de droit canonique, Université Laval, Québec, 1944.

Gibbons, William J., S.J., et al, *Basic Ecclesiastical Statistics for Latin America, 1958*, World Horizon Reports, No. 24, 1958, Maryknoll, N.Y.

Gibbons, William J., S.J., "Developing a Successful Program of Scholarly Research and Publication," a Paper Presented at the Meeting of College and University Delegates, Annual Meeting of the Jesuit Educational Association, Marquette University, April 22, 1957, *Jesuit Educational Quarterly*, Vol. XX, Nos. 1 and 2, June–October 1957.

Gillon, Luc P., "Louvain Goes African," *Worldmission*, Vol. 9, No. 3, Fall 1958.

Goulet, Edward, *The Holy See and the Foreign Missions*, Academia Studies, Vol. III, No. 7, 1945–46.

Goyau, Georges, *La Congrégation de la mission des Lazaristes*, Editions Bernard Grasset, Paris, 1938.

Goyau, Georges, *Les Prêtres des missions étrangères*, Editions Bernard Grasset, Paris; 1932.

Gremillion, Joseph B., "The Church in Latin America," *Commonweal*, Vol. LXVIII, No. 8, May 23, 1958.

Guía de la Iglesia en España, Oficine general de información y estadistica de la iglesia en España 1954 (& Suplemento de 1955), Madrid.

Guía eclesiástica de Chile, Edición de 1958, Arzobispado de Santiago de Chile.

Guía eclesiástica de la República Argentina, Editorial Troquel S.R.L., Buenos Aires, 1954.

Guide de la France chrétienne et missionnaire 1948-49, Centre catholique international de Documentation et Statistiques, Paris, 1949.

Guide to Catholic Italy, Pietro Barbieri and Ulisse Picci, eds., Holy Year 1950 Publishing Co., Rome, 1949 (published for the Catholic War Veterans of the USA).

Harney, Martin P., S.J., *The Jesuits in History,* The America Press, New York City, 1941.

Heck, Theodore, *The Curriculum of the Major Seminary in Relation to Contemporary Conditions—A Dissertation,* Catholic University of America, Washington, D.C., 1935.

Heimbucher, Max, *Die Orden und Kongregationen der katholischen Kirche,* 3 vols., Druck und Verlag von Ferdinand Schöningh, Paderborn, 1907.

Heston, Edward L., *The Holy See at Work,* Bruce Publishing Co., Milwaukee, 1950.

"Historia de los colegios de formácion de la Congregación de misioneros hijos del Inmaculado Corazón de Maria en su primer siglo de existencia 1849-1949, *Colegios Claretianos,* Organo oficial de los colegios internos de la Provincia Claretiana de Castilla, Tomo IV, Num. 18, 16 julio 1949-7 mayo 1950 (número extraordinario), Santo Domingo de la Calzada, España.

Hofinger, Johann, S.J., "Das Problem des Textbuches in Seminarien der Missionsländer," *Neue Zeitschrift für Missionswissenschaft,* Vol. XII, No. 1, 1956, pp. 46-63.

Hofmann, Paul, "Vatican Bans a Biblical Study Approved by Clergy in France," *New York Times,* July 12, 1958.

Holzapfel, Herbert, O.F.M., *The History of the Franciscan Order,* St. Joseph Seminary, Teutopolis, Illinois, 1948.

Homan, Helen W., *Knights of Christ,* Prentice-Hall, Inc., Englewood Cliffs, New Jersey, 1957.

Hong Kong Catholic Directory and Year Book for the Year of Our Lord 1958, Catholic Truth Society, Hong Kong.

Horner, Norman A., *Protestant and Roman Catholic Missions Among the Bantu of Cameroun, a Comparative Study*—a thesis submitted to the Hartford Seminary Foundation in partial fulfillment of the requirements for the degree of Doctor of Philosophy, Hartford, Conn., 1956 (used with permission of the author).

Huber, Raphael, *Modern Missions in Middle America—Political, Social and Religious Problems in Mexico, Central America and the Islands of the Caribbean,* America Press, New York City, 1948.

Huonder, Anton, S.J., *Der einheimische Klerus in den Heidenländern,* Herdersche Verlagshandlung, Freiburg im Breisgau, 1909.

La Iglesia en el Ecuador 1.957—Sinópsis de la jerarquía eclesiástica ecuatoriana y de las órdenes y congregaciones religiosas, editado en la editorial "Pio XII" de la Curia de Ambato, Ecuador.

Index—*1957, Status societatis* (Society of Mary of Lyons, Marists), Tipografía Don Luigi Guanella.

International Fides Service, Congregation for the Propagation of the Faith, Vatican City, various dates.

Janelle, Pierre, *The Catholic Reformation,* The Bruce Publishing Company, Milwaukee, 1948.

Joly, Léon, *Le Christianisme et l'extrême Orient,* 2 vols., P. Lethielleux, Paris, 1907.

Just, Mary, *Digest of Catholic Mission History,* World Horizon Reports, No. 20, 1957, Maryknoll, N. Y.

Katholiek Jaarboek voor Belgie, Annuaire catholique de Belgique, 1953, Centre interdiocesain, Brussels.

Kearns, Robert E., M.M., *The Minor Seminary,* Paper 10B, Maryknoll Conference, Lima, Peru, 1954.

Kidd, B. J., *The Counter Reformation,* Society for the Promotion of Christian Knowledge, London, 1933.

King, Archdale A., *The Rites of Eastern Christendom,* 2 vols., Tipografía Poliglotta Vaticana, Rome 1947–48.

Kirchliches Handbuch—*Amtliches statistiches Jahrbuch der katholischen Kirche Deutchlands,* Franz Groner, ed., Band XXIII, 1944–51, Verlag J. P. Bachern Köln, 1951.

Kittler, Glenn D., *The White Fathers,* Harper & Brothers, New York City, 1957.

Knowles, Dom David, O.S.B., *The Benedictines,* Macmillan Co., New York City, 1930.

Koren, Henry J., C.S.Sp., *The Spiritans*—*A History of the Congregation of the Holy Ghost,* Duquesne Studies, Duquesne University, Pittsburgh, Pennsylvania, 1958.

Lajeunesse, Paul, "L'église catholique en Afrique du Sud," *Revue de l'Université d'Ottawa,* Vol. 23, No. 2, April-June 1953.

Langford, Walter M., "The Role of Catholic Culture in Argentina," *The Catholic Historical Review,* Vol. 26, No. 1, April 1940.

Latourette, Kenneth Scott, *Christianity in a Revolutionary Age,* Vol. 1 ("The Nineteenth Century in Europe, Background and the Roman Catholic Phase"), Harper & Brothers, New York City, 1958.

Latourette, Kenneth S., *A History of Christianity,* Harper & Brothers, New York City, 1953.

Launay, Adrien, *Histoire générale de la Société des Missions-étrangères,* Tequi Libraire-Editeur, Paris, 1894.

Laures, Johannes, S.J., *The Catholic Church in Japan,* Charles E. Tuttle Co., Rutland, Vermont, 1954.

Ledochowski, Wlodimir, S.J., *The Choice and Formation of a Native Clergy in the Foreign Missions*—*A Letter Addressed to the Superior of the Mission of Kiang-Nan, China, from Rome, August 15th, 1919,* P.J. Kenedy & Sons, New York City.

Leo XIII, Pope, "Aeterni patris," August 4, 1879, Walsh, James E., *Maryknoll Spiritual Directory, op. cit.*

Leo XIII, Pope, "Ad extremas," June 24, 1893, *Lettres apostoliques de S.S. Leon XIII,* Vol. 3, Bonne Presse, Paris, 1893.

Leo XIII, Pope, "Depuis le jour," September 8, 1899, Walsh, James E., *Maryknoll Spiritual Directory, op. cit.*

Leo XIII, Pope, "Fin dal principio," December 8, 1902, Walsh, James E., *Maryknoll Spiritual Directory, op. cit.*

Lestra, Antoine, *Le Père Coudrin, fondateur de Picpus,* Lardanchet, Paris, 1952.

Lewis, Carlos A., S.V.D., *Catholic Negro Bishops—A Brief Survey of the Present and the Past,* Divine Word Publications, Bay Saint Louis, Mississippi, 1958.

Lima Methods Conference of the Maryknoll Fathers, Proceedings, Lima, Peru, August 23-28, 1954, Maryknoll, N.Y.

Long, Leonard M., C.R., *The Resurrectionists,* Chicago, Illinois, 1947.

Loughran, Elizabeth Ward, "The Role of Catholic Culture in Bolivia," *The Catholic Historical Review,* Vol. 26, No. 1, April 1940.

Lynskey, E.M., *The Government of the Catholic Church,* P. J. Kenedy & Sons, New York City, 1952.

McCabe, Joseph, *Twelve Years in a Monastery,* Smith Elder & Co., London, 1897 (the author was formerly Father Anthony, O.S.F., an English Franciscan).

McCaffrey, P. R., Ord. Carm., *The White Friars—An Outline Carmelite History,* M. H. Gill and Son, Ltd., Dublin, 1926.

McGucken, William J., S.J., *The Jesuits and Education,* Bruce Publishing Co., Milwaukee, 1932.

McKenna, Stephen, C.SS.R., *Modern Missions in South America,* Academia Studies, Vol. V, No. 4, 1947-48.

McSorley, Joseph, *An Outline History of the Church,* B. Herder & Co., St. Louis, 1949.

Macaulay, Thomas B., *The History of England from the Accession of James the Second,* Macmillan & Co., London, 1914.

Mackay, John A., "A Theological Meditation on Latin America," *Theology Today,* July 1947.

Madden, Marie R., "The Role of Catholic Culture in Venezuela," *The Catholic Historical Review,* Vol. 26, No. 4, January 1941.

Magner, James A., "The Catholic Church in Colombia," *The Catholic Historical Review,* Vol. 26, No. 2, July 1940.

Mallou, T., "The Function of the Seminary Library in the Light of Menti Nostrae," *American Ecclesiastical Review,* Vol. 129, November 1953.

Manning, Timothy, *Clerical Education in Major Seminaries, Its Nature and Application,* Pontificia Universitas Gregoriana, Rome, 1946.

Mariannhill—Half a Century of African Mission Life, Mariannhill Mission Society, Detroit, 1935.

Marinan, Gerard, *The Church in the Smaller Asiatic Lands,* Academia Studies, Vol. VI, No. 1, 1948-49.

Markham, James J., *The Sacred Congregation of Seminaries and Universities of Studies,* Catholic University of America, Washington, D.C., 1957.

Martin, Victor, *Les Congrégations Romaines,* Bloud et Gay, Paris, 1930.

Maryknoll Spiritual Directory, see Walsh, James E.

Masseron, Alexandre, *The Franciscans,* Burns, Oates & Washbourne Ltd., London, 1931.

Masson, J., "La Vocation sacerdotale au Congo et au Ruanda-Urundi," *Bulletin de l'Union du clergé,* No. 127, July 1957, Brussels.

Masson, J., *Vers l'église indigène—Catholicisme ou nationalisme?* Les Presses de Belgique, Brussels, 1944.

Mathis, Michael A., "Modern Missions in India," *Academia Studies,* Vol. IV, No. 8, 1946-47.

Maynard, Theodore, *Saint Benedict and His Monks,* P. J. Kenedy & Sons, New York City, 1954.

Maynard, Theodore, *Saint Ignatius and the Jesuits,* P. J. Kenedy & Sons, New York City, 1956.

Meadows, Denis, *Obedient Men,* Appleton-Century-Crofts, New York City, 1954.

Micheletti, Antonio, M., *Constitutiones Seminariorum Clericalium,* Ex Officina Eq. Petri Marietti—Editoris, Taurini, Typographi Pontificii Ac Sacrae Rituum Congregationis, 1919.

Misi Katolik di Indonesia—Buku Tahunan 1955, Bahagian I-II, Diterbitkan Olek Kantor Misi Pusat, Djakarta.

Missioni cattoliche (Le), Dipendenti dalla Sacra Congregazione "De Propaganda Fide," Consiglio superiore della Pontificia opera della Propagazione della Fede, Roma, 1950.

Monval, Jean, *Les Assomptionnistes,* Editions Bernard Grasset, Paris, 1939.

Monval, Jean, *Les Sulpiciens,* Editions Bernard Grasset, Paris, 1934.

Moss, Doley C., *Of Cell and Cloister—Catholic Religious Orders through the Ages,* The Bruce Publishing Company, Milwaukee, 1957.

Mourret, Fernand, S.S., *A History of the Catholic Church,* 8 vols., B. Herder Book Co., St. Louis, Mo., 1931-57.

Myers, Rawly, *This is the Seminary,* Bruce Publishing Co., Milwaukee, 1953.

National Catholic Almanac, 1957 (USA), St. Anthony's Guild, Paterson, N.J.

National Catholic Directory for Pakistan, 1956, Apostolic Internunciature in Karachi.

Neuvecelle, Jean, *The Vatican—Its Organization, Customs and Ways of Life,* Criterion Books, New York City, 1955.

Nevins, Albert J., M.M., "How Catholic is Latin America?", *The Sign,* September 1956.

Nevins, Albert J., M.M., *The Making of a Priest,* Newman Press, Westminster, Maryland, 1957.

New Schaff-Herzog Encyclopedia of Religious Knowledge, Funk & Wagnalls, New York City, 1908.

Nobels, Albert, *Catholic Mission in the Belgian Congo,* Academia Studies, Vol. VII, No. 3, 1949-50.

Nomina del Clero de la Arquidiocesis de Tegucigalpa, Año 1958, The Curia, Tegucigalpa.

Normae de seraphica iuventute religiose educanda et efformanda in ordine fratrum minorum, Curia Generalis O.F.M., Romae, 1951.

Notes et documents relatifs à la vie et à l'œuvre du Vénérable François-Marie-Paul Libermann, Pour distribution privée, Paris, 1939.

O'Connor, John B., O.P., *Saint Dominic and the Order of Preachers,* Holy Name Bureau, New York City, 1917.

Official Catholic Directory, 1958 (USA), P. J. Kenedy & Sons, New York City.

Ordinamento dei seminari, 2nd ed., S. Congregazione dei Seminari e delle Università degli Studi (Tipografía Poliglotta Vaticana), Rome, 1925.

Ordo examinis annui in domo studiorum C.SS.R., Ilchestriae, Md., 1893, Typis Congregationis SS Redemptoris, Ilchestriae.

Orsenigo, Cesare, *Life of St. Charles Borromeo,* B. Herder Book Co., St. Louis, Missouri, 1943.

Österreichische Priester, Brüder und Schwestern in aller Welt, herausgegeben für die Mitglieder der Pontificia Cleri Consociatio missionalis in Österreich, Missionsdruckerei St. Gabriel, Mödling b. Wien, 1957.

Oursler, Fulton, *The Protestant Missionary Movement,* Academia Studies, Vol. V, No. 1, 1947–48.

Papi, Hector, S.J., *Religious in Church Law — An Exposition of Canon Law Concerning Religious,* P. J. Kenedy & Sons, New York City, 1924.

Parsons, Wilfrid, S.J., *Mexican Martyrdom,* The Macmillan Company, New York, 1936.

Pattee, Richard, *The Catholic Revival in Mexico,* Catholic Association for International Peace, Washington, D.C., 1944.

Pattee, Richard, *El Católicismo contemporaneo en Hispanoamerica,* Editorial Fides, Buenos Aires (1950?).

Paventi, Saverio, *La Chiesa missionaria,* Vol. I & II, Unione missionaria del Clero in Italia, 1949 & 1950.

Peers, E. Allison, *Spain — The Church and the Orders,* Burns, Oates & Washbourne Ltd., London, 1945.

Personal de la Congregación de Jesús y Maria en la Provincia de Colombia, Venezuela y Chile 1953, Editorial San Juan Eudes, Usaquén, Colombia.

Personnel de la congrégation des Missionaires Oblats de Marie Immaculée, April 1954 and November 1956, Maison générale, Rome.

Pius X, Pope, *E supremi,* October 4, 1903, official translation, Burns & Oates, London, 1903.

Pius X, Pope, *Sacrorum antistitum,* September 1, 1910, translation, Open Court Publishing Co., Chicago, 1911.

Pius XI, Pope, "Rerum ecclesiæ," February 28, 1926, *The Encyclicals of Pius XI,* James H. Ryan, transl., B. Herder & Co., St. Louis, 1927.

Pius XI, Pope, *Ad catholici sacerdotii,* December 20, 1935, National Catholic Welfare Conference, Washington, D.C., 1936.

Pius XII, Pope, "Saeculo exeunte," June 13, 1940, *Acta apostolica sedis,* Vol. 32, p. 255, Vatican City, 1940.

Pius XII, Pope, "Humani generis," August 12, 1950, *The Pope Speaks — The Teachings of Pope Pius XII,* Pantheon, New York City, 1957.

Pius XII, Pope, *Menti nostræ* — Apostolic Exhortations, September 23, 1950, Paulist Press, New York City, 1950.

Pius XII, Pope, *Evangelii præcones,* June 2, 1951, individual translations, Paulist Press, New York City.

Pius XII, Pope, "Sedes sapientæ," May 31, 1956, *The Pope Speaks,* Vol. 3, Winter 1956–57.

Pius XII, Pope, "Donum fidei," April 21, 1957, *Worldmission,* Summer 1957.

Placid, P., T.O.C.D., "The Syro-Malabarians—Their Life and Their Activities," *Neue Zeitschrift für Missionswissenschaft,* Vol. XII, No. 4, 1956.

Pons, A., *La nouvelle église d'Afrique, ou le catholicisme en Algérie, en Tunisie et au Maroc depuis 1830,* Librairie Louis Namura, Tunis, 1931.

Pothacamury, Thomas, "The Church in Independent India," *World Horizon Reports,* 1958.

Powers, James M., Bishop, *Memoirs—The Seminary of Montezuma,* Documents and Writings of Most Rev. John Mark Gannon, Chairman of the Bishops' Committee for Montezuma and his Episcopal Associates, Erie, Pennsylvania, 1953.

Rashdall, Hastings, *Ideas and Ideals* (chapter on modernism), Basil Blackwell, Oxford, 1928.

Rashdall, Hastings, *The Universities of Europe in the Middle Ages,* Oxford, 1936.

Reeves, John-Baptist, O.P., *The Dominicans,* Sheed & Ward, London, 1929.

Regan, Joseph W., *The Philippines—Christian Bulwark in Asia,* World Horizon Reports, No. 21, 1957.

Rémy (pseud.), *Goa—Rome of the Orient,* Arthur Barker Ltd., London, 1957.

Repeticci, Chanoine P., *L'Algérie chrétienne, esquisse historique,* Librairie à Notre Dame, Algiers, 1931.

Rios, Dom Romanus, "The Armenian Mekhitarist Benedictines," *Eastern Churches Quarterly,* Vol. IV, No. 2, April 1940.

Roberts, Thomas D'E., Archbishop, S.J., *Black Popes,* Longmans Green & Co., London, 1954.

Rogosh, Andrew, *Rome and the Eastern Churches,* Academia Studies, Vol. V, No. 5, 1947–48.

Roland, Thomas F., O.S.A., "The Augustinian Fathers," *The Catholic News,* New York City, April 11, 1959.

"Roman Catholic Church," *Management Audit,* American Institute of Management, New York City, 1956.

Rondot, Pierre, *Les Chrétiens d'Orient,* J. Peyronnet et Cie., Paris, 1955.

Roscoe, J. E., *A Short History of Theological Education,* Arthur H. Stockwell, London, 1918.

Ryan, Edwin, *The Church in the South American Republics,* Newman Press Book Shop, Westminster, Maryland, 1943.

Ryan, Edwin, "Contribution of the Church to Chilean Culture," *The Catholic Historical Review,* Vol. 26, No. 3, October 1940.

Sackett, Francis D., *The Spiritual Director in an Ecclesiastical Seminary,* University of Ottawa Press, 1945.

Schmidlin, Joseph, S.V.D., *Catholic Mission Theory* (Katholische Missionslehre im Grundriss), Mission Press, Techny, Illinois, 1931,

Schneider, Edouard, *The Benedictines,* The Great Monastic Order Series, Greenberg, New York, 1926.

Sherrill, Lewis Joseph, *The Rise of Christian Education,* Macmillan, New York City, 1944.

Silva y Perez, Carlos, Bishop, *Historia eclesiástica de Chile,* Imprenta de San José, Santiago de Chile, 1925.

Smith, C. Stanley, *The Development of Protestant Theological Education in China, in the Light of the History of the Education of the Clergy in Europe and America, May 10, 1938—a Doctoral Dissertation, Yale Divinity School,* New Haven, Connecticut (unpublished, excerpts used with permission).

Smith, John Talbot, *The Training of a Priest,* Longmans Green & Co., New York, 1908.

La Société de Marie, Congrégation des Pères Maristes, Librairie Letouzey & Ané, Paris, 1923.

Spalding, John Lancaster, *Means and Ends of Education,* A. C. McClurg and Company, Chicago, 1897.

Statistica con cenni storici della Gerarchia a dei fedeli di rito orientale, Sacra Congregazione Orientale, Tipografía Poliglotta Vaticana, 1932.

"Statistique générale du clergé et des congrégations religieuses de la province ecclésiastique d'Haïti au 1er janvier 1958," *Le Bulletin de la quinzaine de la Province ecclésiastique d'Haïti,* Nos. 17–18, 23 fev. 1958, Port-au-Prince.

Stebbing, George, C.SS.R., *The Redemptorists,* Burns, Oates & Washbourne, Ltd., London, 1924.

Sullivan, William L., *Under Orders, The Autobiography of William Laurence Sullivan,* Richard R. Smith, New York City, 1944.

Sylloge—Præcipuorum documentorum recentium summorum pontificum et S. Congregationis de Propaganda Fide, necnon aliarum, SS. Congregationum Romanarum, ad usum missionariorum, Typis Polyglottis Vaticanis, Romæ, 1939.

Taboada, Jesus, "The Catholic Church in Present Day India," *Worldmission,* Vol. 7, No. 4, Winter 1956.

Tettemer, John, *I Was a Monk,* Alfred A. Knopf, New York City, 1951 (the author spent 25 years as a member of the Congregation of the Passion, serving for several years as its Consultor General).

Thauren, Johannes, S.V.D., *Mission im Weltbild und Menschenbild von heute,* Unio cleri pro missionibus, Wien, Österreich, 1954.

Theology in Japan, Information Bureau, Jesuit Fathers, Tokyo, 1957.

Tisserant, Eugène, Cardinal, *Eastern Christianity in India—A History of the Syro-Malabar Church from the Earliest Time to the Present Day,* The Newman Press, Westminster, Maryland, 1957.

Trimingham, J. Spencer, *The Christian Church and Missions in Ethiopia,* World Dominion Press, New York City, 1950.

Tyrrell, George, *Autobiography and Life,* 2 vols., Edward Arnold, London, 1912.

US Catholic Overseas Missionary Personnel, January 1, 1958, Mission Secretariat, Washington, D.C.

Université Saint-Joseph de Beyrouth, UNESCO, Assemblée générale au Liban, 1948.

Vacant, Mangenot et Amand, *Dictionnaire de théologie,* Letouzey et Ané, Paris, 1929.

Van Hemelryck, Marcel, I.H.M., "Congo Seminary Works a Miracle," *Interracial Review,* Vol. 21, No. 8, August 1948.

Variationes kalendarii faciendæ in provincia ecca. Managuensi pro anno domine 1957, Estado del clero, Nunciatura apostólica, Managua, Nicaragua.

Verschueren, J., *La République d'Haïti,* 3 vols., Editions Scaldis, Wetteren, Belgium, 1948.

Veuillot, François, *Les Oblats de Marie Immaculée,* Editions Bernard Grasset, Paris, 1946.

Veuillot, François, *Saint Jean Bosco et les Salésiens,* Editions Alsatia-Paris, Paris, 1943.

Veuillot, Pierre, *The Catholic Priesthood According to the Teaching of the Church,* The Newman Press, Westminster, Maryland, 1958 (Msgr. Veuillot is an official of the Secretariate of State in the Vatican).

von Hoensbroech, Paul Kajus, Graf, *Der Jesuitenorden—eine Enzyklopädie aus den Quellen zusammengestellt und bearb. von Graf Paul von Hoensbroech . . . ,* 2 vols., P. Haupt, Bern und Leipzig, 1926–27.

von Hoensbroech, Paul Kajus, Count, *Fourteen Years a Jesuit—A Record of Personal Experience and a Criticism,* 2 vols., Cassell & Co. Ltd., London, 1911 (the author was a member of the Society's Province in Germany from 1878 to 1892).

Wall, Bernard, *Report on the Vatican,* Weidenfeld & Nicholson, London, 1956.

Walsh, James E., M.M., *Maryknoll Spiritual Directory,* Field Afar Press, New York, 1947.

Waterworth, James, transl., *The Canons and Decrees of the Sacred and Ecumenical Council of Trent,* E. Dunigan & Brother, New York City, 1868.

Watters, Mary, *A History of the Church in Venezuela,* University of North Carolina Press, Chapel Hill, 1933.

Weigel, Gustave, S.J., "Theology in South America," *Theological Studies,* Vol. IX, No. 4, December 1948.

Weyland, Peter, and Ambrosie Manaligod, "A Native Clergy for Mission Countries," *Academia Studies,* Vol. V, No. 3, 1947–48.

Whelan, J., C.S.Sp., "Indigenous Priests for the Missions," *Irish Ecclesiastical Record,* 5 ser., Vol. 65, January 1945.

Williams, Michael, *The Catholic Church in Action,* rev., P. J. Kenedy & Sons, New York City, 1958.

World Almanac, New York World-Telegram, New York City, 1957.

World Crisis and the Catholic, Studies published on the occasion of the Second World Congress for the Lay Apostolate, Rome, Sheed & Ward, New York City, 1958.

Worldmission, editorial, Vol. 7, No. 2, Summer 1956, p. 30.

Woywood, Stanislaus, *The New Canon Law—A Commentary and Summary of the New Code of Canon Law,* Joseph F. Wagner, Inc., New York City, 1918.

Wynne, John J., ed., *The Great Encyclical Letters of Pope Leo XIII,* Benziger Brothers, New York City, 1903.

Yeo, Margaret, *Reformer—St. Charles Borromeo,* The Bruce Publishing Co., Milwaukee, 1938.

Chapter 15. *The Seminaries of the Eastern Churches in Africa, Asia and Latin America*

Informants: Africa—Messrs. Atiya, Badeau, Carpenter, Loutfi, McGill, Maxwell, Philipos, Simon, Tobias, Visser 't Hooft and Waddams.

Middle East—Miss Wysner and Messrs. Anderson, Benedictos, Bridgeman,

Dorman, Grigorios, James, Kraeling, Maxwell, Sarafian, Morton Smith, Tobias, Waddams and Willand.

Southern Asia—Messrs. Dorman, Philipos, Scott, Simon and Visser 't Hooft.

Dr. Tobias was particularly helpful in making available his notes concerning his visits to a number of these seminaries in the years 1952–57 on behalf of the World Council of Churches; as was Dr. Dorman, who obtained information from various sources in the Middle East in connection with the preparation of this Survey.

Addison, James T., *The Christian Approach to the Moslem,* Columbia University Press, New York City, 1942.

Adeney, Walter F., *The Greek and Eastern Churches,* Charles Scribner's Sons, New York City, 1939.

Athenagoras, Kokkinakis, Rt. Rev., "Toward a Pan-Orthodox Association of Theological Schools—An Editorial," *The Greek Orthodox Theological Review,* Vol. III, No. 2, Winter 1957.

Attwater, Donald, *The Christian Churches of the East,* Vols. I–II, rev., The Bruce Publishing Company, Milwaukee, 1948.

Bertram, Anton, Sir, and Harry C. Luke, *Report of the Commission Appointed by the Government of Palestine to Inquire into the Affairs of the Orthodox Patriarchate of Palestine,* Oxford University Press, London, 1921.

Bertram, Anton, Sir, and J. W. A. Young, *Report of the Commission Appointed by the Government of Palestine to Inquire and Report upon Certain Controversies between the Orthodox Patriarchate of Jerusalem and the Arab Orthodox Community,* Oxford University Press, London, 1926.

Bigg, Charles, *The Christian Platonists of Alexandria*—Eight Lectures Preached before the University of Oxford in the Year 1886, Clarendon Press, Oxford, 1886.

Bolshakoff, Serge, *The Foreign Missions of the Russian Orthodox Church,* Society for Promoting Christian Knowledge, London, 1943.

Bridgeman, Charles T., "The Armenian Church in Jerusalem," *Christian East,* Vol. XIII, Nos. 3 & 4, 1932.

Bridgeman, Charles T., "Armenian Reconstruction in Syria," *Eastern Church Studies,* Jerusalem and the East Mission, London, 1928.

Bridgeman, Charles T., *Education for Clergy of Eastern Churches,* American Friends of the Greek Orthodox Patriarchate of Jerusalem, Inc., 1950.

Briggs, Charles Augustus, *History of the Study of Theology,* Charles Scribner's Sons, New York City, 1916.

Brown, L. W., Bishop, *The Indian Christians of St. Thomas—An Account of the Ancient Syrian Church of Malabar,* Cambridge University Press, Cambridge, England, 1937.

Bulletin of the Armenian Theological Seminary of the Catholicate of Cilicia, Antelias, Lebanon, 1951.

Butcher, E. L., *The Story of the Church in Egypt,* Smith Elder & Co., London, 1897.

Dictionary of the Eastern Orthodox Church, The Faith Press, London, 1923.

Dowling, Archdeacon, *The Patriarchate of Jerusalem,* 3rd ed., E. S. Gorham, New York City, 1913.

Every, Edward, "The Sacred Theological School in Halki," *Christian East,* Vol. 14, No. 2; Vol. 15, Nos. 3 & 4, 1934.

Fortescue, Adrian, *The Uniate Eastern Churches,* Frederick Ungar Publishing Co., New York City, 1923.

Glazik, P. Dr. Josef, M.S.C., *Die russich-orthodoxe Heidenmission seit Peter dem Grossen,* Aschendorffsche Verlagsbuchhandlung, Münster, Westfalen, 1954.

Hambye, E. R., S.J., "The Syrian Jacobites in India—A Survey of their Past and Present Position," *Eastern Church Quarterly,* Autumn, 1955.

Hammond, Peter, *The Waters of Marah—The Present State of the Greek Church,* The Macmillan Co., New York City, 1956.

Hardy, Edward R., *Christian Egypt—Church and People,* Oxford University Press, New York City, 1952.

Heyworth-Dunne, J., *An Introduction to the History of Education in Modern Egypt,* Luzac & Co., London, 1938.

Irénikon, Vol. 30, No. 1, 1957, pp. 77–78, Benedictine Priory of Amay, Chevetogne, Belgium (note on the Beit Meri Seminary, of which Msgr. Khat is principal, in "Chroniques religieuses").

Janin, Raymond P., *Les Eglises séparées d'Orient,* Librairie Bloud & Gay, Paris, 1930.

Latourette, Kenneth S., *A History of Christianity,* Harper & Brothers, New York City, 1953.

Marsie-Hazen, Blatta, "The Ethiopian Church," *The Ecumenical Review,* Winter, 1949.

Melady, Thomas P., "The Church in Ethiopia," *Worldmission,* Vol. 7, pp. 263–75, Fall, 1956.

Moore, George Foot, "The Theological School at Nisibis," *Studies in the History of Religion,* George Moore, ed., Macmillan Co., New York City, 1912.

Pankhurst, Sylvia, *Ethiopia—A Cultural History,* Lalibela House, Essex, England, 1955.

Proche-Orient-chrétien, Vol. 3/4, 1953/54, p. 243 (article relating to educational activities of the Coptic Church in Egypt).

Proche-Orient-chrétien, 1955 (article commenting on the contrast between the relations of the Greek Orthodox Patriarchs of Antioch and Jerusalem with the Russian Orthodox Patriarch of Moscow).

Richter, Julius, *A History of Protestant Missions in the Near East,* Fleming H. Revell Co., New York City, 1910.

Rogosh, Andrew, "Rome and the Eastern Churches," *Academia Studies,* Vol. V, No. 5, 1947–48.

Rondot, Pierre, *Les Chrétiens d'Orient,* J. Peyronnet & Cie., Editeurs, Paris, 1955.

Roscoe, J. E., *A Short History of Theological Education,* Arthur H. Stockwell, London, 1918.

Sarafian, Kevork A., *History of Education in Armenia,* Press of the La Verne Leader, La Verne, California, 1930.

Sellers, Katherine W., "Armenian Church Torn by Dispute," *Christian Century,* Dec. 18, 1957, p. 1522.

Trimingham, J. Spencer, *The Christian Church and Missions in Ethiopia,* World Dominion Press, London, 1950.

Waddams, Herbert, "Lesser Eastern Churches," *World Dominion,* Vol. XXXIV, Jan. 1956, pp. 33–38.

Wilkins, Gregory, "Impressions of Ethiopia," *Sobornost,* Winter, 1955–56 (quoted with permission).

World Christian Handbook, World Dominion Press, London, 1957.

Worrell, William H., *A Short Account of the Copts,* University of Michigan Press, Ann Arbor, 1945.

Zananiri, Gaston, *Histoire de l'Eglise Byzantine,* Nouvelles Editions Latines, Paris, 1954.

Chapter 16. The Support Given to Protestant Seminaries by
Foreign Mission Boards

Bates, M. Searle, "The Training of Christian Ministers in Non-British Africa," *International Review of Missions,* July 1954.

Bridston, Keith, *An Ecumenical Survey of the Discussion on Theological Training—A Preparatory Paper for the Consultation on Theological Education, Arnoldshain, Frankfurt, July 1956.*

Cragg, Kenneth, *The Call of the Minaret,* Oxford University Press, New York City, 1956.

Division of Foreign Missions Eighth Annual Report, National Council of Churches (USA), New York City, 1957.

Maddox, James G., *Technical Assistance by Religious Agencies in Latin America,* University of Chicago Press, 1956.

Stewart, William, "Training of the Ministry in South and Southeast Asia," *International Review of Missions,* October 1956.

Strachan, Kenneth, lecture at Mission Executives Retreat, Lake Geneva, Wisconsin, 1954 (mimeographed).

Thomas, Winburn T., and Bishop Rajah B. Manikam, *The Church in Southeast Asia,* Friendship Press, New York City, 1956.

Chapter 17. Recommendations

Informants: Messrs. Beach, Scott and D. C. Smith.

Manikam, Rajah B., ed., *Christianity and the Asian Revolution,* published for the Friendship Press, New York City, by the Diocesan Press, Madras, India, 1955.

Mende, Tibor, *Nehru—Conversations on India and World Affairs,* George Braziller & Co., New York City, 1956.

Monthly Bulletin of the United Nations Department of Economics and Social Affairs, New York City, October 1956.

Report of the Committee on Library Standards of the American Association of Theological Schools, New York City, 1952.

Sub-Committee on the Ministry in Africa—Record of Second Meeting Held in Edinburgh House, London, September 21, 1956, Division of Foreign Missions, National Council of Churches, New York City.

Van Dusen, Henry P., "United Strategy in Christian Missions—The Next Step," *Theology Today,* July 1949.

INDEX